RAISED ON RADIO

Raised on Radio

In Quest of

THE LONE RANGER • JACK BENNY

AMOS `N` ANDY • THE SHADOW

MARY NOBLE • THE GREAT GILDERSLEEVE

FIBBER McGEE AND MOLLY • BILL STERN

OUR MISS BROOKS • HENRY ALDRICH

THE QUIZ KIDS • MR. FIRST NIGHTER

FRED ALLEN • VIC AND SADE

THE CISCO KID • JACK ARMSTRONG

ARTHUR GODFREY • BOB AND RAY

THE BARBOUR FAMILY • HENRY MORGAN

JOE FRIDAY • AND OTHER

LOST HEROES FROM RADIO`S HEYDAY

Gerald Nachman

PANTHEON BOOKS

NEW YORK

To the memory of
Leonard, Isabel, and Judy Nachman,
three other vanished voices
that still reverberate

All rights reserved under International and Pan-American Copyright
Conventions. Published in the United States by Pantheon Books,
a division of Random House, Inc., New York, and simultaneously in
Canada by Random House of Canada Limited, Toronto.

Library of Congress Cataloging-in-Publication Data

Nachman, Gerald.
Raised on radio / Gerald Nachman.
p.   cm.
Includes bibliographical references and index.
ISBN 0-375-40287-X
1. Radio broadcasting—United States—History.   I. Title.
PN1991.3.U6N23   1998
791.44'0973—dc21   98-10355
CIP

Random House Web Address: http://www.randomhouse.com

BOOK DESIGN BY DEBORAH KERNER

Printed in the United States of America

4   6   8   9   7   5   3

Contents

Preface:
Background Music

I SUPPOSE I LED A NORMAL ENOUGH BOYHOOD, BUT YOU couldn't prove it by me. Midway through an attempted memoir, I was chagrined to discover that I had pretty much forgotten or misplaced my entire childhood except for the radio programs that absorbed a fairly alarming portion of those early years.

While I have real trouble tuning in to the major events of my boyhood, which seemed to occur between episodes of *Superman, Junior Miss, Mr. District Attorney, Stella Dallas,* and *The Lone Ranger,* I have almost total recall of the shows I heard. It is no trick for me, and others raised on radio, to hear an announcer's voice or a snatch of a theme song and instantly be able to identify the voice, the show, and the sponsor. The imposing yet ingratiating voices of Ken Carpenter, Harlow Wilcox, Bill Goodwin, Jimmy Wallington, and Ed Herlihy were more familiar to me than those of most of my uncles, aunts, and cousins.

So in a sense this is still a kind of memoir in that many of the shows within these pages were more real to me than my own life—make of that what you will. I was so busy living the adventures of Baby Snooks, Jack Armstrong, Nick Carter, Jack Benny, *One Man's Family,* and the Nelson family that my own life seemed worth little more than a passing glance. Stan Freberg once said, "While other kids were outside playing baseball, I was inside playing the radio." I played plenty of baseball, but my interior life was largely played out within the little box by my bed. It's where my inner child still resides, but I've finally let him out to gambol again among the old shows that I wanted to revisit.

It turned out to be a longer trip—four years—than I planned on when I first set out. What began as a weekend jaunt, a joyride through my favorite shows, turned into a long journey with unplanned detours into programs that I had all but forgotten about (*My Favorite Husband, Sky King, Stop the Music*), was too young to appreciate (*The Goldbergs, Vic and Sade, Information Please*), or for some reason just didn't get or get around to (*Flash Gordon, The Judy Canova Show, Chandu*).

Also, much wonderful stuff had come and gone before I caught the tail end of broadcasting's golden age, from the mid-1940s to the mid-'50s, when I was forced to abandon full-time radio listening for college. I missed more shows than I had realized, which made writing this book not just a rediscovery of old beloved shows but a discovery of those I had overlooked or that had vanished by the time I tuned in—crucial programs like Norman Corwin's poetic docudramas, Rudy Vallee's pace-setting *Fleischmann Hour,* Edward R. Murrow's wartime reports, and Fred Allen's vintage broadcasts.

In listening to certain old shows again, on tape, it was fascinating to find that programs I had been crazy about, like *The Cisco Kid, The Aldrich Family,* and *The Shadow,* were victims of time and didn't bear too many replays. Once you've heard one episode of most swayback westerns and wiseguy detective shows, you've pretty much heard them all. Alas, even the beloved *Lone Ranger* didn't hold me much beyond its promising overture, as yet another tinny plot would unfold.

Other shows, however, sounded better and richer as I listened to them with more alert adult ears, and could savor the writing, acting, and craftsmanship of superb creations like *Suspense, The Great Gildersleeve, Dragnet, The Adventures of Ozzie and Harriet,* and, most of all, *One Man's Family,* a show I had liked even as a boy but realize now why I did, and why this amazing show lasted twenty-seven years.

Certain programs of the period—Jack Benny's, Edgar Bergen's, Burns and Allen's, *Let's Pretend,* and some of the cleverer spook shows—have lost little luster in the intervening half century. Many of the Benny programs might have been written last week; ritualistic as that show was, it never became formulaic, unlike other comedies I was equally addicted to at the time—*Blondie, My Friend Irma,* and *Life with Luigi.*

The highlight of a trip to Los Angeles as a kid of eight was dining at Sportsman's Lodge and being introduced to the announcer Ken Carpenter by my Uncle Carlyle, a hip guy with actual Hollywood connections who, like my father, had grown up in Peoria, Illinois, the home of not just Carpenter but also Jim and Marian Jordan—*Fibber McGee and Molly.* My uncle got us in to see *The Gracie Fields Show,* and it didn't matter that I had no idea who she was—watching a real radio show unfold as it went on the air was thrill enough. My one other live connection to radio was a scary moment at an early Art Linkletter show called *What's Doin', Ladies?,* broadcast from a San Francisco department store, where Linkletter accosted my mother and began pawing through her purse.

I thought I could recall a lot of old radio only to find that what I remembered amounted to only a fraction of the hundreds of series that were on the air. So I've had to leave out many worthwhile programs, since I didn't want to produce an encyclopedia, and as the title suggests, I've included mainly those shows that had an impact on me and my generation or that broke new ground and planted the roots of television.

Rather late in the game, I felt a need to meet some of the people who had actually created the shows I was so devoted to. Many were gone, of course, but many of them were (and are) still around and eager to talk about what turned out to be universally golden times for them, too. I missed a few important people by days—Phil Harris took ill and died before we could arrange a time to meet, and the afternoon I called to confirm an interview with Willard Waterman (the second *Great Gildersleeve*), his wife told me he had died that morning. The writers had the best stories, as writers will, but it was a kick to talk to anyone who had a hand in creating that era—vital people like the elderly Cisco Kid, Jackson Beck, charming soap opera mainstays Mason Adams and Betty Winkler Keane, comic actor Arnold Stang, crusty but twinkly writer-producer Irving Brecher, ever-wry gagmen Bob Schiller, George Balzer, Sherwood Schwartz and Bob Weiskopf, the original Jack Armstrong, Charles Flynn, and ex–Quiz Kid Naomi Cooks, and on and on, all of them generous with their time, memories, and in a few cases, their photos.

But let's return now to where we left off just forty-seven years ago, where, you'll recall. . . .

— GERALD NACHMAN
SAN FRANCISCO, 1998

INTRODUCTION:
BEDTIME STORIES

IT IS EIGHT O'CLOCK ON A THURSDAY NIGHT IN THE MID-1940S. In a bedroom in Oakland, California, the Radio Kid tunes in to *The Aldrich Family* on his little red plastic time machine. He flings himself crosswise on the bed, head dangling over the edge, his finger tracing rosettes in the braided bedspread with the Red Ryder lariat motif. Between bites of Walnettos, he stares at the floor while Henry Aldrich, egged on by his pal Homer, quakes at the prospect of asking out Kathleen Anderson—much as the Kid himself fears telephoning the adorable Jean Anderson, his current seventh-grade passion, with her black bangs, freckles, green eyes, and sweetly lopsided smile.

We fade in now on a Sunday night at the Radio Kid's grandparents' compulsively tidy San Francisco apartment, smelling of cauliflower, chicken soup, liniment, and chocolate cake. The Kid is about to feast on one of Nana's sumptuous dinners while listening to her and Papa's bulky mahogany console radio, with its amber dial and a tuning knob the size of a ship's wheel. The radio brings the family urgent news bulletins from Walter Winchell's *Jergens Journal,* a teletype clattering nervously as Winchell chatters in his terse, hurried, lapel-grabbing New York–inflected big-shot voice: "Good evening, Mr. and Mrs. Nawth Americur and all the ships at sea. Let's go ta press!"

It is now a gloomy Monday afternoon. The Radio Kid, stricken with measles, is imprisoned in the house, the shades drawn, listening to the latest angst-ridden episodes of *Backstage Wife, The Romance of Helen Trent,* and *Young Widder Brown.* The Kid's mother putters downstairs fixing his lunch. Healthy again in a day or so, the Kid plans, like his cowboy heroes, to escape the room by tying two sheets together and lowering himself out of his bedroom window to a ledge over the kitchen door. Or he might simply leap directly onto the top of the garage, make his way to the apricot tree, saddle up and, in the bough of the trunk, gallop into the gathering twilight with one of his faithful sidekicks—Jerry Hyman, Russell West, Kenny Johnson—as they help Red Ryder and the Cisco Kid and the Lone Ranger bring justice to the frontier. . . .

THAT FAR-OFF LAND is where I lived my youth, an arm's length from one radio or another—primarily a rectangular crimson table-model Motorola with a cracked top, split from all the times I smacked the Bakelite case to shake it free of static. From this small box with the diagonal speaker slots I learned much of what I knew about honor, romance, justice, evil, humor, manhood, motherhood, marriage, women, law and order, history, sports, and families. I was told how life was meant to unfold and what America was all about. As I stretched out listening to it, night after night for a decade from young boyhood deep into my midteens, the world seemed—sounded, rather—intimate, manageable, and coherent yet at the same time vast and mysterious and thrilling. I tuned in eagerly every night for more news of life beyond my own humdrum cosmos at 707 Trestle Glen Road.

Listening again to those old programs and twisting the dial once more to the memories and thoughts they evoke, I find they were more than mere radio shows. Nothing "mere" about them. For me, they were basic bedtime stories, more vivid than anything by Grimm, Andersen, or Milne, longer lasting, more indelible. They preserved and fleshed out my fantasies and, in ways both bad and good, protected me from the world beyond the backyard. It all remains locked in my head because I was not only raised with these shows but, in some essential sense, raised *by* them. They helped shape my generation's values and formed notions of what was funny, compelling, inspiring, sentimental, and patriotic.

There was—still is—a mystique to radio unlike that of any other entertainment medium. Its intimacy amounts almost to secrecy. People tend to listen to radio alone. Listening in—eavesdropping—is such a private, vaguely stealthy, literally undercover act. You can take a radio to bed (as I still do) and listen to it in the dark. As a boy, so as to shield the glow of the dial on school nights, I would throw the covers over the radio while catching a late-night *Suspense,* or a distant extra-inning ballgame between the Oakland Oaks and a Pacific Coast League rival, or I might go nightclubbing at *The Chesterfield Supper Club.*

More than going to movies, then largely an adult pastime, I listened to radio from the moment I got home from school and tuned in to two hours of serials between four and six. After a quick dinner break, the radio chattered from seven to ten, often journeying to forbidden lands on *I Love a Mystery,* with its convoluted adventures in unknown places—its eerie mood and exotic locales contrived in a tiny studio in downtown Los Angeles.

When not nestled in deepest Radioland, I discovered the pleasures of reading and cartooning, adjuncts to listening. Radio made me a good listener. At times, I would creep out of bed and sit on the top landing of the stairs listening to the bright adult talk coming from below in our living room. It sounded like a live radio show. Radio was an entirely interior experience, closer to reading than anything else, a quiet, contemplative thing.

Radio was made of words. The comedy shows were almost all wordplay that tickled the ear, from puns to repartee. Radio was my indoor sandbox, where I learned to play with, and to love, language. From radio I grew addicted to stage plays, with their emphasis on speech, more than to movies. It was a verbal age, due mainly to radio, a universe constructed entirely of words.

Radio brought this world to me in fifteen- and thirty-minute chunks. I listened avidly, believingly, ceaselessly. It was all there in that bedroom with the blond knotty-pine wallpaper where I holed up for hours, books piled in a corner, and switched on the daily serials *Superman, Tom Mix, Captain Midnight, Straight Arrow,* and *The Green Hornet,* with its mesmerizing opening, a furious buzzing that accompanied "The Flight of the Bumblebee," which, I later discovered—and which thrilled the classicist in me—was a famous composition and not just a schlocky radio theme. (Likewise Rossini's triumphant *William Tell* Overture and the Philip Morris theme from Ferde Grofé's *Grand Canyon* Suite.)

Radio was America, presented in tones of pure red-blooded wartime patriotism. Radio instilled in me an unabashed love for the idea of America, for its lore, lingo, and popular culture. Radio presented not just programs but America itself, and we listeners bought it completely. Radio made me want to see the places I kept hearing about each night, sparking a wanderlust the way a passing train and paddle-wheeler might have for a boy a century before. Radio was a coming-of-age rite, my own *Life on the Mississippi*. Radio of the late 1940s and 1950s, like rivers and railroads of an earlier time, churned up the brain, the blood-stream, and the psyche.

RADIO AS THEATER VANISHED as swiftly and as totally as had silent films before it, for a similar but reverse reason: Sound killed silent movies, and television finished off radio. Yet whereas talk often enhanced silent movies, TV's pictures didn't necessarily add anything to radio, and usually detracted or distracted; radio isn't frustrated without visuals. Radio created its own visual language through sound effects, vocal theatrics, and music. David Mamet has claimed, "The best way to tell a story on stage is to imagine it on radio," to see if the words alone can carry it. Fred Friendly, the TV documentarian, once re-marked, "Your ear, more than your eye, is what holds you to TV." Radio discovered what the human voice can do to the imagination. Joe Julian, a radio actor, insisted, "No other art form ever engaged the imagination more intensely"—movies for the ears, as someone put it. Radio made listeners collaborators in the truest sense. From a few sim-ple sounds—a door closing, rapid footsteps down a cobblestone alley, howling winds and wolves, galloping hooves, creaking gates and gur-gling rapids, screeching squad cars and wailing trains (countless trains!)—you could conjure up entire landscapes and skylines. Radio combined the power of novels, vaudeville, pop music, and movies. All it took was a rickety screen door closing on *Lum and Abner* or the *"ding!"* of a department store bell on *The Jack Benny Program* to con-jure up an entire setting—a drowsy feed store, say, as opposed to a busy emporium. My little red Motorola was a genie's bottle: Rub the dial, and out popped flying men and woebegone widows and crazed killers and chortling thugs and laughing caballeros. Radio was interactive half a century before it became a cliché.

Radio was life-size—not bigger than life, like the movies, or smaller than life, like television. Radio had no dimensions except, as in novels, the limitless boundaries of fantasy. People were linked to radio in a passionately personal way, took it more seriously, and totally trusted it, much as they did books and newspapers. The direct, unfiltered sound of the human voice, like voices over a telephone on some nationwide party line, compelled you to pay attention. There was no visual clutter to distract; the ear was more grounded, as focused as the eye. The ear was all. Hearing was believing.

No wonder so few radio shows made the successful leap to television—or, before that, to movies—where any illusion was exploded. Watching radio shows on TV was like sitting too close to the stage at a play, where you can see makeup lines, false beards, perspiration and, during big speeches, the spray of spittle. When asked which he liked best, radio or TV, one young boy replied, "Radio—the pictures are better." Listeners also used to *watch* their radios, as if awaiting scenes to pop into view. It was a creative deceit, a kind of *trompe l'ear,* where whites played blacks, Hispanics, and Asians (and, occasionally, vice versa—the first use of "color-blind casting"); adults impersonated kids, dogs, horses, and birds; and men portrayed women, not to mention actors who played several roles within one show.

Our imagination wasn't the whole of it, though. Radio relied heavily on the keenly observed, nuanced, and detailed descriptive powers of gifted writers, not to mention the Industrial Light & Magic wizards of their day—the sound-effects boys, broadcasting's forgotten heroes. Writing and sound had to be punchy, succinct, and colorful. Most of the old shows, both comedies and mystery/detective series, had little fat on them.

Radio's celebrated "intimacy" wasn't simply a matter of its smaller scope, well-worn formats, and day-in, day-out familiarity, further nurtured by soap operas, which provided their own intense continuity. Radio's power to charm lay also in the vast net (as in network) it first spread over the country, literally linking Americans to each other through a coast-to-coast web. It was yesterday's Internet.

Radio did more than amuse America for thirty-five years. It wasn't just something that happened after vaudeville on the way to television. It was an airborne bridge among all other mainstream entertainment forms. Joining theater, films, concert halls, comic strips, touring shows, ladies' clubs, pulp magazines, news, and sports events, it brought together for the first time a tremendous variety of existing entertainments—plus pure radio inventions like the quiz show, the talk show, the game show, the sitcom, and the newscast.

It became everyone's national town hall (Fred Allen even called one of his early shows *Town Hall Tonight,* and Alexander Woollcott called his program *The Town Crier*). Radio, which was virtually Depression-proof during the thirties (NBC's Radio City Music Hall itself was erected in 1932, in the heart of the Depression), became a coast-to-coast Chautauqua tent, plugged-in vaudeville circuit, and neighborhood theater all packed into one elaborate cathedral-shaped console of burnished walnut.

Radio grew into a powerful bully pulpit—or, in the case of the broadcast bigot Father Coughlin, a bullying pulpit. The little box doubled as a handy soapbox for Billy Sunday, Aimee Semple McPherson, Charles Lindbergh, health freak Bernarr Macfadden, and goat-gland "doctor" John Brinkley.

Just as John F. Kennedy later commanded TV, Franklin D. Roosevelt mastered radio, as did his wife, who had a weekly radio slot and who was described by one magazine as "the first lady of the American airwaves." FDR's chummy *Fireside Chats* became his most popular domestic policy, bringing him closer to Americans than any previous president. He spoke to the country informally, as if he were in the same room with us, which in a sense he was. The news commentator Edwin C. Hill said of the chats: "It was as if a wise and kindly father had sat down sympathetically and patiently and affectionately with his worried and anxious children." At one point, Roosevelt was voted radio's most popular personality, ahead of Jack Benny. When FDR met Orson Welles, he said, laughing, "We're the two best actors in America." Radio implanted in the public mind FDR's personality (also Hitler's and Churchill's), through the power of his upbeat, swaggering, aristocratic voice. "The only thing we have to fear is fear itself" was the first sound bite.

During World War II, radio announcers would constantly "interrupt this broadcast" to bring news flashes, often via the somber John Daly. It was from the radio, not the newspapers, that most Americans first heard of such calamities as Pearl Harbor, the Hindenburg crash, and Roosevelt's death, and such triumphs as D-day. The war bonded Americans to their radios as propaganda popped up all over the dial. It seemed as if everyone from Beulah and Baby Snooks to Superman and Fibber McGee had enlisted in the war effort, instructing listeners to save cooking fat and tinfoil, plant victory gardens, buy war bonds, and share rations.

Radio invited you in. Listening to the radio became America's national indoor pastime. A radio-bound nation was regularly transfixed by such crazes as "the Mystery Melody" on *Stop the Music* or the "Mr. Hush" or "Miss Hush" contests on Ralph Edwards's *Truth or Consequences*. When Jack Benny and Fred Allen's mock feud made headlines after they met face-to-face at the Hotel Pierre in New York in an insult duel, it climaxed a decade of intraprogram sparring. One year, much of the country went searching for Gracie Allen's fictitious "lost brother." Radio was not just a time killer. It was a way of life, even though Fred Allen's crusty New Englander, Titus Moody, once observed, "Well, bub, I don't much hold with furniture what talks."

Radio gave me, as it did the country as a whole, a center. It connected us by the welcoming sound, drifting out of windows on summer nights, of Eddie Cantor ("I love to spend this hour with yoo-oo. /As friend to friend, I'm sorry it's throo-oo-oo . . .") or Charlie McCarthy ("I'll clip ya, Bergen—so help me, I'll *mow-w-w* ya down!") or Gene Autry ("Ah'm back in the saddle aginn . . ."). The shows told us what time it was; clocks were reset and movie times juggled to accommodate *Amos 'n' Andy.* Even more than vaudeville, movies, or pop songs, radio created national jokes, jingles, characters, and whistleable theme songs.

OLD RADIO SHOWS are not nostalgia pills, they're time capsules.

Radio became the ultimate populist medium—entertainment by, for, and of the people. It helped give the country a unified sense of itself. It created a common culture no matter what your class, city, or heritage; immigrants learned English by listening to the radio. The history of radio in the 1930s and 1940s is an informal history of pop Americana. Like the automobile, it changed us in fundamental ways. Moreover, the volatile chemistry of car + radio + ballads even altered the country's courtship habits.

Radio changed the face, and upped the stakes, of not merely show business but news, politics, media, promotion, and, most glaringly of all, advertising. Radio was the first information superhighway, but it began as a dusty one-lane back road that, within a decade or two, had become a sprawling, coast-to-coast entertainment turnpike. Radio also subtly homogenized the country—it gets the credit, or the blame, for partially smoothing out regional dialects by broadcasting a standard speech via velvet-toned announcers, speaking in a pleasant but unplaceable voice. Suddenly, everybody tuned to the same shows and heard the same jokes, was pitched the same pills, soaps, soups, cereals, and cake mixes, fell in love with the same stars, and got the same news the same night. Noted Gilbert Seldes: "Radio—cheap, accessible, and generous in its provision of popular taste—has come to be the poor man's library . . . his club. Never before has he met so many famous and interesting people, and never before have these people been at once so friendly and so attentive to his wishes."

Sepia photos show families grouped around a Stromberg-Carlson, gazing at the squatting console. Radio of the thirties and forties was an invited guest, unlike that pushy fifties interloper, television. Nobody was embarrassed to claim radio as a proud piece of the decor with a rightful place in the living room, alongside the sturdy, handsome Victrola and the homey, wholesome family piano.

UNLIKE OLD MOVIES, OLD SONGS, and even old plays, old radio shows have been mostly dismissed, washed aside by TV's tidal wave. Yet radio lives on now not merely in memory but, here and there, like traveling ghost bands of Tommy Dorsey and Glenn Miller; it springs up wherever radio buffs gather. This vibrant, burgeoning subculture meets at conventions where fervent believers re-create old shows. People dial in reruns on one of the hundreds of stations that play old shows or run *When Radio Was,* a nightly hour syndicated to three hundred stations and hosted by Stan Freberg, vintage radio's last star.

For the acutely radio afflicted, however, nostalgia is not a leftover seventies fad or a passing trivia game but an ongoing condition. We long for old radio, real radio—not just call-in shows, soapbox radicals, fragmented pop music formats, and twenty-four-hour news loops that dominate the airwaves and hog the spotlight. With its politicized talk-show hosts and factionalized music stations, radio now separates us where it once united us. What remains stored in the cramped studios of memory is more vividly current and forever. Nothing that today's hard-breathing Hollywood wizards can concoct is able to impress those of us for whom the pinnacle of virtual reality was reached half a century ago with *The Shadow.*

Old radio tells us where we came from, who we were and are today, and how we got this way. All kinds of phrases, now imbedded in the language, came from radio: "gangbusters" (as in, "He came on like gangbusters"); "B.O." (body odor, as banished by Lifebuoy); "soap opera," "Fibber McGee's closet"; "the hit parade"; "the $64(000) question"; "Just the facts, ma'am" and, to be sure, *dum-de-dum-dum;* also, "amateur hour"; "stop the music"; "the Shadow knows"; and "truth or consequences."

Other phrases still resonate: "Only the names have been changed to protect the innocent"; "Who was that masked man?"; "Faster than a speeding bullet"; "Happy trails"; "Say good night, Gracie"; "Stay tuned" and "Don't touch that dial!"; "On, you huskies!"; "Meanwhile, back at the ranch"; "Have gun, will travel"; "Keep those cards and letters coming in"; and "Can you top this?" The prototypes include such lingering legacies as Ozzie and Harriet (terminally wholesome couple or family), straight arrow (square and incorruptible, from the Indian hero Straight Arrow); Tonto (devoted sidekick); Jack Armstrong, the all-American boy (young male jock do-gooder); the Bickersons (squabbling twosome); and Mortimer Snerd (hopelessly stupid). Merely hearing the old NBC chimes is like biting into a Proustian cookie. Yet despite radio's remarkable hold on the nation for three decades, it's thought of now almost as a frivolous, faintly embarrassing craze somewhere between pinball machines and marathon dances.

Television buried dramatic radio with a finality from which it never recovered. TV absorbed radio, simply gulped it whole—its personalities, formats, methodology, sponsors, and audience. Radio survives now in packs of cassettes (The *Our Miss Brooks* Collection, etc.) available in Wireless or Signals catalogs and from mail-order houses (from Radiola, Radio Spirits, Radio Yesteryear, and others), curios for curious yuppies or for their sentimental parents and grandparents, who refuse to kiss off the past. The recordings capture a vital show business era that is no more—ancient vaudeville acts, excerpts from famous forgotten Broadway plays and movies and musicals on thousands of dramatic broadcasts, rare big-band air checks, and the debuts of unknown voices who became epic names.

Of course, it is possible to make too grandiose a claim for radio, which was, after all, simply cheap entertainment, much of it silly and trashy. Radio was a toy that grew up from a World War I message-sending device into a gadget, then a fad, and, finally, into what one broadcasting historian labeled an "empire of the air"—a lost empire now, whose influence has been underrated, largely ignored, and almost forgotten. The author of a Mary Pickford biography argued that silent films are the only art form to be invented, developed, and abandoned by the same generation, but surely radio also qualifies for this unhappy distinction. Today, speeding along the traffic-clogged superhighway of fax machines, cellular phones, computers, E-mail, cable television, and CD-ROMs, it is as if radio's golden era had never existed. In obituaries of show celebrities, lengthy radio careers are often passed over in a line or omitted entirely. That entire wireless world, a vast, vivid, bustling culture, a true vox Americana, is as remote today as the Incas and the Druids, evaporated into the night air.

Tuning in again to these old shows, reading about them, or talking to many of the people who created the real radio city—actors, announcers, writers, directors, musicians, and sound men—has been a little like reconstructing a once-mighty civilization, long buried, from unforgettable fragments of memory that, half a century afterward, still reverberate in the air. *Listen!*

IN THE 1920S, WHEN HE WAS A TEENAGER, THE writer-producer-director Norman Corwin said radio was a kind of dream in which earthlings were visited by friendly aliens from a nearby planet:

"At the very dawn of broadcasting, there was a breathless wonder that is hard to convey to anyone born after radio had become a common and a custom and later a rundown thing," he recalled. "I first heard of the invention as a kid in Boston, when my brother Al, who kept abreast of miracles, told me of a small device by which in the privacy of one's room sounds from afar could be caught on an aerial wire, conveyed to something called a Galena crystal, thence to a coil of wire, and at last to an apparatus called earphones. The human ear did the rest."

In this boyhood recollection from a 1979 speech before an audience of radiophiles, Corwin continued his remembrance of things past:

> *Electricity wasn't necessarily a factor in our home, because we didn't have any. Illumination was by gas mantle. Not even a battery was needed—nothing. God did it all. The sound came through the air, inaudible to the naked ear, with the speed of light and passed through solid objects—yes, wood, stone, plaster, cement, and the human body! You could shut all your doors and windows and still the sound would penetrate as mysterious as time. I just didn't believe it when I was told, but my brother wouldn't lie to me. So I figured he had fallen for some fiction by a leg-puller in the neighborhood.*
>
> *And then I heard the real thing. One of the boys down the street, Harold, had made a crystal set out of a cylindrical Quaker Oats box, around which he had wound a coil of cotton-covered wire. It might have been a gallstone taken from Aladdin, so magical were its properties to me. Harold picked at the crystal with the tip of a thin wire called a cat's whisker, seeking out sensitive*

Overleaf, top: The young David Sarnoff; *bottom:* the young William Paley

areas, his face intent, as if he were listening to word from beyond the grave. Suddenly, his eyes brightened—"Listen!" And he whisked the earphones off and he handed them to me and, oh, yawning heavens! A concord of sweet sounds! There, clear, sharp, undeniable, and beautiful, was the beep-beep-beep *of a code sender. I shivered with the thrill of it. Though I subsequently never learned Morse Code, neither did I learn to forget the wonder of transmitting impulses over airy distances.*

THE FIRST ACTUAL SCRATCHY "broadcast" occurred on Christmas Eve, 1906, when the inventor of something called a "high-frequency alternator," one Reginald Aubrey Fessenden, spoke over the airwaves and played a violin interlude. It was Dr. Lee DeForest, working out of the Parker Building in New York, who first devised a way to make ions audible, which he promptly dubbed an "audion" tube and tried to peddle to the navy. The navy thanked him very much but told him the battery would leak, making it impractical, so DeForest went back to his drawing board. In 1907, he had perfected the audion enough to transmit a yachting race fourteen miles.

And where was Thomas Edison while all this was going on? Scoffing, mainly. In 1921, when a former Edison employee-turned-announcer named Tommy Cowan needed to fill airtime at WJZ in New Jersey, he decided to play some recordings and went out to Edison's home in West Orange to borrow a phonograph and some discs from the master, who had a sign on his door reading, I WILL NOT TALK RADIO TO ANYONE. Edison, irked that he had failed to invent radio—which he considered a byproduct of the lightbulb—lent Cowan a phonograph until he heard the scratchy recordings over the Westinghouse station and demanded it back, saying, "If the phonograph sounded like that in any room, nobody would ever buy it." Cowan brought in live opera singers instead.

Another luckless man who staked a claim to radio patrimony was Herbert Armstrong, who, after losing a bitter lifelong legal wrangle with Lee DeForest, quietly shuffled off to invent FM radio (which he called "the Yankee Network"). The National Broadcasting Company's usually forward-looking founding father, David Sarnoff, ignored his invention at first and then, to avoid paying an FM licensing fee, simply put him out of business by tying him up in lawsuits, as he later would with TV pioneer Philo T. Farnsworth. The obsessed Armstrong spent his life battling RCA and eventually jumped to his death from a bedroom window, radio's most tragic forefather.

Credit radio's popular boom to another generally unknown hero named Frank Conrad, who in the spring of 1920 began broadcasting music and ball scores from a barn he used as a research lab at the Westinghouse Company in east Pittsburgh. The "wireless telephone," as it was known, was further legitimized when KDKA broadcast the election returns of Warren G. Harding's win over James M. Cox. So excited were ham wireless operators (an amateur wireless set cost a mere ten dollars) that a Pittsburgh newspaper began advertising radio equipment "which may be used by those who listen to Dr. Conrad's programs." Westinghouse picked up on the idea, and regular broadcasts began in a shed atop a sixth-story building on November 2, 1920, from a 100-watt transmitter. Westinghouse's main purpose in developing radio was not, as it is now, to make money by selling time to advertisers but by selling radio sets.

The first studio at KDKA was once described by another pioneer, broadcaster Robert Saudek, who began his career there and later went on to develop TV's landmark *Omnibus,* as resembling "the inside of a burlap-lined casket. Burnt orange, a favorite decorator color in 1922, was chosen for the draped-silk meringues that billowed from the ceiling to disguise light bulbs. The door was very heavy. A sign on the wall framed the single word *SILENCE.* A tall vase of gladioli stood in the corner. And in the center of this still room stood the working part, a microphone whose unruffled, impersonal, inscrutable self-confidence gave the whole place the feeling of an execution chamber."

Like DeForest, radio's other inventors were purists and pulpit-thumping zealots, who saw radio as a new religion, promoting its future in much the same rosy language as today's goggle-eyed prophets promote the information superhighway. As early as 1906, however, radio's founders feared for the nation's privacy, sounding like members of the ACLU. One finger-wagger worried: "One could be called up at the opera, in church, in our beds. Where could one be free from interruption?" Indeed, radio did, in its gentle way, roust people out of bed and interrupt the country's tranquility (but then so did earlier intruders, the telephone and the phonograph), replacing parlor games, story-telling, and musicales with electronic versions of the same thing.

An early daily log of WOR in Newark, the voice of Bamberger's Department Store (most early stations were housed in department stores, hotels, and newspapers as promotional outlets), reveals a lineup sure to thrill a ladies quilting society. The day included tips on "Packing the Weekend Bag," classical recordings, an address by a minister entitled "The Man with a Handicap," a talk to the Boy Scouts, another speech on "timely vegetable garden topics" by a New Jersey horticulturist, and an early sign-off at 6:30 P.M. with "good-night stories for the children by Uncle George of the *Newark Ledger.*" Many stations ceased broadcasting one night a week, called "silent night," so people could pick up signals from around the country. Some worried that leaving a radio on might start fires.

In the first flush of commercial radio's birth, in the early 1920s, there were concerts, debates, opera recitals, recitations, lectures, and poetry readings galore, but the novelty of simply hearing a distant event wore off quickly. Radio was nothing if not earnest in those first years, however, determined to civilize the unwashed or know the reason why; many stations broadcast morning calisthenics to get listeners off to a fit start. Walter Damrosch's *Music Appreciation Hour* was piped into 125,000 classrooms, and *The Farm and Home Hour* tried to bring a touch of the poet to farmers. A station surfer in 1930 would have found himself tuned to such stirring fare as *The American School of the Air* and *The Standard School Broadcast,* which for decades brought classical music into classrooms around the country.

George Washington Hill, the eccentric, outspoken tycoon who headed the American Tobacco Company, quarreled with all this high-minded programming. "Symphonic music has no place in a mass medium," he groused, certain that there must be a better way of blowing smoke rings by the public. Not long after, radio and cigarettes found each other, a fond alliance that would continue into the 1960s.

Radio reigned for only thirty years, two decades fewer than TV has now ruled. Like television, it was born of high hopes that it would bring culture to the masses and spread democracy around the globe. Radio did bring a new culture to the public, even if *Fibber McGee and Molly, When a Girl Marries,* and *It Pays to Be Ignorant* were not exactly what Marconi had in mind. He and the other founding fathers had spoken grandly of radio's vast potential for educating the nation and uplifting the populace with the Finer Things. America, being America, stubbornly resisted the Finer Things and decided it would rather have a good time. Madison Avenue was happy to comply.

By the mid-1930s, however, it wasn't enough to be able to pick up *Götterdämmerung* from the Metropolitan Opera in New York City, catch the election returns as they clattered in from Washington, D.C., or hear the Boston baseball scores on the day the game was played. Listeners wanted something more amusing, entertainment they could identify with and that wasn't just good for them. That something else turned out to be a couple of funny, unlettered but lovable black guys out of Chicago bemoaning their life in the big city. That early show, *Sam 'n' Henry,* evolved in a few years into *Amos 'n' Andy,* which set the intimate, folksy tone and comic agenda for radio's next thirty years. Good-bye, King Lear. Hello, Kingfish. It also inaugurated the pop superstar era: Prior to radio, Freeman Gosden and Charles Correll were playing a Chicago club called McVicker's with their blackface act, earning $250 a week in 1927. After two years on the air, they earned $5,000 a week on tour and were America's first broadcasting headliners.

Radio was so widespread by 1922, with crystal sets popping up in every home like minicams in 1992, that secretary of commerce Herbert Hoover—who muttered that his own son had "gone daft on wireless"—decided radio needed controlling before it fell into advertising's greasy hands. By 1932, one out of three homes had a radio, some of which were the most expensive piece of furniture in people's houses— splendid domed cathedral consoles made by Stromberg-Carlson, Philco, Majestic, and Atwater Kent. The boxes themselves were wondrous instruments, known in the trade as highboys, lowboys, consoles, tombstones, and chairsides, often finished with filigree detailing. The ornate Philcos were beautifully designed by Norman Bel Geddes, Albert Mowitz, and Edward L. Combs; Combs dreamed up the famous "Model 90 Cathedral" that most people think of when they think of big fancy old-time radios.

At first, all the free music on radio sent record sales plummeting, but the rise of variety shows—free promotion for new pop tunes—soon had them soaring again, at which point the American Society of Composers, Authors, and Publishers stepped in to license airplay; a dispute between radio and the rigid, often autocratic ASCAP resulted in the birth of BMI (Broadcast Music Incorporated).

People feared the spread of this mysterious new force suddenly seeping into every aspect of American life. Many newspapers stopped printing, or charged for, radio logs, which they considered free advertising. But advertisers couldn't stay away. "It is inconceivable that we should allow so great a possibility for service and for news, for entertainment and education . . . to be drowned in advertising," fretted Hoover. Most listeners didn't mind the commercials; they even rather liked them, in fact—they embraced the whole babbling package. To harness electronic capitalism, a Federal Radio Commission was established, but radio remained, as now, a freaky hybrid hard to control; while it operated in the public interest, it wasn't a public utility. The argument still rages over whose air—or cyberspace—it is, anyway.

The idea of advertising on the new medium was bemoaned by station owners, educators, and anyone who was repulsed by the notion of hawking goods over the air. An article in a trade magazine in 1925 asked, "Who Is to Pay for Radio, and How?" and held a contest asking readers for their ideas. The entries included charging for log listings, volunteer listener contributions, and government licensing, but the winner was a reader who proposed a tax on the vacuum tubes themselves.

WEAF in New York City was the first commercial station to sell advertising to sponsors, who bought time on little ten-minute lecture programs. A leading journalism trade paper was aghast: "Any attempt to make the radio an advertising medium, in the accepted sense of the term, would, we think, prove positively offensive to great numbers of people. The family circle is not a public place, and advertising has no business intruding there unless it is invited." President Hoover didn't like the idea of having one of his addresses tainted by advertising: "If the President's speech is nothing but meat between the sandwich of advertising for patent medicines, who will want the sandwich?" *Printers' Ink* announced: "We are opposed to [radio] advertising for the same reason we are opposed to sky writing. People should not be forced to read [or hear] advertising unless they are so inclined."

WEAF, forced to create its own live programs when forbidden by law to play phonograph records, became a major showcase for New

York entertainers and bands, often named after the sponsor (the Champion Sparklers, the A&P Gypsies, the Clicquot Club Eskimos, and, to be sure, the Eagle Neutrodyne Trio). Within a few years, stars would open their shows with sales-pitch greetings like, "This is Bob 'Pepsodent' Hope" and "Jell-O, again, this is Jack Benny." WEAF also devised the ingenious idea of using a sponsor's name to title a program, leading to *The Eveready Hour,* radio's first major variety show, "brought your way by the National Carbon Company." In another major innovation, National Carbon hired its advertising agency, N. W. Ayer, to put the show together. Advertising not only swamped radio but soon controlled it. The ad agencies in Chicago and New York ran radio, creating and producing all the programs. (Today, of course, the networks own the shows and simply sell airtime to sponsors.) All the pieces were now in place for a couple of junior tycoons named David Sarnoff and William Paley.

Sarnoff, a twenty-one-year-old whiz kid working as a wireless operator for the American Marconi Co. out of Wanamaker's Department Store, became an overnight hero when he transcribed distant dots and dashes from a rescue ship churning the Atlantic toward a sinking vessel on its maiden voyage—the *Titanic.* The incident, Sarnoff later said, "brought radio to the front, and, incidentally, me." Maybe not so incidentally. Sarnoff, already something of a self-promoter, claimed he was the only wireless operator to pick up the distress signals—a report later disputed. One historian thinks it more likely that Sarnoff simply copied the names of survivors from a list that the rescue ship, the *Carpathia,* was relaying to another Marconi station, adding that the incident taught Sarnoff "how events could be shaded or maneuvered to suit his purposes."

Whatever the true story, Sarnoff's star was already rising at the Marconi company; at one point he was entrusted with the task of delivering bouquets and candy boxes to Marconi's New York mistresses. Between deliveries, the young visionary saw the commercial possibilities for what he called "a music box" and wrote a famous report in which he outlined a plan that "would make radio a 'household utility' in the same sense as the piano or phonograph." If it was placed in a parlor or living room, he wrote, listeners could "enjoy concerts, lectures, music, recitals, etc., which might be going on in the nearest city within their radius." He calculated it could bring American Marconi $75 million a year.

Clever idea, but it was dismissed or lost in the daily flurry of interoffice memos in the Marconi office hierarchy. In 1919, undaunted, Sarnoff tried again to propose his scheme for a "radio music box" after a merger of Marconi and the Radio Corporation of America. This time, the head of the new company perked up at Sarnoff's prediction that, in the first year, about 100,000 radio music boxes might be sold for seventy-five dollars.

As a test run, Sarnoff arranged to broadcast the July 1921 Dempsey-Carpentier championship heavyweight match, which was heard by some 300,000 presumably rapt listeners—each one a prospective customer with seventy-five dollars burning a hole in his pocket. In fact, the fight was telephoned in from ringside by a sportscaster to an engineer, who jotted down the jabs and then announced the action over the air to the multitudes. The widely broadcast Democratic convention of 1924 that nominated the flamboyant Al Smith further whetted people's appetites (what a concept: politics as entertainment!), along with the opportunity to call up popular songs like "Barney Google" whenever one might be in the mood. America was hooked on sonics.

Five years later, the National Broadcasting Company was founded by Sarnoff after he had finagled AT&T into giving up its own ideas of transmitting radio signals and, instead, lease its phone lines for $1 million a year to the new network. NBC was then divided into the Red Network (for its glitzier, commercial shows) and the Blue Network (for more prestige shows). When the FCC forced NBC to divest itself of two entities in 1941, the Blue Network was sold off and, in 1943, became ABC when it was bought by the man who made Life Savers; in 1927 there was even an Orange Network of Pacific Coast stations.

Before all that, though, the Red and the Blue divisions merged for a momentous launching of a nationwide radio hookup with a four-hour broadcast from the Waldorf-Astoria Hotel in New York. Walter Damrosch conducted the newly formed NBC Symphony, Will Rogers delivered a monologue from Independence, Missouri, that included an impression of Calvin Coolidge, and in Chicago, diva Mary Garden sang "Annie Laurie." Thus was born the radio variety show. Performers who cashed in on the boom called it "electric money," and Rogers remarked, "Radio is too big a thing to be out of." Radio had shown it could create stars and national heroes literally overnight.

Sarnoff, a runty, remote, frosty-eyed boy tycoon—the Bill Gates of the 1920s—was the network's technician and field manager, and a self-proclaimed "General"; he was only a reserve officer but with all the chutzpah of General Patton. Pat Weaver, the revered NBC programming innovator who worked for him for years, later wrote that Sarnoff was a publicity-seeking "monster" who cared only about radio as hardware; Weaver called him "General Fangs." The joke on Wall Street, recalled Weaver, was that if RCA stock opened at ten and Sarnoff dropped dead, it would close at a hundred. Sarnoff, a Russian-born Jew, defended his hard-nosed work ethic: "I realized I couldn't compete with gentiles in a gentile industry if I were merely as good as they were. But if I were, say, twice as good, they couldn't hold me down."

His major rival, William Paley, was no Jazz Age techie like Sarnoff but, rather, a refined would-be cultural commissar with an all-seeing CBS eye for talent that rivaled Sarnoff's corporate wizardry. In 1929, the year after NBC was formed, Paley—then a twenty-seven-year-old playboy on a $50,000-a-year allowance in search of a business to play with—signed the family cigar firm, the Congress Cigar Company, to a fifty-week contract with WCAU in Philadelphia, to sponsor an innocuous musical show called *The La Palina Hour,* named for its best-selling stogies. When cigar sales soared, Paley began to build what would become the Columbia Broadcasting System. With family money, he snapped up a failing chain of sixteen radio stations, which, in two years, had grown to seventy stations and earned a $2 million profit.

As one historian said, Paley had "an instinctive sense of popular taste," but he also went after affiliates as ruthlessly as Sarnoff, if not more so. Paley outmaneuvered the General by devising an arrangement that allowed stations to use, free of charge, as many CBS programs as they liked; NBC charged affiliates for unsponsored shows. In exchange, Paley had the use of any show produced by an affiliate. Paley, an instinctive showman with a talent for making and acquiring stars and a flair for promotion (he kept PR wizard Edward Bernays on retainer), had a more creative programming touch and simply more innate charm than Sarnoff. Paley became a major influence on U.S. pop culture by seeking out and signing vaudeville headliners in the early 1930s, when people were listening to their radios about five hours a day.

Phil Cohan, who wrote and produced shows for Paul Whiteman and Jimmy Durante, was drawn to CBS and remembered the atmosphere: "Bill Paley was associated with Broadway people and he liked good taste. CBS attracted people like Norman Corwin and [the conductor] Johnny Green and me because we felt that was the place to be. Whereas Mr. Sarnoff was a genius in his own way at NBC, it was just one entity of the RCA corporation. It was a pure business thing, so there was a whole different attitude. Paley would come down once in a while; you had these very intimate studios at 485 Madison. You'd see him in the doorway, interested in what you were doing. He was right there."

Paley loved playing talent scout, as in the anecdote in which he supposedly heard a singer being played on a kid's portable phonograph player aboard a cruise ship and sent a wireless to his office reading, "Heard vocalist called Bing Crosby. Please sign." In the hope of luring listeners away from *Amos 'n' Andy,* which ruled dinnertime radio from 7 to 7:15 P.M., Paley flung Kate Smith, Morton Downey, the Mills Brothers, and Bing Crosby on the air opposite the beloved comics; even Crosby only nicked them. Lawrence Bergreen wrote that "without [*Amos 'n' Andy*] it is doubtful that NBC . . . would have survived the Depression. *Amos 'n' Andy* was the show that proved the networks were as popular as they claimed to be . . . delivering a vast audience— an estimated half the nation every evening—to a grateful sponsor."

Just as Milton Berle was TV's best commercial for TV itself, so Amos and Andy became radio's premiere pitchmen in its first decade. Once the novelty of broadcasting had worn off, what drove radio sales were personalities—and Amos and Andy were broadcasting's most famous brand names in America's burgeoning cult of celebrity. Until then, radio had been a pleasant diversion, made up largely of innocuous musical programs, but in 1929, when *Amos 'n' Andy* went network, it became a national obsession and then a necessity. Sales of radios shot up 23 percent in a year, and when the show's popularity slumped a few years later, falling off by about 25 percent, so did radio sales.

New stars were needed in a hurry and almost anyone would do, from nonentities to national heroes. Stars from other fields were first in line, but almost anybody who made a splash, no matter how ill-suited, was handed a show—Babe Ruth, Charles Lindbergh, Mrs. Roosevelt, Max Baer, Elsa Maxwell, Dunninger. The nation was up to its ears, so to speak, in ready-made radio celebrities. If you were gifted, all the better, but name recognition was at least as crucial as talent; ways could be found to wrap a format around the most unlikely or unsuitable celebrity. Radio was an astonishingly elastic form, able to expand to fit stars like Helen Hayes and to shrink to the size of the Sad Sack or whoever caught the country's fancy that year.

As in TV today, a blockbuster hit at the start of an evening guaranteed a lead-in to the rest of the network's shows, but in 1930 there was a practical reason for listeners remaining tuned to one station. It was less a matter of loyalty than logic: Changing stations created static and loss of sound quality, so people found it easier on their ears to heed the advice of staff announcers fond of warning, "Don't touch that dial!"

The upstart Paley conducted famous "raids" on mighty NBC for such monster names as Al Jolson, Jack Benny, Burns and Allen, Red Skelton, Edgar Bergen and Charlie McCarthy, and Eddie Cantor, and he also became a major producer of what came to be called "theater of the mind," programming dramas by experimental and renegade radio dramatists Norman Corwin, Arch Oboler, and Orson Welles.

But a crucial behind-the-scenes player, and the man perhaps most responsible for Paley's early programming success at CBS, was Arthur Judson, a highly regarded Philadelphia impresario who managed Ezio Pinza, Jascha Heifetz, Bruno Walter, Vladimir Horowitz, and Georg Szell. Judson's attempt to sell his services to NBC had been rebuffed by Sarnoff, and after a misguided attempt to create his own network, he formed the Columbia Phonograph Broadcasting System with the idea of mass-marketing records. Judson, however, needed a network to air them—and quickly, for Sarnoff had just begun his own Victor Talking Machine Company. Hearing records broadcast over the air was a vast improvement over listening to them on squawky phonograph players cranked either too tightly or too loosely until a crackly voice finally emerged, tinny and distorted, through a clunky horn.

Judson, eager to retaliate for Sarnoff's brush-off, went to Paley with the idea of producing records to be played exclusively over CBS. When Paley agreed, Judson hired conductor Howard Barlow who, with the

Metropolitan Opera orchestra, staged a spectacular two-hour concert heard in sixteen cities to launch CBS with a new work by the composer Deems Taylor called "The King's Henchmen," for which Edna St. Vincent Millay wrote the narration. Even so, the young network floundered until a patroness ponied up $45,000 to pay AT&T, which bought Paley enough time to get the fledgling CBS off the ground with the support of two other backers; Paley was down to his last $1 million.

The radio revolution was now nearly complete—CBS had become a true nationwide hookup with its 1929 purchase of the West Coast's Don Lee network—and needed only a promotional genius to create a total coast-to-coast coup. Such a man was Frank Stanton, the third member of radio's troika, in whom was merged a passion for pop psychology with a keen marketing instinct. Dr. Stanton, as he was always called (as if in reply to Sarnoff's military title; the Ph.D. was in industrial psychology for a thesis entitled "A Critique of Present Methods and a New Plan for Studying Radio Listening Behavior"), devised a statistical rating system that measured listening patterns—a primitive Nielsen survey.

In 1937, Stanton codeveloped a program analyzer that gauged audience reaction moment to moment and pretested shows and commercials with focus groups on a gizmo nicknamed "Big Annie," a sort of seismo-polygraph. Stanton's touchy-feely approach to peddling programs and products eventually elevated him to the status of guru, although his analyzer was roundly derided, even by one of his cohorts, who once said of Big Annie: "It defies a hundred marketing rules . . . it's lousy research. The sample stinks, it's not representative of any group. It's not large enough. It's an unnatural situation. The way people register their opinions is unnatural. You can go on and on and show why it shouldn't work. But it works. Our batting average is 85 percent."

In fact, nobody knew by this point who was really running the show(s). The weak, fledgling FCC was trying to please the networks, who were playing footsie with the affiliates, who were dependent on the networks, who had surrendered the job of producing shows to the ad agencies, who were trying to please the sponsors, who were in turn beholden to boards of directors and stockholders. Whatever the case, free enterprise had taken over and radio's land rush was on.

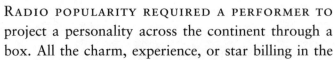

RADIO POPULARITY REQUIRED A PERFORMER TO project a personality across the continent through a box. All the charm, experience, or star billing in the world couldn't make listeners warm up to someone with whom they didn't feel literally at home. Inexplicably, lowbrow comedians like Abbott and Costello and Red Skelton became hits on the air, while theatrical headliners like Bert Lahr, Al Jolson, Groucho Marx, and Danny Kaye failed. Even Jimmy Durante and Ed Wynn, celebrated as they were in radio, never equaled their stage, film, or TV stature, far too flamboyant for so understated a medium.

Although radio became the elephant's graveyard of many a fading or desperate vaudevillian, it was also the Last Chance Saloon for ex-screen stars (John Barrymore), aging Broadway legends (Fanny Brice), resourceful burlesque headliners (Joe Penner), and overripe top bananas (Abbott and Costello)—and also for second bananas who found a lifetime annuity in comedy-show walk-ons.

After the grueling road-show life of one-nighters and split bills, however, radio seemed a snap for transient vaudevillians, but the fallout among many ex-vaudevillians was painful and scary. Radio was trickier than it sounded. Some ex-vaudevillians survived for decades, but many others used themselves up in a few months, stuck in a character or a sketch that didn't lend itself to the new, casual medium, where people sat around in bedrooms and kitchens in their bathrobe and slippers. Said Studs Terkel, a onetime actor on *Ma Perkins,* "Now you could attend vaudeville in your underwear." Not until TV did major stage and screen clowns like Milton Berle, Phil Silvers, Jackie Gleason, and Lucille Ball find their footing. Bob Hope put it best: "When vaudeville died, TV was the box it was buried in."

In radio's formative years, rather than develop their own talent, net-

Overleaf: Ed Wynn, surrounded by *(clockwise from top left)* Jimmy Durante, Eddie Cantor, Milton Berle, and Red Skelton

works went with whatever unformed performer landed at the front door—performers like Billy Jones and Ernie Hare, a vaudeville singing team who converted themselves into "The Happiness Boys," so named because the boys were sponsored by the Happiness Candy Company, the first stars identified with a product.

Jones and Hare were radio's original superstars—their show was a half hour of snappy songs and patter punctuated by their trademark, and apparently irresistible, theme song, "How d'ya do, everybody, how d'ya do/Don't forget your Friday date/Seven-thirty until eight/How d'ya do, everybody, how d'ya do." The boys were nothing if not adaptable: When the candy firm dropped them and a stocking company adopted them, they evolved into "The Interwoven Pair"; when that association ended, they reincorporated as "The Flit Soldiers" after an insect-spray sponsor came to the rescue, and later evolved into "The Best Foods Boys" and "The Taystee Loafers." In one form or another, whether as singing candy bars, socks, or bug repellent, they lasted through the 1930s.

The Happiness Boys—ruddy, compact fellows who not only resembled each other in height and weight but had been born on the same day to mothers with the same maiden name—were less innocuous than their billing suggests. They told corny jokes and sang jaunty comedy ditties, often in dialect, accompanied by a piano or an occasional chorus, but their simple, hummable tunes often had clever, satirical, self-mocking lyrics and endless verses. One of their songs dealt with the newly liberated 1920s woman ("She's the Sweetheart of Six Other Guys," about a gal who smokes, drinks, swears, and—gasp!—parts her hair); another laments talking pictures that made dozing off in movie theaters much more difficult. Some of the numbers still seem funny and unexpectedly barbed, such as a derisive duet sung by the duo in a heavy Yiddish accent about Henry Ford apologizing, presumably for one of his anti-Semitic slurs, in a Dearborn, Michigan, newspaper.

Radio's premier comedy shows often sound fresher today than the dramas, partly because the comics' personalities haven't dated. References may have grown moldy, along with the shtick, but in many cases the dialogue is solidly crafted and pays off regularly in laughs that have nothing to do with nostalgia. Funny is funny, even sixty years after the fact. And when the shows seem embarrassingly weak, it's usually the fault of the writing and not the period; they probably sounded just as bad then.

Radio jokes had to be verbal: the early or lesser shows were heavily dependent on puns, malapropisms, double-talk, mangled syntax, tongue twisters, and spoonerisms; one survey claimed that 40 percent of all comedy routines was made up of puns—and that figure sounds low. There was an entire school of spoonerists, who would pop into comedy shows and dish out five-minute nonsense monologues comprised of inverted syllables recited at a dizzying speed, a guaranteed laugh-getter.

What couldn't be seen had to be evoked with a funny voice or skillful delivery. If many of the old sketches read like labored routines, they were given comic life by the nimble vocal styles of radio's vast gallery of resourceful oral clowns. The *Fibber McGee and Molly* show, to name one, was blessed with such vocal masters as Arthur Q. Bryan and Bill Thompson, who gave voice to the simpering, mush-mouthed Wallace Wimple. Only one of these great dialecticians, Mel Blanc, ever rose to stardom, but others included June Foray, Peter Donald, and Teddy Bergman. Most of these stunt voices, so to speak, toiled anonymously week in and week out. Entire shows were malaprop-centered, notably *Easy Aces,* but also, to a lesser degree, *Amos 'n' Andy.* Many cameo characters' entire routine was confusing words, sputtering non sequiturs, or conversing in pidgin English—a vast gallery of stage Germans, Italians, Irish, Swedes, Jews, and blacks.

There was a major comedy explosion in America in the 1920s, not unlike those in the 1960s and 1980s. When the Depression closed scores of vaudeville houses, it let loose a mob of comedians with nowhere else to go but into the new, untried, but tantalizing medium of radio. Vaudeville clowns known as Baron Munchausen (Jack Pearl), Ish Kabibble (Merwyn Bogue), the Mad Russian (Bert Gordon), and Parkyakarkus (Harry Einstein, father of Albert Brooks) hurriedly tried to reinvent themselves for radio, settling for ritualistic weekly five-minute appearances on shows run by vaudeville's top bananas. They would pop into programs and do their shtick—jokes based largely on the mispronunciations and misunderstandings of foreigners that struck upwardly mobile second-generation Americans as funny—before departing to fond applause.

Those who were primarily verbal comics (Jack Benny, Fred Allen, Bob Hope, Burns and Allen) or singer/comics (Eddie Cantor, Bing Crosby, Jimmy Durante) made the tricky transition from stage to studio. Vaudeville comics who were essentially visual—not unlike all of those doomed silent-screen actors with squeaky voices—didn't last long, but most took their turn at a studio microphone for an additional five minutes of fame. Many a famous funny face washed out after a season.

Among those who languished were one-line comic wonders like Joe Penner, who beat the "Wanna buy a duck?" thing into the ground in record airtime (he actually did say something else: "You na-a-a-a-sty man!," his backup catchphrase). Penner, a funny guy even without that line, was named comedian of the year in 1934. Two years later he was gone, and five years after that he died, at age thirty-six, in showbiz limbo. Jack Pearl was another radio flash-in-the-pan whose Baron Munchausen character was an amalgam of all the stage Germans (called "Dutch acts") who overran burlesque, most famously Weber and Fields and Smith and Dale. Pearl's "Vos you dere, Sharlie?" made him an overnight sensation and a virtual overnight has-been. It was his best and just about only idea, and—as Jack Benny had warned him might happen—the Baron wore out his welcome quickly. George Burns once observed, "The problem with relying on catchphrases is that they get very old even while they're still new."

Radio, although it looked like easy money compared to the rigors of stage life, swallowed comedians whole who had been able to milk an entire career on the vaudeville circuit out of a few routines. As Burns noted after his own radio debut, in vaudeville he could get seventeen years out of seventeen minutes of material that in radio lasted him exactly seventeen minutes; most vaudeville acts were ten minutes, tops. Not even Bert Lahr, the premier burlesque comic of his time (along with Bobby Clark, another radio reject), could adapt to the mike; he was so nervous that he twisted the buttons off his shirt. Despite that funny, unforgettable bawl of a voice, Lahr mugged away his chance before a studio audience while people at home wondered what all the guffawing was about. Two major stage comics who failed to hang around early radio were Groucho and Chico Marx, who did a short-lived show in 1932 called *Flywheel, Shyster and Flywheel,* playing a pair of flimflamming lawyers. George Jessel also languished.

RADIO WAS THE WRONG PLACE for baggy pants comics, yet Ed Wynn played the airwaves like one of his zany *Ziegfeld Follies* shows. With his falsetto old-lady giggle and girlish lisp—accessorized with owlish spectacles, funny hats, and floppy suits—Wynn had the necessary comic vocal props to pierce radio's one dimension even with gags out of Joe Miller's Jokebook (Wynn: "He can only eat soft foods as he has a Pullman mouth" . . . Announcer Graham McNamee: "A Pullman mouth?" . . . Wynn: "No lowers and very few uppers").

To Wynn, the feeble joke was only an excuse for his patented goofiness. After he went into acting in late middle age, he called himself "a method comedian," which he defined as a comic more dependent on how a joke is presented than on the joke itself. The drama critic Joseph Wood Krutch perfectly described the ephemeral appeal of a nonsense comic who seemed almost beyond analysis, writing: "No one can exceed him in solid, impenetrable asininity, but no one can, at the same time, be more amiable, well-meaning, and attractive."

In his Texaco fireman's hat (talk about product placement—imagine Tim Allen doing *Home Improvement* in a Black & Decker T-shirt), Wynn was the first major comic to switch from vaudeville to radio. It gave him a huge head start on the competition, but his first show bombed and he didn't return for a decade; as *The Fire Chief* he eventually caught fire in the early thirties. Wynn's first flop was a version of his Broadway hit *The Perfect Fool,* which he wrote and staged and which gave him a lifelong identity. It was the first Broadway show ever broadcast, full of the wild and crazy stunts that caused fellow visual comics to stumble over their outsize clown shoes.

Wynn realized he needed live bodies to play to and, out of sheer desperation, pioneered the use of the studio audience and the announcer-straight man, using sportscasting legend-turned-straight man Graham McNamee as a foil for his doofus gags, most of them puns. When in 1932 he finally returned to radio after his *Perfect Fool* fiasco, Wynn rounded up a makeshift audience comprised of anyone hanging around the station—cleaning women, office staff, visitors—who could be herded into the studio to provide warm bodies, charging admission and mixing with the crowd as they entered the studio. Indeed, Wynn's first *Fire Chief* broadcasts were actually done from the New Amsterdam Theater on the set of his Broadway show, and during each broadcast he was constantly in and out of makeup and costumes, as often as seven times a show.

(Those first radio studios were primitive affairs. To make room for people, ushers would set up fifty or a hundred folding chairs, and early audiences watched from behind a six-ton soundproof glass curtain, a sort of sneeze guard, to protect radio listeners from being infected with random noise. Laughs, it was felt, might interfere with the listeners' enjoyment of the show, which left comics in a vacuum. As Jack Benny once recalled of his old days in radio, "You couldn't hear them laugh behind the glass, so I'd watch them until everybody had their mouth shut, then I'd go on to the next line.")

Well into the 1940s, Wynn's *Fire Chief* show was a steady barrage of outrageous puns and creaky *College Humor*–style gags, all delivered in the star's breathless cracked voice, which is so high-pitched it slips into a kind of Jewish yodel. "The waiter ate twenty-two hotcakes right off the griddle," says McNamee, Wynn's willing Ed McMahon, laughing at even the setup lines. Gasps Wynn: "How waffle!" Or, Wynn: "The maid was in the kitchen listening to *The Lone Ranger*!" McNamee: "The Lone Ranger was in the kitchen?" Wynn: "Maybe he just dropped in to polish his Silver!"

What's surprising is that this grown-up child of burlesque lasted on radio as long as he did—a quarter of a century, on and off—and had a respectable TV revival without ever changing his fundamental "perfect fool" persona until his last years, when he finally removed the dunce cap and became a serious actor in films and TV (*Playhouse 90*, *Requiem for a Heavyweight*, *The Twilight Zone*).

His actor son, Keenan Wynn, once sadly reminisced that his father was always a reluctant radio star. "Unfortunately, he became a big success in radio and was suddenly locked into it. He had to come up with fifty-five jokes a week." Wynn, among vaudeville's most visual comics, found himself forced to rely on a silly voice just to survive, driven to entertain to keep his fans happy. "My father," recalled Wynn, "would perform in a men's room if someone recognized him."

THE NEVER-SAY-DIE Milton Berle had a surprisingly long run on radio for such a vaudeville fish out of water. He defied the critics and, through sheer persistence and more talent than was always recognized, became a regular on six different if undistinguished shows from 1934 to 1949, beginning when he was a twenty-six-year-old boy wonder on a show with the cumbersome title *The Gillette Original Community Sing.* It began in Boston and ran a year before going network in a shapeless forty-five-minute format that opened with him singing "Let's All Sing Like the Birdies Sing," as the audience twittered, "Tweet, tweet-tweet, tweet-tweet."

In each show, Berle relied on his manic anything-for-a-laugh delivery, but radio for him was a fifteen-year warm-up act for television, where he triumphed over all. As Steve Allen once wrote, "It is not correct to say that [Milton Berle] has more talent than energy. Part of his talent *is* his energy."

Berle was well aware that he wasn't meant for radio, and wrote in his autobiography, "Reading from a script didn't feel as good to me. I was too used to winging it in front of a live audience . . . I did okay, but I never felt I was getting across at my best."

"For a guy who never made it big in radio, I was always on (the air)," he added, a succinct review of his radio career. In 1948, itching to get into TV, he tried to negotiate for a television version of the *Philip Morris Playhouse*; the cigarette company decided against TV and also dropped his radio show. Berle, crestfallen, slunk back to the agency that handled the Gillette show and hustled a variety hour called *The Texaco Star Theater,* a forgotten forerunner to his famous TV show two years later.

The show ran on ABC Wednesday nights, and the reason for its success, acknowledges Berle, was head writer Nat Hiken (more famous later for creating *The Phil Silvers Show*). Hiken rounded up a cast of adept second bananas—Arnold Stang (also Berle's scrawny TV stooge), Pert Kelton, Frank Gallop, and Al Kelly, the double-talk guy; its high point each week was a sketch called "The Berles at Home," a battling husband-and-wife Bickersons riff. This final radio show legitimized Berle as a draw and became his launching pad into television under the Texaco flag. The sponsor signed him up in 1948 for thirty-nine radio shows on ABC and thirty-nine TV shows for NBC. Berle was off and mugging but not as cocksure as he seemed, wondering, "Radio was here to stay, but was television?" Yet he hit TV running and never looked back, taking care to build himself a runway into the studio audience, just as he'd done in vaudeville. Berle's reputation—and nickname—as the "Thief of Bad Gags" began with a mock feud between him and a comic named Richie Craig, who once said of Berle, "I'm still not sure whether Milton Berle sounds like all comedians or all comedians sound like Milton Berle." In brief, Berle was not sui generis; he was the entire genre embodied in one loudmouthed guy—the manic comic who won't shut up until you laugh.

Much of his appeal on radio, which later carried over into video, depended on his self-deprecating manner. He made mincemeat of the jokes, the show—and himself, taking us into his confidence that he knew, and he knew that *we* knew, how second-rate it all was. His what-the-hell-it's-only-a-stupid-show attitude helped the program limp along and gave Berle his rapport with listeners. Irving Brecher, who began his career writing gags for Berle and went on to create *The Life of Riley*, says, "Berle wasn't a hit on radio. He couldn't get a rating. He worked too fast."

Vaudeville performers like Berle and Bert Lahr were used to working up an audience, taking their time to build a performance, playing the crowd, and feeling their way through a show, moment by moment. They had the leeway and the luxury to fill or tighten according to the vibes, to throw out what wasn't working and toss in something that might, to alert the audience when something funny was about to happen. According to Arnold Stang: "Berle did everything—he told the bandleader how to play, the singers how to sing. He was just an overpowering personality."

MAYBE THE BEST WAY TO fathom the radio appeal of lowbrow clowns like Abbott and Costello is to note that they found their groove early and stuck to it doggedly, first on stage, then in radio, and finally in films and on TV, which revived their reputations.

On radio *The Abbott and Costello Show* remained true to the team's vaudeville roots, indulging in formulaic two-man repartee, often disguised in a bare-bones sketch. If they went Christmas shopping, it was just an excuse on which to hang one-liners, timeworn laugh cues triggered by then-mirth-provoking references to a girdle or somebody's mother-in-law. A reference to a mohair coat led inexorably to Lou's line that Moe must not have any hair left.

Although regarded by some as a low-rent Laurel and Hardy, their classic stooge-straightman act was hugely popular, with its roots in ragtag burlesque, where survival of the fastest and loudest was the law. To break up the formula, Lou would play, in falsetto, his kid brother Sebastian. The first bit they ever did in radio became their most memorable, the classic "Who's on First?" routine that nailed down their place in comedy history and enshrined them in baseball's Hall of Fame, where their exchange still runs on a continuous loop. It was supposedly written into a radio contract that they must perform the bit once a month on their show.

Bud Abbott was the definitive straight man; Lou Costello, the bewildered dunce confused by language who had begun his career as the dummy in Dutch acts, where the basic joke was an immigrant who doesn't comprehend English. They met as two singles in search of a partner, Costello looking for a smoother straight man and Abbott in need of a permanent opposite. Abbott's wife, Betty, first envisioned them as a team and brought them together in 1935, when they were wedded for life as Abbott and Costello. (In vaudeville, the straight man's name almost always went first and usually entitled him to 60 percent of the take, to compensate for his reduced status as a laugh-getter and to ensure his loyalty.) Unlike a lot of burlesque acts, they "worked clean," which helped later when they moved into radio, and gained them a following in films among kids and adults. As Costello's daughter said of her father, "He was a little boy in a grown-up's body."

The team's persistent broadcasting career included five years as floating guest stars, breaking in as a replacement for Henny Youngman on Kate Smith's show in 1938. Youngman chose them, he said. "I closed my eyes and I saw they could do it on radio"—unlike a lot of slapstick acts. "Who's on First?" led to a contract with Smith. At first, however, they were said to sound too much alike, so Costello raised his voice a few notches.

In the summer of 1940, they filled in for Fred Allen and two years later had their own show on NBC, which ran for five years. Illness and a feud forced them off the air (in the 1945 season, they spoke only on the air); Costello had rheumatic fever and Abbott became a heavy drinker. They were replaced that year by the arranged comic marriage of Jimmy Durante and Garry Moore.

Abbott and Costello were so hot by the mid-1940s, grinding out three or four movies a year, that they considered buying Universal Studios, which their films helped rescue, but eventually wound up broke and unemployable, with tax and gambling debts and both men in ill health. It was Costello who, not long after his baby son drowned in a swimming pool, decided to end their twenty-one-year career. He died in 1959 at the age of fifty-two. Abbott hung on until 1974, when he died at seventy-eight, alcoholic and still broke.

"Who's on First?" went a long way toward keeping their names alive, although their films have had a steady video afterlife. The baseball bit is quintessential Abbott and Costello, with Lou playing the rumpled mischievous fatso, the pudgy kid forever in trouble (with his trademark bawl, "I'm a *ba-a-a-ad* boy!"), and Bud the slender, behatted, sarcastic, chiding father figure. In fact, they performed many more clever routines, but always using the same hook of Lou misunderstanding Bud's point ("Should I back up?" "Go ahead," etc.), or simply his language.

Their many movies and TV guest shots (plus a short-lived television show that was simply a compilation of ancient vaudeville bits) endeared them to new audiences and had a lasting impact on such unlikely disciples as Jerry Seinfeld, who has acknowledged that their routines inspired him and his TV series. Abbott and Costello, he said, "were a seminal influence in my life. We're always joking about how we do stuff from *their* show. George [Jason Alexander] and I will often get into a riff that has the rhythm from the old Abbott and Costello shows." Praising their timing and byplay, Seinfeld observed, "To me, comedically, they were very sophisticated"—not just the daffy knockabout team seen in clips from such zany films as *Abbott and Costello*

Meet Frankenstein. It was Bud Abbott who perhaps best summed up their comic methodology: "We let a molehill become a mountain."

OF ALL UNLIKELY VAUDEVILLE COMICS, the invincible Red Skelton made the most successful leap into radio, mainly because he had goofy voices—verbal funny faces of a sort—and vocal pratfalls to fall back on in his gallery of clownish burlesque characters: the Mean Widdle Kid, Clem Kadiddlehopper, Willy Lump-Lump, Deadeye, San Fernando Red, and his "Guzzler's Gin" pitchman, who grows progressively drunker on his own product. (Jackie Gleason later stole the idea in a thinly veiled TV version.) Skelton, a former circus clown who struggled with scripted material, was as farcical as radio ever got. He was so addicted to clowning that after the show was over, he would often caper for another hour or so just for the studio audience.

The Skelton show not only was written by committee, like many a comedy show, but often sounded it. There was little continuity in the script, which was interrupted every few lines with the sound of Skelton cracking up at his own jokes or at his or someone else's fluffs. As a Catholic kid from a small town in Indiana, Skelton was always something of an outsider in the tight-knit circle of radio comedians, many of them streetwise New York Jews who had grown up together in delis and resorts. Edna Skelton, his wife, managed Red's career (much like Danny Kaye's take-charge wife, Sylvia Fine) and hired gagmen, whom she purposely kept apart, requesting that each writer submit a separate script, after which the Skeltons would clip jokes and glue them together as if assembling a ransom note.

As Jack Douglas, one of those writers, recalled only too well: "The scripts would be in terrible shape by the time they went to mimeo. And no wonder. Christ, I'd go over there to deliver a routine and I'd see Skelton on the floor, cutting and pasting things. And he cut so quickly with the scissors you knew damn well he was probably cutting off the most important lines in the whole routine. When I'd go over to the house, he and I and Edna would be sitting around his big dining room table; he'd want me to read stuff aloud because he couldn't read it. Well, not couldn't—but it would take him a lifetime to read four pages."

The gag writer Ben Freedman added: "Red was suspicious of anything new and didn't always understand the humor of it right away. He might have to mull it over for a couple of weeks or perhaps months. Later, he'd pull it out of the joke file and offer it as something he'd just originated and put it in the script, and then say, 'Now why can't you guys come up with something like that?' If any of us dared to say we already had, he'd blow his stack." Larry Rhine says of Skelton, for whom he created Clem Kadiddlehopper, "You just stayed out of his way. He felt they were all his characters and he didn't want to divide up the honors with the writers." Skelton rarely saw his writers until rehearsals. "When the script was finished, it was delivered to him by messenger," recalled the gagman Milt Josefsberg. "Moreover, there were no discussions or conferences on the telephone, since Red had a phone phobia and refused to talk to his writers, or practically anyone else, on that instrument."

The actress Shirley Mitchell, who worked with several comedians— Eddie Cantor, Jack Benny, Lucille Ball, and Jim and Marian Jordan— says Skelton is the only comic she would classify as a problem. "He wasn't a tyrant, but he was just so undisciplined. He never did the same line twice the same way, but he's a genius. Red was like a child. His first wife, Edna, watched over him like a little boy." Skelton was a fifteen-year-old usher at a Kansas City burlesque house when he met Edna, and she remained close to him as a writer and business manager long after their divorce. "She brought me up from $50 a week to $7,500," he once said.

Despite Skelton's temperament, and lame-brain sketches, his radio show lasted long enough for him to segue into TV, his natural turf. Sherwood Schwartz, who worked for him in TV, remembers that Skelton was by then so radio-trained that he nearly flopped on television. Schwartz recalls: "I had grave reservations when CBS asked me to do the Skelton show, because I knew he was crazy—talented but crazy. I'd heard he was particularly vicious with writers. He was in deep trouble when I joined him, because he was doing a show that was 80 percent verbal and 20 percent mime. I changed the format and added much more mime and turned the show around in a few months. I just allowed him to be funny—that's the job of a writer. You can't *make* a man funny. You find the part of him that can resonate. In radio I always wrote visually anyway."

Schwartz explains that one of Skelton's trademark habits on TV, breaking up at his own jokes, was really a survival technique. "He didn't do it to get a laugh but so he could look at the script on the floor. He couldn't remember a joke." In seven years, Schwartz never had a meeting with Skelton, reflecting the comic's refusal to acknowledge that he needed writers. Max Shulman, the humorist, once said he was discouraged from becoming a radio comedy writer when he noticed how comedians would refer to "my writers" as if talking about "my neckties."

Recalling his Skelton years, Schwartz continues: "Red never gave any credit to anyone. Noncredit never bothered me—I've given away credit so people could get into the Writers Guild. It was not just Skelton's neglect of writers but his attacks on them. On talk shows, he'd always say how useless they were. He never understood the philosophy behind a show." When Schwartz finally left, the comic considered it a betrayal. Schwartz's brother Al was then writing for the show as well, and after someone broke the news to Red, said Schwartz, "They told me how those little beady eyes of his narrowed and he yelled, 'Then fire that other fucking Schwartz, too! And from now on I don't want any more Schwartzes working on my show.' My brother Al, who was a trusting, innocent soul, didn't get it. I told him, 'Look, we're talking about a six-year-old child.' "

Well into his eighties, the childlike Skelton ("I dood it") still trotted out those ancient preradio circus characters in concerts and bid audiences farewell with his meek little wave and humble "God bless," endearing him forevermore as what Steve Allen termed his "professional nice guy–little boy that is one more of his characters . . ." Although Skelton's shows were bottom-rung radio comedy, at the opposite pole from Fred Allen and Jack Benny, he got away with it merrily until his death in 1997.

LIKE RED SKELTON, Eddie Cantor had the common touch, but the reasons for his radio popularity eluded those too young to have seen his movies or stage act. Even so, his energy and eagerness to please made him a radio fixture from 1931 to 1949. His career spanned radio—in 1924 he had even made an experimental talkie for Dr. Lee DeForest, *A Few Moments with Eddie Cantor.*

Cantor, once billed the "Apostle of Pep," was a classic low-comedy hustler who, by moving his show from city to city, juggled three careers at once—on the radio, on the road, and on the screen, each outlet feeding the other. Without skipping a beat, he rehearsed and headlined a 1941 Broadway show, *Banjo Eyes,* while doing his weekly radio program. As his biographer, Herbert G. Goldman, reported, the canny Cantor also managed the careers of people on his show and took 10 percent. Yet he campaigned against high agents' fees, demanded better working conditions for chorus girls, and hung out a shingle as a "radio consultant." He had ten fingers in every pie.

A giant Broadway star when he entered radio, Cantor continued to trade on his stage and movie persona, which over the air was devoid of much crossover charm: His much-imitated skipping, hand-clapping, eyeballing stage business was totally lost on listeners. Ninety percent of Cantor's appeal, like Jolson's, was his singing; the rest was mechanical comic filler comprised of standard bits and pieces studded with guest stars like John Barrymore.

In one such sketch, Barrymore joins Cantor, playing half of a vaudeville team—"Grogan and Krausemeier." The idea, used by nearly all the major comedy shows, was to parade a highfalutin guest (often British) from theater, films, the opera, even politics, and thus reveal the celebrity as a good sport, a man of the people who enjoyed slumming in radio. It was really a subtle form of back-scratching. The host got to rub elbows with "real" artists, giving the comedy shows a classy veneer. On one Cantor show, for instance, Leslie Howard sang, "If you knew Susan, like I know Susan, Ah, me, ah what a wench!" and on another, Lauritz Melchior crooned, "Aïda, sweet as apple ceda."

The comedy writer Hal Kanter began his career peddling jokes to Cantor. Kanter—famous for saying "Radio is theater of the mind; TV is theater of the mindless"—reminisces: "I'd listen to his show and say, 'I can write jokes as funny as that,' so I walked from my rooming house to his show, and told the guard, 'Mr. Kanter is here to see Mr. Cantor, figuring he'd see me because of our names, although his real name was Iskowitch. I was seventeen years old and had the nerve of a burglar." Cantor wouldn't hire Kanter but one of Cantor's writers, Hugh Wedlock, Jr., hired him to write jokes for him at ten dollars a week, jokes which Wedlock would resell to Cantor. "So I became a ghostwriter to a ghostwriter."

For years, Cantor was dependent on a man named David Freedman, whose joke files were legendary and who became a life-support system for many early radio comics. Joke merchandising was a heavy industry in early radio. Freedman, recalled the comedy writer Carroll Carroll, himself a walking joke file, had an "atelier of puns, quips, funny sayings, and vaudeville yocks" stored in files that lined the walls of his three-story Central Park West penthouse, where young men combed magazines in search of gags for all occasions, which were then neatly collated, filed, and cross-indexed, to be switched and reused at will—to wit, a joke about a fat man eating a hot dog at a football game was filed under "fat," "football," "food," and "frankfurter." Freedman and other part-time gag writers would sit around Freedman's place schmoozing, spritzing, and cobbling together entire monologues for comics.

Freedman found crafting jokes for radio much tougher slogging than writing for vaudeville. "On the stage, if the material is funny, audiences can be made to laugh at any sort of low character, grotesque, or buffoon," he said. "You can't push such a character on the radio, however, because a radio character is a guest in the home. And people don't want to receive 'mugs' in their homes." Perhaps, but no such comic niceties detered such low-comic mugs as Wynn, Berle, Abbott and Costello, Skelton, or Durante.

Cantor's on-air character was once described as an "impudent little scamp," but the imp often came across as desperate, dated, and hokey. On none of his various shows—*The Chase and Sanborn Hour, The Camel Comedy Caravan, Time to Smile, The Eddie Cantor Pabst Blue Ribbon Show*—did Cantor exhibit an especially funny delivery or voice, but he made up for it by projecting himself with a mechanical freneticism. Despite the liberal use of guests and wacky burlesque relief like the characters of the Mad Russian and Parkyakarkus, or a comic violinist virtuoso named Rubinoff, Cantor was caught in a comic time warp, yet he lasted until he moved over to TV in 1949.

By then, he was thought to be used up, but at fifty-eight he had a brief rebirth on *The Colgate Comedy Hour,* on which he suddenly found himself on friendly terrain. The critic Ben Gross wrote that "Cantor came into his own for the first time in the many years he has been on the air . . . the dynamic comedian that he was in the days of the *Ziegfeld Follies.* He sings, he dances, he acts with cyclonic energy." Three years later, an exhausted Cantor, saddled with a heart condition, returned to radio as a glorified DJ on a network show, reduced to rerunning old radio routines between records.

Mary Jane Higby, a soap opera actress who worked with him early in her career, recalled how Cantor would "do anything for a laugh. If he thinks the material is dying he's apt to slug you"—or, as several actresses discovered, goose you on the air. To old-time vaudeville comics, she noted, "silence was the sound of failure." As one radio historian put it, "Cantor believed laughter was contagious"—the premise behind TV laugh tracks. A worried, uncertain Cantor, refusing to shake his stage ways, demanded a studio audience—indeed, depended on it for survival, doing dress rehearsals before a live audience to test-market the gags; he would hastily alter the broadcast version if something died during an afternoon rehearsal.

To ensure his radio acceptance, Cantor proclaimed his lovability, patriotism, and cozy family life. He was an activist entertainer who entertained troops, was the first president of Actors Equity, helped found the broadcasting union AFRA (American Federation of Radio Artists), headed the Screen Actors Guild, and made weekly charity appeals.

But for all his public good works, Cantor had few fans among his writers. "I hated Cantor," says Bob Weiskopf, who worked for him early in his comedy-writing career. "He was a bad man. The five daughters all hated him. He was chasing women around while poor Ida would sit in her room crying. He was also cheap. But all the mothers loved him. My own mother refused to believe he wasn't a nice man." Some of his daughters were hurt by eighteen years of jokes at their expense. "Long-suffering" was Budd Schulberg's term for Ida, who once described herself as the best-known "non–show business person in show business." Despite his oft-expressed devotion to home and hearth, Cantor had a long, well-known (within showbiz circles) affair with the comedian Joan Davis. The endless jokes about his doting wife, Ida—who in real life spent much of her time gambling at Las Vegas—and their five unmarriageable daughters led you to think that his family was his best, perhaps only, gag.

Mort Lachman, who went on to serve twenty-eight years with Bob Hope as head writer and producer, also began his comedy writing career with Cantor.

"We had a very personal relationship," Lachman recalls. "He would use me to annoy the writing staff to prove he didn't need them—it was very weird. He would take me to the show with him and bring me to his house; he didn't know I was married, and I think he was trying to marry me off to one of his daughters." Lachman agrees that Cantor was not a born comedian. "He begged for laughs, and that bothered me. I was a purist in those days; today, I beg. He was a difficult man to work with, a very limited talent, but he got the most out of what little he had."

Like Ed Wynn, Cantor happily indulged in sight gags over the air, breaking eggs and squirting seltzer. His theory: If the studio audience was laughing, listeners would presume some terribly hilarious goings-on. Harry Von Zell remembered how Cantor would jump up and down and prance around, as on stage. "And if there was a passage of music, or a segue of some kind, he would literally dance away from the mike, like he was putting on a regular circus performance."

Cantor had a rack holding thirty costumes, including baggy pants and ladies' dresses, recalls Arnold Stang, "and he was constantly changing costumes for the studio audience. He was a frightened little man—very strange, self-centered, egotistical, and arrogant. I don't know what was funny about him to this day." After a rehearsal in front of an audience, says Stang, Cantor would steal all the other actors' best laughs, change the script, and reassign their lines to himself. Stang finally left. "I told him, 'I'm not going to keep breaking in your material for you.' And in many cases, he wouldn't get a laugh with it, because it was written for my character."

The frantic Cantor was a one-man comic band—straight man, singer, monologuist, host—and was a hit almost at once, earning eventually twenty thousand dollars per show, an enormous amount then, even for a star. Like Berle, he endeared himself with windup energy and seemed to will himself to radio stardom.

He was also one of the first big stars to step through the dial and appeal directly to his audience, person to person, blurring the line between star and human being. With his do-gooder boosterism and pro-family stance, he became an early role model–celebrity, especially among Jewish listeners. If he wasn't a great entertainer at least he could be a great humanitarian. "To Jews," wrote Herbert Goodman, "Cantor seemed to many the epitome of *Yiddishkeit*—a blend of model citizen and personal humanitarian. . . . He made one feel good to be a Jew. He would have made a great politician." Indeed, Cantor was a rough version of today's performer-cum-politico. While he believed in his many causes, he also used them to fan the cause of Eddie Cantor. Like other stars with mega-egos—George M. Cohan, Al Jolson, Frank Sinatra—he could be kind or cruel. One day he would volunteer to pay a staff writer's salary while he attended dental school; the next day he would steal a comic's catchphrase and make him feel honored to be victimized by so great a personage as Eddie Cantor.

Cantor also was the master, if not the originator, of the heartfelt appeal, which planted the first seed of celebrity do-goodism. Before there were mawkish Jerry Lewis telethons, there was Eddie Cantor on radio asking you, in his imploring manner, to give generously to the March of Dimes, the Heart Fund, the Boy Scouts of America, the National Myopia Society, or whatever charity tugged at his heart that week; he was an early supporter of statehood for Israel. When he ran out of charities, he began adding "drive-safely" farewells and public service spots promoting Flag Day, Brotherhood Week, churchgoing, and Americanism in general. American Legion essay contests were heavily promoted by Cantor, with such topics as "How Can America Stay Out of War?" Cantor would end a typical show with, "It's nice to hang out the flag on Flag Day, but why just on Flag Day? Why not give our flag a permanent wave!" As his biographer writes, "He had become less a comedian than an ambassador of good will, less an entertainer than a lecturer."

In an in-house memo designed to keep Cantor in line, Young & Rubicam, the ad agency for Cantor's show, dealt with his urge to display his public-spirited side: "We are all of the opinion that we should present Cantor to the public strictly as a funny man, and try to avoid any publicity that would indicate that Cantor ever has a serious thought or is guilty of a serious deed."

Over the years, he had been an outspoken advocate of various causes, an avid FDR advocate who dined at the White House, and an early crusader against Hitler. He began a drive in 1938 to get five hundred Jewish children out of Germany, and even denounced Henry Ford, a known anti-Semite, as un-Christian and un-American. Even so, Gary Stevens, a CBS publicist in the 1930s and later an entertainment columnist, called Cantor "a professional weeper. He wasn't phony in his on-air appeals but he certainly exploited it."

Cantor not only pioneered the Moment of Candor that all but suffocated broadcasting in the 1980s and 1990s—he called it his "serious spot"—but also delivered what might have been the first truth-in-packaging commercial. He confessed he didn't drink coffee, but that if he did it would certainly be Chase and Sanborn. He might also be credited with initiating cross-programming, purposely scheduling a Dinah Shore song opposite a commercial on Fred Allen's rival show. Shore was one of many Cantor radio discoveries—Deanna Durbin, Bobby Breen, and Eddie Fisher were others. Eddie Cantor may have lacked true radio charisma, but in his doughty, irrepressible, and insistent way, he was as resourceful a broadcaster as David Sarnoff.

LIKEWISE, MUCH OF THE roughhouse magic of Jimmy Durante escaped listeners who hadn't seen him in glorious person. Even so, he was a huge hit on the air, because most listeners already had seen him on stage, where he tore up a song or a piano or the whole joint. The nightclub was his natural setting, but he reigned in every venue and medium—even radio, where he radiated charm invisibly.

Durante's raggedy Brooklyn voice was, like Louis Armstrong's, the essence of his irrepressibly anarchic spirit. Da Great Durante could deliver a line with enormously lovable oomph and innate comic finesse, and his croaking ballads simultaneously made you grin and your eyes brim with tears. In the words of Lou Clayton, his early partner, "You can warm your hands on this man."

Durante was pure, complete, unabashed entertainer, a man possessed with the desire to please at all costs; and he aged beautifully, unlike many entertainers, never wearing out his welcome. His dynamic presence and rumpled personality broke the sight barrier. The very idea of a man who sounded like Durante actually singing, in that ramshackle voice, was enough to make anybody laugh. As he used to say, "I got dat note from Bing—and boy, was *he* glad ta get rid of it!"

His growly delivery, with overenunciated words and precisely rendered mispronunciations, was a joke unto itself—all of it embellished with one of his many Duranteisms, always shouted in a voice of pretend anger: "Dem are da conditions dat prevail," "I'm sur-*round*-ed by assassins!," and—slapping his pants with his palms or striking a profile that revealed his prominent proboscis in all its splendor—"*Ev*-rybody wants ta get intah da act!" After a particularly good line, or even a groaner (it hardly mattered in Durante's case), he would proudly yelp, "I got a million of 'em! A *mill*-ion of 'em!"

The man oozed charm, no matter the medium or the material. Durante transcended dumb songs and lousy jokes by infusing them with a gentle, joyous spirit that had to be heard (or, far better still, seen) to be believed. Twenty years after his death, his spirit had a brief revival on the soundtrack of *Sleepless in Seattle,* when yuppies who had never heard of anyone called Schnozzola were newly delighted; as on radio, it wasn't necessary to see him on screen to be embraced by his spirit. Even now, especially now, he seems an unlikely and wholly remarkable character, a Bowery leprechaun who captivated every audience he ever faced—or didn't face. The critic Gilbert Seldes got it about right when he wrote that Durante "offers himself where others exploit themselves. [He] communicates so unfailingly the laughter that rises out of love." Nobody was ever remotely like him.

Durante seems to have been born disheveled—he lost his hair early and soon grew into a homely snaggletoothed guy with a squat, bowlegged stance, raspy voice, and an innate flair for malapropisms nobody ever had to write for him: "cazzamaclismic," "catastrascope," "exubilant." Durante seemed built for radio, a natural-born Mr. Malaprop. When writers tried to invent mangled syntax for him—called "mals" by the gagmen—he even stumbled over the mistakes; Durante, who spoke in the street slang and cadences of his youth, had to mess up words on his own or not at all.

Bob Schiller wrote for Durante during his last season on radio, 1949. Durante had entered radio in 1943 on *The Camel Comedy Caravan,* where producer Phil Cohan teamed him up with a promising new comic named Garry Moore to revive Durante's diminishing fame; the team broke up when Moore left to emcee *Take It or Leave It,* but

Durante went on. Schiller recalls: "Durante was not a very bright man—he did what his handlers told him to do—but he was just a joy. He'd come in, make a few changes, and leave. We'd write the show at the ad agency. Jimmy was like Ed Wynn. They weren't real people; they were clowns. Durante would walk in, say hello, and you'd laugh."

Durante reveled in his destruction of the language. "I don't split infinitives," he would say. "When I go ta woik on an infinitive, I break it up in little pieces." He once said, "I'm smart enough to know dat the day I starts talkin' good English, back I goes to da pianner!" Durante had such a unique speech pattern that almost two decades after his death, you can hear him uttering a line, sensing which words and syllables he would accent. "Da whole idea of my act," he told Maurice Zolotow, "is that I come out and I'm supposed to be mad at my musicians. Ever't'in' else comes outta dat." Were Durante to reappear on TV now, nobody would know what to make of him. Critics might assume he was a performance artist making a profound statement about man's chaotic state as he smashed a piano to smithereens, or that he was mocking the act of crooning when he sang such infectious non-songs (many of his own devising, often in duets with unlikely partners such as Ethel Barrymore or Helen Traubel) as, "So I Ups to Him," "I'm Jimmy, That Well-Dressed Man," "A Dissa and a Datta," "Didja Ever Have the Feeling That You Wanted to Go, and Still Have the Feeling That You Wanted to Stay?," "Umbriago," and "I Know Darn Well I Can Do Without Broadway But Can Broadway Do Without Me?"

He perfected a style of patter song, reminiscent of George Burns's act, of interrupting a nonsense song with jokes. Durante once explained, in his unique style, how it all worked: "I like to tell a joke wit' a song, 'cause I avoid the monogamy of just tellin' straight jokes. When I finish up da joke and den pick up on da song again, it's like givin' da joke a boost over da fence." Most radio listeners knew what Durante looked like, a constant source of jokes on his shows, but his voice told the whole story. When he moved to TV, he would exit upstage into diminishing pools of light, a bittersweet farewell, crooning, "We've had a few laughs, now it's time for toodle-oo. Au revoir, auf Wiedersehen, and inka-dinka-doo . . ." with a final fond doff of the hat to "Mrs. Calabash, where-*ev*-ah ya ahr."

As to the mystery surrounding the identity of Mrs. Calabash, various talmudic interpretations speculate that it was a pet name for his deceased first wife; a racehorse (taken from the name of a pipe smoked by Sherlock Holmes made from a calabash gourd); a lost love; the widowed mother of a little boy who wrote Jimmy long letters; a little girl in grade school who snubbed him; or a nickname for Lou Clayton, one of Durante's original partners, who died young. Durante's second wife, Margie, said that Mrs. Calabash referred to all of his lonely listeners. Whoever Mrs. Calabash was or was not, as George Burns once noted, "She gave Jimmy one of the most important things any entertainer can have—a great finish."

— 3 —
THE ANTICOMEDIAN

IF BUSTER KEATON WAS, IN JAMES AGEE'S WORDS, "the most silent of the silent comics," then surely Jack Benny was the quietest of all the radio comics. Benny was at his funniest at his most serious, doing as little as possible for a laugh. Only George Burns, his crony and comic Boswell, rivaled him as a straight man, but Burns was never meant to be funny, whereas Benny evoked laughs as jokes flew at him from every direction.

There was a further, even subtler difference. Burns was a traditional straight man, but Benny, a kind of anticomic, was a comedian in the guise of a straight man. Benny lasted longer than almost anyone else in radio because he was so mild-mannered, the Clark Kent of comics. Often the less Benny reacted, the funnier he was, for beneath the silence he was a seething pot of humiliation, exasperation, and buried anger that from time to time burbled to the surface in his ineffectual yelp, "Now *cut* that out!" Benny was revered because he was artless, daring to do the minimum in a medium that most comedians felt demanded maximum noise and speed; he was the comic personification of less is more, an extension of his blasé vaudeville persona.

George Burns once said of Benny, "No one was better suited for radio than Jack. Radio consisted of sound and silence. That was it. While the rest of us were trying to figure out ways of using sound, Jack was smart enough to figure out how to use the silence. No one ever got more out of nothing than he did." In Burns's words, "Jack Benny changed radio. He did something no comedian had ever done before—he eliminated most of the jokes."

Jokes seemed to him too obvious a device. Milt Josefsberg, the long-time Benny writer, said the only way to get a joke past Benny was to cloak it as a character trait. One of his writers once noted, "Jack said the word 'joke' as though he were afraid the gods of comedy were

Overleaf: Jack Benny (*third from left*) with writer Bill Morrow, comic Artie Auerbach ("Mr. Kitzle"), and writer Ed Beloin

going to wash out his mouth with soap." During his elder-statesman period, Benny once remarked that many radio comics became victims of their jokes. "The joke is the simplest method of drawing laughs and most comedians—in fact, almost all—use it too often. Because of its simplicity and repetition, the gag tends to dull the audience. The constant use of this method is the cause of so many failures among comedians who start their careers with great promise and then suddenly flop."

Ernst Lubitsch, who directed Benny in the movie *To Be or Not to Be,* once told him: "You think you are a comedian. You are not a comedian. You are not even a clown. You are fooling the public for thirty years. You are fooling even yourself. A clown—he is a performer what is doing funny things. A comedian—he is a performer what is saying funny things. But you, Jack, you are an actor playing the part of a comedian and this you are doing very well. But do not worry, I keep your secret to myself."

Although he came out of vaudeville (as a teenage violinist in an act called Salisbury and Benny, and good enough to attract an offer to tour with the Marx Brothers), young Benny Kubelsky had a modern sensibility and a staid midwestern manner, the first of a new species of comedian whose laughs derived from situation and characterization. He appealed to high-, low-, and middlebrows, because he didn't attempt to appeal to anyone. He played a nonentity, a long-suffering guy who, it was once said, practiced the fine art of self-humiliation. When Benny first began, he cast himself as a womanizer and drinker, but he decidedly was far too timid and genteel-sounding for that.

Benny was the most human of comedians, the least self-consciously "funny" funny man. His humor came out of familiar characters' relationships with him. Because the audience knew the characters, lines that weren't necessarily funny per se became laughs in the context of Benny's persona. In George Burns's words: "Jack said his best lines took five years to write, because that's how long it took for the audience to really get to know the character."

Analyzing his character's universality, Benny said: "I take on the frailties of all men. They accept my character as they would a character in a play. They accept what you do on the stage, because they're educated to accept the character." He added, "I always play up to my audience. We feel we represent the audience. In us, they see themselves." For Josefsberg, Benny had more audience identification than any other entertainer.

Jack Benny was a middle-aged, middle-American, middle-class Everyman, a droll, unhurried comedian. As opposed to most comedians of that era, or even this one, he labored to maintain a certain decorum. He hated to be caught in the act of being funny: "When your audience sees you working for a laugh, they're all tired out when you get to the laugh. For that reason, we try to make our show as off-hand as possible Our motto is: Be nonchalant!" In vaudeville, Benny had used his face sparingly, rarely mugging, and this helped him become a hit on radio so effortlessly. Shrewdly, he used silences to compel an audience to pay attention.

Benny originally had planned to make his living as a musician and segued into comedy through a violin act called, variously, "Ben K. Benny: Fiddle Funology," "Jack Benny: Fun with a Fiddle," and "Jack Benny: Aristocrat of Humor." He didn't converse on stage full-time until a navy show in 1917, when the writer gave him a line, which he embroidered; by the end of the run he had the main comedy part. "That was the first time I realized I could do comedy." One of his first laughs was, "I know all you sailors complain about the food. Well, you've got no right to complain. The enlisted men get the same food as the officers get . . . only *theirs* is cooked."

From then on, as with Henny Youngman, his fiddle became a prop, and he was first introduced on radio not as a vaudeville comic but as a "popular master of ceremonies." He wasn't a huge vaudeville star, too understated for most audiences—the very thing that would make him so ideal for radio. He was heavily influenced by stage comic Frank Fay's easy, conversational, fadeaway style.

Like many performers, Benny tried to ignore radio at first, considering it a fad, but a chance encounter with Ed Sullivan in 1932 changed his mind. At the time, Sullivan did an interview show with news, sports, and guests, sort of a Broadway column of the air twenty years before he stumbled into TV, and he asked Benny to appear on it. Based on that appearance, Canada Dry gave him a show, billing him "the Canada Dry comedian." Benny was intrigued by radio, yet wary. "I don't know anything about radio," he had told Sullivan, who said, "Nobody does"

(Sullivan's own success was stunning evidence of that), an accurate summation of the anything-goes quality of the medium in the early 1930s.

Many comics were mike-shy, with good reason. As Burns once told Benny, half kiddingly: "Jack, there's absolutely nothing to worry about. Nothing at all. Just forget about the fact that more people are going to hear you on the radio than heard you during your entire career in vaudeville and that if they don't like you, your career is probably over." Instinctive genius or not, Benny later recalled that "radio was not the soft touch my agent had promised. Those were kind of nervous days for me."

Although he was a nervous man personally, a nail-biter and a pacer, Benny's career never seemed in doubt; even on stage he exuded serenity. At the time he plunged, or perhaps waded, into radio, he was starring in Earl Carroll's *Vanities* for fifteen hundred dollars a week, but got out of his contract. Burns claimed Benny never felt he needed radio, as other vaudevillians did, but Benny said, "I gave it all up just to get into radio. I could see [vaudeville] was nothing—radio was the thing. I knew you had to get into it, the same as I knew I *had* to get into television." When he surpassed Eddie Cantor in popularity in 1937, he established radio's supremacy over vaudeville, became a fixture for fifteen years, and finally a national treasure.

Many comics viewed radio as an easy gig, a sort of one-year stand or open-mike vaudeville, but Benny took the long view and adapted himself to it. Radio, he intuited, was different, and he approached its unique dynamics with respect. Harry Conn, then the highest paid comedy writer in the business, developed the lasting Benny format that used the show's regular cast as believable larger-than-life characters in an ongoing show-within-a-show, a kind of *sitcom vérité*. Conn advanced the comedy-cum-variety show format by turning it into a neatly disguised situation comedy.

On his debut in 1934, Benny had been flat, tentative, and awkward, delivering an unfunny monologue without benefit of an audience, and the jokes deservedly landed with a thud, a far cry from the suave, polished Jack Benny of only a few years hence. When Canada Dry dropped him, Chevrolet quickly picked him up and he again began razzing the sponsor. Columnist Heywood Broun wrote, "In days to come, a grateful people [should] erect a statue to Jack Benny, with the simple inscription: 'In memory of the first man to take the curse off radio commercials.' "

Such high-level attention instantly elevated Benny above the common rabble of radio comics. General Foods jumped on board with a dessert that hadn't been selling and pitched the product by changing the name of the show to *The Jell-O Program,* which ran at 7 P.M. every Sunday night for twenty-one years. Benny owned that half hour; CBS promised him 7 P.M. as long as he wanted it, and he now had a free hand. "I warned them I wouldn't make ridiculous claims about Jell-O. I intended to make fun of it and predicted I would sell a lot of Jell-O." To make sure, he opened with, "Jell-O, everybody!" General Foods, which took it all with a brave smile, once measured that sponsor identification for Jack Benny and Jell-O was 91 percent, a mark never topped in radio. When an insurance company that planned to use him in its ads found he was liked by 97 percent of the public, Benny asked, "What did I do to that 3 percent?"

Benny sensed that he didn't need to do that much on radio to get his laughs. By the late 1940s, his radio character was so well established that many of his reactions didn't require even audible responses. The critic Tom Shales called him "a living caricature of preening ego" that satirized us all. "He was the joke and we were the joke." Everyone knew at any given time precisely what Benny was thinking, creating a built-in laugh by using straight lines that writers built upon over time. Sight-deprived listeners could imagine Jack's nonplussed look, his anguish and confusion, whenever he was pushed too far—he was *always* being pushed too far—by a clueless Dennis Day, a pesty Mel Blanc, a nasty Frank Nelson (with his bitchy, "*Oo-ooooo,* would I!"), a sassy Rochester, a garrulous Don Wilson, a snippy Mary Livingstone, or a loudmouthed Phil Harris.

Benny's reaction was often internal: He was always swallowing his enormous pride, wrestling with his conscience, or trying to cope with the insanity and inanity that swirled about him. He perfected the use of the interior monologue, which took us deep into his fevered psyche as we heard him fretting and pondering and plotting. Everything and everyone irritated him. The world was out to get him, bug him, mock him, make his life miserable, or get a rise out of him, as if there were a worldwide conspiracy to spoil his day.

Discussing the interior monologue, Benny said, "Many comedians open with a monologue. I also did monologues—but in a different way. You might hear my footsteps, clicking along a sidewalk . . . and you'd hear me talking to myself, thinking out loud, often spoken as I was returning home." Heard over his clicking shoes on the sidewalk, a typical Benny monologue would unspool as he ruminated in a cheery inner voice: "Gee, the neighborhood sure looks nice . . . I *love* those weeping willows on Claudette Colbert's front lawn . . . And, gosh, how *nice* W. C. Fields' swimming pool looks. What a clever idea, having marbles in the bottom. No, they're not marbles, they're olives. . . ."

Although it took years for him to assemble just the right cast, his fully developed subsidiary characters became as crucial as the star. The program was all about Jack's pals, his "gang," and his supposed world. He used the real stuff of his own showbiz life to concoct a fantasy radio life. It was almost like visiting his home, where many shows were set. Benny's unique show-within-a-show idea, largely abandoned when he went on TV, prefigured Garry Shandling's avant-garde *It's Garry Shandling's Show* on 1980s TV. Shandling freely acknowledges he stole the idea from the Burns and Allen TV show, but in fact it was first done by Benny, and Burns swiped it from *him*. There were faint traces of Benny and Burns in Jerry Seinfeld's TV show, where Jerry played himself, a comedian, and bookended the plot with snippets from his stand-up monologue.

The Benny program created such a feeling of credibility that listeners liked to believe it was all true. To his chronic annoyance, many people truly thought Jack was cheap, drove a Maxwell, kept his money in a vault, and refused to give his servant a day off. Some wrote in to protest his unfair hiring practices, and one man even offered to buy his antique car. Larry Gelbart, the comedy writer, has written: "So complete was [Jack Benny's] achievement, so convincingly had he painted himself as a giant of pettiness . . . that the world paid him the ultimate compliment of accepting the artist as his own creation. It was tantamount to believing that both of Picasso's eyes were set on the same side of his face."

Benny's show took listeners inside Hollywood and, with its casual references to Los Angeles landmarks, made it all both familiar and exciting, especially the way movie stars would casually drop by Jack's house for a visit. The Benny show seemed even more authentic because of all the in Hollywood jokes—references to Mulholland Drive (a local lovers' lane), and kidding references to the May Company, Sportsman's Lodge, the Brown Derby, the La Brea Tar Pits, and Forest Lawn that made listeners in Duluth and Poughkeepsie intensely curious about Los Angeles. For L.A. tourists, it was thrilling simply to lay eyes on the May Company and discover that it really existed.

Radio, a far more informal setting than theater or vaudeville, was ideal for shows where people gathered, hung out, and, as on Benny's show, discussed putting the show together—a somewhat Pirandello-esque notion. In *Sunday Nights at Seven,* a book by Benny's daughter, Joan, with excerpts from her father's unfinished memoirs, he tells how he discovered the key to the show's intimacy: "Our audience totaled 30 million, but it really consisted of small family groups. I felt that now I understood the medium. I would play to those family groups and get them to know me and my family (the cast) as real people with real problems. Exaggerated people, yes, but fundamentally honest and true to life."

Fred Allen, Benny's longtime make-believe archenemy, was in fact his greatest admirer, and once wrote of him, "Practically all comedy shows on radio owe their structure to Benny's conceptions. He was the first to realize that the listener is not in a theater with a thousand other people. When they tune in to Benny, it's like tuning in to somebody else's house. Benny was also the first comedian to realize you could get big laughs by ridiculing yourself instead of your stooges." Benny once told Gisele MacKenzie (his onetime post-TV stage partner and rumored girl friend), "I give all the jokes to others, honey, but it's still 'The Jack Benny Show.' " Another similarity to *Seinfeld* is that Jerry, like Jack, played a comedian who was the least "funny" person on the show.

Benny's age, vanity, and penny-pincher jokes became so refined over time that eventually they weren't even jokes. The merest reference to money in Benny's presence was sufficiently funny to draw laughs, the result of a career-long setup of what Benny called "acceptance"—a form of audience affection as important to a comic as great jokes, giving punchlines a built-in cushion. Benny created a goodwill reservoir that came from a lifetime rapport with his audience. Nobody could make an audience feel as relaxed as he could. Other comics might prod, bully, or coax people into laughing, but Benny pretended he didn't care one way or the other and just happened to be strolling by when we joined him.

On the Benny show, the nuts ran the asylum while Benny, as their helpless administrator, tried to retain control. He was unable to get from one end of the show to the other without being humiliated by his underlings—not to mention Frank Nelson's gallery of snide clerks, waiters, and floorwalkers (Benny: "Excuse me, are you the ticket agent?" Nelson: "Well, what do you *think* I am in this cage—a *canary*?"). His proper British next-door neighbors, the Ronald Colmans, were especially appalled by Benny's vulgar displays of vanity, stinginess, status-seeking, and general gaucherie and gall. Everyone Benny encountered each week—violin teachers, bums, mechanics, bank guards, railroad announcers, even parrots—were dedicated to getting the star's goat. Benny's irritated responses were funnier because he wasn't a fictional character but was meant to be portraying himself.

The cast ridiculed Benny to his face. He was a star, as he kept reminding them, but one clearly without honor on his own show or even in his own house. Benny not only was making fun of himself but, in effect, ridiculing the entire celebrity ethos. Even guests humiliated their host each week, but so politely that Benny was never quite sure if they meant it; his ego was too big to grasp such a possibility. He tried ignoring the raspy wisecracks of his man Friday, the rascally Rochester.

Benny wore well because he surrounded himself with a gifted comic support system, each one amusing in his/her own way and three of whom—Phil Harris, Dennis Day, Mel Blanc—wound up with their own shows. Day, a versatile, underrated comic and mimic, starred five years on *A Day in the Life of Dennis Day*. Harris linked up with his wife, Alice Faye, on a show that lasted six years. Blanc's solo attempt, on which he played a fix-it shop owner, died after a season. Josefsberg noted that Benny was "absolutely devoid of jealousy" of fellow comics and a great booster of young comics, from Danny Kaye to Johnny Carson. Only a secure performer would let lesser comics get all the laughs.

To some, it was curious that Mary Livingstone played Benny's sarcastic girl friend when everyone knew they were married—perhaps a shrewd artistic decision by Benny, sensing that Mary could zing him more efficiently if they weren't married on the show (she often zinged him privately as well). At first, she was cast as yet another of radio's giggling man-crazy lamebrains, which changed when Dennis Day arrived and cornered the dimwit jokes. Day's character was inspired largely by his high-pitched, daffy-sounding voice—a perfect example, Benny insisted, of how all the best radio characters developed out of the actor's voice. "I made sure the characters I gave them all fit their speaking voices."

Indeed, Phil Harris's roguish bandleader grew out of Harris's brash sound. The character's randy life-style and rude manner were a new concept, according to Benny: "With all his coarseness, there was a quality of sophistication about the Phil Harris character that made him different not only from every other character on our program—but from every other character on radio. When we began featuring him, we shocked a lot of people. He was wild. He lived for pleasure. He did not believe in sin. He was completely immoral. The character was so written and so well played that you knew Phil Harris was probably the greatest fornicator of all time. When he made his first speech, usually a simple 'Hiya, Jackson,' he somehow got across the idea that he had come to the studio right after having experienced a most satisfying orgasm."

Benny added: "Harris radiated vitality, *joie de vivre,* and a sheer gusto in animal pleasures that made him unique. His voice went with the braggadocio. Everybody knows at least one person who is in some way like Phil Harris." In a typical Harris gag, Jack asks him why he's gazing so sadly at the ocean and Phil sighs, "What a shame. All that chaser going to waste." The sleazy Harris character was the only one on the show whom Benny treated as an inferior.

Mary Livingstone was an uneasy fit, an untrained performer who did the show for a lark at first; but her character grew so familiar that she couldn't quit. "Mary seemed almost completely devoid of any desire to be a performer, much less a star," claimed Josefsberg. "She had no definable function on the series." To give her something to do, they would have her read funny letters from her sister Babe or recite inane poems. Originally, she played the seventeen-year-old president of the Jack Benny Fan Club of Plainfield, New Jersey, but she was thrust into a major role when an actress missed a dress rehearsal. To her credit, however, Mary could impart a nice note of disdain to her delivery that deflated whatever was left of Jack's ego.

Over time, her early mike fright grew phobic and finally, when tape was introduced, she insisted on reading lines from home, which were then spliced into the final transcription. Now and then she fainted after shows. Veteran Benny writer George Balzer recalls, "I'd say Mary disliked performing every week, but not enough to give it up. You can faint on call, you know. I always felt Jack wasn't as concerned as he might have been." Balzer smiles knowingly. "It was a good attention-getter, let's say . . . she was a tough gal." Livingstone, no company favorite, was something of a snob, who treated the cast more like hired hands than colleagues. At home, she wore the pants. The Bennys' matchbooks were engraved MARY LIVINGSTONE, although outside the house she preferred to be known as Mrs. Jack Benny. After her death, Burns is reported to have said, "I often wondered if Jack knew Mary had very little talent," but Josefsberg noted simply, "Jack was happy if Mary was happy."

Dennis Day was a mere "kid" when he joined the show in his early twenties, a timid Irish choirboy named Owen P. (Eugene) McNulty whom Benny supposedly hired for his naïveté. Called in by Benny over the intercom to audition, Day piped, "Yes, please," which cracked Benny up and was just the quality he wanted in a fresh-faced singer to replace army-bound Kenny Baker, who in turn had replaced tenor Frank Parker; Benny always insisted the show's singer be a tenor—there were six in all.

Day, the most faithful Benny retainer among the radio gang, remained with Benny thirty-five years, never aging beyond the naif stage (he was Benny's Gracie Allen), as in this typical exchange: "Dennis, aren't you going in swimming?" . . . "No, the last time I went in swimming a big crowd gathered around me and pointed at me and laughed at me" . . . "Well, maybe you had a hole in your bathing suit . . ." "Ooohhhhhhhh, *bathing suit!*"

Everyone razzed Jack except announcer Don Wilson, who was alone in respecting the employer-employee relationship. Explaining why he had chosen Wilson, Benny said, "He had a warm voice, he could read a commercial with laughter in his throat, and he proved a great foil to play against." Wilson was Benny's whipping boy, whom he attacked with fat jokes, but Wilson took his revenge by sneaking commercials past Benny on the show—or the show-within-the-show, or maybe the show-to-be (it got confusing if you thought about it)—while Jack stood by stewing.

The integrated commercials, of which Benny's were among the first and most clever, forced you to listen because they weren't walled off from the show. Benny first tried the noninterrupting commercial as a running gag at the start of the 1946 season, when the Sportsmen Quartet first spoke and then sang the Lucky Strike slogan, "LS/MFT" ("Lucky Strike Means Fine Tobacco"), sneaking it into the show whenever possible, to Benny's continued annoyance.

Another canny, appealing innovation was the show's series of ongoing self-references, as when Dennis kept trying to sing a song even though Jack tried to prevent it, until, driven nuts by his shenanigans, Benny gave in. Such routines became as ritualized as a Japanese tea ceremony.

When Eddie Anderson joined the show in 1937, his Rochester was very much of a racist shuck-and-jive stereotype—he drank gin, chased women, shot craps, and even carried a razor. But never did he bow and scrape, and something in his voice bespoke a mock wide-eyed innocence. (On one notable show, Rochester accidentally struck Benny while helping him train for a boxing match with Fred Allen, provoking letters from outraged Southerners, who, recalled Benny, "took it as an attack on the white race" by an uppity Negro. Benny, a self-proclaimed "political innocent," was stunned.)

Years later, the Rochester character came to embarrass Benny, who admitted he had been "a traditional Negro dialect stereotype. He had a molasses drawl and he *yassuh-boss*ed me all over the place. He was such a drawling, lazy, superstitious stereotype even the original Uncle Tom would have despised him." In a 1938 show, Rochester retains tinges of a minstrel black, immersed in racist dialogue during a trip west as he tries to get off the train in Santa Fe, mistaking it for 125th Street in New York:

Rochester: *I thought I was back in Harlem.*

Benny: *Harlem? I told you before, all those people at the station were Indians.*

Rochester: *Indians? Well, just the same, I saw a papoose eatin' a pork chop.*

Benny: *Well, what of it? He can be an Indian and still eat a pork chop.*

Rochester: *I know, but he had it between two slices of watermelon.*

Benny asks if his pants are pressed. Rochester says he forgot, adding, "Gee, I'm lazy. Don't I remind you of Stepin Fetchit?"

Even though Rochester was caught in a stereotype, something in his character played against it, as when Benny refers to the fact that Rochester totes a razor. "Yeah," he says, "but it's only a Gillette and I'm all out of blades." Also, Rochester was written and acted as an equal, more Benny's pal than his valet. "We just played Roch as a normal funny guy," reflected George Balzer. "I was not aware of his being apprehensive" about the role. Prior to Anderson's Rochester, Benny Rubin attempted a Pullman porter that really amused Benny, but writer Bill Morrow wisely objected, warning, "Jack, the studio audience will not laugh at a white man playing a Negro."

World War II sensitized Benny, and after 1945 Rochester gave up watermelon, gin, and razors. He still stepped lively, though, all the while laughing up his sleeve at his boss's feeble delusions of dignity. Rochester eventually was promoted to butler, a sort of black Jeeves, whose full name was Rochester Van Jones. Originally he'd been hired for a one-shot appearance as a porter called Syracuse, but Benny felt he could get more comic mileage out of "*Rah*-chester," which to his ear had a funnier sound. Rochester's cheeky character was quickly established during an early meeting aboard a Chicago-bound train:

Jack: *Hey, porter, porter!*

Rochester: *Yessuh.*

Jack: *What time do we get to Albuquerque?*

Rochester: *What?*

Jack: *Albuquerque.*

Rochester: *I dunno. Do we stop there?*

Jack: *Certainly we stop there.*

Rochester: *My, my! Albuquerque?* (laughs) *What they won't think of next! I better go up and tell the engineer.*

Neither Benny's use of Rochester nor Eddie Anderson's high-pitched gravel-voiced portrayal of the character ever received the abuse heaped on Freeman Gosden and Charles Correll's *Amos 'n' Andy* as a demeaning depiction of blacks—which is ironic because, while Rochester worked as a servant for a white man, Amos and Andy, albeit simpler souls, were homeowners and businessmen. But Rochester was openly, loudly, and gleefully rude, a servant who plainly did not know his place. Benny was "boss" in name only.

Maybe because Rochester was a hipper, lippy, contemporary black character, the racial issue never really arose for Benny, whose sniping manservant enjoyed equal status, perfectly embodying the line that no man is a hero to his valet. In any case, the two always seemed at home with each other, observed one critic, who further speculated that Rochester functioned as a kind of surrogate Mammy for Benny. Rochester's steady barrage of wisecracks was revolutionary for a black servant on the air—not duplicated until Robert Guillaume's TV show *Benson* in the 1980s—although there may have been an unconscious unstated servitude in the fact that of all the cast regulars, only Eddie Anderson, who stayed with Benny twenty-one years, used a fictitious name on the show; in films, he was always billed as Eddie ("Rochester") Anderson.

Benny diffused any latent criticism by his unbigoted private attitude and actions. He went out of his way not only to protect Anderson but to promote his career; he liked to boast that Anderson was the highest paid black performer in radio. When Anderson first joined the show in 1937 (prior to which his biggest role was Noah in Marc Connelly's *Green Pastures* on Broadway) and the cast, crew, and musicians went east, a New York hotel manager tried to get radio's leading black actor to move to another hotel after a couple from the South objected. Benny's producer and brother-in-law, Hilliard Marks, assured the manager Anderson would be glad to find new quarters. Next morning,

Marks and the rest of the company, some forty-four people, accompanied Anderson out of the hotel.

Jack Benny was not a man to toy with. He was then earning nearly $400,000 a year, an enormous salary in radio—or anywhere—in 1937, plus whatever he made in movies, of which there were more than people are aware—such as *Love Thy Neighbor* (with Fred Allen, based on their "feud"), a 1929 version of *Singin' in the Rain,* and the movie nobody saw but everyone remembers because Benny razzed it ever after, *The Horn Blows at Midnight.* George Burns once said it wasn't such a bad movie, but Benny convinced everyone it was, mining comic gold even out of a box office flop. Like most radio comics, he was unable to translate his radio persona into screen terms. *Buck Benny Rides Again,* based on his parody cowpoke, is really a Jack Benny show on film. Perhaps because he was the least physical of comics, he met a fast dead end in movies, especially when he played a character. Only one film really survives, *To Be or Not to Be.* Benny was too typecast as himself.

Jack Benny was suave by comedian standards of the 1930s and 1940s; in fact, he was almost effete. Benny often remarked on his famous stage and TV sashay, once telling an interviewer: "People are always taking advantage of me, and I've always thought it's because there's a tiny bit of effeminacy in me. I don't mean I'm a pansy, but the vanity and the pouting and the sulking in the character I play—it's like a woman." Benny discussed his swishy walk on the *Tonight* show when Johnny Carson would refer to Jack's saunter or his delicate stance, one palm laid primly alongside his cheek, eyes rolling in a manner that now looks decidedly poof. He had also played Charley's Aunt on film, and on TV often reverted to drag scenes, à la Berle. Benny once noted that Bob Hope had the same sashay but *cupped* his hands, while his own hands dangled demurely. Steve Allen, commenting on Benny's TV persona, said that his "pretend conceited swagger seemed to say, 'Here I am, folks—eat me up!' He walks like a headwaiter bringing someone to a good table."

Mainly, the Benny character seemed neuter, although his vanity—about his age, fame, blue eyes, and thin skin—might now be read as feminine or gay, as might the eternally thirty-nine jokes, which began when he was fifty-five and worked because he looked younger than his age; there were endless staff debates among writers on whether Jack should ever turn forty, but they never caved in. If you were a kid then, you didn't get the joke—thirty-nine seemed pretty old.

Many steady listeners never realized Jack Benny was Jewish, for he was the least "Jewish" of the classic Jewish comics. His show had a nonethnic quality, with the exception of Mel Blanc's Mexican, Sy, and Mr. Kitzle, who made everybody Jewish—Nat King Cohen, Ed Solomon, Lum and Adler, etc. "With Mr. Kitzle's routines," wrote Josefsberg, "we used the same philosophy that guided us in Rochester's humor: Don't do any jokes that were specifically 'Jewish' or 'black' jokes." Mr. Kitzle, played by Artie Auerbach, was first heard at a baseball game hawking franks—"mit de peekle in de meedle 'n' de mustard on top," which soon became a national catchphrase.

Benny, like Burns, didn't arrive via the Borscht Belt and didn't sound like a Catskill refugee, partly due to his flat midwestern voice. Radio rarely, if ever, acknowledged a star's Jewishness—unlike today, when comics flaunt it on talk shows and sitcoms. Benny had such a "non-Jewish" persona that he was able to neatly appropriate a reliable vaudeville standby, cheap-Scotsman jokes, but so skillfully retooled it for his own purposes that nobody ever thought of Benny as a tightfisted Jew.

He claimed the cheapness jokes defined his character more than anything else: "I found we could get away with leaving out Phil Harris, Rochester, the fiddle, the Maxwell, Mary Livingstone, but the listeners wanted stingy jokes." He tried rationing them to one per show, but other comedians kept doing tightwad Benny jokes. A cheap-joke sampler: Jack plays a one-hundred-dollar Stradivarius—"one of the few ever made in Japan"; he stays at a New York hotel "that underlooks the Park"; a rock hurled through his window tells him to leave town, and he muses, "Gee, just a note—no ticket."

Even popular mainstream Jewish comics like Cantor, Wynn, Berle, and Burns rarely referred to, let alone joked about, their Jewishness over the air. Only George Jessel, in routines like his telephone calls to Mama, exploited his Jewishness, but Jessel barely made a ripple in radio because dialect comics were soon regarded as vaudeville throwbacks; Jessel also lacked warmth. Though Benny didn't look, act, or sound "Jewish," there was a prickly edge to his kvetchy character that made him not really gentile, either. To a woman who asked why most comedians were Jewish or Irish, he said, "Madam, have you ever met a funny Lutheran?"

Benny's appeal was universal. One of his very few detractors was the popular radio comic Phil Baker, who plainly didn't get it. "Jack never does anything but stand there, touch his face, stare and say, 'Well . . .'," complained Baker. Burns's response: "Phil thought anyone could say, 'Well.' The sad truth is no one could, except Jack, and get a laugh. The audience pushed Jack. The audience made 'Well' a hit. Jack had this tremendous talent, but he looked like he didn't. He always looked so amazed when an audience laughed at him. His expression would indicate a perpetual question: 'Why are you laughing at me?' " When Louella Parsons said Benny would even be funny reading the phone book, he read it on the air—to steady laughs.

Steve Allen once described the nuts and bolts of the nebulous business called "timing" that Benny was invariably lauded for: "A split-second delay here, a rushed word there, can make a joke misfire. Benny never missed. Sure-footed as a cat, he walked his confident way through a monologue or a sketch, feeling with the delicate sensibility of the true craftsman just what was the best possible moment to speak, what was the most advantageous time to remain silent, regarding the [studio] audience with a large, baleful eye."

Benny also used his famous gaze as a timing device to control a routine's rhythm and prevent other actors from stopping a laugh by speaking too soon. After Benny felt he'd milked a laugh enough, Don Wilson related, he turned away from the audience and faced the person who had the next line—the actor's cue to speak. Noted Burns, "There was no hurry with Jack; he played all the waits."

AFTER AN UNBROKEN twenty-three-year run on radio, where he was king—in Josefsberg's phrase, "one of the few constants we could rely on in a rapidly changing world"—Benny reluctantly left radio for CBS-TV in 1954, having worked on both for three seasons. His last regular Sunday radio show, episode 1,838, was broadcast May 22, 1955, but the show continued in reruns until 1958.

Jack Benny's TV career, which began with a forty-five-minute special in the fall of 1950, was successful, but it never equaled the radio version artistically or viscerally, as Benny himself conceded: "It seems so long ago, and I don't just mean long ago in years but also in spirit. It was a time when Americans were emotionally involved with their radio personalities. Television has never made this kind of direct emotional impact on us." He went on, "In radio, people loved me in a different way. They could *see* on radio all my pauses. I came at them gently— quietly, through their ears. I suggested subtle images to them, picture jokes. Now [in TV] I became something else—too much."

It wasn't that Benny was bad on TV, he just wasn't as purely or as quintessentially Jack Benny. His movie parodies tended to rely on cos- tumes, often with Benny in a dress or some other outlandish, un- Bennyesque getup; he had a latent zany streak that he indulged on TV. Whenever Benny appeared in a make-believe guise—as Buck Benny, say—he was never as funny, but audiences by then laughed because it was Benny, in the way that when Uncle Jack puts a lamp shade on his head, everyone howls—not because it's that funny, but because it's lov- able old Uncle Jack.

It just wasn't as funny to *see* his famous buried vault (a hollow- sounding radio vault was funnier than a 3-D version with crocodiles and quicksand added), his tortured violin teacher rolling his eyes, or the choking Maxwell spewing smoke. On TV, the ancient Maxwell looked less like a rattletrap than an antique auto. All suffered by comparison to their imagined radio counterparts, along with little visual disap- pointments in the cast, like the fact that boyish Dennis Day was a middle-aged man with thinning hair or that Don Wilson wasn't as mirthfully Falstaffian as he'd been painted on radio, or that Mary sounded cuter than she looked.

TV broke up that old radio gang of his: Dennis Day, Mary Living- stone, and Phil Harris appeared less often on the TV show. Also, busy guest stars could no longer breeze in and read their lines. Apart from costume fittings, makeup, and light cues, they had to memorize dia- logue and blocking. Sets tended to dictate, scale down, and alter hal- lowed, tried-and-true radio bits.

Benny tiptoed into television, doing two shows the first year, gradu- ally escalating to thirteen shows, until by 1954 he was on TV every other week while still doing thirty-nine radio shows a year. Not until

1960 did he begin a weekly TV show. In 1964, for the first time since his first show thirty-two years earlier, Jack Benny was dropped by a sponsor, beaten in the ratings by rival *Bonanza,* and returned to NBC. Curious about *Bonanza,* Benny watched the first half hour of the western and was so hooked that he missed the first twenty minutes of his own show. "I knew I was through," he conceded. Yet though he had much less impact on TV than he had had in radio, Benny wound up surviving all the major comedians on the tube except Lucille Ball.

While Benny exerted ultimate authority over each of his radio shows, their crafting was a fairly democratic process in which the unusually agreeable star was only allowed one vote during debates with his longtime staff of four regular writers (Josefsberg, Balzer, John Tackaberry, and Sam Perrin), who met at Benny's home at 1002 North Roxbury Drive to lay out each week's offering.

Bill Morrow, his head writer for years, once commented on how relaxed the whole process was: "We put down no set ideas to cramp us. We went places, enjoyed ourselves, and *incidentally* wrote something about it. Our good times were reflected in our shows. Our audience, in fancy, traveled with us and had good times with us." Benny paid his writers many times scale, was never afraid to admit he was wrong (almost unheard of among major stars), apologized on the few occasions he blew up, and was once so racked with guilt that he told Josefsberg he'd underpaid him for material he had trotted out at private events for years. During a threatened writers' strike, the star promised to walk out with his gagmen.

Josefsberg finally left Benny after twelve years because of creative conflicts with other writers, not with Benny, with whom he remained close. In writers' battles, Benny always acted as mediator, but the pressures of TV and Benny's age caused more squabbles toward the end. He protected his writers from guest-star temperament. When Groucho Marx handed back a script he disliked, Benny said, "Well, then, we won't use him." Most actors grow misty discussing his generosity; Elliott Lewis once recalled the time he got a check from Benny double or triple his fee, with a note enclosed from Benny, reading, "The enclosed is because I never would have dreamed you could have gotten that big a laugh on the line." Said Lewis, "He was always like that."

George Balzer, one of two surviving writers from the longtime radio foursome, lives in the same modest Van Nuys home he bought when he wrote for Benny during their twenty-five years together, longer than any other Benny writer. (Josefsberg once said that for comedy writers in TV, two years was a career and three a miracle.) Balzer stayed with Benny because it provided the best comedy climate in radio. "The chemistry on that show was a kind that comes when you feel secure. How can anyone write with a dagger hanging over them, with the star yelling at you and picking on you?"

By the time Balzer arrived, the show's format was firmly in place, although he recalls, "We really had no format. We could do anything." Balzer outlines their usual weekly routine: "When we'd finish the show on Sunday we didn't know what we were going to do the next week. Monday was a day off. On Tuesday, we split into two teams and began calling each other for ideas. We'd set on a possible idea and then call Jack and ask what he thought of it. Often he'd say, 'Well, it *sounds* okay, why don't you go ahead and write it?' Wednesday morning at 10 A.M., we'd start to work in earnest, usually writing either by my pool or Sam's. When we'd finish we'd call the other team and tell them what our segment was. I'd ask what *they* had."

Each team wrote half the show. "By Wednesday night we'd have four pages of a script. Thursday evening, if we had any real issues to resolve, we'd call Jack and then give it to the script girl, who made six copies. Friday, we'd meet at Jack's house, go into the library, and Jack would read it to himself. If it was a good script, he'd say, 'Okay, let's go from the top.' "

By 3 P.M. Friday, the script would be finished and on Saturday morning the cast met for a cold reading, then the writers and Benny would break for lunch at the Brown Derby. If Benny was outvoted on a joke by the writers four-to-one, recalls Balzer, smiling, someone might say, " 'Well, Jack, the four of us *could* be wrong.' If Jack felt strongly about something we never forced him." Benny was confident enough to allow himself the luxury of a joke not everyone might get if it broke him up, rather than spell it out and ruin it. "If we have to lay it out for them, I'd rather not do it," he would say. "If we can't devote fifteen seconds in a half-hour program for our own amusement, we're in the wrong business." His popularity gave him the leeway to be audacious, as on the show on which he spoke only one line: At the very end, a tour bus he's riding passes his house and the guide says, "We are now passing the home of Jack Benny," whereupon Benny spoke his one line: "Stop the bus, driver, here's where I get off."

On Sunday, the cast and writers would meet again in the studio and run through the script at the mikes for timing purposes, after which the show was frozen. "When we said, 'There it is,' nobody—*nobody*— touched that script. That was it." Benny himself never changed a line without consulting the writers.

When Benny went to TV, he took Balzer and Perrin with him, and Josefsberg and Tackaberry remained behind, rewriting old shows—or, in Balzer's tactful phrase, "refreshening" them. "They weren't real happy about it."

Balzer goes on, "After he died, a lot of people would say to me, 'What's it like not writing for Jack?' and I'd say I never *stopped* writing for Jack. Not a week goes by that I don't think of a situation that would be right for the show. The other day, I imagined that the cast goes out for a bite and on the way back they realize Jack is missing. They turn around and he's down on his hands and knees, and he says, 'I lost a quarter,' and Dennis says, 'Oh, boy, look what I found—a dime!' And Jack says, 'Well, give it to me—and you can owe me the fifteen cents.' . . . And the next day Dennis gives it to him." Balzer rarely listened to rival comedy shows. "I had no other favorites. The Jack Benny show was my life."

The Benny show was built in large part on running gags, several of which ran twenty years. Balzer, who came up with two classics that enjoyed extremely long runs (Mel Blanc's "Sy/Si/Sue/Sew" bit and his railroad announcer's "Anaheim, Azuza, and Cuc. . . . amonga" line, now commemorated by a seven-foot bronze statue of Jack Benny in Rancho Cucamonga), explains: "Running gags cannot just be started. You gotta look at a script and say, 'Hey, on page four we just wrote a line that could be a running gag." Many twenty-year running gags began as one-timers, like Sheldon Leonard's shady racetrack tout who popped up every few shows to give Benny odds and tips on everything ("Hey, Bud, take the Super Chief—it's got a good rail position . . . it's a sleeper"), or the annoying racetrack announcer, or Jack's wise-ass parrot (typical of his purist comic mind, Benny had a strict rule that the parrot could only repeat words actually heard during the show).

Benny was regarded by his peers as mainly a great comedy editor who knew instinctively what lines to rewrite or cut, when a setup was unclear to listeners, and how to punch up a line with a word, a sound effect, or one of his famed Pinteresque comic pauses. He had a rare sensitivity to comic nuances. Balzer maintains, "Every line has a rhythm. If you have one word too many or too few, it's not funny—de-da de-da de-da de-*dum*. For instance [referring to the famous your-money-or-your-life? gag], "If Jack says, 'I'm thinking, I'm thinking,' it isn't as funny as 'I'm thinking it over.' *It* is the key word. So you have to go out there and get the laugh—and be careful you don't pass it up on the way."

The legendary Pause Heard 'Round the World—when that famed holdup man demanded, "Your money or your life?"—was in fact a standard six-second laugh, not two or ten minutes, as often reported. George Balzer agrees. "The reason it got so much PR is that [critic] John Crosby liked it so much he made it the theme of several columns" he wrote about the Benny show, using the line as an ideal example of the show's wit. "[Crosby] said it was the biggest laugh the show ever got." Benny could give examples of several jokes that drew much longer laughs, but as the "Your-money-or-your-life?" legend grew, so did the length of the laugh. It may seem longer in retrospect because the joke, which first aired on March 28, 1948, was repeated in other forms and became almost a running gag itself.

There is also a wonderful legend of how the line was hatched: Nobody could come up with a punch line to the holdup man's question. Josefsberg suggested a few that Tackaberry shot down, whereupon Josefsberg sniped, in the manner of comedy writers the world over, "Dammit, if you don't like my lines, throw out a couple of your own. Don't just lay there on your fat butt daydreaming." To which Tackaberry muttered, "I'm thinking it over."

— 4 —
Nesting Instincts

THERE WERE FAMILY SHOWS—MARRIED WITH children—and then there were shows about childless couples, or where the kids were mostly off-mike presences, such as *The Phil Harris–Alice Faye Show,* on which their daughters got lost in the comic shuffle.

The George Burns and Gracie Allen Show was pretty much a two-person operation. It wasn't as comically textured as Jack Benny's show, lacking the gang of regulars that populated the Benny program and gave it that warm, close-knit feeling. The Burns and Allen show, however charming and witty, didn't advance the radio comedy form as Benny's did. Burns and Allen relied largely, often brilliantly, on Gracie's sublimely inside-out logic, which extended the dizzy-dame cliché with detours into the back roads of her mind that made it seem original, never demeaning. Much of this had to do with the writing, but also, in a subtle way, with George's gentle, uncritical, affectionate attitude toward Gracie and her endearing daffiness. She was never a ditz like other radio dimwits—*My Friend Irma,* say, on which Marie Wilson played the ultimate dingbat, or Jane Ace, who radiated less sweetness. Burns never put Gracie down; he just heard her out and let us decide what he was thinking as well as what might be pinwheeling through her convoluted brain.

Gracie was different from the usual female flake. For one thing, she came across not as a flighty dope or blond nitwit but as a lovable eccentric. Burns preferred to call her "off-center." Gracie always arrived at the truth, but in a wacky roundabout way, and in the end she was usually proved correct—and, like Rochester on the Benny show, enjoyed the last laugh. Burns and Allen had been around show business long enough to realize that a character—an act—needed warmth to wear well, and the fact that audiences knew they were happily married in life created a built-in rapport echoed by their lullaby theme song, "Love

Overleaf, clockwise from top left: Goodman and Jane Ace (*Easy Aces*), Jim and Marian Jordan (*Fibber McGee and Molly*), George Burns and Gracie Allen

Nest." They had always been reality-based, even in vaudeville, where they were said to be the first comedy team not to appear in costume.

Gracie had a funny, instantly identifiable radio voice, high-pitched and squeaky (too squeaky for radio in the mind of one NBC executive who tried to nix her), yet never shrill, like Portland Hoffa's, or sing-songy, like Jane Ace's and Sade Gook's. It was a countermelody to Burns's sandpaper baritone; in real life, it was an octave lower. Her singing voice was surprisingly endearing—as well as just plain surprising—in musicals like *Damsel in Distress* and *Honolulu,* where she displayed what a total performer she was, not just a funny voice. Allen did three movies sans Burns—*The Gracie Allen Murder Case, Mr. and Mrs. North,* and *Two Girls and a Sailor.* At Burns's urging, they made twenty-eight films together, nearly all forgotten—with titles like *College Holiday* and *College Swing.*

When the team first entered radio, Gracie was decidedly the star, and the first offer they had, from Eddie Cantor, was for her to appear alone on his show. Even though they were a popular vaudeville team, Burns took the snub in stride and let her appear solo as Cantor's foil.

Their debut on Rudy Vallee's *Fleischmann Hour* quickly followed, but it ate up most of the act—or, as Burns later wrote, nicely summing up the fear of all vaudeville-turned-radio stars: "On one show we'd done about half our act; we still had half an act left and only twenty years to fill." They were a fast hit, for the same reason that kept them popular until Gracie's death. In Burns's summation: "Women understood her. Men thought they were married to her. And everybody knew somebody just like her." Three months after *The Fleischmann Hour* they had their own show, *The Adventures of Gracie,* playing an unmarried vaudeville team, but it wasn't a hit until the title and format were changed to *The George Burns and Gracie Allen Show* and they portrayed themselves. Although he grew into the role of straight man (in vaudeville, he had been the intended funny one), Burns, after making her the lead, was at first envious of Allen's greater renown.

In fact, Gracie Allen took little interest in the radio show and could have done it in her sleep. She made few creative contributions beyond her own enchanting personality, and usually didn't attend rehearsals (her stand-in was Jack Benny's former girl friend, Mary Kelly), which, according to the writer George Balzer, helped her maintain her guileless sound. As Burns told Leonard Maltin, "I had the talent off stage, and Gracie had it on the stage. I was able to think of it and Gracie was able to do it. And that's what made us a good team."

Allen's timing was flawless and second nature. "Because Gracie made playing Gracie appear to be so easy, she never received the credit she deserved as an actress," Burns once said. On TV, she never won an Emmy, probably because everyone, including actors who should have known better, assumed she was just playing herself. For Gracie, reading lines into a microphone didn't count as work, and even TV eventually bored her. She didn't believe she was funny, Burns said, but considered herself an actress rather than a comic and never told jokes offstage; her idea of a serious career was shopping.

Yet, like Mary Livingstone, she had serious mike fright and grew to dread the weekly ordeal. For the first year, the couple went on the air without an audience because Gracie considered audiences an invasion of privacy. During their debut season, paper was taped over the glass doors of the studio to keep visitors from peering in. After a while, they tried doing the shows from a 1,000-seat studio at the Willard Hotel arranged to resemble a vaudeville stage, with footlights in front of the mikes to shield Gracie from the audience. Burns claims that the audience was asked not to laugh or applaud their jokes. Gracie hid behind an oversized mike to keep from meeting their eyes.

Despite her acute fear of radio, she didn't flinch from the spotlight and, recounted Burns, "did everything necessary to make her character popular," such as putting her name on a syndicated advice column called "I Always Say—Sez Gracie Allen," and running for president in 1940 against FDR on the Surprise Party ticket, which included a whistle-stop campaign and mock press conferences. It was also partly a device to boost their radio show's sagging ratings after eight soaring years.

A running gag on their program about Gracie's lost brother turned into a national search for the missing man, the sort of stunt that both radio and the country loved. The media picked up on the hunt, other comics joked about it, actress Grace Moore ad-libbed a line about it in a Broadway play, and a congressman even referred to it in a speech. Burns, always quick to exploit a publicity bonus, hired the Burns Detective Agency to look for his brother-in-law, and wherever they toured, Gracie would turn up at a local newspaper to see if her brother had been turned in to the lost-and-found department. It was literally a running gag: She even pursued him on other shows, dropping in to ask if anyone had seen her brother. The joke lasted for years, to the annoyance of Gracie's real brother, George Allen, a San Francisco accountant.

Burns once explained the seeming contradiction between the private Mrs. Burns and the public Gracie: "One of the reasons Gracie was able to do so much publicity is that she never took it personally. She believed it was the *character* people wanted to interview and photograph, not the actress. As far as she was concerned, that was all part of the act. I still don't believe she ever completely understood that it was the person they were interested in." He observed, "Her ability to create a believable character made everything else work." She also knew where to draw the line, once refusing to pose next to an insane asylum.

As Burns pointed out in interviews, the audience wouldn't allow him to abuse Gracie in any way; he claimed she was the first comedienne to ever dress like a lady. He regarded her with bemused and confused fondness, as many men do their own wives even in more enlightened times, and audiences could identify easily with the fictional relationship. Burns called her "the national symbol of misunderstanding," and the government once even promoted a safety program with the slogan, "Don't be a Gracie Allen."

There was a crucial difference between dumb and Gracie. Burns often said, "Gracie didn't think she was dumb. When she said silly things, you didn't understand she felt sorry for you"—as if you were the stupid one. "She didn't tell a joke; she explained it," as in this classic exchange: "George, do you have any old light bulbs?" . . . "I throw them away, Gracie, why?" . . . "My sister could use a few" . . . "What for?" . . . "She puts them in all her lamps. It's a big saving" . . . "A big saving?" . . . "Of course, George. If you put in new bulbs, they just burn out and you have to change them."

As a biographer put it, Burns never became "the long-suffering husband who ultimately loves Gracie in spite of her befuddlement. George loves Gracie because of it. We were never forced to watch George roll his eyes and bemoan his fate," as Goodman Ace did with his own eternally befuddled wife, Jane. "He loved Gracie just the way she was and wouldn't change her." If Burns had returned Gracie's loony remarks with wise-guy zingers of his own, it wouldn't have worked; it would have upset the delicate comic balance and put too much of a strain on the jokes.

Had they not been married, the act might not have lasted. But there is always an extra layer of interest when a showbiz twosome is a couple in life—fans love to speculate to what extent the fictional relationship reflects the real one. Whatever the truth of their private life, it was never tarnished by gossip, and while Gracie flirted with men on their radio show, Burns never revealed his actual wandering eye. He remained indulgent and forgiving toward his wife, the most loyal and stolid of husbands. We felt that they loved each other and that it wasn't just an act, as in the troubled case of, say, Lucy and Desi.

Even so, their marriage was not quite as idyllic as portrayed. Burns, catnip to women and a ladies' man before marriage, had a series of girl friends afterward but remained faithful in his fashion and made sure never to fall in love. Ever the pragmatic showman, he didn't dare risk breaking up perhaps the most successful husband-and-wife team in show business history. Like many couples of the era, especially entertainers, they had an arrangement: To keep Gracie content, and to assuage his own guilt, Burns would periodically give his wife a lavish gift that was in effect a payoff for her looking the other way. Gracie was known to have once said, whether blithely or bitterly, "I wish Natty [George's real name was Nathan Birnbaum] would find another girl friend. I could use a silver fox jacket."

Originally on the show, Burns and Allen had played an unattached twosome, doing what Burns termed "flirtation routines" as they had in vaudeville. But listeners tired of this after a few years, since it flew in the face of reality, and their ratings dropped. Burns hit on the problem— "Our jokes were too young for us"—and promptly fixed it. From then on, they played their married selves, with kids, living happily ever after in the ratings.

They started out as a team and Burns was meant to be the funny one but, as he recalled, "Even her straight lines got laughs. I knew right away that there was something between the audience and Gracie. They loved her and so, not being a fool and wanting to smoke cigars for the rest of my life, I gave her the jokes." The Burns and Allen show kept the title stars at the center of things. The only other "characters" were announcer Bill Goodwin, a handsome chap who played a ladies' man, plus each week's guest.

Burns hated to leave radio. "I loved being in radio more than any other part of my career. . . . Radio was that place where performers who couldn't do anything except talk, could talk." But Burns and Allen were even more popular on TV without noticeably altering the old format, though Burns made a major change that broke the fourth wall—stepping out of character and, indeed, in and out of the scene, to address the audience, narrate the plot, and deliver an opening monologue; on one show, George waved to the audience from a dramatic scene. (He liked to claim that he stole the idea from *Our Town*.)

Burns and Allen on TV remained largely a video version of the couple's radio show, where there had been few surprises and no vapid singers or rowdy bandleaders to spice things up, apart from a Mel Blanc character called the Happy Postman (recycled as long-faced Mr. Beasely on TV). Gracie, however, balked at TV, pleading migraines and a desire to resume her life of lunching and shopping. Despite her film career, she distrusted the camera, but Burns cushioned the move by promising they'd shoot her from various sides and let her choose a favorite angle.

The relaxed, no-sweat nature of both the Jack Benny and Burns and Allen radio shows—as opposed to the boisterous tone of Milton Berle, Jackie Gleason, and most other TV-born comedy shows—worked beautifully in the early years of television, when nobody had any better ideas anyway and TV was either "radio with pictures," as they used to say, or, in the case of the variety shows, videotaped vaudeville or photographed musical revues. You almost didn't have to watch Benny's or Burns's TV shows at all; it was possible to face away from the set and get just about everything.

In the end, though, the couple relied for laughs almost extensively on Gracie's illogical logic and on Burns's unfailingly good-humored, loving, equally deadpan responses. George's matter-of-fact manner was as quietly funny as Gracie's non sequiturs; her silly piping responses sounded even funnier set against the gravelly Burns's questions and nonplussed responses, as if he were some bystander who had wandered over to befriend a befuddled but beguiling woman and found he couldn't get away. It was a deceptively simple but seductive format that remains fresh, effortless, and inspired to this day.

SOMEWHERE IN THAT same neighborhood resided *The Phil Harris–Alice Faye Show,* the most successful spin-off from *The Jack Benny Program,* on which Harris had been the epitome of the wild-and-crazy bandleader. He played a stock radio character, the carousing musician/announcer, who still exists on TV in watered-down fashion (Ed McMahon, Doc Severinsen, Paul Schaffer, Kevin Eubanks, et al.), but who has less to do today than did his radio forefathers—band leaders like Harris and Ray Noble (conductor on *The Edgar Bergen and Charlie McCarthy Show*). His function is essentially the same, though—to gently needle the star while acting as foil and/or whipping boy.

Harris had broken into radio years before Benny's show, doing a nightly fifteen-minute remote from the Coconut Grove in 1932; it was here that the dashing bachelor conductor later met Alice Faye, then married to Tony Martin. George Burns also met him around that time, and wanted him for his show, but Burns waited too long and Jack Benny got to him first. Harris worked for Benny until 1952; the Harris–Faye show ran until 1954.

A loudmouthed hipster from Nashville, Harris was a pop star in his own right, a singer of such novelty hits as "That's What I Like About the South," "The Preacher and the Bear," and "Some Little Bug." But his larger-than-life persona couldn't be contained on the Benny show, so he and his gorgeous, retired movie-star wife, singer and actress Alice Faye, who played an ex–film star on the show, moved up the block from Benny. Their show even followed Benny's, and occasionally a plot would pick up on their show where it had left off on Benny's show. So he could make it to his own show in time, Harris usually appeared in the top half of the Benny program.

Phil Harris's brazen character didn't work as well on his own show—probably a case of too much of a good thing. Faye was too ladylike, the very thing that made her such a sensual singer in films and on the show, where each week's plot was interrupted for a ballad by her and a comedy song by Harris; many plots involved their long-suffering sponsor, Rexall, and its riled radio CEO, played by the omnipresent

Gale Gordon, yet another example of making the sponsor part of the fun. Harris and Faye brought with them from Benny's show a character who never appeared there but was constantly referred to—Frankie Remley, an even brassier and boozier musician than Harris. It was left a little unclear whether Remley was a comic creation or a real person—as indeed he was, the guitarist in the Harris orchestra; like other Benny characters, he was half-fictional.

Remley (played by Elliott Lewis) was someone Harris could ridicule and humiliate, but the guzzling and womanizing macho twosome wore a little thin; the one-joke concept fit more amusingly into a quick three-minute segment on the Benny show. The boorish booze hound was a tried-and-true device that drew instant, easy laughs.

The type finally seems to have exhausted its comic welcome, and become politically incorrect, but Harris was acceptably funny because on the Benny show he only *talked* about his drinking; he never appeared drunk on either his own or Benny's show. He stood in stark contrast to the uptight, probably teetotaling Benny, whom he irreverently hailed as "Jackson," provoking Benny's disdain toward a man he plainly despised as a lush and a letch, a vulgarian even lower down on the social ladder than himself. In life, Harris was a fairly soft-spoken man, unlike his preening radio persona, who, upon glimpsing himself in a mirror, invariably drawled, "Oh, you *dawwwwg*!"

The show came most vividly to life when Frankie and Phil (or "Curly," as Remley called him) encountered the wisecracking street-wise Brooklyn delivery boy, Julius, played by the reliable Walter Tetley as a tougher version of his Leroy role on *The Great Gildersleeve*. Harris recognized Elliott Lewis's contribution to his show's success. "Elliott and I were like clockwork," he once said. "It was so easy—it just used to flow." Comically, Harris worked much better on the show with Lewis than with his wife. Faye, never much of a comedian, mostly stood by, like a Laurel and Hardy wife, making cracks, but her zingers never carried much sting. The pair weren't a natural comic fit like Burns and Allen, Jim and Marian Jordan (*Fibber McGee and Molly*), or Goodman and Jane Ace.

Although it was technically a family show, with allusions to the couple's daughters Phyllis and Alice Jr., most episodes featured Phil and Frank getting in and out of scrapes; Faye always seemed removed from the action. Years later, the writer Ray Singer said, "Remley was the backbone of the show—he spoke for us." Remley in effect became the Phil Harris on the Harris-Faye show—a crude, hard-drinking guy that Harris, now a family man with two young daughters, could no longer play on the air. As a settled-down husband and father, Harris lost some of the comic vinegar on his own show, where he was portrayed as a semiliterate stumblebum. The first two writers on the show were fired because their jokes, based on the rakish Benny-show version of Harris, were borderline risqué.

Singer recalled, "*The Phil Harris–Alice Faye Show* was a writer's paradise, because Phil was the kind of guy who loved living, and didn't want to be bothered with work or anything else. He left us alone. We never had to report to him." Harris and Faye, who lived in Palm Springs, drove in on Fridays to rehearse. The writers would rewrite on Saturday, Harris and Faye would do the show Sunday, and go back to Palm Springs. "He never knew what was gonna happen. And it was left in our hands. It spoiled us for everybody else."

OF ALL THE COMIC couples who resided in radio, only *The Bickersons* dared reveal the down and dirty underbelly of married life. Other couples squabbled, but the Bickersons were out for blood; and unlike many others, they had no children to get in the way of their violent verbal warfare.

The Bickersons were a perfectly matched couple always spoiling for a fight. While in *The Honeymooners* Ralph and Alice Kramden—obviously inspired by John and Blanche Bickerson—were a struggling blue-collar couple who lived in a wretched Brooklyn flat, the Bickersons were more comfortably middle-class. Both gave as good as they got, they never retreated an inch, and there were no "You're-the-greatest!" closing clinches; the routines always ended with John's defeated "Aw-w-w-w, Blanche." Yet their sketches lacked the emotional texture of those in *The Honeymooners* or the mellowing influence of an Ed Norton to calm the domestic waters. If the Kramdens had been no more than a caterwauling couple, they would have seemed far less lovable.

Forty years after the couple was first heard as a weekly sketch on *The Edgar Bergen and Charlie McCarthy Show,* even people who never heard the originals still refer to "The Bickersons," a phrase now synonymous with spiteful spouses. The name is invoked metaphorically in references to every sort of wrangling twosome, from TV movie critics Gene Siskel and Roger Ebert to political candidates.

The shows were a one-note brawl, a nonstop barrage of rather labored insults said to have been inspired by creator-writer Philip Rapp's own quarrels with his wife, Mary. "I've hidden under a lot of tables in my day," said Rapp's son, Joel, who claims his parents often squabbled in public. "My father would scurry off to the typewriter while the dialogue was still fresh," he recalled. Phil Rapp said that the Bickersons were an antidote to saccharine couples like Ozzie and Harriet and Jim and Betty Anderson on *Father Knows Best.* "It just made me sick," he remarked in 1980. "There was so much sweetness. This was not marriage as I knew it."

Played by suave actor/announcer Don Ameche, John Bickerson was in a permanent state of seething exasperation, while wife Blanche (Frances Langford) alternated between victim and viper. They indulged in a thirty-minute insult-fest more interested in drawing guffaws than in revealing anything amusing about the dark side of wedded bliss; but then marital spats are like that.

Even though their show lasted only two seasons, they remain the generic war-between-the-sexes comedy team, and well into the 1970s Don Ameche was still doing *Bickersons*-like commercials. Langford, though one of the finer band singers of the 1940s, is destined to go down in show business history as America's favorite nag; in 1951, Lew Parker played opposite her in a summer version.

Mr. and Mrs. B went at each other like Jiggs and Maggie—loud and venomous, but with less mitigating charm or believability, as in this typical segment from a 1948 show, which began, as always, with Blanche being awakened by John's snoring:

Blanche: *You used to be so considerate. Since you got married to me, you haven't got any sympathy at all.*
John: *I have, too. I've got everybody's sympathy.*
Blanche: *Believe me, there's better fish in the ocean than the one I caught.*
John: *There's better bait, too.*

Blanche: *I don't see how you can go to bed without kissing me good night.*
John: *I can do it.*
Blanche: *You better say you're sorry for that, John.*
John: *I'm the sorriest man who ever was born.*

NO TWOSOME WAS MORE PERFECTLY attuned to middle-class 1930s sensibilities than *Fibber McGee and Molly,* whose show portrayed an endearing couple at the opposite extreme from the wicked Bickersons. The show, which seamlessly blended vaudeville high jinks with radio's cozier atmospherics, came along at the right time—a home remedy for a shaken, insecure, Depression-era America that needed reassuring that its values were still intact, alive and well at 79 Wistful Vista.

It was a hard show to dislike, despite—or maybe even because of—its old-fashioned comic devices and broadly drawn characters taken from Jim and Marian Jordan's vaudeville career and updated by the inspired writer Don Quinn, who drafted the premise, much of the shtick heard on the show, and Fibber McGee and Molly themselves. Quinn, who had written for *Hellzapoppin*'s Olsen and Johnson, wrote the show on his own for years, not dependent on a revolving door of gagmen, the way most radio comedies were put together.

Fibber McGee was in the long tradition of American braggarts and bumblers, the ineffectual husband who shouts and sputters while his wife looks on indulgently. He was originally a teller of tall tales in the tradition of frontier humorists Mark Twain, Josh Billings, and Artemus Ward, but by the 1940s McGee had, like Huck Finn, been "sivilized" by Quinn and was more inept mainstream American male than cracker-barrel yarn spinner. Now he simply exaggerated, dreamed up goofy get-rich-quick schemes, and fumed.

Molly's sweet nature and amiable kidding of her husband's bungling ways and corny wit (her aside " 'Tain't funny, McGee" became a national byword, along with her astonished "Heavenly days, dearie!") were also in the standard vein of sitcom humor that still prevails, with politically corrected shadings. Even shows as vulgar and as far-removed from *Fibber McGee and Molly* as TV's *Married . . . with Children* are but crasser, trashier 1990s versions of the McGees—a hapless boob of a husband and his brighter, long-suffering, eye-rolling wife.

The McGees began in 1935 as *The Smith Family,* once described as a more amusing *One Man's Family,* and so it might well have remained had the Jordans not met Quinn. He was a former cartoonist who contrived a show for them called *The Smackouts,* about a motormouth grocer and his wife who were always "smack out" of everything, necessitating wild fibs and convoluted excuses by Fibber. Henrietta Johnson, the wife of an agency head, was a fan of *The Smackouts* and called it to her husband's attention. He wanted to put it on the network for the usual thirteen-week tryout, but the Jordans felt they needed more time to establish their characters and agreed to do the show for a paltry $250 a week if the agency would give them twenty-six weeks.

Fibber and Molly were situated midway in radio demographics between the sophisticated urban/suburban comedy shows of Fred Allen, Jack Benny, Bob Hope, Phil Harris, Burns and Allen, Ozzie and Harriet, and Goodman and Jane Ace and the more small-town humor of *Lum and Abner* and *Vic and Sade.* It was easy for people to identify with the goings-on at 79 Wistful Vista, caricatured though they might be. In a sense, it was more of a comic strip than a show, and in the first months the Jordans even dressed in character.

McGee was a frustrated homeowner trying to get through the day but constantly beset by pesky neighbors and petty annoyances, of which the famous cluttered front closet—the most famous running gag in radio—became a hallmark; indeed, it was a microcosm of the show. People too young to have heard *Fibber McGee and Molly* know all about that closet, with its cascading junk, usually followed by McGee's muttered vow: "Gotta clean out that hall closet one of these days." The sound was produced by shoving items down a portable staircase. The closet joke was no accident but a calculated attempt by the Jordans and Quinn to find a running gag to compete with a rival show's squeaky-spring bit that paid off every week. Over twenty years, it became the most recognizable sound gag in the world, largely because it was transformed into a sight gag in the listener's mind.

Radio comedy resounded with sound gags of every sort, especially on *Fibber McGee*—not just sound effects, but bits like McGee's alliterative outbursts and knee-slapper similes ("Them springs are tighter than a forty-dollar girdle after a spaghetti dinner"), Mayor La Trivia's sputtering spoonerisms, and the names of recurring characters (Mrs.

Wearybottom, etc.). To this vocal silly symphony was added a cacophony of giggles, fits, muttered oaths (McGee's "Dad-rat the dad-ratted . . ."), spit-takes, and explosions set off by actors portraying a steady stream of blowhards, wiseacres, and wheezing old-timers, like The Old-timer himself, always one-upping McGee's tall tales with, "That ain't the way I heee-e-e-ard it, Johnny—the way I he-e-e-ard it was, 'One fellow says to t' other feller, he *sa-a-a-a-ys* . . .'" McGee was surrounded by characters whose sole purpose was to deflate his every word and deed, people with fanciful Dickensian names like Throckmorton P. Gildersleeve, Doc Gamble, Mayor La Trivia, Wallace Wimple, and Otis Cadwallader.

Jim Jordan didn't do voices, but Marian Jordan did—best of all the nagging, tee-heeing kid Teeny, who badgered McGee with questions ("Whatcha doin', mister, huh? Whatcha doin', huh?, huh?") and endlessly repeated "I betcha"s, capturing the essence of a pestering little girl. Teeny wasn't a brat, but McGee wanted to brain her, because she saw through his boasts, ploys, and ego.

McGee's main bit, usually opposite Gale Gordon (as Otis Cadwallader), was confused alliteration, such as "Don't call me a phalanx, you soggy, sap-headed serum salesman!" Or, more elaborately, "I was the top tin can designer for the Town Talk Tuna Company. I turned out tuna tins by the ton. I had a type of tin in two tones of tan that was the talk of the tuna trade, but one tan turned tones too tawny, so I had to tone down the tawny tan . . ." That might not bring down the house now, but in the context of the show, the character, and perhaps the times, it produced a surefire payoff; part of the joke was simply to see how long McGee could extend the alliteration or rapidly recite it.

Radio comedy was a verbal steeplechase. Quinn was able to work another switch on his alliteration skills by having fat-headed, blustering La Trivia get snarled up in a sentence, such as: "Why, yes, Mrs. McGee, I suppose you would call a part-harm, petrol-packing possum—that is, a pot-farmed, possum-pinking partridge!"—only to give up and stomp out to applause.

Fibber McGee and Molly spawned radio's first successful spin-off, *The Great Gildersleeve,* and later hatched a second hit, *Beulah*—not to mention singer Perry Como and a wacky drummer in the Billy Mills Orchestra named Spike Jones. Gildersleeve could outbluster even

McGee. The program wasn't big enough for the two of them, but it was an amiable parting and the new show went on to a long life on its own, starring Harold Peary, who originated the character of George Gildersleeve, who owned a girdle factory.

Much of the comedy on *Fibber McGee and Molly,* as on many of the more primitive sitcoms, was simple insult humor, a harmless volley of verbal blows with the gloves on. The radio historian Jim Harmon tellingly noted, "Fibber could only let out his full aggressiveness against Gildersleeve. Partly it was the 'you old horsethief' kind of masculine humor that says in effect: We are such good friends, I can say *anything* to you without you becoming permanently offended. But there was a strain of real hostility, too."

When TV arrived, the Jordans resisted the temptation. "They were trying to push us into TV and we were reluctant," Jim Jordan said later. "Our friends advised us, 'Don't do it until you need to. You have this value in radio—milk it dry.' We never made the change, because Marian had a heart attack." They wound up their career in fifteen-minute sketches on *Monitor*—"Just Molly and Me"—and were set to sign for three more years when Marian Jordan died.

The show's lasting charm, however, was in the unspoken but enduring affection Fibber and Molly seemed to feel toward each other despite his stubborn fulminations and her skeptical Irish nature. (Hal Peary said, "They were as homey in person as they sounded.") Molly forgave McGee his every illusion and self-delusion, waiting for "Himself" to calm down and admit what a jerk he'd been. Surpassing all the other husband-and-wife comedy teams, perhaps including even George Burns and Gracie Allen, Fibber McGee and Molly were radio's most identifiably loving couple.

IT GOES WITHOUT SAYING that most of radio's comedy shows were rampantly sexist—a procession of dumb Doras, nice Nellies, and battling Berthas—but then so were the times. It's difficult to find any character type of any gender, age, nationality, religion, or color that was not a comic stereotype—white males included, usually portrayed (as they still are, never out of fashion) as bumbling, patronizing husbands and fathers, stuffed shirts, mama's boys, or macho jerks. So it's a useless exercise to indict this character or that show. Easier, wiser, and fairer is to write the stereotypes off to lazy writing and leftover vaudeville attitudes.

In radio, and later in TV, every comic female was either miserable, crazy, or unable to function without a man. Then, once a woman snagged a guy, she made *his* life miserable and crazy. Nearly all the comedy writers were, of course, men, who reflected the prevailing attitudes and platitudes of the day, magnified for laughs. Nobody seemed to object much, or really even to notice.

Women were the most hopelessly stereotyped—even more so, in a sense, than blacks—simply because women were the most visible minority on the air during that era; blacks barely existed. There was almost a formula, a sort of First Law of Sitcoms, that if a comedy involved only a couple, almost invariably the woman was a dodo. If, however, there were children, then the woman was suddenly imbued with brains and wisdom and the man became the dummy. Many of the most beloved major female comic characters (with the clear exception of Baby Snooks) were adorable ding-a-lings, from the addled Gracie Allen, Portland Hoffa, and Jane Ace to Marie Wilson's Irma Peterson on *My Friend Irma* and Effie Klinker, the old-maid puppet on the Charlie McCarthy show, in constant pursuit of a man.

Other archetypal fictional heavy-breathing women were Vera Vague (Barbara Jo Allen), a recurring man-hunter on the Bob Hope and Jimmy Durante shows, and the saucy Southern belle Leila Ransom (Mary Jane Croft), whose life was devoted to ensnaring would-be lothario Throckmorton P. Gildersleeve.

Shirley Mitchell played dingbats of every sort—characters like Alice Darling, a ditsy Rosie the Riveter who was Rudy Vallee's sweetheart, comic Joan Davis's pretty foil on TV's *Joan Davis Show*, and even Amos's wife on *Amos 'n' Andy*—one of several white performers in early radio who doubled in black roles. It never occurred to Mitchell that those characters were featherbrains. "It was work. We never thought about the intent," she says. "We weren't that aware, as people are now. I never resented playing a bimbo. What I played didn't bother me—and it still doesn't! The bottom line was, it was a good job."

Only a handful of female comic creations rose above stereotype. There was Mary Livingstone, who showed no interest in her asexual radio beau, Jack Benny, and razzed him unmercifully. Most liberated of all was Eve Arden's Miss Brooks, who remained mildly interested in the dim bulb Mr. Boynton, mainly because he kept hanging around. The few well-matched and companionable pairs included Fibber McGee and Molly, Vic and Sade, and the sensible Ethel and Albert, the most normal of all radio couples.

JANE ACE, QUEEN of the malaprops on *Easy Aces,* was a linguistic first cousin to Gracie Allen, whom she predated by a few years. She also shared Gracie's fear of microphones so that one had to be built into the card table the couple sat at during their broadcasts. Jane Ace had a lazier, flatter, and more ruminative voice than Gracie Allen, often lapsing into a monotonous, almost whiny cadence. Gracie never mangled a phrase—it was her logic that was so brilliantly twisted.

John Crosby wrote of Jane Ace: "She is a woman of sunny amiability who takes an extremely literal and subjective view of everything around her. That makes things very easy for her and extremely difficult for anyone else. There are a lot of Mrs. Malaprops in radio, but none of them scrambles a cliché quite so skillfully as Jane . . . and she got there ahead of most of them." Besides the malapropisms, Jane's scrambled thoughts resulted in dipsy-doodle lines: "I'll say he's not guilty, whoever he is. If he's nice enough to pay me three dollars a day to be his jury, the least I can do is recuperate, doesn't it to you?" Asked by a friend what she's been doing, she says, "Just fine, thanks."

Jane (Epstein) was the invention of her husband, Goodman Ace, who created and wrote the show and played opposite her during its fifteen-year run, humoring his wife's funny if at times labored and unlikely mispronunciations with good-natured asides, often groaning in a fond, faintly patronizing way, "Isn't that *aw-w-ful?*" Ace good-humoredly tolerated his wife's private Janeisms. When asked how Mrs. Ace was, he liked to reply, "Fine, if you like Jane." Millions seemed to.

Easy Aces began in Kansas City in 1930, an offshoot of a show that Ace did on a local station reviewing movies and theater at ten dollars a show. He was then a critic for a local paper who had begun in radio reading comic strips on the air, à la Mayor Fiorello LaGuardia during a New York newspaper strike. By then, he had also begun selling jokes to

Jack Benny, whom he met in his critic's job. When columnist Heywood Broun's network show failed to come on one night, Ace ad-libbed with his new wife for fifteen minutes and, *Easy Aces* lore has it, they charmed listeners with their chatter about a recent local murder and the couple's addiction to bridge, then a national craze. The title of the show-to-be was thus a double play on words.

That show established the conversational format similar to that of *Vic and Sade*—with occasional drop-in characters, such as their good friend Marge (Mary Hunter), whose common sense and affection for Jane gave the show much of its warmth. Marge, who chuckled heartily at Jane's lines, acted as a sort of early laugh track, one writer noted. In its early days, the lack of music (apart from the show's theme, "Manhattan Serenade") and sparse sound effects made it seem as if you had put your ear to the wall and were listening to people yakking away in the next apartment. It all sounded far more lifelike than the similar but more sketch-oriented Burns and Allen scenes.

Easy Aces had frequent bright moments, which explain Ace's reputation as a comic guru who later ran a highly regarded comedy writing workshop at CBS and for years wrote a column in *The Saturday Review*. He later wrote for TV's *Kraft Music Hall* with Perry Como (earning $10,000 a week and making him TV's highest paid writer), whose nonchalant on-air manner was largely Ace's doing. "Goody gave Perry a tone," said TV producer Lester Gottlieb. "It was an established fact that, man for man, Goody Ace was the best guy you could get to work on a comedy-variety show." Ace, considered the comic equal of cronies Groucho Marx, Jack Benny, and Fred Allen, wound up as a commentator on NPR's *All Things Considered*.

The *Easy Aces* shows were simply laid out and nonchalantly paced, often formulaic, but word mavens delighted in Ace's ability to play with the language. "Urbane" was the word most often used to describe their show, wrote Ace's nephew Mark Singer in *The New Yorker*. His primary comic device was putting droll, double-edged malapropisms in his wife's mouth, several per show, like these jewels: "I must have the intentional flu," "He's a big clog in the machinery," "Long face, no see," "A fly in the oatmeal," "I'm a human domino," "She had a face that would stop a crook," "Mother, you're so pessimistic—why can't you be more of an optician?" "Make it short and sappy," and Mrs. Ace's standard: "You have to take the bitter with the batter." At least one phrase, "Time wounds all heels," made it into *Bartlett's.*

After the show's initial run, Ace tried to remake the show in 1948 as a half-hour program called *mr. ace and JANE,* about an ad man who lived next to a radio announcer. The new version allowed Ace, a long-time ad-baiter, who once lost a sponsor when he zinged Anacin's switch from tin to cardboard boxes, to bite his favorite hand. Not surprisingly, the revived program only lasted a year. As Jane might say, it was all harmful fun at the time.

IF *EASY ACES* PATRONIZED ITS FEMALE LEAD, it sounded like a feminist tract next to *My Friend Irma,* which starred Marie Wilson as radio's preeminent dumb Dora. Wilson, in real life a curvy blond sexpot, spoke in a voice that sounded as if she had a permanent head cold, portraying a sweet, vacant dame—a characterization so terminally sexist that the show is almost unthinkable now. Wilson played Irma Peterson, a naive, childlike ingenue; Cathy Lewis, the "My" of *My Friend Irma,* played her smart, patient, long-suffering roommate Jane Stacy, whose life was devoted to getting her dim friend out of trouble. Irma's boyfriend, Al (John Brown), was a luckless gambler reminiscent of Nathan Detroit. Gloria Gordon was the girls' motherly Irish landlady, Mrs. O'Reilly, and Professor Kropotkin was played by Hans Conried, who had a lucrative career in radio, movies, TV, and on stage playing an array of vaguely European short-tempered characters—"stack blowers," as they were called in the trade.

What drew men to the show was Wilson's sexy nasal voice and the sparky-sounding Lewis, later played by Diana Lynn in the inevitable film version, now better remembered, if at all, as the movie that introduced Dean Martin and Jerry Lewis.

My Friend Irma was state-of-the-art dumb blonde, but the other reigning radio female caricature was the wife/girl friend/mom as shrew. To this was added a million mother-in-law jokes that infested the airwaves, memorably embodied by the Kingfish's dreaded mama-in-law on *Amos 'n' Andy,* Wallace Wimple's "big ol' wife, Sweetie Face" on *Fibber McGee and Molly,* and that ace battleax Blanche Bickerson. Say what you will about Sapphire, Sweetie Face, and Blanche, they weren't your usual numbskull radio wives.

FALLING SOMEWHERE BETWEEN the beleaguered Blanche and the bewildered Irma was the Liz Cooper character on *My Favorite Husband,* the forerunner of *I Love Lucy.* It was a sort of "I Love Lizzy," costarring Lucille Ball and Richard Denning as Liz and George Cooper, your basic Average American Couple from Minneapolis.

When the show moved to TV, Liz was played by the comely if far less comical Joan Caulfield, opposite Barry Nelson, but it lasted only a few seasons before being quickly superseded in 1951 by a zesty little item called *I Love Lucy,* an instant and constant hit featuring Ball and her real favorite husband, Desi Arnaz.

Ball and Arnaz wisely took with them to TV their *My Favorite Husband* team—writers Bob Carroll, Jr., and Madelyn Pugh and producer Jess Oppenheimer—but Lucy's comic DNA can be traced back even further: *My Favorite Husband* was inspired by a novel called *Mr. and Mrs. Cugat,* about a Latin bandleader and his kooky wife. (Xavier Cugat, then married to Abbe Lane, sued the show, which quickly changed the couple's name from Cugat to Cooper.)

My Favorite Husband (1948–52) had many of the basic elements of *Lucy:* Ball portrayed what would be her later TV self—a frantic, endearingly spacy wife trying to compete with her husband, though on the radio show he was an obliging banker. Going back to the early 1930s, Ball had played a series of comic redhead bombshells in movies opposite Bob Hope and others and was an early Charlie McCarthy female foil.

Desi's TV presence spiced up the radio concept (he wouldn't have made a terribly credible banker), not just giving the show some Latin heat but adding a crucial ingredient that utilized rather than fought against his real persona. Casting Desi as a Cuban bandleader fending off his wife's showbiz ambitions went back to the original book about the Cugats. Somehow the concept had been overlooked by bandleader Ozzie Nelson and Harriet Hilliard, his real-life band-singing wife, who was revamped on radio as an obedient hausfrau.

The Coopers' good friends, George's grumpy boss and his wife, the Atterburys, were forerunners of Fred and Ethel Mertz. They were played by Gale Gordon and Bea Benaderet, who were set to repeat their roles on TV, but Gordon was bound to *Our Miss Brooks* and Benaderet to Burns and Allen. In a typical episode that would be right at home on *I Love Lucy,* Liz and Mrs. Atterbury want to play on their husbands' office softball team over the men's objections to such a foolish notion; the little woman's place is in the home, obviously. In her most classic *Lucy* mode, Ball whimpers and weeps and carries on until the men agree to let them play. The wives, totally ignorant of the game (naturally), read a book on baseball and get advice from an expert, make the squad, and mess up the game. Liz inadvertently saves the day by being hit on the head by a pitched ball that sends the winning run home and shows up the men—by a fluke, interestingly, not by any innate ability.

Ball's Liz Cooper is a less loopy Lucy, but the radio show became a kind of out-of-town tryout for the TV smash. When Ball was asked to adapt the show to TV, she said, "Only if Desi plays my husband." It was Lucy's ploy to keep the traveling bandleader with the wandering eye at home, over protests from TV executives worried about a sit-com featuring a Cuban husband. During the summer, the couple took the concept on the road, in an act that included husband-and-wife sketches, to see how it played. It proved such a hit that the following fall, the pilot for *I Love Lucy* was shot during Ball's last year of *My Favorite Husband.*

What few listeners have any reason to remember is that, in a unique reversal of the usual chronology, *I Love Lucy* had a brief run on radio in the 1952 season, with the same cast, characters, and concept as the TV show that had premiered the previous fall. Like other shows that overlapped for a season or two on radio and TV, *Lucy* was hedging its bets in the scary new world of video; six of the *My Favorite Husband* scripts later turned up as *Lucy* TV episodes. (It's hard to find an early TV show without radio roots, including *My Little Margie* and *Howdy Doody,* considered a total TV creature.)

Jess Oppenheimer related in his memoirs how he tried to animate Ball on radio: "Lucy was relatively stiff working in front of an audience. She just didn't have the wildly antic quality that I was looking for. I had been trying for weeks to get her and Dick Denning to loosen up and act out the jokes and reactions . . . instead of just standing there waiting to read the next line when the laugh subsided. I knew how effective this could be from watching Jack Benny do his radio program. I remember telling Lucy, 'Let go. Act it out. Take your time.' But she was simply afraid to try." He gave her tickets to Benny's show, and "instantly she got the idea, starting to ham it up behind the mike much more broadly than before. There were times I thought we'd have to catch her with a butterfly net to get her back to the microphone. The audience roared their approval and Lucy loved it." It was the birth of Lucy Ricardo.

PEG LYNCH'S INSIGHTFUL and realistic *Ethel and Albert,* with Lynch and Alan Bunce, was a real leap forward in domestic comedy—a light-hearted, clever, well-observed, daily fifteen-minute show about the amiable travails of a recognizable suburban couple, the Arbuckles, of Sandy Harbor and, only occasionally, their little girl, Susy; the first Albert was Richard Widmark. The sitcom, which ran from 1944 to 1950, even managed a rare successful transfer to TV in 1951. While the show is little remembered today, it was a skillfully written series that bridged the domestic comedy of a vaudeville-based era with a keen modern sensibility. Lynch made her comic points without stooping to female stereotypes, insults, running gags, funny voices, or goofy plots.

"I realized that I didn't have to sit down and knock myself out every minute to try to think of something funny," she told Leonard Maltin. "All I had to do was look around me." Lynch had the underrated knack of taking the small irritations and minutiae of home life and shaping them into a wry comment on domestic life without stretching the facts, much as Jean Kerr and Erma Bombeck later did in print. Ethel and Albert sounded like the couple next door (as their show was called in a second radio version in 1958); he was irritable but loving, and she was a worrywart but bright and capable. Jerry Seinfeld, in defending the position that his show was about "nothing," said, "The little things are the big things. That's the secret of this show." Similarly, Peg Lynch's nothings added up to something gently amusing, smart, charming, and recognizably human.

– 5 –

TREADMILL TO POSTERITY

FRED ALLEN WAS THE DAVID LETTERMAN OF radio: caustic, flip, hip, antinetwork, antiadvertising, antiratings, and disdainful of all show business cant and custom. During the 1930s and 1940s, he ridiculed audiences and rivals, gleefully took on the media, and became the most self-referential comedian of his time. Unlike Letterman, however, Allen wasn't just in it for the laughs. Although he tried to play by the rules of radio, Allen was an engaged and committed satirist laced with outrage and a bleak outlook. When Allen entered radio in 1932, his show had a brash, bright, fizzy new sound, a peculiar mix of verbal comedy and topical wit that had never been heard before.

The show's form was vaudevillian in style—often, as on his famous "Allen's Alley," populated by stock comic types—but its content was acerbic and geared to radio, mocking politicians, news events, advertising, movies, and radio itself, all the hallowed institutions of the day. Allen, alone among his contemporaries, was considered an intellectual, a comic radio radical, a sort of *National Lampoon* of the airwaves.

A CBS executive said, after auditioning Allen in 1929, that he would "never do for radio." He seemed at first too bizarre and savvy for so homey, often corny, a medium. Much of his satire was aimed both at radio's on-air conventions and off-air constraints. Before it became de rigueur, he took generous and regular swipes at mawkish soap operas, treacly kiddie shows, noisy quiz programs, talentless amateur hours, insipid husband-and-wife chatfests, banal interviewers, and mindless commercials. But he saved his most savage attacks for radio's fearful vice-presidents and agency men and their hack mentality, which gave him so much grief. He skewered them in such sketches as one about a lowly gag writer named Gulliver Scribble and a failing comedian, Kenny Dank, who tries desperate ploys to raise his ratings from −2.2. One of Scribble's proudest "gems"—"My sister married an Irishman."

Overleaf, top: Fred Allen; *bottom, from left to right:* Kenny Delmar, Peter Donald, Minerva Pious, Parker Fennelly, and Portland Hoffa (*Allen's Alley*)

"Oh, really?" "No, O'Reilly"—runs into trouble with the censor, the ad agency, and a test audience, none of whom like or get the joke.

Bob Hope also was famous for his topical humor, but Hope was always more interested in being a patriot than an incisive social commentator like Allen, radio's truest satirical gadfly. Some of his shows were cut off the air before they were finished—often because they simply ran overtime, but occasionally because his cracks about NBC executives cut too close to the bone. Allen never understood why shows had to end precisely on time, and once when they cut him off the air in the middle of a sketch, he returned the next week with the end of the sketch and this explanation: "Well, there's a little man in the company we work for. He's a vice-president in charge of program ends. When our program runs overtime, he marks down how much time is saved. He adds it all up. Ten seconds here, twenty seconds there, and when the vice-president has saved up enough seconds, minutes, and hours to make two weeks, he uses the two weeks of our time for his vacation." Allen was not a man easily cowed.

This was a long way from *Fibber McGee and Molly*. Even so, much of Allen's satire now sounds tame, due to its topical nature. A brilliantly cutting joke about the NRA has lost its sharpness today; what made Allen so daring in 1938 is what dates him in 1998. The most vital radio comedians fifty years later are the character comics (Jack Benny, Gracie Allen) or the comic characters of *Amos 'n' Andy, The Great Gildersleeve,* and *Lum and Abner.* Even so, much of Allen's stuff is still on target, like the time he mocked radio stations' habit of nervously identifying themselves every few minutes: "If they did that in theaters, people would burn up," he said. "Imagine a man coming out every half hour during *Hamlet* and saying to the audience, 'This is the St. James Theatre on 44th Street. You are listening to Maurice Evans and Kathryn Locke. We return you now to the Gloomy Dane.' "

Allen's breezy scripts elevated banter into incisive commentary, like another crack about network vice-presidents, whom he dubbed "molehill men." "A molehill man," he said, "comes in at 9 A.M. and finds a molehill on his desk and his job is to turn it into a mountain by five o'clock." Network and advertising executives made his life miserable, but Allen got prime material out of his mythic squabbles with them. Radio was run by ad-agency vice-presidents suddenly anointed impresarios. When one agency man asked him to change a script, Allen exploded in a memo: "You no-good bald-headed sonofabitch, where were you when page 14 was white?"

Sylvester (Pat) Weaver was the lone exception to Allen's antipathy to radio executives. Weaver, who later launched television's *Today* and *Tonight* shows, was assigned to the Allen show, which he approached with trepidation, only to discover that in person "Allen didn't look or act like the ogre he was supposed to be. He was a man of medium height, frowning eyes, and a slightly rumpled pompadour. He made a lot of irreverent remarks to his cast and crew but they were always funny. Several were mildly sarcastic, but I saw no indication of the slightest bit of cruelty. No one seemed to be afraid of him."

Yet the dour Allen remained an outsider with an outsider's nervy instincts. He was such an influential innovator that thirty years later, Johnny Carson was swiping his stuff—specifically, "The Mighty Allen Art Players," which Carson revived as "The Mighty Carson Art Players." Carson also stole Red Skelton's pickled pitchman for Guzzler's Gin, which originated as a sketch on Allen's show and was *first* stolen by Skelton.

Fellow comics and wits James Thurber, S. J. Perelman, Robert Benchley, Groucho Marx, and H. Allen Smith respected Fred Allen's high professional standards, satirical skills, and unique ability to create shows that carried some sting. Groucho Marx wrote a gushing fan letter: "Beyond a shadow of a doubt you are America's Voltaire, England's Ring Lardner, and Spain's Heinrich Heine." Thurber said of him, "You can count on the thumb of one hand the American who is at once a comedian, a humorist, a wit, and a satirist, and his name is Fred Allen."

To mollify network VPs and also to ease the sting, Allen framed his cutting commentary on such sacred subjects as Mother's Day, unions, the FBI, J. Edgar Hoover, the Marshall Plan, FDR, and the WPA within a homespun setting that made his scathing social satire accessible to a general audience. As a workaday vaudevillian, Allen was used to pleasing a wide audience, one city at a time, and learned to tailor his satire to suit the public. That fine balancing act cost him many nights' sleep in fights with network executives who didn't get his intellectual digs and often assumed they must be risqué. Despite an incisive comic intelligence, however, Allen couldn't resist slapstick wordplay. When Port-land Hoffa, his wife and foil, would ask, "Shall we go?," Allen would respond, "As the little boy's lips said to the bubble gum—the time has come to blow," a typical segue as the pair headed up "Allen's Alley." He had a great ear for patois, clichés, and dialects, together with a pro-nounced weakness for excruciating puns, strained alliteration, and wacky similes that harken back to an earlier tradition of frontier humor built on exaggeration and word cartoons, such as Senator Claghorn's "Stand aside, son! Ah'm busier than a flute player's upper lip durin' a rendition of *William Tell.*" Other Allenisms: "His hat was so tight he had to butter his ears to put his hat on" . . . "They were as quiet as a small boy banging two pussywillows together in a vacuum" . . . "A worm is a nudist caterpillar." He once asked a character, "Have you got vertigo?" and the man replied, "Only two blocks."

Nonetheless, several of his better cracker-barrel wisecracks hold up now ("The scarecrow scared the crows so badly they brought back corn they had stolen two years earlier," or his description of eagles as "Tenth Avenue canaries"), and a few have become classics. It was Allen who first made the joke, stolen by nearly every comic in America, about starting a fire by rubbing two Boy Scouts together, and who originally addressed an ad lib to a bald bass player, "How much would you charge to haunt a house?" His definitive line about Hollywood is still quoted: "You can take all the sincerity in Hollywood, put it in a flea's navel, and have room left over for three caraway seeds and an agent's heart." "Agents," he once said, "get 10 percent of everything except my blinding headaches."

But a lot of the lines sound labored today—"He was the first grocer to put bifocal cellophane on apple pie so that nearsighted customers could see what the lower crust looks like"—and a few make you wince, such as his Asian sleuth in a Charlie Chan parody, "Detective One Long Pan," who spoke in stock pidgin-Chinese, "Prease bling me my tlusty lewolver." The widow of Chan's creator, Earl Derr Biggers, tried to sue Allen. Once, in a make-believe commercial about a skin-whitening cream, he used a drawling black man for the "before" voice, followed by a Scandinavian voice endorsing the product.

So although he is remembered as a daring satirist, much of Allen's material was safe, traditional, broad, and strained, notably his reliance on silly names like Pincus Quagmire, Lotta Spunk, Judge Nullen Void, Dr. Rancid Squirm, Eustace Gwelf, and Urquhardt Pollen; it was a burlesque habit he never broke. Two running characters were Socrates Mulligan and Falstaff Openshaw, a Bowery bard who spoke in shaggy verse. Allen was addicted to verbal cartwheels, such as the spoonerisms spun out by Roy Atwell ("Rends, Fromans, and Countrymen, end me your lears").

Like his cronies, he traded heavily in what the critic John Crosby termed "the automatic joke," which dwelled ad nauseam on Jimmy Durante's nose, Bing Crosby's wealth, Bob Hope's golf and womanizing, Jack Benny's parsimony, Eddie Cantor's daughters, etc. It was an early instance of a showbiz syndrome that still infects late-night TV—trotting out guests for courtesy calls, incestuous cross-pollinating plug-athons—but he tried to fit celebrities into the show rather than building the show around the guest. He was the first to use guest stars like Orson Welles creatively. On a 1940s show, he and Welles did an inspired five-minute version of *Les Misérables* (four decades before Tom Stoppard's *Five-Minute Hamlet*), in which Welles has all the lines as Jean Valjean and Allen's Javert is reduced to knocking on doors and blowing a police whistle.

It was considered an honor to be asked to appear on Allen's show, even at a lower fee than bigger shows were paying. Leo Durocher was cast in an Allen version of *Pinafore,* Charles Laughton played a soap opera scene, Helen Traubel sang a jingle, Rodgers and Hammerstein were plaintiffs in a courtroom drama, Bea Lillie belted out an aria from *Rigoletto,* Met tenor Lauritz Melchior did some gospel, and Shakespearean actor Maurice Evans warbled "Ragtime Cowboy Joe." Regularly, Allen parodied a prestigious University of Chicago Round Table program.

Few outside radio realized it, but Allen was less comedian than writer, despite his vaudeville years as a juggler-cum-comic, like W. C. Fields. Allen's Dickensian youth was not dissimilar to Fields's—broken home, alcoholic father, hand-to-mouth struggles—and bred the cynical worldview that gave his humor its edge; an early surefire Allen joke was, "Let X equal the signature of my father."

By the time Allen got into radio he was thirty-eight and had developed confidence in his own comic sense, plus a well-defined world view, unlike many aging vaudevillians busily looking over their shoulder at their stage pasts. He wasn't a clown, but his querulous voice was made for radio, with a whinnying laugh and whine as recognizable as W. C. Fields's. It imparted a dry, deadpan topspin to lines, even when they weren't that funny—a sardonic singsong twang that made them sound amusing and persuaded his first sponsor to hire "the man with the flat voice." Allen's haggard pickle-puss face was wasted on radio, and never stood a chance on TV, but somehow his voice implied how he looked.

His first program, *The Linit Bath Club Revue* (Linit was a bathing lotion), was a dark horse when it debuted in 1932 but became the season's upset winner. The early shows were performed in a void, sans audience, which suited Allen just fine, enabling him to control the lines and timing, much as a humorist does on paper. Like Jack Benny, he came at radio with both trepidation and respect, perceiving that it was as different from vaudeville as talkies were from silents. The two comics were also similar in their respect for the home audience, their keen intelligence and editing instincts—and, most of all, for their willingness to let others on the show get the laughs. Benny, however, was the butt of the jokes, while Allen rarely was. He seemed to be above the banter even as he was engaged in it, more observer than participant; the person who made the most fun of Allen was Jack Benny. Interestingly, four of radio's major comedy stars—Jack Benny, George Burns, Edgar Bergen, and Fred Allen—were straight men. Allen could deliver a funny line flawlessly, but most of his dialogue consisted of such "hilarious" cracks as, "You don't say?" "Is that right?" and "Yes, I suppose it is."

Other radio comics were in awe of him, especially those in his own radio rep company. He worked everyone hard, as he did himself, holing up all week to bat out scripts before going to an all-night deli on Sixth Avenue to thrash them out with his cowriters, often tumbling into bed at 4 A.M.: He earned those famous eye pouches. Yet despite the all-night sessions, Allen was considered a generous boss. He gave announcer Kenny Delmar the rights to the Senator Claghorn character that Delmar played but which Allen had created (recycling an earlier blowhard, Senator Bloat).

When Allen began in radio he earned a paltry thousand dollars a week, which included the salaries for his supporting cast. In those early shows, Allen tried to bend radio to his purposes and to establish it as a branch of theater, both to make the show more accessible to new listeners and to create the musical revue of the air he had in mind. He may have been radio's first, maybe only, true *auteur* comic.

By his second show, Allen had established his smartness credentials with a send-up of Eugene O'Neill called "Slice Yourself a Piece of Life," presented by the Drooping Walrus Dramatic Players. As in his earlier Broadway revues, Allen's shows assumed a level of literacy by the audience, including parodies of *Lysistrata* and Sherlock Holmes. Critics quickly recognized a new voice and style, several cuts above other variety programs. Even in his twenties he had been considered a comic's comic, and often doctored others' acts. The producer of *The Linit Bath Club Revue* later recalled, "After six weeks, everyone was talking about Fred Allen."

Arnold Auerbach, an Allen writer, remembered Allen at work in an undone bowtie and shirtsleeves, glasses down on his nose, and a wad of Tuck's five-cent chaw in his cheek. With an eyeshade and arm garters, he reminded Auerbach of "a cantankerous small-town newspaper editor." A Broadway columnist remarked that Allen wore expensive clothes that looked rumpled because he crammed his pockets with notes and news items. But despite the seeming jumble, Allen had a system, a kind of early pocket organizer, scribbling ideas as they came to him on a folio made up of carefully creased sheets of paper folded into squares, like an old reporter's makeshift notebook.

In a letter to a friend (written in his peculiar lower-case newsman's style), Allen provided a revealing peek into the frantic scene necessitated by getting a live comedy program on the air—and off—in time: "after the two days spent writing them and two days rehearsing and cutting and consulting with the bosses about what is what, you don't feel so funny when it gets around to nine o'clock on friday night, for every second counts and we try to cram so much stuff into the half hour that we can't let down for a second. you should be around some night just before the broadcast when we are trying to take out 45 seconds. the guy with the stopwatch and i are cutting out odd words. by the time you get to the mike you're afraid to unbend or change a word lest the thing run over . . ." If time got tight, Allen often cut his own lines to preserve the "Alley" residents' jokes, endearing himself to the cast.

He held a low opinion of most comedy shows, confiding to a colleague, "i wonder what thoughts are rampant in the minds of the morons who bark the same jokes over the networks week after week. the only way i can figure it out is that the listeners have the same mentality and do not discriminate. . . ."

Studio audiences were a necessary evil to Allen, who traced the people who flocked to radio shows to "a slow leak in Iowa." He felt that they falsely inflated a program's mirth quotient. Even so, he enjoyed talking to people one-on-one during strolls through the crowd for mock quiz-show segments, or in his "People You Didn't Expect to Meet" spot, chatting with folks in odd jobs. He liked people, just not en masse, though strangers cowered before his devastating ad libs. He didn't zing guests, like Groucho, but his repartee intimidated housewives and visiting firemen.

What he craved was intimacy, which he felt a large live audience squelched, once remarking, "It seemed to me that this alleged entertainment should be geared down to the tempo of life in the home. If a visitor banged into your living room and carried on his conversation yelling and hawking his points, in the manner and at a tempo employed by most radio comedians, you would hasten his departure." Allen resisted all attempts to dumb himself down to audiences, fearing that "pretty soon I will be one of those Captain Andy fellows calling everybody 'folks.'" In one testy outburst, he lashed out: "The worst thing that ever happened to radio was the studio audience. We should never have made the change. Somebody like Eddie Cantor brought these hordes of cackling geese in because he couldn't work without a bunch of imbeciles laughing at his jokes. Would anybody with a brain be caught dead in a studio audience? Would anybody with a sense of taste stand in line to watch half a dozen people in business suits standing around reading into microphones?"

Allen didn't disdain all audiences, just noisy ones, but he in some respects was working at cross-purposes with the medium, because the louder audiences howled, the more sponsors and network liked it, figuring that the more raucous the audience, the funnier the show must be. Then as now, studio audiences were primed to laugh by cheerleading announcers or studio aides who begged crowds to howl. Audiences became live laugh machines, set to giggle on cue, just as they do now at

TV sitcoms. Studio audiences rankled him because their responses couldn't be controlled, forcing shows to run over. He was more interested in reaching what he felt was a more discriminating crowd—the silent majority at home he couldn't see. And he found them, despite sponsors who worried he was pitching his shows too high. The first few seasons his show drew 20 million listeners, or three out of every four radio sets. By April 1947 Allen had joked his way onto the cover of *Time,* the supreme accolade. One year later, sunk to twenty-eighth place, he had become television's most visible early victim.

Allen's *Town Hall Tonight* was devised to replace various earlier ungainly names that called attention not to the star but to the sponsor—*The Linit Bath Club Revue, The Salad Bowl Revue* (for Hellmann's mayonnaise), *The Sal Hepatica Revue.* Overall, he did seven different shows for five major sponsors. Most of the time, the nervous sponsors felt his humor was over the heads of small-town America, but everyone looked forward to the star's weekly amble down "Allen's Alley" as characters like Titus Moody and Mrs. Nussbaum popped their head through a door and piped, "Howdy, bub," or, "You vair eggspecting mebbe de Fink Spots?"

Nobody in radio battled censorship like Allen, who refused to back down before idiotic constraints dished out each week by the network and agency people second-guessing each other. Seen from today's anything-goes perspective, the petty edits seem as funny as anything Allen devised on purpose, but the censors were on special alert and clamped down harder on Allen than on other comics, knowing his reputation for pointed satire. He kept a list of the words, lines, characters, and sketches he was forced to delete from his shows, such as *saffron, pizzicating a woman's lavaliere, rabelaisian,* and *titillate,* all considered dirty. A reference to a judge "going to a higher court" was deleted, since heaven was comically off-limits, as were jokes about ministers and marital vows, such as "She promises to love, honor, and lump it till death do them part." Any sexual innuendo was fatal, and when Beatrice Lillie devised a stutter to get around the censors ("Son of a b-b-b-bachelor," or "That's a wh-wh-wh-whole lot of sh-sh-sh-shortening"), comics like Allen and Benny complained that Lillie was getting away with murder.

The slimmest possibility of offending a real person or place drew objections from an Allen censor who once scoured social registers and almanacs to make sure there wasn't a real dowager named Mrs. Biddle Pratt, or a Senator Guff of Idaho (NBC allowed it only grudgingly, fearing there might be a Senator Guff *someday*); a fictitious first mate on the *Queen Mary* was stripped of a cockney accent because, reasoned NBC, the real first mate might object. A town called North Wrinkle had the censor combing maps and atlases to make sure no such place existed. A joke about "wasting an afternoon at the rodeo" was altered, presumably to avoid offending thin-skinned rodeo-goers. A gag about a girl who Allen said could have found a better husband in a cemetery was changed so as not to upset cemetery owners—or perhaps the deceased. NBC trembled when racists objected to black heavyweight champion Joe Louis calling Allen "Fred." To placate advertisers, he had to cut "huckster" and a sketch about a town being blown away when someone ignited a gas leak; gas companies were sensitive. Allen complained to H. Allen Smith in a note, "each week fifty percent of what i write ends up in the toilet . . . practically everything is taboo and we end up with ersatz subject matter and ditto humor."

Allen's mastery of the ad lib caused special problems, for there's no way to censor an ad lib and certain comics unleashed on other shows made the networks nervous. Bing Crosby and Jack Benny were also cited as loose cannons. Comics often snuck in ad libs during rebroadcasts to the West Coast. A female network censor suggested that Allen hold a meeting with Young & Rubicam to have him divulge "his sources of humor"—presumably to plug any possible humorous leaks at the source.

Allen learned how to outfox the censors by a favorite gag writers' survival technique: He would include in each script a few decoy jokes to bargain away, holding on to the lines he really wanted in. Pat Weaver said Allen was "the one person I knew who was neither impressed nor frightened by the power of the agencies."

Even hounded by censors, Allen got away with much more than most radio comedians, but he also *tried* to get away with much more. He took a certain pleasure in his rebel reputation and in making life hot for the censors, both on and off mike. Allen was never a reformer or a radical but a satirist, content to work within the system even if he had no hope for it. In the words of an Allen scholar, Alan Havig, "Jeering was its own reward."

Jim North, an ad executive who worked on several radio shows, says, "Fred couldn't get along with anybody. That was his professional position. I wouldn't say he was feared but people were hesitant to cross him or take him on. He once called a skinny ad guy 'an ulcer with suspenders.' Fred Allen was usually right when it came to show business matters, but the reality was that the client had the last word and could say, 'Screw you, Fred Allen.' "

The Depression first pushed Allen into radio, as it did a lot of road-weary performers, guaranteeing him a season of work without travel, fleabag hotels, broken-down buses, booking hassles, sleazy producers, and tank-town theaters. As Allen observed, a "radio show could not close if there was nobody in the balcony."

He hit his stride on his 1934 show *The Hour of Smiles,* later retitled *Town Hall Tonight* and generally considered his best work. It was a low-budget affair that opened with a march down a mythical Main Street amid whoops, cheers, and band music interrupted by bystanders' remarks. He instinctively realized that setting his big-city satire on Main Street would more readily lure listeners who might otherwise be put off by the show's urbane material. "It seemed to me," he said, sounding like one of the demographically oriented agency men he hated, "that if we had a title that would interest people in small towns, our program would have wider appeal."

An ad agency executive forced him to change the show's title from *Town Hall Tonight* to *The Fred Allen Show* to make it conform more closely to Jack Benny's program, then the model of what a sophisticated show was like. It was felt that *Town Hall Tonight* sounded too small-town, which Allen had intended both ironically and sentimentally. "The colorful allusion had been completely stripped from the program," he later moaned. "We became just another group of actors gathered around a microphone in a radio studio."

Although his roots were deeply imbedded in vaudeville, where he billed himself "The World's Worst Juggler" and "Just a Young Fellow Trying to Get Along," Fred Allen came to radio via satirical Broadway musical revues—sophisticated little shows like, well, *The Little Show,*

The Passing Show of 1922, and *Three's a Crowd,* which starred Allen, Clifton Webb, and Libby Holman, an unlikely trio. Of his radio show, he said, "You could take away the scripts from the cast, cut the best parts out of a few shows, and make a good Broadway revue out of them." These sophisticated revues—satirical, full of witty repartee, atuned to the headlines—were the vital transition that perfectly prepared him for radio.

LONG AFTER HE BECAME A RADIO STAR, Allen would return to old show business haunts for nostalgic visits and as a humbling antidote to the headiness of celebrity. Vaudeville always seemed a sweeter time to him than radio (as radio did to those who left it for TV or movies), and he sprinkled scripts with jokes about his life on the road and savored memories of his scruffy Boston boyhood.

The caricaturist Al Hirschfeld, a lifelong friend of Allen's (whose circle also included the S. J. Perelmans and the William Saroyans), recalled, "Fred loved cheap hotels, absolutely adored them," and Arnold Auerbach added, "He was a permanent transient with the transient's aversion to possessions and long leases." Those cheerless rooming houses, with their peeling plaster walls lit by a single small bulb, were the sort of joint that provided Allen with memorable jokes on radio—"I had a room so small it had removable doorknobs," and, "The room was so small that the mice were hunchback." He disdained big-city life, declined to join the Algonquin Round Table, and vacationed at the same sedate beach in Maine each year, which he said was "so dull the tide went out and never came back." Here he pecked out scripts in happy solitude before the haven, Orchard Beach, became a tourist sandbox filled with autograph seekers. Perhaps with himself in mind, he once defined a celebrity as "a person who works hard all his life to become well known, then wears dark glasses to avoid being recognized."

Even though he came out of the same knockabout school of comedy as Joe Penner, Jack Pearl, and Ed Wynn, Allen was a more learned jester than most. His routines were filled with wild metaphors and acrobatic similes to which he gave newsy twists, such as a nasty 1933 hurricane that Allen described as having "wind so strong in one New Jersey town that it blew two prohibition workers into a speakeasy." Most comics might have been satisfied with that, but Allen added a topper: "Luckily, the wind blew the speakeasy into a church and the bartender was converted."

He was an avid reader of the classics—Twain and Dickens in particular. His trunk was always piled with books, and on tour he kept a copy of H. G. Wells's *Outline of History* with him. His writers included the pre–*Sergeant Bilko* Nat Hiken and the pre–*Caine Mutiny* Herman Wouk, among many less famous others, such as Bob Weiskopf, who later wrote for *I Love Lucy* and *All in the Family*. Weiskopf, who specialized in writing the interview guest spot for Allen, recalls, " 'Allen's Alley' was real torture, because it was patched together with a roomful of writers, not written solo, like other segments. This required brainstorming aloud with other gag writers, with each session a matter of survival of the loudest. Fred liked mixing it up. He used to say, 'From bad comes good.' "

Weiskopf goes on, "I was pretty terrified, sitting in a room with the great man. I did okay because I was good at out-and-out jokes, but one guy was so terrified he didn't open his mouth all season. I was working alone for the first time. It was my favorite show [to write for]. I got very friendly with Fred—our wives were friends—even though you try not to be social with the boss; the boss is the boss. I was with him to the end." Aluding to Allen's dark side, he adds, "To cope with him was difficult—he was a real W. C. Fields character."

George Burns called Allen "an essentially gloomy man," and Jack Benny said: "When you got him off vaudeville, Allen became somebody else, a bitter, frustrated and unhappy man. I couldn't figure out why he was so unhappy about life. He thought life was some sort of miserable trap. I don't know what he wanted or expected out of life or why he was so basically disgruntled about living."

Herman Wouk told Allen's biographer, Robert Taylor, of his devotion to his early boss: "He was a role model and still is. Fred was the most honorable man I ever met. He was the best comic writer radio ever developed, and we were handing in what must have seemed to him mediocre material. I was twenty-one years old and making two hundred dollars a week, a remarkable salary for the Depression. Not once did he tell us our contribution wasn't good enough. We never had a contract. 'Do you want to try it again for another year?' Fred would say, and that was that. The purpose of having youngsters like myself around was simply to eke out the sheer volume of material." Everyone, Wouk included, was heavily rewritten by Allen, who treated his staff like idea men providing raw material he could reshape.

Allen's workaholism and weekly grind made him feel he "lived in a fog, a bedlam." Despite a staff of three writers, Allen cowrote or rewrote by hand, in tiny letters, all fifty pages of each show. His head writer, Harry Tugend, would submit ten pages, and "even if he liked it, he'd feel a need to rewrite it," or toss it out for a new idea, tinkering with a script up to final rehearsal.

Allen, like Benny, hired first-rate writers and prudently employed his wife—an old vaudeville ploy used by married acts as a way to double their income and expense money: If the comic's wife had any talent, it was so much gravy. Married couples in radio seemed to have a built-in added appeal. Six of radio's must popular comedy shows were husband-and-wife teams: George Burns and Grace Allen, Jim and Marian Jordan, Goodman and Jane Ace, Ozzie and Harriet Nelson, Jack and Mary Benny, and Allen and Hoffa.

Portland Hoffa, a version of the Gracie Allen archetype, played a naive secretary in a quavery, addled voice, addressed the host as "Mr. *Al-l-l-*len," and read daffy letters from home, as did Gracie and Mary Livingstone. Even though she was Allen's sidekick, Hoffa seemed the least defined character among the regulars, and at one point there was a thwarted attempt to drop her from the show. She began as Allen's anonymous stooge, or "wooge" as she called it. She was, to quote one writer, "a decorative adjunct . . . a generic little girl" who fed him setup lines, but she evolved into a lovably daffy dame. She was always welcomed by such typical Allen lines as, "Well, as I try to make both ends meet in this tight vest, if it isn't Portland!"

"I had no desire for show business," Hoffa readily admitted, "but I got the breaks." Allen had carefully nurtured her latent comedic skills from her days as a chorus girl in *The Passing Show of 1922* and was fiercely protective of her. In a letter to an agency vice-president who told him the sponsor's wife thought Portland should be dumped, he exploded: "You tell him that Portland is my wife, that she makes my life livable, and that her presence on the show is not a matter of negotiation. We're a family and we work as a family. If he doesn't want Mrs.

Allen, he doesn't want Mr. Allen. I'm telling you and you tell him—never mention this subject to me again."

Even by show business standards, the Allens were considered a slightly eccentric pair. Not only did they keep to themselves, but they would rather walk or take a subway than grab a taxi. Allen never learned to drive, worked out at a nearby YMCA instead of a nicer gym across the street, lived for years in a theatrical hotel, and dined at the same Italian restaurant the same night each week. An NBC executive wrote, "We speak of creatures of habit—Fred is a rigid mold of habit." Arnold Auerbach added that for Allen, "life was ritualistic in its regularity. His week—immutable, symmetrical as the solar system—revolved around a single sixty minutes—the hour on Wednesday when *Town Hall Tonight* was on the air. He lived for Portland and for the program."

If Jack Benny's show was about his actual radio family, Allen fashioned his radio gang out of a handful of deft dialect comics who—as a money-saving device—could play assorted characters, a quartet who found fame years later as inhabitants of "Allen's Alley": Peter Donald, Minerva Pious, Parker Fennelly, and Kenny Delmar, who also covered as announcer and straight man. Their alter egos were Ajax Cassidy, Mrs. Nussbaum, Titus Moody, and, most celebrated of all, Delmar's Senator Claghorn, an inspired name still synonymous with Southern windbags, who contributed "That's a joke, son!" to the American idiom.

For Allen, ethnic humor was a handy comic tool left over from vaudeville, like daffy names, but by 1945 it felt old. After the war, certain Jewish groups weren't pleased by Mrs. Nussbaum, and at first Allen had to fight to keep her on the show. Jews were also shocked when Allen first uttered the word *shmoe* (a laundered locution for *schmuck,* Yiddish for "penis"). Yiddishisms had not yet permeated the airwaves, as they would a generation later on late-night TV.

Nonetheless, Mrs. Nussbaum was hard to resist when she opened the door and delivered her trademark opener: "You vair eggspecting mebbe Cecil B. Schlemiel?" (or "Emperor Shapiro-Hito," "Dinah Schnorer," etc.). Pious, a keen dialectician, played her with warmth, spirit, and self-mockery. With mangled references to "rutabagels," "Rudyard Kaplan," and "Weinstein Churchill," she was as charming as Leo Rosten's literary immigrant Hyman Kaplan.

"Allen's Alley" was really just another excuse for Allen to bounce news items off recurring characters, but the Alley's residents had larger-than-life personalities. Also, it took advantage of Allen's favorite comic forum—the man-in-the-street interview (revived by Steve Allen on TV), then newly in vogue, when Roper, Hooper, and Gallup pollsters were on every corner, clipboards in hand.

Delmar's Senator Beauregard Claghorn was a fierce defender of Southern pride, who never drove through the Lincoln Tunnel, drank only from Dixie cups, and wore Kentucky derbies. Delmar was a radio veteran—he had played the secretary of state on Orson Welles's *War of the Worlds*—but his yakkity Claghorn character was so popular it resulted in spin-off items: compasses that only pointed south and a record entitled *That's a Joke, Son!* What made Claghorn so funny wasn't just the anti-Yankee jokes but the dithering frenzy with which Delmar portrayed him.

Half the fun of "Allen's Alley" was the weekly ritual of Allen and Hoffa moseying down the imaginary side street encountering familiar characters. Allen: "Well, here we are, back in Allen's Alley, Portland. I wonder if the Senator's home. Let's knock. (*rap-rap-rap*)" . . . Claghorn: "Somebody—ah, say, *some*body pounded mah plywood!"

Fennelly's Titus Moody was Allen's favorite character, the definitive weathered, tight-lipped New Englander who espoused the host's skeptical, old-fashioned values: "Effen I ain't a rube," Titus said, "I'll do till one gets here." Titus to Allen: "My granny used to play the zither." Allen: "Was your grandmother good?" Titus: "When Granny'd play 'Can She Bake a Cherry Pie, Billy Boy,' you could smell cookin' comin' outta the zither."

Fennelly, who claimed, "I was born old," had perfected the type in previous radio incarnations; Cliff Arquette and Bill Thompson played a version of Moody on *Fibber McGee and Molly*—The Old-Timer. The character reappeared decades later on TV selling pies with Fennelly as the pipe-puffing, crusty Pepperidge Farm man. Before Allen finally arrived at the magic formula that paid off in 1942 as "Allen's Alley," he tinkered with the idea for years in several formats, first as "Town Hall News," then "Passé News" (a riff on Pathé newsreels), then "The March of Trivia" (*The March of Time*), all based on news items Allen scoured for absurdities.

"Allen's Alley" gave the transient nature of Allen's shows a hook and a continuity his earlier programs had lacked; the trade-off was that the Alley characters grew predictable. Benny had his circle and Fibber McGee and Molly their Wistful Vista neighbors. Most comedy shows had a crew of much-anticipated drop-ins whose familiar greetings were met with authentic warm applause. It was one of radio's most reliable ways of bonding with its invisible audience.

The ethnic mix of an Irishman, a Jew, a Yankee, and a son of Dixie helped give the show its cosmopolitan flavor. By 1942, many comedy shows were sunnily ensconced in Los Angeles, the site of all the inside-L.A. jokes that replaced the New York jokes about the Dodgers, the Automat, the Sixth Avenue El, the Bronx Zoo, Macy's *vs.* Gimbel's, sidewalk vendors, and rude taxi drivers.

Jack Benny's long "feud" with Fred Allen bounced between their two shows and fueled both stars' comic images for a decade. Allen was the ideal man for the role of Benny provocateur. His barbs echoed Benny's in-house needlers. Without insult humor, radio comedy might have gone out of business by 1925, or as Allen had announcer Harry Von Zell cannily observe on one show: "You know how all these programs start, Fred. If the announcer doesn't insult the comedian, people don't even know it's a comedy show."

The Allen-Benny mock feud was the most successful in radio (and gave rise to Hope and Crosby's copycat feud), pitting two of the country's most popular comics against each other in what became a well-milked long-running gag, a mutually beneficial insult marathon that grew wilder by the month. "That guy's so cheap," said Allen in a typical sally, "he'd put his finger down a moth's throat to get his cloth back." Benny had less to work with—Allen, despite his radio presence, had a pallid comic persona—so his comebacks were mainly about Allen's baggy eyes or nasal twang. Each time one comic appeared on the other's show, ratings zoomed, all of it climaxing in a heavily hyped face-to-face confrontation at the Hotel Pierre in New York, by which time the feud had pretty well played itself out; the face-off was anticlimactic, but a glorious publicity coup. Listeners enjoyed the not very lethal badinage. Allen: "The first time I met Benny was in Elyria, Ohio. He was doing a monologue with a pig on stage" . . . Hoffa: "A pig?" . . . Allen: "Yes, the pig was there to eat up the stuff the audience threw at Benny."

The first shot was fired in 1936 by Allen on his year-end show, following violin prodigy Stewart Canin playing "The Flight of the Bumblebee," which prompted Allen's relatively innocuous jab, "You play 'The Bee' so well—Jack Benny ought to be ashamed of himself." For the benign Benny, it was almost a compliment, he explained later: "He probably said that, knowing I was listening to the show, just to make me laugh." The feud went on for six months before either comedian telephoned the other to discuss it. For the stars it was a running gag that got out of hand when the media seized on it and turned it into a papier-mâché battle.

It may sound toothless now, but listeners relished hearing two comics dueling across the dial, as if Jay Leno and David Letterman were to begin lobbing comic grenades back and forth today. Allen theorized that the feud caught on because at the time "radio was fraught with politeness"—honeyed crooners, genial announcers, sappy soap operas, and banter that barely left a flesh wound.

Benny and Allen also shared mediocre movie careers and once costarred in a picture neither liked, *Love Thy Neighbor.* Allen made five movies in all, halfhearted affairs like *It's in the Bag, Thanks a Million,* and *We're Not Married,* opposite Ginger Rogers, in which they play a husband and wife (modeled on radio's *Dorothy and Dick* and *Tex and Jinx*) who host a jolly morning talk show but loathe each other off-mike; Woody Allen later replowed the same ground in his movie *Radio Days.*

Like most radio comics who tried to cross over into movies and, later, TV, Allen's physical presence wasn't as funny as his voice alone; a biographer wrote that Allen didn't photograph well, observing that "his attitude toward the camera was shy and vigilant." In an early film short, *The Collector,* he looks deflated, slouchy, and flat-footed, as he did on his later unhappy TV appearances. His literate jokes don't amuse the camera, which he appears to be dodging, and his relaxed radio timing is stilted. Of all the great radio comedians, only Bob Hope matched his radio success in movies. Benny, Allen, Burns and Allen, Bergen and McCarthy, Brice, Berle, Durante, Wynn, *Amos 'n' Andy,*

Fibber McGee and Molly, Lum and Abner, The Goldbergs—all were cinematic flops to one degree or another, for a variety of reasons.

It didn't help that Allen also hated Los Angeles, but the city inspired his sharpest cracks—"To me, it all looks like Waterbury on a rainy Sunday." He called the Hollywood Bowl "Carnegie Hall on the half-shell," said, "Hollywood is a place where people from Iowa mistake each other for stars," and defined an associate producer as "the only guy in Hollywood who will associate with a producer."

FRED ALLEN NEVER made the transition to television, not only because he distrusted the new visual medium ("They call it a medium because nothing on it is ever well done," he said, a line since appropriated by one and all) but because his wit was too verbal and cerebral. One of his favorite targets was a manic giveaway show, *Pot o' Gold*, which he parodied as "The Tub o' Silver," but he was put out of business by just such a show, *Stop the Music*, which held America in thrall from week to week awaiting the name of the "Mystery Melody."

Opposite *Stop the Music*, Allen's 1948 ratings collapsed from 28.7 to 11.2, while the quiz show leaped from 0 to 20 within months; even Bob Hope's show fell from 23.8 percent in 1949 to 12.7 by 1951. Allen—suddenly a ghost of radio past—toppled almost instantaneously, a major victim of the giveaway fad that overtook radio in the late 1940s as a desperate ploy to keep listeners tuned in and deflect their attention from the dreaded tube that had begun creeping into homes like an invasion of one-eyed body-snatchers.

Allen tried to fend off the alien form with satire, but it failed him for the first time in his career. His instinctive comic response, called "Cease the Music," offered listeners two floors of the Empire State Building, 4,000 yards of used dental floss, 800 pounds of putty for every member of the family, the gangplank of the *Queen Mary*, and 12 miles of railroad track to the first caller. Interestingly, however, he caved in and actually awarded $5,000. Then he got mad and lost his sense of humor. Edgar Bergen, also on opposite *Stop the Music*, simply retreated from radio for a season, but Allen was drawn into the fight—not just out of survival instinct, but out of a deep resentment at how radio was being ruined by what amounted to tawdry "bank nights," the movie theaters' frantic response to TV. The sad truth was that Allen's small-town world—even Allen himself—was being overwhelmed. The critic Harriet Van Horne wrote that *Stop the Music* had "tumbled Fred Allen from the plush pew reserved for Hooper's Top 10 to a camp stool in back of *Lum and Abner.*"

It was hard to believe that people once had actually scalped free tickets to the Allen show. On one of his last shows, in October 1948, Allen attacked the quiz phenomenon in a thinly veiled crusade that didn't hide his true anger. He referred to contestants as "a herd of morons," adding, "Many winners are so dumb that they can't find their way out of the building." He sourly advised a young would-be broadcaster that a good way to break into radio would be to shoot a quiz-show MC, adding: "A lot of listeners will be grateful to you for killing the m.c. and good will is important if you hope to survive in radio."

A year later, with the gag writing on the wall, he narrated a program called "The State of American Humor" and delivered a grim obituary on radio comedy that included an embittered interview with announcer Ben Grauer, who said, "Then you see little hope for humor in radio?" Allen responded, "I never thought I'd live to see the day when I'd have to compete with a washing machine. Ice boxes are replacing actors and musicians. The idea seems to be, if you can't entertain people, *give* them something. If that's not a sorry comment on contemporary entertainment, I don't know what is." He also got in a well-aimed jab at TV: "In the beginning, television drove people out of their homes into saloons [to watch it], but now people have sets in their homes and TV is driving people back into the saloons."

Grauer, hoping to end on an upbeat note, chirped, "But it's a new source of humor, Fred," only to have Allen grump, "Aw, new source of humor! So far it's nothing but a throwback, reviving the vaudeville approach to everything from mugging to juggling"—conveniently forgetting that radio was founded by the ancestors of those very same muggers and jugglers, himself among them.

Allen, bitterly and too easily, blamed his old nemesis Madison Avenue, but he was simply worn-out. He had, after all, survived longer than almost everyone else. When his show was trimmed from an hour to thirty minutes, in 1945, he was forced to compress sketches and banter, and much of the unforced quality went out of the show. After so long, burnout was inevitable, especially for a man of Allen's intense nature. Arnold Auerbach admitted as much: "After 200 broadcasts, freshness and enthusiasm inevitably wane; formulas resurface; set patterns emerge. In one season of radio, we would tell more jokes than Weber & Fields probably told in ten years." In fact, his show had become somewhat predictable and, for all its topicality, had a shopworn feeling by the late 1940s. The last regular *Fred Allen Show* aired on June 26, 1949, nearly eighteen years after he had arrived on radio as a breath of fresh air.

Despite his reluctance to enter TV, he proposed a video version of "Allen's Alley," but it never happened—his hangdog face and acidic personality didn't have a chance in the jolly family-centered universe of 1950s TV, where seldom was heard a discouraging, let alone disdainful, word. Pre-cable TV, with precious few exceptions (Sid Caesar's shows, *Saturday Night Live, SCTV, The Smothers Brothers Comedy Hour*) was never as receptive to biting satire as radio. Radio was, and remains even now, TV's off-Broadway.

Allen wound up as one of several rotating stars of *The Colgate Comedy Hour,* but it was largely a defensive tactic. "I'm fending off oblivion," he told colleagues who wondered why he deigned to go on TV in ill-suited formats. "The Fred Allen of *What's My Line?,*" Steve Allen said, "was not the real Fred Allen." The real Fred Allen said of TV, "They're just photographing vaudeville," and, more famously, "Imitation is the sincerest form of television."

Bob Weiskopf, who was there at the end, reflects on Allen's demise: "He made a big mistake. He thought that when TV came along, he could use his radio scripts. He did a few TV scripts, though, that were really very good. But Fred was impatient. If he'd have stuck around he'd have made it." What stymied him, Weiskopf believes, wasn't just TV itself but that "he couldn't figure out how to stage 'Allen's Alley' " for television; incredibly, he considered reviving "Allen's Alley" with puppets. Perhaps because Allen "had a way of thinking visually," adds Weiskopf, TV was superfluous. "He could act vocally. In radio, voice was movement." He made a halfhearted stab hosting, of all things, a TV game show, *Judge for Yourself,* on which a jury gave thumbs-up or -down to new performers, but the expected peppery repartee never happened. With undisguised bile, Allen called TV "a device that permits people who haven't anything to do to watch people who can't do anything."

In fact, TV became a medium for neovaudevillians like Jackie Gleason, Sid Caesar, Martin and Lewis, Dick Van Dyke, and Lucille Ball, or for reborn burlesque bananas like Sid Caesar, Abbott and Costello, Martha Raye, and, most of all, Berle. Allen fell between the cracks. Just as many radio comedians leaned too heavily on the visual, Allen's humor was too verbal for TV. When you think of Fred Allen, you don't think of how he looked but how he sounded and what he said; when you think of Lucille Ball, you can't remember a thing she ever said that was remotely funny, but you remember the face, the takes.

What Allen lacked was TV presence. Pat Weaver said, "It broke my heart to watch him on TV. If I had been able to put him on the *Tonight* show, his ability to ad-lib would have made him even more legendary than he is." He wasn't lovable enough for the 1950s, but would have been just right for the cynical and ironic 1990s.

Finally, Fred Allen became a kind of comic emeritus. He joined the writing and performing staff of radio's last gasp, *The Big Show*, a $100,000-a-program extravaganza hosted by Tallulah Bankhead and featuring mighty headliners—Ethel Merman, Fanny Brice, Groucho Marx, Jane Powell; Allen worked on the scripts.

He hosted a few episodes of TV's big show, *The Colgate Comedy Hour*, a Sunday-night rival to *The Ed Sullivan Show*, with rotating comic hosts like Martin and Lewis, Cantor, Durante, and Wynn, but the first shows—and his doctor—convinced him to give it up. It wasn't just that TV was a new medium; the entire atmosphere and procedure were foreign to him, plus he had to work with performers he didn't respect. It wasn't fun anymore.

As he wrote to Herman Wouk in an exhausted voice: "outside of a panel deal or some easy show that i could ad lib, i don't think i can cope with the furor most of these musical revues stir up. i have only done the tv guest dates to keep occupied. it has been a new experience doing what other comedians have wanted. for almost 18 years i was telling them what to do on my own show. most of the revues are assembled to the accompaniment of the bloodiest bedlam you can imagine. it is almost impossible to be relaxed working with comedy material you barely know."

He also wondered if anyone still cared. "Radio," he wrote in a melancholy voice in his memoirs, *Treadmill to Oblivion*, "smelled of yesterday's levity." Another time, feeling less immodest about his own great contribution, he called his show "a history of this country done in a comedy mode." *Treadmill to Oblivion* became the best selling book on radio ever written, due in part to Allen's drumbeating. He paid for newspaper ads himself and, anticipating today's talk-show author tours, plugged the book all over radio and TV. A Boston critic offered an Allenesque compliment: "It's a shame that television has no place for Allen. He has been reduced to writing books."

Fred Allen died on St. Patrick's Day 1956, while taking one of his regular midnight strolls up 57th Street from his suite at the Warwick Hotel. Herman Wouk eulogized his former mentor in the *New York Times,* saying: "Without a doubt his great contribution to life in America came in the marvelous eighteen-year run of weekly satiric invention. . . . His was the glory of being an original personality, creating new forms of intelligent entertainment. He was without a peer and without a successful imitator." Wouk went on: "He had a deep reticent love of life and of people which is the source of every true satirist's energy. Fred's wit lashed and stung. He could not suffer fools. But his generosity to the needy, his extraordinary loyalty to his associates (in a field not noted for long loyalties) showed the warmth of heart that made his satire sound and important. In Fred Allen the voice of sanity spoke out for all Americans to hear, during a trying period of our history, in the penetrating tones of comic satire. Because he lived and wrote and acted here, this land will always be a saner place to live. That fact is his true monument."

— 6 —
Wise Guys Finish First

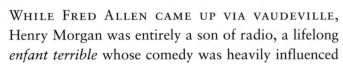

WHILE FRED ALLEN CAME UP VIA VAUDEVILLE, Henry Morgan was entirely a son of radio, a lifelong *enfant terrible* whose comedy was heavily influenced by Allen. But there was a brazen, combative, in-your-face, slightly sour New York quality about Morgan, who gradually did himself in professionally, whereas Allen, a more pragmatic and less pugnacious showman, was able to distance himself—and his real subversive purpose—by speaking through other characters. Allen masked much of his contempt on the air, but Morgan's disdain was undisguised.

So Morgan was radio's first true rebel, a confrontational satirist who shortened his career because—like many comics who go for the jugular, from Lenny Bruce to Roseanne Barr—he didn't know when to quit. He lost sponsors, rankled the network, and resigned from shows before fading from the scene much too soon. He tangled with network censors, like Allen, but unlike Allen, he lacked the clout to win; to the end, he was considered an upstart. The announcer Ed Herlihy, an old Morgan friend from Boston, says: "He was ahead of his time, but he was also hurt by his own disposition. He was very difficult. He was so brilliant that he'd get exasperated and he'd sulk. He was a great mind who never achieved the success he should have."

Morgan endeared himself to a cult of admirers with his flat ho-hum greeting, "Good evening, anybody," delivered in a bored shrug of a voice, followed by his cynical theme song, "For He's a Jolly Good Fellow." His second banana was Arnold Stang, who played a nerdy guy named Gerard who spoke in a Brooklyn squawk, a character later repeated by Stang on Milton Berle's TV show. Morgan chose the greeting as a kick in the pants to Kate Smith's cheery and—to Morgan—fatuous "Hello, everybody!" He signed off each time with a shaky promise to "be back at the same cigar stand next week."

Overleaf, clockwise from top left: Bob Elliott and Ray Goulding (*Bob and Ray*), Arnold Stang and Henry Morgan, Edgar Bergen and Charlie McCarthy with Freddie Bartholomew.

Morgan took no prisoners. By 1947, a year after he went network, radio comedy was on its last legs and had nothing to lose by unloosing anarchic spirits like Morgan and Bob and Ray, who helped put what was left of radio out of its misery. Executives stopped meddling so much and ad libs were almost encouraged—anything to raise comic spirits from the grave. A typically devastating Morgan parody of quiz shows called "Take It, for Heaven's Sake, Take It" features a maniacally laughing announcer ("I have a lady in the balcony—but you should have seen the one who got away!") and an MC who fawns over semiretarded contestants as audiences applaud everything, especially anyone who mentions Brooklyn. Radio quiz shows were sitting ducks, but Morgan's satire has a decidedly hostile edge to it; at one point, he shoots a contestant for not knowing the capital of the United States.

In his tossed-off 1994 memoir, *Here's Morgan!*, published the year before he died, Morgan explained his comic modus operandi: "I couldn't abide reading the junk the clients provided so I ad-libbed them in a kind of breezy, off-handed fashion that sometimes bordered on the insulting." But nearly everything he said sounded like an insult. Morgan's autobiography, like his shows and indeed his whole career, is a series of cranky mutterings in which he devotes more space to a trip to Bangkok than to his career in radio, as if radio were something he'd just as soon forget. He lived a throwaway life, spent largely at celebrity saloons like Toots Shor's, Bleek's, the Absinthe House, the Barberry Room, and Sardi's, before fading away in middle age. Arnold Stang says, "He was a masochist, a neurotic man. When things were going well for him, he would do something to destroy himself. He just couldn't deal with success. He'd had an unhappy childhood that warped him a little and gave him a sour outlook on life. He had no close friends." Stang says that Morgan finally fled to Canada to escape his first wife, who kept him deeply in debt and refused to give him a divorce. Even so, Stang adds, Morgan was "very ambitious," although he spent little time furthering his catch-as-catch-can career, in which he would walk out on shows—he once quit his TV show in midseason and went to Europe, says Stang—or go out of his way to insult sponsors to their face. Stang recalls that Morgan once threw Lee Myers, the head of Bristol-Myers, out of the studio. "If you're trying to commit suicide, that's a good way," says Stang. If Fred Allen bit the hand that fed him, Henry Morgan tried to bite off the whole arm.

On his NBC *Henry Morgan Show* (which also included Art Carney, Pert Kelton, and Betty Garde), Morgan didn't just fondly rag his sponsors but took them on aggressively, making them the butt of his humor. The comic commercials are more clever than the surrounding sketches; his innate antagonism toward sponsors' stupid claims and insipid writing inspired him to comic highs. He insisted that Life Savers cheated people by not filling in the holes in the center, and he supposedly incensed the founder of his sponsor, Adler Elevator Shoes, until Adler realized everyone was talking about Morgan's anticommercials, in one of which he cracked, "*You* might like them, but I wouldn't wear them to a dogfight." After Adler came on to defend his shoes, Morgan apologized, "You're right, Mr. Adler. I *would* wear them to a dogfight." Morgan wrote, in defense, "When they started with me they had two stores and inside of a year they had fourteen. Something happened then that I don't think has happened since, either on radio or TV, viz, the audience *paid attention* to the commercials." In one commercial for—or, rather, against—Eversharp's Schick, Morgan tells, in a booming *March of Time* voice, of several men who, because they saved time using a Schick injector razor, came to bad ends: One man arrived early for a train and had time to read the paper, which made him so angry he toppled onto the tracks and was killed; another fellow came downstairs too soon and caught his wife on the couch with the ice man. After a shave-a-thon, the winner is asked how his face feels; "Bloody," he says. It's amazing the sponsors put up with it as long as they did.

Morgan was a total original, maybe too obstinately so—"swellheaded," an ex-owner of WMCA remembered him. He took pride in coming to work late and in being fired a lot, as if being fired were a comic badge of honor. He twitted weather reports with forecasts, predicting "Muggy, followed by Tuggy, Weggy, Thurggy, and Frigy," and "Dark clouds, followed by silver linings," and "Snow, followed by little boys with sleds." At his best, he was a man inspired: On an early show in Duluth he played Chinese music and sang along, put on sound effects records (especially car crashes), and interviewed himself in various dialects for a man-in-the-street interview, because, he explained, during winter there are no men on the street in Duluth.

This sort of glorious nonsense, first heard in New York City on WOR in 1940 (described by Morgan as "a sprightly farrago interrupted every few minutes by snatches of slightly cuckoo phonograph records"), quickly attracted a local following that included Robert Benchley (later his drinking pal), James Thurber, and Fred Allen, who tried to browbeat NBC into giving Morgan a network show. He finally got an unsponsored network show in 1945 on ABC, where it followed Allen's, and went on the air with this announcement: "*The Henry Morgan Show,* sponsored by [*pause*] *The Fred Allen Show*!" That show lasted three years, then switched from ABC to NBC for Camels and Bristol-Myers, just as radio was beginning its decline. With Allen gone by the end of 1949, Morgan had most of the satirical field to himself, but his scorched-earth policy burned him up.

Born Henry Lerner von Ost, a wealthy banker's son, and cousin of the lyricist Alan Jay Lerner, Morgan had come up through the ranks—studio page, announcer, and band-remote announcer. At one point, part of his job had been to fill in for announcer Norman Brokenshire, a prominent drinker who occasionally, reported Morgan, "forgot to leave the bar at 21 in time to announce his own program." To keep awake between tunes at WOR, he began amusing himself with ad libs that failed to amuse all the stations along the network. WOR gave him a fifteen-minute show buried on Saturday morning that he found himself better at winging than writing. He made wisecracks between wacky records (Spike Jones, mainly) once a week, which spread to three times and then to six days a week, though he was still listed and paid as a staff announcer—the youngest in the country, he maintained.

On his first WOR show, Morgan included an intermission for listeners to diaper the baby, a bagpipe serenade of "The Daring Young Man on the Flying Trapeze," and an overdue tribute to the shirt-makers of America. Listeners loved Morgan's sarcastic, disgusted, don't-give-a-damn attitude, so different from most jolly, upbeat radio comedians. He was briefly blacklisted, due to his ex-wife's left-wing associations, but disarmed the House Committee on Un-American Activities in the 1950s, then reemerged yet again on a midnight–to–3 A.M. show from Hutton's, a New York restaurant. In the 1980s, Morgan was brought back by WOR to host an interview show, and on WNEW he had his last hurrah—or, rather, Bronx cheer.

Morgan spent the last thirty years of his life in semiretirement, wasting away on TV panel shows like *I've Got a Secret* ("You try to be funny on those, you're dead."). He attempted a short-lived TV talent-scout sendup, an early *Gong Show,* where he presented a man who tap-danced on Jell-O, a lady woodchopping champ, and a farmer who played the castanets by flexing his biceps. Barely contained by radio, he was far too free a spirit for TV.

Mostly, Henry Morgan was a victim of bad timing, a transition figure in radio who was simply too acerbic for the generally amiable post-war era—"one of the few really outspoken people in radio," he wrote in his memoirs. "I grew up thinking it was American to be outspoken. I've since learned it's un-American. If I was bringing up a kid today, I'd teach him to nod."

BY ANY RATIONAL MEASURE, Bob and Ray should have been washed up along with the rest of radio in the 1950s, but they hung on until Ray's death in 1990, ending a partnership of almost half a century. In various formats, and rarely sponsored, the pair were at once anachronistic and contemporary, finding new ways to mock a medium whose original satirical targets had long since surrendered or died and gone to radio heaven.

Bob and Ray's comedy transcended time and radio. It hardly seems to matter that *Anxiety!* was a send-up of *Suspense,* a show twenty years earlier, because it was enough like TV's *Amazing Stories* and other current spook shows. Their parodies were generic enough to span generations. A specific show may have expired, but its TV counterpart lingers on; melodramatic dialogue, clueless characters, and wheezing dramatic devices are ageless. In an appreciation, Kurt Vonnegut wrote: "Their jokes turn out to be universal, although deeply rooted in old-time radio, because so much of life presents itself as the same dilemma: how to seem lusty and purposeful when less than nothing is going on."

Robert Brackett Elliott and Raymond Walter Goulding were true radio offspring whose entire career consisted of mocking radio in all of its vast, unending inanities and banalities. Their work was never done. They just followed their ears wherever they led them—from "Jack Headstrong, All-American American" to arrogant sportscaster Biff Burns ("This is Biff Burns saying until next time, This is Biff Burns saying, 'So long' ") to mush-mouthed critic Webley Webster and mumbly farm reporter Dean Archer Armstead. Elliott once said, "Our original premise was that radio was too pompous."

Bob and Ray debuted in 1946 as staffers on Boston's WHDH, where Bob played records and Ray did the news in the morning, ad-libbing bits after the ball games and eventually creating their two-man repertory of bores, boors, dolts, jerks, nerds, and windbags. They had been hired at WHDH nearly simultaneously. "We found out almost instantly that we were on the same wavelength, and after the news, we'd bat it back and forth a little." Their original ad-lib show, said Ray, "kept spreading, like a fungus." Ray's specialty was falsettos and gruff blowhards; Bob's was nasal twerps and fatuous frauds. Bob's classic befuddled newscaster was the ubiquitous Wally Ballou, or "—ly Ballou" as he was always known, coming in a split-second before his mike was live on the cut-in and introducing himself in a snuffly voice as "winner of over seven international diction awards." Like all Bob and Ray people, Wally was always a beat out of sync.

Between routines they inserted equally hilarious commercials and special offers from "The Bob and Ray Overstocked Warehouse," such as Chocolate Wobblies, chocolate Easter rabbits that had been stored too close to the heater, with a guarantee that each Wobbly had somewhere inside it a purple ribbon.

In 1951, they left Boston for New York and, through Ray's older brother, were hired to fill in for Morey Amsterdam's show, *The Gloom Dodgers,* after which they went network on NBC, moving to a rival network in the late 1950s with this cheeky introduction: "Bob Elliott and Ray Goulding present the CBS Radio Network."

They created new parodies while revamping and refining their standbys, working half extemporaneously and half scripted; one staple, "Mary Backstayge, Noble Wife" (their sendup of the radio serial *Mary Noble, Backstage Wife*) was usually all ad-libbed. Although they began 90 percent unscripted in Boston, by the 1950s they would rough out ideas on tape before going on the air. Several of the routines were supplied by Tom Koch, a *Mad* writer.

Their influences were Fred Allen, *Vic and Sade,* and a 1930s satirical radio team, "Colonel Stoopnagel and Budd," played by Frederick Chase Taylor and Budd Hulik. Bob was also a young fan of Raymond

Knight's *KUKU Hour,* a show he would attend with his parents. Knight played Ambrose J. Weems, who ran a radio station and commented on events with a sidekick named Mrs. Pennyfeather. Knight did another show—*Wheatenaville,* set in a small town—that was a major influence on Elliott. Later, he and Knight became friends, and Knight was hired by the team as a writer in the early 1950s. It was one of the few times they had ever used outside help for a crowded schedule that included two radio shows a day and a fifteen-minute TV show; Elliott wound up marrying Knight's widow. John Crosby, the most influential radio and TV critic, gave the young team a rave that launched Bob and Ray nationally, at which point (1953) they began bouncing from network to network, station to station, and format to format for the next thirty-seven years. They were unusual for comedy teams in that neither half was a straight man, and like Henry Morgan, Jean Shepherd, and Stan Freberg, their satirical peers, they came of age in radio, not in vaudeville.

The two men, who seemed so inseparable that even some lifelong Bob and Ray devotees were unsure which was which, kept fine-tuning their parodies, retiring "Mary Backstayge" and their first soap sendup, "The Life and Loves of Linda Lovely," replacing Mary with "Garrish Summit" and "The Gathering Dusk," their masterly parodies of *Dynasty* and *Dallas,* doing in five minutes the work of more elaborate TV soap opera parodies like *Soap, Mary Hartman, Mary Hartman,* or *Fresno.* "Garrish Summit"—which began, "There in stately splendor, far removed from the squalid village below, the beautiful people fight their petty battles over power and money"—was the story of the Murchfield clan, headed by stuffy but powerful grand-dame heiress Agatha Murchfield, whose fortune was founded on lead ingots. Her ne'er-do-well brother, Caldwell (whose entrance was invariably announced by Agatha, "Here comes my ne'er-do-well brother, Caldwell"), tried to wrest away her wealth with various nefarious schemes. Agatha was so rich that she sent her watch out twice a year to have it reset for Daylight Savings Time.

Bob and Ray took a sure, unhurried approach to the pomposities of nearly every radio life-form that stood before a microphone. They never translated very well to TV, yet their 1970 revue, *The Two and Only,* ran for five months on Broadway and later toured. In fact, they were superb comic actors who worked in a small circumference but whose funny, pliable faces—cartoons of the voices they lampooned—were also made to be viewed. Larry Josephson, who produced their Carnegie Hall concert in 1981 and their later NPR revival, says that despite their success they were insecure about their fame. "They never thought they'd fill Carnegie Hall, and I could've filled it three times over."

Their acting was mostly vocal, but seated before the microphone, they suddenly would grow quite lively. *The New Yorker*'s Whitney Balliett, observing them at work at a U-shaped table in their WOR studio in New York, described the scene. Prior to the show, Ray would loosen his shoelaces as Bob chose the sound effects from a case; all the while, both of them were continually clearing their throats. "The moment [the show] started, Bob and Ray seemed to draw closer at their table and a bell of intense concentration descended over them." Bob always sat to the right of Ray. "They became extremely active; they lifted their shoulders and eyebrows, kicked their feet, and swayed back and forth in their chairs. Their in-place motions suggested the furious twitchings of dreaming dogs. They also looked at one another steadily as they slipped in and out of various voices, and when they were finished the tension dissolved immediately in a barrage of throat-clearings."

Kurt Vonnegut observed, "Bob and Ray, who could have looked like anything, looked as wistfully funny as they sounded, and secretly wise. Moreover, they seemed as unlikely a pair of pals as Laurel and Hardy. Ray was the big bluffer. Bob was the smaller, more intellectual, more pessimistic, more easily disappointed one." Their humor was too cerebral and surreal for the screen, large or small; Vonnegut compared their work to Dali's limp watches. "Bob and Ray's humor," said Andy Rooney, "isn't like a joke that depends on remembering the last line. Their sketches are just as funny in the middle as they are at the end."

Their satire was also Benchleyesque, gently cutting without turning crude or cruel, with an inherent civility nearly unknown now among satirists. Bob and Ray were quiet minimalist wits in an age of maximum farcical noise, and the more far-out or gross their rowdy comic colleagues grew, the less Bob and Ray seemed to notice—they were always true to themselves and to their private comic vision. In fact, the wackier the concept—the McBeebee twins, who speak simultaneously; the dawdling spokesman for the Slow Talkers Association; the Komoda

Dragon expert who repeats what an interviewer has just asked; the owner of a cranberry processing plant who never heard of cranberry sauce—the more calm their approach. Somehow it all sounded not only unforced but improvised, which it originally was.

Revered is not too strong a term to describe their hold on a faithful following that stuck with them through thick and, mainly, thin, from five-minute sketches on NBC's *Monitor* in 1956, their national break-through, to a daily show for CBS in 1959 to a four-hour afternoon broadcast on WHN in New York in 1962. While the team never had a huge audience, they always seemed to catch on somewhere. As Andy Rooney observed: "A lot of people think, as I do, that they appreciate Bob and Ray more than anyone else does." Perhaps one reason they remained a cult hit is that they were ambivalent about their careers, according to Josephson: "They had to decide at some point whether to put up with all the showbiz bullshit or to be true to themselves, and they decided on the latter. They'd been screwed over by so many broad-casters."

Genuinely shy men (Goulding evaded most interviews), Elliott once said, "By the time we discovered we were introverts, it was too late to do anything about it." He also said that "maybe the secret of our suc-cess is that we emerge only every few years. We don't saturate the pub-lic, and new generations seem to keep discovering us." He surmised, "I guess we're the longest-running team on the air, or maybe even in show business." Goulding once said, "We've spent all these years trying to entertain each other. And that's a good way to earn a living." They rarely disagreed, and while they thought enough alike to finish each other's sentences, the men were never chummy.

The more of a blabbermouth radio became, the richer grew Bob and Ray's satire. One reason they're still funny, in an era of entertain-ment overload and high-tech dazzle, is that radio really never did die— it just became sillier and more self-imitative. It became television. The broadcast interview, Bob and Ray's basic format, grew even more prevalent as newscasts, talk shows, and mind-numbing experts flooded the airwaves with babble, playing deliciously into their hands.

In most Bob and Ray sketches, the obtuse meets the overblown, as on "Speaking Out," a phone-in opinion program ("I think the prince of Wales should be a civil service job"); the "Bob and Ray Mystery Tune" (winners receive eighteen dollars "in cash" plus a free breakfast at Rudy's House of Dry Toast); "Down the Byways," in search of small-town Americana (à la Charles Kuralt), whose host once visited "one of the last of the small-town grouches"; "The Employment Office of the Air"; and "Mr. I-Know-Where-They-Are," who dug up long-forgotten nobodies such as rodeo star Tumbleweed Gargon or child film star Fat Baby Moxford. Their one dip into political humor was the browbeating Commissioner Carstairs, a takeoff on Senator Joseph McCarthy who popped up from time to time on "Mary Backstayge."

Most takeoffs on commercials merely exaggerate, but Bob and Ray, masters of understatement, twitted commercials by deftly tweaking the language. They delivered earnest spiels for Monongahela Metal Foundry ("Steel ingots cast with the housewife in mind"), Height Watchers International, and the Kretchfield Braid & Tassel Company ("The company that dares to stand behind its fringe for two full years"). For two years, they did a real commercial for Piels Beer, playing Bert and Harry Piel, who drew more laughs than drafts of beer.

Bob Elliott (the short moon-faced one with the big baleful watery blue eyes, who played all the adenoidal characters, led by Wally Ballou) and Ray Goulding (the burly one with the shaggy eyebrows, the swoopy Julia Child-ish voice of "Mary McGoon" and other biddies as well as pompous captains of industry) were the last of radio's true wits. "Comedians" sounds too loud and obvious for their droll, low-key parodies that are so on the nose they're only a notch more idiotic than real radio. Bob and Ray's rubes and boobs, their gee-whiz scientists, smug reporters, and bloated businessmen, are radio versions of characters who might have stepped out of Sinclair Lewis or Ring Lardner.

The duo wore as well as any humorists can hope to, never turning angry, cruel, snide, bitter, or self-satisfied. They didn't bludgeon their targets to death; they kidded human folly and bombast without feeling a need to destroy their objects. They attacked everything with a feather, tickling subjects into submission as if encouraging their hapless cast of characters and listeners to return for more fun another day. Their final series aired on National Public Radio in 1990, just before Ray's death— not a bad run for a pair of low-budget satirists. Fifty years after Bob and Ray began in Boston, they're still contemporary and funny. Little has aged except their listeners.

WHILE WILL ROGERS CLAIMED to detest radio, calling it "that thing," he had little reason to. Rogers was the sort of personality radio was made for. With his relaxed, shambling, cud-chewing style, Rogers endeared himself to listeners as he had on stage and in movies, where he played himself—a sort of country slicker.

Rogers's homespun monologues and wry homilies needed no production values—no bells and whistles, no shtick, funny hats, sidekicks, music, or even audience, although he maintained: "To have to line up there and try to get some laughs, I want to tell you it's the toughest job I ever tackled."

He mused aloud, as if extemporaneously, and listening to him was more like eavesdropping. He didn't play to audiences the way most comics do. He was just a natural-born crowd pleaser who adapted without fuss to radio, just as he had gone from rope tricks to the *Ziegfeld Follies* to movies to newspaper columns, and then on to radio variety shows like *The Eveready Hour,* where he built his greatest constituency.

His political comments could have been declared off limits by the FCC, which banned political satire from the sacrosanct airwaves, but Rogers got around that by never submitting a script, claiming his remarks were spontaneous; the FCC looked the other way. It might have been dicey for the agency to censor a national hero who, at his death in 1935, had become perhaps radio's most beloved personality, using nothing but his mind, his mouth, and a mike.

Rogers arrived on radio's *Gulf Show* already a full-blown star from his touring years, on Broadway, and in movies, but it was radio that brought him to everybody all at once and cemented his stature, though he was to die only a few years into his radio career. He played the role of rube, the only part he ever really played, both on screen and on the air, an act that everyone was on to. Andy Rooney, TV's desktop Will Rogers, has referred to Rogers's "apparent averageness," but adds, "He wasn't. Everything he did was calculated. He gave the impression he was just a simple common man," but his aw-shucks style was his public role, like a character out of Frank Capra.

Rogers, on the air and everywhere he spoke, personified the anti-intellectualism that America still harbors. Americans are suspicious of book learning, especially in their entertainers, and love to believe that great stars evolve from the people and, like Forrest Gump, are just nice folks who got lucky. But Rogers didn't crawl out of the haystack one morning and start making incisive wisecracks. He pretended to hide his light under a bushel, one firmly planted by him very early.

What shone through everything he did, however, was his essential Americanness (he never let audiences forget he was one quarter Cherokee), his basic decency, and his horse sense. In no way was he common, but he had the common touch and appealed to America's best instincts. His career timing was as perfect as his comic timing: Rogers entered radio in the middle of the turbulent twenties, for which he was a sober antidote. He then stood by during the Depression as the country's conscience, a soothing headache tablet for the National Hangover, reminding America of its roots. He was a constant, a man whose mere presence cheered people up. When he died at fifty-six in a plane crash over Alaska, said Stephen Chodorov in his Will Rogers documentary, "it seemed like the passing of a president."

SINCE TALK WAS, AND REMAINS, radio's essential element, a man like Alexander Woollcott was to the manner—or, in his case, mannered—born, the very opposite of Will Rogers's rural storyteller.

Woollcott was the rare writer who actually gained in translation to radio, since he was a performer at heart who knew instinctively what emotional chords to strike over the air. His prose, like the man himself, was excessive and theatrical; his criticism, florid and ferocious—one of his many sobriquets was "Old Violets and Vitriol." By turns effusive and fulminating, he gushed and bawled like a baby or attacked with a razor-edged bludgeon. Beyond his passions, he was a man of vast interests and curiosity (he once called himself "taster-at-large to the American public"), with a reporter's nose for sniffing out lurid items and murder yarns, plus an actor's ability to rattle off an anecdote with consummate skill. In life as in print, he was a self-created character and self-made star, and he took to the airwaves with an almost perverse glee.

His show, *The Town Crier,* began with a ringing bell and the bellow of announcer Paul Douglas crying, "Hear ye! Hear ye! Hear ye!" followed by the host's understated greeting: "This is Woollcott speaking." Owing to his girth and his need to switch eyeglasses on the air, he required a special microphone.

It might seem that an elitist like Woollcott was an unlikely radio star, but the flip side of this flowery, cape-wearing Wildean snob was his firmly held belief that, despite his shameless name-dropping, he was a man of the people. Perhaps it was merely another hue in his performer's coat of many colors, but Woollcott was a good enough actor to make audiences buy his populist pose, quite the opposite of his scathing print personality as withering cosmopolitan critic.

The weekly half-hour program on Mutual was a grab bag of opening-night reviews, book blurbs, theatrical news, scandal, trivia, murder yarns, and fanciful tales about World War I or life in America. Nothing was above or beneath him—his town crier's bell tolled for all, from the latest bon mot overheard at the Algonquin Round Table to a bit of fluff garnered from a small-town weekly. The great Kaufman and Hart play that he inspired, *The Man Who Came to Dinner,* captured his peculiar blend of precocious, lavender-scented self-involvement, mawkish sentimentality, scheming blackmailer, and generosity.

The Town Crier made a household name out of a name that, prior to 1929, had been known mainly among New Yorkers as a smarty-pants spoiled brat. Woollcott wisely abandoned that persona over the air, where he became more of an avuncular fellow, like a man seated before a crackling hearth telling tales to his gathered family. His unlikely network sponsor, Cream of Wheat, warned him against "off-color stories," and the head of the company almost canceled its sponsorship over the word *pubescent,* which some listeners were convinced was dirty.

Whereas in person or in print he could be patronizing, on the air Woollcott assumed the cozy personality of part village gossip and part kindly professor, referring to listeners as "my children" and "my dears"—spoken partly in irony, for Woollcott, a transvestite, was not only childless but said to be virtually sexless. He even adopted a flatter midwestern accent on the air, quite unlike his more distinguished, higher-pitched theatrical voice (one writer said he sounded like a man with "truffles on his tonsils"), as he read from Shakespeare or recited the Twenty-third Psalm for some dying old lady, told ghost and Christmas stories, delivered jokes, discussed language, history, and gothic mysteries (a particular Woollcottian obsession), and promoted favorite performers and new faces with equal fervor.

Woollcott was a one-man show who cast his web wide enough to dragoon friends and colleagues from the worlds of theater, literature, society, politics, and films, all of whom considered an invitation to share his microphone an honor. He dropped names in his gabby reports on the Great White Way, but he later produced them in the studio. For anybody on Broadway, at the mercy of Woollcott's whim as *New York Times* drama critic, a request to appear alongside Woollcott amounted to a command performance. At the show's peak, six million people tuned in each week. "I saw in him a unique personality," CBS's William Paley said in explaining his unlikely, not to say risky, choice for a national town crier. "He had a quality I felt would appeal to a mass audience." It was like hiring Truman Capote to host a prime-time talk show.

His radio show began on WOR in New York in 1929, joined CBS four years later, and lasted until his death in 1943, when he was earning $3,500 a show. He died a few days after a broadcast on which he suffered a massive heart attack during a round-table book discussion and scrawled I AM SICK on a piece of paper. One of the guests, the mystery author Rex Stout, later said he knew it was serious because otherwise the persnickety Woollcott would have written I AM ILL.

RADIO'S MOST MEMORABLE SHOWS usually possessed a unique element that broke the mold and raised them above their rivals—a creative leap of faith that contradicted the genre or the medium itself. In most cases, once the mold had been broken, it resumed its former shape. With Jack Benny, it was the idea of a show within and about the show; with *The Lone Ranger,* it was the notion of a lawman in an outlaw's mask; with *Dragnet,* it was a show about the mundane day-to-day life of a cop. And with the *The Edgar Bergen and Charlie McCarthy Show,* it was the audacious, preposterous, silly, semisurreal concept of a ventriloquist headlining a radio show. It sounds impossible, almost a joke, a sure recipe for disaster—and it was indeed an avant-garde conceit—but what Bergen must have shrewdly realized or soon discovered is that what mattered wasn't the ventriloquist, or even his dummy, but what went on between them: the banter and their relationship, of a boy and his father, which gave it a familial feeling.

The patter on the Bergen-McCarthy show remains funny today, among the wittiest of all the major comedy shows, on a level with Jack Benny, Fred Allen, and Burns and Allen. In fact, Bergen and McCarthy outlasted them all in radio, with a twenty-year-run that ended only in 1956, when the improbable team held the melancholy distinction of being radio's last major comedy stars without their own TV show.

Part of what gave his radio show its special spin was Bergen's constant mocking of his own ineptitude, which became the show's favorite running gag and subtly elevated the act. Listeners delighted in such self-deprecating and self-referential comedy. Indeed, self-deprecation is the trait that links Benny, Bergen, and Hope, although Benny's and Hope's self-mocking was more complex, always at war with their boastful airs. Bergen's civility and modesty, his gentlemanliness, were the perfect counterpoint for Charlie's scheming wisenheimer.

Once you saw Bergen away from radio—in a movie or on a stage—you realized what a lousy ventriloquist he truly was, but radio allowed studio audiences to concentrate on the jokes without being distracted by his ventriloquist's skills or lack of same. Even so, he made personal appearances to establish the visual reality of the bratty McCarthy character, a dummy who is (1) not dumb or endearing at all and who is (2) dressed inexplicably in a tuxedo and wears a monocle. One might have well wondered why a smart-mouth street kid was done up like a diplomat, totally at odds with his impudent Irish personality.

Bergen's most amazing illusion was to turn a puppet into a lifelike personality, with all the characteristics of a real comedian and the ego of a living celebrity. Thanks to radio's illusionary powers, it didn't matter that he was carved of wood, for Charlie had the aura of a human being and the fame of a major star. There were said to be listeners—maybe some of the same ones who fell for Orson Welles's Martian landing in New Jersey—who thought Charlie McCarthy was a real person. In her autobiography, *Knock Wood,* Candice Bergen observes that her father treated Charlie like a human being, as in those movies (*The Great Gabbo,* etc.) in which a dummy comes to life or takes on the persona of his creator. In rehearsals, recalls the writer Carroll Carroll, it was always Bergen who blew his lines, never Charlie.

Charlie's good-natured lamebrain pal, Mortimer Snerd, who came along in 1939, was much more your traditional dummy—quite literally so. In creating Snerd (whose inspired name is a likely derivation of *nerd*), Bergen went the other way, creating the dumbest dummy who ever was, in counterpoint to the quick-witted Charlie. Mortimer functioned much like Gracie Allen's character—a seeming dope whose inside-out logic makes sense. Bergen's widow, Frances, claimed that Snerd was his favorite creation. "There was a sweetness about him," she said. "Edgar used to say that Mortimer was stupid but that he had an advantage over most of us because he knew he was stupid."

A typical exchange between Mortimer and announcer Don Ameche reveals how sharply written the shows were:

Ameche: *Everyone has the impression around here that you're ignorant.*
Snerd: *Awww, you're just sayin' that to make me feel good.*
Ameche: *Mortimer, don't you want to be somebody?*
Snerd: *I am somebody.*
Ameche: *In order to go anywhere, you've got to buckle down and put your shoulder to the wheel.*
Snerd: *Uh-h-h, which wheel?*
Ameche: *Any wheel!*
Snerd: *Which shoulder?*
Ameche: *Let's put it this way—look at Abraham Lincoln.*
Snerd: *Uh-h-h, where's he sittin'?*
Ameche: *When he was a boy, Abe Lincoln used to split rails.*
Snerd: *So what? When I was a boy, I used to break windows.*
Ameche: *And there was another boy in Philadelphia who discovered electricity. Can you tell me what his name was?*
Snerd: *It was, um, uh-h-h, Mister uh . . . I know his last name begins with a capital.*
Ameche: *Concentrate!*
Snerd: *Yup, that's it! No, it's a shorter name than that.*
Ameche: *I'll see you again sometime, Mortimer.*
Snerd: *And then some other time I can see you. If we change off like that we won't get so sick of each other's company.*

Bergen always treated Mortimer kindly but was forever taken aback by Charlie's wicked cracks—yet the shy, polite, erudite Bergen never tried to do verbal battle with Charlie, who treated "the old boy" with thinly veiled condescension, like many a modern child, sniping at him in asides to listeners. Bergen represented traditional values, decency, courtesy, and the system, while Charlie laughed behind his back at his foolish old-fogy ways. Bergen did his best to reason with him and to engender some respect in the rude boy, playing benign Gepetto to Charlie's wayward Pinocchio. Indeed, the relationship between McCarthy and Bergen partly mirrored the classic Collodi fairy tale in that Bergen treated Charlie exactly as if he were "a real boy" (with a make-believe pal named Skinny Dugan), the main difference being that Charlie was disrespectful and unappreciative and had no desire to be anything other than what he was—a cocksure loudmouth who ogled girls and talked back to his father, or, in this case, father figure. It was unclear what the benign Bergen's precise role was. He lectured Charlie in a kindly, avuncular, schoolmasterly manner, with a soothing Scandinavian lilt in marked contrast to Charlie's high-pitched bray.

Bergen (born Edgar Berggren) had worked his way up from tents and vaudeville to the Palace in 1930 and then to Manhattan nightclubs, where he became an unexpected hit. While performing at the Chez Paree, he was seen and touted by Noël Coward, who got him booked into the elegant Rainbow Room. With his saucy repartee, Bergen was the first entertainer to take ventriloquism uptown and out of the mouths of birthday party performers and two-bit vaudeville acts, the first one to make ventriloquism fit for adults.

Bergen described Charlie's metamorphosis from lowbrow street kid to high-hat sophisticate: "We were booked to play the Helen Morgan Club in New York and I didn't think a newsboy was quite the thing for a nightclub. I asked *Esquire* if I could make a dummy of their mascot, Esky. At first they thought it was a good idea but then they changed their minds . . . so there was nothing left for me to do but make Charlie the man about town, and that's how he got his top hat, monocle, and tails." In 1937 he was quickly snapped up by Rudy Vallee for his *Fleischmann Hour* show and became an instant hit, though Vallee nearly got cold feet at the last moment about booking a ventriloquist. "Everyone looked down on ventriloquists," Bergen once recalled. "Vaudeville was dying and we thought we were through." He revamped the act for radio and became radio's most unlikely headliner.

Bergen got his own show almost at once, with Don Ameche and Dorothy Lamour, the first of various movie queens Charlie was forever in hot pursuit of. Mortimer joined the act two years later and, in 1944,

Bergen added spinster Effie Klinker, his least successful puppet, maybe because her voice was a lot like Charlie's. Charlie and Mortimer were mouthpieces enough.

Charlie often went head-to-head with famous guest stars, most notably W. C. Fields, whose running gag on the show was to threaten to chop Charlie up for firewood, a gate-leg table, "a woodpecker's snack bar," or whatever woodsy insult Fields could imagine. Fields, who disliked everything about radio but the money, relished sparring with McCarthy because it gave him an opportunity to unload both barrels on a "child" who gave as good as he got. Charlie was in many ways Fields's nasty illegitimate son, and their periodic confrontations developed into yet another of radio's famous mock feuds.

Perhaps because Charlie was only a puppet, he could get away with more, but Bergen's mouth once got them both into trouble during a famous "Adam and Eve" sketch (written, oddly enough, by horror maven Arch Oboler), with Mae West as a wicked Eve who outsmarts the snake and seduces Adam (Don Ameche) with the promise of "forbidden applesauce" and other double entendres. The sketch resulted in letters from outraged listeners and decency groups, and a ban on further West radio appearances; NBC is said to have outlawed even the mention of her name on the air. What upset churchgoing listeners wasn't the biblical parody so much as the fact that it had the bad luck to air on a Sunday show.

Bergen, a taciturn man who had planned to be a doctor, was a loner, reserved and inexpressive; his daughter Candice called him "an emotional hermit." She writes that beneath his staid Scandinavian stock, he had a "renegade" seed that took root in Charlie. Bergen let the puppet do all the talking in interviews, both out of shyness and to preserve the illusion; at the start, he would only attend parties with Charlie on his arm—all that Bergen had to say he said through Charlie. He married late in life, at forty, living before then with his mother and his puppets. When the famous dolls were eventually joined by a live little girl, she recalled, "The sibling rivalry this established was certainly unique, considering I was the only child and the sibling was, in truth, my father." As a little girl trying to please a stern but adored parent, she longed to be up there performing with her daddy and grew to hate her famous "brother." She tells how she was forced to share a nursery with her imaginary brother (the press invariably called her "Charlie's sister"), who assumed life-size proportions in the Bergen home, with his own tiny bed and wardrobe.

The natural heir to Charlie's crown was Jim Henson's Kermit the Frog. Henson, a devotee of Bergen and McCarthy, dedicated *The Muppet Movie* to Bergen's memory, and much of Kermit's cocky persona, not to mention many inhabitants of *Sesame Street,* can be traced to Charlie and Mortimer, the Muppet clan's spiritual ancestors. When Edgar and Charlie were guests on *Sesame Street* and arrived for rehearsals, recalled Bergen's widow, the *Sesame Street* staff stood and stared in awe. "It was as if they were in church," she said. Although puppets became TV's first major stars—on shows such as *Kukla, Fran and Ollie, Time for Beany,* and *Howdy Doody*—they were kid-oriented; Charlie was too sophisticated for the peanut gallery of the 1950s' afterschool TV.

When Bergen died in 1977, he was a largely forgotten celebrity who, in his daughter's description, had grown bewildered, slightly senile, and "pulled into himself" more than ever. Even in his heyday, however, he would go off by himself in a private plane—wanting, like another famous Swede, to be alone. There was a meager attempt to revive his career on TV in a 1956 quiz show, modeled on *You Bet Your Life,* called *Do You Trust Your Wife?,* on which Bergen and Charlie bantered with contestants, like Groucho, but it lasted only a season. Bergen wasn't much of an ad-libber. In his last live appearances, he would forget lines, but he came out of retirement for one final show at Caesars Palace, where he captivated the audience with his favorite radio routines and then, as if contented that he hadn't lost it, died in his sleep at seventy-five, the day after the farewell run ended.

Charlie and Mortimer live on, not merely in memory but in their semihuman form, at the Smithsonian Institution. After Bergen's death, the family found three old Charlie McCarthy heads in his safe—the original redheaded one from his tent-show days, one with an angrier face and, in a lovely Dorian Gray touch, a third wooden head with an aging Charlie wearing a fringe of silver hair.

— 7 —
JOKES, INC.

BOB HOPE PARLAYED THE ROUTINE SKILLS OF A song-and-dance man into one of the great American show business careers, using radio as his route from stage to screen to legend, fading only when his superpatriotism came home to haunt him during the Vietnam era.

Hope was the consummate entertainer, an amazingly adaptable performer who shifted easily from vaudeville to Broadway to radio to movies to concerts to TV—all with the same jaunty, larky ease. One of his few career stumbles was a failed screen test for MGM in 1930 that delayed his film career. If he had done nothing else but movies, Hope would leave a memorable body of work, from classic farces like *Monsieur Beaucaire* and *Paleface* to the beloved *Road* pictures with Bing Crosby to sophisticated comedies like *The Facts of Life* and *That Certain Feeling* to gentler comedies and light biographies like *Sorrowful Jones, The Lemon Drop Kid, The Seven Little Foys,* and *Beau James.*

All of this, mind you, while maintaining a hugely popular radio show for fifteen years—followed by another quarter century as a TV star, not to mention a raft of best-selling joke-studded memoirs from World War II on (*I Never Left Home; Have Tux, Will Travel; Don't Shoot, It's Only Me;* etc.). For decades, Hope was everywhere at once, even in a comic book that captured his swaggering persona—a cockier, more dashing switch on Jack Benny's boastful buffoon; and no newsreel was complete without a shot of Hope cutting up on the golf course with Crosby or Ike. He hosted the Academy Awards so long, beginning when they were broadcast on radio, that it was the equivalent of a Supreme Court appointment; when he was finally replaced by Johnny Carson, it seemed to many an act of treason. And no comic since Hope has been as courted by presidents, each of whom, upon taking the oath, needed to be blessed not just by a Billy Graham prayer but by a Bob Hope punch line. By the 1950s, he was in training for American icon-

Overleaf: Bob Hope

hood. He retired reluctantly at ninety-three, but only after growing nearly deaf and blind.

Hard though it is to believe now, for any kid coming of age in the 1940s and 1950s Bob Hope was America's most famous dirty comic, reportedly censored weekly by NBC for nasty lines that got cut off the air. Although he loved blue material at banquets and roasts (where he often indulged in his little-known skill at dialects, notably black and swish), most of the on-air tales were apocryphal but made him seem daring and wicked. It wasn't the actual lines that established his naughty persona so much as Hope's provocative delivery. Off-mike and generally unknown to listeners of that rose-colored era, moreover, Hope was one of show business's leading philanderers, with girls in every port—and, around Los Angeles, on nearly every block. In the 1940s he was as potent as any rock star. A former Hope comedy writer, Sherwood Schwartz, recalls, "There were always five or six young pretty girls hanging around in the corridors outside Hope's room, sort of like today's groupies."

Hope took Jack Benny's schnook character to a flashier level and ran with it on radio, using only his voice and superbly crafted jokes to build his character into the sleek, fast-talking Don Juannabe he later played in films and, less skillfully, on TV, where he often seemed to be on autopilot, breaking up endlessly during listless sketches, his eyes furtively searching for cue cards. Steve Allen remembers a party during his TV reign when Hope gave a speech that cracked everyone up. At one point, Allen turned around and spotted Hope's cue-card man, Barney McNulty, kneeling down in the mud behind some bushes flipping the cards while shining a flashlight on the lines.

All that came long after his reign on radio, where, with a silky effortlessness he glided from joke to joke, guest to guest, show to show, decade to decade—singing, joking, MC'ing, and enacting radio versions of his movies. He once noted: "I've been lucky. It's just *never* stopped. I never had a slow time, except once when I didn't think Paramount would pick up my option. Then I fell into the whole USO thing." Fell? Leaped would be more like it.

From his first broadcast for the troops at March Field air base in California, on May 6, 1941, Hope discovered an audience that identified with his red-blooded male humor. It wasn't all altruism and patriotism. The GI camps were ideal both for Hope's professional and personal purposes: Not only were servicemen a large, laugh-starved captive audience that responded loudly to inside military jokes, but Hope was their kind of horny guy. When he leered at this or that Miss Whoozis, it wasn't just for a laugh.

As chronicled by Arthur Marx, the coauthor of seven Hope films, in an unauthorized biography, Hope's ulterior motive for his overseas trips and on-the-go schedule was to provide camouflage for his love nests of far-flung mistresses, often plucked from a waiting bevy of starlets or the latest Miss World contest (Marx claims Hope rigged pageants to crown whatever girl he fancied). In Hope, every sexed-up soldier sensed a soulmate. Though he truly loved GIs—telephoning relatives of injured men overseas when he got home—he also needed them, for they roared at every joke. Steve Allen observed, "Bob Hope is never as popular as when there is a war going on."

Like Howard Stern, Hope was much discussed and quoted the morning after each Tuesday night's show, sandwiched between the *Fibber McGee and Molly* and Red Skelton shows. The next day, junior-high boys' rooms across the nation were thick with cigarette smoke and delicious tales of what lascivious lines Hope had allegedly gotten off the night before to "sweater girls" like Jane Russell, Terry Moore, Marie ("The Body") MacDonald, Anita Ekberg, or Jayne Mansfield. He wisely did nothing to discourage the stories, which turned up in all the columns, fueled by his secret womanizing and bad-boy penchant, as in this exchange (swiftly drowned out by organ music) with Dorothy Lamour when Lamour said, "I'll meet you in front of the pawnshop," and Hope, after replying, "Okay," added, ". . . and then you can kiss me under the balls." Another time, Lamour said, "Don't take me seriously, Bob. I was just pulling your leg." To which Hope reportedly ad-libbed, "Listen, Dottie, you can pull my right leg and you can pull my left leg, but don't mess with Mr. In-Between." A more typical shade of light-blue Hope humor is this exchange, fairly ribald for 1940s radio:

Hope: *Some park.*
Girl: *Some park.*
Hope: *Some grass.*

Girl: *Some grass.*
Hope: *Some dew.*
Girl: *I don't.*

His prophetic opening line on his first show, *The Rippling Rhythms Revue,* was, "This is the voice of inexperience, Bob Hope." A critic called him "easy to take but hard to remember." Hope and Wilkie Mahoney, a writer for *Uncle Billy's Whiz Bang,* a girls-and-gags magazine, wrote the show themselves; the other regulars were tenor James Melton, singer Jane Froman, and bandleader Al Goodman. His female foil was a beautiful blonde Georgia comedienne named Patricia "Honey Chile" Wilder, who reappeared later on his successful Pepsodent broadcasts—his first of many luscious straight women (some of whom were also occasional lovers), among them Janis Paige, Joey Heatherton, Barbara Payton, Gloria DeHaven, and Marilyn Maxwell, with whom he had a serious long-term affair and whom he wanted to marry.

He became a far more viable radio commodity after costarring in a hit Broadway musical in 1933, *Roberta,* and appearing in the star-packed film, *The Big Broadcast of 1938.* By 1939, he had joined the ranks of Allen, Benny, and Bergen, placing fourth behind them in a critics' poll. A year later, he was first; one reviewer called his jokes old but said he "wore well" due to his "self-joshing," another trait that marked his style.

A weekly seven-minute monologue on a short-lived 1938 Dick Powell show, *Your Hollywood Parade,* was Hope's real breakthrough, but he had earned it. As his wife, Dolores, recalled, "He used to rehearse a whole week for those seven minutes. He'd been terrified at first and not at all sure of himself, but within a few weeks he had all the poise he needed. The response had given it to him and I'm sure the response came because he was so refreshing—a wit instead of a buffoon." The show failed, but Hope got national exposure—and also a great theme song, thanks to a huge career- and ego-boosting review from Damon Runyon, who wrote an entire column about Hope's duet with Shirley Ross of a tune he had sung in *The Big Broadcast of 1938* called "Thanks for the Memory." Runyon gushed, "What a delivery, what a song, what an audience reception!"

Hope then met an advertising man named Ed Lasker, son of the tycoon Albert Lasker, owner of the Pepsodent company, who gave him a second chance to host a show; radio was a forgiving medium. On his first broadcast, to ensure boffo laughs, Hope (like Ed Wynn and Eddie Cantor years earlier) dressed up in a cowboy costume for a western-parody number. "It just seemed too strange to talk into a microphone in a studio instead of playing it for real in front of an audience."

He hired eight writers to keep him supplied with gags, and paid them out of his salary of twenty-five hundred dollars a week. "No comic had ever tried to maintain a staff that size," he said. "But I wanted to be Number One, and I knew that jokes were the key. I was willing to pay for it and I must say, looking back, I got much more than I paid for." His forte, he realized, wasn't funny voices and faces but a polished delivery.

That original staff included Mel Shavelson, Norman Panama, Jack Rose, Sherwood Schwartz, and Schwartz's brother Al. The writing crew eventually grew to fifteen, and nearly every comedy writer in the business seems to have put in time on the celebrated Hope assembly line that the comedian commanded like a CEO. As his longtime agent, Jimmy Saphier, once said, "If Bob hadn't become an actor, he could have been the head of General Motors."

"All these comedy minds were necessary if I was going to carry out my plan, which was almost unheard of at the time," Hope has said. "It was to go on the air every week with topical jokes written right up to airtime. Even if they weren't all good, they would give the Pepsodent show an immediacy I find missing today, when so many shows are taped in advance. And we had no canned laughter then to cover the clinkers or create hilarity on cue. We had to be good, or else. It was life or death, sink or swim." He added, "We used to preview the Pepsodent show on Sunday nights, throwing in every joke we thought might have a chance. The studio audience laughs told us which were funny."

During the three hours before the repeat West Coast broadcast Tuesday at 10 P.M., he and his writers ground out new jokes to replace those that hadn't worked the first time around. Mel Shavelson remembered rewriting frantically between broadcasts until a line got a laugh, with Hope throwing new jokes out as fast as he got them. "He finally agreed on a joke just about thirty seconds before it went into the sketch and it laid a big egg, but that's how immediate it was. . . . One little incident could change the whole feeling of an audience, so it was the greatest training ground for a comedy writer there could be." Larry Gelbart adds: "They weren't one-liners, they were half-liners. It was almost like writing bumper-stickers."

Writers put together a ninety-minute script, which was then pruned to thirty minutes. Ideas for each week's show were written on a large blackboard. "In those beleaguered days," Hope said, "the competition among the writers was so fierce, each one would try to outdo the other by handing in more jokes. Finally, they realized they were each writing almost twenty pages of comedy a day, a suicidal pace. They made a pact to cut down the material. They figured that if they all cut down by the same amount, one page a day, I would never notice what was happening."

The writer Mort Lachman recalls that Hope, unlike more selfish comics such as Cantor and Skelton (who once told Jack Paar, "God tells me what to say"), was always secure about his talent. "Bob had been in vaudeville and on Broadway, so he enjoyed writers—and yet he was the most capable ad-libber of all of them. He could *do* it." Hope also liked audiences, says Lachman, and not all comics do; they fear them. Moreover, Hope was unusually cool under fire. Once, recalls Lachman, a show ran short a few minutes and Hope, told he had to fill time, remembered five jokes cut from the monologue and smoothly recalled them all—in their correct order.

Hope braved network censors over double entendres and risked being cut off the air. NBC executive Walter Bunker, charged with bleeping Hope—which called for instant reflexes—recalls: "When he went to say the word I'd bloop him right out and cut back in again right after. I think he was surprised that we'd do that. But radio listeners weren't like audiences today. They were easily shocked by anything slightly risqué, and you could lose 'em easily." On the other hand, the writer Hal Goodman claimed, "If he didn't want a joke to get a laugh, like something you'd fought to keep in but he didn't believe in, he'd deliver the line badly just to prove his point."

Hope expected writers to devote themselves as fully to the show as he did. "Not everyone could do it," says Lachman. Hope might call from South Bend, Indiana, on the eve of a banquet at Notre Dame and, as if dialing room service, order up two football jokes and a Catholic priest joke. It was part of every Hope gagman's job; the boss also figured he owned every joke his writers thought up, even the rejected ones. All jokes became his property and were stored away in the vast files he has kept for half a century, indexed by topic and date, that filled a two-thousand-square-foot vault on his sprawling Toluca Lake estate until he donated them to an archive in 1998.

Although he made a conscious effort to hire the best (and most extensive group of) writers in the business, Hope, a natural comic actor, was not merely the product of his writers. Over time a character emerged from the one-line barrage: Hope as the intrepid smart aleck and failed Romeo who was all bluff, Hope as the luckless con man everyone saw through, Hope as the ridiculous poseur. In his schizoid character, Hope the patsy—whether coward, klutz, con artist, or cad—keeps making a liar and a fool of Hope the fast-talking, skirt-chasing wiseacre.

He never pretended to be a natural clown, but like Benny he was a superb technician with a sure sense of what worked for the well-defined Bob Hope character, which Steve Allen once noted has a particularly American edge: "He is the perennial wiseguy whose braggadocio is made palatable by the fact that in the last analysis *he* gets it in the neck. The average middle-class American would never envision himself as a New York neurotic Woody Allen, a wild and crazy Steve Martin, or a leering Groucho Marx; he would probably picture himself as something like Bob Hope." In short, he was far more than the sum of his monologue. As Hope himself said, "The character that's now known as Bob Hope didn't leap, full-grown, from some writer's typewriter. It developed over several seasons—like a weed. . . ."

Hope's radio image as a sly, sexy, modern city boy with a gift of gab, a kind of joke-peddling Harold Hill, was fleshed out even further when he teamed with Bing Crosby in *The Road to Morocco, The Road to Singapore,* etc., where Hope played the perpetually failed lover boy to Crosby's cool romancing crooner who got the girl without batting a pale eyelash. (Offstage, they were pals who even traded girlfriends but remained fiercely competitive otherwise; Hope was authentically envious over Crosby's Oscar for *Going My Way.*)

The *Road* films grew out of Hope and Bing Crosby's mock on-air feuding, when they would appear on each other's shows and Bob would razz Bing about his money, his racehorses, his sons, his toupee, and his ears, while Bing would counter with gags about Bob's Oscar envy, lack of sexual prowess, his ski-jump nose, and golf mania. It all became as ritualized as a sumo wrestling match:

Crosby: *As I live, ski snoot!*
Hope: *Mattress hip!*
Crosby: *Shovel head!*
Hope: *Scoop nose!*
Crosby: *Lard!*
Hope: *Yes, Dad!*

By the late 1940s, however, the dueling-golf-stick gags had worn so thin that a *Variety* critic, in a sigh of despair, said Hope's show epitomized "radio's sad saga of sameness." He added, "Apparently it's just too much to expect that Hope would veer an inch from his time-tested routine. His answer, it goes without saying, is: Why get out of the rut as long as there's pay dirt in it? Who's going to outlive the other, Hope or the listening public?"

Hope struggled to keep up to date even in his twilight years in TV, when he was trading on old triumphs, cashing in goodwill chips, and celebrity-dropping with that year's favorite new faces—few of whom he seemed to recognize. To stay hip, he would slip into the back row of neighborhood movie houses to see new films and stars. "We're contemporary all the time," he boasted, in a mid-1980s interview, when plainly he was sliding into history. "Last year, we did a show that was a satire on TV. It got a 38 rating. Didja see it? I had five gorgeous gals on it." In interviews, he automatically shifted into his jaunty on-air mode. It was hard to know where the public and private Bob Hope divided, or if they ever did.

Hope's topical humor was in the tradition of Will Rogers. He arrived warm on the heels of Rogers in 1935 (the year the cowboy laureate died) in various revues before nailing down his Pepsodent program. He was far less political than Rogers or, to be sure, Mort Sahl;

while Sahl used a scalpel, Hope brandished a rubber knife—his political zingers were as lethal as Johnny Carson's: "Senator McCarthy got off a train in Washington, D.C., and spent two days at Union Station investigating Red Caps. McCarthy is a new type of television show—it's sort of a soap opera where everything comes out tattletale gray."

By radio comedy standards of the time, Hope's patter seemed topical, since many of the references were to current affairs even if they were really just setups for polite gags. He could *sound* ultrahip just by mentioning a fad like Metrecal, or politicians and labor leaders like Dean Acheson, John L. Lewis, Walter Reuther, or James Petrillo (the musicians' union boss). Hope wisely intuited that topicalizing jokes would make ordinary—and especially old—lines seem fresh. But for Hope, the joke was always the thing. He was far too much the ambitious careerist, the give-'em-what-they-want pro, to sink his political barbs below the surface.

It was on radio that Hope polished his joke-a-second style (more like six or seven a minute, according to one laugh meter), learning how to top jokes, to cushion bad jokes with "savers" (a technique perfected earlier by Milton Berle) and, most of all, to throw away jokes, artfully building his routine into the seamless tommy-gun monologue that made his name. Despite his on-call staff of jokesmiths ("You wouldn't say that if my writers were here," he liked to say, a steal from Jack Benny), he was a lightning ad-libber and born stand-up comic.

"My method, as it developed in early monologues," Hope once wrote, "was to deliver a series of one-liners, joke joke joke. It was a style similar to Winchell's staccato delivery. I would zing a joke and then start on the next line and wait for the audience to catch up. Then I'd ad-lib, 'Laugh first, figure it out later.' I'd say, 'Which one are you working on?' The style chews up jokes in carload lots." Once told that Hope was taking six writers with him on the road, Groucho Marx cracked, "For Hope that's practically ad-libbing."

Hope had also learned how to let his voice convey his entire persona within the confines of a standard comedy show with guest stars, an orchestra leader–foil (Skinnay Ennis, then Les Brown), a singer (Frances Langford), announcer, and regular sidekicks—the man-hunting "Vera Vague," Barbara Jo Allen, and the surreal Jerry Colonna, a pop-eyed wild man with a walrus mustache. Called "Professor" by Hope,

Colonna bellowed songs in a comic caterwaul and, in the early days of the show, went around saying, "Who's Yehudi?," a non sequitur tag line to an old joke. Colonna brought a whacked-out touch to Hope's show. In a typical exchange, Hope asks, "Professor, did you plant the bomb in the embassy like I told you?," to which Colonna replied, in that whooping five-alarm voice, "Embassy? Great Scott, I thought you said *NBC*!"

Hope's persona was easy to write for, remarked Dick Cavett, who began as a TV comedy writer: "The sound of the line is as important as the joke it contains, at least with the great comics. You need funny ideas, but there is something about the great comics' voices." He cited Hope, Benny, Allen, and Groucho Marx—all of whom had voices that could transcend a joke or propel it with twice its intrinsic worth.

"I know how to snap a line, then cover it, then speed on to the next," Hope once remarked, referring to his trademark way of "covering" a line by talking over the laugh ("But I just wanna say . . ."), as if he didn't mean it as a joke. Eventually, he became almost too efficient, removed from the occasion, and rattled off lines mechanically, with a kind of rote indifference. Or, as Steve Allen put it, "It was as if he was saying, 'These are the jokes, folks. Laugh or not, I don't care.' "

In a rare moment of self-analysis, Hope once likened his craft to a ball game: "You have to get over to the audience that there's a game going on and that if they don't stay awake they'll miss something, like missing a baseball someone has lobbed to them. What I'm really doing is asking, 'Let's see if you can hit this one!' That's my whole comedy technique. I know how to telegraph to the audience that this *is* a joke, and that if they don't laugh right now they're not playing the game."

Show business itself was almost a game for Hope, or maybe a nineteenth hole. The breezy comic custom-tailored himself to radio after the labor-intensive vaudeville circuit: "Working in radio was wonderful," he once reminisced. "You could just stand there in front of a radio audience, tell a joke, get a laugh, and then kiss the joke [off] and get another laugh. When the show was over, I'd just walk out, toss the script in a wastebasket, and go right to the golf course. I didn't have to worry about makeup, costumes, or anything like that."

Larry Gelbart has mainly pleasant memories of working for Hope, often at close range for long periods on trips to hospitals and bases, earning seventy-five dollars a week. "He was a funny man and I laughed at him constantly," said Gelbart, whose experiences traveling with Hope through Korea provided the source material for Gelbart's *M*A*S*H*. "I never felt exploited or put upon by him. He never called me in the middle of the night for jokes." He vividly recalled once running a sketch past Hope while one of the star's mistresses sat nearby making negative remarks until Hope was convinced the piece needed rewriting.

Hope liked to brag: "I had the best staff of writers in the business, all young kids right out of college"—another of whom was Sherwood Schwartz, who spent the first half of his career in radio, where he broke in with Hope during the show's second year. Schwartz wrote for half a dozen major radio and TV shows before creating *The Brady Bunch* and *Gilligan's Island,* not to mention *I Married Joan* and *Mr. Ed.*

Of his former boss, Sherwood Schwartz remarks, "One thing I remember is, he'd never do a joke about his mother-in-law. He *liked* his mother-in-law. And for some reason, he liked jokes where people were standing on each other's shoulders. Bob liked to do jokes that were familiar to him, especially about whatever female star was hot at the time." It was just such narrow specifications, however, that caused Schwartz to leave the show after the war. "Writing for Hope was a dead-end street for creativity. Unless you fit the form, you couldn't do fresh ideas. But it was terrific training. I learned not to use superfluous words—how to take a joke and reduce it to its irreducible minimum. Tight! Tight! Tight!" The typical monologue, Schwartz continues, had about sixteen jokes, "and no joke could be more than two lines long. For instance, if the joke involved a car you'd never say 'blue Cadillac,' because blue isn't necessary to the joke. You avoided anything that would detract from the main subject of the joke."

Hope's radio ratings fell nearly as rapidly as Fred Allen's, diving from 23.8 in 1949 to just over half that, 12.7, in 1951, and by 1953 he was down to 5.4. Pepsodent jumped ship. Finally, with TV looming and in a last-ditch attempt to hold on to his radio audience in 1953, he began a curious daily half-hour après-breakfast show for Jell-O at 9:30 A.M., along with his weekly half-hour show, until, inevitably, he drifted into TV. Like Jack Benny, Hope approached TV cautiously, but he made the transition in 1949 more easily than most radio comedians.

Since he was already a film star, the cameras didn't worry him, although three cameras on a set annoyed him ("It's like trying to do a nightclub act with three waiters with trays walking in front of you every time you reach the punch line"). What worried him was that TV would steal time from his twin passions of golf and girls. Also, writers had to learn how to create sight as well as sound gags, which meant that he had to devise shows built around sketches, not just deliver a joke-crammed monologue. Paramount tried to delay his entrance into TV, fearing that it would cut into his big-screen audience.

Hope stayed on radio as long as he could, but his exit was hustled along when he opened the 1950 radio season on Tuesday nights opposite a man later nicknamed "Mr. Tuesday Night"—Milton Berle in his new and, as it turned out, milestone TV show, *The Texaco Star Theater.* Berle moved as many TV sets out of stores as *Amos 'n' Andy* had sold radios twenty years before, leaving much carnage in his path. What finally pushed Hope into TV was money: an offer from Frigidaire to do eight $50,000 specials a year—in addition to his weekly radio show.

Out of radio, too, grew Hope's fabled tours of GI camps, the live remotes from everywhere, which established him as not just the gung-ho all-American wise guy but as a patriot and tireless globe-trotting ambassador of good cheer. From there, it was only a shuffle step to immortality, but Hope never quite left behind the stage roots that accounted for his need to go on entertaining after he turned ninety, by which time, sadly, he had become a comic robot. As an old-time comedy writer observed: "People forget that Bob originally was a small-time vaudevillian. Despite his later success, I think somewhere inside him he still feels like a small-time vaudeville hoofer who got lucky."

— 8 —

For Your Listening and Dancing Pleasure

"There was surely more to World War II than singing. But if you were a child then, the war was all voices on radio—in news broadcasts, of course, but, in memory, mostly voices singing."
—D. J. R. BRUCKNER,
in a New York Times *review*

THE MUSICAL VARIETY SHOW WAS RADIO'S FIRST best idea, an easy-listening format that sprang fully formed from the basic vaudeville bill of fare of the mid-1920s. This multi-cell show business life-form not only spawned new singers but bred announcers, who took to ad-libbing wisecracks, which in turn begot comedians, who eventually opened up the microphones to every sort of performer.

The first music heard on the air were starchy musicales, called "potted palm music"—piano recitals, opera singers, string quartets, etc. (in just six months of 1923, WJZ in New Jersey aired 1,260 music and vocal recitals). Typical was *The RCA Victor Hour,* soon copied by similar Philco/Edison/Bakelite/City Services/Brunswick "Hours."

Long before public broadcasting, networks, and even sponsors, proclaimed themselves firmly on the side of Art—an aspect of early radio's "lust for respectability," to quote one historian. He adds that second-rate sopranos were readily available to sing pre–World War I blockbusters like "In the Good Old Summertime," "Let Me Call You Sweetheart," "After the Ball Is Over," and "A Bird in a Gilded Cage," plus generous selections from Sousa, Gilbert and Sullivan, and waltz kings Franz Lehár, Rudolf Friml, Sigmund Romberg, and Victor Herbert. It was the Muzak of its day. The prime mover was NBC's musical consultant, Walter Damrosch, a conductor, lecturer, and classical music crusader—someone called him America's "musical statesman"—who began a series of young people's concerts, a cause later taken up by Leonard Bernstein on TV; it was Damrosch who persuaded Andrew Carnegie to build a hall in New York City.

The Atwater-Kent Radio Hour, the first big packaged show, pre-

Overleaf, clockwise from top left: Rudy Vallee, Jo Stafford and the Pied Pipers, Jessica Dragonette with Rosario Bourdon's Orchestra

sented unknown classical singers in their debuts and plugged Atwater-Kent as the truest vocal transmitter. *The Palmolive Hour* took the format farther, airing excerpts from Broadway shows. *The Collier's Radio Hour,* sponsored by the popular magazine, expanded on that by adding sports, drama, and current events to music and comedy, creating broadcasting's first "magazine" format.

The effect of free music on radio not only brought opera and concerts to the masses but sparked the recording industry, which for years feared radio would destroy it when sales fell in the phonograph, sheet music, piano roll, and piano businesses; meanwhile, saxophone, mandolin, and banjo sales boomed. But Victor and Brunswick, the two leading phonograph companies, soon recognized the promotional value of radio programs, which were, in essence, hour-long singing commercials for record players.

Still, radios soon began to outsell phonographs. Thomas Edison decided that radio was fine for news, speeches, and sports events (in the long run, he turned out to be right) but said it distorted music—although he was half-deaf himself. "The radio fad will pass," he predicted, "and people will once more return to the phonograph." *His* phonograph. Many felt that talking pictures, another twenties fad, would render radio mute, or at least passé. E. F. Albee, head of the Keith-Albee vaudeville circuit, refused to let performers under contract go on the air, even though, it turned out, radio actually lengthened vaudeville's life span when new radio stars, who had left the stage, went back out on the road in personal appearances.

Opera and singing stars, accustomed to screaming multitudes, stayed away on their own, unwilling to perform before an audience of dead air. The diva Alma Gluck sniffed, "Radio is a nuisance; they are perfectly darn foolish things to have around, and besides the squawks, most of what one hears over them is terrible." The great tenor John McCormack, on first entering a padded studio, proclaimed, "I can never sing here!"—but by the end of the week, he'd been converted. His on-air rendition of a new Irving Berlin song, "All Alone," was snapped up in stores on wax, and in a hundred thousand copies of the sheet music, convincing remaining skeptical divas and doubting tenors that radio was, in fact, their best friend.

One of the first live opera broadcasts was at the Manhattan Opera

House in 1923, hosted by a failed tenor named Milton J. Cross, who went on to host more than eight hundred weekly broadcasts of the Metropolitan Opera for forty-three years on NBC, sponsored most of that time by Texaco, which brought opera to millions who had never heard one before. The Met's early antiradio policy ended in 1931, when regular broadcasts began and Cross became the "Voice of the Met." His resonant voice was an instrument in itself, one that produced a burnished announcer-profundo sound. Cross was a veritable talking playbill who synopsized convoluted plots and provided biographical notes, between-acts trivia, and an intermission quiz with celebrity opera buffs; "Mr. Opera" himself didn't miss a curtain until 1973, when his wife died.

The NBC Symphony broadcasts were conducted for seventeen years by Arturo Toscanini, who was lured out of retirement in Italy in 1937 at the age of seventy by David Sarnoff during the network culture wars; Sarnoff promised to start a symphony orchestra if Toscanini would conduct it. Requests for tickets to the maestro's studio concerts, which played to five million homes each week, reached fifty thousand a month; *New York Times* music critic Olin Downes was the learned commentator. With Leopold Stokowski in Philadelphia and Serge Koussevitzky in Boston conducting on CBS, radio listeners had choice seats at weekly symphonies of the air. Much of Toscanini's reputation rests on those live radio concerts which comprise only a fourth of his total sixty-eight-year career—but they number two hundred broadcasts, over half of them recorded, plus national tours. He finally gave up conducting at eighty-seven, when, at the end of a shaky radio-TV concert in 1954, he dropped his baton and left the podium for good.

Radio and classical or semiclassical music became natural allies as the air was filled with programs that cried "distinguished," broadcasts like *The American Album of Familiar Music*; *The Voice of Firestone* (led unstintingly for some thirty years by Howard Barlow and the equally indestructible John Charles Thomas, the Pavarotti of radio); *The Railroad Hour* (hosted by Gordon MacRae); the much-loved, long-lived *Telephone Hour* (with conductor Donald Voorhees); *The Longines Symphonette*; and, to be sure, the Saturday *Metropolitan Opera Broadcast*, still on the air—as is its equally revered pop opposite, *The Grand Ole Opry*. They are radio's two hardiest survivors.

THE GRAND OLE OPRY was originally a promotional broadcast for the National Life and Accident Insurance Company, which built a robust 1,000-watt station in downtown Nashville in 1925 whose call letters, WSM, stood for the firm's motto, "We Shield Millions."

At WSM, the show's announcer was George Hay, a former Memphis reporter who became the show's talent scout, producer, and promoter of "hillbilly" music, to which the *Opry* brought a gradual grudging respect from city slickers. Hay, nicknamed the Solemn Old Judge, scoured the Ozarks, and then the whole country, in search of local fiddlers, pickers, and singers, finding them in churches, barbershops, gas stations, farms, front porch swings, and back-roads radio stations. One show a week could barely contain them all. At the close of the first show, an eighty-year-old fiddling dirt farmer, Uncle Jimmy Thompson, cried, "Fiddlesticks! A man can't get warmed up in no one hour." The *Opry* soon expanded to four hours, and Saturday-night marathons now run six hours, plus a Friday show.

City fathers fretted that the broadcasts would hurt Nashville's proud reputation as the "Athens of the South" (country music had long been synonymous with amateur nights), but Hay persisted in presenting his good-humored barn dance. On an early broadcast he found the ideal earthy handle for the show after a harmonica player named De Ford Bailey had imitated a chugging locomotive, and said: "Now, folks, you gotta admit that sounded mighty real . . . and classy. Our program can't be called grand opera. But, folks, I don't see why we can't call it 'opry.' So from now on we will be presenting *Grand Ole Opry*." And so he did, and so it was.

From its humble studio the show moved to a theater, then to the Dixie Tabernacle, then to the War Memorial Auditorium, and finally, in 1941, to its hallowed hall, Ryman Auditorium, which seated 3,600 and from which it broadcast for thirty-three years, until it moved in 1974 to new theme-park quarters at Opryland, USA.

During the 1940s and 1950s, the NBC network carried a half-hour segment of the *Opry*. A singer had not arrived in country music until being granted an audience on the broadcast, whose alumni form country-western's core family, from Roy Rogers to Roy Acuff to Roy

Orbison. A few months after Hank Williams debuted on the *Opry*, June 11, 1949, yodeling his plaintive "Lovesick Blues," he was a country-music legend (and three and a half years later he was dead, unable to handle the worshipful fame that the show had conferred).

Even older than the *Opry*, by eighteen months, was its predecessor, *The National Barn Dance*, George Hay's original show on Chicago's WLS, which had more ballads ("heart songs") than backwoods jams and grew so popular that it became the only show in radio to charge admission, surviving until 1957. Another, more Southern-fried, version of the *Opry* was *Louisiana Hayride*.

THE EVEREADY HOUR, which debuted in 1923, was the earliest, if primitive, all-out musical variety show and established the format for the next decade, if not forever: comedy sketches, musical selections, a monologue or a dramatic piece, studded with guests from stage and screen, plus an ingratiating "host" who brought the acts on with a kindly word. On a typical *Eveready Hour* program, an announcer proclaimed, "Tonight, the sponsors have included in the program actress Elsie Janis, who will present hits and bits of former years, and guest Arthur H. Young will tell some of his experiences while hunting wild animals in Alaska and Africa with bow and arrow." Pretty exciting lineup.

Rudy Vallee, who streamlined the variety format, is mainly remembered today as a campy crooner who sang through a megaphone and his nose, made a few movies, and played the stuffy boss in *How to Succeed in Business Without Really Trying*. Not a half-bad legacy—but only half of it, for Vallee was, in fact, not only radio's first crooner but its first impresario as host of *The Fleischmann Hour*, a smoothly executed program that invented the radio and TV variety show as we think of it now. After Vallee's signature "Heigh-ho, everybody!" the band swung sweetly into the theme song, "My Time Is Your Time." In his honeyed, haughty voice, Vallee beckoned listeners thusly: "We earnestly crave your attention and we strive earnestly to please you." With one foot in the door, the curly-headed young tenor then opened with a solo, which led to the evening's guest star, followed by a monologue, another song, and a comedy sketch—everything neatly glued together with Vallee's suave, somewhat self-important manner. Always the youthful well-mannered fellow, he presided over the show like a snooty maître d', bidding listeners a fond farewell with "Au revoir and goodnight."

The ambitious leader of the Connecticut Yankees, a former cheerleading, flapper-chasing, raccoon-coat-wearing Yalie, Vallee was the first Ed Sullivan, whose power and influence in the 1930s equaled that of the real Sullivan on TV and Florenz Ziegfeld on Broadway. He was a Sol Hurok of the air responsible for launching as many major radio careers as anybody in show business. By the early 1930s, his show had replaced the Palace Theater as the prestige booking of vaudeville. It was the first show to revolve around a single host. With his curiously appealing pinched voice, Vallee parlayed a mediocre house band at the Heigh Ho Club (hence his famous opening) into a dominant position as a star and pop hit-maker.

Vallee also introduced to the country a new sound in singing, called "crooning," that was vilified as (to quote one enraged religious leader) "a degenerate form of singing . . . no true American would practice this base art. I cannot turn the dial without getting these whiners and bleaters defiling the air and crying vapid words to impossible tunes." Someone called it "a plague of saccharine slurring and callow boop-a-dooping." The New York Singing Teachers Association asserted that "crooning corrupts the minds and ideals of the younger generation." Others found Vallee's sound sexy and "radiophonic." Via radio, an okay singer could be changed overnight into a sublime charmer.

The ever-modest Vallee later said, "Ninety percent of the natural-voiced singers who followed in the wake of my meteoric success in radio might never have made it had I not demonstrated that the public was ready to eagerly accept crooning." Once, however, when a reporter rudely asked, "Are you a crooner?," Vallee sniffed, "I am not. I have been opposed to the word for a long time." The *New York Times* weighed in with an editorial that pleaded for tolerance, saying, "They sing like that because they can't help it," and tried to calm readers by maintaining, "Their style is beginning to go out of fashion. Reproving crooners is futile for singing teachers or anyone else. Crooners will soon go the way of tandem bicycles, mah jongg, and midget golf."

A new singer named Bing Crosby, who would take crooning to new levels of depravity, was once backed to the wall on the subject, but wriggled free with a Nixonian response: "I am not a crooner." Morton Downey, Russ Columbo, and Kate Smith all issued similar firm denials, but in fact crooning was a natural outgrowth of singing into a mike in an intimate, mellow fashion as if whispering sweet nothings in the listener's ear. In fact, it was almost a technical necessity when singing into a sensitive carbon microphone, to prevent a harsh high note from shattering a filament. Braying or belting on radio irritated eardrums, maybe one reason that singers like Al Jolson and Ethel Merman were radio also-rans while lesser voices, belonging to the Vaughn Monroes and Vaughn de Leaths, were stars. Other velvety singers of that era and ilk included Annette Hanshaw, Gene Austin, Frank Munn (the "Golden Voice of Radio"), and the pretty and prettily named Jessica Dragonette, the "Queen of Radio" from the late 1920s until the late 1930s, who once drew 150,000 people to one appearance in Chicago's Grant Park.

Arthur Tracy, the "Street Singer," was by 1931 radio's hottest troubadour, singing, in his light alluring voice, songs like "Marta, Rambling Rose of the Wildwood," "When I Grow Too Old to Dream," and "Red Sails in the Sunset." An announcer brought him on with: "Down the corner and 'round your way comes the Street Singer to sing you his romantic ballads of yesterday and yore." At the end, the announcer bade him farewell: "And there he goes, the Street Singer . . . back again tomorrow night to serenade you." Along with most 1930s on-air crooners, Tracy remained a musical footnote, buried until his 1937 hit "Pennies from Heaven" was revived on the soundtrack of the 1981 movie of that name, and at eighty-two the ageless Tracy reemerged in cabarets to warble a few final choruses of "I'll See You Again." He died at ninety-eight in 1997.

Few now recall Tracy, Munn, Hanshaw, Austin, de Leath, or Dragonette, but in 1935 they were the reigning pop singers; Monroe survived the longest on radio and records. De Leath, the first "First Lady of Radio," was a warm, chatty, matriarchal Kate Smith credited as the first true radio "crooner" when she warbled "Old Folks at Home" into a mike in 1916 as a demo for Dr. Lee DeForest. In early radio, and even later, breeziness always won out over bravura. Whether it was newscasting, sportscasting, or performing, radio soon learned to loosen its necktie and slip into something more comfortable.

Because NBC, Vallee's network, was then the only coast-to-coast hookup, virtually any new song he performed on his show became an instant hit, among them "S'posin'," "Marie," "Lover Come Back to Me," "Coquette," and his signature tunes—"Goodnight, Sweetheart," "The Whiffenpoof Song," "I'm Just a Vagabond Lover," and "Let's Put Out the Lights and Go to Sleep." When Vallee introduced a new singer, like Alice Faye, people listened seriously. He first brought Johnny Mercer's name to the airwaves with a rendition of "Lazybones" sung with black inflections.

On *The Fleischmann Hour* (which ran from 1929 to 1939) and later on *The Sealtest Show* (1940–42), Vallee paraded a dazzling array of stars-to-be or stars from other venues making their radio debuts. Eddie Cantor, Edgar Bergen and Charlie McCarthy, Burns and Allen, Milton Berle, Bea Lillie, Dolores Grey, Victor Borge, and Noël Coward were first heard by a nationwide audience under the respected Vallee imprimatur.

Not unlike the later, clunkier Ed Sullivan, Vallee took pride in presenting scenes from hit Broadway shows, lavishing them with ornate introductions separated by lush musical interludes, all of which gave listeners the feeling that they were tuned in to one classy program. He was the first to commission dramatic segments—as opposed to lifting scenes from hit plays—from new writers like Norman Corwin. It was on Vallee's show that *The Aldrich Family* evolved from sketches based on its Broadway success into a long-running radio hit of its own.

The Vallee show premiered two days after the stock market crash of 1929, and, even though Fleischmann stock had fallen from 101 points to 28, Vallee's stock soared and the show was wildly popular. As with most of radio, Vallee made the show up as he went along. The first program was broadcast from an organ loft at the Paramount Theater between the band's stage appearances, where he re-created the sound of a supper club by inserting band remotes from his own club, the Villa Vallee, with clinking glassware and rattling dishes. Graham McNamee read the commercials and the show went on to run 520 consecutive weeks.

The innovations didn't kick in until after two years of semi–big band (thirteen pieces) numbers interspersed with Vallee's vocals. The show realized its power in 1932, when stars began clamoring for a spot with Vallee, who presented the major names of the day—Fanny Brice, who first did her Baby Snooks character on the air here, Carmen Miranda, Bob Hope, and Red Skelton. None of these performers made a splash in radio until they got their own shows, but their guest shots with Vallee gave them credibility. Others first unveiled on radio by Vallee included Orson Welles, Mel Tormé, and Larry Adler.

A notorious ladies' man, Vallee would pluck girls out of a chorus line and give them a chance. He spotted Alice Faye in the chorus of George White's *Scandals*. "She was a cute lovely blonde with a smile warm enough to melt the heart of an Eskimo," he said, with "an instinctive gift for handling light rhythmic songs, and great authority, combined with tremendous physical appeal." Needing a girl singer, Vallee had an affair with Faye that ended his marriage and then hired her, although he'd only heard her perform solo at a cast party, where he was smitten by her imitation of Maurice Chevalier singing "Mimi."

With Sealtest, his 1940s show took on a less formal, more traditional air. It was directed by Ed Gardner before Gardner took over as proprietor of *Duffy's Tavern* and became a star himself. Announcer Jimmy Wallington parried with guests and John Barrymore was wheeled in to costar. The two aging roués made an unlikely, often uncomfortable team, with Vallee playing foil to Barrymore's clownish self-mocking ham, who made fun of his shabby reputation as a drunk, a lover, a scene-chewing Shakespearean actor, and a moldy theatrical reprobate.

Rudy Vallee was merely the most resourceful of the big-band leaders who took to radio in the 1930s. Most were content simply to set up shop and play—groups led by Vincent Lopez, Tommy and Jimmy Dorsey, Jack Teagarden, Glenn Miller, Woody Herman, Jan Garber, Bunny Berigan, Noble Sissle, Benny Goodman, and many others, who usually came on late at night and played listeners to dreamy sleep from this or that remote hotel, supper club, ballroom, or lake resort.

A handful of resourceful radio bandleaders reinvented themselves, like Vallee, as talent agents, most famously Horace Heidt, a little-known conductor who ran an amateur night called *The Horace Heidt Show,* a copy of Major Bowes's *Original Amateur Hour.* Other conductors turned their bands to more enterprising gimmicky uses, namely

Spike Jones, Sammy Kaye, and Kay Kyser, a bouncy Southerner who presided over *Kay Kyser's Kollege of Musical Knowledge.*

Crooning was not radio's only corrupting musical influence of the 1920s. There was also jazz, considered as ruinous to youth as rock was in the 1960s and rap in the 1990s. The "race music" of its day was taboo until Paul Whiteman made it respectable and then fashionable; even his last name probably helped smuggle jazz across the color line. Whiteman, with Ferde Grofé, orchestrated jazz (something of an oxymoron) for airplay by smoothing it out, squaring its free-form spirit, and neatly boxing it to fit into a radio format. By the end of the Jazz Age, jazz itself finally found a home on radio.

KATE SMITH—WHO LIKED TO SAY, "I'm big and I'm fat, but I have a voice, and when I sing, boy, I sing all over!"—was never considered a radio impresario like Rudy Vallee, but she was equally influential as the happy hostess of *The Kate Smith Show,* produced by Ted Collins, Smith's longtime Svengali. Her variety show first launched on the air, among others, *It Pays to Be Ignorant,* Abbott and Costello, and singer Bea Wain, later a star of *Your Hit Parade.*

Collins, a one-time announcer and Columbia Records scout, kept Smith at arm's length from the public, securely wrapped in patriotic bunting. John Crosby wrote that she was "presented as a sort of American institution, like Thanksgiving." On her TV debut, following a shot of crashing waves on rocky shores and a cut to the flag, he said, "I half expected her to sing the Constitution in C-sharp minor." "Kate was a wonderful gal, but Collins was a tough uncle, very sharp and totally ruthless," recalls Jim North, an ad executive who dealt with the show.

Behind her lasting image as the mighty pop diva whose "God Bless America" turned her into a sort of singing Statue of Liberty—the song was almost adopted as a new national anthem twenty-three years after Irving Berlin had written it and shelved it as too "sticky"—Smith had a robust three-decade radio career that stretched from her 1931 debut on *Kate Smith Sings* through a 1959 show called *Kate Smith Calls.* For ten years, between crooning and calling, she also did a popular daily noontime series of chatty fifteen-minute uplift sermonettes called *Kate Smith Speaks,* which was eventually slimmed down to five minutes a day. In

1976, she popped up for one last hearty laugh on *The Hollywood Squares.*

Radio and Kathryn Elizabeth Smith were an ideal fit, not just because of her Wagnerian voice and image and earthy regular-gal manner but because of her size: She could hide out behind the mike. Smith took refuge in radio after an early career as a fat-girl foil for vaudeville comics like Bert Lahr. Critics cruelly joshed her in their reviews, and even her theme song, "When the Moon Comes Over the Mountain," conspired against her 235-pound shape. Collins saw behind, and around, the hefty Virginia singer subtitled "the Songbird of the South," rescuing her from Margaret Dumont status and packaging her all-embracing voice and down-home style for records and radio, where she gave recipes for fried chicken, baked squash, and peppermint ice cream, and signed off each show with "Thanks for listenin'!" She meant it.

One critic said of her, "Whatever the opposite of the blues is, that's what she sang." When she met the king and queen of England, FDR presented her thus: "This is Kate Smith. This is America." It was hard to resist the matronly Smith's massive vocal presence. During the 1940s, she and Jack Benny had radio's only no-cancel contracts in broadcasting. Her semiregal bearing and imposing stature led to her being crowned the ultimate "First Lady of Radio." As TV critic Tom Shales wrote, "Kids who grew up to the sound of Kate Smith's voice privately felt that this is what Mom would sound like if only Mom could sing. If all the Moms could sing together."

THE RADIO MUSICAL VARIETY SHOW reached its heights with *Kraft Music Hall,* which took various forms over a long life under different proprietors. Bing Crosby made it his home base for eleven years, starting in 1935, and rode it to the top with cohosts Connee Boswell, Peggy Lee, Ginny Simms, and Mary Martin. Crosby's loose, ultracool style gave the show a nonchalance perfectly suited to radio, solidifying even further his hold on movies and records. At one time, in the mid-1940s, Crosby was the leading film star, radio star, and recording star, a status nobody else has ever equaled. Tony Bennett put it this way: "Crosby dominated in radio like Elvis and the Beatles combined—he had *hour* shows"; other pop singers, even Sinatra, had, at most, quickie, low-budget quarter-hour programs (*Songs by Sinatra,* etc.).

The trademark laid-back Crosby banter and tossed-off asides were largely the work of Carroll Carroll, perhaps radio's busiest continuity/comedy writer, who gave Bing Crosby his urbane, breezy character, an easygoing chatter that segued out of his crooning. It set the tone for other variety shows that copied its back-fence congeniality.

"He seemed to have an ear for the way I talked," wrote Crosby in his autobiography, crediting Carroll with the cool, wry persona that came to be called Bing Crosby. "He encouraged me to incorporate as many of my own words as possible into the script. He'd send a script around to my home and I'd try to rewrite the speeches he'd written for me. And I'd try to put in little jokes if I could think of any. Many of them were clumsy and pointless, but once in a while I hit something mildly amusing and Carroll wouldn't delete it if he thought it had a chance of getting a laugh. . . . It was the next thing to ad-libbing."

Crosby, of course, was only partly a singer. He was at least half a comedian, a man who never seemed to take singing all that seriously. Unlike Sinatra, he didn't seem to worry much about lyric interpretation; it was as if he were singing for the sheer joy of it, like Jolson—as easily as swinging a golf club. A song was not an art form to Crosby; it was fun—part of his persona, but not the whole of it. Pop singing can be divided roughly into "AC" and "BC": Before Crosby, singers sang at you; after Crosby and radio, they sang to you. One great singer, Ruth Etting, wasn't drawn to radio, explaining, "There's no satisfaction singing into a microphone." But Crosby managed to sing into a microphone and make the mike vanish, as if it were eavesdropping on him. From his earliest films, he radiated a twinkle that told people he also didn't take his lover-boy baritone role that seriously. While Sinatra was erotic and aloof, Bing was pipe-and-slippers comfy. Bing was a kidder and, like his idol Jolson, even whistled while he worked. Tom Shales observed, "Crosby didn't sentimentalize himself. He did it in a stroll. It was a particular American way of dealing with fame and glory; he made it look disarmingly attractive. He was not your everyday superstar." He sang with great warmth and even urgency, and during the war became an early voice from home with sentimental renderings of "I'll Be Seeing You," "I'll Be Home for Christmas," and, of course, "White Christmas." Yet he often seemed to be mocking himself just a little. Once, during a duet, he advised a performer to sing lower down in the register, adding, "That's where the money is." He specialized in casual tunes, odes to the simple life, such as "Moonlight Bay," "Ol' Buttermilk Sky," "In the Cool, Cool, Cool of the Evening," "Lazy," "Mississippi Mud," "Gone Fishin'," "Great Day," and "It's a Good Day." He sang in the sunshine, or perhaps sunbeams simply sought him out.

"Crosby was a very shy man who needed liquor to buoy him up," recalls the ex-CBS publicist Gary Stevens, who says he helped sober him up before his first CBS show; Bing's roommates, Jimmy Dorsey and singer Jimmy Reis, fed him enough coffee to get him to the studio and through the broadcast. Says Stevens, "He was kind of a scatterbrained little-boy-lost then, a very difficult guy to know, reclusive, very cold to 90 percent of people he knew. He only came alive around music or to get to a bar. But a perfectionist and a real craftsman on the air."

His Kraft radio show was unusually adept at cross-pollinating Crosby with cultural blue bloods (opera stars, concert musicians, classical actors). "Those longhairs go for humanizing in a big way," he noted. "I'd sing an aria with them and they'd sing a scat song with me." Major stars were eager to join the nation's leading singer in a duet and a few minutes of jaunty Crosbyesque badinage; it was a stamp of pop approval. Carroll explained that the show's attitude was to "treat opera as if it were baseball and baseball as if it were opera."

Kraft Music Hall became a major showcase for jazz musicians, but it can also claim three major comic discoveries: Victor Borge, Jerry Colonna, and Spike Jones. Borge, who had begun by warming up audiences before Rudy Vallee's show, broke in with his still-famous verbal punctuation routine, which was scheduled for twelve minutes but wound up running the length of the show, after which the head of the agency ordered that Borge be signed to a long-term contract; the comic had sealed his entire career within thirty minutes. Colonna was a former trombonist in the John Scott Trotter band on Crosby's show when he was written into an opera parody to bellow an aria in a dead-pan screech that became his trademark on Bob Hope's show. Jones, Trotter's drummer, was asked to devise a series of suitably bizarre arrangements, using auto horns, washboards, breaking glass, screams, cowbells, slide whistles, tin pans, and gunshots to back up bazooka-playing comic Bob Burns "music" solos, which hatched Jones's series of "music depreciation hours" with his wild and crazy City Slickers.

Crosby, like Hope, loved radio's free-form format, and he made radio even freer and easier—indeed, he helped remake it in his own open-collar image. When Crosby wanted to tape his show, the sponsor, the agency, the network, and, claimed Crosby, the entire radio industry, balked, fearful the program would sound canned. So the sponsor canned Crosby instead and in 1946 brought in Al Jolson—a frequent Crosby guest in search of a comeback, whose appearances revived his postwar career, led to *The Jolson Story,* and made him a star all over again. A decade earlier, in his prime, he had hosted the *Shell Chateau,* an extravagant variety showcase.

When Crosby finally split with Kraft (dumping Carroll Carroll in the process, without batting an eye; "very complex man" was Carroll's tactful response), he opened a competing music hall in Hollywood called *Philco Radio Time,* and when Philco pulled out, it became *The Bing Crosby Show,* which was fully transcribed and brought Crosby an additional $40,000 a week from the independent stations that bought the transcriptions (three aluminum discs that recorded ten minutes per side at 33⅓ RPM). When he switched from discs to tape, it wasn't strictly an aesthetic decision—Crosby also had an interest in a small new magnetic tape company named Ampex.

CBS's main argument against taping shows was that performers might be able to sell their shows to individual stations rather than use the network. Hope soon followed Crosby's lead to Hollywood, followed by Jack Benny and then by virtually every major radio comedian except Fred Allen, a New York habitué. Transcription was a godsend for a master ad-libber like Groucho Marx, who could jab and jabber with contestants on *You Bet Your Life* as long as he liked until he had accumulated enough zingers for a twenty-seven-minute show. Comics with a risqué turn of mind could get off any suggestive line and, if it proved too blue, snip it out when the show aired. Taping, a radical notion, also allowed a star to record a show from anywhere he happened to be appearing and, in Crosby's case, make it sound as seamless as his crooning by editing out jokes, gaffes, or ad libs that fell flat before a live audience.

Transcriptions led to an accidental invention of another controversial concept. Bob Burns, "the Arkansas Traveler," was a guest on the Crosby show and tossed off some off-color stories about life on the farm. "They got enormous laughs," reported sound technician Jack Mullin, "which just went on and on. We couldn't use the jokes, but writer Bill Morrow asked us to save the laughs. A couple of weeks later we had a show that wasn't so funny, and he insisted that we put in the salvaged laughs. Thus the laugh-track was born."

The downside of taping shows was that it made for sloppier performances when entertainers knew that sketches, songs, and banter could be fixed with a quick splice or repeated. Ironically, shows that had been done live for decades were remarkably fluff-free. And just as the anti-tape contingent feared, tape took the spark out of shows. "There wasn't as much fun for the listener, either," Carroll Carroll observed. "There was no ever-present peril of a possible boo-boo to lend spice to a dull affair."

Bing Crosby hit listeners where they lived with his innate no-sweat manner, his "Oh, *yeah-h-h*"s, sport shirts, golf hat, pipe, and outdoorsy Southern California air—even the flip nickname itself, allegedly given him as a boy when he shot off imaginary guns with loud cries of, "Bing! Bing!" Crosby stayed on the air, in one form or another, to the bitter end in the early 1960s, and for eight consecutive years was radio's number-one personality. As jazz critic Gary Giddins said of him once, paraphrasing a Mel Brooks line about a fictitious pop singer: "I am them, they are me. We are all singing, [but] I have the mouth."

ALTHOUGH HE STARRED in *Shell Chateau* in the 1930s and was the original and future host of *Kraft Music Hall,* perhaps the country's greatest all-time pure performer, Al Jolson, was never at home on radio. His free spirit was hobbled by a microphone cord.

Jolson wasn't a comic. He was a wide-open theatrical singer who sang with his whole body—prancing on his feet, imploring with his shoulders and expressive hands, rolling his eyes, and shooting his eyebrows as he flirted outrageously with the audience; each listener felt he was singing directly for him. Radio frustrated him in every way; its limited time frame cramped his style and he couldn't take forty-five-minute encores. Inhibited though Jolson was by radio, his talent was so enormous that his voice embodied the invisible Jolie and radiated electricity. His power was reduced by half on routine variety shows, but 50 percent of Jolson was equal to 100 percent of just about anybody else. You felt his presence in every song.

In a sense, Jolson had anticipated radio when he built runways wherever he sang onstage, a way to get closer to the audience. His hypnotic musical spirit took over when he sang and held listeners rapt by his sheer intensity. He made the most of all the vocal tricks he had mastered on stage—sobbing notes, breaking words, slurring consonants, stretching vowels, and riding the emotion of a phrase. In tunes like "Liza," "Keep Smiling at Trouble," and "Let Me Sing and I'm Happy," that jubilant voice rebounds off walls. He was as much orator and revivalist preacher as singer. Indeed, in many songs he segues without a break into talk-singing—as one critic noted, "almost as if he found the tune itself inhibiting."

He was capable of the most basic simpering, groveling sentimentality, tender and pleading, a kind of cantorial sound that is part Kaddish and part Caruso. When Jolie sang, it was all stops out. Like Rudy Vallee, he used radio as if it were a megaphone. His trademark whinnying *nyahh-h-h-h-h* wasn't just shtick but a way of filling silence with the music of his own personality, as if he were overdubbing himself; he abhorred a vocal vacuum, and when he didn't warble, he whistled.

Jolson wasn't much of an actor—his banter on the Kraft shows is strained and wooden, especially alongside his exuberant singing. Conversation seemed to bore him, mere words in between the music, and you sense him straining at the microphone cord on the air when he makes small talk with guests. In Eddie Cantor's words, "[Crosby] treated radio as if it were an instrument of introduction to your living room. Jolie treated it like an imposter." On radio, a critic added, "he sang all too obviously to the studio audience. The radio audience sensed it, and resented it." Radio was too high-tech for a primitive like Jolson, who needed to look in the audience's eyes. He could reach any balcony, but a kitchen in Kankakee was only a distant rumor to Jolson, whose own voice box was the only transmitter he believed in.

"Radio didn't know how to use Jolson," George Burns observed. "I know he hated doing live radio and at that time there wasn't anything else." Jolson was also uncomfortable with radio's nonchalant quality ("I'd like to do radio just like pictures," Jolson once said, "and leave the imperfect stuff on the cutting-room floor"). He couldn't find a way to control the great unseen audience or how to focus his energies. Audiences had been putty in his hands when he would bestride a Broadway stage, yet here they were huge but elusive, an amorphous mass of ether. Burns put it best: "Jolson was too big to fit inside a format."

THE *YOUR HIT PARADE* FORMAT was simplicity itself—a ranking of the week's top ten songs sung by a rotating cast of regulars led for several years by Frank Sinatra, augmented by swoons and whoops from studio bobby-soxers. Radio, and mainly *Your Hit Parade,* took Sinatra from big-band star to superstar. The other voices on the show included Bea Wain, Buddy Clark, Ginny Simms, Dinah Shore, Martha Tilton, Dick Haymes, Johnny Mercer, Eileen Wilson, Georgia Gibbs, Lanny Ross, Doris Day, Andy Russell, plus two rookies who made the transition to TV—Dorothy Collins and Snooky Lanson.

The *Hit Parade* singers were fleshed out by guest vocalists, "Lucky Strike extras," and commercials made famous by the hypnotic babble of auctioneers L. A. (Speed) Riggs and F. E. Boone chanting incomprehensible numbers as they "*sol-l-l-d* A-merican!" and delivered the familiar pledge—"LS/MFT: Lucky Strike Means Fine Tobacco"—stamped on every pack.

Your Hit Parade was on radio from 1935 to 1959, hitting its peak of popularity during the war, when listeners sat around radios on Saturday nights cheering for their favorite songs to win, place, or show. The program's most exciting moment was the announcement of the "Number One Hit Parade song of the week!" introduced with fanfare, drumroll, and vocal flourish by announcer André Baruch. You felt a little tingle as the top song on the charts was named, followed by a groan if it turned out to be the same song as the previous fourteen weeks. Every song on the week's *Hit Parade* was given a triumphal send-off with rippling harp strings as Baruch cried, "And now! In the number-seven spot! Peggy Lee sings 'Sentimental Journey'!"

Long before the onslaught of Top 40 formats, *Your Hit Parade* was the sole oracle of pop music trends—a kind of weekly Grammy Awards. At first, the songs were the stars; singers, who earned a hundred dollars a show, weren't even credited. How songs were surveyed and selected was a secret highly guarded by the agency that ran the show, which insisted that its system was beyond reproach and, as Baruch stated smartly each week, was the result of a tally of sheet-music sales, listener requests, and jukebox selections "coast to coast." In fact, it was fairly random, an allegedly "scientific" sampling put together by hundreds of "song scouts" across the country who talked to DJs, bandleaders, and record and sheet-music sales clerks and then reported the week's best-selling tunes. The show, in turn, boosted record and jukebox sales, so the show's hits became self-perpetuating.

The program had a rigorously spare approach—no patter, no sketches, nothing except the week's hits and a little continuity (written for a time by Alan Jay Lerner). The 1950s video version was a more elaborately produced affair, with each number framed by an inventive, often gimmicky, dramatic or comic device. *Your Hit Parade* played better on TV than radio, one of the few radio shows that can make that claim. It found catchy ways to display the songs, and because the show's roster of famous singers was replaced with a permanent cast of four, the show had more personality than it had on radio.

Most of the arrangements were straightforward, played by the Lucky Strike Orchestra and backed by a dreamy Hit Paraders chorus ("So long, for a while/That's all the songs for a while/So long to *Your Hit Parade*/And the tunes that you picked to be played/So long-g-g-g-g . . ."), led by a revolving door of conductors over the years: Lennie Hayton (the show's first leader), Al Goodman, Peter Van Steeden, Harry Sosnik, Ray Sinatra, Abe Lyman, Harry Salter, Leo Reisman, Axel Stordahl, and, in 1949, Mark Warnow, who gave the show more of a shape during his eight-year reign; Lyn Murray led the chorus and acted as musical director.

When Sinatra joined the show, tickets were scalped outside the studio to teenage girls, whose screams so annoyed listeners—and Lucky Strike baron George Washington Hill—that all tickets required the bearer to be at least twenty-one years of age. (Hill took a hands-on approach to any musical show sponsored by his company. For programs that featured the Lucky Strike Dance Orchestra, all selections had to be run past him—he approved not simply the "extras" but all the tempos. Supposedly, secretaries at his American Tobacco Co. offices were enlisted to dance with each other to see how danceable the songs were in practice.)

Sinatra left the show in 1945, by which time he had conquered radio, as he had records, by seducing listeners even more hypnotically than Crosby, his boyhood idol. As the critic Henry Pleasants writes: "He sang more [than Crosby]. He sustained more. He achieved a wider dynamic range. But he and Bing had much in common—the intimate way with song and listener and the mastery and exploitation of the microphone." Sinatra acted songs far more than Crosby, finding their sorrowful dramatic depths. Crosby was more the Irish comedian; Sinatra, more the Italian tragedian. He tempered Jolson's go-for-broke style and joined it to Crosby's intimate approach. Like Vallee, Sinatra considered the mike an instrument that, says Pleasants, he played like a sax or a trombone that became "an electronic extension of his own vocal instrument," learning to hear his voice as the "mike's ear" does, sensitive to every emotional inflection; he established a connection between singer and listener.

After a break, Sinatra returned to the show in 1946 and was costarred with a perky new blonde band singer, Doris Day. Sinatra also brought in his record conductor, Axel Stordahl, to lead the show's orchestra and he began to take control over his own arrangements. He finally left the show when forced to sing dreadful novelty tunes like "Mama Will Bark" with a howling dog (sound man Donald Bain) doing backup.

Bea Wain, *Your Hit Parade*'s hot canary from 1939 to 1944, with a year off in 1943, was, coincidentally, married to its announcer, the dapper, French-born André Baruch. She recalls, "Before me, everything was in one tempo," due to sponsor Hill's dictum, "but we always slowed down the ballads to sing them as they were meant to be sung." The show was put together by committee, she explains, so the singers had no input—they simply came in, were assigned songs, and sang them with a forty-five-piece orchestra in what is now the Ed Sullivan Theater. "Not even we on the show ever knew what numbers one, two, and three would be," continues Wain, who maintains, "They were legit surveys. We weren't told until the dress rehearsal that day."

She doesn't recall any jealousies or displays of temperament among the singers, including Sinatra, of whom she says, "I never felt any sense of competition. Sinatra did his own thing, and of course he was wonderful, but he had an entourage. I was too busy thinking what I had to do to worry about anything else. You minded your own business because you had to produce. There was no time for coyness." The other male singers were, she noticed, envious of Sinatra's worshipful cult of young girls. By the time *Your Hit Parade* moved to TV, Wain had left it. She can't recall any unhappiness when none of the radio cast was chosen for the TV version. "In this business, you don't get unhappy," she says firmly, sounding the "be happy-go-lucky" attitude of a bygone show business epoch. Eventually the rise of big-city DJs, who functioned as local hit-makers, greased by payola, made *Your Hit Parade* irrelevant, and in 1959 the show sang its swan song.

YOUR HIT PARADE WAS ONLY ONE of countless music shows that filled the airwaves with an army of long-forgotten voices and journeyman house bands that were dutifully acknowledged each week in the hastily read credits but who rarely achieved public recognition—conductors and groups destined to labor just beyond the audio spotlight yet whose names still have a power to evoke the era: bandleaders Billy Mills, Wilbur Hatch, John Scott Trotter, Archie Bleyer, Bernie Wayne, Al Goodman, Lud Gluskin, Frank DeVol, Billy May, Carmen Dragon, and Ray Noble. (Noble was one of radio's legion of bandleader stooges to cross over from podium to straight man, in his case as Edgar Bergen's only live sidekick; Noble, a gifted composer—"The Very Thought of You," "The Touch of Your Lips"—was a proper Englishman who played Ronald Colman to Charlie McCarthy's Irish-American brat.)

From radio's horn also tumbled a cornucopia of trios, quartets, quintets, and choruses—the Jubillaires, the Jordonaires, the Modernaires, the King's Men, the Merry Macs, the De Marco Sisters, the Mariners, the Jeff Alexander Orchestra and Chorus, the Ray Charles Singers—all as interchangeably melodious as they were anonymous; a few, like the Pied Pipers (with Jo Stafford), left their imprint. Ray Charles's itinerant chorus of eight would travel from show to show, with occasional stops to sing, live, the Campbell's Soup jingle ("*Hm-mmm good*"). Musicians and stars dropped into studios at neighboring shows to watch rehearsals, adding to the general camaraderie.

Margaret Whiting sang on radio for a decade as both a regular guest on the Eddie Cantor, Red Skelton, and Bob Hope shows and as cohost of two fifteen-minute shows, *The Oxydol Show* (with Jack Smith, the Andrews Sisters, and Frank DeVol's orchestra) and *Club 15*, with Bob Crosby and his fourteen-piece band; Carroll Carroll, once again, was in charge of banter, on loan from Bob's brother.

Whiting almost made it onto *Your Hit Parade* at the age of fifteen but was fired after four weeks by George Washington Hill, who found her style a little too hip for his taste. "I didn't sing enough on the beat. In my early years, I was taking liberties when I sang," says Whiting, an early Johnny Mercer protégée. "Bea Wain and the others on *Hit Parade* were square singers who sang exactly on the beat. Like Vaughn Monroe. I sang on the offbeat or the backbeat." She was devastated, since *Your Hit Parade* was *the* show to be on. Radio's musical shows were casual affairs, she explains. The singers would come in after lunch, read the script in a room, meet at three o'clock to run through their numbers with the band, and come back to do the show. "There wasn't time to take it home and learn it," chorister Ray Charles recalled. "It was a very fast operation all the time."

Whiting goes on: "It seemed simple, but there was an art to it. The bands were the best musicians you could get, and the scripts sounded natural, like we were having fun. It was a joyous, easy, wonderful time. They were all relaxed performers. I can't recall any temperament or flare-ups at all, except when a comedian didn't want some line cut."

Your Hit Parade's ritzy uptown rival was *The Chesterfield Supper Club*, starring pop singers Perry Como, Jo Stafford, and Frankie Laine. Its most memorable feature was a cigarette girl—that charming relic—who chirped, "Good evening! Cigars? Cigarettes?" at the top of every show as the band played "Smoke Dreams," the Chesterfield theme, backed by a group called The Satisfiers, "They satisfy" being Chesterfield's slogan.

Jo Stafford was a ubiquitous singer on radio in the 1940s and 1950s, a rotating host of *The Chesterfield Supper Club*, a regular on *The Railroad Hour* with Gordon MacRae, and finally, a star on her own show for a season before becoming a recording luminary. Stafford followed two older sisters into radio and the girls became a trio on a local station, KHJ, before she went solo with Tommy Dorsey in 1939 and became a star with the Pied Pipers. Her intimate, longing style seemed especially suited for radio. "I can't think that radio, as such, shaped my style," she says, "but radio gave you a combination of freedom and discipline that a recording session gives you. You have nothing else on your mind. You could concentrate completely on what you were doing. You didn't have to worry about reading lines or lighting. We rehearsed the show the same day, in the morning. In those days, you had musicians who could play anything and you just plunked the music down and they'd play it fine."

Stafford says most of the songs she sang were supplied by music houses, which viewed music shows as a blatant promotional tool. "I wouldn't introduce a song just to introduce it. That's only in the movies. It usually started with the publishers, who were plugging a new song." Tony Martin recalled for Leonard Maltin how "the song pluggers went after all of us at the same time," working their way down the pecking order from Crosby to Columbo to Lanny Ross to him. Payola was invented long before the rock 'n' roll era.

It is hard to hear Stafford's sentimental voice, even now, and not think of World War II and radio; she was America's Vera Lynn, forever linked to yearning wartime ballads. "It must be so, because so many people have talked about that. For many guys, I was a conduit—from them to me to Joanne or whoever their girl was at home. Something about my sound made them glad to be sad." In England, she says, hospital radio stations always played her recording of "Yesterdays." "That nostalgic sadness was the last thing they wanted to hear before they went to sleep at night."

The war was a boon to radio performers—especially girl singers like Stafford, Dinah Shore, Kay Armen, Georgia Gibbs, Connee Boswell, Joan Edwards, and Jane Froman—who began touring camps and canteens, meeting their male fans face-to-face en masse for the first time, and recording transcriptions for overseas broadcasts (the famous "V discs"). CBS's Frank Stanton boasted, "Radio fare has not been rationed. Radio is the one product that can be produced for the armed forces without depriving the civilian." On wartime music shows like *Mail Call* and *Command Performance,* however, no song requests were allowed, for fear they might be an enemy code. Likewise, the wartime rule against GIs on quiz shows bidding their mom "Hi!" remains intact over half a century later on talk shows, where guests still often ask, anxiously, "Is it all right if I say hello to my wife?"

Virtually every singer who had a hit song or two won his or her fifteen minutes of fame, literally, usually in the form of a quarter-hour show—singers like Curt Massey, Johnny Mercer, Dolly Dawn, Harry Babbitt, Tex Beneke, "Whispering" Jack Smith, Dick Haymes, Eddie Fisher, and Bob Crosby, who finally made his mark in radio headlining the smart little *Club 15* show. His aim was to showcase rising girl singers and he came up with a few: Kay Starr, Peggy Lee, and Gisele MacKenzie.

BAND REMOTES HEIGHTENED RADIO'S long-distance appeal, as a far-off voice cooed, "And now from the Tulip Room atop the Sheraton Hotel in Topeka, Kansas, it's Jack Culpepper and His Topeka Top-Hatters." Suddenly you were out there in Kansas, fox-trotting.

The big band era is said to have begun in 1935 with Benny Goodman's broadcasts, but in fact it got under way three years earlier, when CBS began carrying regular remotes from the Glen Island Casino where Glen Gray and the Casa Loma Orchestra played. Other shows, like *Saturday Night Swing Club,* gave new bands, like Bunny Berigan's, an airing. Big-band shows were cheap and easy—just tune up an orchestra, turn on the radio, and drop in. All you needed for a dance was a floor, a punch bowl, and a radio. Since every major hotel had an orchestra (Carmen Cavallaro at the Hotel New Yorker, Georgie Hall from the Grill Room of the Taft Hotel, and on and on across America), broadcasting dance music became a cheap and efficient way to fill time on the air, promote a hotel, and, to be sure, further the name of a band, its singers, and new songs. A 1935 show like *Let's Dance,* featuring Benny Goodman and Xavier Cugat in a three-hour swing-fest, made Goodman's name nationally famous virtually overnight, along with something called swing.

The big-band shows created instant hits, not to mention "singing sensations" (Bonnie Baker, Lee Wiley, Martha Tilton, Ramona, Helen Ward, Helen O'Connell, et al.), dance crazes, catchphrases, and sign-offs like conductor Ben Bernie's "Yowsa, yowsa, yowsa" and his closing "Good night, lads and lassies, cheerio, a bit of a pip-pip and pleasant dre-e-e-eeams." In no time, everybody was jumping on the big-band wagon—guys like Paul Tremaine, whose orchestra serenaded listeners from somewhere in radio cyberspace called "Lonely Acres," a serene paradise located in Young's Chinese Restaurant.

Each band's theme became a built-in hit—Harry James's "Ciribiri-bin," Bunny Berigan's "I Can't Get Started," Eddy Duchin's "My Twilight Dream," Louis Armstrong's "When It's Sleepy Time Down South," Jimmy Dorsey's "Amapola," Ted Weems's "Heartaches," Skinnay Ennis's "Got a Date with an Angel," Frankie Carle's "Sunrise Serenade"—and led to national bookings, record contracts, and movies. Major careers sprouted from this musical seedbed and quickly spread the word about such first-rate black jazz groups as the Chick Webb band, which radio put on the mainly white map. The record producer John Hammond discovered Count Basie one night while listening to the radio en route to Chicago, tuned to a tiny station at the top of the dial, and finally traced Basie to Kansas City.

Every conductor yearned to be the next Vincent Lopez, who started the craze with his orchestra at the Pennsylvania Grill—or if not Lopez, then surely Guy Lombardo, who broadcast from the Roosevelt Grill for twenty-five years before finally moving to the Waldorf-Astoria, where he began presiding over New Year's Eve as if he had invented it.

Lombardo came to prominence in 1929 with music so stolid and on the beat that it became, perhaps unfairly, the working definition of square—or, in the slang of the day, "strictly from hunger." Lombardo and his oddly titled Royal Canadians was the bubbly Lawrence Welk of radio—much mocked but unquenchable. Through radio, he became the world's richest bandleader and outlasted many other bigger and hotter radio bands, indeed the big band era itself. Lombardo refused to change his syrupy style or be influenced by radio and record people who tried to update him with songs he felt were wrong for his distinctive style—the "sweetest music this side of heaven."

As much entrepreneur as entertainer, Lombardo soon realized that the sweeter the music, the sweeter the pot and the bigger the home audience—giving rise to sugary aggregations led by Ted Weems, Jan Garber, Hal Kemp, Shep Fields, Ben Bernie, and Ozzie Nelson, all purveyors of the "businessman's bounce" anyone could dance to, unlike hipper swing bands led by the likes of clarinetists Artie Shaw, Woody Herman, and Benny Goodman. Lombardo, defending his swaying style, said without apology, "That's what people wanted, so that's what we gave them. Every time we changed styles our ratings went down."

Aside from the big-name bands, each network maintained—and moved around at will—a house orchestra and/or symphony orchestra, a few dance bands, and maybe a string ensemble, not to mention organists and a couple of full-time musical directors and arrangers. To keep them all busy, every major variety show, drama, and sitcom had its own assigned orchestra that played shows on and off, added musical bridges between scenes, and gave programs their live exciting sound. CBS kept a staff of studio conductors on call, people like Lyn Murray, Ray Bloch, Johnny Green, Abe Lyman, Peter Van Steeden, and André Kostelanetz; ABC's musical director was Paul Whiteman. Musicians at NBC hung out between shows at Hurley's Saloon, awaiting word from a musical contractor as to when and where their services were needed next.

While music filled radio's air, the lyrics to songs gave network censors a whole new cesspool of innuendo to splash in. Most songs were innocuous enough, but the more sophisticated lyricists—Cole Porter, Lorenz Hart, Noël Coward, Ira Gershwin—kept network vice-presidents up nights parsing double entendres.

In his monumental compendium *The American Language*, H. L. Mencken noted: "The radio is almost as prudish as Hollywood. Late in 1934 its [executives] actually forbade the verb 'to do' in songs, feeling that it was a bit too suggestive." In this case, of course, they were probably right: Porter wasn't just suggesting fornication, he was all but describing it, using "love" as a euphemism for sex in songs like "Let's Do It." Sheet-music publishers began printing two sets of lyrics, one for radio and one for cabarets, records, and parlors. After that, almost any song with the verb *do* in the title—"Do It Again," "You Do Something to Me," "Do, Do, Do"—was outlawed. The first song censored on radio was "Little Red Riding Hood," for the salacious line, "How could Red Riding Hood have been so very good and still keep the wolf from the door?"

Even the tender "These Foolish Things" had its lyrics altered from "gardenia perfume lingering on a pillow" to the awkward, decidedly unsensual "a seaplane rising from an ocean billow," and "silk stockings thrown aside" were exchanged for "a glove you threw aside." A comic novelty song called "Keep Your Undershirt On" was also nixed, and "Body and Soul" was banned from Boston and NBC, but some stations played it after a line was changed from "My life, a hell you're making" to "My life, a wreck you're making." When Bea Lillie sang "Miss Otis Regrets," she had to leave out the line "Down lover's lane she strayed." The word *bed* was taboo, forcing the writer of "Let's Turn Out the Lights and Go to Bed" to sanitize it to "Let's Turn Out the Lights and Go to Sleep."

In the 1930s, each record had to be identified as a recording (that is, an "electrical transcription," or ET), which carried a stigma for networks that prided themselves on being live; delayed rebroadcasts were rare. All that changed in 1940, when the FCC relaxed rules on announced transcriptions, which caused ASCAP to boycott stations; the only music that listeners heard that year was in the public domain. The war relaxed the rules further when so-called V-discs carried shows to armed forces overseas, but there remained such a taboo against "canned" radio shows that some artists stopped recording and others recorded under *noms de wax:* Benny Goodman became "Bill Dodge," Tommy Dorsey was "Harvey Tweed," Fats Waller turned into "Flip Wallace," and the opera singer Jan Peerce sang as "Randolph Joyce."

All of which paved the way for disc jockeys, who became the scourge of postwar radio. Small stations began clandestinely interspersing live music with records (despite the label warning "Not licensed for radio broadcast") or playing old records after it was ruled in 1940 that if a broadcaster bought a record, he was free to play it without paying royalties. Stations even tried to palm off records as live orchestras, and one Paterson, New Jersey, DJ had a fictitious chat with Paul Whiteman before playing a Whiteman disc. Out of all this came, in 1942, the musicians' union strike and the dispute with ASCAP that drove all live music off the air—replaced by Stephen Foster tunes and a capella singers humming "ooo-ahh" accompaniments.

Martin Block on New York's WOR led the way in the late 1940s and 1950s as the informed host of *The Make-Believe Ballroom,* which had begun in 1941 as a musical interlude between reports from the Lindbergh trial. Block filled the "live music" void with smart, vivid patter as he spun platters by a variety of bands and vocalists; a moonlight counterpart on WNEW, *The Milkman's Matinee*, was an all-night juke-box manned by Stan Shaw. Around the country, inexpensive make-believe ballrooms—basically do-it-yourself remotes—sprang up, with hosts like Peter Potter and Al Jarvis in Los Angeles, Jack Sterling and John Gambling in New York, the young Steve Allen in Phoenix, a female phenomenon in Chicago named Halloween Martin, and Frank Cope in San Francisco, whose *Alarm Klok Klub* from 5 to 8 A.M. ran an astonishing thirty years without rewinding. They all became person-ality DJs with rabid local followings, since they were able to tap into their own audience's tastes. Even ex-"live" musicians defected and became network or syndicated DJs—Rudy Vallee, Tommy Dorsey, Duke Ellington, Benny Goodman, Jack Teagarden, and Paul Whiteman spun backstage stories better than most of their peers, who were un-comfortable behind a turntable. The key was not the song but being able to sell the song to the listener. In their final years, music shows cut back on bands, and even Crosby had to make do with the Buddy Cole Trio in his last regular show in 1954.

Gradually, the DJs began to intrude on the discs, until the songs sounded more like backup music for the host's banter. This eventually gave way to robot DJs, who were just plugged into the Top 40 charts, which in turn led to today's characterless DJs and syndicated formats—the worst of all possible musical worlds.

— 9 —
THE CHILDREN'S HOUR

 IF MANY A LISTENER'S ADULT ATTITUDES WERE firmly sealed by the age of ten, it's because by then we had been thoroughly brainwashed by radio's wartime and postwar propaganda that turned kids into crime-busting, anti-Communist, Nazi-bashing, junior G-men vigilantes. Most adventure heroes of the airwaves seemed to have rolled off the same assembly line—sworn to uphold liberty, administer justice, rout the common enemies of mankind (i.e., the common enemies of America), and remain, throughout, champions of goodness and honor.

Even then, however, in that pre–V chip era, grown-ups, shrinks, and parent groups grumbled that kids might be too heavily influenced by the violence inherent in these shows that pitted superheroes and their sidekicks (often kids) against supervillains: Some fifteen hundred murders took place each week on the air, according to one body count. Women were virtually banished from these battles for law and order. If they popped up, they were either helpless victims, helpful junior assistants, or dragon ladies, but even female heavies were rare. The major heroine crime fighter in radio was a ten-year-old girl, Little Orphan Annie. This was men's—and teenage boys'—work.

The networks issued somber rules of conduct for kids' shows: "Cowardice, malice, deceit, selfishness, and disrespect for the law must be avoided . . . the hero and heroine must be portrayed as intelligent and morally courageous. . . . Cruelty, greed, and selfishness must not be presented as worthy motivations . . . conceit, smugness or unwarranted sense of superiority over others less fortunate may not be presented as laudable . . ."

If few of these shows made the delicate move from radio to TV, even fewer survived the chancy transfer from funny papers to radio tube—comic books for the ear like *The Adventures of Superman, Little Orphan Annie, Red Ryder, Tarzan, Buster Brown, Mandrake,* and

Overleaf, clockwise from top left: Charles Flynn (*Jack Armstrong*), Bud Collyer (*Superman*), Nila Mack (*second from left*) and the cast of *Let's Pretend*

Terry and the Pirates. A truckload of presumably invincible comic-strip icons vanished quickly, in a season or so. This distinguished list of on-air casualties included *Li'l Abner, Harold Teen, Bringing Up Father, Joe Palooka, Dick Tracy, Popeye, Gasoline Alley, Skippy,* and *Smilin' Jack.* They flopped for different reasons, but their common flaw was that few could sustain the flavor and style of the comic strip that had given them birth. Translating visual humor into audible comedy, or comic-strip adventure into thrills for the ears instead of the eyes, was as fragile a process as the reverse—turning radio shows into movies.

Blondie, while a big-screen success with twenty-seven sequels, seemed a pale copy of its colorful cartoon self on radio, where it sounded forced and manic. As on film, Penny Singleton was Blondie and Arthur Lake played the inept Dagwood Bumstead, a prototype for clumsy, clueless sitcom husbands-to-be who mysteriously wind up with capable, adorable wives. Somehow, you needed to *see* Dagwood's twin cowlicks, his wacky schemes, mountainous sandwiches, sofa naps, his frazzled boss Mr. Dithers, Blondie's sweet simple patience, the hapless postman, Daisy the dog, the kids, and their neighbors Herb and Tootsie Woodley. On radio, the comic strip just sounded shrill and surprisingly charmless.

The Adventures of Superman, however, became an instant radio classic superior to its many imitators, would-be Supermen like Spider-man, Plastic Man, and Captain Marvel, many of whom also posed as mild-mannered guys who changed, quick as a wink, into superheroes. For certain young, mild-mannered listeners, the Clark Kent aspect of the fable was more interesting than the Superman business, except for the endlessly repeated tale of Superman's origins. (The radio show itself was born in 1938, soon after Jerry Siegel and Joe Schuster's creation landed with a bound in Action Comics.)

Although he never quite made it to radio in his own show, appearing only as a frequent guest hero on *Superman,* Batman was somehow different, because he was in reality "millionaire playboy Bruce Wayne," though few kids knew exactly what a playboy was. It was confusing, for *playboy* had a mildly disreputable sound, associated with real-life roués of the day like Porfirio Rubirosa and Ali Khan. Socially conscious playboys nevertheless abounded in radio: Lamont Cranston (*The Shadow*) was a well-heeled playboy with a social conscience, as was publisher Britt Reid, aka the Green Hornet. It was almost as if Donald Trump were to lead a secret life fighting crime in New York dressed in fruity blue tights and boots (no doubt where rumors started that Batman and Robin were more than just friends). A playboy hero seemed implausible. Why would a millionaire want to dress up in a tight-fitting suit and swing from buildings in order to right social ills? Perhaps it was a kind of hobby, like racing cars or polo.

The pro-Batman contingent preferred him over Superman because Batman had no "superhuman" powers, which struck some kids as nonsense except for the part about X-ray vision, which had its own appeal for horny preadolescent boys. It seemed never to occur to the Man of Steel to use his X-ray gifts to undress Lois Lane with his eyes—not that Superman would ever do such a thing, let alone Clark Kent. What made Batman superior to Superman was that he relied on his own derring-do and lived by his wits. He needed no superhuman powers, which robbed Superman of true dramatic tension: If Superman could do anything and had ten times the strength of mere mortals, where was the challenge? The only element that endangered the Man of Steel was that nifty kryptonite angle.

Superman's enemies were mainly lugs, but Batman faced whimsical villains like the Joker and the Penguin, far more entertaining than Superman's major nemesis, a tiresome mad scientist, Lex Luther; Superman's most lethal demon wasn't a person—it was a green rock. It was a vast disappointment when Clayton (later Bud) Collyer, the machismo voice of Superman, became the grinning MC of *Beat the Clock* and other goofy TV shows beneath the dignity of a superhero: The Man of Steel had feet of clay. As it happened, Collyer's identity as the voice of Superman was kept secret for six years, until a courageous *Time* reporter took his life in his hands and squealed on the Man of Steel.

Clearly, Superman and Clark Kent were mirror images of the same humorless hunk. An unwritten radio rule was that all superheroes were without a grain of wit, just big boring chiseled chunks of righteousness. What's more, they were asexual beings. There were no women in Batman's life, and that lingering, halfhearted relationship between wet noodle Clark Kent and Lois Lane, radio's most ruthless tease, seemed not just sexless but pointless. It never occurred to kids (boys, anyway) that there was anything romantic in the air—one reason all the sexed-up *Superman* movie and TV versions badly miss the point. It was also hard to figure how Lois could hunger for Superman but refuse to give Clark Kent the time of day when it was obvious that they were the same guy, except that Clark wore glasses. Superman was oblivious to Lois Lane, of course, because it was a firm given that radio superheroes never messed with women. It was clear to listeners that Lois just wasn't his type, even though she swooned and Superman would hold her under one arm, like a newspaper, as they flew through the air. Female listeners, and possibly male cross-dressers, may have felt a slight thrill when Clark Kent stepped into a telephone booth and disrobed as he declared: "Off with these clothes—this looks like a job for . . ." (*voice drops an octave or two*) ". . . Superman!"

As with *The Lone Ranger,* much of what we recall today about *Superman* was its inspired opening (*"Faster than a speeding bullet . . . more powerful than a locomotive . . . can leap tall buildings in a single bound. Look! Up in the sky! It's a bird! It's a plane! It's . . . Superman!"*), which any child of the period can still recite, although the original show had a slightly different, wordier, version: "Boys and girls—your attention, please," cried a staff announcer. "Presenting a new, exciting radio program featuring the thrilling adventures of an amazing and *in*-credible personality. Faster than an airplane! More powerful than a locomotive! Impervious to bullets! (*sound of roaring hurricane*) Up in the sky, look—it's a giant bird!" Sound of boy's voice: "It's a plane!" Announcer: "It's SU-perman!"

More intriguing than Superman's adventures were the atmospherics of the show—the city called Metropolis, i.e., New York, which conjured up the Gothic aura of an underworld captured in the Fritz Lang movie of that name. Later cardboard TV and film versions of Superman didn't approximate the radio show or even the cheesy feel of the Saturday morning serials, with their fiendishly grinning, bald-headed Tojo-like villains meant to strike terror in our hearts, the typical Yellow Peril heavies of World War II.

Reporter Clark Kent, furthermore, never seemed to write any stories, but would-be boy reporters overlooked that, satisfied by city-room scenes with gruff editor Perry White and Jimmy Olsen, the ageless pipsqueak copyboy. It was puzzling how a mighty New York newspaper could be staffed by two reporters, one editor, and a jittery copyboy, barely enough for a New Hampshire weekly.

AS FOR THE GREEN HORNET, he seemed a bit—well, foreign, perhaps because of his faithful servant, Kato, with his Asian accent, whose vocabulary was limited to "Yes, Mr. Britt," and "Right away, Mr. Britt." After Pearl Harbor, Kato underwent a miraculous nationality transplant, from Japanese to Filipino. On TV, a suddenly energized, karate-chopping Kato was played by a newcomer named Bruce Lee.

During the war, all evil was encapsulated in the Far East on exotic series like *Terry and the Pirates* (what pirates?) and *Chandu the Magician,* not to be confused with *Mandrake the Magician.* It all seemed a tad farfetched, especially *The Green Hornet,* whose most engaging moment was that change-of-garb scene, a clear *Superman* rip-off, when "daring young publisher Britt Reid," of the *Daily Sentinel,* would switch into his Green Hornet outfit. At the close of each show, a *Sentinel* newsboy would bawl, "Extree! Extree! Read all about it! Green Hornet still at large!" Why a hornet? And why green and not yellow?

During the costume change, an urgent voice-over (Mike Wallace was one of the show's announcers) explained, as if every kid didn't know the drill by heart: *"Stepping through a secret panel in the rear of the closet of his bedroom, Britt Reid and Kato went along a narrow passageway built within the walls of the apartment itself. This passage led to an adjoining building which fronted on a dark side street . . ."*

Shows like *Chandu, Terry and the Pirates,* and *Little Orphan Annie* also were full of secret panels, approximated at home by nailing orange-crate planks across an unused side door in the garage, which opened onto a weed-choked path alongside the neighbor's chain-link fence. Such a secret place was ideal for stealthy reenactments of radio shows and their visual counterparts, the Saturday morning serials. Any sort of cubbyhole, deserted pathway, or crawl space would do, allowing you to creep unnoticed, flattened against a wall, cap pistol in hand, stalking the dreaded villain.

OVALTINE WAS THE MAGIC elixir that fueled *Little Orphan Annie,* whose comic-strip appeal eluded kids to whom she seemed a glum, badly drawn heroine, a fairly dreary strip by Harold Grey full of wooden characters like Punjab; even Annie's faithful dog, Sandy, looked like a lawn sculpture. Only on Broadway, cutened up and sugar-coated, did Annie ever seem alive and endearing. Maybe the concept of a girl heroine was too hard for boys to swallow. What remains most memorable about the show was announcer Pierre André peddling gotta-have Little Orphan Annie mugs that now fetch exorbitant prices at collectible shows: "Hey, boys and girls, you'll want to get your Orphan Annie Shake-Up Mug for chocolaty shakes and malts! Yessir, real shaker-uppers, kids!"

Little Orphan Annie opened with a dorky song *("Who's that little chatterbox/The one with the pretty auburn locks?/Who can it be?/It must be Little Orphan Aaaa-nie . . ."),* and the tales that followed were much toned down from the reactionary screeds of cartoonist Grey, whose panels were full of antileft, vaguely anti-Semitic, rhetoric (one 1930s strip depicts hook-nosed spies with bushy beards in Hasidic attire—hats and long black overcoats).

The show's tomboy heroine—played by Shirley Bell, who also barked Sandy's "arf"s—was much closer to spunky Nancy Drew than Grey's streetwise scrambler. Her equally golly-gee pal Joe Corntassel was played for a time by Mel Tormé; it was hard to take seriously a show that included a character called Joe Corntassel. As in most kids' adventure serials, and in many adult adventure series, villains were reliably identifiable by foreign accents of some vague derivation—German, Italian, Asian, Russian. Most of them were spies, Nazis, or, best of all, Nazi spies.

ANOTHER CLASSIC HERO, "Jack Armstrong, the All-American Boy," was a peppy preppy given to humorless heroics at Hudson High, where Jack was an all-sport letterman and all-around square-jawed fellow in the can-do Frank Merriwell tradition. Each episode began with a rousing male chorus singing, *"Wave the flag for Hudson High, boys/Show them how we stand!"* etc., and then, with rising inflection and heavy reverb, an announcer would cry, *"Jack Armstrong! Jack Armstrong! Jack ARMstrong! The Al-l-l-l American-n-n boy!"*

Jack was supposedly named by writer Robert Hardy Andrews after the bulging biceps on the Arm & Hammer baking soda box. Andrews once said of Armstrong: "He was a decent fellow, had a sense of responsibility, and didn't preach like Horatio Alger. In short, if you were like him, you were a pretty good kid." Andrews, who had written countless soap operas, was asked to devise "a soap opera for kids."

The show debuted in 1933 in a five-day-a-week format, played at first by Jim Ameche (Don's announcer brother), but it was Charles Flynn who nailed down the role for good in 1939. As early-radio entrepreneur Carl Amari has put it, "The seventeen-year-old Flynn took the part and was still kicking sixty-yard field goals in 1950."

Actually, by then Jack was kicking un–all-American subversives, aided by his cousins Betty and Billy Fairfield (once played by Dick York) and Uncle Jim Fairfield, bringing down Commies, Fascists, mobsters, and random forces of corruption and evil afoot in the world. One of the things that made *Jack Armstrong* unique among boys' shows was that the kids on it who experienced unreal adventures sounded like actual kids. The guardian figure of Uncle Jim further grounded the show emotionally, creating a surrogate family.

When Charles Flynn took over as Jack Armstrong, he had been rejected for the lead in *Skippy,* a show based on the famous comic strip, but he had done a few soap operas and played Chester Gump on *The Gumps.* Flynn's parents were actors, and his mother wrote for the soaps, so he was born to his calling. Something in Flynn's earnest voice embodied what he calls "the epitome of all that was right" in the teenage hero, whose name became synonymous with noble, idealistic young Americanism. "I was a good sight-reader and I had a teenager's voice, very straight and dramatic," recalls Flynn, now a sturdy-sounding eighty, who believes that an integral part of the show's fame was its affiliation with the sponsor, at the time a new cereal called Wheaties, which rode to success on Jack Armstrong's broad shoulders. "Do I still eat Wheaties? You bet I do!" says Flynn, laughing. "It put my kids through school. By golly, I owe 'em something."

Young Jack matured when World War II began and his problems at Hudson High seemed passé. "He grew up overnight," Flynn says, then laughs. "Jack Armstrong single-handedly won the war." Young Armstrongs at home were encouraged to join the Write a Fighter Club and become penpals with soldiers and sailors. (The show followed in the intrepid footsteps of *Terry and the Pirates.* Between the clang of Chinese gongs and the clamorous babble of Asian voices, Terry Lee and his buddy Pat Ryan battled "the Japs" on behalf of Quaker Puffed Wheat and Rice "shot from guns," followed by an announcer who sketched in the scene: "Now, then, gang, here's the picture . . .")

After graduation, the show changed to *Jack Armstrong of the SBI*, a short-lived sequel that cast Jack as a G-man. Flynn, who still does voice-overs for navy training films, says the shows now sound "so dated." Maybe so, but whenever people discover his valiant past, they ask him to sing the Hudson High anthem—and like the true-blue guy he remains, Charles Flynn gamely responds.

EVEN THOUGH THE PREMISE of a flying detective sounded slightly absurd, *Captain Midnight* (like colleague *Hop Harrigan*) earned the devotion of radio-obsessed kids. It wasn't necessarily because of an unlikely hero named Midnight or the concept (crime fighting in the skies); it was because of all of the offers, primarily the generous array of handsome decoder jewelry.

The show was sponsored, like *Little Orphan Annie,* by Ovaltine, a "food supplement" that, the announcer claimed, helped cure nervousness, listlessness, crankiness, and "under par" feelings. It featured the humorless iron-jawed Captain ("I don't understand why two mugs would resort to such knavery"), head of the "Secret Squadron"; his sidekick Ichabod Mudd ("Icky"); and two young Jack Armstrong–like junior assistants, Chuck Ramsey and Joyce Ryan. Joyce could scarcely utter three lines without exclaiming, "Gee-min-ee!," and Icky's favorite expletive was "Loopin' loops!"

In a typical episode, Chuck's model airplane is stolen by the bad guys, who are in fact out to purloin "the crown ruby" worth $100,000. After the model plane and the jewel are recovered, announcer Pierre André bids all would-be Secret Squadron members farewell with a hearty, diminishing, "Happ-e-e-e-e lan-n-n-dings!"

THE BEST KNOWN—OR, AT LEAST, the most significant—outer-space show was *Dimension X* (intoned in diminishing reverberations, *"Dimension* X-X-X-X-x-x-x-x-x . . ."), considered by sci-fi experts the first science-fiction show for adults. It was the *Star Trek* of radio, praised for its basic dramatic strengths.

The series of "adventures in time and space, told in the future tense" lasted only one season, 1950–51, but it commissioned scripts now considered classics, adapted by Ernest Kinoy from such masters of the form as Ray Bradbury, Earl Hamner, Jr., Robert Heinlein, Isaac Asimov, Robert Bloch, and Kurt Vonnegut; sonorous Norman Rose narrated. Bradbury's *Martian Chronicles* was first heard here, along with his *Mars Is Heaven,* an early taped show.

Its more successful successor, *X Minus One,* landed on NBC in 1955 and lasted three years. Lovers of the genre can still recite that series' heart-pounding opening: "*Countdown for blast-off—X-minus five . . . four . . . three . . . two . . . X-minus one . . . FIRE! From the far horizons of the unknown come transcribed tales of new dimensions in time and space. These are stories of the future, adventures in which you'll live in a million could-be years on a thousand maybe worlds. The National Broadcasting Company, in cooperation with Galaxy Magazine, presents X-X-X-X-X . . . Minus-minus-minus-minus . . . one-one-one-one . . .*" The show's jets burned out in 1958, but a relaunch was attempted in 1973, when favorite old shows were rerun monthly; the mission was scrubbed a year later.

Buck Rogers in the 25th Century was the earliest space hero (he was first sighted on November 7, 1932, also adapted from the comics), in which a boy winds up in the fifth dimension and awakens five centuries hence on the planet Niagara. Buck's archenemy was Killer Kane (whose female accomplice was the evocatively named Ardala Valmar), the girl was Wilma Deering, and the friendly master (not at all mad) scientist was Dr. Huer, who devised such dazzling-sounding inventions as a "gyrocosmic relivator."

The telltale sound of Buck Rogers whooshing into outer space was achieved by happy accident. Irving Reis, regarded as a creative genius at CBS, had begun as an engineer, and when the show needed to come up with the sound of Buck's rocket roaring across the heavens, Reis remembered a troublesome air duct on the twenty-first floor that nobody could silence, and he placed a microphone in front of it. Suddenly, listeners were strapped aboard Rogers's spaceship zooming through eternity. To reproduce the echo effect for the opening cry of "Buck Rogers of the 25th Cen-tur-EEE . . . eee . . . eee," announcer (and later film star) Paul Douglas would shout into an open piano.

Buck's faithful Tonto was Black Barney, a doltish Martian and reformed space pirate, who was played by several actors, the last of whom, John Larkin, wound up starring in *The Edge of Night* on TV. Buck fought his final intergalactic battle with Killer Kane in 1947, after which Buck and Wilma floated off together to live happily ever after in some cozy corner of the cosmos.

Flashing across the airwaves three years after Buck Rogers, in 1935, came *Flash Gordon,* Buck's comic-strip rival, drawn by Alex Raymond. The show, produced by Himan Brown, is perhaps most notable now for the fact that the original Flash Gordon was Gale Gordon (no relation to Flash), who went on to a flashier career in sitcoms. Flash himself had a bigger career on screen in a Saturday-matinee serial starring Buster Crabbe, who also doubled as Buck Rogers.

Lovers of radio space-fantasies disdainfully acknowledge the existence of *Space Patrol, Tom Corbett, Space Cadet* (i.e., "Spa-a-a-ace Cadet"), *Buck Rogers in the 25th Century,* and *Flash Gordon,* all of which John Stanley, the author of books on horror and science-fiction films, labels "kiddie sci-fi." Tom Corbett was basically Jack Armstrong in a space helmet, circling the galaxies in search of extraterrestrial evildoers. Its half-life continues on in the term *space cadet,* to denote twentieth-century dingalings (whence also *spacey*). Tom was followed into the radio beyond a few years later by the more mature Buzz Corey, commander-in-chief of the "Space Patrol," a sort of interplanetary Mod Squad, aided by his ace junior sidekick, Happy (whose main contribution was his favorite expletive, "Smokin' rockets!").

"When you talk about radio sci-fi, you're talking about a very limited number of shows," according to John Stanley. "Most of them were just mysteries with some sort of fantasy tacked on." Radio really wasn't as good a medium for science fiction as movie serials, comic books, and TV. Futuristic high-tech wizardry has to be seen to be thrilled to. Inventive as they were, sound-effects men were unable to make you "see" the flashy paraphernalia—burbling laboratories, blinking control panels, etc.—that created the 1940's sci-fi appeal. It sure wasn't the stories.

THE G-RATED KIDS' SHOWS, as opposed to what might have been considered the more action-packed PG programs, were led by the venerated *Let's Pretend,* the *Masterpiece Theater* of children's shows. The

Saturday morning staple was produced and hosted by its very own fairy godmother, Nila Mack ("She was a mother hen to all the kids, but I was terrified of her," recalls one-time child actor Arnold Stang; "I couldn't speak around her"). Jimmy Lydon, who played the movie Henry Aldrich, recounted auditioning for Nila Mack. "She was a very nice lady but a big imposing lady." Like all newcomers, he had to read "the dog story" for her—about a little boy whose dog is run over. "On the last page I had to cry and scream, which I'd never done before—I was a total amateur—but I screamed my head off and got the job. And that was radio—you did whatever you had to do to get the job."

Let's Pretend was sponsored by Cream of Wheat, whose warm, buttery jingle created lifelong Cream of Wheat eaters (*"Cream of Wheat is so good to eat/That we have it every day/We sing this song, it will make us strong/And it makes us shout hooray!"*). The ditty echoed the theme song that opened each show: *"Hello, hello/Come on, let's go/It's time for* Let's Pretend./*The gang's all here and standing near/Is Uncle Bill, your friend/The story is so exciting, from the start right to the end/So everyone, come join the fun/Come on and let's pretend!"* At which point, Uncle Bill Adams would bellow, "Hello, Pretenders!" and the excited audience of moppets would shout back, "Hello, Uncle Bill!"

For fifteen years, *Let's Pretend* rolled out weekly enactments of classic children's stories performed by a stock company of polished junior actors. The tales ventured well beyond the classics. Mack & Co. staged hundreds of tales that standard storybooks never got around to, enhanced with rich production values, a live orchestra, and original songs: "Princess Moonbeam," "Jorinda and Joringel," "The Yellow Dwarf," "The Six Swans," "The Donkey, the Table, and the Stick," plus the then-obscure "Little Mermaid."

THE BUSTER BROWN GANG, later rechristened *The Smilin' Ed McConnell Show* for its big, jovial gravel-voiced star ("Hi, kids, better come a-runnin'!"), was a sugarcoated commercial for Buster Brown Shoes. It was a variety-show version of a weekly *Buster Brown* drama that ran in the early 1930s, whose shoe-company theme song went, *"I got shoes, you got shoes/Everybody's got to have shoes/But there's only one kind of shoes for me—/Good ol' Buster Brown shoes!"*

Conrad Binyon, who appeared frequently on the show, remembered Smilin' Ed as "a genial father figure who sat and played the piano during the entire show while emoting the voices for the imaginary characters"—Froggy, the invisible infuriating gremlin; Squeaky the mouse; and Midnight the cat—all of whom cohabited peaceably. Said Binyon, "Ed in effect would talk to himself, his different-voiced characters bantering among themselves."

For the show's weekly tour de force—following an adventure with Ted and Tad—Froggy, Squeaky, and Midnight would join forces in the hope of so confusing McConnell and other windbag regulars on the show (prissy poet Algernon Archibald Percival Sharpfellow, cowboy Alkali Pete, jock Mr. Jim Nasium) that they would stammer and scramble their words in a madcap fashion while kids in the studio howled with glee. "I had strong muscles!" Jim Nasium would cry, to which Froggy would croak, ". . . between your ears!" When the fiendish Froggy would "plunk his magic twanger," he would appear and croak, "Now I'll sing my song, I will, I will." And so he did, he did—in the green flesh if you happened to be watching the program in person.

The Buster Brown Gang and *Let's Pretend* were the prototypes for many other kids' shows, some of them fairly treacly affairs, such as *Big Jon and Sparkie,* a daily show, and its more elaborate Saturday-morning companion, *No School Today,* a ninety-minute extravaganza that arrived each week to the merry theme of "The Teddy Bears' Picnic." The shows were hosted by Jon Arthur, whose "magic spyglass" peered into bedrooms all over America (after which Big Jon would caution listeners to make their beds, brush their teeth, and clean up their rooms). Sparkie was an elf who, Pinocchio-like, wanted to be a real boy. The weekend show featured riddles, fairy tale adaptations, and a "movietime serial."

Children's radio's most famous myth involved the beloved New York kiddie show *Uncle Don,* whose host, through the 1930s and 1940s, spun tales and nonsense songs of his own devising, such as his theme: *"Hibbidy gits, has bah/Rainbow, ree, Sibonia/Skividee, hi-lo-dee,/Horney-ka-dote, with an alikazon/Sing this song with your Uncle Don!"* Don Carney allegedly cracked into an open mike at WOR, "That oughta hold the little bastards for a while!" Never happened, claim radio scholars, who report that it was simply a great story spread via a Kermit Schaefer *Bloopers* album (others say it happened but didn't go over the air). Some sources insist the line *was* once uttered, in 1930, but on station WIP in Philadelphia by one "Uncle Wip," who was promptly dismissed.

For kids, listening to the children's radio shows and serials was like retreating to a secret clubhouse or shinnying up into a tree house in the clouds. Late-afternoon and Saturday morning radio was a haven where live adults were not welcome, where kids were no longer helpless peons but heroes, or junior heroes, and where grown-ups—villains aside, of course—were good guys who did not treat you like a child. A lot of homework, contrary to parents' outcries, could be done while tuned to *Superman, Jack Armstrong,* or *Captain Midnight.* The shows created a Disneyland of the mind, an endless E-ticket ride to your own frontier-land, tomorrowland, adventureland, and fantasyland. But you never had to be accompanied by an adult to enter radioland.

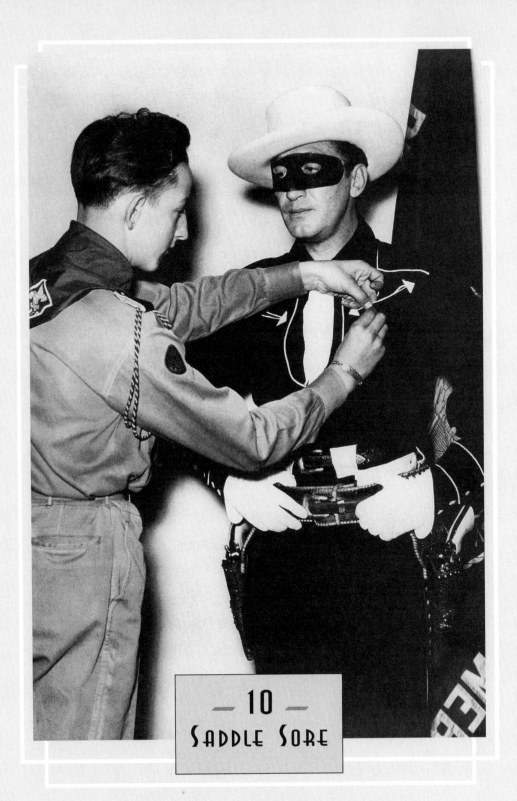

— 10 —
Saddle Sore

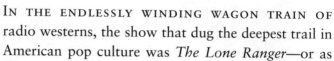

IN THE ENDLESSLY WINDING WAGON TRAIN OF radio westerns, the show that dug the deepest trail in American pop culture was *The Lone Ranger*—or as young schoolyard cowboys often called him, "The *Long* Ranger," suggesting one lean and lanky dude.

In the mind's eye, he cut as imposing a figure as the Virginian, any John Wayne hero, or such textbook legends as Buffalo Bill, Davy Crockett, Kit Carson, and Daniel Boone. What's more, the show's introduction implied that his saga was torn from "the pages of history." Even grown-ups who didn't much like westerns found the Lone Ranger mesmerizing—not necessarily for the shows themselves, but for the concept and the show's ornate framework. Here was a western hero who was 90 percent packaging.

The Lone Ranger may have been the first "adult western," a phrase that began to be heard in the 1950s to describe movies like *High Noon* and *Shane,* not to mention the 1958 radio program often cited as the first grown-up horse opera—*Gunsmoke. Gunsmoke* was decidedly better written and acted, but *The Lone Ranger* was mythic—the first such show to employ a loner hero and moody effects, a kind of *noir* western.

The Lone Ranger shows sound no less hackneyed today than others of the era, yet something elevated the program above more ordinary sagebrush series with Tom Mix, Hopalong Cassidy, Red Ryder, Roy Rogers (anointed "King of the Cowboys"), and his slick rival, Gene Autry. Radio's leading cowpoke crooner was specifically devised to knock Rogers off his throne, and ran a spread with the highly suspect name Melody Ranch. Gene and Roy were mildly entertaining Hollywood creations, with comic sidekicks, campfire ballads, plus, in Roy's case, the galling idea of a romantic interest named Dale Evans, who came out of nowhere to assume her place as Queen of the Cowgirls.

Overleaf: Brace Beemer (*The Lone Ranger*) receives an award from the Boy Scouts

Alongside such nonsense, *The Lone Ranger* seemed very much the real thing.

Other heroes wore masks (Zorro, Batman), and others bent the law for their own purposes (various Robin Hoods), but none in western lore had near the appeal of a "lone ranger." That was the show's basic grabber, along with the fact that—unlike Messrs. Zorro and Hood—the Lone Ranger was modest almost to a fault, so pathologically shy that he refused to stick around for even a simple thank-you. Rather, he galloped off into the horizon toward his next adventure, leaving behind only a silver bullet to identify himself. Incredibly cool.

You always wondered how he kept himself supplied with silver bullets and whether he used them in actual gunplay or just as a calling card. With his own silver mine, he was independently wealthy—perhaps another of those millionaire playboys who chose to do good, like Bruce Wayne/Batman and Britt Reid/the Green Hornet. The show was full of tantalizing totems to dazzle the imagination—the mask, the silver bullet, the hero's speedy white steed, Silver, and the Masked Rider of the Plains's rallying cry, "Hi-yo, Silver—awa-a-a-a-ay!" Pretty riveting stuff, and the show hadn't even begun yet. There was intense debate in sandlot re-creations whether it was "Hi-yo" or "Hi-ho." The former sounded more western than the Englishy "Heigh-ho!" (The official cry, by the way, is indeed "Hi-*yo!*") Legend has it that the name Silver was chosen because the show was first sponsored by Silvercup Bread.

To complete the daring trio, there was Tonto—an Indian, supposedly the sworn enemy of the cowboy—two outcasts riding together as compatriots toward a common good. The program's concept was a jumble of intriguing genre contradictions: a lawman in an outlaw mask, a humble hero, a bullet from Cartier's, and a sidekick who is a *friendly* redskin—the hero's "kemo sabe" ("faithful friend" in Potawatomi lingo); *The Lone Ranger* was the first politically correct western.

Tonto, it turns out, was played by an elderly British Shakespearean actor named John Todd, who often doubled in other roles to make up for his lack of lines as the monosyllabic Tonto; Todd had actually brushed elbows with Buffalo Bill while traveling in a road-show *Hamlet*. By the time announcer Fred Foy joined *The Lone Ranger*, John Todd was getting on in years and, because he had so few lines, tended to doze off during episodes. "We'd have to keep one eye on his chair," Foy recalls, "and once he nodded off during a show and Brace [Beemer, who played the lead] had to improvise a monologue."

One puzzling aspect of the series was why Tonto, such a wise, quick, and astute fellow in every other way, could never get his pronouns straight no matter how long he was exposed to the Lone Ranger's impeccable English. Tonto's major grammatical errors might be so simply corrected, you thought, if only he could learn to change *him* to *he* and *me* to *I*, but then he wouldn't have sounded "Indian" enough. It was explained that while Tonto may not have had perfect command of English, he spoke Spanish and several Indian dialects.

(If Mexicans on westerns were either evil or comical, "Injuns" were, if not wicked, subservient—until *Gunsmoke*, which treated its Indians more as peace-lovers than sworn enemies. The sole exception was *Straight Arrow*, whose hero was, in fact, not an Indian at all but Steve Adams, a white cattle rancher in redface. Adams, it seems, had been brought up by Comanches and "when danger threatened innocent people, and when evildoers plotted against justice," he would vanish into a cave at the Broken Bow Ranch and, Clark Kent–style, fling off his dusty ranching duds and emerge as . . . *Straight Arrow,* a bronzed brave atop his golden palomino Fury, crying "Kaneewah!")

Turning out a coherent script each week even for a western potboiler was trickier than it sounds, especially in the case of *The Lone Ranger,* whose hero, by virtue of the fact that he *was* alone, had nobody to talk to. This meant that the writer, Fran Striker, had to devise ingenious ways to push plots along by having the hero mumble asides to Tonto (as noted, not a great conversationalist) or to Silver, as if talking to himself—and, of course, us, thus: "Silver, Thunder Martin is in trouble! We need to make it into town by nightfall. This could be a showdown. Up, big fellow!" Or he might be forced to address nobody in particular to make a complicated plot point: "This looks serious. If I don't locate that lost deed and get to Clarabelle's in time, the sheriff will think Tonto lied to them. But first, I've *got* to untie myself by sawing this knot in two on the sharp handsaw hanging just over my head (*grunt, grunt*). There! I'm finally free at last!"

Then, lastly, there was that riveting back story of how he came to be. The "Lone Ranger" was literally just that; it was not simply a pretentious handle he'd come up with to dazzle people, like his more mundane Wild West colleagues.

As we were regularly reminded, the Lone Ranger was a former Texas Ranger whose buddies had all been wiped out by the dreaded Butch Cavendish gang—and he alone had survived with the aid of a caregiving Native American who nursed him back to health, at which time he devised his catchy moniker. "Me . . . Tonto," the Indian introduced himself to the wounded Texas lawman, John Reid. Nestled in the arms of Tonto, Reid gasped, "What happened to the other Rangers? They were all my friends. One was my brother." Tonto broke the bad news and unwittingly gave him immortality when he said, "Other Texas Rangers all dead. You only Ranger left. You *lone* Ranger now."

To which Reid replied: "From now on, Tonto, my identity shall be forever buried with those brave Texas Rangers who died at my side. I'll *be* the Lone Ranger." Thus was the concept meticulously worked out by the show's creator, lawyer-turned-radio-mogul George W. Trendle. To launch his first station in Detroit, WXYZ (a financially troubled CBS affiliate), Trendle devised a western that would appeal to adults as well as kids, with a wholesome, larger-than-life hero who had a code of honor he remembered from his boyhood. In truth, the Lone Ranger could be something of a windbag, a Dudley Do-Right who often mounted a soapbox to deliver ringing orations on the American Way. In a typical script, he rumbles, in that slightly patronizing jut-jawed tone of his, full of heroic pauses: "Yes, Dan . . . you have a great heritage. You live in a land of equal rights for all . . . governed by laws that are the best for the greatest number . . . to strengthen and preserve that heritage is the duty and privilege of *every* American." The Lone Ranger was a little to the right of *Mr. District Attorney,* a kind of Joe Friday of the plains. In Striker's original draft, the LR was a laughing macho Robin Hood, but Trendle nixed the humor in favor of a less dashing, far more formal hero. Trendle envisioned the Lone Ranger as a "guardian angel" and "the embodiment of granted prayer."

What ennobled him was that he seemed aloof and above the fray—a snob, almost, who, rather than hang around to take his bows after he'd brought the bad guys to justice, beat a hasty retreat. He was utterly humorless—no comic sidekicks for him—and had no time for obsequious thank-yous and small talk. Was it humility, boredom, timidity, or arrogance? He disliked having grateful townsfolk slobbering all over him, that was clear, but it seemed impolite for him to exit so quickly. Yet you never tired of the famous fade-out: "Who *was* that masked man, anyway?" "Why, don't you know? That was . . . the *Lone Ranger*!" As if there were lots of other cowboys on white horses sporting black masks who handed out silver bullet mementos and had Indian assistants.

Trendle had hired Fran Striker, author of an outdoors show with the lumbering Bob-and-Rayesque name of *Warner Lester, Manhunter,* to put flesh on this western hero who would embody all the classic virtues. "First of all," Trendle once said, defining his hero as a kind of grown-up Boy Scout, "our man is a clean fighter. He never attacks from behind. Then, he is tolerant, completely without racial prejudices—just look at the way he treats Tonto. He is kind to animals—why, he'd give his life for Silver. He respects womanhood and he's religious—but without indicating that he belongs to any special church. As for smoking, drinking, and using profanity, they're completely out. Of course, it goes without saying that he never makes love, and certainly he doesn't ever kiss a girl—not on radio or TV. The kids, you see, don't go for mushy stuff." He would also eschew slang, decreed Trendle. "And even more important, our hero is a bug on good grammar. When he says 'who' or 'whom' or 'shall' or 'will,' you can bet your boots that he uses those properly." Despite this goody-two-shoes job description, *The Lone Ranger* played to some 12 million listeners a week.

Trendle and Striker deserve some kind of posthumous literary recognition for their inspired creation. Striker, working fourteen hours a day six days a week, not only turned out 156 *Lone Ranger* scripts a year, that ran Monday, Wednesday, and Friday nights, but 365 daily comic strips, twelve juvenile novels (for the "Big Little Books" series), and edited and supervised thirty episodes of two *Lone Ranger* movie serials.

Behind the heart-pounding opening theme (from Rossini's *William Tell* Overture), perhaps the best known in radio, the opening lines were narrated with ever-rising galloping excitement by several announcers, the last of whom, Fred Foy, later turned up on TV in the 1970s as Dick Cavett's ABC talk-show announcer. Cavett would occasionally request that Foy repeat his Lone Ranger spiel and he would happily oblige.

Watching him speak those memorable words, forever emblazoned on the brain, was a rare thrill.

The pulsating preamble itself, which every schoolboy knew almost by heart, had the patriotic cadences of the Pledge of Allegiance or the Gettysburg Address. Return with us now to those thrilling days of yesteryear as we listen to it once again. It opens with the sound of gunshots and hoofbeats, and then: *"A fiery horse with the speed of light, a cloud of dust, and a hearty hi-yo, Silver! The Lone Ranger!"* (bridge music—Liszt's "Les Préludes"). *"With his faithful Indian companion, Tonto, the daring and resourceful masked rider of the plains led the fight for law and order in the early western United States. Nowhere in the pages of history can one find a greater champion of justice! Return with us now to those thrilling days of yesteryear. . . ."* Inspired writing, by any measure, which gave the western its historical luster and literary tone.

The show debuted on Trendle's small three-station hookup on January 30, 1933, and was expanded nationwide in 1937. It was such an instant success that the program led to the formation of the Mutual Broadcasting System, an outgrowth of the half-dozen stations that originally signed on to air the hit western. The series ran until May 27, 1955, whereupon it went into thirty years of reruns, spun off the TV series (which itself remains in reruns, starring Clayton Moore and a real Indian, Jay Silverheels), two movies with Moore and Silverheels, and one fairly dreadful mid-1980s remake.

Red Ryder was a sort of seedy *Lone Ranger* clone: Red wore red shirts and had an Indian as a faithful companion, a mini-Tonto named Little Beaver whose dialogue was limited largely to "You betchum, Red Ryder." Red's horse was called Thunder, as opposed to the Lone Ranger's "great white horse with the speed of light," and his cornball cry was, "Roll-l-l-l on-n-n-n, Thunder!" Nice try, Red.

When *The Lone Ranger* began, sound effects were fairly primitive, with sound men dropping to their knees to slap their thighs and chests to mimic the sound of hoofbeats (just as kids did), or using short-handled sink plungers in a gravel box. Separate studios were used to create the sound so it wouldn't drown out the dialogue and so that a proper balance could be found—early sound mixing. Four men were needed to produce sounds on *The Lone Ranger,* but actors often played several roles and even the sound men sometimes uttered a few lines.

In some ways, it was just another schlock western, but to those who refused to miss a single chapter, *The Lone Ranger* took on the aura of art. Not even the fairly faithful TV version had the hypnotic power of its radio predecessor. The original series was led during its glory years by Brace Beemer (itself a name to conjure with; Beemer had wisely dropped his first name, Marcus). He proved an ideal choice: A strapping six-foot two-inch man with a naturally rumbling voice, Beemer was a much-decorated war hero who as a teenager had served in France with the Rainbow Division and was wounded in action; at fifteen, he was the youngest soldier to serve overseas in World War I. He became an outdoorsman and horse breeder at whose ranch in Oxford, Michigan, Silver and Scout were stabled between personal appearances in rodeos and parades.

Beemer had been the studio manager at WXYZ when he was asked to narrate the show. After Earl Graser, the original Lone Ranger, died suddenly, Beemer was drafted and played the part for seventeen years, until it left the air. Beemer left the air with it and returned only a year before his death, at sixty-two, to do a few commercials. Foy, a close friend of Beemer's, says, "He fit the role perfectly. To me, he *was* the Lone Ranger, on and off the air. You wouldn't have been disappointed to meet him, as you often were when you encountered radio heroes in real life. He was tall, handsome, and rode well; he used to ride at Madison Square Garden. Brace wouldn't do anything to tarnish the Lone Ranger image. I guess the character sort of takes you over."

Only Fred Foy still lives on, recalling the show that became the defining event of his career. Since *The Lone Ranger* was told in large part via narrative, Foy, albeit unheralded, was as much a character on the show as Beemer. Foy, whose voice retains much of its old vigor, has concluded his career doing voice-over commercials for items that call for a certain excitement, such as a collection of fifty famous operas.

People who meet Foy invariably ask him to repeat his famous introduction, which he willingly does. "As soon as they find out [who I am], they say, 'Can you do it? Can you do it?' I don't mind. It's wonderful to be remembered."

If *Sergeant Preston of the Yukon*—officially and more grandly entitled *Challenge of the Yukon*—seemed vaguely reminiscent of *The Lone Ranger*, with its throbbing classical theme music (von Reznicek's *Donna Diana* Overture), it's no wonder. Sergeant Preston, with his trusty husky, Yukon King, was really the Lone Ranger on ice.

Preston, a Canadian cowboy, came out of the same Wild West shop in Detroit, WXYZ, as the Lone Ranger, and was created by the same team, George Trendle and Fran Striker, who decided to spread themselves farther north—and just a bit thin. The show harkened back to an earlier Mountie radio epic, sans dog, called *Renfrew of the Mounted*. The stern, steely voice of Preston belonged to Paul Sutton, and John Todd, aka Tonto, played the Inspector; Jay Michael announced.

Sergeant Preston aimed too closely at duplicating the somber manner of the Lone Ranger, and there was more than a passing similarity to the characters—crabbed sourdough prospectors and hard-bitten old ladies who said, "Tarnation!" The show was as boring as a slow sled ride across Alaska, made sillier by all of those astonishing rescues by King, with whom Preston had in-depth conversations that echoed the Lone Ranger's heart-to-heart chats with Silver.

RADIO'S OTHER MAJOR GROUNDBREAKING western, *Gunsmoke*, moseyed into town late in the game, in 1952, when radio was hanging on by a few soap operas, mysteries, and private-eye shows, many of them repeats. Although the pilot show had been written in 1949, by David Friedkin and Morton Fine, its innovations had less impact than they might have had ten years earlier, when westerns were aimed at adolescents, not adults. *Gunsmoke* was a classy western, with more mature plots, writing, and characterization than almost anything on radio, and CBS carried it for eighteen months. Even the sound effects strived for realism and the sound men were credited ("sound patterns by Tom Hanley and Ray Kemper"); a twenty-piece orchestra, led by Rex Khoury, featured original music. Its reach for realism included a reference in the intro to "the smell of gunsmoke."

Indeed, John Dunning, in his encyclopedia of radio, superbly evokes the program through its sound effects alone: "When Marshal Dillon went out on the plains, you didn't need a narrator to know what was happening. You heard the faraway prairie wind and the dry squeak of Matt's pants against saddle leather. . . . When Matt opened his jail-cell door, you heard every key drop on the ring. When he walked the streets of Dodge, his spurs rang with a dull clink-clink, missing occasionally, and the hollow boardwalk echoed back as the nails creaked. Buckboards passed, and you heard them behind the dialogue, along with muted shouts of kids playing in an alley, and from the next block the inevitable dog was barking."

The original vague idea can be traced to CBS's William Paley, who asked producer Harry Ackerman to "develop a Philip Marlowe of the early West." Recalled Ackerman: "We experimented in writing scripts with [Matt Dillon] as sheriff for a while and I think in one version we had him as a private eye. Then we finally settled on him being a marshal."

Each radio episode began with a terse lead-in recited by William Conrad, who, with a squint in his voice, originated the role of Marshal Matt Dillon (originally Mark Dillon) that he later lost on TV to strapping, cleft-chinned, telegenic James Arness. Casting a squat, baggy-eyed, multichinned, mustachioed actor as a western hero—*that* innovative TV's *Gunsmoke* wasn't. The radio version ran until 1961.

Gunsmoke scripts, complex and full of psychological insights, led to several imitators—*The Six-Shooter, Frontier Gentleman, Fort Laramie, Luke Slaughter of Tombstone*—and, in 1958, the successful *Have Gun, Will Travel,* which again broke the stereotype with stories about a frontier dude, a well-spoken gun for hire, Paladin, who handed out calling cards and enjoyed the finer things in life, including women, whom most radio western lawmen shied from like a horse approaching a rattler. The show was also an oddity in that it originated on TV before coming to radio.

Characters on *Gunsmoke* broke the ironclad bad guy/good guy molds of the genre by playing against type—a heavy with a good side, or a good woman with a bad past, such as the show's female lead, prostitute-turned-saloon owner Kitty Russell. There were crazies, sociopaths, and amoral murderers. In one episode, two bullies cut off the ear of a donkey with a timid owner, and in another show a woman at close range shoots the men who wrongly lynched her husband. Producer-director Norman Macdonnell refused to prettify the Old West and, speaking of the aura he tried to capture, said, "Life was straightforward, bone-simple, and honest."

The show had a highbrow audience; one of its biggest fans was the esteemed *New York Times* theater critic Brooks Atkinson, who praised its dramatic integrity. A writer with the show remembered how listeners "would sit around discussing the show's moral aspects." Most moral of all was Macdonnell's taciturn, slightly grumpy hero, Marshal Dillon, who lived by a code that was more finely shaded than that of most western heroes. Dillon was a proto-Bogart figure, a cynical man ("a sad, lonely man," Macdonnell called him) who had lived and who viewed the world as a more complicated place than did Roy, Gene, Hoppy, Red, Cisco, or the Lone Ranger.

Gunsmoke was swept aside in the early 1960s as networks began to cancel entire blocks of shows, not just specific programs, and the program ended unceremoniously, without the dignity of a decent burial in a farewell episode. One day it was simply over, leaving its ardent listeners in the lurch, typical of how long-running beloved radio shows often came to abrupt, inconclusive ends. Listeners were told only, "This concludes the current series of *Gunsmoke* on CBS Radio."

There was great bitterness among the stock company when CBS chose an all-new cast for the TV version, led by greenhorn Arness, and in 1957 Liggett & Myers dropped its radio sponsorship (some claim that the Marlboro Man was modeled after Arness); a live orchestra was replaced by canned music. *Gunsmoke* slid into TV without a hitch, riding in confidently on the wave of good publicity from its three years on radio. Conrad produced and directed the first twenty-six episodes, then left the show. Macdonnell took over and remained there for nine years, until 1964.

Comparing the radio and TV versions, Macdonnell once said, "In radio I think the show was more authentic. The original characters were more extreme. They've mellowed with age—maybe they mellowed too much. They didn't used to be quite so warm [in radio]. Kitty was more of a madam, Doc was more of an abortionist, and Matt smoked big black cigars, drank rye whiskey, and very often a man rode into town who could shoot faster and straighter than Matt Dillon."

Parley Baer, whose radio Chester was more hillbilly than the better-remembered Dennis Weaver TV version, recalled: "I never felt about any other series as keenly as I did about *Gunsmoke,* or loved it as much; the others were the same way. *Gunsmoke* gave the listener a respect that westerns up until then hadn't." The show even hired a woman writer, Marian Clark, to develop stories with a female slant.

As Conrad recounted it, "There was great character development. God, we'd go in with eleven-page scripts and take all the time in the world to do it, taking an incident and making it a story. It was basically a story of *that* man, and someone else he cared about very deeply. We all felt we had something, and we treated it very carefully."

The series was a transition program between the comic-book qualities of much radio adventure shows and the gritty realism of early 1950s plays, movies, and even TV—the era of Brando, James Dean, Sidney Lumet, Martin Ritt, John Frankenheimer, Arthur Miller, Rod Serling, and Paddy Chayefsky. Recalled John Meston, one of the main writers, along with Lester Crutchfield, who did the lighter scripts: "Radio had just about come into its golden age. The mistakes and all the hard knocks were pretty well behind it, and TV had not yet made serious inroads." Sums up a regular *Gunsmoke* hand: "It was just goddamn well done."

THE CISCO KID WAS THE FLIP SIDE of all this sagebrush sincerity, a western lite—or in Cisco's case, maybe a comic Denver omelette, although he had impressive literary credentials. Identified at the top of every show as "O. Henry's famous Robin Hood of the Old West," Cisco was originally more of a wicked rogue with whom those alien varmints, women, figured heavily.

In "The Caballero's Way," O. Henry cast him as an outlaw hero, a Latino Lone Ranger, a love-'em-and-leave-'em womanizer, but by the time he galloped off the page and into radio in 1942, to tacky organ accompaniment, he was just a charming rascal who romanced willing señoritas—all of whom swooned, "Oh-h-h-h, Ceesco!," the closest thing to an orgasm on radio. After each adventure, Cisco (originated by gringo Jackson Beck) and the paunchy Pancho (Louis Sorin) hot-hooved it out of town, laughing at one of Pancho's lame jokes. It was as if the Frito Bandito had joined up with Sancho Panza. Indeed, Pancho was played for many years by Mel Blanc, who doubled as the monosyllabic Mexican Sy on Jack Benny's show and as Pedro on *The Judy Canova Show,* where his catchphrases were "I *thee*-eenk" and "Pardon me for talkeen een your face, señorita."

Beck—who later supplied the voice of Bluto in the *Popeye* cartoons and, much later, became the basso voice-over for Little Caesar's Pizza—says of the part he played for two seasons: "It's a great character, and you can't really murder it, so you just go with it." He didn't speak Spanish ("I was helpless in Spain") and did the character somewhat tongue-in-cheek, one of several accents he picked up living in New York. (Although Cisco is now a stereotype, Beck says, "I was careful not to be offensive.") Apart from *Cisco* and many other shows he did, Beck also left his mark doing the *Mark Trail* opening: "*Battling the raging elements! Fighting the savage wilderness! Striking at the enemies of man and nature! One man's name resounds from snow-capped mountains down across the sun-baked plains . . . Mar-r-r-rk Trail-l-l-l!*"

WHAT REMAINS MOST MEMORABLE about the Tom Mix show, more portentously entitled *The Tom Mix Ralston Straightshooters,* wasn't the show but its fervent pitches for premiums (whistling rings, belt buckles, badges, decals, posters, neckerchiefs). The gewgaws were neatly dropped into the show—or, as on *Little Orphan Annie,* were the plots written around the premiums?—with its jaunty theme sung to the tune of "When It's Roundup Time in Texas": "*Hot Ralston for your breakfast/Starts the day off shining bright/Gives you lots of cowboy energy/With a flavor that's just right/It's delicious and nutritious/Made of golden western wheat/So take a tip from Tom/Go and tell your mom/Shredded Ralston can't be beat!*"

For some kids, Mix seemed *too* much of a straight shooter. A wooden character whose exploits were a curious, unsatisfying blend of old West and new, Tom played a sort of six-gun-toting private detective at the TM-Bar Ranch who worked alongside Sheriff Mike Shaw (one more grizzled Gabby Hayes–like old coot) to solve mysteries.

The two genres mixed uneasily. To lighten things up, there was a stereotypically excitable black cook named Wash, who began every line of dialogue directed at Mix with "Mist' Tom! Mist' Tom!" Mist' Tom's true sidekick, however, was Tony the Wonder Horse, a star in his own right from the rodeo circuit, who had major billing and possibly his own press agent. Radio writers labored in vain to give distinctive equine personalities to a herd of otherwise interchangeable super-nags—Trigger, Thunder, Silver, Scout, Amigo, Fury, and Tony.

Kid listeners were slightly baffled by the exact status of Tom Mix, an allegedly legendary cowboy, for it was hard to deduce whether the Tom Mix we were hearing was the actual famous figure or just an actor playing Mix (he was portrayed by various actors, among them Russell Thorson, who later came into his own as Jack on *I Love a Mystery*). Furthermore, just why the heck *was* Tom Mix so famous? It kept a few would-be loyal Mix listeners from becoming totally dedicated Straight-shooters. About the time we made Tom Mix's acquaintance on radio, unbeknownst to us he'd been dead eight years (killed in an auto wreck), but his name lived on in the "Big Little Books," a sportswear line, and Saturday matinees that reran his 1930s films.

Mix was much more interesting in real life than on his radio show—a soldier of fortune and latter-day Buffalo Bill who had been a Rough Rider at San Juan Hill with Teddy Roosevelt, was wounded in the Boxer Rebellion, fought on both sides during the Boer War, and was injured in World War I. Mix then went on to ride the rodeo circuit as its "World Championship Cowboy," which led to his Hollywood career and a touring Wild West show. Radio was just a sideline, and indeed, when the show began in 1933, Mix nixed an offer to play himself, content to remain a legend, where the money was better.

He was portrayed by various actors, including, at the end, Curley Bradley, who once recalled Mix's attempt to flog his flagging legend through the radio show. "When Mr. Mix was alive, and he wanted his name perpetuated, the best way he knew how was for children to remember him, because he was a children's idol," said Bradley. "He made out a plain old handwritten letter to Mr. Danforth, who owned the Ralston Purina company, saying he would never do another commercial for any other company except Ralston, and gave him exclusive radio rights to the Tom Mix title. Far as I know, he was never paid anything to do that. He was just that kind of a feller."

Indeed, such was the credo instilled into every cowboy feller—and listener—who rode the radio range, notwithstanding the fact that most real cowboys had been semiliterate amoral saddle-tramps. There was the National Lone Ranger Council of Honor "to encourage America's youth to adhere to the principles and clean living and good citizenship," not to mention Gene Autry's Cowboy Code: "A cowboy never betrays a trust; a cowboy is kind to small children, animals and old folks; a cowboy is clean about his person, and in thought, word and deed; a cowboy is a patriot," etc.

After Pearl Harbor, the *Tom Mix* show proclaimed that the program would project only patriotic and "clean thinking" themes into American homes, along with "wholesome entertainment" that would be an "inspiration for better living." Even radio premiums went to war: *Tom Mix Commando Comics* was the Straightshooters' official organ, and Kix offered a Lone Ranger Blackout Safety Belt. Routine cattle-rustlers and stagecoach bandits were replaced by such polecats as spies and saboteurs. In May 1945, Tom mounted the soapbox and vowed, "We've shown Hitler and his gang that we know how to lick bullies and racketeers, but we've still got a big job to do for our brothers, and our cousins, and our uncles, and our dads who are still fighting the Japs." It was easy to spot the bad guys on westerns in the 1940s because in lieu of black hats they sported Asian or German accents.

— 11 —
Valued Families

RADIO GAVE BIRTH TO THE SITUATION COMEDY and hatched several of television's most famous family programs—*Father Knows Best, The Life of Riley,* and *The Adventures of Ozzie and Harriet,* which together defined the genus *sitcom americanus.* Situation comedy was a totally new comic form. It ventured beyond crude gag-oriented sketches and involved listeners in middle-class lives not so unlike their own—simple homey incidents inflated into domestic farce. Fibber McGee's visit to the optometrist for new eyeglasses was a far cry from Ed Wynn or Red Skelton, and Chester A. Riley was even further removed. Radio's early clowns exchanged their baggy pants for suits, work duds, and robe and slippers.

Radio was the massest of mass entertainment, and its audience, mostly middlebrow and increasingly suburban, was amused and flattered at seeing itself reflected in shows that made light of its travails but never questioned the all-American family unit. *The Aldrich Family, A Date with Judy,* and *Vic and Sade* didn't know from divorced parents, single mothers, illegitimate kids, swinging singles, and biracial broods. Radio sitcoms didn't prattle on about the nuclear family because it had not yet been threatened.

Radio sitcoms might have wacky characters and wildly improbable situations, but everyone returned to the fold at show's end and all was well that ended well, with a peppy promise to be back next week (same time, same station, same family), after which, say, Henry and his pal Homer would warble their show's jolly theme on *The Aldrich Family:*

"Oh, the big red letters stand for the Jell-O family!/Oh, the big red letters stand for the Jell-O family!/That's Jell-O—yum-yum-yum!/ Jell-O pudding—yum-yum-yum!/Jell-O tap-i-oca pudding, yes, sirree!" Note the repeated "family" theme; also, the subtle implication that if *The Aldrich Family* can make you feel good, so will Jell-O puddings.

Overleaf, clockwise from top left: Fanny Brice (*Baby Snooks*); Eve Arden (*Our Miss Brooks*); Jackie Kelk, Ezra Stone, Katharine Raht, and House Jameson (*The Aldrich Family*); Ozzie, David, Harriet, and Ricky Nelson

The program, which lasted fourteen years, set the tone for sitcoms to come. Most of the episodes focused on Henry, the adolescent son, and his troubles with girls, grades, and growing up, all very much in the wildly popular Andy Hardy vein. More significantly, although this was the first major show about teenagers, it kept one foot in the past: Henry's father, Sam Aldrich, was no palsy-walsy, sweater-wearing, football-tossing Ozzie Nelson—he was more in the gruff but understanding Judge Hardy mold; stern Mrs. Aldrich didn't sound like a barrel of laughs, either. At the end of one episode, Sam Aldrich turns to his wife in bed and says, in that benevolent chuckle one rarely hears on sitcoms now (not to mention the Panglossian sentiment itself), "Well, dear, things usually turn out for the best"; one radio scholar called the *Aldrich* shows "secular parables."

This landmark sitcom had several lives: It began as a 1938 Broadway hit by Clifford Goldsmith, *What a Life!,* which was featured on Rudy Vallee's *Fleischmann Hour* before becoming a weekly sketch on *The Kate Smith Show,* graduating to summer replacement for Jack Benny, and finally getting its own slot in 1939.

The show was hopelessly bland, neither quite zany nor lifelike, and Henry's teenage girl problems and peccadilloes, heard on tape today, lack the charm, spice, or whimsy of rival shows like *Junior Miss* or *Meet Corliss Archer*—possibly because the young female is more complex than the male. If girls seemed to lust less avidly after the boys on these shows, it's only because the boys were such unromantic wimps— squeaky-voiced geeks named Oogie, Dexter, Haskell, and Archie, who could barely pick up the phone and dial for a date. Geekiest of all was Homer Brown, Henry Aldrich's pal, played by Jackie Kelk, a Broadway child actor who ran the gamut of teenhood on radio: Kelk also played Jimmy Olsen on *The Adventures of Superman,* Terry of *Terry and the Pirates,* and Chester Gump on *The Gumps.* Ezra Stone (Henry), a dark-eyed Jewish kid (born Ezra Chaim Feinstone), who went on to become a theater and TV director and directed the short-lived 1951–52 TV version, looked nothing like a gawky all-American boy next door in the studio audience's minds. Recalls Kelk: "It was a big shock to people who came to see the show in the studio, because I looked more the part; I was slight and skinny. Ezra was this fat little man in a vest who smoked cigars."

As *THE ALDRICH FAMILY* gave rise to endless copycat sitcoms that tended to focus on female Henrys, radio for preteen males became an early covert semisexual experience. Young boys had serious crushes on the terminally pert teenage girls who populated family comedy shows with the ever-so-perky voices of 1940s radio, the land of the fresh-scrubbed soda-fountain coed. Each of those anonymous actresses (delectable creatures all, one felt certain) was a surrogate girl friend for adolescent boys' desperate but barren sex lives. Most alluring was Barbara Whiting's Judy Graves of *Junior Miss*. The show, based on a popular series of *New Yorker* stories by Sally Benson, which became a Broadway hit and a movie, aired Saturday mornings and was listened to by kids who were still in bed, right after *Big Jon and Sparkie;* it caught preteen boys in a priapic zone between childhood and manhood. It was also easy to be smitten, if not aroused, by Judy Foster of *A Date with Judy,* not to mention the nubile young heroine of *Meet Corliss Archer,* based on the hit stage comedy *Kiss and Tell.*

These fluffy shows spun from cotton candy—and their sweet but brainless heroines—were indistinguishable from one another, with the possible exception of *Junior Miss.* Equally inane though it may have been, apart from Judy's prickly father (played by radio and TV's inveterate grump, Gale Gordon), *Junior Miss* was set in New York City and had fascinating references to Schrafft's, Fifth Avenue, Bonwit Teller, Radio City, Macy's and Gimbel's, Bloomingdale's, Rumpelmayer's, the Plaza, Central Park, the ice-skating rink at Rockefeller Center, and those curious twin East Coast phenomena—doormen and taxi drivers.

Junior Miss had three radio incarnations—first in 1942, starring Shirley Temple in what was her first ill-fated grown-up effort, canceled after one season because of the lavish twelve-thousand-dollar an episode budget (most of it eaten up by Temple's salary); again, in 1946, when paltry scripts did it in; and finally and most successfully in 1948, when it starred singer Margaret Whiting's kid sister Barbara, who was sixteen when she took over the role of Judy Graves. (In the movie, she had played Judy's ditsy sidekick, Fuffy Adams.)

"In radio in those years you did everything," recalls Barbara Whiting. "You just changed your voice a little and you could do sixteen different characters," a freedom that ruined TV careers for many fine radio actors who, like Whiting, didn't resemble their voices; Whiting was chubby when she first played Judy Graves. "In radio, you can be fat, thin, whatever. I had a case on Dick Crenna [boyfriend Oogie Pringle], but he didn't even know I existed." The show was a six-year success, even though, she laments, "nobody ever paid attention to *Junior Miss,* because we were on in the morning, after *Let's Pretend"*— the kiddie ghetto.

Not quite. Young males were titillated by the saucy virgins heard on these teenage shows, stirring up what Philip Roth later identified in Jewish boys as *"shiksa* lust": the tantalizingly Protestant souls of Judy Graves and big sister Lois; Judy Foster, given prepubescent life by bouncy-voiced Louise Erickson, and girl friend Mitzi, or the adorable Corliss Archer, portrayed by another promising radio date, Janet Waldo, who remained Corliss for ten years. Radio's teen circuit was so incestuous, and the shows so interchangeable, that Waldo and Erickson played secondary characters on each other's show.

All the teenage boys were jerky variations on Henry Aldrich—Judy Foster's Oogie Pringle, Corliss Archer's Dexter Franklin, Judy Graves's Haskell Wexler, Bronco on *The Great Gildersleeve,* Walter Denton on *Our Miss Brooks,* and Archie Andrews. Archie was forever torn between those twin Loreleis, Betty and Veronica, two more vocal vixens who flirted from afar. Girl listeners presumably were left to fantasize about Jack Armstrong, Superman, and the Lone Ranger.

John Crosby once wrote that the problem with radio's teenage boys is that they weren't truly bad. "There aren't any Huck Finns in radio," he wrote. "Judging from radio, the lads still get into mischief, but they never get into it deliberately. For Homer and Henry and Oogie and Archie, I see no hope whatever of future brilliance. Week after week, they get into one jam after another, always by accident, never by design. Modern boys—I'm judging by Oogie and company—are a bunch of namby-pambies. They never *try* to get into trouble. They try to stay out of it. . . ."

It's a long, winding garden path from *The Aldrich Family* to *Married . . . With Children* and *Roseanne,* but structurally only an Ezra Stone's throw. There's now a cruder, even cruel, edge to the jokes and to subject matter, and middle-class families have less in common—or maybe middledom just has more stratifications. Different times, themes, tone, and, to be sure, dialogue, but in the end it's the same sitcom, plot devices, and often-sentimental resolutions.

EVEN MORE SO THAN *The Aldrich Family,* the radio show that most set the style, tone, and agenda for radio (and for TV) situation comedy was *Father Knows Best.* Its very title announced an almost avant-garde premise for the time—that the stumblebum era of Dagwood Bumstead, Chester Riley, and even Ozzie Nelson (a transition figure, stranded between father-knows-best and -worst) had vanished. From then on, fathers were no longer lovable lunkheads but sage, stable breadwinner-philosophers. Into father Jim Anderson's sturdy no-nonsense wingtip shoes later stepped TV's Ward Cleaver, Andy Taylor, and Steve Douglas of *My Three Sons.*

Anderson and his wholesome circle were firmly rooted on radio for five years. The show starred Robert Young, the fresh-faced epitome of decent upstanding American manhood, fatherhood, and husband-hood—an MGM star of the thirties who had established his decency credentials on screen in films like *Claudia, The Enchanted Cottage,* and *Those Endearing Young Charms.*

The show had a homier, more realistic, less jokey feeling than *My Favorite Husband* and *The Adventures of Ozzie and Harriet,* which it most closely resembled. Jim Anderson wasn't quite as wise a sage on radio as he evolved into on TV, where he became an all-knowing fount of wisdom, but he was no dunce, either. Wife Betty was cast in the helpful Harriet Nelson mold. We were now in the era of the indulgent smile, the warm chuckle, the wise nod, and the twinkle of recognition. Sitcoms had turned a corner into dullsville, with more sit and less com.

Writer Paul West was largely responsible for the placid, benign tone of *Father Knows Best,* which had begun on a rowdier note when Ed James first devised it. "It was an entirely different show at the beginning," West recalls. "I'd heard it a few times and I didn't like it. It was very quarrelsome, a lot of bickering." West, a gentle, mild-mannered fellow himself, de-squabbled the script and, he says, patterned the family after his own—he had four children. Radio people thought the show too nice to be true, and it did hit new levels of vacuity: On a typical episode, teenage daughter Kathy, infatuated with the new family washing machine, finds excuses to launder everyone's clothes and mistakenly washes Dad's briefcase; as the show ends, Young groans, "Oh, no-o-o-o!," the exit line on many a radio sitcom.

West recalls, "They didn't think it had enough sharp edges. When people would say life isn't like that, Bob [Young] always used to say, 'No, of course, but that's how we'd *like* it to be.' It won awards as a comedy show, but we never thought of it as a comedy. It was a family drama. None of the shows I worked for [*The Adventures of Ozzie and Harriet* and *The Great Gildersleeve*] were big ha-ha shows. Even *Gildersleeve* was not a big joke show."

Robert Young, says West, who also wrote for the show when it moved to TV, was as nice a guy to write for as his fictional counterpart. "He never questioned a word. He'd have read the phone book if we'd have put it in front of him."

ALTHOUGH MISS BROOKS didn't have a literal family, her extended Madison High School family in *Our Miss Brooks* made her as much a mother figure as any sitcom matriarch. She was never portrayed as a romantic figure, probably because teachers, even zippy modern ones like Connie Brooks, were still considered asexual schoolmarms. Her undefined relationship with Mr. Boynton was a standoff, treated comically rather than romantically. An unmarried woman on the air wasn't permitted to have a real sex life, which didn't really change until TV's *Mary Tyler Moore Show* demonstrated that a single woman could enjoy sex without being a tramp.

Most female comic characters on radio were either virgins, vipers, vixens, vapid cutie-pies, or spinsters—with the enduring exception of Eve Arden's Miss Brooks, the first bright, independent, unmarried, working female comic character on the air. Quick, outspoken, and funny, even sophisticated, Miss Brooks possessed one of the fastest tongues of either gender, regularly cutting everyone down to size with a withering wisecrack or flippant aside. It's safe to say that *Our Miss Brooks* did as much to raise the image—if not the salaries—of teachers in America as did Robert Maynard Hutchins.

Certain men's taste in women during that era may well have been influenced by early and steady exposure to Eve Arden's Connie Brooks. She was smart, sexy, and took no guff from guys, whether it was her wet noodle of a beau, Mr. Boynton, or her huffing and puffing boss, Mr. Conklin, portrayed by the perpetually fuming Gale Gordon. Gordon moved into the principal's office after a respectable run of dramatic roles in radio, from *Gang Busters* and *The Shadow* to *Sherlock Holmes*. He created historic radio characters out of two landmark hotheads—the seething, blustering Mr. Conklin and the sardonic Mayor La Trivia of *Fibber McGee and Molly* before earning lasting fame as Lucille Ball's TV nemesis.

Eve Arden, the thinking man's Lucy, was a favorite of CBS's William Paley, who encouraged her to do the show despite her own doubts about the original scripts. Arden's voice never matched her prettified surname, supposedly inspired by a jar of face cream. Given her lemony voice, tart rejoinders, and puckered expression, Arden should have stuck with her real name, Eunice Quedens. In films, she started out as a sassy showgirl in *Stage Door*, playing the streetwise pro with a cat on her shoulder; it typed her as everyone's pet smart-mouthed gal, a master of the dry aside, sidelong look, and permanently arched eyebrow.

Miss Brooks was acerbic but nice, a combination that rarely exists in female comedians. Arden was a snappy lady in the tradition of Joan Blondell, Rosalind Russell, and Celeste Holm, but as striking looking as Rhonda Fleming or Lucille Ball, who had turned down the role. In retrospect, it's impossible to think of anyone else playing the role, but Arden was a second or third choice. Producer Harry Ackerman wanted Shirley Booth. "All she could see was the downside of the underpaid teacher," he recalled of Booth. "She couldn't make any fun of it." *Our Miss Brooks* was several notches above most radio comedies of the period, but what really raised it above the competition was Arden's softly muttered put-downs of the clowns, loudmouths, and fatheads—mostly male—who surrounded her on campus. She stood out amid the banal Betty Andersons and Harriet Nelsons.

Given today's smart aleck sitcom characters like Murphy Brown, it's easy to take Arden's Connie Brooks for granted. But she was her own woman fifty years ago—decidedly female and nonthreatening, yet a feminist before it was in fashion. Miss (Ms.?) Brooks was feminine, single, and marriage-minded but never man-crazy, like most sitcom women, or antimale. Although too sharp for the thick Mr. Boynton, she patiently waited for him to exhibit real interest. Her attitude seemed to be: If it works out, fine; if not, it's his loss. Their twenty-year relationship on radio and TV never led anywhere—not even to the bedroom. They might indulge in a little light smooching, but half the time they addressed each other, like lovers in a Jane Austen novel, as "Miss Brooks" and "Mr. Boynton." On rare cozy occasions they'd slip into something a little more comfortable—"Connie" and "Philip."

Much of Miss Brooks's unique appeal was that, unlike most of the rattlebrained females that surrounded her in radio comedy, she treated men with refreshing suspicion—but as undeserving equals. She tolerated the befuddled, hopelessly square Mr. Boynton (played by Jeff Chandler, then known as Ira Grossel, on radio and briefly on TV, until Robert Rockwell took over) but was clearly superior to him. She humored the perpetually enraged Mr. Conklin and pitied the inept, crinkle-voiced Walter Denton, played by forever-young Richard Crenna (perhaps the only radio juvenile to later establish a significant movie career), who tripled as Oogie Pringle ("Boy, Judy, do you look *sna-a-zzy!*"), the resident nerd on *A Date with Judy,* and as Marjorie's boyfriend, Bronco, on *The Great Gildersleeve*—wherever the services of a squeaky-voiced teenage boy were required. At one point he played seven different teenage boys simultaneously.

Crenna is surprised that Arden wrote so little about the show in her autobiography, but he says Miss Brooks didn't much resemble Miss Arden. "There was not a lot of Brooks in her. She had a wonderful sense of humor, but I wouldn't say she was particularly sardonic. She never played the comedian offstage—she didn't need to be the funniest person in the room, unlike so many comics, who find it difficult to get off. She went out, got the laughs, and went back to her ranch in the Valley. She was just a wonderfully unselfish actress, and was just so up all the time; she made you feel good to be around her."

He recalls that the cast liked to socialize, and that he once lived with the Gale Gordons. "We all couldn't wait to get together for rehearsals, we were so enamored of the show." It was such a devoted cast, relates Crenna, that after Ira Grossel went on to stardom as Jeff Chandler in TV's *Cochise,* he insisted on playing Mr. Boynton on radio five more years, until his contract ran out, earning a fraction of what he earned as Jeff Chandler. When Crenna turned thirty, he decided he'd played seventeen-year-old Walter Denton long enough and announced he was leaving the show. "Eve was adamant, saying, 'Dick has just *got* to play Walter Denton on TV.' She begged me, 'Help us get it off the ground. Just do it for one year.' So I did it for a year, and then *two* years, and then *three* years," whereupon they gave her a new boyfriend and made other changes. "It lost its momentum," says Crenna, which allowed him to finally make his escape—into TV's *The Real McCoys* and then to *Slattery's People,* an adult at last.

As for Miss Brooks's surrogate family, her pupils and colleagues, they loved and respected her while she looked on with mild disdain, too dignified and polite to say anything truly mean—except out of the corner of her mouth to us, her sympathetic listening audience. She also confided in her kindly landlady, Mrs. Davis, and Minerva the cat, but most of all it was we who were her secret allies. This most capable and charming of quasi-moms truly was *our* Miss Brooks.

RADIO'S QUIRKIEST FAMILY SHOW—if indeed it can even be called that, or classified at all—was *Vic and Sade,* an eccentric small-town serial created and written during its entire fifteen-year run by Paul Rhymer, a former reporter once fired for writing feature stories about people he had neglected to interview.

The humor of this peculiar yet passionately adored show, which ran from 1931 to 1946, was an acquired taste; people either loved it or didn't quite get it. It took a while to appreciate the show's slightly askew state of mind, throwaway humor, and between-the-lines wit. The episodes consisted of the spectacularly picayune doings of the Gook family and their zanily named but unheard friends, family, and neighbors; we're talking now of Dottie Brainfeeble, Jake Gumpox, Smelly Clark, and Ishigan Fishigan of Sishigan, Michigan.

Each show was self-contained, usually a two- or three-way discussion with conversational detours and cul-de-sacs about, say, what flavor ice cream they should order or whether Vic would attend a niece's piano recital. A casual remark easily built into a major discussion. "Their horizons were so small," said Bernardine Flynn, who played Sade. In a 1972 tribute to the show, she discussed the intricate nature of Rhymer's dialogue. "Banal as the words were, and as ordinary as the conversations may have been, it's like music that's been beautifully woven into a tapestry of rhythm."

To contemporary ears, the program—about the humdrum lives of a crotchety, semicockeyed bookkeeper for a kitchenware company, Victor Gook, his put-upon and slightly nagging wife, Sade, and their perpetually cheery teenage son, Rush—sounds like a warped *Our Town* or a wry Bob and Ray soap opera parody. Its off-the-wall whimsy, at times quite thick, struck an unexpected nerve in the thirties and forties, especially on radio, where whimsy was virtually an unknown commodity. As Bob Brown, the show's longtime announcer, commented on the tribute show: "Set amidst a welter of tears that began at nine in the morning with *John's Other Wife* and ended at four in the afternoon, *Vic and Sade,* with its warm daily vignettes with no cliffhangers to worry about, was an island of sheer delight in a sea of tears."

Paul Rhymer's original comic mind was much admired by James Thurber, John O'Hara, and Sherwood Anderson, who claimed that he had captured small-town American speech patterns and concerns as well as any novelist working the same midwestern ground. Vic and Sade Gook's unnamed hometown outside Peoria (based on Rhymer's native Bloomington, Illinois) was a woozier Winesburg, Ohio. Its echoes can clearly be heard in the whimsical stories concocted by Garrison Keillor about the citizens of Lake Wobegon; "The Iowa State Home for the Tall" sounds like a Keillorism but is vintage Rhymer.

Ray Bradbury, in his introduction to a collection of *Vic and Sade* scripts, wrote that Rhymer "collected bits and pieces of mediocrity from all our commonplace occurrences, all our inane conversations, all our bored afternoons and long evenings when all we could think of to do was trot down to the YMCA to watch the fat men play handball."

In a typical episode, Uncle Fletcher explores the commercial possibilities of his latest invention, "hyena grease." In another, Vic tries to compose a letter to his brother-in-law, finds he has nothing to say, and simply fills in the note with items from the newspaper, irritating Sade, who flounces off to bed early. There are no raised voices, just occasional hurt feelings and pouts.

Most of the humor was in the references to ongoing off-mike characters, past events, and family effluvia and trivia, such as one of the Gooks' favorite dishes—"beef punkles." As on *Lum and Abner,* a sort of Ozark *Vic and Sade,* the jokes were small; mostly, you smiled at the interplay of characters often speaking at cross-purposes—"Wheels within wheels," Rhymer put it. Flynn remarked, "People interrupted each other, and rarely did anyone finish a sentence, which was rare [in writing] then."

When the show expanded to thirty minutes, the phantom characters were given voice, and a studio audience added, which Idelson said upset the delicate balance of the three Gooks talking amongst themselves. "The half-hour version didn't gain anything. Paul knew how to handle three people in a ten-minute frame. You didn't need to hear the off-mike characters, because they were bigger than life—caricatures—and you had your own idea of how they sounded. The one-sided phone calls and their letters told you all you needed to know."

The shows began with a lazy lead-in by announcer Brown: "*Well, sir, get ready to smile again with radio's homefolks, Vic and Sade. . . . It's about eight-thirty on a warm evening in early autumn as we join our friends at the small house halfway up in the next block . . .*"

Characters hailed from places like Seepage, Ohio, and Vic belonged to a lodge called the Sacred Stars of the Milky Way (Drowsy Venus chapter), in which he was Exalted Big Dipper. Vic had a habit of calling Sade and Rush by any pet name that came to mind, such as "Kneecap," allowing Rhymer to indulge his flair for not just the nonsensical but the non sequitur—now and then a bit tortured ("You could've cut off my nose with a pound of butter").

The leads were played from the very first show by Art Van Harvey, a former grain broker, adman, and vaudevillian, whose vague, weather-worn voice belied a pointed wit, and Flynn, a Broadway actress who played Sade with a dying-swan voice similar to that of Jane Ace of *Easy Aces.* Flynn once recalled, "The hardest thing was to keep a straight face. And the more we rehearsed, the funnier it got." During one episode, she said, "the engineer was on the floor and the announcer had to leave the room. I can tell you it wasn't easy."

Billy Idelson was the sweetly obedient fourteen-year-old son, Rush (who calls his father "Guv," a typical Rhymer touch), perhaps broadcasting's last well-adjusted teenager. The only other voice heard was that of dithery Uncle Fletcher (Clarence Hartzell), whose eccentric ramblings became a regular part of the show.

Vic and Sade was an original absurdist comedy that somehow raised the trivial to the significant. One of the Gooks' friends runs a restaurant that serves only bacon sandwiches; Sade goes to washrag sales but only to browse; Vic attends all parades. Perhaps its basic appeal lay in the show's ability not just to mimic but also to elevate and celebrate small talk at a time in America when a family's conversation was often its primary source of entertainment.

"None of it was derivative," reflected Idelson in 1972, by which time he was a writer and producer of Bob Newhart's TV show. "Paul had this completely fresh, unique way of looking at the world. It has the timeless quality of all great literature." Idelson joined the show reluctantly. "I'd just done *The Gumps* and I hated radio acting and I went into this screaming tantrum when my mother sent me to *Vic and Sade*. It was only for four days, so I said I'd do it, and I wound up staying twelve years. But I knew right away this was an entirely different thing than anything I'd done. I was confused, because I liked it! It's a crime that Procter and Gamble destroyed all the recordings." (After a brief, misguided revival on TV in 1957, with a new cast sitting in wing chairs, *Vic and Sade* finally succumbed.)

It's difficult to choose a "typical" excerpt from the show, since every episode was typical and, at the same time, none was. A show entitled "Mr. Gumpox and His Bride" opened this way:

Vic: *I heard a little gossip today. Mr. Gumpox's bride got in town . . . Mrs. Kleeberger—Ike Kneestuffer's secretary—was down to the depot this noon to meet her mother, an' there was Brother Gumpox takin' a lady off the same train.*
Sade: *Well, well, well. Mr. Gumpox has been writin' to matrimonial agencies for years an' at last he's got a wife . . . I'd give my hat to see her.*
Vic: *Don't imagine she's any ravin' beauty—woman that a garbage man got through a matrimonial bureau.*

In even this brief exchange, chosen from some 3,500 scripts, you can sense how Rhymer captures the sound of small-town life, the language and the languor. You can see the kitchen, sniff those simmering beef punkles, and sense an old married couple utterly at ease in their own company, with all the little shorthand references and private jokes that pass without mention. You become a fly on a wall overhearing lives being played out.

One of the recurring phrases on the show was "stuff happens," a phrase more recently revised to the less elegant "shit happens." Stuff happened on *Vic and Sade,* often from out of left field. Listeners rarely knew how a sentence would end, let alone an episode—and it was this "stuff"—the lint, loose change, paper wads, keychains, and chewing gum of daily life Bradbury refers to—that Rhymer used to construct his oddly compelling little show, which he began writing when he grew bored knocking out continuity for music shows.

In an introduction to another collection of scripts, Jean Shepherd—the beloved radio monologuist on New York's WOR who, during the 1960s and 1970s, spun his own droll yarns of growing up in Gary, Indiana, all very much in the Rhymer-Keillor mold—believed the show remained largely a cult classic because it was buried amidst daytime soaps. Shepherd felt it deserved a wider nighttime audience. "The Lone Rangers and the Green Hornets are forever being dredged up as examples of 'The Golden Age of Radio,' while unfortunately the true gold is rarely mentioned, if at all. I remember nothing of the Lone Ranger except 'Hi-yo, Silver!,' which is not much of a line if you think of it, but Smelly Clark's Uncle Strap taking his lady friend to Peoria for a fish dinner somehow got me where I lived."

Shepherd points out Rhymer's skill at weaving a fifteen-minute episode called "Caramels on a Hot Day" out of nothing more than caramels, a summer afternoon, and a bored teenage boy. His work resonated, said Shepherd, "because Paul Rhymer created true humor. Practically every episode had little shafts of insight, and often sadness, that would come and go like the brief hints of darker things we all have in our lives."

THERE HAS NEVER BEEN a sitcom about a truly abusive parent or a really miserable child, but the closest to a family comedy about a bad seed was *The Baby Snooks Show.* By nearly any measure, Fanny Brice's Baby Snooks—or "Schnooks," as Brice Yiddishized her off-mike—should have been a radio disaster. It was a total burlesque creation that originated in one of Brice's old *Ziegfeld Follies* shows in a sketch written by Moss Hart, perhaps the least likely man to have fathered Baby Snooks (although another source claims that the writer Philip Rapp created her). In any case, Baby Snooks was the grandbaby of all comic brats, from Dennis the Menace, Eloise, and Madeleine to Lily Tomlin's Edith Ann, a one-note version of Brice's needling tot. Snooks was a pest but cute and, like all maddening kids, knew every trick to beguile, and just which buttons to push, to bedevil her exasperated father.

The character may have seemed a noisy one-joke idea based on Snooks driving Daddy (Lancelot Higgins—played by Englishman Hanley Stafford in a constant state of red-faced apoplexy) to a screaming fit. Yet Brice was wonderfully adept at giving voice to her irritating moppet without making Snooks obnoxious. To quote *Variety*'s veteran critic, Hobe Morrison: "Snooks was not nasty or mean, spiteful or sadistic. She was at heart a nice kid. Similarly, Daddy was harried and desperate and occasionally was driven to spanking his impish daughter. But Daddy wasn't ill-tempered or unkind with the kid. He wasn't a crab."

During the show's seven-year run, from 1944 to 1951, during which Snooks aged from four to six, Brice employed the entire range of annoying attitudes in every little girl's pestering arsenal that drives parents berserk—from petulant to persistent to self-pitying. When all else failed, she would pipe up with her innocent but infuriating, "*Why-y-y, Daddy?*" Fanny Brice meant nothing to young fans of the show, but grown-ups were intrigued by a family comedy starring a major stage personality who made the switch from Broadway to radio in what must have been seen as a comedown for so grand a onetime *Follies* star.

Everett Freeman, who produced the show, said, "I never got a performance out of her during rehearsal," where Brice gave desultory readings but reassured him, "I can't do a show until it's on the air, kid. Don't worry." She invariably came through in performance, said Freeman. "While she was on the air, she *was* Baby Snooks." During a broadcast, recalled George Burns, she was "squirming, squinting, mugging, jumping up and down."

Brice (born Fanny Borach) didn't see the show as a step down. In fact, she took Snooks so seriously—was "possessed by her," someone said—that, in a throwback to her burlesque days, the comic dressed in a baby-doll dress for the studio audience and refused to wear glasses to read the script for fear of ruining Snooks's image; the script was printed three times its normal size.

Brice was so devoted to the show that she took a pay cut in its last two seasons, but it was almost driven off the air when Milton Berle came on opposite her. The show also took a few critical knocks when it took a preachy turn in its last year. The world's most famous brat even cut a series of Capitol albums for kids that might have been approved by Mr. Rogers, with titles like *Crossing Streets, Truthfulness, Kindness to Animals,* and *Table Manners.* Radio's meanest widdle kid was going straight. In 1951, while writing her memoirs, Baby Snooks's real-life mama, Fanny Brice, died of a stroke.

THE GREAT GILDERSLEEVE was the first non-nuclear family sitcom, about a kindly unmarried uncle who is the guardian of two children—a teenage niece, Marjorie, and a nettlesome nephew, Leroy. Perhaps because of that, the show holds up better than many other radio sit-coms, feels closer to us in time, is less gimmicky, and seems a little more honest than most. As radio chronicler Jim Harmon said of the show's complex middle-age, rotund, small-town Romeo, "The superficial aspect of his character was his blowhard act, but beneath it all, you could sense he was sincere and earnest, wanting to help himself and others, but finding that his enthusiasm always exceeded his abilities." The not-so-great Gildersleeve was wonderfully vulnerable.

The character was created by Harold Peary in 1937 on *Fibber McGee and Molly* as McGee's nemesis ("You're a *har-r-r-rd* man, Gildersleeve!" an irked Fibber would mutter), the only one who could outbluster "Himself," as Molly called McGee. The portly Gildersleeve (Peary *sounded* portly) was such a hit that he got his own show in 1942, generally considered radio's first spin-off character, and stayed with it until 1950 when he outsmarted himself and lost the role of a lifetime to Willard Waterman, a journeyman actor who sounded so amazingly like Peary's Gildersleeve it was almost impossible to tell them apart. A *Gildersleeve* writer, Paul West, recalls: "Hal wanted a piece of the show, and his agent, MCA, was so sure they wouldn't con-tinue the show without him that they sold him on the idea he was irre-placeable. Even though he'd worked with him before, Hal forgot that Willard Waterman was waiting in the wings."

Hoping to recycle himself on *The Harold Peary Show,* Peary played a radio crooner named Honest Harold (the better to display his singing voice), one of whose pals is a kid named Marvin, a less rude Leroy. As merely a *good* Gildersleeve, Peary was again giggly and ingratiating, but his unique voice, laugh, and the hapless bachelor character were too closely identified with Gildersleeve. Happily for the sponsor, Kraft, if not for Peary, *The Great Gildersleeve* was one of the shows in which the lead character became more important than the star, hence the seamless transition from Peary to Waterman.

But Waterman refused—out of respect, he claimed—to imitate Peary's famous trademark laugh. "Hal used that [laugh] before he ever did Gildersleeve," Waterman said. "I decided that I would not use it. And I never did use the laugh as he did it. The character had to laugh, though, so we used what the writers called the 'Gildersleeve social chuckle.' " Though some felt Waterman's version of Gildersleeve was more human, the actors were interchangeably charming and amusing, most noticeably in the subtle ways they deployed Gildersleeve's sliding, insinuating titter (Peary called it a "dirty laugh") to indicate a vast range of emotions: fear, disgust, humiliation, and secret glee.

Like most radio family comedies, the show (created by John Whedon and Sam Moore) gave off a sunny glow—but then it was set in "Summerfield"—and featured several indelible supporting characters whose purpose was to butt heads and egos with Gildersleeve: Gildy's ostentatiously wealthy, loutish neighbor Bullard (Gale Gordon yet again); the waspish, wicked Judge Hooker (Earle Ross), who regularly browbeat the essentially soft-hearted Gildy; his barber and buddy, Floyd, who offered unwanted advice; plus all the women in his complex life—Marjorie; Birdie, the maid who saw through all of her boss's self-delusions; and lady friends like Leila Ransom and Eve Goodwin, who could easily twist him around their little fingers. Even the most timid character, the mumbly milk-toast druggist Mr. Peavey (superbly underplayed by Dick Legrand and Forrest Lewis), could deflate Gildy with his woundingly dubious, "Well, now, Mister Gildersleeve, I wouldn't say that."

Gildy's main family goad was his whiny nephew, Leroy ("Aw gee, Unc, for corn's sake!"), portrayed by Walter Tetley, who by age sixteen had played teenagers on some 2,800 broadcasts and continued to do so well into his adult life. Leroy regularly caught his uncle shading the truth or dodging dicey situations and took great delight in calling his bluff and bluster, whereupon Gildersleeve would emit the sputtery equivalent of a spit-take and snarl, "*Le-e-e-roy!*"

The show's appeal stemmed in part from its complicated title character—a sometimes silly but at heart decent and at times profound man who did his best in a trying situation as part-time parent and full-time bachelor. *The Great Gildersleeve* was the only comedy show that dealt seriously with an unmarried middle-aged person's love life; not even the eligible Miss Brooks did much courting. Gildersleeve, however, had a healthy male libido, and thought himself very much the ladies' man even as he trembled in the presense of any attractive single woman.

In one particularly skillful script, Gildersleeve falls hard for a woman he sees in a restaurant and feels sure she is his soul mate. He cadges an invitation to a dinner party where the woman of his dreams will be, reduced to using the loathsome Judge Hooker as a go-between, only to be reminded by the judge that only a scoundrel would crash a party in order to steal the host's date. Gildy realizes it's a pretty crummy ploy but plows ahead anyway. Finally, barely able to speak, he attends the party and is introduced to the woman, who turns out to be the wife of the guest of honor, a military hero who's been at war for two years. Gildersleeve is devastated and skulks away, defeated yet again, sighing his fluttery defeated swoon.

The episode, unusually adult for a radio sitcom, is honestly conceived and nicely observed, written with equal parts of humor and poignance, even a touch of poetry, as the giddy Gildy sees his unrealistic hopes dashed. We feel his guilt, his boyish adoration, his determination to woo the woman or know the reason why, his anxiety, and, finally, his disappointment and resignation. It's a small jewel of a show, typical of *The Great Gildersleeve* and of situation comedy at its most enchanting.

BY UNANIMOUS ACCLAMATION, radio's most huggable household was the Nelsons'—Ozzie, Harriet, David, and Ricky, a squeaky-clean nuclear family to gladden the hearts of the Christian Coalition.

The Adventures of Ozzie and Harriet was often—and still is—denigrated as the very definition of vapid, but it was expertly crafted and structured. While it didn't aspire to more than an effortless amiability, it achieved that with great consistency. It's easy to disparage the show today, but there was a genuine pleasantness about it that made it hard to hate. Like *Leave It to Beaver* and *The Brady Bunch* a generation later, entire childhoods were defined by it. Subsequent TV generations grew up on *Father Knows Best* as an impossible family role model, but kids and parents of the 1940s and 1950s had those perfect, well-scrubbed, ever-smiling Nelsons: the bemused, slightly dazed Ozzie; the lovely and sedate Harriet; the irrepressible and irreverent Ricky; and his repressed, well-meaning older brother, David, forced to play straight man to an unfailingly funny kid brother.

The unspoken appeal of certain radio comedy shows was their way of creating a funnier and fuzzier sense of family than many listeners found in their own homes. The average household lacked the easygoing banter and bonhomie that ran through surrogate family radio shows set in small towns with names like Centerville, Summerfield, and Springfield.

One of the charming aspects of *The Adventures of Ozzie and Harriet* was that it allegedly mirrored the Nelsons' actual lives: The set for their TV house was modeled after their own home, and all the actors on the show played themselves. They were "America's favorite young couple" in the opening credits, later amended to "America's favorite family." Jack Benny had laid the groundwork for reality-based comedy on his show, but the Nelsons further blurred fact and fiction when the real Nelson sons took over for child actors in 1949—in Ricky's favorite word, neat.

The show was lovable for reasons hard to explain or perhaps justify now. It wasn't terribly clever, or original, merely good-natured, ever so perky, and, to be sure, homey as heck. As on most radio (and TV) sitcoms, Harriet was the brains and power behind the throne who easily and shrewdly untangled her inept male brood's lives. The show inspired a comedian to concoct a succinct parody comprised solely of "Hi, Dad." "Hi, Rick." "Hi, Mom." "Hi, Dave," ad nauseam. It hurt a little to laugh, because it ridiculed a family that America had adopted.

Ricky was the acknowledged smarty-pants, but in fact Ozzie, in his quizzical, distracted way, was funnier than he was ever given credit for.

Harriet and poor David were gentle foils, walk-ons in their own house, where nothing out of the ordinary ever happened, which may partly explain its popularity. The Nelsons bore no resemblance to any family yet captured the essence of familyness.

Theirs was the Holiday Inn of sitcoms—no surprises, at least not until Ricky learned how to play guitar and everything fell apart. The program could take any minor domestic incident and effortlessly wring a mildly entertaining half-hour show out of it, with the emphasis on the mild. What drew America to the Nelson family was the relaxed camaraderie between parents and children that everyone wanted to emulate. Most fathers of the forties and fifties were formal, even autocratic, less of a chum like Ozzie. Though Ozzie was called Pop, he behaved more like a big brother, with his boyish voice, crew cut, and love of football tossing and ice-cream cones.

Life with the Nelsons—as the show was eventually called on TV, to which it made the easiest transfer of almost any radio situation comedy—was cheerful and utterly free of any anxiety. Harriet was a gentle, compliant mom, modest of manner, with a wry note in her voice, yet sexier than most mothers encountered at that time by young boys. She was a Mother Superior of the Suburbs, kind but firm, with an unmussed demeanor that every wife and mom must have secretly resented. The real Harriet, however, had not always stood by in an apron behind a plate of cookies; she had once sung with Ozzie's popular cookie-cutter band. David and Ricky, with their cutting repartee, completed the snug family portrait. Most of all, the Nelsons seemed a well-balanced unit at a time when most dads ran the family show.

Firstborn sons strongly identified with David, the stolid, obedient, well-behaved, and somewhat boring big brother, who fed his kid brother straight lines. Without Ricky, the show might not have run as long as it did, but his deadpan comebacks spiced up the otherwise vanilla-flavored episodes full of Protestant ritual, which had a certain exotic appeal to non-WASPs.

The Nelsons, however terminally idealized, were unlike the kooky, cartoony domestic comedies of the Henry Aldrich–Archie Andrews–Corliss Archer–Judy Graves ilk. Whenever David or Ricky got into some minor mess, Ozzie was always there with a fond moral reminder, closely followed by Harriet, in her spotless apron, with a comforting glass of milk and a platter of doughnuts.

For all of its sugarcoated reputation, *The Adventures of Ozzie and Harriet* often touched on real domestic issues. In "Nobody Likes a Yes Man," Ozzie tells Thorny that he and Harriet are off to the sports and boat show, only to be reminded by Thorny that Harriet always seems to be doing things to please *him*. Ozzie suddenly realizes how selfish he's been and, racked with guilt, offers to go to a flower show with Harriet. She's aware he's only doing it to be nice, but the gesture itself is enough to show her he cares. It's one of those small marital moments made funny and affectionate without turning the whole thing into an obvious object lesson.

The show mirrored Ozzie's idyllic memories of his own youth in Ridgefield, New Jersey, a tranquil boyhood where he became the youngest-ever Eagle Scout at thirteen, the start of what a biographer called "a lifetime of overachieving": He went to Rutgers, became varsity quarterback, and attended law school with tuition money earned by leading a "sweet" big band that first brought music to the fabled Glen Island Casino on Long Island Sound. It was at a gig there on New Year's Eve in 1931 that he first clapped eyes on a beautiful dancer and hostess, a would-be singer named Harriet Hilliard (née Peggy Sue Snyder, a name straight out of *Ozzie and Harriet*), whom Ozzie hired to sing with his band. They did duets and, as in some Dick Powell–Ruby Keeler musical, fell in love.

What brought Ozzie and Harriet to California in the early 1940s was *Sweethearts of the Campus,* a musical that first featured them as a couple and led to their network debut on Red Skelton's show in 1940. The idea was that Nelson would lead the orchestra while Harriet played the female characters, such as the mother of Skelton's Mean Widdle Kid, but the ever-ambitious Ozzie began writing sketches for the band and then for the star himself. An unlikely trio, Skelton and the Nelsons got on famously, both on and off the air. When Skelton was called into the service in 1944, the show's innovative producer, John Guedel, suggested over lunch at the Brown Derby that Ozzie and Harriet star in their own show, replacing Skelton and playing themselves. Two kid actors (Tommy Bernard and Henry Blair) would impersonate their young sons, David, eleven, and Ricky, eight; Blair was sixteen at the time. Guedel just felt the couple would click. "He was kind of droll and she was funny, with a lot of warmth; she had a Myrna Loy quality. I just felt they had the right personalities, so I said, What the hell, I'll make a record. Ozzie wrote the first show and we used almost all of it. Pretty soon he was directing, and he was good."

Guedel soon dropped out, sold the show to Nelson, and took a royalty. "I cocreated it with him, but I had other shows, so I got him some writers. I had the format, but he was 85 percent responsible for the success of the show. He wasn't a slick guy at all—he had a midwestern quality. He was a very polite but persistent guy."

On the Nelson's ninth wedding anniversary, October 8, 1944, announcer Verne Smith first chirped: "From Hollywood—International Silver Company presents *The Adventures of Ozzie and Harriet*! Starring young America's favorite couple—Ozzie Nelson and Harriet Hilliard!," as Billy May's band swung into the familiar theme composed for the show by May, who also wrote the musical bridges that gave the show its bright, bouncy sound.

The debut show's introduction set them on course: "Ozzie and Harriet have just finished their usual summer orchestra tour with the many annoyances and discomforts that go with a theatrical career on the road. . . . As our scene opens they are getting settled in their new home at 1847 Rogers Road. Here they are . . ."

"The living room looks great the way you've arranged it."

"Thanks, dear. I'm glad you like it. I tried to make it look as near as possible to page 53 in *House Beautiful* . . ."

Thus began a series that would establish not just Ozzie and Harriet but the master mold for countless situation comedies to come. Even in that opening exchange you can hear the relaxed, even mundane, tone that remained steady for the next twenty-three years. For two seasons, the show included musical numbers and the King Sisters, but gradually Ozzie Nelson, the touring musician, segued into Mr. Nelson, the bemused homeowner of 1847 Rogers Road. Years later, a real-life friend of David's asked Ozzie, incredulously, "Is it true that you used to be a bandleader?"

Ozzie hired good gag writers—too good, in a sense—such as Jack Douglas, who had written for Skelton, Hope, and Cantor, and proved too much the wacky gagman for the cozy show Ozzie envisioned. The show faced a classic comedy dilemma: The jokes got big laughs and were painful to cut, but they were the wrong kind of laughs. Ozzie bit the bullet. "I realized that eventually we would have to get into more believable situations with stronger audience identification." He also dropped a goofy couple—"Mr. and Mrs. Waddington," a henpecked husband and harridan wife—who were too broad. Enter Thorny, Harriet's "mother," and Emmy Lou, based on the teenage girls who hung out at the Nelsons' tennis club pool. The Thornberrys were also borrowed from life—the Nelsons' real-life neighbors, Syd and Katherine Thornbury. The omnipresent Janet Waldo played Emmy Lou; Barbara Eiler eventually took over the part and wound up marrying Ozzie's brother, Don, a staff writer responsible for Ricky's famous catchphrase, "I don't mess around, boy."

The Nelson boys messed around on the set, jealous of their performing counterparts. The idea of having them play themselves on the show came about by accident when Bing Crosby and his son Lindsay appeared on a Nelson show on which the real David and Ricky first played themselves and proved to be naturals. In exchange, Ozzie and his real sons did the Crosby show. The Nelson clan was suddenly in demand for guest shots on superstar shows with Jack Benny, Fred Allen, and Eddie Cantor, where they seemed a fresh breeze from suburbia.

The boys turned pro fast, questioning lines that didn't sound like them, and Ozzie became facile at working their lives into scripts. The real Ricky was a hit with his brash comebacks, which got out of hand when he began ad-libbing. Ozzie took him aside and scotched that idea, saying, Ozzie-like, "Son, there is no such thing as a child comedian." Yet he once cannily observed, "It's a cruel hard fact that a punch line delivered by a little guy of eight will get a much bigger laugh than the same line delivered by a boy of twelve." Ricky became the program's half-pint star, so much so that Harriet said, "It'll be a wonder if David doesn't murder Ricky in his bed some night."

Writing for the Nelsons, says Bob Schiller, was like being one of the family. "They really *were* just like the people on the show. We'd go to their house, and halfway through the evening Harriet would roll out a serving cart with ice cream in bowls that had our names on them—I still remember that—with a plate of cookies she'd baked." Nelson constantly emphasized plots over gags. "He was the only one I know who worked hard on stories. It was always easy to fill in the jokes later."

Another Ozzie and Harriet writer, Paul West, recalls Nelson as "one of the most unforgettable characters I met in radio. He was very bright—a former Phi Beta Kappa, with a sharp business mind. He was a very single-minded man, but he operated the show like a family." West remembers how deeply involved in the scripts Nelson got. "We were writing about *his* family, using their real names, so it was a personal thing to him." He wanted to make it as human as possible. "Ozzie would always say, 'I don't want to be the dumb cluck husband with a Phi Beta Kappa wife.'"

Nelson's quest for the appearance of reality extended to the credits. Sol Saks, who spent three years writing for the show, once pointed out that Nelson didn't want to credit the writing staff on the grounds that it "would dispel the illusion that the dialogue was spontaneous and the incidents were actually happening."

The show was a marzipan version of the Nelson's home life. Ozzie and Harriet were caring but no-nonsense parents—he, in particular, was given to lengthy lectures, while Harriet wielded the big stick. He was a workaholic, unlike his lackadaisical radio/TV self, and she was a stranger to the kitchen, having spent much of her band-singer life on the road, eating in greasy spoons and dining cars; when the pair became stars, all of their meals at home were prepared by servants. The Nelsons had a butler, a cook, an upstairs maid, and, eventually, a chauffeur and gardener.

When the show moved to TV, Harriet's home became a fantasy dollhouse, except that the dinner guests were not the Thornberrys but the Fred MacMurrays, Art Linkletters, and Charles Corrells, and they hung out not at the corner soda fountain but at Chasen's and Don the Beachcomber's. When David arrived, the Nelsons traveled with an entourage unlike your normal American family's—an arranger, a secretary, a nurse, a servant, and fourteen musicians.

The writer Sherwood Schwartz recalls that "Ozzie was a strange man, far to the right of Pat Buchanan, yet he was absolutely honest. A handshake with him was better than a contract with other people. He was deeply sincere; you could trust him. Integrity was a big thing with him. When *Red Channels* [the bible of the McCarthy era that "exposed" alleged Communists in broadcasting] said we had to get rid of an actor who was listed in the magazine, Ozzie said, 'You say he's a Communist, but I'd like to have proof first. I won't fire him until you show me.' The sponsor said the show was at stake, so the actor quit the show."

While the TV version was so clean you could eat off it, Ozzie took pride that he and Harriet were the first television couple to sleep in a double bed. And despite the show's traditional values, they had somehow raised a rock star in Ricky, signaling the start of their demise as pillars of American domesticity. Like most parents of the mid-1950s, they couldn't do much about it. Ricky seemed to have been kidnapped by an alien cult and had gone from cute cocky kid to sullen rocker with a greasy forelock and curled lip—the first Elvis impersonator.

In his characteristically upbeat autobiography, however, Nelson sounds only one cranky note—on the matter that bugged him throughout his radio-TV career: what was his presumed occupation, other than modeling an inexhaustible supply of cardigan sweaters? "The battered cliché of 'What does Ozzie do for a living?' became a standard ploy of unimaginative nightclub comics and newspaper writers in search of a column," he griped. He had hoped to "put the old bromide to rest" in a sketch he once wrote for the *Tonight* show in which Harriet asks him what he does for a living. "It got a very big laugh from the audience," he related, "and I thought that would be the end of it. But to this day scarcely a week goes by that somebody doesn't sidle up to me and hit me with the old line." Ozzie claimed that because his work was unspecific, audiences could identify with him more readily. More convincingly, he added that in his head, the shows always fell on a weekend.

There's a more plausible explanation: When the show began, he had "played" a bandleader and had become so identified with his role that he felt the audience wouldn't accept him as, say, an insurance agent or a plumber. Somehow it mattered what Ozzie did for a living, unlike other stay-at-home sitcom dads. Most sitcom fathers worked in generic "offices," but precisely what they did was rarely mentioned. Actually, Ozzie Nelson was ahead of his time—a sitcom house-husband—but then Harriet didn't work, either. Maybe, like the Lone Ranger, they owned a silver mine.

The show, in any case, proved to be a gold mine, and after five years was among the ten most popular radio programs on the air. ABC signed the Nelsons to the first noncancellation ten-year contract in the history of show business, which gave Ozzie complete control over radio and future TV shows, insulating him from meddling sponsors, network vice-presidents, and ad agencies. After *Here Come the Nelsons* in 1952—their only movie, which Ozzie made to persuade TV executives that they were also visually appealing—the Nelsons journeyed into television as easily as moving out of one house and into another identical place next door (one radio writer said, "They looked exactly like we thought they would"), living happily ever after until 1956, when Ricky bolted for the rock 'n' roll life, David took a fling at acting, and Harriet retired to real-life domesticity.

And so ended the Nelsons' blissful adventures. Ozzie and Harriet tried to revive themselves in a strained 1973 TV sitcom called *Ozzie's Girls,* about two coeds who rent David and Ricky's old rooms, but it barely lasted a season and only underscored how dependent their appeal was on the interplay with their off-mike/off-tube selves.

Ozzie died of cancer in 1975, Ricky came to an early and tragic end in a private-plane crash on New Year's Eve, 1985—a faded rock idol—and Harriet finally succumbed at eighty-five in 1994. By then, Ozzie and Harriet had been off radio more than four decades, but the death of each of the three most endearing members of the family still stung if you had grown up on the same block as those cheery and seemingly indestructible Nelsons.

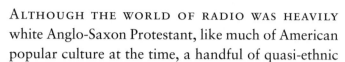

ALTHOUGH THE WORLD OF RADIO WAS HEAVILY white Anglo-Saxon Protestant, like much of American popular culture at the time, a handful of quasi-ethnic shows managed to slip in the back door. Most were comedies, and all were seen through decidedly nonethnic eyes. Even shows that purported to deal with an Irish-Catholic working-class family or an immigrant Italian—*The Life of Riley, Life with Luigi*—had a decidedly WASPy point of view.

Radio's few black actors were restricted to comedies. Norman Corwin, who hired Paul Robeson for one of his dramatic programs, once commented: "Blacks were just not around in radio in those days, just as they were not around in baseball. I remember creating somewhat of a minor sensation at CBS, in my first program for CBS, in 'The Plot to Overthrow Christmas' for Christmas Day 1938. I'd heard a black actor named Eric Burrows read some poetry once and I had him come in. It was the starring role and he was cast in it. Through the corridors, it was, 'Hey, you heard about the Corwin show? He's got a Negro playing the leading role. Holy smoke!' "

Only during the war, on the Armed Forces Radio Service, were blacks given dramatic roles. When blacks were occasionally heard on radio, it was only to play blacks. A black soldier found his way onto *Our Gal Sunday* in 1942, followed by a discussion between the title heroine and her husband about Negro patriotism. On *The Romance of Helen Trent,* Helen was rescued by a black doctor, who became part of the plot, which was punctuated with well-meaning dialogue, like public service announcements, about "the capabilities of the Negro, his unflagging loyalty to his country, and his patience with persecution."

When she first appeared on *Fibber McGee and Molly* in 1944, the character Beulah was a chuckling Aunt Jemima handkerchief-head, not all that far removed from a minstrel show, with her introductory

Overleaf, top: Gertrude Berg (*The Goldbergs*); *bottom:* Hattie McDaniel (*Beulah*)

cry, "Somebody bawl fo' Beulah?" After one of McGee's elaborate tantrums, she would shake her head and laugh, "Luh-*uhhve* dat man!" On her own radio show two years later, *Beulah,* she shed her Aunt Tomming and, played by Hattie McDaniel, took on more authority working for a white-bread suburban family, the Hendersons, who were so bleached that it's hard now to recall them.

The original voice of Beulah Brown on *Fibber McGee* was falsetto, supplied by a man named Marlin Hurt, who had been raised by a mammy. On the program called *The Marlin Hurt and Beulah Show,* Hurt doubled as Beulah's ne'er-do-well boyfriend, Bill. When Hurt died at forty, a year after the show began, he was replaced by yet *another* white male, Bob Corley; Hugh Studebaker, also white, briefly played Silly Watson, a black handyman and another *Fibber McGee and Molly* refugee.

When Corley left the show, somebody finally had the inspired idea to hire a black woman to play a black woman—McDaniel, one of several Beulahs over the radio show's seven-year run. Later, the part went to Louise Beavers, and finally to Lillian Randolph. Racial ironies abounded: After Tess Gardella, a white actress, was featured as Queenie, the mammy in the 1927 musical *Show Boat,* she starred in *Aunt Jemima,* a radio show inspired by the pancake-mix icon.

Beulah's best friend, who worked for the family next door, was named Oriole, a birdbrain played by Ruby Dandridge (mother of the actress Dorothy Dandridge), who sounded a lot like Butterfly McQueen; indeed, McQueen later played Oriole on TV to Ethel Waters's Beulah. Like *Amos 'n' Andy, Beulah* was chased off the tube after three seasons by pressure from black organizations.

An even deeper irony and humiliation is that blacks who tried to get into radio were forced to sound "more black" in order to play blacks, to assume a sort of black-speak; one of Beulah's stock phrases was "On the con-positively-trairy!" Maidie Norman, a black actress, was turned down for jobs in radio because she didn't "sound like a Negro." Bizarrely, Lillian Randolph was asked "to tone her [Negro] dialect" to play Beulah and Madame Queen on *Amos 'n' Andy.* Wonderful Smith, the "Negro comedy find of the year in 1941" when he played a cook on Red Skelton's show, was dropped from the show, he says, when he "had difficulty sounding as Negroid as they expected." To work in radio as blacks—the concept of a black playing a nonblack was unheard of—actors were forced to demean themselves and endorse the very stereotyping that kept them from working more. *Beulah* later partially redeemed itself by becoming the first TV show with an integrated cast.

Beulah, a name long identified with black movie maids, ran the house, solved domestic dilemmas, and was treated as a member of the family, a concept well ahead of its time. *Beulah* now seems pure white-America fiction, if well meant and perhaps harmless, although it fostered the illusion of the happy black servant—not that Beulah ever sounded contented. She was a reverse stereotype in the same sense as Jack Benny's Rochester—an uppity servant.

Beulah and Rochester were far less subservient than sarcastic—even superior. A false image, perhaps, but hardly degrading. Rochester, Beulah, and Birdie (the housekeeper on *The Great Gildersleeve*) were all portrayed as respected, hardworking, hardheaded employees full of sage advice for their bumbling white bosses, whom *they* barely tolerated, which was all part of the joke.

In those days, many a middle-class home had a maid, and even a maid's room, so it didn't seem unusual to find the situation duplicated in radio families. Gildersleeve's Birdie dispensed unheeded words of caution. Radio's blacks were listened to and considered "part of the family"—a pleasant myth but, at worst, an unrealized ideal. According to the black cultural historian Mel Watkins, "The show depicted an ideal suburban world in which whites and black *servants* lived in harmonious acceptance of the status quo."

When Hal Kanter wrote for *Beulah,* he recalls, "We got a few letters of complaint from groups, but Beulah was really an inoffensive, benign character. Beulah was not stupid. There were stupid characters on the show, but there were a lot of stupid characters on all-white shows, too." He doesn't remember any conversations with Hattie McDaniel about racial matters. "It just was never an issue in those days."

Sherwood Schwartz, who alternated with Kanter writing the show, says, "We were very, very careful" about inadvertent slurs, "and concerned with the image of blacks. We made sure that no blacks were ever unemployed on the show. Beulah was played honestly. The show was interesting because we focused on the black servants; the white household was kept in the background. At that time the NAACP liked the show, but they didn't like blacks playing servants." One of radio's busiest comic actresses, Mary Jane Croft, played Alice Henderson on *Beulah* for three years opposite McDaniel and McQueen. She recalls no ill feelings among the black actors toward their "place" on radio as servants. "They stayed by themselves, I do remember that, but it was like any show—you just came in and did it."

Going all the way back to Gardenia, a maid on the first soap opera in 1932, *Betty and Bob*, radio had a tradition of black housekeepers— Lillian Randolph's Birdie Coggins on *The Great Gildersleeve*, Ruby Dandridge's Geranium on *The Judy Canova Show*, and of course Butterfly McQueen, with her long résumé of wacky maids, all cousins of her flibbertigibbet character Prissy in *Gone With the Wind*. Countless 1930s movies featured black maids—often knowing and sardonic.

Beulah was watered down when she moved to TV in 1950 and was assumed by Ethel Waters; Dooley Wilson played her boyfriend, Bill Jackson. On TV she scarcely uttered a discouraging word, and the show was drained of its original comic spirit. Waters's Beulah, critics agreed, had lost her sassy tongue and a lot of her, well, color. The show ran until 1954.

WHILE BLACKS WERE THE MOST obvious ethnic minority in radio, there were others who helped create a rather thin rainbow coalition. Among comic ethnics there was J. Carrol Naish's wistful, sweet-spirited Luigi Basko of *Life with Luigi,* which opened and closed with a letter to his "dear-a mama mia" in Italy to the strains of "O, Marie"; the tenement-dwelling Goldbergs; a smattering of blue-collar types on *Duffy's Tavern* and *The Life of Riley;* and lovable hillbillies Lum and Abner and Judy Canova.

Radio, needless to say, had no gay characters and few that could even be classified as closet queers, tagged by the code word of the day, *fey*, but Joe Besser came close. Besser, a vaudeville swish comic who years later became one of the Three Stooges, popped up on various radio shows as a character who spoke in emphatic gay inflections in phrases like, "You ol' crazy, *yooooo!*" "Well, get *him-m-m-m*" and "Not so *fa-a-a-st.*" There were also gay overtones to a character on the Edgar Bergen–Charlie McCarthy show named Ercil Twing (played by Pat Patrick), and distinctly lavender tinges to Joe Penner's trademark

"Oh, you *na-a-a-a-sty* man!" NBC executive Walter Bunker remembers that the Jack Benny show once introduced "a fairy window-dresser," but, says Bunker, "NBC wouldn't go along with it after all the window-dressers threatened not to buy Jell-O."

Undeniably the most beloved ethnic radio show after *Amos 'n' Andy* was *The Goldbergs,* a creation of writer-actress Gertrude Berg, whose Molly Goldberg first became an icon of American-Jewish motherhood, then a cliché, and finally an object of derision in books like *Portnoy's Complaint* and *A Mother's Kisses.* Molly, inspired by Berg's mother and grandmother from New York's Lower East Side, opened with her yoo-hooing out a window in Apartment 3-B at 1030 East Tremont Avenue in the Bronx, to wit: "Yoo-hoo! Mrs. Bloom! Is Mickey home? Yes? Tell him he should go vid Sammy, yes?" *The Rise of the Goldbergs,* as it was first called, was about cultural assimilation and the desire to make it in America. It was a new kind of program—a radio "mixed marriage" that wedded the soap opera to the situation comedy, creating the first "dramedy."

In Berg's original script (she wrote her early shows in longhand in the main reading room of the 42nd Street Library—to get away from her family), Molly's husband, Jake, a dress-cutter, goes into business for himself but needs money to rent a loft. Guess who comes through? Molly—a jollier, Jewish version of the gentle, firm, wise Norwegian mother in *I Remember Mama* on stage, screen, and TV (yet never radio, oddly)—came up with money she had salted away in a teapot for a rainy day. Typical for *The Goldbergs,* the premiere episode imparted a life lesson, along with laughter and tears—a classic sitcom formula revisited in 1970s and 1980s TV, where Bea Arthur's Maude was sort of a hip Molly.

Molly Goldberg was a bridge between generations. While she still spoke with an inflection and respected her parents' ways, she had modern ideas and an American sensibility and, to be sure, two American-born kids. What gave the show its humor, appeal, and tension was the pull between old and new, tradition and change. The same concept would spice ethnic generational TV sitcoms—from the 1970s *All in the Family, Sanford and Son,* and *Chico and the Man* to the 1980s *The Cosby Show* and, deep into the 1990s, Margaret Cho's *All-American Girl.* In Cho's show, a hip young fad-crazed Korean-American woman was at odds with a conservative family with ancient Asian values—it was *The Goldbergs* with egg rolls in lieu of matzo balls.

The clash between old and new was more poignantly felt on *The Goldbergs,* however, because in the 1940s memories of repressive European regimes cast a shadow on American life. Consider how Molly meekly but overpolitely asks a mounted policeman directions in Central Park: "Mr. Policeman, officer of the law, Your Honor, could you be so kindly if you would to inform me of the location of where is Fourteenth Street?" Berg noted in her memoirs, "Molly's reaction is the relief of many immigrants at not only having found their way but also of not being arrested for asking a simple question."

While still a teenager, Gertrude Berg began writing playlets to keep guests' children busy at a family-owned upstate New York Jewish resort hotel called Fleischmann's, where she was in charge of the books and the entertainment. The kiddie shows grew into sketches to amuse the parents, and a favorite skit was a bit built around a character named Maltke Talnitzky—a more Orthodox Molly Goldberg—and her no-goodnik husband and sympathetic neighbor. She was a character invented by Berg at fourteen to amuse a meeting of lawyers at the hotel.

In her memoir, *Molly and Me,* Berg explained the rise of Molly Goldberg: "Gradually Maltke began to turn into a woman from an extreme caricature. She became more human when I gave her a new husband, one who wasn't so much trouble and who was a little more helpful. I made her younger, about thirty-five or forty, and I gave her two children, a boy and a girl more than a little like my own two. Her name changed too, Maltke became Molly. And Talnitzky was no longer suitable. It was too much, it was trying too hard. I changed the name to Goldberg because it sounded right. After a while Molly Goldberg began to sound euphonious and so I kept it."

The first scripts, dealing with generational conflict between European-born parents and their Americanized kids (the stuff of much Yiddish theater of the time), efficiently established the pattern of the program, but the dialogue was more heavily Yiddish than in later scripts, to make Molly and Jake sound like immigrants: Molly: "Vat's de matter, so late, Sammy? Let me look on your hands? Playing marbles, ha? A marble shooter you're gonna be? A beautiful business for a Jewish boy!" At times it was almost impenetrable: "You t'rowing in my face vat your brudder Joe helped out vid a copple notes?" Pains-takingly, she wrote every line in dialect.

Berg sent a script to a man her husband knew, Herman Bernie, the agent brother of radio bandleader Ben Bernie, who gave it to the manager of a New York station. The agent offered her a job writing commercials, which emboldened Berg to try a full-length script. The local station liked her proposal and a few weeks later she had her own show, costarring herself. After its first season at CBS the network canceled it, but NBC liked the show enough to put it on the air unsponsored.

Molly herself was a lovely *tsimmis* (stew) into which Berg mixed her mother, grandmother, and hotel guests, from whom she stole some of their Yiddish malapropisms—"Mollyprops" they were called—that gave the show its unique comic flavor: "Enter, whoever"; "If it's nobody I'll call back"; "Come will and come may, I must face it"; "Give me a swallow the glass"; "It's late, Jake, and time to expire"; "We're at the crossroads and the parting of the ways." And always, her imploring, "Tell me, Jake—is it bad?" She referred to some neighbors in her building not by their names but by their apartment numbers ("Mrs. 5-C") or their location ("Mrs. Herman Across the Hall").

Berg wrote all the scripts herself, rising at 5 A.M., taking a break to fix breakfast for her family, finishing by noon, and then going into the studio to rehearse at five in the afternoon for the daily show. To relax, she would walk the streets and watch people, which, Berg said, gave her story ideas; a voice she overheard might suggest a character or plot.

Arnold Stang, who played a neighbor on the show named Seymour Fingerhood, remembers Berg as "a very bright sophisticated woman who got this great cast together because she knew a lot of Broadway actors and people from the Group Theater. She was a very shrewd woman who ran the show with an iron fist, very tyrannical in many ways, but she showed affection and had marvelous judgment. I learned more from her than from any other director." On the other hand, producer Himan Brown, the original Jake, was no fan of Gertrude Berg's. "Berg was only out for Berg," he said many years later, claiming she was the hard-nosed antithesis of her soft-hearted radio character.

The Goldbergs wasn't full of riotous banter, but was rich in comforting and amusing small talk, performed in the comical/quizzical singsong rhythms of New York Jewish family life in the 1930s—light-years away from *The Adventures of Ozzie and Harriet,* yet each was as true to its world as the other. Berg was praised for being less stereotyped than the standard Jewish mama of the mournful, hand-wringing kind found in *The Jazz Singer.* Season by season, she eased up on the Yiddishisms and indulged in fewer "*Oy vey!*"s.

The show changed with the times, and the Goldbergs eventually left the city. By 1945, the show was set in suburbia and Jake was running for the city council against a shady politician with a Southern accent. In the 1950s, episodes revolved around the Girl Scouts and beauty parlors, and fewer programs dealt with the family's economic woes. "The [nightly] radio show had developed into a comedy out of an afternoon tragedy," said Berg. By the 1950s, dialect humor and immigrant travails had become a stale joke to middle-class suburban viewers. *The Goldbergs* lost its first sponsor, but after Palmolive revived the show, it remained a fixture for ten years, drawing fans from across all ethnic lines; it went on tour and, during its height, performed five shows a day at the Steel Pier in Atlantic City, the pinnacle of showbiz success.

The TV version ran four seasons, from 1949 to 1953, despite initial fears that it wouldn't "translate." Although it made less of an impact on TV, the show coasted on its vast carryover radio popularity and worked as well on camera as it had at a microphone, maybe because it was essentially a dramatic, not a comedy, show, and didn't depend on gags and wild situations. Berg tried to maintain the comic flavor and play down its "soap opera" elements.

As with *Amos 'n' Andy, seeing* an ethnic family was infinitely more vivid—i.e., risky—than hearing one, and there was much worry about how a Jewish family would play on TV. Radio had been filled with Jewish types when the Goldbergs arrived, but no Jews had as yet integrated TV's new fifties' lily-white comedy neighborhood. When program executives seemed reluctant to book the show on television, Berg made a personal appeal to the head of CBS, William Paley, who was Jewish, and Paley gave it his blessing.

The TV show's demise was hastened by Commie hunters in the 1950s, who went after the show's Jake, Philip Loeb. Loeb's sin was supporting the End Jim Crow in Baseball Committee. General Motors finally dropped the show after offering Loeb $85,000 to leave, which he refused. Berg, ostensibly for the show's good, let him go and, protesting his innocence, paid his salary for two years, but Loeb rarely worked afterward. Five years later he jumped out of a window, an incident that was dramatized in the film *The Front,* with Zero Mostel in the role of the beleaguered Loeb.

The Goldbergs eventually became a play, *Molly and Me,* and even a movie (*Mrs. G Goes to College*), but the radio show finally bowed to the inevitable in 1950, after a brief revival. Much of what radio had been, its heart and spirit, was *The Goldbergs.*

AMONG NON-WASP SITUATION COMEDIES, *The Life of Riley* has a unique niche. It wasn't particularly inspired, but it had an original concept: a blue-collar family comedy. The show debuted in 1944 and lucked into an endearing star in William Bendix, a movie character actor who was perfectly cast as Chester A. Riley, a gentle lug. "He's for the little guy," as Bendix once put it.

Riley was a simple dese-dems-dose mug, not overly bright and easily ruffled but well-meaning, whose family was forever picking on him and then rescuing him from one of his endless "revoltin' developments." Riley was a clown with heart, but without a guy like Bendix to play him, it's doubtful the program would have lasted. The scripts were often as assembly-line as its factory-worker hero—enjoyable if predictable—but Bendix gave everything a sweaty, grimy-overalls reality, reflecting America's working-class shift from city to suburb, where the Rileys lived.

Irving Brecher had originally conceived the show as *The Flotsam Family,* starring Groucho Marx, of all miscast people; it didn't survive beyond the pilot show. Not long afterward, Brecher saw Bendix in a short film and realized he'd found his Riley. "He was a Brooklyn guy and there was something about him. I thought, This guy could play it. He'd made a few films, like *Lifeboat,* but he was not a name. So I took *The Flotsam Family* script, revised it, made it a Brooklyn family, took out the flippancies and made it more meat-and-potatoes, and thought of a new title, *The Life of Riley.* Bendix's delivery and the spin he put on his lines made it work." It's hard to imagine anybody else, with the exception of Jimmy Durante, uttering Riley's famous catchphrase, "What a revoltin' development *dis* is!" "The character was dumb but vulnerable and sweet. If you're dealing with William Bendix, what else could he be?"

Brecher claims that *The Life of Riley*—which ran from 1944 to 1949—was "the first true situation comedy"—as opposed to *The Aldrich Family,* generally regarded as the first. The Rileys weren't as WASPy as the Aldriches. They were Irish but, like Fibber McGee and Molly, may as well have been Unitarians. "We didn't ever accent the Irish thing," Brecher said. "Riley never went to church or anything like that." It was a case of the title wagging the show.

Riley was canceled after one season but was saved from going off the air by Brecher's creation of Digger O'Dell, "the friendly under-taker." "We needed something to fill about ninety seconds of a show in which Riley was in terminal trouble. I thought, we need someone to come through the door that would scare the shit out of him. I thought an undertaker would do it, then I thought of an Irish name, O'Dell, and Digby somehow came to me."

He told John Brown, who played Digger (along with a slew of other radio characters, including Thorny on *The Adventures of Ozzie and Harriet* and Al on *My Friend Irma*), "I want a very sepulchral voice, quavering, morbid, and he got it right away." Too well, almost. Execu-tives at the Meat Institute, the show's sponsor, thought the character was overly morbid. "A guy named Frank Ferrin at Leo Burnett told me, 'Those pricks in Chicago want it taken out.' I asked him what should we do and he said, 'Fuck 'em!' " As Brecher tells it, the show got hun-dreds of letters from people who loved the character. "The older people told me that Digger took the sting out of death." Listeners waited in glee for the weekly visit of Digger O'Dell and his grave-rattling routine ("It is I, Diiiig-bee O'Dell . . . ah, good morning, Riley. You're looking fine . . ." (ominous chortle) ". . . veddy natural"). It seemed funny even if you were too young to have ever been to a funeral or heard oily undertakers and open-casket clichés.

Riley almost didn't make the transition to TV. A young comic on the rise named Jackie Gleason played Riley in its first video season in 1950; Bendix couldn't get out of a movie contract—a real revoltin' develop-ment for Brecher—and the show nearly wasn't renewed because Bendix felt TV was a fad and wasn't eager to try it. Gleason may have been too brash, too like his Ralph Kramden bully of a decade later on *The Hon-eymooners,* not the blustering softie created by, and personified by, Ben-dix on radio. Gleason's Ralph Kramden was a more complex, rowdier, meaner, fatter, and funnier Chester A. Riley. The televised *Riley* with Jackie Gleason lasted twenty-six weeks, after which Bendix agreed to try TV, but Brecher dropped out when the network wouldn't guaran-tee more than six weeks; so he licensed it to NBC for five years for $600,000.

Brecher wasn't fond of either Riley. Bendix, he says, was not that dissimilar from the Riley character. "He wasn't easy to do business with, because he was suspicious that he was being cheated. He wasn't very bright. Sometimes he'd miss the whole point of something. He'd go to the ball park and everyone would shout, 'Hello, Riley!,' which he hated. His manager came to me not long after that and said he wanted the name of the show changed to *The William Bendix Show.* I said, 'That's not a bad idea. Then when he dies or quits all we have to do is find another guy named William Bendix.' He was affable enough to work with—punctual, and he did his work well—but in a way he was a schmuck."

Brecher elaborates: "In those days, if a product was mentioned on a show, the manufacturer would send me over a sample. Once, we men-tioned Longines watches and they sent me two, so I gave one to Bill. Later, we happened to mention Chevrolet and they gave me a Chevy. So Bendix's manager calls me up and says that Bill wanted to know when he was getting *his* Chevrolet. I said, 'I'm running out of Chevrolets, but I'll send him over a couple of fenders. A schmuck!' "

DUFFY'S TAVERN WAS REALLY "a state of mind," in the apt descrip-tion of broadcast historian John Dunning. Indeed, the show deftly cre-ated the appealingly seedy atmosphere of a real New York dive, with references to pig's knuckles, ale, and "ersters"; you could visualize the sawdust on the floor, the fan spinning slowly overhead, and the faded boxing photos on grease-stained walls.

Unlike the respectable Rileys, the characters in *Duffy's Tavern,* a New York–based blue-collar show, were hangers-on at a Third Avenue bar and grill ineptly run by another dese-dems-and-dose guy named

Archie, played by the show's creator, head writer, and producer, Ed Gardner. Gardner, a character in his own right, who, in a squinty, side-of-the-mouth style, spoke lines like, "Leave me not forget me hospitality."

The tavern itself was a funky dive where the owner never appeared—the show's long-running gag. Each week, Archie began the show by answering the phone and, in a bored monotone, drawling, *"Hello Duffy's Tavern where de elite meet to eat Archie de manager speakin' Duffy ain't here . . . oh, hello, Duffy."* When the absentee Duffy checked in each week with his hassled manager, Archie unreeled the latest problem to befall the hapless saloon, perpetually on the brink of bankruptcy, and to tell Duffy (i.e., us) who the show's guest would be.

A former saloon pianist, transient writer, radio director, and adman, Gardner (a non-Irishman, born Friedrich Poggenberg in, yes, Astoria, Queens) cast himself in the lead role when he couldn't find a suitable actor, or so legend has it. Gardner had been the producer of a CBS show called *This Is New York,* hosted by the composer and music critic Deems Taylor. On that show, Gardner had also played a guy called Archie, who pestered the highbrow Taylor and his truly elite guests.

Duffy's Tavern was clearly an Irish pub, but just as on *The Life of Riley,* there wasn't much particularly Irish about the habitués apart from their names (Miss Duffy, Finnegan, Clancy). The common bond was not their church or their forebears so much as it was their working-class status. These were people whose New York accents defined them as surely as Eliza Doolittle's cockney.

When the show debuted in 1941, Gardner was married to Shirley Booth, who created the role of Duffy's wisecracking, man-hunting daughter, Miss Duffy. When the pair divorced two years later, Booth must have won partial custody of the character, whom she renamed Dottie Mahoney and took with her to other shows.

Abe Burrows, who helped create the series, said of Booth: "Shirley was an amazing Miss Duffy. Here was an elegant actress who came from Hartford doing the best New York accent I have ever heard. If you aren't born in New York, it's very hard to fake this sound. Through the years I auditioned people for *Duffy's Tavern.* They would often step up and say they were New Yorkers, but after two minutes I'd know they were faking it. Shirley Booth's ear was perfect." Florence Halop, sister of "Dead End Kid" Billy Halop, replaced Booth, the first of many later Miss Duffys.

Other Tavern regulars included Finnegan (Charlie Cantor), a retard who began every sentence with "Duh . . ." and whose weekly greeting was, "Duhhh-*yuhhh*-hiyuh, Arch"; Eddie, a loyal black waiter; a house pianist named Fats; and an Irish cop called, of course, Clancy. (The dopey Clifton Finnegan character was supposedly an inside-radio dig at *Information Please*'s intellectual host Clifton Fadiman, with whom Gardner was said to be feuding.)

Although *Duffy's Tavern* was hardly a groundbreaking show, it won a Peabody Award for its treatment of a black character, Eddie the waiter (played by Eddie Green), the only continuing male black character in a radio comedy at the time other than Rochester. Eddie was a far more deferential character than Rochester, but he didn't play as big a role in the show, and he was the only character who called Archie "Mister Archie."

Guests would pop by to shoot the breeze at Duffy's, a joint known for its bad food, nonservice, and fly-specked ambience, all nicely indicated by Gardner's mangled syntax, Miss Duffy's Brooklynese, and the theme song, "When Irish Eyes Are Smiling," heard tinkling over the opening on a player piano. A knock-off version was later attempted on TV when Carroll O'Connor left *All in the Family* to open "Archie's Place," but it didn't last long. The original Archie's place finally closed in 1951, after twelve years, and on one of the last shows a bitter Gardner got in several good shots at TV, radio, NBC, and sponsors.

Abe Burrows returned to *Duffy's Tavern* as a guest five years after he began writing it as a Gardner protégé. Burrows, who went from radio to Broadway and, legendarily, the musical *Guys and Dolls,* owed much of his success to Gardner. Burrows traced his skill at writing the *Guys and Dolls* street characters to his days on *Duffy's Tavern,* populated by Damon Runyon types. "The people on that show were New York mugs, nice mugs, sweet mugs, and like Runyon's mugs they all talked like Ladies and Gentlemen. That's how we treated the characters in *Guys and Dolls.*"

Gardner took pride in Burrows's success on Broadway and became the godfather of Burrows's son James, who thirty years later helped to open TV's most famous tavern on *Cheers,* a yuppified 1980s *Duffy's.*

Lou Grant, a writer on the show, claims it's no coincidence that *Cheers* reminded radiophiles of *Duffy's Tavern*. "Think about it," Grant postulates. "Sam, the ladies' man, was like Archie, who was always chasing women. Diane and Rebecca were Miss Duffy, who was always looking for a man, and the token dope, Coach, and then Woody, was like Finnegan."

"Ed was a crazy man," Grant says of Gardner. "He'd change writers like he changed clothes, and he was always looking for a premise." After Grant sent him a story line, "He told me, 'I'll hire you for two weeks.' He'd hire anyone for two weeks—a guy parking cars, you name it—if they could come up with a good premise for the show. He used a lot of jokes from two brothers who ran a pharmacy, in exchange for Benzedrine." One ex-writer said it wasn't unusual to walk in and find Gardner had hired his interior decorator, a trumpet player, or some guy he'd met in a bar who had cracked a joke he liked. "We can use you on the show," he'd tell virtual strangers he thought amusing. "He'd hire anybody for fifty dollars," adds Bob Schiller, Grant's writing partner on the series. Gardner's barber at the House of Rothschild fed him lines supplied by his prolific teenage son, a prospective comedy writer. The lines were so good that Gardner finally hired the boy, a seventeen-year-old at Fairfax High School named Larry Gelbart, who went on to write *M*A*S*H, City of Angels,* and *Tootsie.*

Hazel Shermet, the last Miss Duffy, got on fine with Gardner. "He was caustic and a perfectionist but fun to work with," she says. "I thought I'd do the show two weeks but ended up lasting two years. Nobody did Miss Duffy like Shirley Booth, but I did it with a higher voice." Rehearsals were few, leaving the cast tense by airtime. "We didn't read it through more than twice, if that," Shermet recalls. "For me it was a breeze. Ed was always happy with me, so I'd just do a rehearsal and go off shopping." "

Gardner also used her as a hostess to entertain guests who flew to Puerto Rico to do the show during its final three seasons, Gardner's ploy to avoid paying U.S. taxes. "He'd call you at all hours. Once he called me at 11 P.M. and said, 'Ray Milland wants to go swimming with you. It's part of your job.' " She said good night and went back to sleep.

Larry Rhine, who later wrote for the show's disastrous TV version, remembers Gardner's inability to adapt to television. "It went right down the toilet. He couldn't act and he wouldn't learn camera. The show was shot at the Hal Roach studios, where Roach would tell Gardner, 'These are moving pictures, Ed. You gotta move,' but Ed would sit on his stool and say, 'Just give me my jokes, like George Burns.' Ed thought he could do TV, so he left radio, but he was a bad actor and knew it."

For all the anxiety that went with being a radio comedy writer, it also granted one membership in a very small, close-knit club. Bob Schiller estimates there were no more than 150 full-time gag writers in America during the mid-1940s; good writers could write for any comedian. Rhine, whose career spans Ben Bernie and Phil Baker of *Take It or Leave It* ("I wrote all his ad libs") to *All in the Family* and *The Brady Bunch,* says, "You learned the rhythm, the style. I could write thirty minutes for Jackie Mason right now. You just write through their sound." Rhine tells a famous comedy-writer's story about the time George Burns, who produced TV's *Mr. Ed,* objected to a joke and told a writer, "The horse wouldn't say that." Rhine: "And you know what? We had to admit he was right."

Schiller adds, "We were all enormously competitive. We'd always count how many jokes we got on the air each week. The next week you'd walk down the street and people in the business would tell you what they liked on the show—or didn't like." It was quite a cachet to be working on *Duffy's Tavern,* which Schiller said was thought of as a quality program. "It was good, it was bright, and it had both high- and lowbrow appeal. It was like *Information Please*—the intellectuals loved it, and for guest stars it was like going on the Larry King show—if you got on *Duffy's Tavern,* you were validated as a celebrity."

In 1943, the sponsor, Schick, insisted that the show, despite its well-defined midtown Manhattan flavor, move to California. Although the scripts were heavily one-liner-laden, the charmingly cheesy characters gave the show a defined New York City tang. Despite its eventual huge success on radio, the show didn't find a sponsor for a long time. The agencies, Abe Burrows wrote, thought it "too New Yorkish, too sophisticated. We heard all the old bromides: 'How will it go with people in Kansas City?' 'The rest of the country doesn't care about New York.' " Maybe not, but they cared about what happened at *Duffy's Tavern.*

AMONG ALL THE URBAN middle-class radio comedies, the backwoods humor of *Lum and Abner* struck a certain rustic comic nerve in America. The two Ozark characters were droll, well drawn, and understated. Their comedy had a tranquil simplicity, unlike the rowdy humor of programs like *The Judy Canova Show*, a *Beverly Hillbillies* precursor with Canova migrating to the city after growing up in Cactus Junction; the rube wit of Bob Burns's *Arkansas Traveler;* or the corn-pone comedy of *Grand Ole Opry*.

Chester Lauck and Norris Goff, Arkansas natives, wrote and played not just the title characters of Lum Edwards, the level-headed partner, and Abner Peabody, the hotheaded, eccentric half of the team, but all the other male characters in the town of Pine Ridge, Arkansas—Squire Skimp, Grandpappy Spears, Cedric Wehunt. On the show, which ran, remarkably, from 1930 to 1953, Lum and Abner were partners in a sleepy general store called the Jot 'Em Down Store, where absolutely nothing happened, yet you could all but see the glow from a potbelly stove and a horsefly crawling across a sack of feed. At the Jot 'Em Down Store, time moved in slow motion. This air of lassitude was part of the humor, most of which dealt with the owners' cracker-barrel ruminations; Lauck and Goff could squeeze a half-hour show out of a busted pencil.

For the first nine years, Goff and Lauck wrote every word themselves; finally, Roswell Rogers came in to help while the boys made a film. Rogers would rise early, write each day's script in the morning, and then race from the San Fernando Valley to NBC. Like *Amos 'n' Andy* and many other shows, it lost its slow-paced charm when it went from fifteen minutes a day to a weekly thirty-minute program with an audience. Rogers once said, "I was against it but Chet wanted to do it. I thought the characters would change." He was right: The show left the air after a year. As a serial, "a story would take two or three months to tell," Rogers said, but a self-contained half-hour forced him to devise a new comic plot each week, taxing his inventive resources.

It's hard to recall a single plot, gag, gimmick, or subsidiary character on the show, for Lum and Abner's charm was largely in their folksy byplay, wry wit, and backwoods expressions ("By dogies!"), the sort of homespun humor that later captivated visitors to Mayberry RFD, on TV's *Andy Griffith Show;* Sheriff Andy, Barney, Gomer, Aunt Bea, and Opie would have fit right into life in Pine Ridge. The little unprepossessing show assumed such mythic stature in the South that the town of Waters, Arkansas, proudly changed its name to Pine Ridge in 1936, more evidence of radio's power not only to enchant listeners but to enter their lives.

THE JEWS HAD MOLLY GOLDBERG, the Irish had Duffy and Chester A. Riley and Fibber McGee and Molly, the blacks had Amos and Andy and Beulah, the South had Lum and Abner—and the Italians had Luigi, one of the last immigrants on radio's showboat. *Life with Luigi* pulled into homes in 1948, at a time when ethnic humor had all but disappeared from the air.

The show, originated and directed by Cy Howard (creator of *My Friend Irma*) and starring the character actor J. Carrol Naish (who was actually Irish—Joseph Patrick Carrol Naish), was about a gentle little Italian, Luigi Basko. Luigi ran an antiques store in Chicago's Little Italy next door to a restaurant, the "Spaghetti Palace," owned by Pasquale, Luigi's noisy countryman whose sole purpose in life was to marry off his fat, giggling 250-pound daughter Rosa to Luigi. The only real problem Luigi found in his adopted land was the loutish Pasquale, played by Alan Reed, aka Teddy Bergman, radio's man of a thousand voices.

At the top of each show, Luigi would begin a letter home to his "mama mia," describing his latest American adventure in loving tones full of tender feelings about his new country, where every ethnic slight had a silver lining and a patriotic moral; nobody ever called Luigi "wop" or "dago," and he never had any run-ins with the mob. All misunderstandings were gently worked out, and the worst Luigi ever had to say about America is "Wotta country!"—the same phrase of wonder and amused disbelief uttered forty years later by Russian stand-up comic Vladimir Smirnoff in his takes on America's funny customs.

The show celebrated nationalistic pride and the immigrant experience as related by a grateful and patriotic European—just the message that postwar America wanted to hear. The culture clash was muted in mixups among Luigi, Pasquale, and Jimmy, Pasquale's young clerk, a native Chicagoan who explained peculiar American folkways to the bewildered but willing Luigi. When he attends an English-language class—like the one in Leo Rosten's *The Education of H*Y*M*A*N K*A*P*L*A*N,* of which *Life with Luigi* is a kissing cousin—the teacher, Miss Spalding, asks him who invented the light bulb. Luigi replies, "Marconi." When Miss Spalding objects, Luigi claims, "Marconi invent-a everything!" "Thomas Edison invented the light bulb," replies Miss Spalding politely, but Luigi is unfazed: "Well-a then, Marconi invent-a Edison."

Luigi, although Italian to the core, is fiercely American. On the show's premiere broadcast, he discovers a statue of George Washington in his shop but refuses to sell it to a woman from the "Americana Society," who wants it for a charity auction. Luigi, who already owns nineteen statues of Lincoln, talks to the bust of Washington: "You a-fine man, you a-rich man. You-a give up plan-a-tation when people ask-a you to become their presidente. Now I wrap you up warm so you don't-a freeze like at-a Valley Forge." Like *The Goldbergs* and, less obviously, *Amos 'n' Andy, Life with Luigi* was also a weekly civics lesson. When he clings to his statue of Washington, the lady from the Americana Society tells him, "Mr. Luigi, patriotism isn't measured by statues. It's something we feel." Reluctantly, Luigi sells the Washington statue to the Society's representative, but then tries to buy it back. "Why, Mr. Luigi?" the lady asks him. "You-a used to him," he says. "Maybe you not know what is a-like to have-a George Washington in your house." He goes to the auction but is outbid by the bank, which pays a thousand dollars for the statue—and then returns it to Luigi, who stammers, "This-a is impossible!" The lady from the charity says quietly, "In America, Mr. Basko, *every*thing is possible."

— 13 —
We'll Be Right Back
after These Words

RADIO COINCIDED WITH—INDEED, WAS LARGELY responsible for—the rise of advertising in America, and while there was cynical talk of "hucksterism," few minded the advertising that brought Americans their favorite radio shows for free. In many cases, the commercials became identified not just with shows but with specific announcers, who became longtime product spokesmen. In the case of kids' shows, the link was forged even more strongly through rings, badges, belt buckles, and other "valuable" premiums.

Advertising agencies created and produced programs, hiring the talent and staff and assuming total responsibility for what went over the air, the better to control its content. The networks simply found it too expensive to produce shows, which created a vacuum the ad agencies happily filled.

Even more than through magazines and billboards, it was via radio that advertisers burrowed their way into the American psyche. On network radio, the directors, writers, and cast members auditioned for ad men, not producers. Not only that; many early stations were themselves owned by companies as promotional outlets. In the words of one aghast critic, it was as if "the editor of a newspaper had to farm out the writing of the news, page by page, to the corporations whose advertisements appeared on those pages." Shows that went unsponsored were carried by the networks. The euphemism for unsponsored was *sustaining*—often the more prestigious fare presumably above the commercial fray, such as forums, workshops, and newscasts.

In 1922—when radio-set ownership had increased in one year from about 50,000 receivers to something like 800,000—WEAF in New York City devised an ingenious and rather radical concept whereby each station would subsidize itself by selling advertising for specific shows. It was called "toll radio" and soon became the normal way of

Overleaf, clockwise from top left: Don Ameche, Harold W. Arlin, Ed Herlihy, Ken Carpenter and Don Wilson doing business in the infant industry. General Sarnoff begrudgingly went along with the idea of toll radio—advertising booths along the unpaved information superhighway of the 1920s—if only as a way to keep government off NBC's back.

Presto!—instant sponsor identification: *The Palmolive Hour, The Wrigley Revue, The Eveready Hour,* not to mention groups that became singing advertisements: the Ipana Troubadours, the Goodrich Zippers, the Clicquot Club Eskimos, the Champion Sparklers, the Gold Dust Twins, the Vick's Vaporub Quartette, and a Smith Brothers act called Trade and Mark. By comparison, today's athletes sporting brand-name tennis shoes and headbands seem the height of good taste. Imagine singers now calling themselves the Snapple Rolling Stones or Levi's Sex Pistols.

In the early days of radio, big business was leery of advertising on a medium where people couldn't *see* the product. It was then an article of faith that nobody would buy a car—indeed, anything—sold over the air. Yet when gossip columnist Louella Parsons was sponsored by Campbell's Soup, she personally plugged the cream of tomato soup one night and (advertising legend has it) caused such a run on the stores the next day that Campbell's ran out. It wasn't long after this that sponsors began to wield their power over broadcasts, also anxiously combing scripts for detrimental references, real and imagined.

Mel Blanc remembered that when he was performing on three shows with three different cigarette sponsors, he had to be sure to smoke the correct brand for each job—Lucky Strike for the Jack Benny show, Chesterfield for Bing Crosby, and Camels for Abbott and Costello. It wasn't out of loyalty or tact; it was required. "Absurd, isn't it?" he recalled. "Especially since this was radio; who could tell which brand you were smoking? But the companies were so insistent that actors complied with inspectors, who carried out their duties with Gestapo-like zeal," said Blanc, who was once stopped by a cigarette cop for puffing Pall Malls on a Lucky Strike show, even though both brands were made by the same company. Mary Livingstone had it written into her contract that she could smoke Parliaments rather than Lucky Strikes. Programs sponsored by Luckies insisted on using the word *lucky* in lieu of *fortunate.* One actor on a Philip Morris show was forced to stuff his Lucky Strikes into a Philip Morris box.

Commercials were not only fondly ingrained in the national psyche but often were neatly and cleverly folded into the body of the show, most famously on *The Jack Benny Program* when Don Wilson would pester Benny to let him tell the audience about the glories of Lucky Strikes, followed by a jingle sung by the Sportsmen Quartet, all of which Benny barely tolerated, shooing Wilson away. It made you feel better about Lucky Strikes, and, more important, it made you listen closer—and perhaps one day light up a Lucky. Sponsors were better sports then, and endured kidding by Benny, Fred Allen, Henry Morgan, Arthur Godfrey, and others. Perhaps they also just liked being in on the fun, a guest at the party, not the bullying intruders they seem today. On *Fibber McGee and Molly,* announcer Harlow Wilcox would expound so exuberantly on the glories of Johnson's Glo-Coat that McGee took to addressing him as "Waxy."

Your (Lucky Strike) Hit Parade was a textbook example of a program's product tie-in that made everyone harbor warm thoughts about Lucky, especially when the company launched its patriotic World War II battle cry, "Lucky Strike Green has gone to war!" In fact, the slogan was a shrewd device that allowed the company to dump a new green Lucky Strike wrapper that American Tobacco Company tycoon George Washington Hill hated, a classic case of making lemonade from a lemon. It took years for advertising to woo magnates like Hill, who, when he finally came aboard, became one of radio's major boosters. He believed in personal salesmanship, and finally realized that radio was the way to get his cigarette sales force's foot in America's door. He even sent packs of Lucky Strikes to radio stars, and filmed short sales films with Jack Benny and his cast for use in the field.

Hill, a flamboyant character who wore a sombrero festooned with fishhooks (and on whom the novel and film *The Hucksters* were based), also devised a way to sell more cigarettes to women by claiming that smoking was a great weight-loss program, via the slogan, "Reach for a Lucky instead of a sweet!" Radio's other marketing genius was Albert Lasker—who dreamed up the miracle Pepsodent ingredient "irium" (*"Sweet Miriam, sweet Miriam, now she's using irium . . ."*), which was touted in commercials as a newly discovered chemical element. "I invented irium," Lasker liked to say. "Tell me what it is!"

Another of radio's mystery minerals was "solium—the *sunshine* ingredient," which made clothes "whiter than white" when washed with Rinso.

Radio commercials never seemed quite the noisy pests they are today—ingratiating allies of the show they sponsored rather than raucous interruptions to be zapped into silence. Until vintage radio's last years, shows had a single sponsor and listeners tolerated commercials, but sponsors seemed less strident then, and some even had a sense of humor about themselves. The lasting benefit to Madison Avenue was intense product loyalty. Certain stars became identified with their commercials, and often remained faithful for decades.

If you could plumb the psyche of anybody over fifty-five, it would be a safe wager that Wheaties still benefits by its ancient connections to Jack Armstrong, just as Bob Hope equals Pepsodent, Johnson's Wax profits subliminally from its fond links to Fibber McGee and Molly, you can't drink a cup of Maxwell House without thinking Burns and Allen, and Ovaltine still means Little Orphan Annie. For years you couldn't think of Ma Perkins without conjuring up Oxydol (the intro made sure by referring to "Oxydol's *own* Ma Perkins"). Ozzie and Harriet were forever joined at the hip with "International 1847 Rogers Brothers silverware" (their address was even 1847 Rogers Road). *The Aldrich Family* was embedded forever in memory with Jell-O's "six delicious flavors." The Abbott and Costello show opened with, "C for Comedy, A for Abbott, M for Maxwell, E for [bandleader Skinnay] Ennis, and L for Lou Costello. Put them all together, they spell Camel!" Many mid-fifty and over listeners still can't pass a display of Wheat Chex without hearing Tom Mix warbling the jaunty Ralston theme. Each product had a built-in celebrity endorsement.

Most of the big shows were named after their sponsors, not their stars, which changed when newspapers balked at providing free advertising in radio logs for *The Chase and Sanborn Hour with Edgar Bergen and Charlie McCarthy, The Kraft Music Hall with Bing Crosby,* and *The Pabst Blue Ribbon Show with Eddie Cantor.* Likewise, it was *Philip Morris Playhouse, The Fitch Bandwagon, The Pepsodent Show Starring Bob Hope, The Texaco Star Theater, The Tom Mix Ralston Straightshooters,* and *Lux Radio Theatre.*

Like those raised on TV, radio babies still can sing jingles they heard half a century ago. A sponsor's image then was dependent largely on the programs it supported, and one measure of the power of those ancient tie-ins is that half a century later, the radio generation has vaguely pleasant feelings toward Sal Hepatica ("for the smile of health") and Ipana ("for the smile of beauty") and Alka-Seltzer and Anacin ("with a combination of medically proven active ingredients"). Few listeners were ever quite sure what an "analgesic" was, but everyone knew it cured "pains of neuritis and neuralgia"—whatever *they* were, something only old people need worry about. Those who came of age with radio hold warm spots in their heart for Ironized Yeast, Sloane's Liniment, Peet's, Bisodol, Feen-a-mint, Wildroot Cream-Oil, Jergens Lotion, Haley's M-O, Camay, Dreft, Drene, Duz, Doan's Pills, Serutan, Dr. Lyon's Tooth Paste and Tooth Powder, and Vitalis.

Likewise, nearly every radio baby can still sing or whistle the peppy Rinso White tune and, like Johnny, the grinning bellhop, bellow: "Call-l-l-l for-r-r-r Philip Mor-r-r-*reees*!" Products of that period even provided punch lines—many jokes involved Air-Wick, Sen-Sen, Metrecal, Burma Shave, Ex-Lax, and Carter's Little Liver Pills.

The words to dozens of radio jingles still tinkle merrily in the brain as clearly and indelibly as old pop tunes—indeed, someone once called them radio's own folk songs: "Super Suds, Super Suds/Lots more suds with Super Suh-*uh*-uhds!" . . . "Halo, everybody, Halo!/Halo is the shampoo that glorifies your hair/So Halo shampoo, Halo!" . . . "Roy-*al-l-l-l* Pudding! Rich, rich, rich with flavor/Smooth, smooth, smooth as silk/More food energy than sweet fresh milk!" . . . "Be happy—Go Lucky! Be happy—go Lucky Strike today!" . . . "Good health to all, from Rexall!" . . . "Get Wildroot Cream-Oil, Charlie" . . . "I'm Chiquita Banana and I've come to say/Bananas have to ripen in a certain way/When they are flecked with brown and have a gol-den hue/Bananas taste the best and are the best for you!"

The Chiquita samba was a sheet-music best-seller, played on jukeboxes and records, the work of songwriters Garth Montgomery and Len Mackenzie. Two more jingle geniuses, Alan Bradley Kent and Austin Croom-Johnson, wrote the famous Pepsi-Cola opus: "Pepsi-Cola hits the spot!/Twelve full ounces, that's a lot/Twice as much for a nickel, too/Pepsi-Cola is the drink for you!/Nickel, nickel, nickel, nickel/Trickle, trickle, trickle, trickle."

Many sponsor tag lines are also stuck in the mind, in the same pop-trivia file with old political slogans and comic catchphrases, such unforgettable lines as: "Tide's in . . . dirt's out!" . . . "Out-standing!—*and they are mild*" . . . "Look sharp! *(ringside bell clangs).* Feel sharp! *(another bell).* Be sharp! *(final bell)*—Use Gillette Blue Blades, with the sharpest edges ever honed" . . . "Whiz-z-z! The best candy bar there *iz-z-z!*" . . . "A little dab'll do ya" . . . "Push pull, click click! Change blades that quick" *(ping!)* . . . "The time is ten o'clock. B-U-L-O-V-A, Bulova watch time" . . . "LS/MFT—LS/MFT—Lucky Strike means fine tobacco!" (followed by a tobacco auctioneer's actual mesmerizing chant, "*Hey twenty-nineninenineninenineninenine, roundemroundem-roundem roundemroundem, am I right at thirtythirtythirtythirtythirty,*" etc.) . . . "*Bromoseltzer-Bromoseltzer-Bromoseltzer*" (in a chugging rhythm, the Little Antacid That Could) . . . "L-A V-A, L-A V-A." And, of course, Lifebuoy's—and every schoolboy's favorite basso profundo taunt—foghorn warning, "Be-e-e-e-e *Oh-h-h-h!*"

As with sponsors, the opening and closing themes were integral to—in many cases, the best-remembered parts of—radio shows. Great care was taken to frame programs with readily identifiable theme music, narratives, and sound effects, a sort of overture for the program to come; station surfing then required much more effort. Many a radio theme followed stars to their graves—Jack Benny's "Love in Bloom" and "Hooray for Hollywood," Burns and Allen's "Love Nest," Bob Hope's "Thanks for the Memory," and Jack Webb's *dum-de-dum-dum,* as familiar as the first four notes of Beethoven's Fifth.

JUST AS THESE SHOWS' opening themes, commercials, and jingles linger vividly in memory half a century later, so do the specific announcers who gave them resounding voice: Ken Carpenter, Dwight Wiest, Art Gilmore, Ken Roberts (Tony Roberts's father), Ed Prentiss, Ed Herlihy, Jim Ameche (Don's brother), André Baruch, Jimmy Wallington, Rod O'Connor, Durward Kirby, Del Sharbutt, Harry Von Zell, Michael Fitzmaurice, Verne Smith, Hy Averback, Art Baker, Dan Seymour, Bill Goodwin, Charles Stark, Howard Petrie, Ken and Wendell Niles, Glenn Riggs, Frank Gallop, Ben Grauer, Jay Jostyn, Dick Stark, George Ansbro, Dick Joy, and Fred Foy. The names still cast a nostalgic glow. Some announcers even developed signature greetings, like Norman Brokenshire's hearty, "How do you do, ladies and gentlemen, how *do* you do?" These jubilant and somber voices still resonate in our heads, from Ed Prentiss, so muscular sounding that he wound up as the voice of Captain Midnight, to the so-called personality announcers—the fellows from the Hail Fellow School of Broadcasting. A lifetime later, you can still hear a snatch of a commercial and identify the show by the announcer's voice.

In the 1920s and early 1930s, the announcer was, claims one radio historian, "a genuine American hero" whose "splendid diction could have a more beneficial effect on the national literacy than ten thousand schoolmarms with their drills and chalkboard grammar lessons." The further back you go, the more syllable-perfect announcers had to be. An early test for announcers required them to render the following excerpt without stumbling or slurring: "Penelope Cholmondely raised her azure eyes from the crabbed scenario. She meandered along the congeries of her memoirs. There was kinetic Algernon, a choleric artificer of icons and triptychs, who wanted to write a trilogy. For years she had stifled her risibilities with dour moods. His asthma caused him to sigh like the zephyrs among the tamarack." Announcers came from everywhere—they were former singers, out-of-work actors, moonlighting ad salesmen, part-time sound men. There were even a few women announcers in the 1920s, until it was somehow decided, by the male hierarchy, that a baritone voice was more to be trusted, more appealing and listener-friendly. There are, even today, few, if any, female staff announcers in radio or TV.

The first star announcer was a young red-hot at New York's WEAF named Graham McNamee, a singer and ex–semipro baseball and hockey player whose magnetic voice and dramatic flair were tempered with an easygoing personality that set him apart from the mellifluous voices that dominated the microphones of the 1920s, some of whom affected an unctuous theatrical inflection. With his cheery American manner, eye for color and detail, and dynamism, plus the vital ability to fill time during slow-moving games, McNamee fell naturally into sportscasting, which he soon ruled. From there he went on to become

Ed Wynn's announcer-straight man—a natural progression for announcers, who fell into sidekick roles and had to learn the delicate art of the care and feeding (and occasional razzing) of comics. Three of the best at it were Frank Gallop, whose grand, richly sardonic voice regularly cut Milton Berle down to size; Harry Von Zell, deadpan jester in the court of Eddie Cantor and Burns and Allen; and Don Wilson, the most jovial member of Jack Benny's subversive circle.

Sidekick announcers walked a fine line between hired man and hired gun, laboring in the shadow of the star while taking potshots at him. In time, it became standard on comedy shows to make the announcer part of the sketches, an idea introduced by Eddie Cantor when he had Jimmy Wallington (later Von Zell) step in as straight man. The concept didn't really carry over into TV except in the case of talk shows, when radio refugees like Steve Allen sparred with Gene Rayburn and bandleader Skitch Henderson, a tradition now considered de rigueur on TV talk-variety shows; the announcer and/or bandleader stooge is in every late-show job description.

No radio orator is more closely associated with the golden age than Ed Herlihy, who for sixty-three years on NBC read commercials, hosted shows, and introduced soap operas, game shows, detective classics, kids' programs, political forums, and, basically, announced whatever needed announcing. Herlihy's friendly yet authoritative voice was, if not the unofficial Voice of Radio, the official Voice of Kraft Foods, first on such shows as *Kraft Music Hall* and later on *Kraft Video Theater.* Once, while in line in London at the British Airways counter, Herlihy recalls, "I was complaining about something and I guess projecting a little and some lady behind me said, in a thick British accent, 'Excuse me, but aren't you the gentleman who sells cheese?' " Herlihy, who claims, "I've probably done more commercials than anyone in radio," has said that even people too young for radio recognize his name and voice—not just from radio but as the narrator of countless Universal-International newsreels during the war and long after.

Herlihy recalls the luxurious life at NBC, where the announcer's lounge had a hostess who announced visitors. "It was like a gentleman's club," he says, with showers and a writing table. "Oh, we were big shots." He rubbed elbows with announcing gods Frank Gallop and Graham McNamee, who, he says, once offered him a thousand dollars to marry a wife he wanted to ditch. Herlihy, like most of radio's announcers, never took a voice lesson. "We were all individuals and had our own styles. McNamee had a brilliant light baritone and was the first personality guy, but he didn't associate with us. He was a big star." One of Herlihy's mentors was Ben Grauer, and another was Ralph Edwards, whose *Truth or Consequences* Herlihy announced for twenty-seven years, often taking part in stunts. He was also the announcer on radio's final blowout, *The Big Show*, the lavish last-ditch effort to reassert the primacy of radio in 1950.

Like all announcers, Herlihy became adept at the art of "filling"—when a show ran short and he would have to say nothing, with great authority, for seconds or even minutes. He once had to fill for seven minutes by telling listeners about the following week's show—and then the preceding week's show. "Shows always played faster than they did in rehearsals," he explains, "so I was always prepared to filibuster."

Another of radio's busiest and most recognizable voices belonged to George Ansbro, an NBC staff announcer for fifty-eight years before retiring in 1990 at the age of seventy-five. Ansbro could sound somber when the occasion demanded it, as it did five afternoons a week for the eighteen years he served as announcer on *Young Widder Brown*. Or he could be jubilant for his weekly shout, from the far reaches of the Ritz Theater, "I have a lady in the balcony, Doctor!" for his chores on *Dr. I.Q.* Ansbro simply did his job in a crisp, polished, workmanlike way for as many shows as required his services—soaps, comedies, detective dramas. "I never went a week without a paycheck, though some were pretty small at first." When networks stopped using staff announcers, he segued into TV.

Ansbro, a tall, distinguished man in his late eighties, lives in New Jersey and is writing his memoirs with the working title *I Have a Lady in the Balcony.* He began as an NBC page, worked his way up through the ranks to tour guide and then junior announcer, free-lancing at big-band remotes for Jimmy Dorsey, Eddy Duchin, and others. He did everything then, including "hitchhikers" and "cowcatchers," announcerese for fifteen-second promos between shows.

Announcers in Ansbro's day were minor celebrities, accorded VIP treatment at nightclubs and restaurants. As David Brinkley wrote in his memoirs, "NBC believed it was only fitting that after 6 P.M. all announcers speaking on its network were required to wear tuxedos. Formal dress, yes, even though the audience could not see them, but it was felt that announcers would take their work more seriously and their words would carry greater weight and authority."

Jim Backus (radio's insufferable rich boy Hubert Updyke III on *The Alan Young Show,* reborn as Thurston Howell on TV's *Gilligan's Island*), broke in as an NBC announcer. "Being a radio announcer at that time [1936] was indeed a glamorous, prestigious profession," he wrote in his memoirs. "But the reign of the announcer as numero uno was fairly short-lived. The advent of the comedians who reigned supreme demanded announcers who were more informal and relaxed. Our role models were such hallowed names as Milton J. Cross, Alois Havrilla, and André Baruch—these were the giants who walked the earth—not to mention Del Sharbutt and Harry Von Zell, and of course the most thunderous of them all, Westbrook Van Voorhis, the mere mention of whose name stayed eagles in their flight. His voice could shatter a shaving mug at twenty paces."

At NBC, Ansbro hung out in the announcers' lounge, passing the time schmoozing with Ford Bond and Graham McNamee, playing Ping-Pong and checkers, and learning about jobs via an exchange that the announcers dialed regularly. At one point, Ansbro was up for the voice of Johnny, the fabled Philip Morris mascot, but the sponsors found a real bellboy, Johnny Roventini, a midget page who worked in the lounge of the Palmer House in Chicago and possessed the unforgettably riveting piping voice that turned into a lifelong career "stepping out of store windows all over America." (A favorite old announcers' story: One night when Groucho Marx was dining out, a waiter dropped a tray of glasses and Marx cracked, "I think I just heard Johnny stepping out of another store window.") Ansbro didn't envy celebrity announcers like Wallington, one of those said to "have a smile in their voice." Indeed, many announcers actually grinned as they spoke to achieve that very ear-to-ear grin effect.

Bill Owen, a longtime ABC announcer (*Discovery, Ellery Queen's Minute Mysteries*) who grew up admiring Don Wilson, Harlow Wilcox, and Wallington ("They always sounded so intelligent to me"), learned how to make listeners salivate while delivering, say, a Campbell's Soup commercial. He says, "I'm in love with the English language—I always felt announcers had a mission to preserve the language—and if a word is onomatopoeic you can have some fun with it—'creeeeamy rich,' for instance. You can overdo it, and some announcers will milk it, but it should still be conversational. You're a combination of an actor and a salesman."

Art Gilmore, for seventeen years *Dr. Christian*'s announcer—and, like many of his cohorts, tall, handsome, and imposing, with a mane of white hair—recalls: "The day I heard the voice of Ted Husing I thought, *That's* what I want to do! I'll work for nothing." Many nearly did. Gilmore, who had the same college speech coach as Edward R. Murrow and whose license plate reads GAB4PAY, began working for a Tacoma, Washington, station five days a week for fifteen dollars a month. One memorable night Gilmore got the hiccups just before *Dr. Christian,* but cured it twenty minutes prior to airtime with a teaspoon of vinegar, an old announcer's remedy. Gilmore, whose voice is perhaps even better recalled as the voice of some ten thousand movie trailers and scores of newsreels, says, "The announcer's life is a pretty lonely job. You're sort of the Lone Ranger—you do your job and you go home. The announcer isn't part of the show." Gilmore usually went out with the crew, not the cast.

Don Stanley, *Dragnet*'s first announcer, agrees: "You were all by yourself much of the time, but many announcers kind of liked it that way. I still enjoy it; it was a great life. I didn't start out as an announcer, but I was the last man out the door at NBC. I literally turned out the light."

IN WOODY ALLEN'S *RADIO DAYS,* young Woody feverishly solicits donations, ostensibly for a Jewish cause, to raise cash for a decoder ring, but in fact radio trinkets were so cheap anybody could afford one who had a dime, a quarter, or fifty cents, max, and a handful of box tops from Pep or Kix.

The box tops were the hard part, forcing kids to ingest all sorts of foreign substances, such as Shredded Wheat, which boys and girls choked down for months to qualify for a Tom Mix item from Ralston Purina—a bent-nail horseshoe ring you had to own or die, or a replica of some crime-fighting tool indispensable to Sky King or the Green

Hornet, which glowed in the dark. If a premium didn't glow in the dark, it wasn't much good.

Radio premiums were the predecessors of today's baseball-card fetish, collected with an avidity known only to the truly obsessed. Most were as cheesy as a Cracker Jack "prize," but that didn't discourage kids from sending their quarters and cereal flaps to "Checkerboard Square." Less sentimentally remembered are the adult premiums that cluttered the soap operas (no less tied into the plots than the kiddie prizes), such as a packet of seeds to grow your very own bed of Ma Perkins peonies, a weird can opener invented by Lorenzo Jones, or a recipe book "by" Mother Barbour, the matriarch of *One Man's Family*.

The point wasn't merely to possess something used by one of your heroes. The true kick was becoming a part of some secret club. But in lieu of handshakes, oaths, and rituals, all that was required to belong was an official totem—be it a cardboard Captain Midnight Secret Squadron "code-a-graph," a Sky King "sign-a-scope," a Jack Armstrong pedometer, or a "magic cat's eye ring." The ultimate premium was a glow-in-the-dark Lone Ranger silver bullet that included a tiny reflecting mirror and a secret compartment for messages. Anything involving a secret compartment was certifiably nifty. The silver bullet may even have had a teeny compass tucked inside it or a sliver of a mirror; the more microfeatures packed into a premium, the better.

Out of every radio speaker tumbled a veritable cornucopia of chintzy but crucial slide-whistle rings, key rings, siren rings, magnet rings, signature rings, flashlight rings, six-shooter rings, movie rings, microscope and periscope rings, weather rings, Navajo treasure rings, flying saucer rings, Rin-Tin-Tin rings, gold ore rings, and rings with mirrors that enabled the wearer to see if the enemy was creeping up behind him. Among the better ones: an Orphan Annie Altascope Ring with a magnifying glass; a Buck Rogers Repeller Ray Ring; a Green Hornet Ring with a secret compartment that glowed in the dark, all concealed beneath an engraving of a hornet; a Captain Marvel Rocket Raider Compass Ring; and a Melvin Purvis Secret Scarab Ring. Half these rings had secret compartments into which one might tuck tiny maps or microfilm. The magnifying glass, standard equipment on many rings, was not only for reading documents but for starting a fire in the wilderness—or, if you were tied up by Nazis, for burning a hole in the ropes binding your hands and allowing you to escape.

It seemed as if every show offered a ring of some kind, or some sort of a decoding device that, of course, owed its popularity to the war effort. You often stayed tuned in less for the tale than for the cryptogram at the end, which only those owning official decoders could crack. The message, alas, always turned out to be something discouragingly stupid, such as, "Drink Your Ovaltine Today," or, "Be a Good Citizen," but all of that (as well as the fact that the item was made from some cheap wartime alloy) was overlooked in the excitement of receiving anything by mail after long weeks of unbearable patience. Finally, a small brown parcel arrived from Battle Creek, Michigan, home of Kellogg's cereals and premium paradise, you ripped open the box with hot grubby little hands, and suddenly you were the member of a secret society numbering only, say, a select few hundred thousand.

Contrary to popular belief, there never was a "decoder ring," according to expert Gary Alexander, whose private ring collection was auctioned off for $90,000 at Sotheby's in 1995. "People mix these things up," he explains. "There were decoder badges, however." The Captain Midnight decoder was the most popular; it came with a little built-in whistle. Alexander recalls one secret message that, when he was a kid, totally baffled him: " 'All men are created equal.' What did that mean?" You wanted something exciting, not a fortune cookie platitude—something more like "The Japs will attack Tuesday at 4:48 P.M." Which explains why Alexander's Orphan Annie Altascope Ring, the Hope Diamond of radio premiums, went for $11,000 at Sotheby's. With a miniature bomb sight, the ring was comprised of separating dovetailed brass leaves with pinholes of varying diameters, which, when opened and aimed at an aircraft, told you (by peeping through the hole) how far away a plane was. Leapin' lizards!

The most popular prize ever offered was a curious anachronism— the Lone Ranger atomic bomb ring, a rare bauble from the Kix Collection, c. 1947. The ring had red tail-fins at the base of the miniature bomb, which, when removed, allowed you to peer in the dark and see tiny explosions going off inside the ring, simulating nuclear fission. Exactly how the Lone Ranger got mixed up with the Atomic Energy Commission remains a mystery.

— 14 —

A Voice
of Another Color

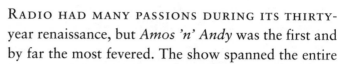

RADIO HAD MANY PASSIONS DURING ITS THIRTY-year renaissance, but *Amos 'n' Andy* was the first and by far the most fevered. The show spanned the entire golden age of radio, from 1928 to 1960, an astonishing run that survived fluctuations in racial attitudes and adapted to the times until the civil rights movement overtook its innocent world and finally put Amos Jones and Andrew H. Brown out of the taxicab business after thirty-two years.

No matter how the show eventually came to divide Americans, nobody disagrees that *Amos 'n' Andy* was radio's first big hit. But it was far more than that; it was a show that, because it transfixed the nation, also transformed and transcended the medium itself, and first alerted skeptical advertisers to radio's vast appeal and drawing power. More than any other program, *Amos 'n' Andy*—created and played by Freeman Gosden and Charles Correll—revealed that radio was not just an amusing new form of vaudeville but had unlimited and largely untapped commercial potential. The show came along at the absolutely right time, when networks were hungry for new ideas, the country was in a receptive mood, and advertisers were eager to find a program that would prove to clients radio's potential to engage millions. This quiet, unassuming little comedy show out of Chicago, about two luckless but lovable black guys, gave broadcasting the breakthrough megahit it needed to reveal radio as a major medium, a moneymaker, and, mostly, a new art form for the masses.

When the sponsor, Pepsodent, had a huge spurt in sales, other companies were persuaded that radio was no longer a fleeting craze but a hot market, and clambered aboard (an hour of advertising then cost about four thousand dollars). The show was also responsible for the first threatened sponsor boycott when Amos's wife, Ruby, nearly died

Overleaf: Freeman Gosden and Charles Correll (*Amos 'n' Andy*) in 1935 (*top*) and in 1952 (*bottom*)

and the show received eighteen thousand letters from people vowing to switch from Pepsodent to Colgate if she didn't recover; Ruby survived, and so did a toothpaste empire.

In its heyday, the show charmed nearly everybody—some 40 million people, a *third* of the nation, from the White House on down. Calvin Coolidge refused to be disturbed between seven and seven-fifteen, when the show was on six nights a week at America's dinner hour. Plumbers reported that water flow dropped dramatically during that time, after which pipes were flooded; factories staggered shifts so workers could catch the show; phone lines went suddenly still every night at seven. A year after it debuted, Amos and Andy impressions were in every mimic's act.

The team's favorite expressions became catchphrases of the day—lines like "Ain't dat sumpin!" "Check and double check," "'Splain dat to me," "Holy mack'el!" "Ah ain' goin' *do* it, I ain' goin' *do* it!" "Ah's regusted," and "Buzz me, Miss Blue." George Bernard Shaw made their triumph international when he famously said, "There are three things I shall never forget about America—the Rocky Mountains, Niagara Falls, and *Amos 'n' Andy*."

Amos 'n' Andy altered not only America's entertainment habits forever but also the country itself. Listeners during the Depression, when the show was riding high, realized they could stay home and be as amused as they could spending money for a vaudeville show, a nightclub, a dance, or even a movie. Radio had been readily available, but suddenly it seemed indispensable. *Amos 'n' Andy* sold radios in 1930 the way Milton Berle later peddled TV sets Tuesday nights in 1950.

To miss an episode of *Amos 'n' Andy* in the 1930s and 1940s was a little like not watching *Seinfeld* or *The Simpsons* in the 1990s—one felt slightly out of it. People didn't just want to hear them, they *had* to hear them. Newspapers ran recaps of the previous night's show. Within a year, it had become an obsession. To make sure audiences on both coasts heard the show at a convenient hour, *Amos 'n' Andy* devised the repeat broadcast, a major innovation. The show also produced the first tie-in products—*Amos 'n' Andy* records, dolls, and toy taxis, a candy bar, animated cartoons, and a daily comic strip that crudely caricatured Amos and Andy as minstrel types with pop eyes, thick lips, and darker skin than their svelte women; Gosden and Correll supplied the strip's dialogue, but without their voices to infuse the words with personality and warmth, it lasted only seventeen months.

In 1929, the main hurdle that an upstart new network called the Columbia Broadcasting System had to overcome was what to program opposite this newest national mania at the end of a mania-packed decade. No matter what William Paley threw at it—singing rages like Bing Crosby, the Mills Brothers, and Kate Smith—the show was unshakable and, for the next three decades, a vivid piece of Americana.

Andy's wedding to Madame Queen, to take one episode, had the country on the edge of its coast-to-coast seat for weeks when the ceremony was interrupted just before the preacher pronounced them married. Were they legally wed? The press agonized, bringing in judges and lawyers to render legal opinions. It became an early media event, like Tiny Tim's wedding to Miss Vicki on the *Tonight* show—except, of course, it was all fictitious.

The original *Amos 'n' Andy* show was deceptively simple and succinct—a mere ten minutes, plus commercials. Ben Gross, the longtime New York *Daily News* radio critic, was struck by the show when he first heard it in 1929: "These boys are different from any other comedians you ever heard. They're great; but there's one thing odd about them: They don't have any jokes." Freeman Gosden proudly remarked on that fact: "We were after the creation of character, not gags. We believed that once you establish your characters, if they're likable, the public will become fond of them. All you have to do is put them into recognizable situations. You don't have to have a laugh in every line to be funny." The characters held listeners because they were funny but also layered and contradictory. Amos and Andy's essential humanity triumphed over all and trumped even their most severe critics.

NBC's vice-president of programming once put his finger on the show's enduring popularity: Gosden and Correll, he observed, were canny showmen who "gave the audience very little in that fifteen minutes every night. You could relax listening to them. They didn't force a lot of humor on you. They never gave too much—just eased along. And this was their secret. They were real students of entertaining by radio."

Like soap opera writers, the team learned how to pace shows so that episodes kept listeners anxious over a weekend, as in an episode when

Andy was about to be convicted of murder and his girl friend fainted. Gosden and Correll orchestrated their plots with artful precision, stopping the action for a day or so if something in the news was distracting listeners. The series was set in real time, so holidays and news events were in sync with events on the show until it went weekly, in 1943. *Amos 'n' Andy* was radio's first major reality-based comedy show.

While most people now remember the radio show less well than its TV counterpart, the two shared a crucial ingredient evident almost from the earliest episodes: an inherent vulnerability that went beyond humor. No show drew warmer laughter than *Amos 'n' Andy*. Although other comedy shows may have been at times more clever or witty, none was as gentle, as consistent, or as durable. This can only be traced to the innate taste and sensibility of Gosden and Correll, who possessed an unusual racial sensitivity in an era when nobody thought it odd that white men would portray blacks—not even when they blacked up to play Amos and Andy on tour.

With age, the program developed more finesse. Gosden and Correll's 1928 *Sam 'n' Henry* show in Chicago, before it went network as *Amos 'n' Andy*, reveals characters with thicker drawls and labored jokes. It was just a vaudeville act on a barren landscape. All the dialogue was written in dialect, the focus of its humor. Someone once typed out the dialogue in perfect English to see if it sounded as funny; it doesn't. The black lingo made detractors wince even though it was simply a comic technique, not a comment on blacks—no more cruelly intended than a Brooklyn accent, a Southern drawl, or a western twang. The mispronunciations, a major part of the laughs, were pure comic malapropisms as vital to Amos and Andy, Molly Goldberg, Mr. Kitzle, and Mrs. Nussbaum as to Archie on *Duffy's Tavern*, Chester Riley of *The Life of Riley*, or even midwesterner Fibber McGee. Radio comedy would have quickly dried up without malapropisms. Any comedy, even one about black life, needs to be cut a certain poetic slack.

Ironically, the raucous black sitcoms that dominated TV in the 1970s and 1980s—*The Jeffersons, Diff'rent Strokes, Sanford and Son*—were not just filled with the kind of ancient vaudeville stereotypes that eventually drove *Amos 'n' Andy* off TV, but they had far less of their wit, richness, and goodwill. In fact, those boisterous black sitcoms make the best case of all for *Amos 'n' Andy*. *Time*'s critic William

A. Henry III wrote that "the flavorsome street life of *Amos 'n' Andy* would look far less offensive today than when it was measured against the sanitized blandness of *The Donna Reed Show* and *Father Knows Best*. Such characters as Lightnin' and the Kingfish may have been inelegant, but they had an enviable vitality."

Even though Amos and Andy were broke, they weren't lazy; they were merely strapped for money in the Depression era that gave them birth, as were many of their listeners. It was this bond between two struggling small businessmen and their hard-up audience that deflected the sort of harsh criticism that surfaced when the show emerged on TV in the more prosperous 1950s. Amos and Andy's Fresh-Air Taxicab Company ("Incorpulated") was a going enterprise, even if the pair only had one rattletrap cab with no windshield, hence the company name. Amos was industrious and upright, had a family, and, if anything, was too sterling a citizen—nice, if comically innocuous: responsible, thrifty, and thoroughly middle-class in attitude. In time, interestingly, the bland Amos proved too meager a source of humor and was relegated to walk-ons in his own show, except for the annual Christmas show where he explained the Lord's Prayer to his daughter, Arbadella. Young listeners in the 1940s wondered why the show was called *Amos 'n' Andy*. Where was Amos and how had this Kingfish fellow assumed the lead? Why wasn't it called *Kingfish 'n' Andy?*

The show was simply taken over by characters who went their own way. In his ultimate con job, George (Kingfish) Stevens squeezed Amos out, took over the comic action, and dominated the show—if not his own harassing wife, Sapphire. While Sapphire, a name that became synonymous in black culture with a hectoring female, might be regarded as a stereotype, she was essential, the only person capable of whittling her husband's outside ego down to size; and if she didn't, her bombastic mother did. Sapphire was a black Alice Kramden. The Kingfish, likewise, was merely another of radio's countless henpecked husbands, and what made his blowhard character even funnier was hearing him cower in Sapphire's presence as she took the wind out of his sails. She was a long way from the cliché jolly mammy figure in films of the time.

Andy's thickheadedness—no worse than that of scores of white radio stooges—was balanced by his good nature. Andy wasn't stupid;

what he was, mostly, was guileless. Andy was a perpetual naïf, swallowing the Kingfish's outlandish bait-and-switch schemes, but always against his better judgment. When he took the bait, it was usually to do the Kingfish a favor. Andy was full of basic horse sense, more often duped than dumb; mainly, he lacked the courage and skepticism to overrule his sensible inner voice. Andy also had flashes of wit he was never credited with, heard in mumbled asides. Because he spoke slowly he was mistaken for a dope, but anyone would look dumb up against the wily Kingfish.

Amos 'n' Andy, however, was all that most whites knew about blacks, a fact that enraged the show's critics. Somehow, Jack Benny's valet, Rochester, and his female counterpart, the wise and loving Beulah, escaped the black wrath that tarred Gosden and Correll's show, most likely because Eddie Anderson and Hattie McDaniel were black. *Beulah* beat *Amos 'n' Andy* to TV by eight months, and though she was more of a stereotype, the show remained largely immune from attack. In his close study of the show, Melvin Patrick Ely wondered why, if *Amos 'n' Andy* was "nothing more than a heap of racist clichés," was it so beloved by whites *and* blacks. The show sent a mixed message even to blacks and was so benign that it defused heated arguments against it. Also, it was not just funny; it had a sentimental streak. Had the show been created and performed by blacks, it might never have been thrown on the defensive, for many ethnic acts were performed by German, Jewish, Irish, and Scots comics who made rude fun of their own heritage.

While *Amos 'n' Andy* was in the tradition of ethnic vaudeville and could trace its roots to minstrel shows, it presented a slippery target, depicting Amos and Andy as lower-class and nonthreatening but never subservient. Amos, Andy, the Kingfish, and their pals were decent, law-abiding, upwardly mobile guys who could pass any family-values test. Kingfish bent the law but never broke it and Andy was a ladies' man who wanted to settle down but avoided being trapped by duplicitous girl friends. The show's heart was in the right place, nobody could deny that; even Gosden and Correll's primitives, Sam and Henry, were depicted sympathetically.

Amos 'n' Andy was a transitional act that toyed with black stereotypes, maybe at times exploited them, but it also left racism behind and ventured into modern life—going from a black-and-white world into one with gradations of gray. The men lived within a virtually all-black world and yet they seemed very much of the larger white world beyond, unique and independent spirits.

The Kingfish was a small-time black hustler but so funny, deft, and brilliant a swindler that he transcended race; listeners admired his con, gift of gab, and bravado. (Huey Long, the garrulous Louisiana politician with the florid oratorical style and scandalous reputation, was nicknamed the Kingfish after his four-flushing radio counterpart.) Andy isn't fooled because he's black but because he's too eager to make a fast buck. Likewise, the fast-talking lawyer, Calhoun, is more glib than he is black. Of all their characters, only the dim, slow-footed janitor was a true Lightnin'-rod for racist charges.

Amos and Andy were not meant to represent anything more than themselves—"deliberate anachronisms," in the words of Bart Andrews and Ahrgus Juilliard in their history of the show. They point out that Amos and Andy were only black on the outside and that any of the show's plot lines would have worked as well on *The Life of Riley* or *I Love Lucy*. The problem unique to *Amos 'n' Andy* is that politically incorrect sparks fly when traditional comic devices collide with black characters.

Amos 'n' Andy remains a Rorschach blot in which you can see virtually any evil or good to support all arguments pro or con. While it's possible to criticize this outlandish scheme or that gullible or conniving character, the reality is that the show made white America feel a closer kinship with blacks and helped whites view African-Americans in a new, more realistic, flattering, and nonthreatening light. Amos and Andy were never objects of derision. Whatever your skin color, you rooted for them. Laughter is the ultimate leveler.

FREEMAN GOSDEN—SLENDER, handsome, refined—and Charles Correll—stumpy, jowly, crude—first met in Durham, North Carolina, when Correll, then working as a piano player for silent movies, was sent there from Chicago to stage a show at an Elks Hall. Although Gosden was a twenty-six-year-old Southerner from Richmond, Virginia, and Correll a thirty-five-year-old Northerner from Peoria, Illinois, they hit it off, became roommates and, while staging amateur acts for the Joe Bren theatrical company for six years, teamed up as traditional song-and-dance men (Correll at the piano, Gosden on uke) in an act called "The Life of the Party." The two were only interested in radio as a stepping-stone to big-time vaudeville; Gosden still worked occasionally as end man in a minstrel show.

In 1925, while they were performing in a weekly late-night slot for a Chicago station broadcast from a small studio off the hotel dining room, someone at the *Chicago Tribune* heard their act and offered them jobs at $250 a week to harmonize each night on the paper's station WGM (for "World's Greatest Newspaper") at the Drake Hotel. The station manager then asked them to craft a show based on one of the *Tribune*'s, and America's, most popular comic strips, "The Gumps," but the team suggested crafting their own creation—"a couple of colored characters"— hoping to bring to radio what Mutt and Jeff had to the funny pages. "We chose black characters," claimed the pragmatic Gosden, "because blackface comics could tell funnier stories than white comics." Mutt was short and Jeff was tall, so they came up with the vocal equivalent—one of the voices would be high and one low. Thus was born, within a week, *Sam 'n' Henry*, which became an almost immediate local hit; a year after it debuted, fifteen thousand listeners turned up to gawk at them at a Chicago factory carrying Sam and Henry toys. It was a new form, as revealed in a billboard ad that read FOLLOW THE RADIO COMIC-STRIP. The spare fifteen-minute nightly serial (no sound effects) had faint sociological overtones: The first episodes depicted Sam and Henry headed north to make their fortunes in the big city like so many black Southerners who had come north after World War I looking for work. On the opening show, January 12, 1926, they drove a mule-drawn wagon to the depot:

Sam: *Henry, did you evah sees a mule as slow as dis one?*
Henry: *Oh, dis mule is fas' enough. We gonna git to da depot awright.*
Sam: *You know, dat Chicago train don' wait fo' nobody—it jes' goes on—jes' stops and goes right on . . . Ah hope dey got fastah mules dan dis up in Chicago.*

Their story became a black pioneer saga as Sam and Henry strike out for higher ground, start from scratch, and create a livelihood out of a ramshackle taxi. It was classic Horatio Alger stuff that grabbed listeners almost from the start, as thousands tuned in six nights a week to the welcoming intro of station sales-manager-turned-announcer Bill Hay.

When NBC beckoned after two years and 586 episodes, the *Tribune* balked, demanding control, so Gosden and Correll left WGN and *Sam 'n' Henry,* which the paper owned. The *Tribune* had rejected their then radical idea to record the shows, a daring concept, and syndicate them to thirty-five other stations as a "chainless chain." They moved to a rival station, the *Chicago Daily News's* WMAQ, and recycled *Sam 'n' Henry* as *Jim 'n' Charley,* which became *Tom 'n' Harry,* and, finally, *Amos 'n' Andy.* Gosden later said that the name Amos came from the phone book and had a nice biblical ring; Andy, Correll added, sounded "pleasant, round, and juicy," like the roly-poly guy who played him. They tried countless combinations before finding two names that were euphonious and alliterative. Initially, Amos was the innocent and Andy the crafty one, a dynamic that changed once the mighty Kingfish arrived, whereupon Andy became the stooge.

A New York newspaper noticed the show, as did a Chicago adman named William Benton (later of the Benton & Bowles ad agency), who decided that the popular Chicago-based radio team would be just the thing to launch a new toothpaste, Pepsodent. He persuaded his boss, Albert Lasker, who persuaded NBC, and the new show premiered on NBC August 29, 1929, when Amos and Andy moved from Chicago's South Side to New York's Harlem.

NBC gave *Amos 'n' Andy* a major buildup—and their stars a major salary, $50,000 a year, a nice raise from their former $250-a-week wages in Chicago—but the first shows failed to live up to the hoopla and critics were unamused. Those early episodes were far less polished and nimble than the show that became a legend, closer to vaudeville routines (Andy: "What was yo' ancestors?" Amos: "Ah don' have no sisters."), and the stories stall; they might do ten minutes on a word that neither man knew or could pronounce.

Their original studio, in the Chicago Merchandise Mart, was laid out like a living room, with a fireplace, easy chairs, and a wooden table where Gosden as Amos, Lightnin', the Kingfish (later), and Correll as Andy sat facing each other at a single mike. Nobody was ever allowed inside the studio to watch them at work. The first shows were written in half an hour on the day of the broadcast; later ones took three or four hours to polish. There was little or no rehearsal, since the men knew the characters as well as their own and wanted to sound spontaneous.

They traded off subsidiary characters, often playing seven or eight per show, some 150 characters in all by 1935, when they began hiring other actors and their first actress, in 1939, who was white, to play Ruby, Amos's wife. Ruby, Madame Queen, the Widow Parker, and other female characters were major presences on the show without ever appearing—heard from indirectly, by reference, letter, or telephone. Depicting black females as wives or fiancées was rare in an era when young black women in radio sketches were often portrayed as sexual playthings.

Their audience grew to 40 million listeners at a time when, apart from a few guests like Fats Waller, Cab Calloway, and Louis Armstrong, there had been no black stars, let alone shows, on network radio. Local black music shows thrived in big cities, but nationwide there was a literal blackout, plus an unwritten agreement that fan magazines would not publish photos of black performers. All black voices were performed by whites, a phenomenon known as racial ventriloquy.

Prior to Amos and Andy, "blackvoice" acts were staples of ghettoized local programs with names like *The Burnt Cork Revue, The Corn Cob Pipe Club,* and *The Show Boat,* inspired by the sturdy 1927 Broadway musical vessel. Major teams like Mack and Moran ("The Two Black Crows") were surrounded by imitators—Slick and Slim, Moonshine and Sawdust, Sugarfoot and Sassafras, Buck and Wheat, and Watermelon and Cantaloupe. Pick (Malone) and Pat (Padgett) did an act called "Molasses 'n' January." Gag books entitled *Coon Jokes* and *Darky Jokes* kept white comics well stocked, and every home with a piano had songbooks of "coon songs" such as "He's Just a Little Nigger But He's Mine, All Mine" and "Hottest Coon in Dixie"; even Irving Berlin wrote his share of "coon" tunes.

It was into this demeaning cartoon world that Gosden and Correll arrived in 1926 with *Sam 'n' Henry,* whose likely roots were characters originated by the black comics Flournoy Miller and Aubrey Lyles in a musical comedy, *The Mayor of Dixie,* the basis for two Sissle and Blake revues, *Shuffle Along* and *Runnin' Wild.* Much of what Gosden and

Correll did was inspired by Miller and Lyles, who might have become the original Amos and Andy had they not been black. Eventually, CBS, hoping to create its own *Amos 'n' Andy*, gave them their own show twice a week, now lost in history. Correll's son Rick observed, "Blackface was acceptable, but black skin was not." Not even when totally hidden on radio.

A TYPICAL WHITE BOY WHO grew up in the center of Richmond, Freeman Gosden came from a family with black servants, of whom one, nicknamed "Snowball," was a boyhood pal. Since he was the better mimic, Correll relied on him for "authenticity," but to establish his own credibility Correll claimed he had "researched" black life in the Chicago ghetto. His major research, it's safe to say, was studying blackface acts that toured the Peoria theater where he ushered.

Amos and Andy, unlike many blackface acts, didn't drink, gamble, or cheat on their women—or eat pork chops, fried chicken, and watermelon. Gosden boasted that ministers and mothers praised the show's wholesomeness and "cleanliness." To quench any flickering protests, and for goodwill purposes, Gosden and Correll posed with black groups to promote their affection for and knowledge of urban blacks. A black newspaper, the *Philadelphia Tribune,* praised them as role models in their ability to re-create black culture; "Some of the imitators" of blacks, it noted, "are better than the original article." The leftist columnist Heywood Broun wrote that the pair went beyond racial or even comic considerations and could be enjoyed simply as "living, breathing persons." Many felt *Amos 'n' Andy* wasn't just funny but cathartic and universal and mirrored "life itself." One exuberant columnist called their humor "Shakespearean." A San Francisco reporter wrote that Gosden and Correll "never slur or make fun of the colored race, and portray their characters in a human, appealing manner at all times."

A lot of the media coverage, however, undid their best efforts to tone down the show's racial aspects by referring to the team as "darky comedians" or by showing them blacking up before a broadcast, a photo op fantasy—there was then no live audience. *Amos 'n' Andy* thus became unfairly synonymous with the worst excesses of racial humor when careless reporters and listeners confused them with their shameful minstrel ancestors. To whites, all blackface comics were created equal; the best was the same as the worst. Gosden and Correll were blamed for the ignorance of insensitive fans, as when James T. Farrell's hero Studs Lonigan praises the show: "You would have laughed yourself sick at them. They're so much like darkies. Not the fresh Northern niggers, but the genuine real Southern darkies, the good niggers, lazy, happy-go-lucky, strutting themselves out in titles . . . just like in real life."

As if to reveal just how boldly inventive they could be, Gosden and Correll performed a routine on tour in which Amos and Andy flung off their nappy wigs and raggedy costumes to reveal themselves as Freeman Gosden and Charles Correll, performing snappy songs and patter as their pre–Amos and Andy selves. A special makeup, under a sensitized light, turned their black faces white. Then, to top even this bit of racial hocus-pocus, they reverted back to their Amos and Andy voices and ended with a routine in whiteface using black voices; the crowd ate it up.

As Melvin Patrick Ely observed in his look at *Amos 'n' Andy* as a social phenomenon, "Gosden and Correll leap[ed] back and forth across the color line in a manner both cavalier and surreal—indeed, in a way that caused the line, in the last minutes of each show, to blur altogether."

What made Amos and Andy unique and utterly different from their "coon show" predecessors was that they were absorbed by—and into—the national life, which took them out of their minstrel-black skins and into the white listeners' world. True, they inhabited an all-black community, but they weren't isolated from the country's real concerns, which the two comics were plunged into when the Depression struck only two months after *Amos 'n' Andy* went network. Indeed, *Amos 'n' Andy* reached its greatest popularity during—and due to—the Depression, when the characters' financial woes reflected the nation's but were funnier; they were worse off than most, but ever determined and optimistic.

In February 1932, Amos delivered one of his pep-talk sermonettes on the "Repression": "Times like dese does a lot o' good, 'cause when dis is over, which it's bound to be, an' good times come back again, people's like us dat is livin' today is goin' learn a lesson an' dey goin' know whut a rainy day is. People is done always say, 'I is savin' up fo' a rainy day,' but dey didn't even know what dey was talkin' 'bout."

When FDR shut the banks, Amos patriotically explained it to Andy and the Kingfish: "Mr. Roosevelt means bizness, an' he's gettin' action, so you see, dis bank holiday is really a great thing fo' the country."

Amos and Andy had by now become barometers of the national climate as their misadventures were blended into what was going on, day to day, around the American neighborhood. The show was an anomaly—a kind of topical soap opera. Accidentally, Gosden and Correll had invented both the sitcom and the soap opera when they were the first fifteen-minute feature on the air and the first to broadcast six nights a week. Their show had the flexibility to be timely, which kept it fresh, and yet it retained the leisurely pace, tone, and continuity of a daily serial. The humor came both out of its rounded characters and off the front pages. As innocents, they were able to fold topical, social, and even political humor into their escapades, as when Andy called socialists "social-risks" who "puts ever'body in de same basin"—a little like Peter Finley Dunne's sage bartender Mr. Dooley.

The show was also a rare look inside black society, even if glimpsed through a comic white prism. Noted Mel Watkins: "The daily routines of ersatz black folks had never received such exposure and scrutiny in the media . . . until Bill Cosby's more realistic but ironically less representative Huxtables in the 1980s." For decades, in fact, Amos and Andy were radio's only nonservile blacks. Fred Allen, radio's reigning sophisticated wit, wrote admiringly of Gosden and Correll that "their vocal changes, and the fading in and out of the characters as they come and go, are uncanny. Most people cannot appreciate the skill involved." Here's a prize example of that skill in an excerpt from the 1950s that evokes the show's flavor, wit, and warm appeal:

Sapphire: *George Stevens, I done made up my mind that I'm gonna have a husband that dresses good, knows nice people, and is got a steady job.* [Kingfish's "job" was running the lodge hall.]
Kingfish: *Sapphire, you mean to say that you is gonna leave me?*
Sapphire: *George, I know why you're a no-good bum. It's on account of your association with Andy Brown. Why don't you meet a nicer class of men?*
Kingfish: *Well, I ain't got da opportunity to meet 'em. Dey is all workin'.*

Sapphire: *Well, that Andy Brown is the cause of it all. What has he ever accomplished?*

Kingfish: *Well, yesterday, he had a run of thirteen balls in da side pocket without leanin' on da table.*

Sapphire: *Now, that's exactly what I mean—Andy hangin' around a pool table all day. Why don't he go to a cultured place like a public library?*

Kingfish: *They ain't got no pool table there.*

Whatever the show's artistic merits and national popularity, its premise divided blacks, especially black newspapers. As early as 1931, a group of black attorneys tried to get an injunction to have it taken off the air at the same time that a Harlem fund-raiser sent Gosden and Correll a telegram thanking them "for being friends of the Negro race." The issue descended into a nasty food fight among black newspapers. One called it a terrible example to black youth; another claimed it was one more example of whites' curiosity about the black demimonde. The *Pittsburgh Courier,* a leading black paper, tried to get the FCC to yank it, accusing it of the "exploitation of Negroes for profit." The black *Louisville News* editorialized that, while it "yields to none in race pride," it was "unable to work up a sweat over *Amos 'n' Andy.*" The respected *Chicago Defender* attacked the *Courier* and invited Gosden and Correll to perform at a picnic for thirty thousand black children.

A columnist in Harlem's influential *Amsterdam News* ridiculed the *Courier:* "When they complete their tally of [anti–*Amos 'n' Andy* show] signatures, we will know precisely how many halfwits there are in the race." The *Courier* finally abandoned its crusade; during a dark Depression year, the issue was hardly a major concern to most blacks. One of its young reporters, Roy Wilkins, later the NAACP's most distinguished leader, originally defended the show, calling it inoffensive, and scolded blacks who denigrated it, writing that the show "has all the pathos, humor, vanity, glory, problems, and solutions that beset ordinary mortals and therein lies its universal appeal."

In the late 1930s, William Paley finally gave up trying to beat Gosden and Correll and enticed them to leave NBC at twice their salary in exchange for rights to the show. Gosden said, "That was the beginning of a beautiful friendship." Also the beginning of a slow demise. Paley lured them to CBS with a complex tax plan that turned the team into a corporation. The Fresh-Air Taxi Cab Company was now truly "incorpulated," to the tune of $2.5 million a year, with prospects of a profitable TV version just around the corner.

After its high of 40 million listeners in the early 1930s, the show's popularity began to fall by the end of the decade. It not only left NBC for CBS but moved to California from Chicago, and the sponsor shifted from Pepsodent to Campbell's Soup. *Amos 'n' Andy* was no longer a two-man operation—other writers were hired, along with black actors Johnny Lee, Eddie Green, and Ernestine Wade as Sapphire. In 1936, they added guest stars and did one show a week as a minstrel act featuring their lodge brothers.

Selling CBS the show had proved a bad idea. In 1943, eight months after Gosden and Correll took a leave of absence when their ratings suddenly dropped to a low of 9.4, they were moved into a thirty-minute Sunday night slot at CBS. That ended their unique and classic fifteen-minute nightly series and turned the show into a standard weekly thirty-minute variety show, on which they became just another act. *Amos 'n' Andy* had gone from Harlem to Hollywood. The new version seemed out of sync with the show's leisurely character. It sounded strangely snappy and slick, and crowded with outsiders—the Jeff Alexander Orchestra and Chorus, an audience, and a new announcer, hearty Harlow Wilcox, who replaced the languid Bill Hay. Meant to compete with the fast-paced comedy of Bob Hope, Jack Benny, and Fred Allen, the show had a revised glitzy format and a new sponsor, Rinso (whose twittery "Rinso white! Rinso white! Happy little washday song!" was piped by little diva-to-be Belle Silverman—later Beverly Sills). Musical bridges were used between scenes, with comic *wah-wah*s from the trumpets.

Even in its streamlined CBS format, however, the lead characters hadn't changed. On one show, Kingfish is still trying to fix Andy up with a rich, overstuffed woman so he can skim off a 50 percent marriage broker's fee, and Andy was ever gullible, but warily so, and still torturing the language ("Ah's gettin' nupulated"). The banter remains crisp and effective, the plot neatly structured, and every joke scores. When Andy balks at being married off to a fat woman ("Ah couldn't even get mah arms 'roun' her"), the Kingfish scoffs, "Oh, sho' ya can, if ya jes' time it right. Whatcha do is, yo watch her breathin' and catch her on de *in*-hale." Kingfish adds, "You jes' judgin' her on de surface, Andy. Wah, underneath all dat fat, she's prob'ly very skinny."

Hal Kanter, who wrote for the show in the late 1940s, vividly recalls Gosden and Correll as diverse personalities. "Freeman was the boss man. He would pace while Correll typed. Freeman was smarter and the voice of authority. Freeman was a rather sophisticated old-school Southern gentleman and a very shrewd businessman, astute and talented and a little bit of a snob, and probably anti-Semitic. Charlie Correll was more down-to-earth and blue-collar—he'd been a brick-layer—and much easier to talk to."

Kanter says of the show's racial factor: "*Amos 'n' Andy* had a running gunfight with the NAACP for thirty years, much to the shame of the NAACP. Because of that, we lost a lot of native folklore." Liberals like the NAACP's Roy Wilkins, who had enjoyed the radio show in the 1930s, changed their mind in the pre–civil rights 1950s. The times had changed it for them.

ALTHOUGH THE IDEA of taking *Amos 'n' Andy* to television had been around since 1945, it took five years for Gosden and Correll to cast the show with black actors they felt would flesh out the richly imagined characters. They agreed that after an embarrassing film debut in *Check and Double Check*, they couldn't black up and re-create the roles on TV. Vocally and physically they had been fine on screen, but the 1930 movie, a primitive talkie, bogs down in a lifeless plot and extraneous characters, who intrude on their usual two-character byplay—a glaring early example of a hit radio show with sharp verbal wit unable to find a visual equivalent on screen; they seem on alien turf.

Briefly they considered using both blacks and whites in blackface in the TV roles (dubbing the voices themselves!), but after seeing *Anna Lucasta* by the American Negro Theater, the team realized there were able black actors for the parts. It's startling how closely their choices approximated the visual images listeners had carried in their heads for decades, most of all Tim Moore's creation of the Kingfish, so indelible to this day.

Gosden and Correll helped produce the TV series, assisted by other white writers from their radio show (Bob Ross, Bob Connolly, and Bill Moser—the latter two wound up on the suburban side of the tracks writing for *Leave It to Beaver*), plus a white director. Perhaps to assuage all their consciences, CBS hired the black comedian Flournoy Miller—half of the minstrel-show mold for Amos and Andy who had felt badly ripped off in the 1930s and threatened a plagiarism suit—as a writer and "racial consultant." (Gosden and Correll also were listed as consultants, but CBS played down their involvement, hoping to defuse the program's newly enraged critics of the postwar 1950s. It didn't work.) Miller, their envoy to the black theater community, recalled an actor named Spencer Williams, Jr., for the role of Andy. Alvin Childress, a bartender in *Anna Lucasta,* wanted the Kingfish part but finally agreed to play the lackluster Amos, who acted as the show's narrator. Childress was regarded as too light-skinned, so makeup men were told to darken him up, which he tried to resist; alert viewers could detect a color change at his neckline.

Black performers told Gosden, Correll, and Miller that the only man for the role of George "Kingfish" Stevens was a veteran vaudevillian named Tim Moore. When they finally tracked Moore down in his hometown of Rock Island, Illinois, where he had retired, the sixty-two-year-old actor emerged from a life of fishing to audition for the part; Cab Calloway and the great Count Basie singer Jimmy Rushing, known as "Mr. Five by Five," were also tested. Johnny Lee, as fast-talking jivester Calhoun, and Nick Stewart's Lightnin' rounded out the TV cast, with rotund Amanda Randolph repeating her radio role as the Kingfish's mama-in-law from hell.

Shooting began in October 1950 on the pilot show, a rewrite of an old radio episode about a rare nickel worth $250 that Kingfish tries to pry loose from Andy. Amos was his usual peripheral self. The show's eventual director, Charles Barton, was a veteran of Abbott and Costello and *Ma and Pa Kettle* comedies. As a onetime director, producer, and actor in black films of the 1930s and 1940s, Spencer Williams played an ex-officio role as assistant producer and dialectician. Even so, there were stories of Gosden and Correll taking black actors aside to coach them on their dialects, and at one point Barton tried to bar Gosden from the set.

Not until the show appeared on TV, of course, did its white radio fans realize how middle-class *Amos 'n' Andy*'s world looked—or, rather, how gentrified it became. The sets and clothes were purposely designed to read respectable middle class, not ghetto, and even the dilapidated taxicab was upgraded. Kingfish was always dressed in a three-piece suit, and many of the men, primarily the Kingfish and his attorney, Algonquin J. Calhoun, looked prosperous. They wore vests and had offices; they went on vacations, had dinner parties, and lived what seemed utterly American—not invisible, fringe, or ghetto—lives. No other blackface act had ever inhabited the real world; black comics before *Amos 'n' Andy* were merely isolated jesters, performers rather than people.

For white Americans, *Amos 'n' Andy* didn't deepen the stereotype, which was the usual claim—it did quite the opposite. The show was a first peek on TV at a bustling black community. Blacks were depicted as judges, executives, doctors, and businessmen; the title characters were only part of a larger, thriving, and admirable society. In one episode, Kingfish casually refers to the *Wall Street Journal*. For whites who came of age in the 1940s and 1950s, this was all eye-opening stuff.

When William Paley took *Amos 'n' Andy* to TV from radio, he fully expected it to be the first major comedy hit, never anticipating the attacks it would endure. Five days after it debuted on TV, black leaders were calling it "a comic anachronism insulting to blacks." What perhaps did most to sabotage the TV version was the character of Lightnin', a painful throwback that some felt out-farfetched Stepin Fetchit.

Amos 'n' Andy was doomed on TV from the start. The show premiered the very week the NAACP held its annual convention, when a protest letter was drafted threatening to boycott Schenley Distillers, which owned the show's sponsor, Blatz beer, even though Schenley had donated to black organizations, which cynics claimed was an effort to buy off black viewers when *Amos 'n' Andy* came to TV. When Blatz pulled out in 1953 after two years, CBS had the excuse it needed to cancel the series (despite a 1952 Emmy nomination), due to renewed pressure from the hard-nosed NAACP chairman, Walter White, who also found the classic film musical *Stormy Weather* objectionable. In its third season, the TV show went to syndication—but stayed on radio—and the series remains in limbo today but is available on videocassette, one outlet selling forty thousand *Amos 'n' Andy* videos in six months. Eddie Brandt's Saturday Matinee in Los Angeles says that three quarters of the videocassettes' renters are black.

Many lifelong devotees, of all hues, feel the show was unfairly driven off TV. Just as in radio it was blessed with perfect cultural timing, bad timing killed it off on TV. The irony was that the show made one of the purest, smoothest, and most successful transitions from radio to TV of any situation comedy. It was thirteenth in the Nielsens in its first season, with a cast made up of some of the best black comic actors available—one reason it divided the black show-business world.

The NAACP made a strong plea for the TV show's demise, with a list of reasons why *Amos 'n' Andy* should be removed from the air, a list that today seems overly harsh and humorless. The NAACP stated that the show revealed Negroes as "inferior, dumb, lazy, and dishonest . . . dodging work of any kind"; every black is "cast as either a clown or a crook," and doctors and lawyers are "quacks, thieves and slippery cowards"; black women are "cackling, screaming shrews." Those same charges, of course, might have been leveled at the white characters in *The Honeymooners, Sergeant Bilko, The Bickersons,* and all of Red Skelton's gallery of incompetents and nincompoops.

GOSDEN AND CORRELL WERE CRUSHED by attacks on their beloved characters. Correll responded to the accusations in 1972 by saying, "We weren't kidding race. We were kidding people—human nature—things that happened to anybody and everybody. Our characters depicted cross-sections of life. Everybody knew a wheeler-dealer like Kingfish, living off his wits; or a blustering Andy, who never learned from experience. I knew a lot of people like that—they were relatives of mine."

The issues around the show remain unresolved—*Amos 'n' Andy* was far more than what it has unfairly and too simply come to be remembered—an embarrassing footnote to black history and a shorthand term for racism. The issues, much like the show, are complex, subtle, and filled with paradoxes. For instance, while blacks could only play blacks on the air (invisible or not), black roles provided jobs in radio that were scarce. Likewise, black listeners were starved for any show that reflected their lives, although an early black-produced series,

A Harlem Family, failed. Listeners searching for black entertainers had to settle for musical shows.

There has never been a single black party line on the show. In 1973, long after Ernestine Wade originated Sapphire, she recalled, "It was a happy experience. I know there were those who were offended by it, but I still have people stop me on the street to tell me how much they enjoyed it. And many of those people are black members of the NAACP." Wade considered Sapphire just one of many black types in her repertoire; on some episodes, she played three different women.

The distinguished black actor Canada Lee, however, claimed that "a virtual iron curtain" divided blacks from most radio shows. "Where is the story of our lives in terms of the ghetto slums in which we must live? Who would know us only by listening to Amos and Andy, Beulah, and Rochester?" Most black actors who worked regularly in radio or TV claimed not to be offended. For them, of course, it meant survival— or as Hattie McDaniel wryly remarked in her own defense after winning an Oscar as Mammy in *Gone With the Wind:* "Either I can play a maid in a movie for seven hundred dollars a week or I can *be* a maid for seven dollars a week." Black entertainers, looking for any entrée to white America, used *Amos 'n' Andy* to further their own careers: Duke Ellington's band appeared in *Check and Double Check,* and dancer Bill Robinson and other prominent black stars took part in *Harlem's Salute to Amos 'n' Andy.*

Shirley Mitchell, who played several comedy parts on radio alongside black actresses, recalls that a few black women in radio, such as Lillian Randolph, "felt a deep resentment about their roles. These were really good black actors and they had to play dumb parts." Eddie (Rochester) Anderson, who rarely spoke out on anything, remarked to *Variety* in 1949: "I haven't seen anything objectionable. I don't see why certain characters are called stereotypes. . . . The Negro characters being presented are not labeling the Negro race any more than Luigi is labeling the Italian people as a whole. Beulah is not playing the part of thousands of Negroes, but only the part of one person, Beulah."

It made whites who loved the show feel better about laughing at it to hear that a lot of blacks liked the show. But Erik Barnouw attacked that cozy idea by insisting that *Amos 'n' Andy* told whites that blacks on the show "were lovely people, essentially happy people, ignorant and somewhat shiftless and lazy in a quaint, lovable way . . . better off where they were," maintaining that the show "made poverty somehow charming and fitting. The nation needed the fantasy." Melvin Patrick Ely added: "To depict black characters . . . whom whites could care about on a human level at least nibbled" at the fantasy, but he argued that "The series comforted most white listeners more than it challenged them. To convince oneself that *Amos 'n' Andy* was true and humane and that blacks liked it was an easy, cheap way to get some moral reassurance . . ."

By now, the radio and TV shows have been blurred so long in the public mind that *Amos 'n' Andy* has become a buzzword and *cause célèbre* in black cultural history. Despite its insouciance, it remained for some a hurtful reminder. "In private, as in my household, the show was relished," conceded Mel Watkins. "But the comic exaggeration was a public embarrassment for many African-Americans who had struggled to middle-class respectability."

The show became a victim of opposing forces, but then blacks also disagreed, and still do, over *Porgy and Bess, The Adventures of Huckleberry Finn, Green Pastures,* and other white depictions of black life. Many blacks felt that Diahann Carroll's bleached-out sitcom *Julia* was a form of whiteface and that *The Jeffersons* was a 1980s minstrel show without the songs. Yet few issues divided blacks as did this seemingly innocent comedy that was comically accurate but inaccurate as a full picture of black life.

The main case against the show is that *Amos 'n' Andy* was, for far too long, the only TV program about blacks. The whole issue might never have exploded had there been a black soap opera or sitcom. Until *I Spy,* there were no black spies, cops, cowboys, private eyes, or families to balance a show about a couple of bumbling black guys some saw as clowns but others found endearing. Not until *Sanford and Son* in 1971 did another all-black TV series appear.

Roy Wilkins decided that the TV version was too "burlesque," although in fact it was far less burlesque than it had been when he liked it. He felt that blacks and whites had grown since then and "what was endured and even chuckled over is now seen in its true colors, and resentment is evident on all sides." Wilkins vetoed a boycott, however, aware that many blacks loved the show.

Major black comics were appalled when it got the hook. Redd Foxx said, "It was comedy, man, it was laughs. That's what it's all about . . . get some laughs and you're not hurting anyone. Whatever they were doing, they were doing for an era. And they made it possible for me to do something so that after me, other young comedians could do something, and after them others." Flip Wilson said, "I watched it when I was a child and I thought it was funny—and I didn't object to the dialect." Younger black comics, like Richard Pryor, called the show "an outrage." Bill Cosby, after becoming TV's first black superstar, mounted the barricades against *Amos 'n' Andy*.

Jesse Jackson, however, went so far as to say that the show (and also *Beulah*) made blacks proud: "Black people had enough sense to appreciate them as funny people playing at their roles. . . . There was a tradition in our community of funny people. It did not dominate black life to the extent that it has been projected." The black scholar and writer Henry Louis Gates, Jr., insisted that the TV show "transformed racist stereotypes into authentic black humor." The NAACP's Walter White believed that the show's warm and fuzzy quotient only proved that in order for blacks to be acceptable to whites, they had to be cuddly.

The man who issued the edict to ban the show from the airwaves, Sig Mickelson, was the liberal head of CBS-TV's news and public-affairs division. His attempted compromise with the NAACP, to make the show "acceptable," fell apart when the group claimed there was no way to salvage *Amos 'n' Andy* without rebuilding it from the ground up using black writers; CBS had even suggested bringing in black academics like Kenneth Clark to study the show. Those uneasy about the program wanted to rewrite it as a social document, but *A Raisin in the Sun* it was not. A point too often lost on its sincere critics—who demanded a brighter Andy, an honest Calhoun, an industrious King-fish, and a sweeter Sapphire—is that the nature, purpose, and duty of comedy is to poke fun at people, even black people.

A screening for twenty NAACP executives turned into a PR disaster that convinced CBS the show was a lost cause. Walter White felt any compromise was a sellout and the NAACP head was in no mood to be placated after his losing twenty-year war against the radio show. Thurgood Marshall, the NAACP's chief counsel, said, "*Amos 'n' Andy* and everything like it has to go." He referred to it, pointedly, as "this continuing harm." Arthur Spingarn, one of the NAACP's highest-ranking white members, attempted a naïve, if not laughable, compromise: to include a disclaimer before each show, saying it was all a caricature, not reality; to "minimize" the Kingfish's role; remove all "stereotyped corruptions" of speech; and to run jingles touting "good intergroup relations." He suggested that at the end of each show, Amos, Andy, and the Kingfish sit down and "converse with each other in correct English, and with perfect diction," and exchange "a few good-natured comments" about that night's episode. No major changes were ever made.

The NAACP won the battle when the show was canceled but perhaps lost the war when *Amos 'n' Andy* went into syndication in a hundred markets, twice as many as had aired it when it was on the network, and eventually it was seen on 218 stations here and abroad, including Kenya and Nigeria. In 1997, the head of the NAACP, Kweisi Mfume, said, "If it was bad thirty years ago, it's equally bad now. The only thing worse than selling the tapes is somebody wanting to buy them or view them. We are providing fuel for bigots who like to believe that series accurately depicts black people."

Removing the show from the air was a Pyrrhic victory for blacks; its controversial demise very likely frightened off potential sponsors and networks for black shows. After it left CBS, there was nearly a decade of no blacks on TV at all, until Nat King Cole's short-lived nightly fifteen-minute songfest in 1961, Bill Cosby's much-ballyhooed costarring role in *I Spy* in 1965, and Diahann Carroll's lily-black *Julia* in 1968. A Harlem resident said that during the 1950s he was forced to turn to *The Shadow*, which he called "the closest thing to a spade they had on the air."

At eighty-three, shortly before his death in 1982, Freeman Gosden—who had tried to remain above the fray with a wounded and cautious silence—finally told a Chicago reporter: "I don't think blacks as a body resented the program. That certainly wasn't what we intended, nor did we ever feel it when we were on the air." A friend of Gosden's said, "It bothered him the rest of his life that *Amos 'n' Andy* fell from public esteem."

THE RADIO SHOW LASTED, remarkably, until 1960, but by 1954 it was all pretty much over for Gosden and Correll on radio. Their last big fling, *The Amos 'n' Andy Music Hall,* was a sterile, stilted packaged show with canned applause and no sponsor. Amos, Andy, and the King-fish spun records and killed time between discs and a weekly "mystery guest," such as Kay Kyser ("Evenin, folks, how y'all?" . . . "Why, it's Mr. Kay Kyser!").

It was sad to hear two onetime radio giants introducing the Ames Brothers latest hit, announcing the Crew Cuts singing "Crazy 'Bout You, Baby," and shilling for Kay Starr's new disc ("What we got fo' de folks now, Andy?"). Gosden and Correll, ever the troupers, did their best to squeeze in some jokes about the records themselves: "What is dis heah RPM on de label, Kingfish?" . . . "Dat stands fo' revolution" . . . "What does dat mean?" . . . "Ya know, Andy, like when da earth revolves aroun' da sun" . . . "How long has *dat* been goin' on?" It was a heroic last stand when you realize that *Amos 'n' Andy* entered radio in the Charleston era and hung around until the early days of rock 'n' roll.

On their twenty-fifth anniversary in 1953, an hour-long radio program paid Gosden and Correll tribute in "The Life Story of Amos 'n' Andy"; it was hosted by Edward R. Murrow and had cursory walk-on regards delivered by Bing Crosby and Jack Benny, who sounded a bit embarrassed to be included, plus a historic bipartisan appearance of David Sarnoff and William Paley, praising the team's fine work. The whole thing had rather a bleak ring about it, a eulogy posing as a gala.

Gosden and Correll's contribution was possible to treasure but difficult to measure in 1953, when America still took *Amos 'n' Andy* for granted. Nearly half a century later, the show seems more remarkable than it must have then. Is there any radio or TV comedy today that could captivate a nation for more than three decades? *Amos 'n' Andy* was the show that did just that, more deserving of being cherished for its sly, charming self than for being chastised—in the safely enlightened sanctuary of hindsight—for what it was not.

— 15 —

Radio Noir—
Cops and Grave Robbers

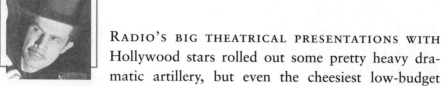

RADIO'S BIG THEATRICAL PRESENTATIONS WITH Hollywood stars rolled out some pretty heavy dramatic artillery, but even the cheesiest low-budget detective show could afford ornate scenic descriptions laid down by a grim narrator. On many detective shows—*Sam Spade, Boston Blackie, The Adventures of Philip Marlowe, The Adventures of Nero Wolfe, The Fat Man,* and *Mr. and Mrs. North* (a thinner *Thin Man*)—the hero would sketch in the scene in rich detail, as in this excerpt from *Sam Spade,* with Howard Duff speaking to us in the typical voice-over fashion that took us inside Spade's mind:

"What I found on the roof did surprise me a bit. It was a rope and grappling hook, human-fly type, which fitted in with the circusy aspect the caper was beginning to take on . . . but I would never have taken Sylvia for a stunt-woman. . . . I took a few quick knee bends to get in shape for what lay ahead . . . slid down the banister to the top floor, somersaulted into the elevator and rode it down to the lobby, no hands. Pausing only to acknowledge the applause of the scrubwoman, I skated on over to the phone . . ."

Sam Spade, set in evocative San Francisco, was the archetype, starring Duff as the cynical private eye with a wandering eye, a lingering thirst, a weakness for arch metaphors and wise-guy slang who addressed his presumably slinky secretary, Effie, at the top of each week's show. To Sam and company, cases were "capers," women were "dames" (or just "blondes" or "redheads"), a cop was a "gumshoe," a "flatfoot," or a "shamus." Most were narrated in the then-standard Hollywood tough-guy manner by two-bit Bogeys who disdained the police, always depicted as plodding, well-meaning stumblebums who were no match for the dashing private detective with his brash manners and wry insults. Their colorful vocabulary was full of strained meta-

Overleaf, clockwise from top left: Raymond Edward Johnson (*Inner Sanctum*), Brett Morrison and Gertrude Warner (as Lamont Cranston and Margot Lane in *The Shadow*), Jack Webb (*Dragnet*), Arch Oboler directs Alla Nazimova (*Everyman's Theater*)

phors and overwrought similes, now the stuff of parody—phrases like "you might as well try to start a conga line in a cathedral"; one tough case was "like trying to follow a grain of rice in a Shanghai suburb." Femme fatales inspired writers to literary heights—in one, a woman is described as looking like "118 pounds of warm smoke"; another had a voice "like a furnace full of marshmallows."

Listeners now like to flatter themselves about their fanciful imaginations, but narrative was one of radio's most refined elements and made the shows different from, and often superior to, location-bound movies. Billy Wilder admits that he stole such common radio devices as the interior voice-over for movies like *Double Indemnity* and *Sunset Boulevard.*

Yet the great radio detective shows failed to last the way comparable movies of the era have. They're almost totally forgotten, even though they used the same eerie ambience, plot devices, stereotypes, language—and, in many cases, actors. When you look at a noir film now, a classic like *Night and the City*—or just close your eyes and listen to it— it's highly reminiscent of radio private-eye dramas, all of which seemed to have been "shot" in grainy black-and-white, populated with cardboard heavies, wise-guy heroes, and slinky, sloe-eyed babes with insinuating voices. Everybody speaks hard-boiled Mickey Spillaneish or ersatz Raymond Chandlerese, cast in the same cynical, unsentimental mold as Dashiell Hammett's Sam Spade—incorruptible and rigorously true to himself but never self-righteous.

A passage from an episode of the highly regarded *Adventures of Philip Marlowe,* which debuted in 1947 starring Van Heflin (replaced by a grittier Gerald Mohr), seems to come straight from the pen of Chandler sketching in a still, moody Los Angeles air: "I listened a while to the wailing seagulls. All at once I'd realized that the wind had died, the Santa Ana had blown itself out. The red wind was done. It was over." Clipped first-person narrative was supplanted by an even more intimate, more melodramatic second-person style, as in, "You're in your office looking out the window one day when a dame walks in and asks if you have the time. Suddenly, you think to yourself . . ."

The writer George Wells refers to another radio device, called "the look-see system," in which a character points out details of a scene to a friend in order to inform the blind listener, as in: "Irene, do you see what I see? There's a little man in dark glasses wearing a red raincoat walking his poodle next to a police car parked outside that cigar store."

The private-eye shows, concisely plotted and tightly written if overly fond of trick endings, were the ancestors of today's much-longer-winded TV cops and robbers. The heroes were far closer to being free spirits, quasi-vigilantes who led double lives as reporters, gourmands, ministers, or playboys; some were lone wolves—rogues like Michael Shayne, Boston Blackie, and, well, Richard Rogue—prowling for action; a few were exotic and came with literary credentials: Charlie Chan, The Saint, Harry Lime, Mr. Moto, Bulldog Drummond, and, to be sure, Sherlock Holmes. One had even been to college and was a professional man, Perry Mason; the show ran during the day on radio and was an anomaly—a sleuth surrounded by soap operas.

Two other genre gumshoes were *Nick Carter, Master Detective* and *Richard Diamond, Private Detective,* the first played through its entire run by Lon Clark and the second by singer Dick Powell, who somehow made the transformation from dewy-eyed, pomaded Warner Bros. tenor to lighthearted but tough-talking PI, with a stop along the way as Philip Marlowe in the movie *Murder, My Sweet,* which set him up for his radio role. The show hinted in the opening at Diamond's tuneful past, with Powell whistling the theme song and occasionally even crooning to his girl friend, making him the first singing detective.

The radio audience's addiction to cop shows coincided with the real-life rise of gangsters and criminals in the twenties and thirties, when newspapers dramatized their exploits with lurid, detailed stories that provided the grist for radio's ceaseless cops-and-robbers mill. The actress Elspeth Eric, who played many gun molls on cop shows, regularly received letters from prisoners who had fallen in love with her on-air seductive dames.

The private eyes' female confederates and confidantes were the mature older women of radio, all of those assistants, secretaries, and "companions" of dashing detectives—Lamont Cranston's efficient Margot Lane, Nick Carter's equally adroit Patsy Bowen, Sam Spade's sweetly discombobulated Effie, Steve Wilson's sexily businesslike Lorelei Kilbourne, and George Valentine's (of *Let George Do It*) flip Brooksie. None of these sidekicks did a whole lot of typing, but they could plug a gangster at a hundred feet, were always available for hair-raising assignments, had witty rejoinders, and sounded incredibly stylish. It was easy to be seduced by these older Real Women, whose knowing repartee dripped with what even a twelve-year-old boy recognized as innuendo. (Aural sex, you could call it.)

Lurene Tuttle, who played Effie Perine, Sam Spade's loyal, long-suffering secretary, once spoke to the subject of their much-speculated-about relationship: "In the original *Maltese Falcon,* Effie was just as much of a wisecracker as Sam. She was almost a female Sam. I discussed this with Bill Spier, who directed and wrote the show. He and I decided that it would enhance Sam's character, make him even more masculine, if Effie were very kind and sweet and good—a soft little creature, you know, just a dear good little girl. He went around and made love to a million other girls, but he always came back to Effie."

Candy Matson (Natalie Masters), who worked the San Francisco waterfront on a popular West Coast series, was the only female private eye of note, and even she had to endure such descriptions as, "Figure? She picks up where Miss America leaves off. Clothes? She makes a peasant dress look like opening night at the opera. Hair? Blonde, of course. And eyes? Just the right shade of blue to match the hair."

Private eyes tended to be dapper and suave, like the chap in *The Falcon,* derived from a screen character whose nickname was never explained but whose given name was Mike Waring, introduced as "that free-lance detective who is always ready with a hand for oppressed men and an eye for repressed women"—whatever that meant.

Other PIs were noble as well as cynical. Among dozens of them prowling radio's mean streets, the most distinctive were *Boston Blackie* (*"Enemy to those who make him an enemy, friend to those who have no friends"*), about a master thief-turned-New York private eye, based on a series of B movies with Chester Morris, who was the first Blackie on the air, before Richard Kollmar took over; Nick Carter, the generic hero of a series of cheap dime novels; and Mr. Keen of *Mr. Keen, Tracer of Lost Persons* (or, in Bob and Ray's version, "Mr. Trace, Keener Than Most Persons"), who spent much of his time in saloons.

Then there were the public eyes—the by-the-book, humorless, heavy-footed, hard-nosed, unromantic federal agents on *The FBI in Peace and War, This Is Your FBI, Gang Busters, Mr. District Attorney,* and *Counterspy* (*"Washington, calling David Harding, counterspy . . .*

Washington, calling David Harding, counterspy . . ." "David Harding, calling Washington . . .").

Gang Busters, one of the works of radio crime-buster and producer Phillips H. Lord, premiered in 1935 with an episode on the capture and killing of John Dillinger. As Joe Bevilacqua noted in an introduction to a Smithsonian collection of recordings of radio detectives: "The 1930s was the age of the glamorized gangster—Al Capone, Baby Face Nelson, Pretty Boy Floyd, Bonnie and Clyde. Lord decided it was time to glamorize the work of the men who fought the underworld." From roughly 1936 to 1957, actual criminals were sought and often but not always brought to justice. For ten years, *Gang Busters* was narrated by the former superintendent of the New Jersey State Police, one Col. H. Norman Schwarzkopf (father of the 1991 Gulf War general) and later by a retired New York City police commissioner, while cops on the cases provided authentic detail.

Gang Busters began with the sound of shuffling prisoners' feet, followed by a burst of machine guns and the warning wail of a siren, after which a voice would bellow over a loudspeaker: *"Calling the police! Calling the G-men! Calling all Americans to war on the underworld!"* Many of its episodes were told from the villain's viewpoint, giving the programs an extra *frisson* of excitement, and each show began with Lord discussing the case with a law-enforcement official, lending an even thicker air of reality. This was followed by nationwide "crime watch" alarms that alerted listeners to be on the lookout for bad guys at large, all of whom were "armed and extremely dangerous," and gave detailed, scary descriptions of the man on the loose, including scars, moles, and other physical marks. Supposedly, *Gang Busters*'s on-air "wanted" posters led to 110 busts in its first three years.

Lord also produced *Counterspy, Treasury Agent, G-Men,* and *Policewoman,* the godfathers of today's pulpy reality-based TV dramatizations, such as *America's Most Wanted* and *Unsolved Mysteries.* Another Lord production, *Mr. District Attorney,* which ran from 1941 to 1949, opened with a stirring oath in which Mr. DA proclaimed himself *"the champion of the people, defender of truth and guardian of our fundamental rights to life, liberty and the pursuit of happiness,"* delivered in a stentorian voice in what sounded like a vast marbled hall. Mr.

District Attorney, who had no other name, was assisted by a guy with no first name, known only as Harrington.

There was a glut of radio detectives, largely because the shows were done on the cheap for about a tenth of what a comedy show cost. *The Jack Benny Program* budget came to $40,000 a week, whereas *Sam Spade* could be knocked out for about $6,000. No star was required (Dick Powell and Basil Rathbone were exceptions), which is perhaps why they rarely pulled high ratings; Rathbone's classic *Adventures of Sherlock Holmes,* which ran for six years, was again the exception, but then it was a literary classic and a movie spin-off.

Most of the crime shows were, apart from the hero and perhaps a riveting opening, fairly interchangeable. One notable exception was Carlton E. Morse's *I Love a Mystery,* which neatly interwove two related radio genres, the private eye and the suspense program, into a seamless original that became the most respected show of its type. Morse gave the series wit, spirit, and the bantering interplay of three diverse characters, all of which allowed the creator of the compelling but conservative *One Man's Family* to indulge his more fanciful, swashbuckling side. Jack Packard was the valiant leader; Doc Long, the funny and frenetic Texan; and Reggie Yorke, the sophisticated two-fisted Englishman. They were originally played, respectively, by Michael Raffetto, Barton Yarborough (both housebound regulars on *One Man's Family*), and Walter Patterson, who, when the show moved east, was replaced by a newcomer named Tony Randall. The trio of engaging investigators worked out of the A-1 Detective Agency ("No job too tough, no mystery too baffling"), but the original premise took a detour to the Orient and they turned into far-flung soldiers of fortune who had first met after surviving a Shanghai bombing together. Between assignments, the boys hung out in Frisco saloons.

I Love a Mystery, which opened with a train whistle—that most promising of radio sounds—had a long journey, on and off the air from 1939 to 1952, much of it on railroads traveling through exotic lands. The titles of a few of their adventures sum up the lip-smackingly sinister flavor of the series: "My Beloved Is a Vampire," "The Hermit of San Filipo Adavapo," "The Graves of Wamperjaw, Texas," and "The Thing That Wouldn't Die." Even listeners with a limited palate for shaggy ghost stories tuned in for the spooky atmospherics. In one writer's analysis, "*I Love a Mystery* at its best was a vivid, spine-tingling audio version of pulp horror fiction."

One escapade, "The Twenty Traders of Timbuktu," ran twenty-two episodes, for Morse was at heart a novelist who just happened to work in radio. He cranked the show out in magazine-serial fashion, separating each escapade into episodes (just like the Saturday matinee serials it resembled in its love of cliff-hanger endings), some of which got so entangled in plot details that Morse forgot to unsnarl them. Like *One Man's Family,* the shows had a tendency to lapse into more talk than action, but Morse had a knack for creating mood and giving his detectives more depth than most hard-boiled private eyes; the *I Love a Mystery* trio were soft-boiled lugs.

MOST COPS-AND-ROBBERS SHOWS leaned heavily on a narrator, which some writers, like Robert E. Lee, considered a "lame gimmick," but the show that defied the genre was *Dragnet,* whose bored cop-narrator created an understated dramatic aura. The program's unique stark, naturalistic, semiexistential, just-the-facts style, devised by actor/producer Jack Webb, influenced scores of lesser and better TV cop shows, but other shows could never imitate it; they could only parody it, a sure sign of its indelible singularity.

In every way, Webb's show was a stylistic breakthrough, combining the disciplined drudgery of the professional cop whose work is largely legwork with an intriguing pair of grim investigators whose private lives we knew little about. *Dragnet's* unemotional, nonliterary cop talk grabbed you—there were no fancy similes or purple passages in the monosyllabic world of Sgt. Joe Friday and his partner, Ben Romero, first played by Barton Yarborough. He was succeeded by Barry Phillips, Herb Ellis, and, finally and most memorably, by Ben Alexander, who followed *Dragnet* to TV, where Romero was Anglo-ized into "Frank Smith." When Harry Morgan took over the role, he inexplicably became "Frank Gannon."

The partners went about their no-nonsense jobs like "real" policemen—or so the series' heavy emphasis on painstaking methodology and laconic cop talk (just what *was* a "bunco squad"?) made it appear: "Sunday, October ninth, eight forty-seven A.M. It was cool in Los

Angeles. My partner's name is Ben Romero. The boss is chief of detectives Thad Brown. My name's Friday. We were working the daywatch out of robbery when a call came in from Central Division . . ." The initial 1949 series deliberately, even maddeningly, withheld as much personal information about Joe and Ben as possible, tantalizing listeners with only an occasional strained line of levity about Joe's lousy cooking or Ben's sore feet and nudgy wife. No girl friends were allowed on the show to divert Joe's attention and presumably taint or dilute his passionate pursuit of justice.

While Friday and Romero had no off-duty lives, today's reality-based TV cops now spill their guts about their anything-but-drab souls—their troubled home lives and dark pasts, their battles with booze, women, drugs, parents, and children. All of which would have shocked and embarrassed tight-lipped, uptight Sgt. Friday.

With Joe's dedication to law and order and his moralistic curtain speeches, *Dragnet* was like a big-city western with all of Los Angeles as the wide open spaces and Joe Friday as a John Wayne in streetclothes who lived by the book and indeed spoke in police code numbers ("We got him on a 502, but he was also wanted on a 327 and a 1258") when he wasn't delivering moralistic editorials.

Prior to *Dragnet,* Webb had hired out on *Pat Novak for Hire* as the jaded, tough-talking Novak ("I'll dirty you up like a locker-room towel"), and before that he had done a brief hitch in a 1947 show called *Johnny Madero, Pier 23.* Johnny, who prowled the San Francisco waterfront, was far more of the wise guy than Joe, though clearly his ancestor—a transitional figure between the hard-bitten Sam Spade school of private eyes and the even harder-bitten Joe Friday police academy. Both shows were written by Richard Breen in the square-shouldered, squinty-eyed style that became the *Dragnet* stamp. Neither gumshoe had any illusions, but Sam had more fun than Joe, an anti-social drudge who got his only kicks delivering sarcastic lectures to criminals.

Dragnet's famed "only the names have been changed to protect the innocent" became a part of American lore, as did Webb's clipped response to long-winded eyewitnesses ("Just the facts, ma'am"—a phrase Webb claimed he never used on the show until Stan Freberg's dead-on parody, *St. George and the Dragonet,* which became the first million-selling comedy record); the famous four notes of the theme by Walter Schumann—*dum-de-dum-dum;* the initial phrase of the opening narrative: "I was working the daywatch out of homicide . . ."; and the voice-of-doom monotone of Hal Gibney's or George Fenneman's closing summation: "*On August 23rd 1947, in and for the city and county of Los Angeles, Luther Waldo Motley was placed on trial on two counts of mopery . . . in a moment, the results of that trial . . .*" The show was delivered in stark black-and-white sound bites, and at the end, as the villains were led away to jail and their sentences pronounced, the announcer intoned, "*The story you have just heard is true. Only the names have been changed to protect the innocent.*"

The terse scripts were written in a kind of police blotterese that captured the language of crime and lab reports (based on actual cases from the files of the Los Angeles Police Department), and was unique to radio. When the show moved to TV and became an even bigger hit there, Webb added almost nothing—he simply photographed Joe and Frank Smith trudging from dreary, sparsely furnished house to dingy diner to dimly lit coffee shop to drab fingerprint lab. In fact, the neorealistic show was such a total radio creature that it gained nothing from TV—you could shut your eyes and absorb it totally through your ears—and it actually lost something whenever Joe and Frank attempted a bit of jaunty byplay in a halfhearted effort to humanize them. On TV, Webb came off as a humorless stick and Harry Morgan's Frank Gannon looked sheepish. The undynamic duo rarely busted down doors and never romanced bimbos with names like Velda. They were quietly macho; Joe's only emotional outbursts were his self-righteous General Patton–like sermons, often beginning, "Listen, mister . . ." When Webb took *Dragnet* to television in 1951, everyone tried to tell him he had to "make it more visual," but NBC's Pat Weaver, although himself a TV innovator, warned Webb to leave it alone. Years later, Webb told Weaver he had taken his advice: "I shot the first fifty-two shows straight from the radio scripts, with no changes whatsoever."

Today, the TV shows seem limp and laughably flat, like animated radio, which is what they are. Webb's wooden acting is a collection of squints, sneers, and self-satisfied smirks (hilariously mimicked by Dan Aykroyd in the 1987 movie parody), making painfully clear how organic to radio it really was. The flaccid video version—the first TV series broadcast in color, in 1953—became a preachy law-and-order polemic that turned Webb into a police apologist and crusader.

Herb Ellis, who knew Webb in high school and first worked with him in college radio and with whom Webb roomed for a time in San Francisco and Los Angeles, was there at the creation. Ellis, a seasoned radio actor and sometime writer-director, was a regular on *Tales of the Texas Rangers* and was one of various Archies on *The Adventures of Nero Wolfe,* but his primary place of business was *Dragnet,* on which he performed in all but a dozen shows.

"*Dragnet* was created at my dining room table," Ellis recalls, but the show's genesis was a crime lab technician that Webb played in *He Walked by Night,* a 1948 movie with Richard Basehart done in semi-documentary style, with a terse narrative in which the word *dragnet* is heard several times. The pilot script they wrote in 1948 was called *Joe Friday, Room 5,* which didn't sell. "*Dum-de-dum-dum* hadn't been born yet, until we brought in Walter Schumann," continues Ellis, "but we had a march theme of some kind. Everyone at NBC loved it and Lorillard [the cigarette maker] came aboard right away" with Fatima cigarettes as the sponsor. Ellis credits Richard Breen with creating the format, taciturn tone, and everything people think of now as *Dragnet.* "The first *Dragnet* and the last *Dragnet* were very similar," notes Ellis. Don Stanley, the announcer on the first radio episode, says, "I remember all the scrambling to get the show on the air. I didn't even know whether to pronounce it *Dragnet* or *Drag-net.* They were changing it right up to airtime." Webb, remembers Ellis, was "absolutely aware" from the start that *Dragnet* was a breakthrough in the flatfoot genre.

Dragnet was so tightly formatted and stylized that certain actors were flummoxed by Webb's insistence on flat deliveries. "He was a stickler, especially on TV. There were a lot of very good actors Jack made very unhappy," Ellis chuckles. "He didn't want actors, he wanted readers. Actors want to act and they couldn't stand the show's monotonal acting style. They didn't get it."

Peggy Webber, a veteran radio actress and *Dragnet* regular, recalled: "We got along very well because we thought the same way. He [Webb] finally did what I'd been trying to do in radio for years, to fight against the overacting, to make it all seem real. He'd turn the pots [the sound board] way up, tell us to step back from the mike and underplay everything." Webb regularly had actors stand back from the mike, to make them sound more lifelike, and wouldn't employ "voice actors" like William Conrad, whom he accused of "listening to themselves." He told Peggy Webber, "I don't want those rounded mellifluous tones. I want people who sound like people."

Ellis agrees that Webb gradually turned into somber, humorless Joe Friday. "He did become like the character. He became a do-gooder and very conservative. The show turned him into a right-winger. Even though he loved jazz, he was very tightly wound, very driven. He was intent on a career and he wanted stardom." Unlike most actors, Webb didn't mind being typecast as one character for most of his career. "Oh, no," says Ellis. "He rode it as long as he could."

When the TV version was canceled, Webb became Warner Bros.' head of TV production, but, notes Ellis, "He was no good as a mogul." In 1969, he produced a new *Dragnet* movie not much different from the *Joe Friday, Room 5* show he had done two decades earlier that changed the sound and style of cop shows. To the end, Jack Webb was unable to resist *Dragnet*'s siren call.

THE SHADOW WAS A TOTAL aural experience, taking place in the dark night of the soul. In a way, it was the ultimate radio show, and its concept was soon shadowed by other phantom figures: *The Whistler, The Saint,* and the oily guardian of *Inner Sanctum*'s unoiled door.

The Shadow was fairly far-out by radio standards of the 1930s, but by the 1940s the once-offbeat show had settled into a routine formula. By then, Lamont Cranston was established as a detective rather than a freelance playboy, with the Shadow's voice mechanically slotted twice into each show, once before the commercial. By the mid-forties the Shadow seemed but a shadow of his original self, and the program grew less eerie, a mundane cops-and-robbers show with a cackling mystery voice that invariably cornered the bad guys in the final scene.

It debuted in 1931 as part of something called *The Blue Coal Radio Revue* when the Shadow character was the show's narrator/host (later fleshed out) based solely on its vocal gimmick. The plots of the show were pretty thin, but nobody tuned in for the plots. *The Shadow* was the highest-rated dramatic program from the 1930s to the early 1950s; after sinking from sight in 1954, it flickered to life again in the early 1960s in syndicated reruns.

When Orson Welles became Lamont Cranston, not only did he have nothing to do with writing the show, as many assumed, often he didn't even know beforehand what an episode was about. "Not rehearsing—that was part of my deal with Blue Coal, the sponsor—made it much more interesting," recalled Welles. "When I was thrown down the well or into some fiendish snake pit, I never knew how I'd get out." He called *The Shadow* "a part of American mythology." Indeed, anyone growing up then could do a credible imitation Shadow, especially those evil "heh-heh-heh-heh-heh"s in the show's famous opening.

People willingly sat through the flimsy stories for those moments of high camp when the Shadow's filtered voice (first Welles, then, for much longer, Brett Morrison) trapped the villains in a room ("I'll getcha, Shadder—where are ya?"), then cackled them into submission with his hideous laugh. Helpless hoodlums addressed him as "Mr. Shadow." On one episode, it is suggested that the Shadow is not invincible and may be foiled, even destroyed, by an electric eye. "The Shadow can hide himself from the human eye," Lamont tells Margot Lane, his trusted assistant, "but he has a physical being and the photoelectric beam could detect his presence." That was the first time we learned that the Shadow was "a physical being."

The Shadow's hypnotic power—learned "long ago while traveling in the Orient, the power to cloud men's minds so they cannot see him" (one never learned just how this effect was achieved)—was patiently explained each week by the announcer: "*The Shadow, Lamont Cranston—a man of wealth, a student of science, and a master of other peoples' minds—devotes his life to righting wrongs, protecting the innocent and punishing the guilty. Cranston is known to the underworld as the Shadow—never seen, only heard, his true identity known only to his constant friend and companion Margot Lane . . .*" (Just how constant we could only surmise.) Listeners interpreted the Shadow as the Voice of Conscience, who knew "*what evil l-l-lurks in the hearts of men*" and that the "*weed of crime bears bitter fruit.*"

The Shadow, like many another pulp radio drama of the period, never masqueraded as art, but it perfected the knack of intriguing listeners with a catchy, scarifyingly crafted device.

THE SHADOW'S OPENING UNDOUBTEDLY inspired another familiar opening: "*I am the Whistler and I know many things, for I walk by night. I know many strange tales hidden in the hearts of men and women who have stepped into the shadows. Yes, I know the nameless terrors of which they dare not speak.*" Just why the Whistler whistled was never explained, nor was there any need to; it was purely to make your hair curl. Clearly, he wasn't calling for his dog.

The Whistler's wavery warble, with its haunting two-octave minor-key whistle, was performed live each week by a woman, Dorothy Roberts, who during the war would dash in for the dress rehearsal between shifts at Lockheed. The whistle was accompanied by footsteps on what sounded like a damp street; you couldn't see the hazy glow of a streetlight but, boy, could you ever hear it. Many of those menacing voice-overs were read by men whose slithery voices and grim chortles might now seem comically excessive, but when first heard they were frighteningly lifelike and ghoulish.

There were many cardboard spook shows about as subtle as a campfire ghost story—shows like *The Haunting Hour* ("*No, no, stay where you are. Do not break the stillness of this moment, for this is a time of mystery, a time when imagination is free and moves forward swiftly. This is . . .* The Haunting Hour"); *Murder at Midnight* ("*The witching hour—when night is darkest, our fears the strongest, our strength at its lowest ebb. Midnight, when graves gape open and death strikes . . .* Murder at Midnight"); *Nightmare* (hosted by Peter Lorre, who greeted listeners each week with, "*Out of the dark of night, from the shadow of the senses, comes this—the fantasy of fear*"); and *The Witch's Tale*, in which Nancy, the wickedest witch in Salem, sits by a fireplace stroking her black cat, Satan, and spins horror stories.

There were, however, some clever knock-offs, and chief among them was *Escape*, a more action-oriented, streamlined version of *Suspense*, which took place mainly in your mind, whereas *Escape* happened in your gut and took you to actual places for high adventure, adapting tales by Poe, Conrad, Wells, du Maurier, and London. *Escape*, which ran from 1947 to 1954, with and without sponsorship and always without stars, was wilder, wider ranging, weirder, and, to be sure, bloodier than its rivals—man-eating ants, rats overrunning a lighthouse, etc. Its appeal was nicely summarized by the radio authority John Dunning: "Within five minutes, *Escape* listeners were up to their earlobes in alligators."

In the realm of radio noir, it is hard to find a more hair-raising program than *The Mysterious Traveler,* with its morbidly solicitous but nameless host (played by Maurice Tarplin), who welcomed us from a club car of a speeding train. While it wasn't, strictly speaking, science fiction, the show stirred up a chilling brew that blended futuristic fantasy "what-if?" tales with suspense and horror, all accomplished with great style and polish. *The Mysterious Traveler* never had a sponsor in its entire nine-year run, but it had an irresistible spine-tingling opening: *"This is the Mysterious Traveler, inviting you on another journey into the strange and the terrifying. I hope you will enjoy the trip, that it will thrill you a little and chill you a little. So settle back, get a good grip on your nerves and be comfortable—if you can . . ."*

To TRUE MONSTER MAVENS, the definitive horror show was *Lights Out,* whose name played on—indeed, gleefully exploited—the unseen aspects of radio by asking listeners to hear the show in total darkness, warning, "If you frighten easily, turn off your radio now." The original series, which premiered in 1934 and didn't switch the lights back on until 1939, was the brainchild of a near-forgotten spookmaster named Wyllis Cooper, who pioneered in stream-of-conscious horror. Fortunately, Cooper's first shows were forced to air after midnight, lending themselves nicely to spine-tingling audio effects—screeches in the night, footfalls, baying dogs—and, to open the show, tolling bells, and a gong followed by the announcer's insinuating, *"Lights out, everybody! This is the witching hour, the hour when dogs howl and evil is let loose on the sleeping world. . . . Want to he-e-ear about it? . . . Then turn out your lights . . ."*

When Cooper left the show in 1936, it was taken over by a young unknown playwright named Arch Oboler, whose only previous credits had been writing for Rudy Vallee and for the *Grand Hotel* series. Oboler made the show his own by pulling out all remaining terror stops with supernatural tales filled with genuine horror and monsters, employing experimental sound effects and stream of consciousness. He left in 1939, when the show went dark, and resumed it three years later. (Cooper went on to devise another, more literate fright-fest called *Quiet, Please,* which went in for surreal psychological horror stories.) Oboler's first show drew thousands of letters of outrage from terrified listeners, which almost ended his career. "I forgot my responsibility," he later apologized. "Radio had an impact far beyond TV."

Arch Oboler was to radio what Rod Serling became to television. With Himan Brown and Norman Corwin, he was one of the medium's three theatrical giants, and easily its most prolific: Between 1938 and 1948, he produced close to eight hundred works, many of them daring, outspoken, and heavily liberal dramas. Oboler was considered "experimental," with good reason: One script went inside the mind of an ugly man, another overheard the thoughts of a woman awaiting birth, and his most controversial production, Dalton Trumbo's antiwar *Johnny Got His Gun,* revealed the inner life of a horribly injured veteran considered a vegetable.

Oboler—the first playwright to have his own series to play with, *Arch Oboler's Plays*—was a Wellesian wunderkind who wrote for the people in his stock company, many of whom later became film and TV stars. He turned radio into his private toy, and, because *Lights Out* came on so late, when most listeners were asleep, he was allowed more freedom than he would have had in prime time. "I learned to write for a medium which, up to that time, dramatically, at least, had been badly bastardized as a combination of theater and motion pictures," he told Leonard Maltin.

Like Serling and Ray Bradbury, Oboler made fantasy, horror, and science fiction accessible and believably scary by avoiding the outrageous. "I didn't write about little green men," he told Maltin, "monsters with dripping talons and grotesque faces from the special effects department . . . I wrote about the terrors and monsters within each of us." Often his tales had moral implications, but often they had no higher purpose than to scare the hell out of you. Oboler also wrote and produced patriotic series, such as *Plays for Americans.* Like Corwin, Oboler lasted a decade and, like so many in 1948 and 1949, he left radio reluctantly and unhappily. But he was exhausted. "The writing of each play, over these years, has been a nerve-wracking, stomach-turning, head-spinning series of week-after-week crises." Oboler hadn't helped his own cause by attacking the low wages paid writers and blasting the networks, sponsors, and radio itself, which he called "a huge insatiable sausage grinder into which [the writer] feeds his creative life, to be converted into neatly packaged detergents."

Arch Oboler remains the acknowledged Edgar Allan Poe of the genre, and his shows can still send shivers up spines in episodes like "Cat Wife," in which Boris Karloff's wife turns into a wicked woman-sized feline, and "Chicken Heart," about a small heart that balloons until it swallows the world, accompanied by increasingly loud *ka-thump . . . ka-thump . . . ka-thump*s. Some were hideous even by today's gory standards, such as a Hannibal Lecter-like tale in which Peter Lorre plays a man feasting on a brain. As the TV critic Ron Miller recalls, "I used to have to listen to *Lights Out* in my parents' room."

Oboler was a speedy writer who, at his own dinner parties, would excuse himself at 11 P.M. and return at 1 A.M. with a finished script. He often got ideas from listening to sound-effects records, and took special delight in devising grotesque effects. His scare tactics included the sound of a man frying in the electric chair (sizzling bacon), bones being snapped (spareribs or Life Savers crushed between teeth), heads being severed (chopped cabbages), a knife slicing through a man's body (a slab of pork cut in two), and, most grisly of all, somebody eating human flesh (wet noodles squished with a bathroom plunger). Oboler cooked up a delicious pantryful of terror. The series' most celebrated audio effect—a man being turned inside out—was achieved by turning a watery rubber glove inside out to the accompaniment of crushed berry baskets, to simulate broken bones.

One of the Chicago actors on *Lights Out* (before it moved to Hollywood) was Macdonald Carey, who, in his memoirs, recalled the lengths to which Oboler went to manufacture an eerie mood for the cast inside the studio itself: "The stage was the biggest stage at NBC. The director would put the microphone in the center of the floor and there'd be a floor lamp there and a light by the piano. Here's this big, big studio and this one little floor lamp with actors huddled around it in the dark reading their lines. There was a real feeling of mystery about the whole thing. The sound man was in this umbrella of light way off in the corner. They were very, very spooky shows."

Oboler made his mark with the series, and, after leaving it for war work, revived it in 1942—with a revised format and an opening that began, "*It . . . is . . . later . . . than . . . you . . . think*" (with bonging chimes between each word)—and then again for TV, where it ran for three years, 1949–52, hosted by Boris Karloff. But if ever a radio show was doomed on TV, *Lights Out* was it. By 1967, after he had been driven out of broadcasting (his star briefly twinkled once more with *The House of Wax*, the first 3-D movie), an angry Oboler said: "If TV could make money out of showing the rape of their grandmother, they'd show it."

One of the little boys Oboler scared half to death was the postmodern prince of horror, Stephen King, who has called Oboler "the genre's prime *auteur*." King heard *Lights Out* reruns in the 1960s on *Dimension X*, recalling especially Ray Bradbury's "Mars Is Heaven!" "I didn't sleep in my bed that night," he remembered. "That night I slept in the doorway, where the real and rational light of the bathroom bulb could shine in my face. That was the power of radio at its height." Oboler, like Hitchcock, loved merging horror and humor into a gross-out giggle. "Part of Oboler's real genius was that when 'Chicken Heart' ended, you felt like laughing and throwing up at the same time."

Oboler, said King, played on two of radio's prime strengths: "The mind's innate obedience, its willingness to try to see whatever someone suggests it see, no matter how absurd; the second is the fact that fear and horror are blinding emotions that knock our adult pins from beneath us and leave us groping in the dark like children who cannot find the light switch. Radio is, of course, the 'blind' medium, and only Oboler used it so well or so completely." In radio, King observed, we never saw the zipper running down the monster's back.

On TV, King said, *The Shadow* and *Inner Sanctum* overdescribed scenes, whereas Oboler relied on speech, sound, and silence to achieve his effects. He can't forget the gruesome "A Day at the Dentist," in which a dentist extracts revenge from a patient who, years earlier, ruined the dentist's wife when she was a young girl. With the patient strapped in his chair, the dentist drills a hole in him ("to let out some of lover-boy"), but the audience is left to guess where—his brain? heart? genitals? The lone sound of a burrowing drill left listeners very much in the dark indeed. King singles out radio's ability to unlock the door of evil without "letting the monster out," as movies or TV or theater would be forced to, because our eyes demand to know what's behind the door; our ears leave the solution tantalizingly, and horrifyingly, up in the air. Yet in the hands of a master radio storyteller like Oboler, we don't feel cheated. We feel challenged . . . and chilled.

The author of *The Shining, Carrie,* and *Misery* remembers how, when *Inner Sanctum* left radio for TV, it finally made the creaking door visible. "And visible, it certainly was horrible enough—slightly askew, festooned with cobwebs—but it was something of a relief, just the same. Nothing could have looked as horrible as that door *sounded*. . . ."

ANOTHER SHOW "WELL CALCULATED TO KEEP you in . . . suspense" was, in fact, *Suspense*—a chill-a-second series set in the here and now, not in the hereafter or the netherworld, about people in real trouble. Only rarely did it cross over into fantasy, the supernatural, or heavy-duty horror, but it had a weakness for gimmicky endings and melo-drama. Its specialty, to quote John Dunning, was "the slow tightening of the knot." The theme music, composed by Bernard Herrmann, was unusual at a time when radio shows preferred to use classic pieces in the public domain; his eerie, mesmerizing opening used a harp, a flute, and a graveyard bell. Among its staff of eight regular writers were John Dickson Carr and Ray Bradbury, but outsiders like Ben Hecht were also used. "When *Suspense* died, part of my creative soul died," Brad-bury recalled.

Its most famous drama, "Sorry, Wrong Number," repeated eight times during the series' run, was an inspired use of radio to tell a story—about an invalid housewife (Agnes Moorehead) who hears her murder being plotted over a party line and tries in vain to alert some-body, only to encounter busy signals, hapless operators, and a disbe-lieving desk sergeant. It was a scary *pas de deux* between Moorehead and sound man Berne Surrey. When transferred to film, with Barbara Stanwyck, the earplay fell flat. Moorehead, the star who appeared most on the series (thirty-two times), noted the importance of sound to that show: "A mood can be projected expertly in the mere dialing of a telephone." Other landmark *Suspense* episodes were Orson Welles's "Donovan's Brain," "August Heat" with Ronald Colman, "The Dunwich Horror" by H. P. Lovecraft, "Track of the Cat" with Richard Widmark, and "House in Cypress Canyon," about newlyweds whose new suburban home comes equipped with its very own werewolf. In "Dead Earnest," a man who falls into a deathlike near-coma must elude the ever-nearing embalmer's blade.

Suspense became a celebrity showcase, with comics like Jack Benny and Red Skelton turning up in its grisly plots. Comedians especially loved to play heavies and killers. *Fibber McGee and Molly*'s Jim and Marian Jordan appeared in "Back Seat Driver," as a couple whose car breaks down on a lonely back road with an escaped killer crouched in the back seat. Largely because of director William Spier, *Suspense* was a favorite of stars. Spier cut rehearsal time to four hours, partly to keep the actors tense and on their toes; also, the stars were on the air almost the entire show. Major Hollywood names asked to be on *Suspense* because, said a sponsor representative, "it gave them a chance to dig their teeth into a role. Cary Grant acted all over the place."

Suspense began in 1942 and, under various hosts, writers, and directors, had a twenty-year life, 945 episodes in all, and ran five seasons on TV from 1949 to 1954. It was initially narrated by "the man in black," Joseph Kearns, and after 1948 by Robert Montgomery. The program, sponsored most memorably by Roma Wines and Autolite, was led by a pantheon of radio's most respected directors—Spier, Elliott Lewis, Norman Macdonnell, William Robson, Tony Ellis—but it was Spier, called "the Hitchcock of the air," who set the original tone of impending doom and established the show's life-or-death format.

Sound man Surrey was given his head to create the bizarre background for *Suspense* tales. He researched "Donovan's Brain" three weeks before "coming up with his impression of what a severed brain, kept alive in a tank and still experiencing powerful human emotions, would sound like." His solution was to submerge a motor pump and a gurgling oscillator in a jar of water to express a whole range of feelings.

ONE OF THE MASTERS of radio noir was Himan Brown, a savvy innovator and entrepreneur. Out of Brown's restless, relentless mind came such classic programs as *The Fat Man, The Thin Man, Grand Central*

Station, plus his share of potboilers—soap operas like *Little Italy; Joyce Jordan, Girl Interne;* and one of the first network soaps, *Marie, the Little French Princess.* He also took a fling at comedy with *The Gumps,* hiring an NYU pre-law student named Irwin Shaw to write it. But of all of Himan Brown's many successes, his most enduring creation remains *Inner Sanctum,* as much for its squeaky opening door as for the shows themselves. "I'm gonna make that door a star," Brown vowed when he hit upon one of radio's most celebrated sound effects. That he did. Along with Fibber McGee's overflowing front closet, the Whistler's plaintive warble, and the Shadow's laugh, the rusted door-hinge of *Inner Sanctum* is identifiable even to people born long after the show ended. "I didn't have Leonard Bernstein and two hundred musicians doing *The Ride of the Valkyries,*" Brown now says. "All I used was a creaking door. There are only two sounds in radio that are trademarked—the creaking door and the NBC chimes."

Brown's series, with its farfetched tales from the crypt, was compared by many to Poe. Even in its heyday, however, it was a little over the top (but then so was Poe), with its frequent hideous screams in the night. The shows now sound more often campy than scary—not unlike the schlocky spook shows that now drift onto the tube late Saturday nights. They were intended to be nothing more or less than campfire ghost stories featuring the best ghouls Brown's money could buy— Boris Karloff, Peter Lorre, Claude Rains, Raymond Massey, Paul Lukas, etc.

Inner Sanctum's Raymond was the prototype storyteller, whose sepulchral narrative was riddled with macabre allusions and deadly puns. The over-the-edge acting was heavily punctuated by ominous organ chords, chortling villains, and midnight wails; the eerie sound effects were the work of Jack Amerine. *Inner Sanctum* later became a pulp magazine and a series on TV, where it lost its power to make your hair stand on end. The radio version ran for over a decade in various time slots and with assorted sponsors before the creaking door banged shut for the last time in 1952.

Brown attempted to revive the show in 1959 as a daylight series, *The NBC Radio Theater,* called "the last gasp of quality daytime drama," an overly ambitious, unsuccessful series of hour-long shows with a distinguished company of actors that included Eddie Albert,

Celeste Holm, Madeleine Carroll, and Gloria DeHaven. "It was really *Inner Sanctum* in disguise," says Brown. "Great writers writing in the Gothic mode. Nobody believed I'd deliver a one-hour show each week." He did 185 shows before the series was canceled. In 1974, long after radio had been pronounced dead, he tried to resuscitate the lively corpse once more as *The CBS Radio Mystery Theatre.* The show, still fondly remembered by those who hoped it might spark a full-fledged radio revival, was a nightly mix of original and classic creep shows, hosted by E. G. Marshall and featuring many of radio's finest actors as well as new names. Brown gave it his customary all, but the series wasn't carried by enough CBS affiliates, or was shunted into a late-night hour, when its aging core audience was asleep.

Brown, a crusty, crisply alert man in his late eighties, dislikes the nostalgia label that clings to discussions of old radio, feeling it condescends to a still-vibrant form; he points out that some $2 billion is spent on recorded books each year. "I don't see radio in that sense. I don't want prop airplanes; I want jets. You can't produce an old show for today's audiences. Dialogue in 1997 is not what it was in 1937. There is no reason that radio can't accommodate drama now."

Hi Brown was an unabashed radio hustler. When he learned that Listerine wanted a show, he devised *Inner Sanctum.* "You hear a company is looking for a new show and you go out and you peddle," he explains. *Inner Sanctum* was an instant hit. To his great delight, he recalls, "The shrinks said it was scaring people out of their wits." *Inner Sanctum* was originally called *The Creaking Door,* but somebody at the network told Brown, "Nobody's gonna tune into a door." Brown grins. "Little did he know!" He noticed an ad in *The New Yorker* for a series of books published by Simon & Schuster called "Inner Sanctum Mysteries," to which he bought the rights in exchange for plugging the books.

Brown, who began in radio as Jake on *The Rise of the Goldbergs,* not only made a star out of a creaking door but did the same for trains at *Grand Central Station,* which he boasts he produced for $750 a week—"five or six actors, music, sound effects, announcer, the works." (Arnold Stang recalls that Brown was "the biggest cheapskate in radio—he'd use the NBC reception desk to make phone calls.") Brown's Saturday morning series of dramas set at the great station, with its famous opening sound of a chugging train pulling into the terminal, drew a hundred letters a week informing him that the train was an outmoded steam engine rather than a modern diesel. He invariably wrote back, "What does a diesel train sound like?"

Brown talks as if he had originated much of early radio. "I created *Dr. Friendly* way before *Dr. Christian*," he says, and then grins. "And Dr. Friendly did better operations." As both writer and director, Brown was known to be a tough cookie and a hard-driving boss. "I went like greased lightning. I used the least amount of rehearsal of anyone—two and a half hours for a half-hour show"—and he liked to edit right up to airtime. He brushes away *Inner Sanctum*'s many rivals and imitators—*The Whistler, The Shadow,* etc. "They didn't bother me. *Inner Sanctum* was the granddaddy of them all. I felt *Inner Sanctum* was just a wonderful framework for all sorts of things." He smiles. "When that door creaks open, I'm in business!"

Minds over Matter

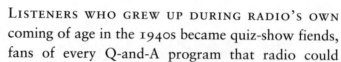

LISTENERS WHO GREW UP DURING RADIO'S OWN coming of age in the 1940s became quiz-show fiends, fans of every Q-and-A program that radio could devise—including the quiz shows' demented child, the game show. Game and "giveaway" shows, with their ferociously grinning MCs, fevered contestants, and fusillade of appliances, dominated radio in its last frantic days, replacing the superior contest of "matching wits." Mind games gave way to mindless greed.

The quiz show appealed to information junkies and cut across generational lines, among them the father of all quiz shows, *The $64 Question,* a simpleminded but engaging program on which the contestants were really foils for the various quizmasters who held the post over the years—performers like singer Kenny Baker and comic Garry Moore; *Dr. I.Q.,* a rigorous third-degree that featured no-nonsense rapid-fire questions and was the *Jeopardy!* of its day; *Stop the Music,* which stopped America in its tracks each week to discover which unsuspecting listener might identify the Mystery Melody and become rich beyond Croesus, or even Charles Van Doren; *The Quiz Kids,* easily the most adorable think tank of them all; *The Answer Man,* a hard-core fact-fest that eliminated the middleman, the studio contestant, hosted by a supreme know-it-all, Albert Mitchell, a factoid wizard; *Noah Webster Says,* a must-hear show for language mavens who hung on every obscure word; and the brilliant, innovative *Quick as a Flash,* which acted out clues in various styles—nursery rhymes, mysteries, songs, news stories, poems, Shakespeare, etc.

The quiz show itself was born in 1923 as a circulation-boosting scheme by a new current events magazine called *Time.* The circulation director, Roy Larsen, persuaded a New York station to give him free

Overleaf, clockwise from top left: Clifton Fadiman (*Information Please*), Groucho Marx (*You Bet Your Life*), The Quiz Kids with Quizmaster Joe Kelly, Ralph Edwards and contestants (*Truth or Consequences*)

airtime for a show called *The Pop Question Game,* hosted by *Time's* cofounder, Briton Hadden; listeners had to answer a question out of the news before Larsen rang a chime.

Early variety shows stayed clear of studio audiences, but quiz and game shows coveted them, learning quickly that a jazzed-up audience, filled with giggling, squealing tourists, made for a seemingly lively show; the hyped audience was built right into the quiz- and game-show concept from the first freeloading housewife. Movie theaters, to compete, offered "bank nights" and bingo games to seduce people away from their radios.

A Kansas City candymaker named Frank Russell exploited the idea in 1933, when a station manager wondered if anyone was listening to a morning show sponsored by Russell's confectionery. To find out, listeners who wrote in were awarded one free chocolate—thus were born the first radio premium and the first ratings sample. When other shows began offering bigger prizes, the FCC clamped down and banned them as "lotteries."

Not long after, a couple of nosy guys in Houston began stopping people on the street and asking them questions, marrying the traditional man-on-the-street interview to the quiz show. It was fun, but better still, it was cheap; contestants—i.e., passersby—were awarded a dollar for their trouble. The show was called *Vox Pop* and went on the road, where it won over the populus. Its credo was that the average man is just as interesting as the average celebrity; he also charges less for his services.

Quiz shows, game shows, and amateur hours were a mixture of the classic American get-rich-quick fever (rife during the Depression), coupled with the ideal of the People, yes—no matter how silly, stupid, or embarrassing; they were also a celebration of Mr. and Mrs. America. While game shows revealed folks' willingness to make fools of themselves, quiz shows redeemed the man in the street and revealed that the average guy wasn't as hapless as he behaved under the influence of Art Linkletter, Bert Parks, or Ralph Edwards.

According to the quiz-show archeologist Thomas A. DeLong, the first answers-for-money program was something called *Professor Quiz,* out of Washington, D.C., in 1937. It sounds like an early draft of

Dr. I.Q. (the grand prize was forty silver dollars) but is most notable now for having boosted the career of an announcer who ribbed the contestants, a red-haired wise guy with a drawl named Arthur Godfrey.

The first quiz show to truly sweep the country was *Pot o' Gold*, in 1939, on which listeners were paid just for answering their phone and then given a chance, via a giant wheel of fortune, to win prizes by answering actual questions posed by a little-known bandleader named Horace Heidt. The program, the first call-in show and the first of many long-distance giveaway shows, featured a segment called "Answers by the Dancers," during which couples dancing to Heidt's music were miked and their remarks broadcast; Heidt later parlayed this gimmick into his own talent-scouts program.

Pot o' Gold deftly skirted the anti-radio-lottery laws by claiming it wasn't a game of chance because it didn't involve a listener's active participation—in legalese, a "consideration"; i.e., it was considered a stroke of luck if you happened to be home to answer the phone. The show also dodged a ban on advertising laxatives by claiming that the sponsor, Tums, a new remedy for acid indigestion (or, as it was first termed then, "overindulgence"), was really a candy; it *looked* like Life Savers. *Pot o' Gold* primed America's economic pump, but the programs that turned America into a nation of moneygrubbing Scrooge McDucks were *Stop the Music* and *Break the Bank*.

The more courtly *Dr. I.Q.* arrived that same year, 1939, out of Texas, the brainchild of a Houston producer named Lee Segall. Segall stationed usherlike aides with roving mikes around a movie house who, when called upon by an MC with a jubilant voice named Lew Valentine, would sing out, "I have a sailor in the right downstairs, Doctor!" or, "I have a lady in the balcony!" It was just the sort of gimmick—and catchphrase—that helped the show to catch on. The brisk, question-a-minute *Dr. I.Q.* distinguished itself from chatty, personality-based quiz shows; even the doctor's identity was kept secret. Dr. I.Q. was all business, and was forever shushing helpful audiences with a scolding, "No coaching, please! Let him answer." If a stumped contestant froze, the quiz doctor would egg him on to take a stab and seemed rather annoyed when anyone refused even to make a wild guess. Quiz contestants in those days were far more shy and less showbiz savvy than today. Many seemed terribly apologetic when they couldn't deliver the right answer.

Once I.Q.'s assistant had introduced the lady in the balcony, the good Doctor would utter his clarion cry, "Twelve silver dollars to the young lady for *this* one!" Like *Jeopardy!* (in essence, a photographed radio quiz), *Dr. I.Q.* was question-driven, but the slightly patronizing Doctor would feign sympathy, groaning if anybody guessed wrong ("Oh-h-h, I'm *aw*-fully sorry, but I think you'll find the answer to that one is . . ."), after which he brightened and proudly awarded "a box of Mars bars and two tickets to next week's production at this theater!"

The most exciting moments on *Dr. I.Q.* were the Tongue Twister ("Which I'll repeat *one* time and *one* time only!"), the Famous Quotation, and the Biographical Sketch, contributed by listeners, in which the contestant's cash prize decreased with each clue recited by the determinedly hearty Dr. I.Q., who was played by three different, equally anonymous interrogators, but primarily by the venerable Dr. Valentine.

Lew Valentine belonged to a new breed of performer, the jolly MC, also personified by men like Bob Hawk, who hosted *The Camel Quiz,* on which the winner was crowned a "Lemac" (Camel, the name of the sponsor, spelled backward) and promptly serenaded by a quartet (*"You're a Lemac now! Yes, a Lemac now! We've got two-hundred silver dollars, built up for this week's scholars . . ."*).

THE MCs FOR QUIZ SHOWS were relentlessly jolly fellows usually named Bob, Bill, Bud, or Bert, much as the house announcers for game shows were the seemingly generic "Johnny Olsen." Joe Kelly was always identified as "genial Joe Kelly," but then all quizmasters were congenitally genial. Most of of them were former actors, aging or would-be comics, failed singers, and ambitious announcers—people like John Reed King, Wyn Elliot, Walter O'Keefe, Dennis James, Bud Collyer, and, most famously, a young, hungry, hyperkinetic singing MC from Atlanta named Bert Parks, who began by warming up audiences and cueing applause on Kate Smith's show and rose to fame not (the way most now remember him) as the Miss America host with the leaping eyebrows but as the most excitable man on radio, who shrieked, "Stop the music!!" and "Do you want to try to break the bank?!" *Break the Bank* chose contestants by an ostensibly random stroll through the audience. In the wake of the TV quiz show scandals, who knows what hanky-panky was afoot, but it sounded excruciatingly exciting as the "bank" roll mounted from week to week, at a princely one thousand dollars a show.

The first quizmaster of *Take It or Leave It,* radio's definitive quiz show, was Bob Hawk, a veteran quizmaster. Hawk, who called himself a "glibmaster," was soon replaced by comedian Phil Baker, who in turn was spelled by onetime Jimmy Durante straight man Garry Moore. Moore and Baker found new careers as quizmasters, much as fading film and stage stars today wind up in sitcoms and soap operas. No less a legend than Groucho Marx resuscitated a waning screen career in the late 1940s by agreeing to host a quiz show that was given little chance, *You Bet Your Life.*

Eddie Cantor also hosted *Take It or Leave It,* as did Jack Paar on the way up, but Hawk was generally regarded as its best MC; Baker, however, played off the contestants better and hyped the questions with the sure touch of an old vaudeville hand. Most of his ad libs were written by the gagman Hal Block, so even this most innocuous of quiz shows was, in a sense, rigged. And nobody ever went away a loser. For one dollar, Baker asked contestants: Who was buried in Grant's Tomb?—which Groucho handily stole as his own consolation query for *You Bet Your Life* losers.

Take It or Leave It, later renamed *The $64 Question*—a phrase soon embedded in the language to indicate the ultimate imponderable—was devised in 1939 by a research director named Peter Cranford for a Georgia education association. Cranford read that radio was desperate for new ideas and methodically set about concocting a quiz show that would give listeners maximum identification. He concluded that a betting game was the answer, a quiz that would double the player's earning each time he appeared, a roulette wheel of the air. His result was *Take It or Leave It,* where contestants tried to parlay the $1 lob question into $64 by answering progressively tougher questions if they dared continue; *Double or Nothing,* a clone, reworked the same idea. Meanwhile, the kibitzing audience was encouraged to egg folks on or plead with them to quit, chanting en masse, "You'll be SOR-eeee!"

Producer Milton Biow sold the idea to a nearly bankrupt mechanical-pencil company called Eversharp, which spent the rest of its ad budget on the new quiz show. It saved the company, maker of the "repeating pencil" ("*Right . . . with Eversharp!*"). *The $64 Question* lasted through the 1952 season, when Biow sold his interest to TV people who inflated and retitled it *The $64,000 Question* and, in time, turned a once-innocent question game into a media frenzy, followed by a national scandal that wrecked the format for decades and tainted the very term *quiz show.*

IN THE MOVIE *RADIO DAYS,* Woody Allen depicts a Quiz Kid as a snippy little twerp, which made for a funny scene but somehow rang false. What made *The Quiz Kids* so popular, even with kids, and endeared them to millions was that they sounded like actual children. That was the awesome and scary part. They knew chemical formulas and Greek mythology the way we knew the names of the Yankees' starting pitchers and Pee Wee Reese's hometown. The Quiz Kids became role models by demystifying intelligence.

The show featured brainy moppets who, despite their polite manners and quick quips, seemed smarter than not just any kid you knew but any adult. *The Quiz Kids,* like *College Bowl* a TV generation later, made intelligence fun as well as respectable. Decades afterward, one woman recalled how, as a little girl who had been rejected as too gawky to be a cheerleader, she would sit in her room listening to the show and, when she got an answer right, applaud herself.

Apart from superbrain Joel Kupperman, the regular brain trust roll call included Naomi (Cooks) and Ruthie (Duskin), Lonny (Lunde), Patrick (Conlon), and "little" Melvin (Miles). Over thirteen years, on radio and TV, some six hundred kids graduated from the show, but only two dozen became regulars. Fifty applied each week, but producer Lou Cowan was looking for more than sheer brainpower (the kids' average IQ fell between 135 and 180). According to Ruth Duskin, who decades later wrote a book about the show, "Poise, originality, humor, modesty, and mike sense were more important than profundity. It helped to be young and/or small—the ability to wow the audience bore an inverse relation to size and depth of voice." She added, "Showmanship was critical . . . showoffs and smart alecks were crossed off at once."

The Quiz Kids began as an attempt by quiz-show mogul Cowan to create what Fred Allen called "*Information Please* in short pants." In that pre–"gifted child" era, smart kids were considered freaks. Cowan scoured Chicago schools for examples of this exotic species of youngster and found four; more important, he found sponsors, Alka-Seltzer and One-a-Day vitamins. After rejecting names like *The Kids Knew, School Kids Questionnaire,* and several inspired by *The Wizard of Oz* (*Quizard of Oz, Quizard of Kids*), Cowan decided on *The Quiz Kids,* which quickly became a catchphrase and opened every Sunday with a clanging school bell and the inevitable theme song, "School Days."

Cowan, called by his peers "the quiet innovator," was then a twenty-nine-year-old six-foot-three-inch University of Chicago graduate who had married into the Spiegel mail-order family and had produced Kay Kyser's boneheaded *Kollege of Musical Knowledge.* He later recalled: "Everyone said it was impossible—you can't get the kids," which turned out to be the easiest part, thanks to a *Chicago Daily News* feature writer who came up with the names of four bright kids he'd written about. That became the demo show Cowan shopped around to ad agencies, all of which agreed that nobody would listen to a bunch of wise-ass kids and that those who did would figure the show was rigged. One agency tried the show as a summer replacement after searching everywhere for the right quizmaster. After four were auditioned, the head of the agency suggested the down-home host of *National Barn Dance,* a folksy midwesterner named Joe Kelly. He was afraid to take the job for fear of looking like a dunce, but as it turned out, his gee-whiz personality and common touch ("Oh, boy!" "'Sakes alive!" "Golly, that's just dandy, kids!" "Put on your thinking caps here") were the winning counterpoint to the panel of perky intellects.

Kelly, introduced each week as "the Chief Quizzer himself," remained disarmingly out of his depth yet ideal for the part: Listeners loved his slightly baffled, tongue-tied manner and understood his awe of the junior geniuses before him. A third-grade dropout and ex-vaudevillian, Kelly had played "Jolly Joe" on a Chicago kids show. He often stumbled over the questions and seemed as gleeful as a proud papa at the kids' lightning responses. His gentle, nonplussed manner and the genuine joy he found in his little wizards took an edge off the high-powered brains on display.

The premiere show began with a typical question: "What would I be carrying home if I brought an antimacassar, a dinghy, a sarong, and an apertyx?" Cleverly, the questions were often phrased in the first person, creating a rapport between Kelly and the Kids. Bumbles and all, the first show brought in 2,600 letters and 250 would-be Quiz Kids; it was welcomed as the best new program of the year.

The show was put together by eighteen people, who took listeners' questions, rewrote them with an entertaining twist, and tried to find a balance in questions that would be tough enough to challenge the Kids but not so difficult that listeners would feel hopelessly stupid. Many were artfully chosen to trick the panel, such as how far a phonograph needle travels playing a ten-inch record (answer: 2½ inches—the needle travels across a record, not around it, as the groove revolves).

Typical listeners' questions that the Kids polished off like Harvard graduate students: Give the difference between a simile and a metaphor; Why is Kim in *Show Boat* so named? (She was born at the juncture of Kentucky, Illinois, and Mississippi); What monarch recently became an Indian? (Satchel Paige of the Kansas City Monarchs brought up to the major leagues by the Cleveland Indians). Half of the fun was in the Kids' wrong but nonetheless edifying or funny responses, or in their footnote ad libs, for the heart of the show's appeal was in the young-sters' likability quotient and quick wit. When Lonny Lunde identified the song "I'm Looking over a Four-Leaf Clover," he added, "If you find a four-leaf clover that's very good luck . . . at least it's supposed to be. I found one and I didn't find any immediate change for the better."

Roby Hickock, who pretty much ran things and acted as mother hen to the Kids, said she would "pray for girls as farmers pray for rain." Ruthie Duskin, its youngest panelist, was the daughter of a high school chemistry teacher and had an IQ of 200; doubters claimed she was a midget. She retired from the show at sixteen, in 1950, after winning $157,000 in U.S. Savings Bonds and appearing a total of 146 times on radio and eleven on TV, not to mention making countless personal appearances and visits to army bases when the show toured. The Kids' main challenge, she later wrote, was "overcoming expectations that you were snotty."

"Joel Kupperman," said Duskin, is the one ex–Quiz Kid whose name almost invariably follows the words, 'Whatever happened to . . . ?' " Quiz Kidder Patrick Conlin put it best: "Joel was the quin-tessence of what they were selling on the show." He was what people meant when they razzed some poor kid as "another Einstein." Kupperman lasted ten years on the show; Naomi Cooks and Lonny Lunde, seven. Two went on to semiprominent careers—Vanessa Brown became a minor TV and film star, and James Watson won a Nobel Prize in medicine. Kupperman, who became a university professor (and has mostly declined interviews about his early life), expressed mild criticism of a misspent youth. "The show may have done some good for the idea that education is a good thing," he told an interviewer in 1982, "but being a bright child among your peers was not the very best way to grow up in America." He had applied to the show, saying, in part, "I would like to be a Quiz Kid. I am not as good at numbers as Richard [Williams], but I am pretty good. Love and kisses, Joel Kupperman. P.S. My grandfather has teeth that he takes out at night but he is smart." That P.S. undoubtedly landed him the job.

Called the "Midget Euclid" by *Coronet* magazine, Joel at six was reading eighth-grade history books and doing cube roots of six-digit figures, which dazzled listeners who couldn't even fathom the questions. On some four hundred broadcasts, he became something of a trained flea, once solving a math problem while playing the piano and jousting with Milton Berle, Fred Allen, and politician Harold Stassen. Kupperman eventually retreated from all the publicity, kept to himself at the University of Chicago and Cambridge, and later denigrated his *Quiz Kids* performances, calling them "calculator's tricks" and "fast, superficial answers." Even so, he emerged on TV's *$64,000 Challenge* as a music expert and won eight thousand dollars. He wound up in philosophy, the author of *Fundamentals of Logic* and *Ethical Knowledge,* and always shunning Quiz Kid reunions. The mother of one Quiz Kid called Kupperman "the Garbo of our group."

Most of the Quiz Kids turned out better than the average child star, though they were subjected to similar commercial pressures—endorsing Quiz Kids games, cutouts, badges, and sweatshirts, making seven Quiz Kids movie shorts, posing for twelve Quiz Kids postcards, cutting Quiz Kids records, and turning up in a Quiz Kids magazine and a Quiz Kids dictionary; none shared in the profits, though.

Naomi Cooks Mann now lives in an elegant Victorian home in the posh Pacific Heights section of San Francisco, where a maid answers the door. Since her *Quiz Kids* days, she has had at least two more lives, as the co-owner of a novelty store and as a writer (two textbooks on writing and a book on her daughter's experience in India, *Seeking the Mother of Immortal Bliss*).

She remembers that her parents had a long discussion about whether to allow her to be on the show. "I was just a smart kid and so I auditioned. It was sort of like a game. It wasn't like working. But it *was* showbiz. The show was cast like a play. I was the cute smart little girl"; each kid had a specialty, and hers was literature. There was always speculation that the kids were too quick not to have been coached. "We were not coached at all," Cooks says firmly—but they were badly underpaid, she still feels. "It's amazing how they got away with it, considering how much talent there was on that show." There were no rehearsals. "To the best of my knowledge, it was totally spontaneous." The kids came in, wriggled into the robes and mortarboards they wore each week, and awaited the bell.

Even though Cooks's parents "made a big effort to tone down" the showbiz aspects, she acknowledged that she "had a different kind of childhood, for sure. People would stop me for my autograph, but my parents tried to keep me unsophisticated. I didn't equate it with being a movie star. It was a notch up from playing a piano recital. Remember, I did it every week for *seven* years; after a while it became a part of my life. I took ballet, piano, swimming. This was just another hyped-up after-school activity."

When the show moved to TV, it lost much of its charm, but remained for a while on radio. Apparently to cuten it up for TV, the producers lowered the general age level—teenagers didn't look as adorable as they sounded on radio, and the girls were asked to wear pigtails until they were nearly teenagers—and answering questions gradually gave way to sounding off on current events and life in general.

The TV show also lowered its standards, introducing such stunts as guest celebrities and a hypnotist who tried to put the kids in a trance. The clown Emmett Kelly tried to speed-read, Naomi Cooks rode a horse, and Melvin Miles arrived via helicopter. With Clifton Fadiman as the brainy new TV Quiz-Kidmaster, the easy chemistry between teacher and pupils vanished. "Fadiman," recalled Duskin, "committed the unpardonable sin: dullness. Because he clearly knew more than the kids, they did not amaze him—nor the audience." In the words of alumnus Patrick Conlon, "At a certain point, people said, 'So what?'

and flipped the channel to *I Love Lucy*." The show, Duskin lamented, "had become almost a parody of itself." In 1954, when the sponsorless video version was playing to near-empty houses, the Quiz Kids were replaced by a smart dog named Lassie. At semester's end, Kelly finally dismissed his gifted video class.

When the TV quiz show scandals broke in 1959, people began to wonder about the Quiz Kids. Lou Cowan, who had gone on to master-mind *The $64,000 Question,* was asked by CBS to resign, left TV under a cloud, and wound up in academia, where he revived his damaged reputation at Columbia before dying in a hotel fire.

Joel Kupperman's mother, Sara, and Quiz Kids graduates agree that the show was only "fixed" in the sense that certain questions played to various panelists' strengths. In Sara Kupperman's recollection, "The producers knew pretty well what Joel knew and the questions were pitched sometimes so that he would have the first hand up." Lonny Lunde insisted it was clean. "Spontaneity was the lifeblood of the show." Duskin, however, pointed out, "By juggling categories and known strengths, it was possible to put a seven-year-old on a competitive footing with a fourteen-year-old." She recalled "discreet inquiries" and "broad brush-up suggestions."

The show's staffers might notice, or delicately ask, what book a certain kid was reading and devise a question around the subject. Or a parent might get a call asking, "Does Naomi know anything about . . . ?" Cooks: "And if Naomi didn't, Naomi certainly found out!" Duskin commented, "I always was somewhat uncomfortable with those occasional phoned feelers." Conlan, who went on to become an actor, said, "It was a game, that's all, and all of us were players." It was never meant to be a Yale entrance exam.

INFORMATION PLEASE WAS EASILY the elite of the genre. With its appealingly snobby air and inside wisecracks, it seemed of another, more glamorous, world. To young listeners especially, the smokey, innuendo-laden community of grown-ups was alien but intriguing— all that scintillating wit from the brainy likes of Franklin P. Adams, George S. Kaufman, John Kieran, and Oscar Levant. The show, a sort of Algonquin Round Table of the air, was elegantly hosted by civilized

Clifton Fadiman, who presided over the panel of sharp-tongued ad-libbers.

The show was thought up by Dan Golenpaul, himself a pretty bright guy who put on lectures and public-service programs and devised the first broadcasting "magazine," called, yes, *The Magazine of the Air,* featuring pieces on theater, sports, music, literature, and current events. Golenpaul's idea for *Information Please* came out of his frustrations at listening to MCs give contestants a hard time for blowing answers. He once explained, "A bit sadistic, I thought. I wish I had these quizmasters and so-called experts in front of me. I'd like to ask *them* some questions. They're probably not much brighter than the average person."

In fact, they were, but Golenpaul, as with *The Quiz Kids,* decided mere gray matter would not be enough; he wanted a panel that was also scintillating and likable. He recruited *The New Yorker*'s book editor, Fadiman, who later said, "It was a crazy idea, and I told him so. No one but Dan had much faith in the program. A shoestring product, it seemed to have no chance of finding an audience or a sponsor."

The first panel was bright but boring, top-heavy with scholars. Only the urbane columnist Franklin P. Adams (aka "F.P.A.") was invited back, soon to be joined by two cohorts with equally sophisticated pedigrees: John Kieran, a mild-mannered sportswriter with a broad range of knowledge, and Oscar Levant, a bad-mannered pianist with a scathing wit whose wisecracks on the show made him a star and boosted his music career; the fourth chair was for the weekly guest. Fadiman and his conferees addressed each other with tongue-in-cheek politesse. "For ten years, with occasional lapses, we called each other Mister," he recalled. "On *Information Please* this worked. People liked it. They *wanted* to feel a certain distance between themselves and the panel."

The show became a surprise hit and, thanks to the panel's press connections, received more attention than it might have otherwise. The guest spot became a coveted seat for artists hoping to plug their latest work and also appear in a prestigious showcase. It allowed celebrities a chance to strut their intelligence: Gracie Allen came off alarmingly well, and Harpo Marx answered with his auto horn. Politicians loved to snag an invitation (but, said Fadiman, they had the dullest minds). The show became a revolving door for such prominent figures of the day as Deems Taylor, Louis Bromfield, Grantland Rice, Christopher Morley, and Russel Crouse.

Fadiman recalled: "The result was that a quiz show turned into a four-man conversation, sometimes good, sometimes ragged, always real. I was well aware that my own talents were as nothing compared with those of Frank Adams, Oscar Levant, or John Kieran. But I was also well aware that I was so placed as to be able to do one thing better than they could do it themselves. That one thing was to prod them into being Adams, Levant, and Kieran."

The very notion of a commercial TV show devoted to sophisticated verbal byplay and intelligence today seems impossible, even preposterous. Listening to it now, what strikes you about the show is its simplicity—just four guys (and an occasional gal) sitting around a dinner table being brilliant together. "No such show could work on TV now," agrees Fadiman today, an astonishingly alert and lucid ninety-three, "because they all have to be mechanically perfect efficient machines to keep things moving. We never worried about time." Fadiman, whose brisk, urbane voice still sounds as if he could host a new season of *Information Please,* believes the show was popular "because my experts were also human beings. So in addition to learning something, listeners met three interesting, entertaining people. I knew their characters so well so I could tease them or set them against one another in a friendly manner."

Fadiman further observes today, "The questions we asked were not extremely difficult or recondite. A very bright high school graduate could have answered them. It was the way the panel attacked them— the puns, the jokes, the tiny bits of extra information they'd throw in. In getting the answers, the audience got a lot of humor, too; they were all genuinely funny people. It was not a highbrow show. The questions on *Jeopardy!* are much more difficult than the ones we chose."

The show was most fun, noted Kieran in his memoirs, when the experts were stumped—Golenpaul's original idea. "It was generally more fun when the answer was wrong, especially if the culprit tried to wriggle out of it. An uproarious error or a brilliant bit of irrelevance was rated far above any dull delivery of truth."

Information Please lasted six months on TV. "We weren't any good," Fadiman frankly admits. Golenpaul, he recalls, "brought in showgirls and gadgets to make it more visual, which only made it a standard show." The quiz was a hit on film, curiously, where about fifty programs were shown as short subjects in movie houses, but the complex dynamics of television had somehow finally stumped radio's experts.

EVEN — OR ESPECIALLY — PEOPLE who hated quiz shows loved the parody quiz, *It Pays to Be Ignorant,* an unabashedly silly program with a streak of surrealism—a kind of *Disinformation Please.* It had a broad burlesque tone and was, in fact, manned by a ragtag panel of aging dumbbell comics—Lulu McConnell, George Shelton, and Harry McNaughton.

Tom Howard was the cranky host and make-believe quizmaster who attempted to retain decorum amidst verbal pandemonium. His daughter had created the program with her husband, the manager of a New Haven radio station. It's amazing that a show satirizing another genre could exist as long as *It Pays to Be Ignorant,* but it was funny in its own right and not just a parody of quiz shows. The hoary gags, groaner puns, and general knockabout quality of the show, with its daffy theme song ("*It pa-a-ays to be ignorant, to be dumb, to be dense, to be ignorant . . .*") endeared it to adults, who had grown up with vaudeville, and to kids, who loved its sheer nuttiness. It featured loony questions, such as, "How many rodents are in the nursery rhyme 'The Three Blind Mice'?" "What color is the White House?" and "What animal do we get goat's milk from?"

The more inane the questions, the more perplexed the panel; and the more stupid, self-serving, and irrelevant their own questions, the more exasperated grew the harried Tom Howard. Its zany non sequiturs and noisy, numbskull frenzy made it unlike any other show of the time. Its endlessly repeated catchphrases never failed to tickle fans. Even today, if someone mentions Sheboygan, Wisconsin—a knee-jerk radio laugh, like Peoria and Brooklyn—listeners recall the excited cry of Mr. Shelton (the knucklehead panelists were always courteously addressed), "I usta—, I usta—, I usta *woik* in dat town!" Or the horny Lulu McConnell, in her whisky tenor, confronting any male guest with a brassy, "Are you married, honey?"

Tom Howard wisely chose his trio of dunces from veteran vaudevillians. "I deliberately picked old-timers for my experts," Howard once explained. "I figured their experience would make the show sound ad-libbed." In fact, it was fully scripted. "I hit 'em in the eyes with the satire," said Howard, "while I kick 'em in the pants with the gags."

WITH THEIR ELABORATE practical jokes and crazy but good-humored style, Ralph Edwards—together with Art Linkletter and producer John Guedel—reinvented the hot foot and the whoopie cushion. If there's a fine line between the quiz show and the game show, an even finer line exists between the game show and the giveaway show, and a still more microscopic border divides the game show and the stunt show. Edwards and Linkletter defined the genre.

Edwards, an ebullient, smiley guy from Colorado, was a well-paid journeyman CBS announcer in New York itching to become a producer and MC when, at twenty-six, he hit upon an idea for a new radio show based on an old game he had grown up playing as a farm boy. The game was called Forfeits and the idea was to stand behind whoever was "it" and chant, "Heavy, heavy, hangs over thy head. Is it fine or super-fine? Tell the truth or pay the consequences." The fine might be a feather or a doily, and if the person didn't guess he would be ordered to do something stupid. Edwards sold the concept to an ad agency, undaunted by the notion of pulling stunts before an audience that couldn't see them. The show, called *Truth or Consequences*, premiered in March 1940 with Edwards and sports announcer Mel Allen.

Each week's show opened with a perfectly timed explosion of laughter, the secret of which Edwards would never divulge: About thirty seconds prior to airtime, two men from the audience (often servicemen) were asked to see who could put on the most female clothing from a trunk, and about the time one of them began squeezing into a girdle, the show went on the air to the sound of giddy howls and the announcer's jubilant, "*Hello, there! We've been waiting for you! It's time to play Truth or Consequences!*"

Contestants got fifteen dollars for answering impossible questions—nobody ever did, of course—and fifteen dollars for partaking of a consequence and being dubbed a good sport, every game show host's highest accolade. A *Variety* critic dubbed Edwards "fleet of tongue, a suave party man and adept at keeping things moving snappily." It was a style he didn't alter the rest of his broadcasting life, first as host of a TV version of *Truth or Consequences* and then later as that excitable surprise party-giver on the even more popular spin-off, *This Is Your Life.*

Truth or Consequences was a national habit that people might have felt a little silly listening to but couldn't rise above. If nothing else, it made you feel superior to the willing clucks who allowed themselves to be made ninnies of nationally; it probably helped that nobody could be seen. Edwards took a special glee in sending people off on fool's errands, chortling satanically, "Aren't we devils?!"

The wackier the stunt the better, such as a Brooklyn construction worker commanded to cry like a baby for its bottle, a man asked to play a piano upside down, a bachelor instructed to diaper a piglet for practice, a golfer who drove golf balls from coast to coast, and a guy ordered to go to bed with a seal at a busy Hollywood intersection. Edwards saw no harm in any of it, saying, "These people aren't psychopathic—they're just everyday lawyers, preachers, salesmen, housewives, cabdrivers—out for a little fun, and perhaps a cash prize." He saw the 1940s show as "a welcome relief from the unhappy news of world affairs" and a throwback to "the long-neglected front parlor, making it once more a friendly room, wherein family ties are formed."

When *Truth or Consequences* first aired on TV, the critic John Crosby wrote: "The radio version . . . was the ultimate in silliness, but at least it was decently veiled. Its television counterpart is a monstrosity of vulgarity." It came back in 1954 on TV with Jack Bailey, resurfaced yet again in an even more unruly format with Bob Barker, and then one last time with Larry Anderson in the late 1980s, an interrupted run of forty years.

Edwards was also a sharp promoter and used the show to raise money for causes like the American Heart Association and the March of Dimes, which made you feel a little better about listening to it. Now and then his more inspired stunts produced news stories, like the time, in 1950, when he convinced a town in New Mexico to change its name from Hot Springs to Truth or Consequences. His "Walking Man" (Jack Benny's footsteps), "Mr. Hush" (Jack Dempsey, originally), "Miss Hush" (Clara Bow), and "Whispering Woman" (Jeanette MacDonald) became mysteries that captivated America and, when they were at last identified, made front pages coast to coast.

ART LINKLETTER'S SHOWS WEREN'T quiz shows, game shows, or talk shows, but some peculiar goulash of the three—a mix of *Truth or Consequences, Candid Camera,* and *Family Feud*—in which the host roamed the audience, played pranks, surprised guests, and labored ceaselessly to have a good time or know the reason why. His unending *House Party* began life in a dreary San Francisco department-store basement, where a wild-eyed Linkletter pawed through housewives' purses, one of his trademark stunts.

Linkletter was a young, hustling can-do guy from California (originally from Canada, born Arthur Kelly) whose toothy grin and innate gift of gab were perfect for his chosen field. After his broadcasting career ended, he became a motivational speaker, an extension of the basic door-to-door salesman style he developed early by working remotes, sports events, store openings, and fairs for local radio stations, interviewing tourists and people in the street, where he refused to take "Get lost" for an answer. By the time he got his own program, he had hosted some nine thousand shows and conducted perhaps five times that many interviews.

Linkletter parlayed a cruise director's personality into a huge success in two hit shows on radio (and then TV)—*People Are Funny* and *House Party*—plus games, books, lectures, and collections of moppet wit called *Kids Say the Darnedest Things,* in which he induced little boys and girls to say the cutest, rudest, or most endearing things and, with any luck, embarrass their families on national radio.

"I was always an originator," Linkletter says, looking back now. "We had 35 departments dealing with family life, occupations, relationships, men-in-the-street interviews." Some of his wackier stunts were somewhat comparable, by 1940s radio standards, to '90s hyper tabloid TV shows. He says, "We had men-in-the-street and now they have men-in-the-gutter. That's a good line—you can use that. Everyone then said, 'My God, what's happening to people?,' just as I say it now when I watch a show like Jerry Springer's."

A favorite device of *People Are Funny* was to take some truism, cliché, or stereotype—husbands don't know the color of their wife's eyes, women are lousy drivers—and put it to the test over the air. "*Peo-*

ple Are Funny was not the kind of show that I would have listened to or watched," the host once confessed. "Art Linkletter the listener or viewer would have tuned out Art Linkletter the entertainer, especially during the program's early years. Although I took pride in making *People Are Funny* the best in its class of program, throughout those years of network success I was painfully aware that it was a very lightweight operation."

Even so, it developed into a very slick operation, and Linkletter managed to walk the line between ingratiating and insulting. The stunts were surprisingly clever, and even the prizes were funny, chosen randomly from a trick list of gifts composed of alternating lavish and booby prizes—or both, like a diamond ring embedded in a fish. He candidly admitted: "Our show was almost embarrassingly slapstick entertainment—squirting water on people or getting them to fall into swimming pools with their clothes on." He preferred *House Party* to *People Are Funny*, he said, because "it gave me the opportunity to develop a confrontation that elicited humor from my participants rather than make them the brunt of the joke, as so often happened on *People Are Funny*."

Linkletter came to loathe the manic TV shows that developed out of *The Price Is Right* and *Supermarket Sweepstakes*—accusing them of hyping contestants, juicing applause, and goosing reactions. His own shows, he claimed, were more warm and human. He looks disdainfully at contemporary TV shows where people stand on their seats, wave their arms, and scream maniacally. "The reason we had such consistent success is that I was and am truly interested in people, and that interest communicated itself to millions of listeners across the country."

Despite Linkletter's unquenchable on-air guile, the veteran of some seventeen man-in-the-street shows had to fight his way into the limelight past the original star of *People Are Funny*, a better-known Art—Baker—who later reappeared in early TV as the white-haired, grandfatherly host of *You Asked for It*. Baker later sued and lost.

When Linkletter and Guedel, a former writer of Laurel and Hardy and *Little Rascals* shorts at the Hal Roach studios, first sketched the blueprint for *House Party* in 1941, Linkletter was an unknown redhot from San Diego who had been conducting similar audience-participation shows at the 1939 World's Fair on San Francisco's Treasure Island. When the fair closed, he hosted *What's Doin', Ladies?* from Hale Brothers Department Store, where one of his announcers was TV game-show-guru-to-be Mark Goodson.

Their most famous show was hatched in a corner booth at the Brown Derby at Hollywood and Vine. Linkletter and Guedel had the same idea but decided to merge forces. Linkletter called his version *Meet Yourself*, but he liked the name of Guedel's show better—*People Are Funny*. "The format was unique and simple," Linkletter explained, "an entertaining study of human behavior based on a psychologist's observations and reactions." At the time, it was a fairly avant-garde concept for radio. "Human nature, that's the whole key," claims Guedel.

Guedel, now a doughty man in his mid-eighties, got the name *People Are Funny* after doodling it on a note pad during a meeting. "The show came out of the title," he recalls. "I wanted to do a show that wasn't ha-ha funny but peculiar funny." NBC put up fifteen dollars for the demo disk—half the cost—and Guedel put up the other fifteen dollars. He was bursting with game show ideas. "We were the first to do [a version of] *To Tell the Truth*—but it was called *Detecto*—and we were going to sue Goodson and Todman over it. We did the first *What's My Line?*, but we did it with individuals instead of a panel. We did *The Newlywed Game,* but we called it *Think Alike.* We beat *Candid Mike* (Allen Funt's *Candid Microphone*—later *Candid Camera*) by six months when we had a soldier pick up his date in a tank and stuck a mike in his lapel. We called it *Hidden Mike.*"

John Guedel claims that he and Ralph Edwards "invented the game show," and he just may be right. The man never rested. Once, listening to *The Quiz Kids,* he thought, "Maybe if there was a panel of ordinary kids people could identify with . . ." and quickly came up with *Paging Young America,* which evolved into the famed "Kids Say the Darnedest Things" segment on *House Party.* According to Guedel, he built the framework for *House Party* in a few hours. Using his marketing skills, the producer designed the show to take place in different rooms of a house. " 'Oh, boy, the sponsors will love that!' " he thought. "And so it became *The General Electric House Party* for the next twenty-six years." Over their half-century partnership, says Linkletter, they never had a contract. The daily matinee soiree on CBS didn't end until 1967 (following a long TV life), beginning each day with the hum of excited housewives and a hearty welcome from announcer Jack Slattery: "Come on in! It's Art Linkletter's *House Party*!"

The show specialized in tracking down missing heirs, a game called "What's in the House?" (with a cornucopia of mixmasters, washing machines, ovens, and waffle irons as prizes), and Linkletter's interviews with kids. Linkletter worked ad-lib and was rarely caught speechless, although he once outsmarted himself when a little boy, asked what he'd wish for if he had one wish, replied, "My daddy back from heaven." Kids also could say the saddest things. Linkletter, though, swears that he never provoked kids into making wisecracks. "Of *course* I egged them on, but I wasn't trying to get them to be smart-asses. I was always a straight man for kids or anyone I talked to. Most game show hosts are comedians who are always looking for a laugh and treat the guests as straight men. Kids have to realize you're not just setting them up." He adds, "I'd never let on that I thought what a kid said was funny, because they weren't trying to be funny. So I would just listen. I'd play games with kids to get them talking, and I always took my time. In TV now, there's just no time to let anything develop. The attention span in TV has been reduced to two and a half seconds."

Although you hated yourself in the morning, you *had* to find out what happened to the poor schnooks Linkletter sent out dressed as trees, or who were told to dress a mannequin in a store window (where half the gags seemed to take place), or were given twenty thousand dollars and ordered to play the stock market for a week, or were asked to register at a hotel with a seal. One regular stunt, which evolved five years later into one of radio and TV's most popular quiz shows, pitted contestants against the cigarette sponsor, Raleigh; the throwaway bit was called *You Bet Your Life*.

You Bet Your Life was a life preserver thrown by Guedel to Groucho Marx in 1947 to save the great comic's slowly evaporating career. Despite great success in films and on stage, Marx had flopped in previous radio shows, including *Flywheel, Shyster and Flywheel,* on which he and Chico played sleazy lawyers; it was a cult hit that Esso was not amused by. Other shows shied away from using Marx as a guest, so he was in a creative funk when Guedel heard him on a car radio freely ad-libbing with Bob Hope on a special that broke up the audience when Hope dropped his script. "I didn't know Marx was such a good ad-libber," recalls Guedel. He shrewdly drew on Marx's verbal spontaneity—the very reason Groucho hadn't done well in radio before: He had a risky habit of veering from scripted material, which, while fun for audiences, drove directors berserk and gave him a reputation as a maverick comic who couldn't be controlled.

Groucho was only fifty-five when his screen career seemed over after the last Marx Brothers film, *The Big Store,* failed loudly. He was dubious about starting over in an alien medium, and going it alone for the first time in a long career frightened him. Guedel remembers, "I figured he'd be great working with people out of an audience. When the people were being funny, Groucho could be the perfect straight man; when the people played it straight, Groucho couldn't miss with his own comedy. With Groucho, I figured we'd be protected from both sides."

When Guedel asked Marx if he could ad-lib regularly, he cracked, "I've ad-libbed a whole Broadway show many a time." Guedel convinced him he could be as funny bantering with real people as he had been badgering scripted ones. He and Marx became partners, each contributing $125 to make an audition disc. It was proposed that Marx appear in his customary greasepaint mustache, swallowtail coat, and horn-rim spectacles so the studio audience would identify him. He declined but finally agreed to grow a real mustache. Contrary to some accounts, Guedel claims that Marx didn't balk at playing a lowly quizmaster, bottom man on the showbiz totem pole. *Newsweek* said assigning Groucho to a quiz show was like sending Citation to a glue factory. He was further chastened by the fact that earlier he had actually auditioned for *Take It or Leave It* and failed. What clicked was the fact, unrecognized at the time, that Groucho was an antidote to every vapid, sugary quiz-show MC on the air—he was radio's first *un*congenial quizmaster.

Guedel (whose original choice for MC was far more conventional: Garry Moore) says that when he suggested the show, Groucho told him, "Well, I've flopped three times on radio. Maybe I could compete with refrigerators." All the networks turned it down. Guedel recounts: "I figured Groucho could insult people and get away with it. Not everyone could do that. Elgin watches bought it, because the head of the company didn't know Groucho had flopped before."

The choice of George Fenneman as Groucho's good-natured whipping boy was pure happenstance. Forty-two men auditioned for the announcing job, but Fenneman impressed Guedel instantly: "Right away, I felt the contrast. George was the guy on the top of the wedding cake. They were the odd couple." Fenneman was as mild-mannered as Groucho was ill-mannered. Marx called him his male Margaret Dumont. Frank Ferrante, who later was to play Groucho in a one-man show, recalled, "George took it as the highest praise. Groucho called him the perfect straight man."

Marx's career wasn't just rehabilitated by the simple little quiz show, it also displayed him in an entirely new light—three new lights, actually: as a man of the people, as himself (a buccaneer banterer with a lethal tongue), and as a wit in his own right who wasn't dependent on scripted gags, props, and plots—or on two lunatic sidekick brothers.

"I needed the work," Groucho explained much later. "I knew I probably wouldn't make it as a quizmaster. I didn't seem the type." He called them "dress dummies." Indeed, when he appeared on the TV version, he was dressed in plainclothes gray, an oddly dignified Groucho.

Flying solo now, Groucho endeared himself to both a new audience, who knew him only from scratchy old movies on TV, and to older audiences, who knew him as the hunched-over cartoon in a morning coat and thick wiggling eyebrows, clenching a stogie. He kept the cigar and mustache for the benefit of the studio audience, but otherwise he was no more comical looking than Fenneman. Perched on a stool, benignly puffing his cigar, he was the very picture of quizmasterly decorum, a decoy for the viper lurking beneath. Groucho had finally tamed radio by deploying his wicked verbal skills and forgoing all the visual shtick on which he had ridden to stardom and to which he had clung for so long.

Behind the mundane quiz-show format, however, was a complex machine that produced the sort of willing stooges who made perfect sitting ducks for Groucho. The guests were not just plucked at random, as it appeared, but were carefully screened by producers. They looked for people with quirky names (such as the most memorable guest, Gonzalez Gonzalez), jobs, personalities, backgrounds, or, in the case of women, physical attributes; the lecherous side of Marx was left intact. He was served up characters to toy with as precisely as if they had been conceived by a clever screenwriter. The sponsor's one proviso was that the show be prerecorded and sent to a censor, due to Marx's reputation for ribald asides.

The early programs weren't as lively as everyone had hoped, considering Groucho's film reputation as an anarchic comic who breaks up the joint with withering wisecracks. Many of the cracks withered, and the quiz lagged, even though the first show was entirely scripted and Marx had mingled with the guests beforehand. Jack Gould in the *New York Times* was not amused, claiming Groucho had been reduced to the level of Art Linkletter and Phil Baker. "Trouper that he is, Mr. Marx works hard and does his best, but the show never really comes off. Somewhere along the line the delightful silliness of Mr. Marx's act has been confused with the exhibitionistic absurdity of the average radio quiz. One happy day Mr. Marx will break into radio; he will be assigned a program without a stylized format."

To fix things, Guedel decided to run the quiz-show segment straight, give Groucho only a few clues about the guests without his ever actually meeting them, and hire gagwriters to better arm the host should his wit fail him. Groucho was fast and funny—in private life, he never let up—but hardly fail-safe, and he felt better going into battle with a few ripostes up his sleeve; writers on the show were disguised as "program staff." Even so, making lines *sound* ad-libbed is its own art. So while everything sounded extemporaneous, it wasn't. What finally saved the show were guests with a high ribbing potential—contestants with, say, twelve children, a silly job, a bizarre hobby, a deadly personality, or a 46-inch bustline.

Moreover, although few realized it at the time—and were later disillusioned to learn—the give-and-take was heavily edited, leaving only the best repartee for listeners; an interview that lasted only five minutes on the air might be the result of a fifteen-minute sparring session. The half-hour show was so artfully edited, in fact, that it helped popularize the use of tape, then a prohibited device. Happily, the no-tape rule was reversed days before *You Bet Your Life* debuted. Guedel has said, "Not even Groucho was as funny as he seemed. He would press at first. He'd keep going-going-going until he got what he was after. Hell, we wouldn't ever have finished a show. It would have been a thirteen-week show. Instead it was a fourteen-year show." The program grew gradually into the burnished, nonchalant give-and-take that endeared it to audiences for so long. It was a primitive example of that later curious TV hybrid—half-interview, half-banter—called the talk show.

Groucho remained skeptical about the show's popularity: "I am now fifth in the national ratings, but I can't find anyone who admits they still have a radio, much less listens to one," he grouched in a letter to Fred Allen in 1950. "The rich people are the ones who have the TV sets. The paupers, or schlepper crowd, still hang on to their portable radios, but unfortunately they're not the ones who buy Chryslers and DeSoto station wagons."

The quiz aspect of *You Bet Your Life* was the least interesting part of the show (which during its mid-1950s peak had a combined radio-TV audience of 40 million), merely a hook on which to hang Groucho's wit. The show's double-or-nothing format featured the it-pays-to-be-ignorant consolation question for couples who won nothing ("Who is buried in Grant's tomb?") and the famous Secret Word ("It's a common word, something you see around the house every day") that, on TV, triggered a bespectacled, mustachioed duck to drop from above as the band played his and the show's "My Name Is Captain Spalding" theme.

Any sting the legendary comedian might have felt about succumbing to a radio quiz show was greatly soothed when the show became a hit and won a Peabody Award, the first time a quiz show had ever won anything. *You Bet Your Life* was also the first radio show to use reruns, thanks to the persuasive Guedel's totally bogus statistic that the average radio listener heard only 3.4 shows during a season; ABC bought his argument. Guedel also devised the first simulcast, using the same soundtrack for both radio and TV versions—sight-gag laughs were cut from the radio transcript, prompting Jack Gould's comment: "To Mr. Marx's credit, this is probably the first radio show that without material change holds interest on television." Its director boasted that it was the staidest TV show ever devised. Sure enough, the most animated thing on screen are Groucho's eyebrows—amazing, considering his perpetual motion in movies; he looks like an insurance man. It was also

TV's cheapest major show, requiring only a curtain, a stool, and a duck on a wire.

The show peppered its list of contestants with celebrities, usually from outside show business (stars were afraid of being publicly humiliated by Groucho, or at least overshadowed), or on the fringes, like Rocky Marciano's mother. It made the best use of contestants of any quiz show. Well-known guests like General Omar Bradley and singer John Charles Thomas were trotted out without fanfare, preserving the egalitarian offhand quality of the show, linking the famous with the obscure, the blue-collar worker with the tycoon, and the urbane with the rube. The only person conspicuous by her absence on the show was Groucho's old film foil Margaret Dumont, who insisted on being paid despite the show's no-fee policy.

Much of the TV show's charm lay in the byplay between the bumptious, needling Groucho and the handsome, genteel announcer, Fenneman, for whom it became the job of a lifetime. "I pinched myself regularly," he once said, astonished to find himself on the same stage with one of the greatest wits of all time, and an idol. Marx ordered him around like a serf—"Get out here, Fenneman!" He took it like a man, which created a congenial tension. Fenneman didn't take the insults personally—or, for a while, at all. As he told Marx's biographer Hector Arce: "At the beginning I was young and resilient, and I didn't have the good sense to know I was being insulted." Later, he realized that everyone was fair game. "It was part of the character he was building for me that became wonderfully saleable in years to come. I'd have to be a clod to bad-mouth the man who made it possible."

The show finally went off the air in 1961, and in 1970 Groucho attempted to get NBC to syndicate the TV version, but the network thought the black-and-white show too lifeless and dated. Guedel salvaged the prints when NBC threatened to throw them out and got a local Los Angeles station to rerun them late at night, paying $54.88 a show. *You Bet Your Life* repeats became a cult, like *The Honeymooners,* and gave the series, and Groucho, yet another life; for Fenneman it meant $200,000 a year in residuals, seven times what he had been paid the first time around.

Marx loved playing the rude quizmaster character in life, insulting whoever crossed his path. Once, after heckling a waitress, to writer-producer Norman Krasna's uneasiness, Marx claimed that his brow-beating was a badge of honor. "You don't understand," he told Krasna. "That waitress will go home tonight and say, 'Do you know what Groucho said to me?' And she treasures it."

STOP THE MUSIC WAS HOSTED BY the irrepressible and inexhaustible Bert Parks, whose never-say-die attitude and chummy, at times clammy, Southern charm set the tone for game show hosts ever after. Parks, who later achieved lasting notoriety as the Miss America pageant's MC, was impossible to avoid on radio, and later on the tube. Like mafia dons, Bert Parks, Bud Collyer, Wyn Elliot, Bob Hawk, and Bill Cullen divided up the game show turf evenly. The job also retrained all sorts of unemployed actors.

The frenetic Parks took the most getting used to, but the man was as persistent as bees at a picnic. When Parks finally broke through in *Stop the Music,* which tested both your musical expertise and your patience, Henry Morgan called it the final nail in radio's coffin; it surely closed the lid on Fred Allen's career.

Stop the Music and similar giveaways were radio's version of the desperate "bank nights" that movie theaters held to lure people away from their TV sets in the mid-1950s, handing out cheap sets of dishes between double bills. They were, sneered critics, a brazen attempt to bribe audiences. What fueled the giveaways was a simple trade-off in which items doled out were plugged with an elaborate description of the product that amounted to scores of free commercials within each show. This practice led to prize-brokering by companies—Prizes, Inc., V.I.P. Services—that were set up as legal fences to distribute the swag to quiz shows, raking off a tidy surcharge for every "donated" prize. The odds were 25 million to one that you'd be called. The FCC pondered hard the philosophical question of whether the shows were, in fact, lotteries before deciding that they were not. But one columnist wondered if radio was selling or buying time.

The show that parlayed all of this national lotto fever was devised by the bandleader Harry Salter with *Your Hit Parade*'s conductor, Mark Warnow, as a way to blend big bands and big bucks into the biggest radio-bang-for-the-buck of all. Their central gimmick was the telephone. The long-distance call had become a minor rage itself during the war. The idea of calling a radio program (even if only Parks's end of the conversation was audible to listeners), plus winning a jackpot by naming a mystery tune, dazzled America. Although callers were ostensibly chosen at random from a bank of operators, in fact contestants were contacted well ahead of time and waited by their phones for hours to hear from Parks.

Stop the Music (*"Starring YOU, the people of America!"*) handed out far fancier prizes than most giveaways—diamond rings, steamship cruises, thousand-dollar savings bonds, fur coats, pianos, and cars. America in 1948 was clearly on a postwar spending binge. "After half a dozen years of rationing and empty shelves," said producer Louis Cowan, "people just hearing the prizes mentioned gained a certain sense of, 'Well, it's great to be able to have these things again.' " One radio historian, however, called it just another instance of radio's "constant search for ways to intertwine program content and products." The crafty Cowan recognized the show's potential. ABC, desperate for a way to put a dent into Fred Allen and Edgar Bergen and Charlie McCarthy's lock on the Sunday hour from 8 to 9 P.M., took a chance and, within a season, sent both major comics scurrying for shelter.

The New York *Daily News* TV critic called giveaway shows "a major calamity" and the *New York Times* critic also lamented the siren call of cash: "[*Stop the Music*] has adopted the press agent's oldest stratagem of strewing coins on the street to attract a crowd." Maybe, but there was something wholly, if not unholy, American about the quiz show, with its democratic spirit, lucky streak, and rags-to-riches theme: The possibility that any schnook sitting on his stoop in Brooklyn or feeding chickens in Omaha could, with the tinkling of a telephone bell, become a national hero and an overnight tycoon appealed to every red-white-and-blue-blooded Yankee. Said Bob Hawk: "A quiz can't be beat. It can't be touched. It stands by itself. It's a people's program. A good quiz should be called *A Program for the Common People.*"

A GI contestant named Knox Burger (now a literary agent) recalled in *American Heritage* that radio giveaway shows were often slightly rigged even in the relatively innocent pre–TV quiz show scandal era. During the war, a civilian was rarely allowed to beat a serviceman. "The uniforms wouldn't be visible to people listening on their radios," he observed, "but radio shows drew their energy from the enthusiasm and applause of the studio audience, and back then *soldier* was a synonym for *winner.* A guy in a suit meant nothing." Thus, before his appearance on a giveaway show, Burger was pointedly told what day Franklin Roosevelt had died—April 12, 1945. "It's a date we think every American should know," the producer remarked, all but winking. Wrote Burger, "The same dynamic that sealed the fate of Herb Stempel on *Twenty-One* was, of course, at work even in 1945."

ANOTHER PROGRAM THAT USED the quiz format as a hook on which to hang a music show, or maybe vice versa, was *Kay Kyser's Kollege of Musical Knowledge,* which found a way to blend two innocuous genres and to showcase a dance band in a day when every big band was trying to make itself heard on radio over its rivals.

Like Horace Heidt and Sammy Kaye, Kay Kyser was just another bandleader filling time on a Chicago station when he developed a bit whereby dancers would try to stump the band; to losers, he gleefully shouted, "That's right, you're wrong!" Playing a loopy North Carolinian, Professor Kyser addressed his rowdy studio audience as *"stoodents"* in a musical/quiz show that blended the goofiest aspect of each genre and turned musicians and contestants into clowns.

Lew Wasserman, the legendary longtime head of MCA, at the time a booker and publicity man with the agency, heard Kyser at the Blackhawk Restaurant and suggested to his new client that he combine his music questions into a "Professor Quiz"–like show. Kyser, a onetime prelaw student with a thick drawl ("Evenin', folks, how y'all? Come on, chillun, le's dance!"), overlaid with ersatz 1940s jive ("Greetings, Gates, let's matriculate"), was an ideal choice. The peppy onetime head cheerleader at the University of North Carolina had a cheerleading personality.

It was a rambunctious classroom led by the irrepressible Kyser, who went on to make campus musical films like *That's Right, You're Wrong* and to record novelty hit songs ("Three Little Fishies," "Praise the Lord and Pass the Ammunition," "Woody Woodpecker"). In the most inventive bit on an otherwise giddy show—which also featured a faculty that included nonzany singer Ginny Simms, class clown Ish Kabibble (who took his name from a nonsense song), and a new voice and future TV talk-show host, Mike Douglas; crooner Harry Babbitt sang titles off-key to stump contestants. Kyser took early retirement at forty-five and went home to North Carolina to become a Christian Science lecturer. Like many radio bandleaders, he was more MC than musician. Once, he admitted during a lecture (confirming many suspicions): "I never learned how to read music or even play an instrument, although I made a lot of money leading a band. I can brag about it now, but I was anxious to hide it back then."

AT THE OPPOSITE END of radio's pursuit of pure knowledge was the greedy pursuit of pure loot, at least partly due to postwar prosperity. It was as if all of those women imprisoned in their kitchens listening to soap operas during the war had themselves finally been liberated in 1945. At the start of *Second Honeymoon*, a show aired from a Bamberger's department store in Newark, New Jersey, Bert Parks would bellow, "Who's the pillar of American society?" and a rabid crowd of women would screech in response, "The housewife!!" The show was a precursor of such capitalist orgies as TV's *The Price Is Right*.

Out of the quiz shows' cornucopia tumbled giveaway extravaganzas—*Break the Bank, Strike It Rich, Queen for a Day, Bride and Groom,* and *What's the Name of That Song?* If soap operas had made homemakers into domestic divas, game shows dragged them onstage to take part in gimmick-laden shows that—in the tear-drenched instances of *Queen for a Day* and *Strike It Rich*—tapped into the misery zone where *Stella Dallas* and *Backstage Wife* had for so long dwelt.

The show that totally blurred the fuzzy line between quiz shows and game shows was *Queen for a Day*, hosted by radio's favorite male sob sister, Jack Bailey, a resolutely jocular fellow despite his gruesome five-day-a-week job. *Queen for a Day* was ostensibly a quiz show but in fact it fronted a charity bazaar that awarded prizes to women who could come up with the most heart-stabbing stories told by the sick and the downtrodden. It was a game show that would have gladdened the heart of Charles Dickens. On one show, a mother of nine requested a washing machine to replace one that broke when it fell on her husband and disabled him—and who, by the way, also needed heart surgery.

The never-say-die Bailey refused to be dismayed or disturbed by anyone's tragedy, no matter how horrific. People listened to the show the way motorists gape at five-car pileups. Bailey had a way of smiling through tears and of jollying sobbing contestants out of their miseries with a chin-up joke before signing off with his jubilant cry, "*I'd like to make EV-ery woman queen for EV-ery day!*" He once explained the emotional pull of the show, which turned the giveaway idea into a benefit: "Many women put on their cards that they'd like an ironer to make their work lighter. Who wouldn't? But the woman who wants an ironer so she can take in ironing to help the family finances, that's a different story."

Strike It Rich was a weepy hybrid of *Stop the Music* and *Queen for a Day*, using the surprise phone call to reward misery via "The Heart Line" from do-gooder listeners, who donated money or prizes of their own; once, virtuoso Fritz Kreisler called up to give away a violin to a kid who had lost his own instrument.

As on *Stop the Music*, the spontaneous outpourings were choreographed. Many years later, producer Walt Framer admitted: "We'd arrange with donors to phone in gifts for a particular contestant. If a widow with six children came on to explain the pressing need for a new roof for her house, we would contact ahead of time a roofer to set up a donation." The roofer got a plug, the poor wretch at home got a roof, and the show didn't have to dole out a penny except for the phone calls.

The tear-streaked *Strike It Rich* MC, first on radio and then TV, was former Broadway and B-movie actor Warren Hull, a Quaker whose heart was so genuinely stirred by the plights of contestants that his eyes grew moist as he bestowed appliances and medical payments upon godforsaken winners—paraplegics, fathers of leukemia victims, the widowed mother of five whose father was killed by a hit-and-run driver, a choir of blind black gospel singers in need of a van for tours.

Hull was himself wounded when critics attacked shows like his and Bailey's for exploiting human suffering; Framer argued that most newspapers were equally filled with human woe. A stone-hearted New York welfare commissioner once took Framer and Hull to court for fundraising without a license and the show was actually found guilty.

IF *QUEEN FOR A DAY* was a tearjerker quiz show whose main effect was torment and heartbreak, *Can You Top This?* was a laugh-jerker that opened with the sound of a guffawing audience. Much of vaudeville's rambunctious anything-for-a-laugh spirit was lovingly captured on this quasi-quiz show on which a panel of old-time vaudeville spritzers and toastmasters—"Senator" Ed Ford ("Good evening"), Harry Hershfield ("Howdee!"), and Joe Laurie, Jr. ("Hel-lew")—held a weekly challenge joke-off to see if they could outdo each other on the studio's Colgate Palmolive Laugh Meter, which rated laughs from 1 to 1,000. There were few duds, or, in fact, any jokes that pulled under 850 on the laugh machine. Listeners received ten dollars if their joke was used and retold by host Peter Donald, plus a five-dollar bonus each time a panelist failed to top it; if nobody could (a rarity), they won a hefty twenty-five dollars. Most of the time, the joke was easily topped. It was a merry show, full of fraternal kidding and free-wheeling joshing among the three aging New York jesters—Hershfield, a cartoonist and after-dinner speaker; Joe Laurie, Jr., a former burlesque performer and editor of *Variety;* and quipmeister Ed Ford.

As explained each week by announcer Warren Wilson, "Our three gagsters have no scripts; they rely on memory and the ability to switch jokes to make them fit the subject." Wilson would announce a topic, such as "Indignation," Peter Donald would tell the listener's joke (often using Irish characters that recalled his "Allen's Alley" alter ego, Ajax Cassidy), and the panelists would submit their entries. Sample Joe Laurie, Jr., joke: "Two friends were talking and one guy says, 'Was my wife indignant this morning! Oh, brother, was she mad.' The other guy says, 'What about?' 'What about? I almost twisted her nose off her face last night.' 'What'd you do that for?' 'I dreamt all night I forgot to shut the water off!' " (it easily scored 1,000 on the laugh meter). The resourceful wags often slipped in bonus one-liners, such as Ed Ford's "I know a fellow whose little boy had whooping cough and he got him a job as a glass blower."

During its eleven years, *Can You Top This?* pulled in six thousand jokes a week, many rich in ethnic accents and all clean; only jokes on religion, politics, and arson were rejected. Moved to TV, the show seemed a stale joke that gained about a 12 on the laugh meter and was gone in a year.

THE MICROPHONE DEMANDED a mellower approach than more pushy performers could master. Radio was a cool medium, where nonchalance reigned and where a faintly amusing man of uncertain credentials and indefinable talents could become a superstar. Just such a man was the star of *Arthur Godfrey Time*.

Godfrey, whose disheveled, folksy-cum-foxy, laid-back manner— "the man with the barefoot voice," in Fred Allen's succinct summation—spawned that peculiar breed which came to be called "talk-show host." He was the first of a long line of personable but only vaguely talented performers as diverse as Phil Donahue, Mike Douglas, and Tom Snyder, who would later be transformed into stars in their own right. Godfrey invented and personified the informal, often aimless, conversational style that would, in TV, become a mammoth industry.

It was Godfrey, moreover, who defined the art of coast-to-coast ad-libbing, navel-gazing, joshing, and star-making. He was a man both revered and feared for his chuckling manner, a man whose idle back-fence chitchat belied a ferocious ego. Yet ironically, his rambling from-the-heart spiels for Lipton's tea and soups turned him into radio's most trusted pitchman; he could make the act of brewing a cup of tea into an orgasmic experience. At one time, his three shows generated 12 percent of CBS's total advertising revenue, and he was reputedly the second most successful salesperson on the air, after hostess and interviewer Mary Margaret McBride. Larry King once said, "If Godfrey talked about peanut butter, I *had* to have that peanut butter!"

Meanwhile, a handful of other father figures waxed poetical or philosophical, homespun fellas like Galen Drake, Ted Malone, and Tony Wons, a full-service guy who sang, gave advice, and read verse in a whispery voice—an estimated ten thousand poems by 1931. In New York, meanwhile, the beloved Eugene Field provided inspirational

Overleaf, top: Major Edward Bowes (*The Original Amateur Hour*); *bottom:* Arthur Godfrey

solace and answered letters from distraught female listeners after break-fast, to the sound of organ music and singing canaries. The understand-ing Dr. John J. Anthony ("Dr. Agony") hung out his shingle at "The Court of Human Relations" and sorted out peoples' troubled personal lives, like today's radio shrinks Dr. Laura Schlessinger and Joy Browne.

Godfrey, an über-patriarch, was partly the creation of CBS's Frank Stanton, the salesman half of the Paley-Stanton partnership, who rec-ognized Godfrey's ability to hawk products under the guise of enter-tainment. Godfrey was the original and ultimate infotainer. He was a uke-strumming pitchman with a checkered background as cemetery-lot salesman, cabdriver, sailor, pilot, and banjo player who had once hosted a show called *Red Godfrey's Ukulele Club*. Essentially, he was an announcer, but with enough personality and chutzpah to imperson-ate a performer. He once confessed, "I knew I didn't have any talents, so I had to make you believe that what I said was true." Stanton stuck by his boy, whom he called an acquired taste. "The traditional comedi-ans in Hollywood did not understand Godfrey's style," Stanton once said. "They were very contemptuous." Jack Benny told the CBS chief, "I can't understand what the hold is that this man has on the audi-ence."

Godfrey's hold on his audience was that he was, or pretended to be, the average Joe, unimpressed with the glitter of showbiz or with politicians and all the other highfalutin pretensions that he ridiculed in his quasi-hayseed manner. In fact, he hung out with celebrities and made sure you knew he was on a first-name basis with politicians. Nonetheless, listeners felt he was one of them ("He was the first star who made us feel he was a friend," said one fan), but as his stature grew he became as pompous as the people he kidded. He also was steeped in greeting-card sentimentality, delivering Hallmark homilies with reverence; one of his favorite phrases was, "May the good Lord willin' . . ."

The freckled, redheaded, tousle-haired schmoozer ruled a major portion of CBS's on-air empire for a quarter century on two different shows, first on radio and then TV: *Arthur Godfrey Time* (also known as *Arthur Godfrey and His Friends*—identified by basso announcer Tony Marvin as "all the little Godfreys") and *Arthur Godfrey's Talent Scouts,* which launched a few careers and sank a few. His cast of regulars included singers Frank Parker, Marian Marlowe, Lu Ann Simms, Janette Davis, Carmel Quinn, Bill Hayes, Julius La Rosa, and a Hawaiian, Haleloke.

Perhaps due to his own dubious talent, Godfrey was uneasy coexisting with major talents. If Godfrey, a control freak, felt that a performer was getting too large a head or becoming too famous, he might delay his entrance on a show. If Godfrey was truly upset, he wouldn't call on the singer at all and then, to rub it in, would dock his paycheck. "He was pretty tough," recalls the singer Betty Johnson.

Godfrey's "aw, to hell with it" attitude and his average-guy act hid a mean streak that emerged when he sacked the stunned La Rosa on TV. Before La Rosa's number, he pretended to razz the singer, saying in his best avuncular manner, "You're doing pretty good, aren't you? Getting big money in the nightclubs and so forth. This show must be a pain in the neck to you." After La Rosa had finished his song, "Manhattan," Godfrey finished the job in these smarmy words: "Thanks ever so much, Julie. That was Julie's swan song with us. He goes now out on his own, as his own star, soon to be seen on his own program, and I know you wish him godspeed the same as I do." Then, the deed done, Godfrey beat a hasty retreat and concluded the program with a chilly, "This is CBS, the Columbia Broadcasting System." What had actually upset Godfrey, La Rosa later claimed, was that he had made a hit record "E Cumpari," with Archie Bleyer, Godfrey's longtime conductor, which, La Rosa admitted, had made him a little "cocky." When La Rosa further declared his independence by hiring his own press agent, Godfrey took it as a blatant act of "nonhumility." His worst sin, though, was drawing more fan mail than the boss.

A few weeks later, Godfrey also dumped Archie Bleyer himself, supposedly because Bleyer had the temerity to record a song with Don McNeill of *The Breakfast Club*, Godfrey's nonthreatening midwestern morning rival; Godfrey treated this as an act of treason. His petulance and arrogance were the stuff of legend. La Rosa recalled that Godfrey told everyone at a cast meeting (which regulars called "prayer meetings"), "Remember that many of you are here over the bodies of people I have personally slain. I've done it before and I can do it again."

The Irish singer Carmel Quinn, who won a *Talent Scouts* show in 1955, only days after she arrived from Ireland, and quickly joined the regular cast, springs to his defense. "I never saw any of that other side," she says gently. "The Arthur I knew was nothing like" the fuming tyrant so often described. "We hit it off from the start. He reminded me a lot of my father, with his red hair, blue eyes, and wit. I had a great time with him and I learned so much from him—that it's all right to be honest. He was very honest, and so good at just making conversation. He listened."

In her endearing manner, the modest Quinn would simply level with Godfrey on the show, and never kowtowed, if only because she had never heard of him when she first auditioned. "The others held him in such awe, and were always trying to please him, but I was very straight with him," she recalls. Quinn left the show in 1961, after Godfrey took ill and others attempted to fill in for him. "Nobody else had his touch. He had a certain something, an instinct for understanding the ordinary woman at home. No one today is as big as Arthur Godfrey was then."

Godfrey's calculated homespun manner was aided by a slightly naughty bedside manner, which made him seem both wicked and benign. His adoring audience was mostly middle-aged women, whom he could make purr with his sincere homilies, patriotism, tales of his flying escapades, love of the outdoors, and the horses he raised on a Virginia farm he often broadcast from—everything sprinkled with a steady supply of mildly ribald innuendo that titillated the bathrobe-clad housewives who sat cradling their midmorning coffee.

In a typical show from a 1946 *Arthur Godfrey Time,* Godfrey drops names in his drowsy drawl like a neighborhood gossip columnist: "Earl Wilson told me last night at Toots's [Shor] that Harry Hirshfield asked the waiter what could he order that would induce heartburn immediately instead of at 2 A.M. . . . That's cute." He joshes with the band, tells jokes, spins stories, discusses a book he liked, reads some cards from listeners, then segues into a rendition of "Comin' Through the Rye," plunking out his own ukulele accompaniment.

The La Rosa incident marked the start of Godfrey's long good-bye. He remained on radio and TV for another decade but never regained his hold on the public's affection after the La Rosa spectacle, unheard-of in its day—or even in our own time. The critic Ben Gross said of Godfrey's fall from grace that while those in broadcasting weren't taken in by Godfrey's jovial act, "radio fans have sentimental views of their air idols. It came as a shock to them that Arthur was not the beloved paternal figure presiding over a contented family . . . a group torn by jealousies, romantic intrigues and petty dissensions."

Godfrey was finished at CBS despite thwarted efforts to reestablish himself, most disastrously as a cohost on TV's *Candid Camera*. Paley sent him a Christmas card each year and Stanton asked him to a cocktail party, which Godfrey declined with a snarl. He did some Chrysler commercials—perhaps his true calling—before retiring to his Virginia farm, but managed a sidewalk reunion with La Rosa one day when they ran into each other in New York in 1974 and warmly shook hands. La Rosa kidded that they'd better not display too much public affection or the press might make an item out of it, to which Godfrey replied with his usual venomous charm, "Fuck 'em," and limped away.

A FAR MORE WHOLESOME and genuine all-bran Arthur Godfrey was Don McNeill, whose early-morning show *The Breakfast Club* preceded *Arthur Godfrey Time* and for three and a half decades was a gentle snooze alarm that roused America from bed each day between 8 and 9 A.M. (9 to 10 A.M. in the late-rising East). His *Breakfast Club* was the on-air equivalent of a warm bowl of oatmeal.

McNeill's Chicago-based show was an authentic taste of the Midwest, or so it seemed to any nonmidwestern ears. Spooning Cheerios in your breakfast nook, you felt much less small-town. From its opening song ("*Good morning, Breakfast Clubbers, we're glad to see ya!/We wake up bright and early just to howdy-do ya*"), the show was hopelessly hokey and often downright silly, but there was something unsynthetic about it, unlike Godfrey's imitation New York–grown corn.

McNeill and Company also were an acquired taste. For six years the show was entitled *The Pepper Pot* and was sponsorless from 1933 to 1939, before McNeill changed the name and began to ad-lib; by 1951, there were plenty of sponsors and a $4 million-a-year budget. It was thirty-five years before the show finally folded up its collective breakfast table in 1968, but even at that late date it was heard on 224 stations; a 1954 TV simulcast version failed.

Breakfast-clubbers looked forward each morning to the "march around the breakfast table"—you envisioned farm wives clumping about big tables, as indeed they did during the "four calls to breakfast," one each quarter-hour; to "Fiction and Fact from Sam's Almanac," with comic sidekick Sam Cowling reciting lousy jokes, worse verse, folklore, nostalgia, and letters from his mailbag; and to regular village gossip from "Aunt Fanny," played by Fran Allison pre–*Kukla, Fran and Ollie,* delivering rambling monologues on wacky relatives and neighbors—folks like Bert and Bertie Beerbower, the Smelsers, and Ott Ort (shades of *Vic and Sade*). It was all simple small-town fun that, in fact, emanated from a big Chicago hotel, with such regular sentimental segments as "Memory Time—a Moment of Silent Prayer," led by McNeill ("*Each in his own words, each in his own way, for a world united in peace, bow your heads and pray*"); and a do-gooder report called "The Sunshine Shower," which asked listeners to write to shut-ins. All this plus unabashedly bad jokes: "Courtship makes a man spoon, but marriage makes him fork over" . . . "The distance from the head of a fox to its tail is a fur piece." *The Breakfast Club* proved you didn't necessarily have to love a show to listen to it. You listened to it because it somehow connected and, quite literally, spoke to you—just you.

Don McNeill exemplified what Arthur Godfrey had also honed to perfection—the art of speaking to one person, as when he bid listeners adieu each day with his cheery, "So long now and be good to yourself!" McNeill would often refer to his wife, Kay, who occasionally pulled up a chair at the coast-to-coast breakfast table for a cozy chat. Even acerbic Fred Allen was a *Breakfast Club* admirer, praising McNeill as "a big friendly fellow whose good nature pours through the microphone, and listeners react in the same way anyone reacts meeting him in person." McNeill didn't shy from charges that the show was as corny as Kansas in August. "Of course we're corny," he happily conceded in 1950. "And why not? Probably most American wit and humor could be called that. As for sentiment, nobody should be ashamed of it. There are too many poker faces in the world today."

SPOTLIGHTING THE COMMON MAN was the life work of Major Edward Bowes, a rather dour fellow in rimless spectacles who, as managing director of the Capitol Theater in New York, began introducing amateur nights to local radio audiences in the mid-1920s.

Bowes, a theater impresario and film distributor, further adapted and streamlined the traditional vaudeville amateur night for network radio in 1934. A year later, reported *Variety*, the Ziegfeld of birdwhistlers and spoon-players was show business's leading earner, grossing $1 million a year with his show, *Major Bowes and His Original Amateur Hour*, originally called *Major Bowes and His Capitol Family*, a modest Sunday morning broadcast. Just how "original" the show was, nobody ever quite determined—local radio stations had presented, indeed lived off, amateurs for years, and three months before Bowes's show went network, *National Amateur Night* debuted on CBS; also, precisely what constituted an amateur was very much open to question.

Major Bowes—he claimed to have been a major in intelligence in World War I, although one source says he was only in the Officers Reserve Corps—did a pretty good juggling act himself. Eventually he had twenty units crisscrossing the countryside preaching the gospel of amateurism (and perhaps secretly hoping to revive vaudeville). He also produced film shorts. But it was the radio show that served as Bowes's nerve center. On it, every week the humorless Major spun his show business roulette wheel and droned in a funereal voice, "Tonight we spin our weekly wheel of fortune for the 5,368th time. Around and around she goes, and where she stops nobody knows." When performers were too awful to be allowed to continue, Bowes would strike a gong, an audio version of the early vaudeville hook and a gimmick later exploited by TV's *Gong Show*, a sort of subamateur hour.

Bowes's show later gave rise to pro/am versions like *Arthur Godfrey's Talent Scouts* and hustling Horace Heidt's *Youth Opportunity Program*, with its WPA overtones, as if Heidt were providing work for roving teenage accordionists who might otherwise go astray. Indeed, Heidt's major find was the squeeze-box virtuoso Dick Contino, whose peppy version of "Lady of Spain" remains to this day amateurism's finest hour.

Bowes's units traversed the country in search of gifted water-glass soloists, hand-saw players, spoon thumpers, and harmonica geniuses; local amateur hours included magicians who described their tricks on the air. The program played to some 20 million listeners in its heyday, inspired copycat versions, and became a radio staple, even though NBC at first resisted the notion that listeners would tune in to hear a bunch of amateurs on the air. The very idea seemed repugnant to networks, which prided themselves on their highly paid professional talent.

One radio historian has recounted how small-time entertainers who had wowed the local Lions Club were encouraged to sell their homes, pack up their banjos, tap shoes, washboards and cowbells and, like showbiz Okies, head east in pursuit of theatrical fame and fortune. Some ten thousand people wrote in each week seeking auditions with Bowes. The list was then whittled down to about twenty, leaving the remaining out-of-work yodelers and wineglass virtuosi out on the street. When *Newsweek* reported that during a single month of 1935 some twelve hundred stranded entertainers needed emergency aid, Bowes ruled that only people from the New York area were eligible. The radio-show winners and "finalists" (never "losers") were judged by an electorate that voted via mail and telephone; winners did an encore, and three-time winners took part in an annual championship. Some thirty thousand voters each week answered the Major's constant request to listeners to "dial JUdson 8-1000; New Jersey residents may vote by calling. . . ."

"All men are at heart critics," Bowes liked to say, describing the show's appeal, "and since time immemorial, they have always felt they can run the other fellow's show better than he can. It gives them a feeling of satisfaction to believe that they may have started someone on the road to success"—someone, perhaps, like the guy who hit himself over the head with two mallets and, by opening and closing his mouth, serenaded listeners with "The Sheik of Araby," one of scores of amateurs adept at playing bizarre instruments of their own invention; as often as not, the program was as much freak show as talent contest.

The Major was a businesslike fellow with a mirthless chuckle who, unlike most MCs, had a gift for nongab. He would welcome his guests, ask what they were going to perform, and if they jabbered too long, would cut them off with a curt, "All right, all right." He was flanked by a bodyguard, to protect the Major against any unruly losing bird-callers, but he had a good heart, notably in his great years during the Depression: Before the show, he took contestants to dinner, gave them ten dollars each and, in an informal preinterview for his on-air chats, tried to loosen up the frightened entertainers prior to their make-or-break performance before millions; he also provided blacks with more opportunities than most network shows did.

The *Original Amateur Hour* got the hook in 1946, when the Major died, but resumed on TV in 1948, headed by the equally bland Ted

Mack. For years, Mack had directed auditions, as well as the show itself, and was imbued with Bowes's selfless quest for talent in any and all forms. He treated frightened amateurs as gently as possible, and when they stumbled and had to start over, Mack would try to relax them with a sympathetic word. The TV show ran until 1952 under Mack's benign hand, and is principally remembered now for its dancing pack of Old Golds—more often than not the niftiest act on the show.

Many were called but few were chosen: Out of the more than fifteen thousand amateurs who had five minutes of fame, some went on to eke out a living in two-bit clubs and country fair circuits, and a few made it later on—Lily Pons, Beverly Sills, Jack Carter, Robert Merrill, Mimi Benzel, Teresa Brewer, and a skinny baritone named Frank Sinatra who appeared on a 1937 show as a member of the Hoboken Four, which drew a record forty thousand call-in votes. Nancy Sinatra claims that, in fact, her father had auditioned for the show as a solo act and the Major grafted him to a trio called the Three Flashes and dubbed the new quartet "The Hoboken Four." In any case, Sinatra willingly piped, "I'm Frank, Major. We're lookin' for jobs. How about it? Everyone that's ever heard us liked us. We think we're pretty good." The other three Hobokeners (Frank Tamburro, Jimmy Petro, and Patty Prince) soon returned with thousands of their fellow amateurs to showbiz oblivion.

THE EARLIEST TALK SHOWS were run by chatty New York couples from around a breakfast table amid clattering coffee cups and clinking spoons. Perhaps the chattiest and best-known pairs were *Dorothy and Dick,* the columnist Dorothy Kilgallen and her actor-husband Dick Kollmar, gabbing away from their sixteen-room Park Avenue penthouse, and *Tex and Jinx,* which featured columnist-commentator Tex McCrary and his chic wife, Jinx Falkenburg, a tennis player, model, and gadabout. Ed and Pegeen Fitzgerald broke the ice in the early 1940s, and Pegeen was still gabbing away on the air into her eighties. The Fitzgeralds always seemed utterly themselves, pleasant people unscarred by brushes with the famous, fatuous, and powerful. The Kollmars and the Fitzgeralds went eggcup-to-eggcup with each other. John Dunning recalled, "Dorothy and Dick considered the Fitzgeralds crude and uncouth; Ed and Pegeen thought the Kollmars aloof and snooty." Another mealtime chatfest, *Breakfast at Sardi's,* was cooked up by host Tom Breneman, who broke bread with stars in a way that, for its day, was tantalizingly up close and personal; he later opened up his own rival West Coast on-air bistro, *Breakfast in Hollywood.*

Mary Margaret McBride (parodied by Bob and Ray as "Mary McGoon") did a solo act, working for a time under New York City station WOR's corporate name "Martha Deane" (where she discussed her nonexistent grandchildren) before moving to CBS and breaking out from behind the mask as her unmarried independent self. While she was "Martha Deane," she became a role model for corporate mother figures and doled out advice to the lovelorn, like Beatrice Fairfax, or to the ovenlorn, like Betty Crocker. McBride had a genuinely homey manner, a compelling interview style, and gave off a concerned air that drew a huge devoted audience to her bubbly recipe of household tips, celebrity chats, and social issues. One writer called her a female Arthur Godfrey, mainly because her sincere manner could sell any product— but only those she believed in and had lab-tested to prove their promises. McBride's personal seal of approval kept sponsors in line— and standing in line, begging for a satisfied nod from her.

The talk-show, now largely the domain of washed-up politicians, would-be actors, ex-announcers, and showbiz-minded reporters, rose to polished heights with Tex and Jinx's show, which opened with the attractive couple conversing about what was in the morning papers. The worldly Tex did most of the talking as the agreeable Jinx chimed in with a wifely word or two; in their first show, *Hi, Jinx!,* he acted as editor and sent her out on assignments. (One of their writers was Barry Farber, a master of the call-in talk show format originated at WOR by Barry Gray.) In the manner of TV's Regis Philbin and Kathie Lee Gifford, Tex and Jinx would discuss that day's theater reviews, or give their own, chat about a party they had attended, and interview celebrities. It wasn't quite the vapid gabble parodied by Fred Allen on his show, and they didn't actually sip coffee or chew muffins on the air, but some of their celebrity "interviews" were closer to press releases. From a conversation with Walt Disney, for instance, Jinx breathlessly reported that he loves his work.

*Your radio friend
Ma Perkins*

MOST RADIO SHOWS WERE AIMED AT A GENERAL audience, but the soap opera was precisely designed with the little woman in mind.

Three things made the soaps—after the news—the most profitable shows on the air. First, they aired during the day, when housewives were the chief radio audience, so they could pitch every sort of item, from Ajax to Ex-Lax, to the very person who let the sponsor get his foot in the door with the ease of a Fuller Brush man. In those days, the lady of the house was always in. Second, they were cheap and efficient to produce: The quarter-hour shows required only a few pages of script per day, and featured an interminable plot with only a handful of characters. Finally and most crucially, soap operas enticed and hypnotized vast numbers of female listeners/buyers indefinitely who, over time, formed intense attachments to both a program and a product; in one survey, 61 percent of the women questioned said that they used the items sold on their favorite soaps.

So the soaps—sorry, daytime dramas—made everybody rich and happy. For ad agencies, they were a license to print money five days a week in perpetuity. For journeyman actors, they created a lifetime annuity for reading lines they could almost recite in their sleep after a while; if ever it was possible for a performer to "phone it in," a soap opera provided that opportunity. And for the networks, they filled their empty daytime logs with profit-making programs that required little effort to get on the air (an average soap cost a meager $18,000 a week) and generated some $35 million a year during wartime, when many men were not at home.

Only the writers truly had to toil, producing convoluted stories like

Overleaf, clockwise from top left: David Gothard and Julie Stevens (*The Romance of Helen Trent*); Dorothy Lowell ("Sunday" in *Our Gal Sunday*); a sound man opens a door during a broadcast of *Stella Dallas* while director Richard Leonard cues Vivian Smolen ("Laurel") and Anne Elstner ("Stella"); Virginia Payne (*Ma Perkins*)

sweatshop workers, but they soon learned to crank out stories through the simple yet ingenious device of slicing the sausage as thin as possible into fifteen-minute episodes that inched the plot forward almost imperceptibly. Not only did plots mark time for days, often dwelling in the same moment for an entire week, but stories even went *backward* in time, recalling incidents from earlier years and former lives. Then there were those agonizing internal monologues when the heroine mulled over her options. Plots dawdled longer than they do even now on TV soaps, where serials must at least create a visual illusion of action. It once took the barber on *Just Plain Bill* four days to shave a customer, and half of one week's serial was spent deciding the proper length of a hemline. Ma Perkins wondered about a bundle that sat on her kitchen table, unopened, for more than two weeks, and Chichi Conrad on *Life Can Be Beautiful* took a two-week bath off-air while the actress, Alice Reinheart, went on vacation.

The snail's pace with which serials are so identified, and have been such a rich source of parody ever since Bob and Ray's "Mary Backstayge, Noble Wife," was all but built into the genre. It was possible to tune out for days, weeks, even months, turn on the show, and find you hadn't missed anything really essential; if you had, the recap brought you up-to-date quickly, and by the closing commercial you'd be sucked back into the plot.

On a soap like *Backstage Wife,* it might take Mary Noble a week to awaken, bid her husband Larry good morning, ponder the nature of his feelings for her, and amble into breakfast, and by the end of the month it's possible that Larry would just be warming up the car to head off for rehearsal. The real artistry of soap opera writing lay in finding a way to end each day's nonevent with a tantalizing cliff-hanger while giving a semblance of movement.

The soaps sprouted from a lighthearted 1925 serial called *The Smith Family,* starring Jim and Marian Jordan in their pre–*Fibber McGee and Molly* days, which emphasized the mundane lives of a couple in small-town America. After a few false starts—*Famous Loves, Polly Preston's Adventures, True Romances*—the form hit its recognizably gloomy stride with Frank and Anne Hummert's first opus, *The Stolen Husband,* a primitive 1931 mock-up for their later, more complex and comical *Betty and Bob*. That year there were three "women's serial dramas"; by 1934 there were ten, thirty-one by 1936, and by 1939 the number of soaps had bubbled to sixty-one.

Gilbert Seldes claimed that "the great invention of radio, its single most notable contribution to the art of fiction, is the daytime serial." He argued that soaps were a new form of theater—a story told in fragments, geared to the audience's household habits, to be heard in segments that wouldn't interrupt your life. The soap opera is founded, he said, "on the assumption of immortality: everyone is expected to live forever, nobody gets any older, time is shrunk or ignored and nothing is ever resolved." Seldes went on, defending soaps' humdrum nature: "We do not expect old friends to be dramatic or amusing every time we see them. The longer we know them, the more content we are merely to be in their company; and if we don't see them for several days, we want to know what happened to them and quite expect them to be a little repetitious when they tell us." Unlike conventional drama, the daytime serial "welcomes irrelevancies and interruptions, postponing the inevitable hour when it must go somewhere." On soaps, inaction is action, despite the semblance of real time, in which characters grow up, marry, have children, divorce, grow ill, and die.

The soaps' much-kidded pokey pace wasn't intended just to stretch out a plot forever but to make the story easier to follow should a devoted housewife happen to have missed a day or be cleaning an upstairs bedroom when a crucial scene occurred. The opening recap fixed that, as did a little teaser at the end of each day's episode that usually ran along these lines: "What will Jenny say when she encounters the handsome young intern, Bryce Bradshaw, in the kitchen of her next-door neighbor Estelle's country home? Will Bryce recognize her after so many years? How will Estelle react to Lance's reference to Troy Gilmore's brother, Ralph, blinded during the war? And what will Jenny say when she learns that the Reverend Renquist knows her secret? Tune in again tomorrow for 'One Woman's Angst.' "

A concerned-sounding announcer functioned as the omniscient narrator's voice, posing questions for listeners to ponder or pointing to possible troubles down the line—not just at the beginning and ending, but also in breaks *between* scenes, allowing one exchange to sink in while segueing to the next: "Paula looks out the window as Carter

leaves abruptly, wondering what she might have said to cause his outburst. As she does so, Wilbur Winstead is coming up the pathway, and
we hear . . ." The announcer was the voice of God, probing and nagging and mulling over this or that action: "Paula ponders the consequences of Carter's decision and doesn't know whether she can cope
with these new responsibilities or whether Aunt Clara was right when
she told her not to wait for him. Will Paula at last find it in her heart to
tell Wilbur what Carter has just told her?"

For the compulsive heartbreak addict, nothing was more satisfying
than an hour or so each day spent in the company of shows like *Stella
Dallas, Backstage Wife, Ma Perkins, The Romance of Helen Trent,
Young Widder Brown, Pepper Young's Family,* or *Young Dr. Malone;
young* seemed to be the operative word in one corner of Soap County.
If nothing else, the soaps made luckless or lonely Depression- and
wartime-era lives seem less bleak than many of those on the air.
Nobody was in more constant misery than Stella Dallas, and yet at the
same time women could draw hope from her strength. Other much-
loved "washboard weepers"—to invoke one of the many disdainful
nicknames given daytime dramas—included *When a Girl Marries, Our
Gal Sunday, Big Sister* (the "girl" triumvirate), *Aunt Jenny's True Life
Stories, Just Plain Bill, A Brighter Day, The Road of Life, The Right to
Happiness, This Is Nora Drake, The Second Mrs. Burton,* and the
much-parodied *John's Other Wife.*

Against the Storm, which debuted in 1939 and ran until 1942, was
an unusual, idealistic, polemical serial written by Sandra Michael that
dared to deal with the war and fascism, one of only two soap operas to
win a Peabody Award, cited as "a case of merit in a field of mediocrity." If a soap opera mentioned the war, usually it was obliquely, a
passing reference to rationing or to someone going overseas, but war's
painful reality rarely intruded on the plot; although more than three
hundred thousand men died at war, only one major soap opera male
ever died in action (Ma Perkins's son). Later on, the soaps made good
use of postwar breakdowns, neuroses, and sundry mental traumas.

Soap operas were roundly ridiculed almost from the beginning, and
some scolds even found them harmful to the national well-being. One
Dr. Louis Berg, a New York psychiatrist, launched a noisy crusade
against the soaps in 1941, accusing them of "pandering to perversity"

by providing an unhealthy, deviant, perhaps evil outlet for the unstable. He compared them to lynching bees and witch burnings. Berg tried to demonize soaps as the work of, if not the devil, anti-American forces plotting to create, he wrote, "a state of anxiety . . . which is the end of all enemy propaganda, for it lays the groundwork for civilian panic in emergencies and saps the productive energies of the afflicted individuals in all their essential efforts." He blamed these daytime serial killers for infecting the general populace with high blood pressure, arrhythmia, depression, and vertigo. Somehow he omitted halitosis, dandruff, irregularity, and the pain of neuritis and neuralgia.

The networks—like the cigarette companies in response to anti-smoking crusaders of the 1990s—hired academics, shrinks, and doctors to write reports maintaining that soaps were *not* hazardous to women's health and indeed were beneficial, because the women they identified with on these shows were capable of solving tough problems and were survivors and role models. There was a case to be made for soaps, persuasively put forth by Madeleine Edmondson and David Rounds in their study of the soap opera ethos, what they call "our own American mythology, disavow [it] as we will." They argue that the soaps' lasting message was not from Camay soap but one that teaches "the only life that can bring happiness is the life of the heart. [Soaps ask] What do we live for, anyway? And is it all worthwhile?" In short, soap operas were novels for the ear—the first audio books, really—that went on for years, decades, in a state that someone called "sustained anxiety."

One of the dominant beliefs of 1940s soap opera—and indeed even of 1990s America—was that people are redeemable (an especially female idea). When soap opera heroines went bad, it was often due to an excess of goodwill. In this pre–*Twin Peaks* era of American life, nearly all of the people who caused trouble in the small towns that comprised the innately incorruptible souls of Soap County were from the big city or were foreigners, often artists and tycoons, and usually male—all of which echoed the nineteenth-century melodrama and the silent films of directors like D. W. Griffith. The do-gooders, known as "helping-hand characters" in radio parlance, were all natives, always older, and thus, wiser—often women who had suffered and survived, although one of the most revered was *David Harum,* based on an 1898 novel about a wry, wise banker and horsetrader.

Soap opera figures rarely went to their nondenominational church, but it was assumed that all lead characters were God-fearing folks. Soap impresaria Anne Hummert's pronouncement to her writers was "I want you to put God on every page," to which the writer Manya Starr asked, "Who's going to play the part?," and was allegedly fired. The serials' major faith was an unswerving, fundamental belief in marital harmony. Eternal misery awaited every soap opera spinster, whereas any bachelor was considered eligible and desirable, and any woman who failed to convert his heathen ways to home life must be some kind of hag. "Marriage doesn't always work out," an older male soap character tells a younger man. "It's a clumsy arrangement at best, but it's the best device there is for keeping the family together. You can't toss that overboard and not be punished for it." Yes, *punished*—burned in Wesson Oil.

In an exchange on *Rosemary,* a character's husband chides her for getting involved in a friend's marital rift. "Darling, it isn't your affair. It's really their affair." Rosemary comments, "It's any woman's affair when you see a marriage being broken up." Later she tells her mother: "I'm so happy to have you home, and it's so nice to sit here and talk to you. Sometimes I think I don't want to get married at all." Mother responds, "That's nonsense. Of course you want to get married. Every girl wants to get married." Clearly, that's what the sponsors wanted: A woman's place was in the home, listening to the radio, and buying endless boxes of Oxydol, bars of Lux, and bottles of Lysol.

Women were not only expected to marry but to be "good wives." Even though women on soaps seemed consumed by the need to please their husbands, the men seem almost peripheral characters—plot devices, almost props—engaged in nebulous occupations whose importance was only measured by its threat to the couple's marital future. Few soap heroines were devoted to a career. Work wasn't sexy, and was (still often is) considered a serious distraction from what soaps regarded as women's true life work—marriage and family. Of course, if the man had work problems, the woman quickly ran to the rescue, because career trouble could wreak household, or romantic, havoc.

Even so, some of radio's major heroines were self-reliant and capable of successful careers when they put their minds to it. The trouble was, their heart wasn't in it. Their heart was at home. On some soaps, a woman who even flirted with the idea of a career was regarded as a semi-floozy, as in this line spoken by one soap husband: "I don't want you to work, darling. I don't want you to have to do a thing—just be waited on hand and foot" (that is, wait on *him* hand and foot). This played into a prevailing princess fantasy for women at home scrubbing floors and bent over hot stoves all day. Interestingly, perhaps deliberately, few women on soaps were ever caught with an actual bar of soap in their hand cleaning the house. Such unseemly tasks only went on during commercials for the benighted Cinderellas listening in at home as they dusted the hearth, for whom radio was a pumpkin able to transport them by golden chariot to a better—or at least cleaner, whiter, more hygienic—life.

Children were rarely heard from on soaps (and babies almost never), or were referred to obliquely, perhaps regarded as unromantic encumbrances to a woman in serials, whose first duty was to her husband—or to landing one. Soaps preached married life but practiced the pursuit of love at all costs. Radio soaps, despite their housebound settings, were essentially romance novels. Not surprisingly, the writers were often women's magazine authors.

For schoolkids who listened to soaps when they could contrive an excuse to stay home ill, the programs were a keyhole peek into the strange world of adults. Soaps ran all day long and included the melodramatic *Backstage Wife*, in which Mary and Larry Noble were always being plagued by some blackmailing producer or calculating leading lady; the heroine of *Young Widder Brown*, Ellen Brown, forever in and out of love with Dr. Anthony Loring, whose life was so dedicated to building a new wing on the hospital he had little time for Ellen, no matter how young or available; the stodgy but riveting *Stella Dallas*, a tale of "mother love and sacrifice" (and "the conflict between a mother's duty and a woman's heart"); and dingbat *Lorenzo Jones*, a soap opera with, of all things, a sense of humor. *Just Plain Bill,* named for genial geezer Bill Davidson, was just a little too plain for some tastes, as Bill dispensed musty advice to his troubled daughter, Nancy, and son-in-law, Kerry Donovan, from a one-chair barbershop in Hartville rarely occupied with a live customer. It always seemed beneath Bill to cut anybody's hair.

Nearly all of the residents of Soap County (whose seat was Chicago, where most daytime serials originated) were white, middle-class, and professional, with a smattering of upper-blue-collar types such as Bill the Barber (the original title of *Just Plain Bill*) and Ma Perkins, who ran a lumberyard in the misnamed Rushville Center, where time stood still. No matter its name, however (Simpsonville, Elmwood, Oakdale, Three Oaks, Great Falls), everyone seemed to inhabit the same cloistered place, where news of the real world rarely intruded. There were no politics, social ills, or cultural life in Soap County, whose characters lived, as they do still on TV, in an eco-pod. All major events dealt with relationships, usually confined to the family circle. One close friend was always present as a sounding board and a shoulder to lean on, acting as the listeners' surrogate—voicing questions on the audience's mind and suggesting solutions to worries confronting the hero or heroine.

Most radio soaps dwelled on what seemed, to young ears, like aging female troubles in a day when post-thirty-five singlehood meant curtains for anybody like Helen Trent, the plucky heroine introduced each day in its famous opening (heard over the plaintive strumming of a mandolin and a man softly humming "Juanita") as a woman who *"when life mocks her, breaks her hopes, dashes her against the rocks of despair, fights back bravely, successfully, to prove what so many women long to prove in their lives: that because a woman is thirty-five or more, romance in life need not be over, that the romance of life can extend into middle life, and even beyond."*

The soaps believed in the pursuit of domestic bliss—as in *The Right to Happiness* and *Life Can Be Beautiful*. That ephemeral but constitutional right to the pursuit of happiness was the bottom line on soaps, and so it remains. In one script, a woman who has just been reconciled with her husband rhapsodizes to her best friend, "I'm so happy . . . I never knew what it was to be happy before—not really happy . . . not deeply, warmly, happy. Happiness is a funny thing, isn't it? . . . I guess I sound goofy, don't I?" Replies the friend: "No, you just sound happy."

The soaps were a daily polemic on behalf of love and marriage, as in this gushing endorsement from one just-wedded female character: "Marriage is such a wonderful thing. No matter how nice your family is—and mine is, darling—or how much they do for you, I don't think you start to live until you're married. I don't think life takes on any real meaning, any real purpose, until that time. All the rest of it has been a sort of preparation for marriage." With that message going out regularly from radio, it's no wonder a generation of women grew up believing devoutly in marriage, often to be disappointed by it: as almost every episode revealed, marriage was no bed of roses. The soaps perpetuated the cycle by offering cures, along with a crying towel.

On *The Romance of Helen Trent,* romance continually eluded the unloved, or maybe overlovable, Helen. She was meant to be a desirable thirty-five but sounded (at least to adolescent ears) much closer to fifty—perhaps on purpose, so that women of any age could identify. Helen, denied wedded bliss, became the soaps' most exasperating tease, leading on needy, semicommitted Gil Whitney for decades until the poor worn-out woman, after twenty-seven years, finally decided to hang it up in 1960; it was the end to radio's most famous chaste woman. Albeit a divorcee, Helen remained officially unsullied until what would have been her mid-sixties, still unsure if a woman could find romance at thirty-five . . . "or more." In one episode celebrated in radio history, Gil, as ever, implored Helen: "My darling, my darling, what can I do?" At which point, legend has it, an anonymous voice cut in from a station somewhere along the CBS circuit, "Aw, for Chrissakes, lay the dame and get it over with!"

Men on radio soaps may have sounded manly, but they rarely acted the part unless they were philanderers out to corrupt the heroine. Love was much discussed, but never sex, maybe because the pure heroines were considered above all that, or maybe the men were too busy with their work to bother. It was impossible to imagine Young Widder Brown rolling around in the hay with Dr. Loring. But then sex was equally restrained in movies, the theater, and even books, until the 1960s. The lack of sex on radio soaps—as opposed to TV soaps, where everyone ruts like rabbits—was to indicate female moral strength, suggesting that women have nobler passions. No wonder so few kids were born on the serials; everyone was either impotent or a virgin. Soap opera offspring were often adopted, neatly doubling the trauma potential.

The soaps divided up roughly into two categories—the romance-novel genre, in which the beautiful young heroine searches in vain for true love and keeps meeting men who don't appreciate her, and the handsome-but-aging career woman, resigned to a life alone, who bravely tries to help others prevent the heartbreak she has encountered, as in a classic of the breed called *Valiant Lady. Our Gal Sunday* went contrary to all this small-town suffering in that the heroine was a Cinderella from Silver Creek, Colorado, who had found her prince, "England's richest, most handsome nobleman," with whom she lived in baronial splendor. Even so, Sunday was every bit as miserable a gal as Stella Dallas or Mary Noble.

Soap heroines were, by birthright, valiant—and ladies. *Valiant Lady* was (to recall its opening) *"the story of a woman and her brilliant but unstable husband—the story of her struggle to keep his feet firmly planted on the pathway to success."* A show like *Ma Perkins* deftly blended both genres: Ma is described in the show's early introduction as "a woman who spent all her life taking care of her home, washing and cooking and cleaning and raising her family. And now, her husband's death pitched her head foremost into being the head of the family as well as the mother." In one description, Ma was the warm, tolerant conscience of the town "constantly at odds with the small-minded residents."

The serials often sounded menopausal chords of middle-age regret, reflection, and a possible second chance. The shows sold hope as feverishly as they did soap—hope for a more attentive or successful spouse, a more appreciative, less selfish child, a more committed lover, or a less meddlesome parent. Soaps dissected midlife crises before the syndrome had a name. No matter what blows life had dealt them and continued to mete out on a daily basis, the women remained undaunted, like Joan Crawford, Bette Davis, and Barbara Stanwyck's movie characters—tough but vulnerable gals struggling in a man's world against man-made wickedness and deception. Women might be cast as duplicitous villains (usually young and beautiful), but they were always strong, able to withstand any form of male deceit and disappointment, creating a paradoxical prototype that embodied all female traits in one—a sort of needy virginal earth mother.

The good men tended to be milksops, unable to resist female wiles, and the women could only accept the inevitable. In the words of one soap heroine, "It's man's instinct to wander. And it's our job to hold on." Usually, it was the men on soaps who were afflicted with disabling (perhaps even castrating) illnesses that rendered them in some way impotent—in any case, less than virile men. Blindness, amnesia, and comas were the most popular crippling maladies; amnesia was as common as a headache, while every headache signaled a brain tumor. Soaps may have appealed strongly to housewives because they were then the only place in America where men were subservient. Even the playboys, roués, and louts seemed controlled by some all-seeing female who ruled the radio roost.

If there *was* one central guiding female force in Soap County, it was unquestionably that of a small, quiet, refined, puritanical, secretive, rather severe woman named Anne Hummert, a former newspaperwoman, Paris correspondent, and divorced Baltimore columnist to the lovelorn. The former Anne Schumacher Ashenhurst, she married her bachelor boss, some twenty years older, in a veritable soap-opera tale. Her urbane husband, Frank, was described as a lean and gangly ex–Texas Ranger; he had been a *St. Louis Post-Dispatch* and *Paris Herald* reporter and was a successful (retired at forty-one) adman responsible for Camay's slogan "For the skin you love to touch" and for devising ads that read like feature stories. The Hummerts wrote and produced the bulk of the major serials. From the humble origins of *Betty and Bob* and *Just Plain Bill,* their empire grew to thirty-six shows, which in the mid-1940s amounted to 10 percent of all airtime. They pretty much had the field to themselves at the start; most daytime radio was filled with shows dispensing household hints and recipes.

To fuel their repertoire of soap operas, the Hummerts employed a bank of sixteen to twenty writers, who worked from a brief outline supplied by the feisty, indefatigable, and high-strung Mrs. Hummert, though the Hummerts were the only ones ever credited (". . . created and written by Frank and Anne Hummert" became a familiar daytime radio chant). Her husband eventually ran the mystery-and-music-program end of the business. The astonishingly prolific but remote Hummerts rang an amazing number of changes on the reliable theme of female unfulfillment, male unreliability, and general domestic knavery; their original guiding inspiration was *The Perils of Pauline.* They once called their formula "successful stories about unsuccessful people."

Frank Hummert elaborated: "They may be very successful in family life, or in the way they manage to help their neighbors and their friends, they're everyday people—[with] stories that can be understood and appreciated on Park Avenue and on the prairie."

But try as they did to corner the soap market, the Hummerts didn't quite succeed in totally monopolizing it. One of their two main rivals for the hearts and souls of housewives was Elaine (Sterne) Carrington, author of *Pepper Young's Family* and *When a Girl Marries*. A high-spirited, buxom, silver-haired Jewish woman, she had a fondness for risqué jokes and liked to sneak double entendres into her scripts. Carrington had a more sexual approach than the Hummerts. According to historian Jim Harmon: "Hers was a revered, harmless, and no doubt beneficial pornography—the make-believe fantasy of women about how marriage and sex might be and perhaps should be, but seldom is after many years." Carrington had no illusions about soaps, yet stoutly defended them: "If they aren't a highfalutin form of art, they frequently contain profound wisdom expressed in universal terms."

Although she was quick to give herself an opening credit at the top of every show, Carrington generally took a less somber attitude toward daytime serials than her radio sisters, reciting dialogue into a Dicta-phone from brief notes and breaking for long lunches. She didn't like listening to playbacks of her own shows, and avoided hearing anyone else's, but defied directors or actors to change a word of dialogue.

Carrington became a soap writer by converting some unsold short stories into scripts for a show that became *Red Adams*, about a teenage boy in a small town and his coming-of-age problems. (The show's sponsor, Beech-Nut Gum, changed its hero's last name because Adams was the name of a rival chewing gum, so Red Adams became Red Davis.) When Procter & Gamble came in, the title was again changed, to the somewhat soapier *Forever Young*, about a family named Young and its leading male character, Pepper, which evolved into *Pepper Young's Family;* the announcer introduced them each day as "your friends, the Youngs."

Mason Adams broke into radio in 1945 as Pepper Young, inheriting the role from Lawson Zerbe and Burgess Meredith, who originated the part, and he played it until the show ended in 1959. In the late 1930s, the show was so popular that for five seasons it ran on two networks, and in 1937–38 on three—a phenomenon rarely duplicated. Adams is more identifiable today after thirty-eight years as the folksy lip-smacking voice of Smucker's jams and jellies: "With a name like Smucker, we'd *better* be good."

"You had to be vocally interesting in radio, but beautiful, mellifluous voices weren't necessary," remarks Adams. "Honesty was more important. If there was a phoniness in your voice it would show up." Adams stayed with *Pepper Young's Family* "probably longer than I should have," partly because it allowed him to go on appearing on Broadway. Carrington would write him out to do a play. Of Carrington, he recalls, "She had been a short story writer but was interested in theater, so if she saw a young actor on Broadway she liked, she'd write in a part for him," as she did for Jason Robards after seeing him in *The Iceman Cometh,* and for Marlon Brando, of whom Adams says, "He couldn't act his way out of a paper bag in radio—you had to be able to *read.*"

"*Pepper Young's Family,*" continues Adams, "wasn't very different from other soaps. You were doing shit day after day, so literature it wasn't, but there were no demands on you and it was interesting work." Also easy—three readings from 1 to 3:30 P.M., then on the air. Little direction was required. Adams remembers the director urging, " 'Squeeze it! Squeeze it!' A lot of actors tap-danced their way through it, but you couldn't really phone it in. You couldn't have contempt for the material. I really enjoyed it. There was such variety!"

The third member of the daytime-tragedy troika was Irna Phillips, a tiny Dayton, Ohio, schoolteacher who taught drama and storytelling to children. Phillips, radio lore has it, was allegedly mistaken for an actress during a tour of a Chicago radio station while on vacation and offered a job—without pay. She went back to Dayton instead but, on a later trip to Chicago, auditioned for a script-writing job and wrote one herself that she starred in, *Today's Children,* which became a staple.

In time, Phillips created three huge hits that later were transferred to television—*The Guiding Light, The Right to Happiness,* and *Road of Life,* plus a hospital drama, *Woman in White.* She was able to write three scripts a day—or, like Carrington, dictate them. Phillips, who prided herself on creating more realistic stories, liked to act out all the parts as she paced the floor and recited the lines, upward of sixty thousand words a week. Under deadline conditions, often scripts would be torn from her typist's hands and, still wet from the mimeograph machine, rushed to waiting actors in an adjoining studio.

Her first success—*Painted Dreams,* in 1930—is considered radio's first true soap, the story of Mother Moynihan (played by Phillips) and her brood. Les White, a former soap opera writer, credited Phillips with creating the soaps' first amnesia plots, first kidnapping, first illegitimate child, and first trial. He added that she paid lawyers for synopses of their trial cases and then filled in fictitious names; she even hired lawyers to write scripts. Two other longtime soap writers, Julian Funt and Milton Lewis, were specialists in medical shows—respectively, *Young Dr. Malone* and *This Is Nora Drake,* which Lewis cranked out for most of its eleven years. It was one of a handful of soaps that ran on both CBS and NBC, until the plug was unmercifully pulled on January 2, 1959, when three other daily series that defined the form also expired—*Backstage Wife, Road of Life,* and *Our Gal Sunday.*

Dr. Christian, the *Marcus Welby* of its day, was the leading medical soap, a beloved nighttime serial that ran from 1937 to 1953, starring the soft-spoken Danish film actor Jean Hersholt as an altruistic, saintly physician with a churchly name who was so busy mending the broken lives of friends and neighbors of River's End that he rarely had time to tend to the ills of paying patients. The good doctor was aided by his loyal nurse, Judy Price (Rosemary De Camp), who opened each show by picking up her phone with a perky, "Dr. Christian's office!" The show's helping-hand spirit, which Hersholt personified off the air in charitable causes, lives on in the Jean Hersholt Humanitarian Award, presented annually at the Academy Awards show to a member of the academy for his or her fine "Dr. Christian"–like works.

If you needed a second opinion, just down the corridor was *Dr. Kildare,* with Lionel Barrymore as grumbling Dr. Gillespie and Lew Ayres as the idealistic Kildare. The 1949 radio show was less popular than the movie that hatched it or the 1960s TV series with Richard Chamberlain and Raymond Massey, but its prayerlike opening vow must have inspired many a kindly young M.D.-to-be: "*Whatsoever house I enter, there will I go for the benefit of the sick, and whatsoever things I see or hear concerning the life of men, I will keep silence thereon, counting such things to be held as sacred trusts.*"

Despite the competition, the Hummerts were the General Motors of daytime radio, pumping out 5 millions words a year. From the Chicago offices of the Blackett, Sample & Hummert ad agency, their programs brought in some $1 million a week in billings and, it's said, 50 million letters a year. The couple leaped on the broadcasting bandwagon precisely when radio was hitching its own wagon to Madison Avenue. They saw that daytime was lying fallow and, in spite of advertisers' resistance to pitching products to what they felt was a nation of non-listeners, literally seized the weekday by populating morning and afternoons with serial dramas.

The team cranked out not just daily serials but programs of every sort, from *Mr. Keen, Tracer of Lost Persons,* to such pearls as *Hamburger Katie, Nona from Nowhere, Wife Versus Secretary,* and mysteries like *Mr. Chameleon* and *Alias Jimmy Valentine.* They later produced two landmark programs, *Manhattan Merry-Go-Round* and *The American Album of Familiar Music,* which played the elevator music of its day. They were all over the dial: The Hummerts not only pioneered soap operas but also persuaded General Mills to sponsor children's shows, an untried idea, and devised the first ones, *Terry and the Pirates* and *Skippy,* based on the comics-page rage of the time, a less neurotic Charlie Brown; *Skippy*'s sponsor was a new cereal called Wheaties.

The Hummerts oversaw every line of their shows. They created such lead-ins as the unforgettable "*Can a girl from a little mining town in the West find happiness as the wife of England's richest, most handsome lord?*" that introduced *Our Gal Sunday* (as the theme music played "Red River Valley"), laid out the plots to shows, and dictated how long each crisis would run, but left it to their bank of writers—called "dialoguers," who earned twenty-five dollars a script—to fill in the blanks, not unlike inkers on the Walt Disney assembly line. Mrs. Hummert also cast every serial herself, and set them mostly in the Midwest, although *Our Gal Sunday* was set at posh-sounding Black Swan Hall. "People seem to like characters from that area best," she once said.

Working out of the couple's home in Greenwich, Connecticut, Anne Hummert knew how to jerk tears from lonely, or simply homebound, housewives. In a rare interview, the reclusive grand dame of the daytime serial described her show's appeal this way: "The silence throbs . . . the empty hours are endless . . . then a friend in need is brought into the room by the turning of a dial. Misery loves company." Proclaimed Mrs. Hummert, "Worry, for women, is entertainment." Nobody ever put it better. In another pronouncement, late in her long life, she told a reporter in a voice described as cultured, almost British: "Nobody can understand the phenomenal success of the soaps without knowing when they were born. It was during the Depression. The housewife was at home worrying about everything. Would her husband lose his job? Where was the family's next meal coming from? They found escape in the lives of the people on the soaps."

As James Thurber described the soap-carving process in a *New Yorker* series: "The Hummerts think up their own ideas for serials. When they do, Mrs. Hummert writes an outline of the plot, suggesting incidents for the first three months or so and indicating key dialogue. Copies of this are given to five writers, and the one whose sample script seems to hit it off best is picked to do the serial. He is given an opportunity to write at least five scripts in advance, and from then on is supposed to stay that far ahead." Shows kept up to six weeks ahead.

Although nearly all the shows were written for women, by women, the iron man of the soap opera was a six-foot, two-hundred-pound ex-newspaperman from Chicago named Robert Hardy Andrews, an unsung radio legend. Andrews, a boy reporter who had been city editor of the Milwaukee *Journal* at twenty-one, became the plow horse of the Hummert stable, churning out episodes at an astonishing clip, writing from noon to midnight in a Central Park West penthouse, fueled by forty cups of coffee and five packs of cigarettes a day. The ex–city room veteran could write under any conditions. He once managed 15,000 words in a night—another time, he banged out five scripts in a day— and on average supposedly turned in between 50,000 and 100,000 words a week. At one point, he was writing seven serials simultaneously, never worked on fewer than five, and he had a hand in some twenty-five others. By the time he retired, Andrews calculated he had written about 30 million words; an awed colleague called him a one-man syndicate. Indeed, when the Hummerts needed someone to write *Skippy* and *Terry and the Pirates*, Andrews was their boy. By 1942, he was understandably burned out, and went to Hollywood as a Warner Bros. screenwriter; on the train west he wrote twenty-seven new soap opera scripts. In a 1935 interview, Andrews theorized that the Cinderella theme drove most soap operas. "In her never-ending story, justice overcomes cruelty and injustice, riches supplant poverty, virtue is rewarded, and romance comes to complete the dream."

For all their fairytale themes, daytime serials had a handful of what might be called prefeminist heroines—divorced or widowed women who worked, such as Ellen Brown, the aging "widder" who ran a tearoom but mostly brooded over how to snag the handsome and semi-eligible Anthony Loring, her presumed soul mate; the somewhat self-pitying seamstress Stella Dallas (each episode was announced as being from the novel by "the immortal Olive Higgins Prouty," also author of the novel *Now, Voyager*), who appealed to martyred mothers of spoiled, ungrateful, grown-up brats as she forever tried to pry a kind word out of her often inconsiderate daughter, Laurel, her "Lollie baby"; Ma Perkins, the unfailingly wise and patient matriarch who ran her lumberyard and was known in soap circles as "Just Plain Bill in skirts"; Helen Trent, who, between romances, was a fashion designer; Joyce Jordan, who was a "Girl Interne" (and later, "Joyce Jordan, M.D."); Senator Mary Marlin, appointed to her husband's seat when he came down with amnesia after vanishing in a plane over Siberia, which one writer said represented the dream of all the women who secretly wished their husbands would intermittently get lost; and attorney Portia Manning of *Portia Faces Life,* whose namesake had all that trouble with Shylock in *The Merchant of Venice,* a popular Elizabethan soap.

If most daytime serials were white-bread, one that was more of a rye roll was a soap opera with an urban setting and Jewish overtones, the chicken-soup opera called *Life Can Be Beautiful* (nicknamed in the trade "Elsie Beebee," after its initials). As "drawn from life by Carl Bixby and Don Becker," it featured in Papa David a kindly Pa Perkins in a yarmulke, a sort of *Goldbergs* refugee. The show was pretty heavy slogging, with its hearts-and-flowers theme music and title that summed up the appeal of all soaps: Life can be beautiful, yes, but usually it's not at all pretty—despite its idealistic opening: *"John Ruskin wrote this: 'Whenever money is the principal object of life, it is both got ill and spent ill, and does harm both in the getting and spending. When getting and spending happiness is our aim . . . life can be beautiful.'"* Actually, the characters on *Life Can Be Beautiful* were more intriguing than those on many soap staples: the waif heroine, Chichi Conrad, whom Papa David rescued from the street and employed in his second-hand store, the Slightly Read Book Shop; gentle, teary-eyed Papa David himself; and the embittered Steven, who loved Chichi although he felt himself trapped in a wheelchair.

Whoever the heroine or hero or whatever the hook, most soaps relied on three or four tried-and-true traumatic devices. Best of all was an epidemic of some obscure tropical fever (usually a rare form of aphasia, apparently transmitted by exposure to radio waves), which was often inserted into a story line when ratings sagged, or just to pep things up dramatically and further snarl the yarn by introducing ex-lovers or scheming heavies from the past.

It wasn't uncommon for soap opera husbands to suddenly vanish into thin air, which allowed the heroine to be courted by other men while remaining technically faithful and tragic. Indeed, it was the ideal soap opera state—a semiwidowed woman with a husband who can conveniently reappear if needed. And let us not forget the evergreen dream sequence, which allowed a plot to tread water indefinitely while a lead actor was ailing, on vacation, having a child, or working in a play or film—or simply until the writers could figure a way to get someone out of the corner they had painted him or her into.

Lastly, there was the classic "meanwhile" device, which permitted a soap opera to float off into an entirely new, often unrelated direction, then suddenly return to the main story, or maybe weave them together. The Hummerts also devised the "recap," without which no soap opera could survive, to unsnarl overly impossibly knotted plot lines.

Soaps had their own unspoken plot signals, conveyed via an eloquent organist through the use of foreboding chords; a "sting"—a sudden stabbing chord that indicated that something dreadful was about to happen . . . right after this message from Rinso; swirling notes to accompany a possible dizziness, life-threatening illness, dream sequence, or disturbing turn of events; a rippling effect to evoke a sinking heart or a sudden chilling moment that left listeners clinging to a precarious emotional cliff—like a letter about to be opened that might reveal the sordid details of *Our Gal Sunday*'s past.

The exception to most of these rules was *Lorenzo Jones,* a frothy soap opera about an amiable crackpot (played by Carl Swenson), a chronically unsuccessful inventor who devised plausible gadgets (an antispeeding device attached to a car, a three-spout teapot for strong, medium, and weak tea), and his long-suffering wife, Belle. It opened with "Funiculi Funicula" played jauntily underneath the credits and an introduction that identified the wacky antihero in announcer Don Lowe's smiling voice as *"a character to the town, but not to his wife Belle, who loves him."*

Lorenzo Jones was an odd duck in that it was told from a male perspective, and was comic relief from the incessant heartache of surrounding serials. Soaps with comic elements—*The Goldbergs, Myrt and Marge, Vic and Sade*—were stuck in the daytime ghetto because nobody knew what to do with them, though they clearly belonged in nighttime slots. *Lorenzo Jones* was written outside the Hummert shop, farmed out to a husband-and-wife team, Theodore and Mathilde Ferro, who were told to create a sort of comic soap opera.

Any serial that was in any way humorous was considered heretical and outside the form, for wit is the natural enemy of the true soap, a germ that no washday detergent can scrub away. Most soap opera banter was of the grinning-through-tears variety. *Vic and Sade* was both a soap opera and an anti–soap opera. In its heart it was a sitcom, but it was programmed alongside traditional serials. In their study of soaps, Edmondson and Rounds observed: *"Vic and Sade* had no feelings. Surface was all, and that surface represented a comic distortion of everyday life. This makes *Vic and Sade* almost an inversion of true soap opera. . . . Nobody was ever intended to establish an emotional bond with Vic and Sade."

Backstage Wife, on the other hand, was a definitive soap opera, with all of the classic elements of the genre. It featured a trusting Iowa stenographer who married above her station—a favorite soap opera theme, rife with built-in class problems—and who became "the wife of a famous Broadway star—dream sweetheart of a million other women," in the words of the show's longtime announcer, Ford Bond, to the organ strains of "Rose of Tralee." *Backstage Wife* had one of radio's longest runs—twenty-four years, from 1935 to 1959—and the title role was played by only two actresses, Vivian Fridell, who originated the role, and Claire Niesen, who portrayed the noblest of all wives throughout her final fifteen years; there were three Larry

Nobles—Ken Griffin, James Meighan, and Guy Sorel, who was married to the longtime star of *When a Girl Marries,* Mary Jane Higby; soap casts were often incestuous.

Larry Noble was a charming, loyal, but somewhat obtuse leading man, devoted to Mary but forever tempted by one of those million other would-be "dream sweethearts" out there—as Larry in turn was seducing millions of would-be dream sweethearts over the air. For years, he was pursued by one of the soaps' leading shrews, Regina Rawlings. Mary stood by him, no matter what—blackmail, stolen jewels, death threats, sexy conniving costars—and was herself forever being pursued by this director or that rival of Larry's. She was the dutiful, fretful wife, and with good reason; as she whimpers in one episode, "I just have the sinking feeling, Larry, that something awful is about to happen." Rarely was our Mary proved wrong.

In a typical sequence, Larry tries to get beautiful young Claudia Vincent a part in his new show, ostensibly because he believes she's talented, but a Broadway gossip columnist writes that Larry and Claudia are an item. Mary endures the ugly speculation and is befriended by the show's producer, roguish financier playboy Rupert Barlow, who has an eye for *her,* but Mary is, of course, only interested in his friendship during this trying time (the thought never crosses Mary's mind that he might have sexual designs on her).

There are polite confrontations during the plot and an occasional outburst, but nothing truly nasty ever happens. Most of the drama, as in many soaps, is in the implied threats. The promise of retribution hangs heavily over each episode; everyone seems to have something on someone else and just may expose them. In soaps, what *could* happen is always far more exciting than what does happen. Over the course of many weeks, the tale of romantic intrigue on *Backstage Wife* plays out implausibly and yet in such tantalizing increments that you're hooked, and as in all good soaps, you absolutely must hear how it ends. It's an afternoon bedtime story. In Soap Country, of course, no story ever truly ends, for the seeds of the next crisis are always carefully planted in the soil of the ongoing one.

By the early to mid-1950s, things had changed within once tranquil Soap Country as trendy new topics like alcoholism, adoption, adultery, illegitimacy, and homicide began replacing amnesia and thwarted romance. The soaps skidded to a halt in the late 1950s, when networks cut daytime programming almost in half, dropping four of its ten most popular shows—*Backstage Wife, Our Gal Sunday, Road of Life,* and *This Is Nora Drake*—and replacing them with giveaway shows rife with soap operatic angst, like *Queen for a Day* and *Strike It Rich.*

The soaps were forced to fade away quietly, without a satisfying resolution. After a record twenty-seven years, *Ma Perkins* simply ended one day, as actress Virginia Payne (who first played the part when she was twenty-three years old but with her contrived tremolo persuaded listeners she was at least twice as old) bid the audience a characteristically brave good-bye, saying primly: "This is our 7,065th broadcast, and I want to thank you all for being so loyal all these years." She read the credits and signed off with, "If you write to me I'll try to answer all your letters. Good-bye and may God bless you." In twenty-seven years, Payne had never missed one of the show's 7,065 episodes.

On that grim Black Friday, November 25, 1960, three more venerable serials soaped up for the last time—*The Right to Happiness, Young Dr. Malone,* and *The Second Mrs. Burton*—but by then many of the shows had died or moved to TV, where the basic form was adapted but little altered, aside from spicing the recipe with increased sex and violence. The remaining vintage daytime dramas scrambled to wrap up their heroines' convoluted lives, as in this excerpt from the final episode of *The Romance of Helen Trent,* in which the perennial nonbride Helen and her beau, senatorial candidate John Cole, stand on a terrace overlooking the sea, as violins play softly.

John: *Helen, I love you.*
Helen (laughing): *Oh, John, you say it like a campaign slogan.*
John: *Helen, you drive me crazy. I know you'll be fighting the men off—men you insist on being nice to without any idea that every one of them has an ulterior motive.*
Helen: *John, that's absurd!*
John: *. . . I'll knock the first man down who looks at you!*
Helen (ecstatically): *Oh, will you!*
John: *You scrappy little wench, you. Helen, will you marry me?*
Helen (startled): *Oh, John.*

John: *Now, don't say it's a surprise. I won't ask you to set a date. I'm going to win this election bare-knuckled first.*

Helen: *Oh, you* will *win it, John. You'll win it because you have everything it takes . . . courage and honesty, toughness and ideals . . .* (hushed) *Oh, John, I love you so much.*

John: *Will you wait . . . six months?*

Helen: *Oh, yes. I'll wait six months. Darling, I'll wait—*

John: *Not* forever, *Helen.* (whispering) *Not unless you're sure.*

Helen: *I'm sure now, John . . . very sure.* (Music plays)

Announcer: *With this broadcast, we bring to an end the present series of* The Romance of Helen Trent.

Note that Helen had found romance yet again but still not *quite* marriage. Things were left slightly open-ended (who could tell what might happen after John's campaign in six months?) as Helen Trent slipped quietly into eternity, her virtue intact forever.

— 19 —
THE ROYAL FAMILY

To CARLTON E. MORSE, THE PROGENITOR, WRITER, director, and patron saint of the Barbour brood who made up *One Man's Family*, radio's preeminent serial, the family was a secular religion. The show, an ode to domesticity, was emblematic of America's ongoing faith in the home as the savior of the nation and the wellspring of its spiritual strength. Not to marry and procreate was sacrilegious, unthinkable, un-American, and downright barbaric to believers in the Barbour family credo.

There was a lot of the preacher in Carlton Morse, and when inspired he could launch into lofty, often pious and patriotic, sermons on how the family was the source of all human goodness and the salvation of civilization; even the organ strains that opened the show sounded almost hymnal. This, of course, was a time before incest, child abuse, wife-beating, codependency, teenage pregnancy, and drugs were de rigueur family problems—they were barely acknowledged in real life let alone on a radio show. On *One Man's Family*, the worst thing to befall anyone was divorce. On an episode when divorce threatens to darken the family doorstep, Father Barbour huffs, "Divorce? Oh, no. There has never been a divorce in the Barbour family, and there never will be!"

Strictly speaking, the show was pure soap opera, with continuing characters and stories made up of intertwined subplots that had no fixed beginning, middle, or end (somehow, Morse kept dozens of characters and stories in his head all at once), but it transcended the soap opera genre by its superior writing and greater scope and by the sheer length of its run, which almost spanned radio's heyday—from 1932 to 1959. Moreover, unlike the families in most such serials, the Barbours were well-off, with a live-in housekeeper and a weekend place, the Sky Ranch, in Burlingame. There is a depth and richness to *One Man's Family* that transcends its own time. Almost any episode plucked at random makes a quick claim on your attention—you need to know

Facing page, from left to right: Page Gilman, Mary Adams, J. Anthony Smythe, and Russell Thorsen (*One Man's Family*)

how things turn out. The characters are written with understanding and insight, and many a twelve-minute segment is a tiny jewel as Morse sketches in complex events and emotions in a few graceful strokes.

One Man's Family really was closer to radio theater than to soap opera, the most distinctive and honored show of its kind (though it had no true rivals). It could be as sentimental, saccharine, and romantic as soap opera, but it was rarely as melodramatic, as full of soap operatic agony, dark, dire events, preposterous coincidences, wrenching plot twists, and the overwrought ladies'-magazine-fiction tone of routine soaps. A man wrote it, for one thing, whereas most soaps were overseen, and written, by women. If Morse's marathon had aired in the afternoon, it surely would have been called *One Woman's Family,* but it came on at night (until its final four years) and had little in common with the sudsy dishrag-twisting serials of the 1930s. It dared to be optimistic, realistic, and philosophical; episodes often included a poem, a prayer, and even a song. Although it sanctified the family, it didn't cater or exploit the presumed woe-is-me sensibilities of female listeners. Barbour women were hardier and smarter and more self-aware than traditional soap heroines.

One Feller's Family, as Bob and Ray later renamed it in their delicious parody of "the Butcher family," wasn't just less lachrymose, it also was more textured and detailed. The show was an open-ended opus, divided into "books" and "chapters," a radio novel that went on, and on . . . and on . . . for twenty-seven years (or 3,256 episodes, concluding at last with Chapter 30 of Book 134)—as did Morse himself, who died at ninety-one, the grand old man of radio. At his death in 1993, he was working on a new adventure serial.

One of radio's most prolific writers, Morse was a workhorse. At one point he was writing his other hit show, *I Love a Mystery* (some fifteen pages a day five days a week), and a half-hour version of *One Man's Family* once a week, while also producing and directing both series. He turned out half a dozen other shows, short stories, novels, and a book on metaphysics. Morse, who had grown up on a farm milking cows, would rise at 4 A.M. and begin writing. "I had to write an episode a day seven days a week for seven to ten years," he recalled at eighty-eight. "The minute I started to write I was lost to the world for two and a half hours"; he never found anyone else to write the shows the way he heard them in his head.

Morse's shows had a literary sensibility. *One Man's Family* was inspired by and somewhat modeled on *The Forsyte Saga*. "An American dynasty," one writer called it. The serial took the long view of life and seemed, even more than conventional soap operas, to be in no hurry. It had a restful, reassuring quality about it, and the methodical pace of family routine itself. Morse never charted his plots, which he made up day by day, unreeling in a meandering free-form style that took months to play themselves out. "I never wrote plot," he explained. "Plot didn't worry me. Plots always came to me out of the relationships."

When one imagined the extended Barbour family, which eventually numbered some ninety characters—most of them descendants of the original One Man—they were always sitting around a crackling fire with Father Barbour in his rocker and Mother Barbour at her knitting, which is how publicity stills invariably portrayed them in fan magazines.

The show was a veritable album of idealized American family life (and at one time even offered make-believe Barbour family scrapbooks to listeners): troubled, occasionally tragic, often joyous, but forever close and tightly, inextricably bound. It was many a mother's favorite show, but even men wanted to belong to the Barbour household.

The show, as Morse eulogized after it finally went off the air, had been a beacon of light, and he likened its demise to "a stranded lighthouse." The metaphor was apt, for the show was set in Sea Cliff, on the fog-shrouded western edge of San Francisco above the Pacific Ocean, strongly enhancing its reality for Bay Area listeners.

The program's basic appeal was its built-in sense of continuity and closeness, the underlying theme of *One Man's Family*—the thing families everywhere, especially during the difficult 1930s and war-torn 1940s, looked for in their own homes and found every week in the snug Barbour living room. Its basic article of faith, espoused by Father Barbour in a celebrated 1938 episode on the eve of world war, might have been ghost-written by Billy Graham: "It's my opinion that the family is the source from whence comes the moral strength of the nation. . . . A well-disciplined, morally upright family is bound to turn out good citizens! Good citizens make a good nation." It is still a potent blend of Americanism—patriotism and patriarchy.

Along with *Amos 'n' Andy* and *The Jack Benny Program*, *One Man's Family* was one of radio's sturdiest pillars, America's surrogate family for over a quarter-century and, with *Against the Storm*, the winner of a Peabody Award. The show survived every national calamity, soap opera trend, and radio upheaval—even TV, on which it ran three seasons in the early 1950s, with Eva Marie Saint as Claudia.

As often happened in Soap Country, many of *One Man's Family*'s ever-growing, intermarrying cast of characters stuck around for decades. J. Anthony Smythe, who was a lifelong bachelor, portrayed Henry Barbour for the program's entire run, and Minetta Ellen was Fanny Barbour from the first show until 1955. Michael Raffetto, a successful ex-attorney, played Paul Barbour, the consoling older son injured in World War I, and was the show's moral focus until nearly the end, dispensing more advice on life and love than Ann Landers.

Many in the cast were infused with a Barbour-like loyalty to Morse. Page Gilman joined *One Man's Family* at fourteen, playing Jack, the youngest and least troubled of the five Barbour offspring, and stayed with the show until he was forty-one, one of several actors who devoted a large chunk of their lives to the series.

In an episode plucked at random—Chapter 6, Book 54—we come upon Mother and Father Barbour celebrating their forty-ninth wedding anniversary by repeating their marriage vows surrounded by a doting clan. It would play like a Hallmark commercial were it not for the skepticism of Henry, who is at his crankiest, mumbling, "Poppycock!" at attempts to sentimentalize the occasion and sighing, "Yes, yes," in his customary fusty sigh, of which a critic once wrote: " 'Yes-yes' are the bywords of Father Barbour. They can imply irony, compassion, kindness, and can hold a world of understanding or a sharp rebuke." The episode ends with Father Barbour sending a bouquet to Fanny, who weeps quietly as the theme drowns out the happy buzz of congratulations and the announcer asks us not to miss the next engrossing chapter, entitled "Father Barbour Plants a Petunia."

Morse, who himself had come from a large family with six siblings who gathered for regular reunions, joined NBC as a writer of adventure yarns. His original proposal to do a show about an ordinary, albeit well-off, San Francisco family was met with little enthusiasm, but his persistence paid off, and *One Man's Family* debuted on May 13, 1932. It went nationwide the following April, one of the first network shows to be broadcast from San Francisco. At the end of the first rehearsal, Morse had no idea what he had, for it was an experimental concept, the first radio show to depict the day-to-day lives of a fairly normal family. Late in life, Morse recalled that inaugural run-through: "I remember Bart Yarborough slapped his script across his knees after the first reading and said, 'Well, there it is, folks, take it or leave it—no bang-bangs! Nobody dead, nobody saved in the nick of time! It's either a flop or a sleeper!' Tony Smythe was the only one who expressed enthusiasm. As we left the rehearsal, he slipped his hand under my arm, squeezed and said, 'Carlton, I think you've done it. It's what radio has been waiting to hear.' "

Morse allowed his scenes to unfold slowly and naturally. On that first show, the twins have gotten into some sort of teenage trouble and are being held in jail. Morse sounds many of the themes he will return to again and again during the show's long run, and the characters seem as familiar on that first show as they would nearly three decades later, with a timeliness that make certain lines sound as if they were written yesterday:

Father Barbour (grunts): *The papers don't print* anything *but crime anymore. . . . What's the world coming to, Glen?*
Judge Hunter: *In a way that's true, Henry. There is a restlessness. It's the younger generation fermenting . . .*
Father Barbour: *Why, even Jack—fourteen years old, mind you— even* he *springs wild-eyed sophistry about "personal rights" . . .*
Paul: *It's the first important step in a tremendous social revolution that's taking place in this country.*
Father Barbour: *Social revolution! Rot. You and your social revolution. . . .*
Paul: *Dad, progress is built on unrest; conservatism, on self-satisfaction.*
Father Barbour: *Why shouldn't I be satisfied? Haven't I worked hard all my life? Haven't I built a business that has put myself and my family in comfortable circumstances for the rest of their*

lives? Haven't I given my children good educations? Haven't I taught them the laws of the land and the laws of God? Why shouldn't I gain a little comfort from the fact that I've done my work well?

Paul: *Dad, don't misunderstand me. I don't belittle your efforts. I mean to say, I think you've lived splendidly according to your own lights.*

IN 1952, FOR A PROMOTION commemorating the show's twentieth anniversary on the air, Mother Barbour wrote a family history that listeners could receive with a copy of "Mother Barbour's Favorite Recipes" (all presumably cooked with Wesson Oil, the sponsor), in which she recalls landmark events in the Barbour saga in such fine and loving detail that you could swear it's the account of a living, breathing family. An earlier promotion featured young orphaned Teddy's handwritten diary. In advertisements for one of their sponsors, the actors are depicted espousing the miraculous cure-all power of Tender Leaf tea balls but are identified only by their characters' names, not their own, an early example of sponsor control and identification. ("Mother Barbour says: 'My family would be lost without Tender Leaf Tea' " . . . "Claudia Barbour Lacey says: 'Holding *my* husband is no problem with Tender Leaf Tea.' ")

One Man's Family was itself a kind of commercial for home and hearth. The saga began with seven Barbours—Henry and Fanny, oldest son Paul, big sister Hazel, the twins Clifford and Claudia, and teenage son Jack. From these fertile seedlings sprouted an entire vast orchard. Father Barbour was a Montgomery Street stockbroker (part of the show's charm and verisimilitude lay in its San Francisco place-names and the mystique of the city itself), which provided the family with its secure estate in the well-heeled Sea Cliff neighborhood.

The show was built like a grandfather clock, and the endless small events that made up the Barbours' complex family life seemed to occur in measured tick-tocks. Mother Barbour, the queen mother of radio's matriarchy, tried to steer her brood with a firm hand, deferring at times to the wisdom of her all-knowing husband, but skillfully guiding him when he veered too far off-course. She was an obedient, understanding but occasionally outspoken wife, who kept Henry in line with gentle rebukes ("Stop fussing, Henry!"). The show's introduction, recited in the bemused voice of the announcer, stated: "One Man's Family *is dedicated to the mothers and fathers of the younger generation and to their bewildering offspring*," neatly covering all the generational bases. At the top of each show, following a teasing snatch of dialogue from the scene to come, the announcer would say, "Hm-hm—so *that's* how it is at the Barbours' today!" It defied you to tune it out.

Henry Barbour was cantankerous but lovable, unswerving in his beliefs, loyal to a fault, and he looked upon outsiders with a skeptical, almost Archie Bunker mentality. He may not have been a racist and a bigot, but he was clearly a conservative class-conscious snob who ran the family like the CEO of a prosperous corporation, grumbling over his children's modern ways and forever muttering, "Nobody ever tells me anything!" Anthony Smythe's amusingly gruff Father Barbour was everybody's grandfather, with his inflexible nature and stubbornly held attitudes, prejudices, and homilies. The man brooked no nonsense, balked at the slightest change in his carefully arranged world view, tried to run his children's lives, and was damnably hard to impress. As John Dunning said of Henry Barbour: "When he took to a cause he was relentless in his attempt to ramrod it past his reluctant family."

Michael Raffetto not only played older brother Paul for most of the run but was also Morse's cowriter early on and, in later years, director; his sincere resonant voice bespoke maturity, insight, and inner resolve, and he possessed a poetic sensibility. Paul, a loner, could sound a tad noble at times, but he, not the crusty, reactionary Father Barbour, was the show's true north. Paul was rooted in the old ways without being a fuddy-duddy, and his war experience (he'd been wounded) gave him the moral authority to lend a sympathetic ear to all who sought him out for help in dealing with parents, friends, or lovers. When Paul spoke, you listened. He was the wisest, and nicest, one in the house, saintly but never as sanctimonious as his father, the gentle big brother everyone wishes for. Paul walked with a cane and lived in a loft in the Barbour house, where he wrote and doled out advice, most often to his female ward, Teddy (Winifred Wolfe), whom he finally adopted but who became so strongly fixated on him that she could never find another man in her life to compare; few women could. Paul, likewise, never found a wife and some listeners suspected that the relationship had incestuous overtones: When Teddy left her husband, she returned to Paul.

Even though the Barbours bred like bunnies, sex rarely raised its head on the show, though careful listeners found it lurking there anyway. In 1935, a letter from a shocked listener in Buffalo, New York, was sent to the president of NBC objecting to conversations between characters that occurred in b-e-d. A nervous NBC executive sent Morse a stern letter telling him to knock off the raunchy bedroom stuff: "I feel that you are treading on very dangerous ground. . . . How far is this sex trend in *One Man's Family* going to go? Several of the bedroom scenes lately could just as well have been living room, dining room or any other room scenes and did not need to suggest the intimate relationship between men and women. I hope you will discontinue this type of presentation before we are asked to do so by our New York office if not the Federal Communications Commission." All highly ironic for a show that was, by every account, the epitome of taste, decency, and family values.

It is difficult now to convey the show's emotional hold on listeners over its nearly three decades, but reading part of an old script can still touch your heart—and not out of sentimentality. The lines carry a powerful sense of family, a bond of affection that was the glue that held Morse's Barbours together. Typical of the subtle tenor of *One Man's Family* is a compelling exchange between Jack and Paul when the two men discuss Jack's confused feelings—his yearning for adventure, mingled with guilt that he's actually looking forward to going away to fight in Korea even if it means leaving his family behind.

Jack: *Paul, were you eager to go to France in the last war?*
Paul: *Yes, of course.*
Jack: *Just as I want to go to the Pacific? I mean there was a feeling that if you didn't get to go you'd lose something out of your life?*
Paul: *Is that the way you feel?*
Jack: *Yes . . . I've got Betty and the three children. . . . If I don't go out into the world right now and do all the things men do, the opportunity will be gone and lost to me forever.*

Paul: *You feel it would be such a great loss . . . never to have experienced active combat?*

Jack: *It's more than the fighting, Paul . . . it's going places . . . experiencing things . . . finding out for yourself the color and texture and bigness of the world we're in . . .*

Paul: *I get it.*

Jack: *The way you say that, I wonder if you* do.

Paul: *Yes . . . you have suddenly come to realize you are a married man with three daughters. . . . You suddenly see domestic duties facing you for the rest of your life. . . . Your army career is giving you one last, glorious fling before you settle down to practicing law and becoming a staid family man.*

Jack: *I . . . I don't know, Paul . . . maybe that is why I want to go. . . . I'd never consciously thought of it that way . . . maybe I do want to store up adventure and action and excitement . . .*

Paul: *For your memories to feed on in the years to come, when you're completely domesticated.*

Jack: *Do you think I'm being disloyal to Betty for being anxious to go? . . . Because I do want to come back to her, and I don't know anybody who's crazier about his children.*

Paul: *You don't have to justify yourself to me. . . . I wouldn't worry about it too much.*

Jack: *Doggone my conscience, anyway!*

Paul: *The Barbours all have them. They can be very inconvenient. . . .*

This passage reveals that Morse also recognized the downside of family life—the burdens, tensions, tedium, and temptations—as well as the domestic bliss the show trumpeted and perhaps oversold. When the Barbours were all together, as at their holiday gatherings, the joy was unrestrained, but when anyone left the household, for whatever reason, it caused a 7.1 tremor in the foundation that Carlton E. Morse had hewn out of bedrock America on that fogbound cliff above the ocean.

RADIO'S PREMIER NEWSCASTERS HAD MUCH THE same dramatic omniscient power as newsreels, probably because some of the same stentorian voices who worked for Pathé, Mutual, and Fox Movietone News doubled on the air—mighty names like Lowell Thomas, Ed Herlihy, and Michael Fitzmaurice, not to mention *The March of Time*'s voice of God, Westbrook Van Voorhis. The other *March of Time* announcers were Ted Husing and Harry Von Zell, but it was Van Voorhis whose oracular voice lives on—and was used to such hypnotic effect in the opening sequence of *Citizen Kane.*

The March of Time, which began on radio in 1931 as a promotion for *Time* magazine, and ran until 1945, featured actors doing the voices of people in the news (the first "reenactments"), with stirring background music conducted by Howard Barlow and Donald Voorhees every bit as triumphal and patriotic as a Leni Riefenstahl documentary. Art Carney created a famous FDR, and during World War II, legend has it, the White House asked the program, in the interest of national security, to stop mimicking the president's voice. Agnes Moorehead played Eleanor Roosevelt, announcer Dwight Weist mimicked Hitler, and Peter Donald was Neville Chamberlain.

Early radio news was a catch-as-catch-can affair, thrown together to broadcast major events—disasters, celebrated trials, conventions, title fights, and the World Series. The watershed event for radio news was a marathon sixteen-day Democratic convention in 1924 that required 103 ballots to nominate John W. Davis as breathless listeners clung to their radios awaiting the outcome.

There were no newscasters as such until wire services began to object to networks and stations ripping them off—literally, right off the news ticker without crediting the source. Rather than be dependent on the news wires, which finally allowed CBS and NBC the right to

Facing page, top: Walter Winchell; *bottom:* Edward R. Murrow

staple together two five-minute newscasts a day, William Paley decided to build his own electronic press at CBS, called the Columbia News Service, with bureaus in New York, Washington, Chicago, and Los Angeles. Newspapers, afraid of being scooped financially, began building and buying their own stations. By 1937, newspapers owned a fourth of all radio stations, and by 1942 a poll revealed that 73 percent of Americans relied on radio for news, versus 49 percent who read newspapers—not unlike today's TV-versus-newspaper ratio. Yet very unlike TV today—though very much like newspapers and magazines— radio was a babble of opinionated voices, along with more even-handed forums such as *America's Town Meeting of the Air, The University of Chicago Round Table,* and the redoubtable *Face the Nation* and *Meet the Press.* In 1933, radio commentators were ordered by an uneasy alliance of newspapers and newscasters, called the Press-Radio Bureau, not to go beyond "generalization and background" and not to report news less than twelve hours old.

A few newspaper-column stars like Walter Winchell, Dorothy Thompson, Boake Carter, and Drew Pearson nonetheless transferred their print persona to the air, but in 1943 CBS tried to muzzle its most opinionated commentators—people like Thompson, Pearson, Murrow, Quincy Howe, and Ned Calmer—and ended up backing down when the FCC denounced the policy. Thompson, in her unblinking style, asked her listeners: "Do you want to hear fearless viewpoints, or don't you? Are all broadcasters to become mushmouths?"

Like the newspapers that most newscasts patterned themselves after, each news broadcaster took on a distinctive voice, part of broadcast journalism's emerging cult of personality. H. V. Kaltenborn was radio's first news superstar on *Kaltenborn Edits the News,* which began in 1925 and from which he handed down Delphic analyses in his clipped, commanding, autocratic style, often without a prepared script, dropping names ("As the president of Yugoslavia said to me . . .") to reveal his insider status and casually crossing the line from news to opinion. Kaltenborn was radio's most respected newsman, but was widely parodied for his overenunciation (*Russia* became "Rush-she-uh") and omniscient manner. NBC's news chief said you could wake Kaltenborn up at four in the morning, whisper *Czechoslovakia,* and he would ad-lib for half an hour on the state of the Balkan republics.

The princely Hans von Kaltenborn (he dropped the "Hans von" prior to World War I), a tall scion of German aristocracy and a Harvard man as well, was the definitive voice of radio news analysis in the 1930s and 1940s—"a professor at large in a global classroom," one writer called him. He had been an editor and editorial writer at the *Brooklyn Eagle,* and possibly launched the first quiz show when he began a radio current-events "bee." He also lectured, developing the stentorian delivery that became his trademark, and led tours of Europe, after which WEAF in New York hired him as a commentator.

His boss, William Paley, drew a fine, often invisible, line between "analysis" and "commentating"; Paley was anticommentator and Kaltenborn's brusque, opinionated analyses, and high-handed manner made him especially nervous. In his memoirs, Kaltenborn recalled being called into a Paley aide's office and told, "Just don't be so personal. Use such phrases as 'it is said,' 'there are those who believe,' 'the opinion is held in well-informed quarters,' 'some experts have come to the conclusion . . .' Why keep on saying 'I think' and 'I believe' when you can put over the same idea more persuasively by quoting someone else?" Kaltenborn tried to comply with Paley's point of view, but it cramped his style and not long afterward he moved to NBC.

The dial was crammed with lesser Kaltenborns of every style and slant: Chipper Sam Hayes ended each broadcast with a jaunty "recap and zipper on the news"; chummy Edwin C. Hill promised "the human side of the news"; Cecil Brown, Alex Dreier, and Norman Brokenshire intoned the news in authoritative after-dinner-speaker style; rigid Fulton Lewis, Jr., gave the news his increasingly right-wing bias; the frank and witty Elmer Davis, a respected Indiana newspaperman with a flat midwestern voice, countered with a liberal take on the day's events in terse, tightly edited five-minute statesmanlike commentaries—an early trusted Walter Cronkite, with Walter Lippmann's insight; another dignified Elmer—Peterson—brought a fatherly personality to bear; newsman Raymond Gram Swing delivered elegant essays on European affairs; William L. Shirer provided his insider's notes on pre- and postwar Germany (his book *Berlin Diary* was a huge best-seller in 1941); and the resolutely upbeat Gabriel Heatter, who first came to notice with his lachrymose reports on the Lindbergh kidnapping and whose gloomy voice, ever-aquiver with hope, insisted in the face of worldwide calamity: "There's good news tonight!.," a line that began as an ad lib and became a much-mimicked comic catchphrase.

DAVID BRINKLEY, WHO BEGAN writing news for radio in 1943, claimed that when TV came along, "All the older guys failed." In his memoirs, he writes: "In the radio years, the networks had a roster of well-known newsmen—H.V. Kaltenborn, Robert McCormick, Elmer Peterson, Lowell Thomas, and others—all of them admired figures accustomed to attracting large radio audiences. But not one of these older, richer, more famous newsmen from radio were able to make the transition to television news programs. Murrow did some great documentaries . . . but never TV news. Why? Because they knew how to read a script on radio but they did not know how to deal with television. They were afraid of it and reluctant to try anything new. Kaltenborn once told me, 'I hate television.' "

Edward R. Murrow, however, combined substance and style as no other newscaster ever had—or has. If H. V. Kaltenborn represented the old school, Murrow represented the new, with a conversational rather than academic style.

Murrow may have been theatrical in his way, but he rarely came across as showy—indeed, he seemed the antithesis of showiness, although in his determinedly downbeat way he was as much the showman as Walter Winchell; he just went at it from a quieter angle. Murrow had taken the leads in some college plays, and in fact, it was his teacher at Washington State who suggested the famous dramatic pause that became his calling card in those reports from London rooftops, the better to pick up the sound of sirens and aircraft: "This [beat] . . . is London." He picked up his basic speech patterns from his Quaker mother, who often spoke in inverted phrases like "This I believe," an echo of which was heard in such Murrow locutions as "Hear it now" and, indeed, in a series he later did on famous peoples' spiritual feelings titled This I Believe.

Edward R. Murrow (originally Egbert Roscoe Murrow) was regarded at CBS as not just serious but, according to one veteran reporter, as something of "a stuffed shirt," despite the red suspenders he affected. Murrow once stymied a bunch of CBS newswriters by asking, "Gentlemen, what do you think is the most important problem facing the world today?" Nobody who had ever worked in daily journalism—as Murrow had not—would ever dare pose such a highfalutin query to fellow journalists.

He never considered himself a writer, and preferred to dictate his broadcasts to a secretary, which might account for their personal, off-the-cuff style. Even so, he was a superb writer, reporter, and broadcaster, all talents that came together for his rooftop newscasts on the London blitz, which established his reputation by bringing to radio listeners what Ernie Pyle brought to readers from the battlefield. The terse delivery spoke volumes, revealing a touch of the poet and a mordant humor. Murrow spoke in short . . . slow . . . quiet . . . understated . . . sentences—made doubly dramatic by the horror all around him. He sent back stark verbal photographs of a city under siege. In one typical piece, he intoned in a grim voice you can still hear, filled with his moral indignation and sadness, "The bombs don't seem to make as much noise as they should"—as riveting an opening line as anything in Stephen Crane. "The sense of danger and disaster comes only when the familiar incidents occur, the things that one has associated with tragedy since childhood. The sight of half a dozen ambulances weighted down with an unseen cargo of human wreckage has jarred me more than the war of dive bombers or the sound of bombs."

He framed the Luftwaffe's attack as a sort of schoolboy prank gone terribly awry: "Last night as I stood on London Bridge and watched that red glow in the sky, it was possible to understand that fire was the result of an act of war. But the act itself, even the sound of the bomb that started the fire, was still unreal. What had happened was that three or four high school boys with some special training had been flying about over London in about one hundred thousand dollars worth of machinery. One of them had pressed a button, and fire and a number of casualties was the result."

Murrow's broadcasts were greatly responsible for stimulating and stiffening America's resolve to enter the war, even if at times his reports veered into unapologetic propaganda. Bucking authority, he went on bombing raids and, in his reports, sent home powerful mental pictures (as TV later did with footage from Vietnam, Somalia, and Bosnia), including an anguished dispatch from Buchenwald: "There surged around me an evil-smelling horde. Men and boys reached out to touch me; they were in rags and the remnants of uniform. Death had already marked many of them, but they were smiling with their eyes."

Murrow gave electronic news a soul and a conscience, yet he wandered into it with no journalistic experience whatever. The slouch hat and trenchcoat were at least partly for effect, for Murrow was essentially an egghead, not a newsman; he never worked for a newspaper, a wire service, or in radio news before going to CBS but, to quote one biographer, he was "an evangelist for radio" and his persuasive manner made him hard to resist. He was perhaps the least qualified reporter on his staff, made up largely of correspondents he hired away from the low-paying United Press, some of whom, like Eric Sevareid, never did grow accustomed to the mike. A biographer noted that Murrow had a great ear for talent. "He always denied he was a reporter—he said he was an executive," said Robert Trout, a CBS senior correspondent. Elmer Davis, in his introduction to Murrow's *This Is London* collection, admitted he was "faintly scandalized" that someone as green as Murrow was such a terrific reporter. A Murrow colleague added, "He wasn't a reporter, he was a great crusader." Sevareid said, "He had a lot of the educator in him."

When Paley hired him at the age of twenty-seven, in 1935, Murrow was head of something called the Institute for International Education, which held lectures by statesmen and debates on foreign affairs at the League of Nations; he was hired to replace a man who had been CBS's "director of talks," lining up interviews with European diplomats. His first job out of college had been organizing student conferences in the U.S. and overseas. There was almost no such thing as a radio foreign correspondent when Murrow arrived; the U.S. foreign correspondents' association turned him away. CBS's Columbia News Bureau was merely a loosely linked chain of part-timers, stringers, and overseas wires that supplied the network with two minutes of news a day.

Much of what he learned on the job he learned from Robert Trout, who taught him mike technique—how to treat the microphone more as a telephone than a transmitting device. "From the start," said ex-Murrow colleague and biographer Alexander Kendrick, he had an on-air authority. "He marched through the news clearly and precisely, as if it had been made for him and he for it."

Under the often-overlooked Paul White, the CBS news division began to expand, but not until Murrow was hired did it flourish and come into its own with a stable of distinguished foreign correspondents—imposing (and, in retrospect, dashing) men with a taste for the good life, a few of them, like Charles Collingwood and Murrow himself, lady-killers: Sevareid, Kendrick, Richard C. Hottelet, Winston Burdette, Bill Downs, John Daly, Larry LeSueur, Daniel Schorr, and William L. Shirer. Shirer was the first man he hired, in 1937, and with whom he had a warm friendship and later a chilly falling-out when Shirer's postwar reports took on a liberal tilt. Paley wanted him out and Murrow was unable, or unwilling, to save him. Shirer said later, "Ed cast his lot with Bill Paley, who was not worth a hundredth of Ed Murrow." Paley later sold Murrow out by canceling *See It Now,* although Murrow and Shirer had, in the words of Stanley Cloud and Lynn Olson, "set in motion a chain of events that would lead, in only one year, to radio's emergence as America's chief news medium and to the beginning of CBS's decades-long dominance of broadcast journalism."

All of the men Murrow hired, noted one radio historian, were created in Murrow's image: "literate, often liberal and prima donnas all," also "sartorially impeccable." Movie star Kay Francis, touring with the USO, said Collingwood was the only man in North Africa who knew where to get a suit pressed; he traveled with a red silk dressing gown. Two Murrow protégés were Rhodes scholars. He briefly hired a woman reporter—against the wishes of CBS, which didn't want any women on the air. Howard K. Smith said, "I met Churchill and I met Roosevelt and Ed Murrow was the most impressive man I ever met. Even if your back was turned, if he came into a room, you knew he had arrived." He had come a long way from Polecat Creek, North Carolina, his birthplace, or from the Washington logging camps where he'd worked after college. (An affair with Pamela Churchill didn't hurt his image, either.)

While Murrow has become the godhead of radio and TV network news, he also inadvertently was the man who first combined serious journalism and show business, a broadcasting trend now run amok. With his innate flair for theatrics, and given the European theater of war as his stage, he transcribed—in effect, televised—dramatic images to listeners in their homes. In one report, he said: "Once I saw *The Damnation of Faust* presented in the open at Salzburg. London reminds me of that tonight, only the stage is so much larger. . . ."

Equally, he could offset an operatic vision of hell with a vividly homey report: "There were two women who gossiped across the narrow strip of tired brown grass that separated their two houses. They didn't have to open their kitchen windows in order to converse. The glass had been blown out. . . ." He was capable of visualizing a scene in a phrase—"The top floors lie in the street"; an office looked "as if some crazy giant had operated an egg-beater in its interior." He spoke of how good it felt, after a bomb attack, to "pick yourself up out of the gutter without the aid of a searcher party." One 1940 report began: "Today I went to buy a hat—my favorite shop had gone, blown to bits. The windows of my shoe store were blown out. I decided to have a haircut; the windows of the barbershop were gone, but the Italian barber was still doing business." And then there was this harrowing phrase from a Christmas Eve 1940 newscast: "Christmas Day began in London nearly an hour ago. The church bells did not ring at midnight. When they ring again, it will be to announce invasion."

Murrow spoke in almost Shakespearean and biblical cadences. Yet he once advised a cub correspondent, "When you report the invasion of Holland, understate the situation. Don't say the streets are rivers of blood. Say that the little policeman I usually say hello to every morning is not there today." He explained his approach—that he tried to make events simple without dumbing them down for listeners: "You are supposed to describe things in terms that make sense to the truck driver without insulting the intelligence of the professor."

The war had made Murrow a star, and after the war he became a confidant of Paley's, in whose eyes he could do no wrong. Paley, who welcomed him home with a huge banquet at the Waldorf-Astoria, wanted to make Murrow a vice-president, but he was uncomfortable as an executive—or as an icon. When Murrow heard there was a Murrow Isn't God Club at CBS, he asked how he could join. He became a reluctant convert to TV—he feared becoming beholden to the camera—although he became even more renowned there than he had been in radio, and he once grumbled, "I wish goddamned television had never been invented." News is about ideas, he said, and how do you put ideas into pictures? He rose to the challenge in his famed *See It Now* report that took on Senator McCarthy. *See It Now* was a video version of his popular 1950 *Hear It Now* radio programs which Murrow's producer, Fred Friendly, called "pictures for the ear." Too late for radio, it ran only a year.

Inevitably, Murrow succumbed to TV's soporific powers as host of the fluffy *Person to Person,* on which, fatal trademark cigarette in hand, he visited celebrities in their homes and asked marshmallow questions. Faking a cozy, chuckly demeanor, he seemed quite another man, awkward and sheepish, an embarrassment to colleagues who had idolized him and felt the show cheapened him. Murrow revealed himself every bit as twittery and awestruck as Diane Sawyer, Barbara Walters, or Morley Safer in the presence of show business legends.

By 1961, he was bored and ignored, and no longer Paley's fair-haired genius. His much-praised TV attack on McCarthy had made him a broadcasting hero—Don Hewitt recalled the night Murrow walked into Sardi's and diners stood and applauded—but also eroded his power at CBS, where his stock plummeted after a speech to broadcasters in which he blasted TV. He had become a tarnished, less marketable network troublemaker; Paley complained that *CBS Reports* shows like "Harvest of Shame," about the plight of America's farm workers, was starting to give him stomachaches. Reluctantly, Murrow left CBS to head the U.S. Information Agency, coming almost full circle to where he had begun less than a quarter-century earlier, as CBS's "director of talks." Four years later, at fifty-seven, one of radio's best talkers was dead.

BEFORE AND EVEN AFTER MURROW, the reigning philosopher king of radio news was Lowell Thomas, who not only covered the news but uncovered it as well. Thomas was an intrepid reporter who went where the news was and related it in a breezy style ("Good evening, everybody") full of unabashed awe and import—a *National Geographic* report with a glaze of gee-whiz journalism that implied if Lowell Thomas wasn't there to witness it, it wasn't worth hearing about. Thomas combined the crisp, grandfatherly authority of a Walter Cronkite with the showboat qualities of a Dan Rather. Watching Rather in a shroud reporting the Afghanistan uprising reminded older radio listeners of Lowell Thomas peering out beneath a burnoose in newsreels from this or that far-flung dateline alongside a llama or the Dalai Lama. If Rather seemed silly, Lowell Thomas never did.

Thomas did his best to walk in the outsized footprints left by radio's earlier leading reporter-swashbuckler, Floyd Gibbons, whose program he inherited. Gibbons was a big, handsome newsman and ex-marine who wore a white patch over an eye lost during the battle of Belleau Wood in World War I. On his 1929 series, *The Headline Hunter,* he spun war stories in a dramatic staccato beat, clocked at 217 words a minute, that must have left a mark on Winchell. There was actually a Floyd Gibbons School of Broadcasting that ran grabby ads asking, "Have *you* an idea for a radio program? Can *you* describe things? Have *you* a radio voice?" Gibbons was too much of a buccaneer newscaster for William Paley, who wanted someone with a calmer, more rational, and distinguished aura, like a knowledgeable and engaging speaker he had heard at Covent Garden, who turned out to be . . . Lowell Thomas.

Thomas was a travel-lecturer-turned-roving correspondent, the stylistic opposite of Gibbons's derring-do, but with his own frontier credentials. A doctor's son from Cripple Creek, Colorado, who grew up peddling newspapers in saloons and later taught college, Thomas had the authority to replace Gibbons, who introduced him to listeners in 1929 as "a gentleman, a linguist, and a scholar." Thomas, Sr., had been a believer in the importance of public speaking, so Lowell grew up reciting poetry by heart and speaking at lodge halls and church suppers. He had prepped for his audition, striving for lightness and likability, by eliciting the help of a young light-verse poet named Ogden Nash and a pop psychologist who gave Thomas a few tips on winning friends and influencing people on the air—Dale Carnegie. The refreshing change from Gibbons's hard-driving style won Paley's ear.

Like Kaltenborn, Gibbons, Ed Murrow, and Walter Winchell, Thomas firmly believed in his own place in history, which he flogged unashamedly with self-promoted exploits in some fifty books and countless travelogues. Yet unlike Kaltenborn, he rarely aired his private views; he had Kaltenborn's dignity but not his godlike bearing. The nightly 6 P.M. radio report *Lowell Thomas and the News* spanned five decades and became an institution (his clean diction was studied in speech classes). In his last years, he broadcast his nightly reports from his home in Pawling, New York, where he still skied into his eighties and remained to the end a genial potentate of the news. Not until 1977, when he was eighty-four, did Thomas reluctantly relinquish the mike with a final hearty, "*So long* until tomorrow!"

IF LOWELL THOMAS WAS THE *New York Times* of the air, Walter Winchell was the *National Enquirer,* an agitated voice on the radio every Sunday night, when families gathered for dinner accompanied by the sound of Winchell nattering away. At his peak, Winchell was a burbling fount of wisdom to those who believed in the world according to the *Saturday Evening Post* and *Reader's Digest.* A TV documentary dubbed him the "Voice of America," and one colleague anointed him "the prime minister of the airwaves." Many listened to him as if he were delivering the last word, exactly how Winchell expected to be heard by the 50 million people who tuned in religiously—in the words of one writer, "the largest continuous audience ever possessed by a man who was neither politician nor divine."

With his twelve-year showbiz background—he began as a kid in a Gus Edwards kiddie revue called *School Daze,* in the same "Newsboys' Sextet" act that spawned Eddie Cantor and George Jessel, before recasting himself as a gossip columnist for a backstage trade sheet called *The Vaudeville News*—he had an innate flair for self-promotion and self-dramatization. Winchell was a one-man precursor of every tabloid TV show now running wild. With his feuds, fast talk, jingoistic fulminations, scoops, and self-serving heroics, he was Rush Limbaugh and *Hard Copy* and Mike Wallace and Robin Leach and *Entertainment Tonight* all packed into one. To create an aura of authenticity, he often led off items with datelines and cries of "*Flash!*" As somebody once said, Winchell could announce the arrival of spring and make it sound like an invasion from outer space.

Winchell—the original Russian-Jewish family name was Weinschel ("sour cherries")—was a cowboy journalist whose in-your-face style lent itself beautifully to radio. He was a totally self-created Hollywood version of a reporter, the popular notion of a hard-bitten newsman. Actually, Winchell was an actor playing a newspaperman, with hat tilted back rakishly (to hide a bald head, which made him look far less formidable) and clattering teletype. He was forever trying to legitimize himself as a "real reporter," but as the columnist Jimmy Breslin once said, commenting on how WW loved to chase police calls in his car, "he was more of a buff than a reporter." All his life, he craved reporters' respect, knowing deep down he was a manufactured correspondent, which only fueled his scoop-crazy mentality and love of exposés.

In fact, Winchell was the laughingstock of real newsmen, yet many imitated him—Leonard Lyons, Louis Sobel, Jimmy Cannon, Jack O'Brien, Irv Kupcinet in Chicago, and Herb Caen in San Francisco were all Winchell acolytes. But the public bought his act, and so did the cops, indeed all officialdom. He stage-managed mobster Louis Lepke's surrender in grand movie style, turning him over to J. Edgar Hoover as if he had personally nabbed him. In his twilight years, he returned for a curtain call to narrate TV's *The Untouchables,* lending just the excited rat-a-tat-tat voice of authority that the mob-hunting series needed (it proved to be the aging paper tiger's last roar). Winchell was the Eliot Ness of radio journalism, blasting away at real and potential enemies of the people and himself.

Even if you hated him, and many did, Winchell was impossible to ignore. He was an FBI groupie, a power fiend, Red-baiter, celebrity sycophant, and a crony of Sherman Billingsley, at whose Stork Club Winchell held court and which he plugged constantly on the air and in print until the club was sued on discrimination charges by Josephine Baker, earning Baker a place on Winchell's long enemies' list. He gave stock tips that influenced Wall Street until the SEC stopped him, while doling out advice and consent to congressmen with the confidence of a Washington pundit, confusing himself with Walter Lippmann. He attacked Hollywood and Broadway stars who he felt had snubbed him. He held famous grudges and swooned over the air, bestowing "orchids" to this starlet or that politician. He could create best-sellers and hit shows (singlehandedly he kept the roundly reviled *Hellzapoppin* alive for five years), and jump-start careers. He reordered the world—and later tried to order it around—to suit his fancy.

His vaudeville training, somebody remarked, taught him how to please an audience. He could read a line with mawkish sentimentality, slip into a hostile sneer when on the attack after "Uncle Joe" Stalin or that week's gangland bad guy, then switch in an instant into a homespun mode for a fond farewell: "This is Mrs. Winchell's little boy Walter saying . . ." He seemed semifictitious, like another of Damon Runyon's fanciful Broadway swashbucklers—and in a way he was one.

Winchell seemed an unlikely prospect for radio. "I talk too fast," he said, as he had even as a kid vaudevillian—the very thing that would give him his rapid-fire on-air identity; he claimed to have once been clocked at 220 words a minute. As someone said, he seemed to embody the sizzle of the 1920s—not just in his style, but in his language. What is too often forgotten about him, lost in the jangle of his personality, is that he was an inventive writer and phrasemaker, coming up daily with original coinages, a few still used today: To marry was to "merge" or be "lohengrined," to divorce was to be "Reno-vated" or "phffft!," to expect a child was "infanticipating," a baby was a "blessed event," and debutantes were "debutramps." Words like *cinemaddict* for movie buff were stolen by *Time,* whose early rococo "*Time*style" was heavily influenced by Winchell. His word for passion—*pash*—later turned up in an Ira Gershwin lyric and "making whoopee" began as a Winchellism for sex. The critic and slang lexicographer H. L. Mencken took Winchell seriously as a vital influence on what Mencken called "the American language."

Winchell personified the classic definition of journalism as "history in a hurry." It wouldn't have mattered how fast he talked, for by the time he came to radio he was a household name, and what he had to say mattered more than how he chose to say it. In radio, as in print, he was an innovator, a total original; there had been nobody like him on the air before nor has there been since. With his tommy-gun bursts of speech, he sounded like Jimmy Cagney delivering the news. Indeed, Marshall McLuhan once compared Winchell's "telegraphic rattle" to "the voice of the symbolic 'gunman' reporter of the big night spots."

After a few guest gigs on Rudy Vallee's show, and MC'ing Alexander Woollcott's program, Winchell was first heard barking the news regularly in 1929 on a forty-two-station hookup sponsored by Gimbel's Department Store, on a show rather cumbersomely and, with characteristic mock Winchellian modesty, called *New York by a New York Representative;* Winchell always loved thinking of himself as the senator from New York City.

On that first show, he greeted listeners by saying, "In case you have never read my drivel in the *Daily Mirror* or the other newspapers with which I am associated, I am the 'Peek's Blab Boy' who turns the Broadway dirt and mud into gold, a terrible way of making a living, perhaps, but some people are radio announcers."

He liked to launch preemptive strikes against himself that reeked of self-praise. He asked listeners to send in criticisms, boasting, "My skin is thick," and adding that "slams only prove that you are not being snubbed." Unabashed in his need to be read and heard, he once quoted an Illinois senator in what might have been his life credo: "Notice me, for heaven's sake, notice me. If you can say something good, say it; but in any event, say *something. Notice me!*"

People noticed him, most of all tobacco tycoon George Washington Hill, who allegedly ordered, "Deliver Winchell to me in the morning." Hill, who hired the public relations wizard Edward Bernays to "build [Winchell] as if he were an institution," promoted the gossipcaster in sensational ads that promised listeners they would "drop their newspapers onto their ears as they sat at their radios." He was introduced each week as "the one and only Walter Winchell, whose gossip of today is the news of tomorrow." Winchell made a different, louder racket than radio had ever heard.

As biographer Neal Gabler noted: "Though an egomaniac, he also had a self-deprecating wit. . . . Now he had to find a way to bring some of that to the radio." Winchell didn't just read a column into a mike but, as Gabler pointed out, created a new on-air persona. "By piling one item on another and by wrenching them all from any context, he created a new context: a dizzying and disorienting bacchanalia, almost prurient in its appeal." John Crosby wrote that he had detected "a definite feeling of guilt connected with listening to Walter Winchell."

The brilliance of his later newscasts—which were introduced, "And now to the editorial room of the Jergens Journal . . ."—was that they sounded exactly like his column, spoken in the same breathless voice in which he wrote, with the identical slangy, cocksure tone: "Dots and dashes and lots of flashes from border to border and coast to coast!" Once he said, "I want to be like a newsboy shouting 'Extra!' " and the newscast was exactly that; as another Winchell biographer, Bob Thomas, wrote, "The Winchell voice on radio defied inattention." On the air, his voice rose an octave. Winchell brought his old showman's razzmatazz to the newscast by turning the globe into an extension of Times Square. For him, Europe was off-Broadway. He advised and admonished world leaders and movie stars in the same hot breath. At the 1934 Lindbergh trial, he was considered "the thirteenth juror," as much of a celebrity as Lindy.

His early broadsides against Hitler and Mussolini were couched in flip Winchellese (Nazis were "Ratzis"), the first of many attacks on Axis leaders. To his credit, he was among the earliest commentators to attack Hitler publicly and steadily. The newscast didn't just make him more money, it let him say things over the air, with a political slant, that were deleted from his *Mirror* column by fidgety Hearst editors. As someone put it, "Winchell, apparently, can sell anything he puts his tongue to. What served to sell Broadway gossip—and still does—serves at least as effectively to sell fervent, quippy patriotics, even straight war news."

During World War II, although he was still considered a mere gossip columnist, 90 percent of his newscasts dealt with political events at home and abroad. WW gave political news his hot insider's spin, revealing world events as if seen through a keyhole, referring to "Joe Goebbels"—his way of cutting everyone down to his size. He spent more time prowling the halls of power on Pennsylvania Avenue than 42nd Street. Anyone who attacked FDR (an occasional Winchell source and fan), or was against the war, made WW's "Drop-Dead List." When FDR died, he eulogized the president for nine minutes, then left the air, shaken; he spoke so slowly many didn't recognize his voice. As one of his intimates observed, "Walter wanted to be taken seriously and FDR gave him legitimacy."

Winchell gleefully took on America's greatest hero of the 1920s and 1930s, Charles Lindbergh ("He wants the British to quit. Apparently he thinks everyone quits as easily as he does. . . . He once quit America. Remember?"). He loved a brawl—"If I didn't love a fight I wouldn't start so many of them"—and Germany and Japan were made-to-order bullies. Winchell took World War II personally. He waded into battles on the air, responding to this senator or that governor ("I repeat, ladies and gentlemen, I welcome their attack"). The newspaper publisher Cissy Patterson called him "a popgun patriot." He used the microphone as a blunt instrument. Warning *Time* not to tangle with him, he snapped at one of its reporters, "Tell your editors that I am the guy who invented the low blow." When threatened with a lawsuit (far fewer than he liked to claim), he boasted, "You want to sue me? Well, line forms to the right, mister." Between the mid-1930s and 1955, remarkably, he was never once found guilty of slander. When network censors began to tone down or delete controversial items, attack-dog Winchell said, "My fangs have been removed." He protested to a radio executive that Roosevelt was "saying the very things you would not let me say," and was told, "Yes, but the president doesn't have a sponsor."

On the air, Winchell became at least twice as famous as he had been in syndication, earning about $200,000 a year. He starred in a movie short, *The Bard of Broadway,* MC'ed a vaudeville show at the Palace Theater at $3,500 a week, and wrote lyrics to a song called "Things I Didn't Know Till Now" (the subhead over one of his column features). Songs were even written about him—"I Wanna Be in Winchell's Column" and "Mrs. Winchell's Boy." He played himself in a movie, *Wake Up and Live,* and Darryl Zanuck hired him to write a screenplay, *Broadway Through a Keyhole,* about the Al Jolson–Ruby Keeler relationship he had shadowed like a house detective. In *Broadway Melody of 1936,* a miscast Jack Benny played a powerful, arrogant, wisecracking, hat-wearing Winchellesque columnist who does a newscast using a clicker instead of a telegraph key. A character says, "He's the eyes and ears of Broadway with his nose in everybody's business." Another film patterned after him, *Blessed Event* (perhaps his most lasting coinage), dealt with a powerful, ill-mannered, scandal-mongering Broadway columnist, played by Lee Tracy.

Herman Klurfeld, Winchell's right-hand man, said of him: "He loved being Walter Winchell. He reveled in it. Every day was a jubilee— and a coronation." Stories of his power and arrogance were legend, like the time he supposedly dropped a dime on the sidewalk and ordered the famous saloonkeeper Toots Shor to pick it up for him. Shor, afraid of annoying him, bent down and retrieved it. To counteract his growing power, he sentimentalized himself on the air in phrases like "your humble newsboy," whose 1933 fifteen-minute show was heard by 25 million people each Sunday night. Nobody who recalls those broadcasts can hear the name Jergens without thinking of Walter Winchell, who signed off each show "with lotions of love."

At first, the radio show confined itself to flashes from Broadway and Hollywood, but Winchell began taking items off the wire-service tickers and pretending they were his own scoops. When the wires forced him to quit using their stories for free, without credit, he began buying items out of foreign newspapers. He broke the story on radio that the prince of Wales might abdicate the throne for Wallis Simpson. In print he had been trivialized because his columns ran in entertainment sections, but on radio he gained new importance by becoming a one-man newspaper of the air, giving equal play to showbiz, world news, sports, and the stock market. Moreover, he no longer spoke in gray type; over the air, each item was a headline.

Gabler, who credits Winchell with inventing "infotainment," remarked, "It was the commingling of [these elements] that now made the program the strange, unique, virtually surrealistic concoction it was. The death of ten thousand people in Ethiopia was followed immediately by a Hollywood divorce or romance. . . . By applying the techniques of show business to news, as radio permitted him to do, Winchell blurred the distinction between the two."

In his famous wrap-up, he would conclude with a bright crack, blind item, joke, or inside comment intended to leave listeners with mouths agape. Any press agent who could fill in that final phrase was in Winchell's good graces for that week, anyway. One of aide Herman Klurfeld's specialties was the "lasty," Winchellese for the dramatic final item of the newscast—a wisecrack, a patriotic salute, a plea to drive safely, a eulogy—such as one of WW's most-quoted lines: "She's been on more laps than a napkin." A few days before each broadcast, his radio associate Ernest Cuneo described Winchell as "cantankerous," by the next night he was champing at the bit and pawing the ground, and by the night before the newscast, "ungovernable." Cuneo and Winchell would wind up in shouting matches arguing over possibly slanderous copy that Winchell hated to change, with Cuneo often leaving the studio in tears until Winchell coaxed him back. Sometimes, just to rile Cuneo, Winchell would restore a deleted line on the air. As Cuneo recalled, "Exactly at 8:58, Walter would enter the broadcast studio, open his shirt, loosen his belt, open the waistband of his pants, and tap on his sound effects key. . . . It was like Man O' War bursting out of the chute."

Bob Thomas described how Winchell would put together his shows:

"The editing of the Winchell broadcast was accomplished with the showmanship of Flo Ziegfeld assembling a Broadway revue. Individual items appeared on separate pieces of paper, and Winchell spread them out on a table before him. Oblivious of his surroundings, he plotted the order of the broadcast, switching the slips of paper dozens of times. As he did so, he muttered comments like, 'That'll teach the son of a bitch.' As air time neared, he began restapling items in a final order."

The famous telegraph clatter was a perfect acoustical accompaniment—the melody to Winchell's steady hum of words—and a typical Winchellian theatrical touch and a brilliant idea: Not only did it add an aura of excitement and authenticity, but the dots and dashes were the aural equivalent of the dot-dot-dots between column items. He operated the key himself, tapping out telegraphic gibberish between stories; "I want the feel of it myself," he insisted, refusing to turn over the telegraph key to a sound man; working the key himself also gave him time to sip water and catch his breath. When a schoolgirl once asked Winchell why he talked so fast, he said, "Young lady, if I spoke slowly, people might realize I didn't have much to say."

He did newscasts with his hat on, as if to put himself in the mood and assume his on-air persona, but also out of superstition. Winchell would become so genuinely excited during a newscast that he bounced in his chair, jiggling his foot to keep time—"as though," said a reporter who witnessed a show, "the whole broadcast were set to a metronomic rapid tempo, as indeed it is." To others, said Thomas, he seemed hunched in a crouch, coiled to spring. The on-air fervor was manufactured with a purpose. On one show, Bob Hope was a guest, and just before airtime Winchell told the comedian he needed to use the men's room. Hope said, "Well, why don't you go down the hall? You've got time," and Winchell answered, "The show's better if I don't." Herman Klurfeld described his on-air style: "He wriggled, waved his arms to emphasize a point, thumped the desk, rocked around in his chair, and scuffed his feet as though beating out a bunt to first," audibly punctuating items with doubting "hmmm"s and "huh?"s. He once told Klurfeld, "Hermy, I want to die doing this."

Everything was manipulated to increase the excitement of the broadcasts. Klurfeld once neatly deconstructed a typical Winchell on-air item made exciting by his phrasing: "Needles, California: Moving across the desert tonight at high speed in a darkened Pullman car is a man under heavy guard. He is Al Capone, chief gangster of them all. He is being moved to a certain prison on the Eastern Seaboard." Klurfeld's analysis: "From the breathless manner in which he delivered it, the train might have been under bombardment. Winchell told the exact truth, but he made the truth sound unique, exciting. Streamliners always move at 'high speed' across the desert, picking up time lost in the mountain passes. Thus, there was scarcely any news in this. And of course the train was dark; they turn the lights out in every Pullman at night. And of course Capone was 'under heavy guard.' It would have been absurd to hand him a railroad ticket and tell him to show up in Atlanta. But why 'a certain prison on the Eastern Seaboard' instead of naming the city? Because every other news service would have covered the story. Winchell wanted a sensational exclusive. That's exactly what he got. The movement of Al Capone was a routine item but Winchell made it a front-page story."

Winchell was insecure about his newscast, unlike his column, and needed to hear from his wife after each broadcast that it was a good show; otherwise, he was morose. Cuneo remembered: "If June was enthusiastic about the broadcast, it had a magical effect on him. He would blossom into great exuberance. If she merely liked it, he was pleased and happy." His secretary, Rose Bigman, said he was his own worst critic. "He didn't think anything [he did] was good." A Winchell aide said he always felt he was on the brink of failure.

Although he had long been a ham, the newscast made him a bona fide star, and he carried himself like one, with a star's salary; his combined audience in print and on the air was more than 50 million, and the $800,000 he earned in one year made him the nation's highest-salaried American. There was no more influential man in the country, a power he used for as much good as ill with his double-barreled cannon of daily bombast and weekly newscast. As a poor boy from Harlem, he was an audible civil-rights crusader, which made his later run-in with Josephine Baker doubly painful and ironic. As a Jew, he was constantly on the march against anti-Semitic slurs, and eagerly took on Hitler.

Cronies once played a practical joke on Winchell by slipping him a mock item off the teletype, just as he was going off the air, which said that Hitler had been killed while inspecting eastern-front defenses.

Winchell went berserk in what an aide called his "Donald Duck indignation." "His eyes bugged; his mouth fell open; his hand shook," recalled Klurfeld. "Damn those bastards!" he screamed. "That fucking Hitler! He couldn't die [earlier] and give me an opening item!"

By 1948, Winchell's audience outranked Jack Benny's, Fred Allen's, and Bob Hope's, and his power grew accordingly. He became a junior G-man, an advance man for Joseph McCarthy in his power to wreck careers, and lives, with a caustic word, a careless accusation or hurtful innuendo. He took pride in having kept the great opera singer Kirsten Flagstad (unjustly accused of collaborating with the Germans) out of the country, and when producer Mark Hellinger asked him about another foreigner under his spyglass, WW, in all sincerity, replied, "I haven't cleared him yet." Ethel Barrymore once said, "It is a mark against American manhood that Walter Winchell is allowed to live." In his broadcasts during World War II, he forever wrapped himself in the flag, sounding regular calls to arms that now make him seem like some raving right-wing talk-show crank—an early Limbaugh, Bob Grant, or G. Gordon Liddy. He began to feel he was being censored. The sponsor, network lawyers, and editors had begun keeping a closer watch on his copy, for he was becoming something of a loose cannon, a situation that grew worse during a long, complex wrangle with Martin Dies, the head of the House Un-American Activities Committee. Always spoiling for a fight, Winchell took any criticism as an attack on his First Amendment rights, vowing to remain "as free as the air, not as free as the airwaves." He threatened the ad agency, "What you fellows want me to do is to begin looking around for another show. You boys don't want me. Our ten-year honeymoon is about over."

Winchell's superpatriot tendencies began appearing with shameless regularity, unfurled like Old Glory during some tired 1920s vaudeville act: "I don't want any part of fascism or Communism," he once broadcast. "I'm just an American—a Yankee Doodle Boy. And if you ask me what an American is, I'll tell you it's Walter Winchell."

AFTER SIXTEEN YEARS ON THE AIR for Jergens, he and the company had a falling out over a commercial Winchell refused to read for a new deodorant, claiming it was beneath him. He told Jergens to let Louella Parsons read it, but they insisted he do it. Despite his ratings, Jergens was ready to dump him, its excuse for pulling out of a newscast that had grown increasingly rabid. Winchell's rant-filled crusades turned rancid as he launched one corrosive attack after another and became bogged down in misbegotten personal wars. As depicted in *The Sweet Smell of Success*—Ernest Lehman's novel and screenplay based directly on a power-mongering Winchell, to whom Lehman had once spoon-fed items as a toadying press agent—Winchell broke up his daughter Walda's romance with a man he disparaged through innuendo in his column and on the air; ●also had her committed to a mental institution.

With a string of showgirl mistresses, a son who later killed himself, and a daughter whose life he almost destroyed, his own domestic life was a mess—despite a home in Westchester, he spent most of his nights at the St. Moritz—but women found him irresistible. One ex–girl friend, performer Jane Kean, boasted, "He was the most vibrant, exciting man I've ever been with."

CBS offered Winchell a TV broadcast, but he turned it down to stay with ABC, for which he began doing a simulcast on TV in 1948. Various sponsors had fought for him—Old Golds and Chesterfield, Lever Brothers, Kaiser-Frazer, and Gruen, which won the bidding war with an offer that topped out at $702,000, making him, said *Variety,* "the highest paid single [act] in show business history," comparing his impact with that of *Amos 'n' Andy.*

The hat and the telegraph key went with him to TV, even though viewers were puzzled as to why he wore a hat indoors; it made him look much less authoritative than he had sounded, even a bit foolish with his loud scattershot style, ferret features, and spectacles, reading items hunched over a desk. Gruen intended the show as a televised version of the newscast—a cross between a city room and a TV newsroom, with cluttered open file cabinets, telephones, a map of the U.S., and clocks showing the time in Paris, Rome, London, etc.

Winchell sat at a table with a typewriter, snapping his glasses off when addressing the viewers directly; his collar was open, his necktie askew, his sleeves rolled up. Jack Gould wrote that watching Winchell, "with the muscles of his jaw flexing in rhythm with the torrent of his words," made it hard to concentrate on what he was actually saying, adding, "Those who were enamored of his radio broadcasts will find him even more fascinating than ever on TV; those who were not so enamored, more disturbing."

According to Klurfeld, TV quickly exposed Winchell's act. "The phoniness of it came through. He'd jump in his seat and he just looked foolish." Desperate for new attention, he started dispensing dubious tips of all kinds—on horses, on the stock market—and his personal crusades and vendettas began to sound even more nagging and mean-spirited. TV had revealed the glint in his eye and the sneer on his lips that radio had hidden from listeners for nearly two decades. "I don't like myself on television," he said, and many agreed. Winchell's son told his wife he feared for his father when he saw him on TV: "I knew that would be his downfall," said Walt, Jr. "The moment they saw this little man on television they would lose all respect for him. And they did." Klurfeld says, "He just looked like a silly old man screaming into a microphone."

He finally fell out with ABC over a libel suit he lost against the *New York Post* when network president Robert Kintner balked at paying punitive damages of thirty thousand dollars for Winchell's claim that the paper, its publisher, and its editor were Communists. When he tried to get ABC to indemnify him against future lawsuits, Kintner said no and Winchell resigned in a snit, foolishly giving up a lifetime radio-TV contract after four years, sure that ABC wouldn't accept his resignation. He was stunned when they did.

The *New York Post* had unleashed a long-running exposé that further damaged his reputation with allegations that he had floated stock on his newscasts as casually as he gave racing tips; it also unmasked his ghost, Klurfeld, for the first time. The *Post*'s circulation went up 35,000 during the series, not long after which Winchell slipped from a weekly broadcast over 365 radio stations and 45 TV stations to a single Mutual newscast; time was running out for Mrs. Winchell's little boy. In 1950, when radio lost a million listeners, he slid from the top ten. Wrote Bob Thomas: "He continued with the same old format but the 'Good evening Mr. and Mrs. North and South America' sounded more strident. His prejudices overshadowed everything. He seemed less like the breathless reporter of old and more like a garrulous, opinionated eccentric."

NBC's David Sarnoff agreed to talk to him, but nothing came of it, and the columnist Jack O'Brien said that Pat Weaver "wouldn't have that yapping Winchell voice on the network." Desperate to be part of the action, he appealed to Frank Stanton, humbling himself by pleading with the CBS president to "consider me for things other than commentating—panels, quizzes, variety? I don't want to be off TV." Stanton never got back to him, and Winchell suspected that Ed Sullivan, his old nemesis, was responsible for keeping him off TV this time. At a press conference, Winchell, in Thomas's account, had called Sullivan "a talentless fraud, a copycat, a person of questionable morals"—and, if that wasn't good enough, revealed that Sullivan had cancer. Sullivan called him "a small-time Hitler."

When Sullivan went on the air to attack Winchell over the controversial Josephine Baker issue—the black singer charged that Winchell had failed to intervene in her behalf when she was asked to leave the Stork Club one night—it was the climax of a long-simmering, twenty-year mutual distrust. Sullivan's dislike was partly fueled by a fierce newspaper rivalry and the fact that he had long stood in Winchell's shadow. Years later, Winchell and Sullivan made up, and during a chance meeting the two graying gladiators exchanged photos of their grandchildren. Sullivan later introduced Winchell from his audience, the TV impresario's grandest tribute.

Although no network wanted him back as a troublemaking newscaster, ABC-TV came up with *The Walter Winchell Files,* on which he narrated dramatizations of New York stories. It was a dud. Then NBC cobbled together something called *The Walter Winchell Show* in 1956, a low-rent *Ed Sullivan Show* with only money enough for one guest star per week ("After all these years, I'm back where I started from—vaudeville," Winchell bravely announced). Driven to show himself the TV equal of Sullivan, Winchell, then fifty-nine, put up $7,500 of his own. When the show was canceled after five weeks, Winchell announced he would expose the ratings system. His last hurrah was a pathetic Las Vegas act that featured him in a simulated broadcast, seated at a table, hat on, shouting items into a mike; for a finale, he danced with a showgirl (hat off at last).

Winchell wound up as an ambulance chaser, cruising around answering police calls with a revolver in his glove compartment in a quest for one last humdinger of a scoop to impress Mr. and Mrs. America. During a 1960 election-night broadcast, he compared Democratic candidate Adlai Stevenson to Christine Jorgensen, saying if Stevenson were elected, it "would mean a woman in the White House." Some wondered if he had lost his marbles. A radio sponsor canceled, and he left Mutual on March 3, 1960, the first time in twenty-eight years that Walter Winchell was without a microphone.

When he couldn't find a New York outlet for his column, he mimeographed it and handed it out at nightclubs. Toward the end, when he was in his seventies and still fighting to regain his credibility, he was spotted at the Columbia University riots of 1964 by TV reporter Jack Perkins, scrambling along the barricades unable to persuade a young cop to let him by. "They don't know me. They don't know who I was," he told Perkins, dazed at the idea that nobody remembered him—or, if they did, didn't care. At the 1964 Republican convention, Perkins recalls noticing an elderly reporter climbing onto a platform for a better view before recognizing that it was Winchell again, with a card stuck in his hatband that said PRESS, just like in the movies. John Mosedale, a Winchell biographer, remarked, "The age of celebrity that he invented eventually claimed him."

When his old paper, the *Mirror*, went under, so did Winchell; no other paper would take him on. "That was really the end of him," said Klurfeld. "His voice changed after that. He didn't speak with the same vigor and snap. He spoke more slowly, in a lower register." His last outlet, in 1968, was a short-lived all-column weekly called *The New York Column*. When John Crosby recognized him in a Miami Beach barbershop looking "very withdrawn, a million miles away," Winchell stirred to life and said to Crosby, "Castro has just invited American journalists to fly down and look at his revolution. Let's go!" Crosby declined and, as Winchell walked away, he seemed to Crosby "the alonest man I ever did see."

LESSER GOSSIP COLUMNISTS of the air were led by the brash, Winchellesque Jimmy Fidler, who mimicked the master's staccato delivery and scoop-crazed mentality in a show that ran, on and off, nearly thirty years and on which he signed off each time with a farewell that sounded more like a threat: "Good night to you—and I do mean *you!*" Fidler, like his idol, was an ex-actor in and out of feuds with stars and studios, several of whom barred him from screenings and soundstages.

He had worked as a movie press agent and edited fan magazines and brought to his broadcasts a fanzine fervor but also an opinionated mouth. He was also the original, if far less finely tuned, Siskel and Ebert, rating movies by a four-bell system.

Fidler had a lot of the bitchy Rona Barrett in him and, not content merely dinging movies, he would clang a bell for or against movie stars whose films or behavior he approved or disapproved of. He was imbued with a moral fervor against divorce and similar shady doings among the movie crowd. John Crosby compared him to a small-town blue-nosed biddy, clucking over this failed marriage and that drunken husband. He liked actors who were nice to their mothers, stayed happily married, and didn't indulge in public spats.

Other Winchell-like features included scolding letters to stars wherein he dispensed career and personal advice as well as "notes from the little black book" along these finger-wagging lines: "Open letter to Mark Stevens. Dear Mark: Ever since the termination of your affair with Hedy Lamarr and your reconciliation with your wife, you've been indulging in public self-recrimination. You've declared to reporters that you made a fool of yourself, that you don't deserve a wife like Mrs. Stevens. . . . The point is, will you let her forget? Certainly she can't if you continue parading your repentance in the newspapers."

Again, like Winchell, when not reporting scandalous affairs involving Hedy Lamarr, Fidler dabbled in punditry and anti-Communism while taking periodic swipes at colleagues like Westbrook Pegler ("Attention, please, to this editorial: I am not in full accord with Walter Winchell's warnings of war"). The controversial Fidler, who had begun in broadcasting in 1932 and zigzagged between networks, formats, and sponsors, was still prowling the radio beat in the 1970s, sniffing out hot scoops that would blow the tinsel off Hollywood.

Fidler, the only male Hollywood gossip on radio, was surrounded by three buzzing queen bees of the airwaves, but the one whose sting stars feared most was Louella Parsons. Her gushy, garden-club-lady delivery makes it hard to imagine Parsons as a menacing movieland presence, as powerful a Hollywood mother hen as Winchell was a Broadway capo. The Hearst columnist was such a showbiz power broker that when she hosted a variety series called *Hollywood Hotel,* bootlicking movie stars fell all over themselves to appear on it—for nothing. When they balked, she threatened them, as when she was overheard to order a reluctant Olivia de Havilland, "Now, Olivia, you get down here or I'll tell a hundred million people what a rotten actress you are." Parsons naturally expected lowly radio actors to do the same, the sort of abuse that led to the formation of the American Federation of Radio Artists.

On Parsons's show *The Woodbury Hollywood News*—which billed her as "Hollywood's best-known, best-loved, and most respected reporter on the latest up-to-the-second Hollywood news"—Louella read items in a stuffy monotone, punctuated by an occasional tsk-tsk: Howard Hughes "is in trouble again," she began one report. "He's being sued by the family of sheriff Pat Garrett . . . Ann Sheridan's ex is remarrying for the fifth time . . . Mona Freeman is expecting . . . Mrs. Hal Wallis is out of danger after emergency surgery . . . Jack Warner received an award for service to his country . . . Mad Man Muntz is going to wed." Louella concluded with a hard-hitting commentary from her "Woodbury Soap Box," commending the studios for protecting stars from poison-pen letters.

Sheila Graham's cultivated British accent was hard to reconcile on the air with her gaudy Hollywood beat (but she was born Lily Shiel, a cockney Jewish orphan in South London who endured a Dickensian girlhood), which she covered with a certain discretion and an occasional private word of advice to wayward stars, neatly hiding her own famous liaison with F. Scott Fitzgerald.

Hedda Hopper, radio's other great movieland tattletale, ostensibly knew the territory from the inside as a former minor player and celebrated hat-wearer who was generally liked by movie people and took herself less seriously than her colleagues: when she blew one, she blew a mechanical bird on the air. Hopper, who had got her start on Rudy Vallee's show in 1939, chased items until 1951, winding up as a right-wing Red-baiter like Winchell.

ANOTHER OVERHEATED REPORTORIAL motormouth, Bill Stern, was a hammy sportscaster who, on his *Colgate Sportsreel,* told thrilling tales of athletic heroism in a voice full of throbbing emotion and exclamation points—tales with O. Henry twists and leaden ironies that revealed the name of the hero in the last phrase. Nobody seemed to care if the tales were true or not, so persuasive was Stern at unfolding them in his taut, over-the-top style.

Stern was a fabulist, a sensational scenery chewer in the manner of other sportscasters of the era—Don Dunphy and Bill Corum at ringside, or Graham McNamee, Ted Husing, and Clem McCarthy with his growly, "Good afternoon, *r-r-racing* fans." Is it any wonder that the quiet, measured Red Barber seemed so civilized and literate among these clubhouse rowdies? Next to them, "the ol' redhead"'s soft Dixie drawl and understated commentary seemed positively scholarly, much like Vin Scully, his protégé and longtime Brooklyn Dodgers partner.

Though scoffed at by his peers, Stern was unabashedly hyperbolic but perfectly attuned to wide-eyed kids, for whom every ball game was a life-or-death duel. With his embellished elegies and eulogies, Stern was a less didactic but equally punchy Howard Cosell. Like Cosell, Stern had flair, even if some of his athletic fables were just that—artfully embroidered fantasies delivered in a dramatic voice that created the lasting and now-troubling myth of the jock gladiator during the Golden Age of Sports. He was introduced by a theme sung by a barbershop chorus to the tune of "Mademoiselle from Armentières": *"Bill Stern, your Colgate Shave-Cream man is on the air/He's here again to bring you stor-r-r-ies rare. . . ."*

Rare indeed. In his caveat-emptor intro, Stern as much as conceded that his yarns were partly or even largely apocryphal, many woven of whole cloth—*"featuring strange and fantastic stories—some legend, some hearsay—but all so interesting that we'd like to pass them along to you."* A onetime Stern writer confessed that half the stories were fabricated, but added defensively, "It ain't easy to dream those things up." The stories invariably wound up with a spellbinding ". . . and so, ladies and gentlemen, the name of that feisty little half-blind sandlot ballplayer who was told he would never amount to much was . . . Harry S Truman." In another whopper, he told of Abe Lincoln's dying words, spoken to Abner Doubleday, whom he had sent for: "Keep baseball alive. In the trying days ahead, the country will need it." Thomas Edison, according to Stern, was nearly deaf because of a baseball that hit him in the ear, thrown by . . . Jesse James.

Many of Stern's tales seemed to involve presidents, such as the father of William Howard Taft, who, Stern reported, wouldn't allow him to sign a major league contract with the Cincinnati Red Stockings. A fan later pointed out that the team didn't sign players to contracts, there was no major league then, and when the club disbanded in 1870, Taft was only thirteen. In one of Stern's more inspired sagas, Frank Sinatra, upon being knocked out as a young prizefighter, was advised to go into singing by sportswriter Grantland Rice, who just happened to overhear the skinny boxer singing in the shower after the bout. Stern ended each broadcast with, "And that's the 3-0 mark for tonight" ("3-0" being the old newspaperman's symbol signifying a story's end), to lend the show its Winchellesque stamp of authenticity. Stern's stuff was full of compelling heroics (he himself had come back from an amputation and drug addiction), by noble sportsmen, each electrifying tale narrated in a tone of reverence that made every story *sound* true, like the one about a horse race won by a dead jockey, or the corpse who scored the winning run in a ball game when a player had a heart attack rounding third base and collapsed on home plate.

Red Barber, the quiet, honorable opposite of Stern's flashy sportscasting style, couldn't stand him: "Bill Stern and I were contemporaries, at times competitors, but we didn't spend much time around each other," he wrote. "I guess you could say we just didn't see anything in the same light. . . . He lost his left leg as a young man, and he has blamed that for much of what has happened in his life. He had a terrible time following the amputation, but often he used his plight to get his way, to evoke pity, to escape responsibilities, to slip out of trouble."

Barber recalled how Stern got a big break doing play-by-play for an Army-Illinois football game and, before the game, told his friends and family to send the head of NBC telegrams saying what a great job he had done. Unfortunately, the telegrams arrived before the game and Stern was fired. He drifted around for years before working his way back and, at last, was rehired by the man who had let him go and now, out of guilt, made him NBC sports director. Stern's main competitor then was the famous Ted Husing, and they maintained a ruthless on-air rivalry, badgering and embarrassing each other whenever possible. According to Barber, the two sportscasting icons would snip each other's mike wires and nail their nemesis' broadcast booth door shut.

Radio's early sports page was put together by men like Stern, Barber,

Husing, and Graham McNamee—most of them dedicated on-air reporters who, more often than not, broadcast games with grace, wit, and, when necessary, pizzazz and poignance. When no baseball game was readily available, they could even "re-create" one from the wire service report by simulating the crack of a bat and appropriate crowd noises, a bizarre, old-time radio art unto itself—embroidering a two-hour game off the sports ticker with fanciful descriptions of a match that took place primarily in their head: "Musial steps out of the box, taps his spikes, steps back in as the pitcher paws the mound impatiently." When the ticker slowed down, or if the tape snapped, there would be a sudden "rain delay."

Radio quickly became a crucial arm of sports in America, spreading the gospel of baseball in the 1920s to 1950s. Radio literally spread the word, starting with its first ball game, heard over KDKA on August 5, 1921, between the Philadelphia Phillies and the Pittsburgh Pirates, with a play-by-play by staff announcer Harold Arlin. Earlier that year, to show that radio had a future (the team owners thought broadcasting games was a threat to baseball), a new thirty-year-old general manager of something called the Radio Corporation of America, David Sarnoff, arranged to broadcast the Dempsey-Carpentier "fight of the century" as an RCA promotion.

An amateur boxer and wireless fiend, J. Andrew White, called that first fight, during which a transmitter exploded in Hoboken. White realized as the fight began that he wasn't sure how to describe it into a telephone, so he winged it from a cramped, sweaty corner of the ring, where he was nearly crushed by a sprawling Carpentier. Some 300,000 people heard the fight, and the publicity about the sportscast was enough to give it—and radio—quick credibility. Early sportscasts were relayed from the arena by phone to a second man at the station, who would rephrase the on-the-scene account in his own words. If anything went awry en route or at the station, the field man had no way of knowing.

It was voices belonging to men like McNamee, Husing, and Stern that lifted sports to the mythic status it still holds today despite all the contemporary off-field and off-court wrangling, cynicism, and law breaking. Husing, like McNamee and Stern, was of the thrill-a-minute school of sportscasting. As a boy, young Ted fantasized that he would one day become a commentator of some sort, and broke in at WJZ in New Jersey, where his colleagues included Milton Cross and Norman Brokenshire. When someone told Husing his voice was too pinched for radio, he had his nose broken to widen it, and broadened his career.

Sportscasting's first major star, Graham McNamee, was a vibrant wordmeister with a personal flair who symbolized, and helped create, America's golden age of sports in the 1920s and 1930s, when hype was the name of the game. McNamee, according to one account, "never arrived at a game without getting himself psyched up for it first. He would literally force himself into a frenzy before every game." In fact, McNamee was neither a natural sports fan nor an expert. He was an entertainer, mainly, who moved on from sportscasting to working as Ed Wynn's stooge. "Honest enthusiasm," he said, is "what the audience wants"—and maybe a dash of dishonest enthusiasm for good measure. It worked. His mail, it is said, came in by the truckload, and after the 1925 World Series he supposedly received fifty thousand letters, many of which decried his inexperience, but he was more interested in providing thrills than stats. As Heywood Broun wrote in praise of his florid style, "Mr. McNamee has justified the whole activity of radio broadcasting. Graham McNamee has been able to take a new medium of expression and through it transmit himself—to give out vividly a sense of movement and of feeling. Of such is the kingdom of art."

McNamee and his partner, Phillips Carlin, came up with the two-man system of sportscasting still in use—one to call the action and the other to fill in the color commentary, spell him at the mike, and give the play-by-play guy somebody to banter with, like a couple of informed fans in the stands. McNamee and Husing influenced a generation of sportscasters—excitable enthusiasts—as well as those who came after them, more sedate, reflective, skeptical, and informed (the Vin Scully–Bob Costas school), of whom Red Barber was perhaps the first and best, combining style, insight, and a painterly eye. Red reported the game but also the poetry. He took pains to learn baseball and its players and to tell it to listeners in a charming, knowledgeable, detailed manner, although one veteran sportscaster believes Barber became too "anti-excitement" and a bit self-important.

The same familial link that passes on the love and lore of baseball from fathers to sons was also handed down through generations via sportscasters to those who grew up listening to baseball games while mowing the lawn, washing the car, or overhearing them through an open window. "Baseball is the radio game," the columnist Jon Carroll wrote. "Its dimensions are wrong for television. Baseball on the radio in a dark room deep in the woods—its appeal is somehow deeper than baseball itself. When I used to drive long distances because I thought it was romantic—sometimes there was a girl at the end of the journey, but often I was just driving—I would often twiddle the dial to find baseball arcing through the night. . . ."

Fans grew up to the serene sounds of polished sportscasters like Lon Simmons and Hank Greenwald, longtime (2,500 games) play-by-play San Francisco Giants announcer, who did phantom sportscasts as a kid in Rochester, New York, listening to the far-off voice of Harry Carey in St. Louis calling the Cardinals games on KOMX; in a pinch, Greenwald would dial in Bob Nelson broadcasting the White Sox on WCFL or pick up the Pirates games out of Wheeling, West Virginia, on WWBA. "I used to take a red pencil and sort of mark on the plastic dial on the old radio, so if the stations faded out I knew where I could get KOMX, or even get WCKY in Cincinnati and pick up the Reds. That was the extent of my research, those little marks on the dial." Greenwald actually practiced by speaking into a wire recording machine and playing back the spool. Players may jump teams every year, but voices like Greenwald's seem to go on forever, becoming part of the midsummer music. The Harry Careys, Vin Scullys, Lindsey Nelsons, Jon Millers, Russ Hodgeses, Mel Allens, Bob Murphys, Ralph Kiners, Lon Simmonses, Ernie Harwells, and Phil Rizzutos sign lifetime contracts with the fans, and owners release them at great risk of mutinous listeners.

"You are there every day," recounted Greenwald. "You are in people's house, in their car, God knows where, talking into their ear. You become part of their family. And you want to be someone in their family that they like. I always felt that the primary voice of every team is the guy on the radio. People, if they are baseball fans, always tend to remember the guy they grew up listening to."

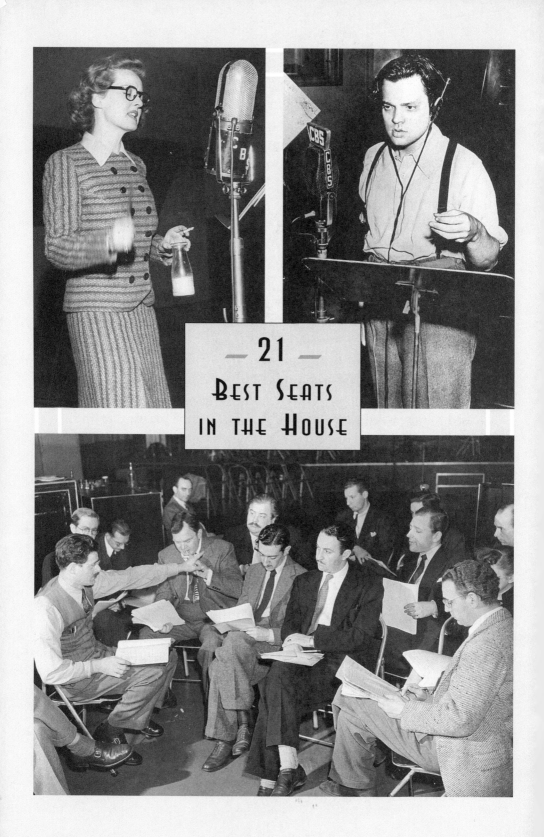

— 21 —

**Best Seats
in the House**

MEMBERS OF RADIO'S FAR-FLUNG AUDIENCE WERE drawn to any radio show that put them in touch with New York and, best of all, Broadway. A tingle passed through you at the sound of trains roaring into *Grand Central Station*—or, as it was announced over the show's coast-to-coast loud speaker, "*Gran-n-n-nd Cen-n-n-n-tral Station-n-n-n*," with its pulsating opening: "*As a bullet seeks its target, shining rails in every part of our great country are aimed at Grand Central Station, heart of the nation's greatest city. Drawn by the magnetic force of the fantastic metropolis, day and night great trains rush toward the Hudson River, sweep down its eastern bank for 140 miles, flash briefly by the long row of tenement houses south of 125th Street, dive with a roar into the two-and-a-half-mile tunnel which burrows beneath the glitter and swank of Park Avenue, and then. . . .*"

It was such heady stuff as this that helped speed dreamy small-town boys and girls to New York City, first in fantasy and then, in many cases, in reality—by train, if possible; always, the destination was Times Square and, of course, Broadway.

On radio's imaginary Great White Way stood playhouses such as *The Lux Radio Theatre, The Theatre Guild on the Air, The Philco Playhouse, The Damon Runyon Theater* (hosted by a Nathan Detroit soundalike named "Broadway"), and *The Mercury Theatre on the Air,* among many; one detective show was called *Broadway Is My Beat.* (Out west, there were *Stars Over Hollywood, Screen Guild Theatre, The Screen Directors Playhouse, Hollywood Hotel* (the first big network show from Los Angeles, hosted by Louella Parsons), and *Hollywood Playhouse.*)

It was thus easy to be seduced by such big-city radio shows as *The First Nighter Program,* hosted by a bon vivant addressed as "Mr. First

Facing page, clockwise from top left: Bette Davis in a radio drama, Orson Welles (*Mercury Theatre on the Air*), Norman Corwin directing the cast of "This Is War" (*Columbia Presents Corwin*)

Nighter," a suave-sounding chap presumably in top hat, tails, and sporting a gold-tipped cane. Beginning in 1930, he was played by a succession of actors that included the ubiquitous Bret Morrison and Marvin Miller (but also Macdonald Carey, Charles Hughes, and, finally, Rye Billsbury). All the housebound Mr. and Mrs. First Nighters mingled with bustling playgoers in the lobby of "The Little Theater just off Times Square," a hubbub that was finally stilled by Mr. First Nighter's hushed whisper, "The house lights have dimmed and the curtain is about to go up on tonight's production. . . ." The opening ran along these lines:

"Good evening, Mr. First Nighter."

"Good evening, Vincent. I see there's a good crowd here tonight at the Little Theater off Times Square."

(Most listeners didn't realize there really *was* a place off Times Square named the Little Theater—in the 1970s the home of David Frost's and Merv Griffin's TV shows, later the Helen Hayes Theater. Radio playgoers assumed the Little Theater was a generic term for some unnamed Rialto playhouse even though the show itself never originated from New York but from Chicago and then Hollywood.)

The distinguished announcer Vincent Pelletier confided: "Well, we can always be sure of a good play with stars like Barbara Luddy and Les Tremayne."

"I'll see you after the first-act curtain, Vincent. Now, friends in the radio audience, we have good seats—third row center, so let's go right in, shall we?"

Before stepping inside, listeners would hear bustling Broadway traffic noises and a hum of playgoers as the First Nighter headed for the theater, remarking as he strolled: "Broadway's buzzing with excitement and eagerly waiting to welcome an opening night performance. There'll be a crowd of onlookers and autograph fans on hand at the entrance to greet the celebrities who always attend a premiere on the Great White Way, so let's not miss a minute of the excitement." As he entered, the orchestra played a jaunty number called "Neapolitan Nights," the same overture each week, even though it was always a *play* we were about to "see," not a musical. After a buzzer sounded, Mr. First Nighter would say, "That's the signal for the first-act curtain," as an usher called out, "Curtain! Curtain!," lending an added surge of excitement.

Every play had three acts, broken up with commercials for Campana, a beauty soap. At the commercial break, a *First Nighter* usher bawled, "Smoking in the downstairs and lobby only, please!" On some shows, the host would point out various celebrities in the crowd, perhaps with a plug for their latest play or movie ("Look, there's Judy Garland, star of the new MGM Technicolor musical *The Harvey Girls*"). Then, after the commercial break, the usher would announce, "Curtain going up on act two, ladies and gentlemen!" It all sounded impossibly glamorous. You were hooked for life on not just radio but on an equally magical thing called theater.

The productions were less exciting than the buzz inside and outside the theater—they were slick and mildly entertaining, fairly formulaic romantic comedies, mostly, that allowed Barbara Luddy, Les Tremayne, Olan Soulé, et al., to portray various characters, all of whom fit into their own pleasing if limited performing styles during the broadcast's long run. The final curtain rang down on *The First Nighter Program* in 1949, with a one-season revival in 1952.

Despite superb supporting casts, it was really "The Les and Barbara Show," a two-person repertory company that provided a lovely sinecure for the two stars. The series demanded of its writers that they strive for "WHOLESOMENESS . . . excessive sophistication is OUT." It was theater by the numbers; one radio historian called it "an audio version of the old *Saturday Evening Post*." Remarking on the speed required to develop a character in a twenty-five-minute play, Tremayne says of his costar Barbara Luddy, "She was a good pro and so was I." Tremayne never felt constrained by the show's narrow dramatic range. "It was satisfying—up to a point." Much of it was largely instinctive. "In radio, you worked by the second," he says, remembering how often he had only moments to shed his First Nighter tuxedo before racing off to do another show.

Tremayne costarred opposite Luddy for ten years, until he was succeeded by Olan Soulé. Don Ameche was the show's first leading man, from 1930 to 1936. Tremayne, a Chicago actor, took over the lead when Ameche left for the movies. "Many of the guys went to Hollywood, but none were very successful except Don Ameche," Tremayne once said. "Some came back, beaten and broken, literally, and very disillusioned."

Nobody seemed to want Tremayne in movies. "Now here I was, on a top show. I was winning awards as the No. 1 dramatic radio actor in the U.S.—and no one was coming to me with an offer! And friends were asking, 'Why aren't you going to Hollywood?' Well, I had no answer to that." He made a test for Warner Bros. in 1940 but never heard anything. In 1943, he left the show to give films a final try, but the sponsor, betrayed a second time, had Olan Soulé slide into his shoes; Tremayne said listeners thought he had died. Almost fifty years later, Tremayne learned how the agency and his own agent had conspired to tell an interested Darryl Zanuck that he was under exclusive contract to the network, which was untrue—it was a ruse programs often used to hold on to premier radio actors to keep them from going to Hollywood.

Tremayne became a free-lance radio actor in New York on *The Thin Man* and *The Falcon,* and was host of *The Hallmark Hall of Fame.* He played on Broadway in *Detective Story,* and then tried Hollywood again working as a journeyman actor in forty films. But he never equaled his *First Nighter* marquee billing, and ended his acting years in broadcasting's green pastures as a regular on TV's *General Hospital.* Likewise, Olan Soulé, who starred opposite Luddy from 1943 through 1953 after knocking around the dial as Jack Armstrong's Coach Hardy and on *Little Orphan Annie* as Daddy Warbucks's Chinese cook, Aha, never reclaimed the fame he had enjoyed on *The First Nighter.*

THE GAUDIEST BIG-CITY SHOW was *The Lux Radio Theatre,* which opened with a sweeping overture and was hosted from Hollywood by the majestic-sounding Cecil B. DeMille. CB was replaced in 1945 by William Keighley, who had an equally impressive impresariolike voice.

The *Lux* show at first functioned as a billboard for Broadway, alerting listeners to new plays, but its mainstays became movies. Each *Lux* production was presented with all the razzle-dazzle of a Broadway or Hollywood premiere. You imagined limos pulling up, arc lights scanning the heavens, and red carpets being unrolled. The show attracted actual autograph hounds, who tried to sneak into rehearsals.

Lux presented *Reader's Digest* versions of famous movies and plays, hour-long reenactments with famous stars who deigned to "appear" on radio (or were forced to by their studios), bringing Hollywood and Broadway right into your bedroom. A writer who adapted movies for *The Dreft Star Playhouse* says it was easy to squeeze a two-hour film into an hour, or even half an hour, on the air. "It was stolen money," laughs Paul West, comedy writer-cum-condenser. "The places to cut would just jump off the page." Too often, however, capsule versions of plays and films gutted the original works and acted more as promotional trailers for them. Boiling a feature film down into a half-hour radio play was accomplished by wraparound narrative and a few key lines. It was cut-and-paste drama.

Writers on radio deadlines also shamelessly stole plots from the classics and dressed them up in modern clothes. True Boardman, a veteran radio dramatist, told Leonard Maltin: "I have written *Hamlet* twice, *King Lear* once, *Julius Caesar* four times, and *Romeo and Juliet* oftener than I should confess. *Faust,* too, has done yeoman work on occasion, as well as the *Odyssey* and the *Iliad.*"

During its twenty-one years, from 1934 to 1955, *Lux* presented virtually every movie and play of note—cut-down, occasionally cut-rate, versions of current comedies, dramas, and musicals, classics, revivals, and even an occasional original. According to *Variety, Lux* and lesser playhouses of the air in just one year, 1938, served up an astonishing 164 stage adaptations, 60 adaptations of prose and poetry, 208 original radio plays, and countless movie adaptations—plus 138 works written for a New Deal program, the Federal Theater Radio Division.

When you survey the hundreds of shows that *Lux* alone adapted, it is a staggering list, a virtual encyclopedia of American theater and cinema, starring a Who's Who of Hollywood and Broadway. For stay-at-homes it was a crash course in the theater of the time, not to mention the occasional Shakespearean work starring film stars with serious theatrical credentials—John Barrymore, Tallulah Bankhead, Leslie Howard, Laurence Olivier. Mutual produced a landmark three-hour *Les Misérables* with Orson Welles; another radio theater, incredibly, once shrank the epic to thirty minutes.

It was sugarcoated culture, perhaps, yet it had a major influence on the theater, and on young, far-off latent playgoers—another example of radio's gift for bringing art to the masses. For most Americans, the *Lux* dramas were their first, perhaps only, exposure to theater, and for many listeners it was their only chance to hear a professional version of Shakespeare with world-class actors.

For young writers like Rod Serling (*Dr. Christian*), Irwin Shaw (*The*

Gumps), Herman Wouk (*The Fred Allen Show*), and Paddy Chayefsky, much radio writing was a crash course in dramaturgy. Arthur Miller wrote for the historical anthology *Cavalcade of America,* and in his autobiography the playwright said he was the show's "utility man," often called upon to knock out a script on four days' notice. "There would be a desperate phone call" followed by a messenger dropping off a book about some historical event. "I would read it by Wednesday evening, cook up a half-hour script on Thursday, and get it to [the producer] by Friday morning," for which he earned five hundred dollars. "It was an easy dollar and allowed me to continue working on plays and stories and took less time than teaching."

The Lux Radio Theatre itself almost flopped after one season, when it had run out of available Broadway plays to adapt to the air, so the show was moved to Hollywood in 1936 and gilded with the DeMille name. Broadway plays didn't lend themselves to paring down as easily as films—at least one of which, *Dark Victory,* was "adapted" for the *Lux* show before it was even filmed. Also, Broadway writers, producers, and directors were not pleased to hear their work slashed in half, or less, on the air. DeMille himself cost Lux two thousand dollars a week, but he attracted stars, usually two per week, most of whom appeared for a flat five-thousand-dollar fee and whose presence gave the humble bar of soap a sudden luster.

An average broadcast, performed at the Music Box Theatre on Hollywood Boulevard (later the Vine Street and Huntington Hartford Theaters, now the Doolittle), cost about $20,000—there were fifty cast and crew members, plus a twenty-five-piece orchestra—but it was worth it: During its long run, *The Lux Radio Theatre* was inevitably among the top ten–rated shows. Each week's production was broken into three 15-minute acts, with anecdotes by DeMille and stilted curtain chats with stars promoting their latest ventures. (Fox insisted that every plug include a reference to studio boss Darryl F. Zanuck.) To pick a few at random, *Main Street* starred Barbara Stanwyck and Fred MacMurray; Clark Gable appeared in *A Farewell to Arms; Men in White* featured Spencer Tracy and Frances Farmer; and Fredric March and Jean Arthur were in *The Plainsman.*

The cast would first meet Thursdays for a run-through, followed by

Friday and Saturday rehearsals and two dress rehearsals Monday before the broadcast itself at 9 P.M. (EST), when announcers Melville Ruick or John Milton Kennedy intoned, "Lux presents—*Hollywood!*" Some of Hollywood's biggest names, however, froze before the mike. Joan Crawford was petrified. Screen legends like Crawford, Gary Cooper, William Powell, Barbara Stanwyck, Lana Turner, Victor Mature, and Paul Muni found themselves without the on-air technique of even minor supporting players. Others adapted so easily that they got their own shows: Jimmy Stewart (*The Six-Shooter*), Dana Andrews (*I Was a Communist for the FBI*), Joel McCrea (*Tales of the Texas Rangers*), Ann Sothern (*The Adventures of Maisie*), Brian Donlevy (*Dangerous Assignment*), Lew Ayres and Lionel Barrymore (*Dr. Kildare*).

Major screen stars, used to scores of takes, were either too mike-shy, too stubborn, or too famous to adapt their camerawork to radio. Arch Oboler sat Gary Cooper down and patiently explained that he needed to speak more intimately to other actors, but Cooper ignored everything Oboler told him and changed the subject to deer hunting. "The man had no concept of radio," Oboler recalled. Tommy Cook, leading radio child actor, adds, "I worked with picture people like Gary Cooper on radio—we did *Pride of the Yankees*—and he couldn't get his own name out. He didn't know who he was on radio or what the hell he was doing. He just couldn't handle it. It was an entirely different technique. You need that voice presence that doesn't overaccentuate and yet still paints a picture. Some picture actors could do it in the face but not the voice." To corral stage and film actors and keep them within mike distance, at least one show employed a three-sided bar that encircled the microphone. Joan Crawford, in her autobiography, revealed the inner fears of movie-star guests new to radio: "All I had to do was speak a few words about music. But I was Joan Crawford. No character to hide behind. I was so nervous they nailed a chair to the floor. Later we used a chrome bar, like a towel rack, for me to hang onto and every line was printed on cardboard. Paper might have rattled in my shaking hand." Bea Lillie recalled in her memoirs that Helen Hayes "shook like a leaf for ten minutes" after her radio debut, that it took Ethel Barrymore years to recover, and that after Claudette Colbert sang two songs, "she broke down and wept."

Sandra Gould, who did several roles on the *Lux* series (between stints as a switchboard operator on Jack Benny's show), recalled that female movie stars received cartons of Lux soap for years, mainly so the sponsor could proudly proclaim, "Nine out of ten film actresses use Lux beauty soap." Every studio ladies' room was well stocked with Lux. Beyond free soap, the show paid better than any other in town, according to Gould—$133 a week. Did radio actors mind that movie stars earned thousands of dollars a week? "Constantly."

Although DeMille was billed as "your producer," he never directed a single *Lux* production—the actual anonymous director for years was Frank Woodruff, followed by others. DeMille played the impresario role with his usual flair, though, often arriving at the theater direct from a set in his trademark boots and jodhpurs. Robert Cummings was on the show nine times and said he never met DeMille, who was known to speak to stars on other shows through his secretary. When the autocratic director refused to pay a one-dollar union assessment to fight a California open-shop law, he was banned from radio.

IT WAS RADIO THEATER that first unleashed Orson Welles, who was nineteen in 1934 when he began auditioning for dramatic shows before landing a part in *The American School of the Air* as John D. Rockefeller on *Cavalcade of America*. Welles also recited poetry on the air at fifty dollars a crack on *Musical Reveries,* sponsored by Crisco; as a commercial spokesman, he billed himself the "Voice of Cornstarch."

For Welles, *The Shadow* was almost a throwaway assignment, because his real interest was *The Mercury Theatre on the Air,* a spin-off of his just-formed Mercury Theatre on Broadway. Welles, by then only twenty-three, used his theatrical company to populate its radio companion, featuring seasoned radio and stage actors Agnes Moorehead, Joseph Cotten, Everett Sloane, Ray Collins, and George Coulouris, the core of his original rep company. "The ones who played in *Citizen Kane* were all from radio," said Welles, who transferred devices to the screen first learned in radio, like the swift segues in which a musical bridge was interrupted with action: In *Kane,* when the snowball hits the young Kane's house, the lyrical music halts in the middle of a passage and he cuts directly to inside the house.

Radio was a major influence on films like *The Magnificent Ambersons,* in which (as on many broadcasts) Welles used an outside narrator and zoomed in on voices in a crowd of townspeople to comment on the action. He claimed his radio innovations exceeded even his screen inventions. He gave narrative as much resonance as dramatic dialogue; for a famous production of *Julius Caesar* he hired political commentator H. V. Kaltenborn to read a narrative passage from Plutarch as if analyzing the action. *The Mercury Theatre on the Air* set the tone and gave radio a theatrical, indeed classical, respectability it had lacked before, with its repertory of serious players and Shakespearean dramas, and its overall aura of quality, all signed by the magisterial Welles's semimocking reference to himself as "your obedient servant."

Arthur Anderson, who appeared in six radio plays for Welles, recalled that a typical *Mercury Theatre on the Air* show consisted of a read-through, a lunch break, a "work-through" with sound effects and music cues, a dinner break, a dress rehearsal that was recorded on giant sixteen-inch acetates and, an hour or so later, after last-minute fixes, the show went on the air live. Anderson related one favorite Wellesian stunt: "The director was about to give the cue when Orson's script dropped to the floor. Pages were scattered all across the entire stage. Well, there was panic. Everybody rushed to pick up the pages of Orson's script, trying to get the pages in the proper order: 'Page one! Have you got page one? Here's page eight!' All this was *sotto voce* and frantic. Just as the cue came and the show went on the air, Orson pulled the real script from the inside breast pocket of his coat. And he went on the air flawlessly. He loved practical jokes."

Welles's most spectacular practical joke was, of course, *The War of the Worlds,* which was just another in his series of plays for CBS in a season that had begun with a truncated version of *Dracula* adapted in a seventeen-hour work session at Reuben's Restaurant; he worked best surrounded by food. He was coasting on the recent triumph of the Mercury Theatre, which had opened with a string of hits that climaxed with his appearance on the cover of *Time* at the age of twenty-three. Even so, he was still mainly a New York theater celebrity. At the time, he was squeezing in a weekly radio series while simultaneously rehearsing two plays, cowriting the movie that became *Citizen Kane,* and preparing Shakespearean productions; radio rehearsals were directed by Paul Stewart until Welles could free himself to take over midway.

Due to the assembly-line nature of radio, and to Welles's overcommitted, overheated, helter-skelter way of working, the show was patched together in a few weeks on too little sleep. "We never seemed to get more than a single jump ahead of ourselves," said John Houseman, Welles's co-producer. "Shows were created week after week under conditions of soul- and health-destroying pressure." The cast would rehearse a week and then he would come in, scrap much of what had been done and make last-minute changes, unnerving everyone.

Houseman recalled there were always two dramas going on simultaneously—"the minor drama of the current show and the major drama of Orson's gargantuan struggle to get it on. Sweating, howling, disheveled, and single-handed he wrestled with Chaos and Time—always conveying an effect of being alone, traduced by his collaborators, surrounded by treachery, ignorance, sloth, indifference, incompetence and—more often than not—downright sabotage!"

The self-dramatizing Welles loved the chaos, added Houseman. "Every Sunday it was touch and go. As the hands of the clock moved relentlessly toward air time, the crisis grew more extreme, the peril more desperate. Often violence broke out. Scripts flew through the air, doors were slammed, batons smashed. Scheduled for 6 P.M. but usually nearer 7, there was a dress rehearsal, a thing of wild improvisation and irrevocable disaster," with programs often running a quarter-hour over or under and last-minute script slashes. "With only a few minutes to go, there was a final frenzy of correction and reparation, of utter confusion and absolute horror, aggravated by the gobbling of sandwiches and the bolting of oversized milkshakes."

Those were the conditions under which all of Welles's radio plays were readied for airtime. "At that instant," recorded Houseman, "with not one second to spare, this titanic buffoonery stopped. Suddenly, out of chaos, the show emerged—delicately poised, meticulously executed, precise as clockwork, and smooth as satin. And above us all, like a rainbow over storm clouds, stood Orson on his podium, sonorous and heroic—a great victory snatched from the jaws of disaster."

Houseman functioned as series editor, choosing the shows with

Welles and helping to write them—at first alone and then later with Howard Koch (better remembered now for cowriting *Casablanca*.) It was Koch who actually adapted *The War of the Worlds* for the air. He was then a young playwright working on his first professional script, the sixty-page adaptation of H. G. Wells's novella, which only consumed about forty-five minutes of actual airtime. Koch said he used "practically nothing" of the original Wells story except the idea, switching the locale from England to Grovers Mill, New Jersey, a real town he decided upon by closing his eyes and sticking his pencil in a New Jersey map. The only invaders the town's residents ever had to fight were sightseers inquiring even years later where the Martians had landed.

The show aired on October 30, 1938. En route to the barber the next day, Koch overheard words like *panic* and *invasion* and assumed that Hitler had taken over another country and war had finally broken out. "When I anxiously questioned the barber," he recalled, "he broke into a broad grin. 'Haven't you heard?' And he held up the front page of a morning newspaper with the headline 'Nation in Panic from Martian Broadcast.' Center page was a picture of Orson, his arms outstretched in a gesture of helpless innocence, and underneath was the opening scene of my play." Pandemonium also broke out in the columns. Columnist Heywood Broun wrote: "We have far more to fear from the silhouette of the censor than from the shadow of Orson Welles." Political pundit Dorothy Thompson wondered how anyone could be duped by such an obvious dramatization ("Nothing whatever about [the show] was in the least credible, no matter at what point the hearer might have tuned in"), but wrote that the show "cast a brilliant and cruel light upon the failure of popular education," showed up "the incredible stupidity, lack of nerve and ignorance of thousands," and "proved how easy it is to start a mass delusion."

Lest people think the scare has been exaggerated over time, the *New York Times*'s lengthy account reveals how real it all was to those who tuned in after the show began and allowed themselves to be swept along in its theatrical path until the end, when Welles stepped out of character as the convincing Princeton astronomy professor who spoke dispassionately from the observatory on the unfolding events to take his usual bow. Here are the opening paragraphs from the *Times*'s account:

"A wave of mass hysteria seized thousands of radio listeners throughout the nation between 8:15 and 9:30 o'clock last night when a broadcast of a dramatization of H. G. Wells's fantasy, *The War of the Worlds,* led thousands to believe that an interplanetary conflict had started with invading Martians spreading wide death and destruction in New Jersey and New York.

"The broadcast, which disrupted households, interrupted religious services, created traffic jams and clogged communications systems, was made by Orson Welles, who as the radio character *The Shadow,* used to give 'the creeps' to countless child listeners. This time at least a score of adults required medical treatment for shock and hysteria." The *Times,* besieged by 875 phone calls, pointed out that the show was listed in the logs as "Today: 8:00–9:00—Play: H. G. Wells's *The War of the Worlds*—CBS."

Much of the public hysteria, hard to believe today, might be traced to the fact that the panicky announcer on the show sounded eerily like Herbert Morrison, the radio newsman who, only a year earlier, had reported the Hindenburg disaster in a sobbing voice. Actor Frank Readick, who played the correspondent, listened to the famous recording of a horrified Morrison reporting the *Hindenburg* explosion— which also occurred in New Jersey, except that in the Welles version, reporter Carl Phillips dies on the air, victim of a Martian death ray.

In Koch's script, Phillips describes the horror visited upon the small town: "This is the most terrifying thing I have ever witnessed. . . . Wait a minute, someone's crawling. Someone or . . . something. I can see peering out of the black hole two luminous disks . . . are they eyes? . . . It might be a face. It might be . . . good heavens, something's wriggling out of the shadow like a gray snake. Now it's another one, and another one, and another one. They look like tentacles to me. There, I can see the thing's body. It's large as a bear and it glistens like wet leather. But that face! It . . . ladies and gentlemen, it's indescribable! I can hardly force myself to keep looking at it, it's so awful. The eyes are black and gleam like a serpent. The mouth is kind of V-shaped, with saliva dripping from its rimless lips that seem to quiver and pulsate. . . ."

In retrospect, of course, it all sounds like what it was—a wildly improbable ghost story, but some people assumed that Hitler was launching gas bombs, as he had threatened to. "Many listeners translated the monstrous creatures into Germans," wrote Koch later. "They assumed that Hitler had developed a devastating weapon and was taking over the whole world. In one terror-filled night our accumulated fears and insecurities came home to roost."

The *Times* account concludes: "Expressing profound regret that his dramatic efforts should cause such consternation, Mr. Welles said: 'I don't think we will choose anything like this again.' He hesitated about presenting it, he disclosed, because 'it was our thought that perhaps people might be bored or annoyed at hearing a tale so improbable.' " Some 6 million people were said to have heard the show.

The program, like so many Welles productions, barely made it to the air. Koch reported early in the week that he couldn't find a way to make the premise credible, and Houseman's secretary agreed that the show sounded infantile. "You can't do it," she protested. "Those old Martians are just a lot of nonsense! It's all too silly. We're going to make fools of ourselves!" For Welles, the show was not his top priority that week. He was busily involved in a massive stage production of *Danton's Death* and had no time to worry about the next week's radio show; Houseman couldn't even get him on the phone to discuss the problems Koch was having on the script.

Finally, the cast gathered at midnight in Welles's room at the St. Regis to hear the first playback. Everyone agreed it was still too dull, but the thing might be salvaged by adding eyewitness accounts to the mock newscast. "All night we sat up, spicing the script with circumstantial allusions and authentic detail," remembered Houseman, then the script was sent to the CBS censor the next day, where certain real places were given new names and sound men began their task of juicing up the show with fake "live remote" touches; they worked especially hard on the crowd noises, on a cannon roar in the Watchung Hills, New Jersey, "battle" sequence, and on the death-ray effect. Despite all that, a sound man told Houseman, confidentially, that it wasn't one of their best efforts.

Houseman said that on the Sunday the show came together, on the twentieth floor of the CBS Building, it produced what he called "a strange fever [that] seemed to invade the studio—part childish mischief, part professional zeal."

While Welles didn't write the script for *The War of the Worlds,* he gladly took, indeed stole, the credit for it away from Koch, who later sued to regain his rightful recognition as its primary author—and won. Houseman credited several factors for its success—from engineer Johnny Dietz's skill at creating the illusion of what Houseman called "imperfect reality" (the disjointed news bulletins interspersed with snatches of dance band music) to the mind-set of listeners used to hearing shows interrupted with news bulletins. But maybe it was Charlie McCarthy who played the most crucial, little-known part that explains the panic that ensued.

The Edgar Bergen and Charlie McCarthy Show was on opposite *The War of the Worlds,* and it was by far the more popular program in that time slot (with a 34.7 Crossley rating, as opposed to Welles's meager 3.6). So most people listening that night were tuned in to the comedy show rather than to the adaptation of an obscure work of science fiction by H. G. Wells, and thus many missed Welles's opening explanation that what they were about to hear was a dramatization.

A little-known singer who came on the McCarthy show at 8:12 on NBC inadvertently caused the panic. When the comedy led into the evening's routine musical interlude, station-surfing listeners were tempted to switch temporarily to CBS, where they picked up *The War of the Worlds* and assumed that the news of the Martian landing was the real thing. This is the most plausible explanation for all those now hard-to-believe morning-after news accounts of listeners spilling into the streets during the show and behaving as if New Jersey had indeed been invaded by marauding extraterrestrials.

What is forgotten is that the historic show was preceded by a lengthy introduction by Welles: "We know now that in the early years of the twentieth century this world was being watched closely by intelligences greater than man's and yet as mortal as his own," he began, which segued into an announcer delivering a bland weather forecast, followed by "We now take you to the Meridian Room of the Hotel Park Plaza in downtown New York, where you will be entertained by the music of Ramon Raquello and his orchestra . . ." (in fact, Bernard Herrmann's twenty-seven-piece orchestra playing a persuasively ricky-tick version of "La Cumparsita"). This is where many people tuned into the show and when the madness began.

What is also forgotten is the second half of the program, when the frightened multitudes (exact numbers mushroomed with each retelling, along with supposed suicides, none verified) abandoned their radios and fled into the streets in terror. Anyone who stayed tuned would have quickly caught on to the stunt. For one thing, there was a break, as an announcer came on to say, quite clearly, "You are listening to the CBS presentation of Orson Welles and *The Mercury Theatre on the Air* in an original dramatization of *The War of the Worlds,* by H. G. Wells. The performance will continue after a brief intermission."

Moments before, a CBS executive tried to respond to frantic callers by going on the air to explain it was all a joke, but Welles wouldn't let him; the station break was only a minute away. Someone claims seeing William Paley arriving in robe and slippers to calm the commotion. "By now," said Houseman, "the Martians were across the Hudson and gas was blanketing the city. The end was near." Ray Collins, as "the last announcer," was gasping for air as a ham radio operation tried to make contact, with his plaintive query: "2X2L calling CQ, 2X2L calling CQ, 2X2L calling CQ. Isn't there anyone on the air? Isn't there anyone?"— followed by five seconds of horrifying silence.

Associated Press bureaus were beset with terrorized callers. Sobbing women called the *Providence Journal* with eyewitness accounts, and a woman in Boston told the *Globe* she "could see the fire" set by the Martian forces. "New York destroyed! This is the end of the world! You might as well go home to die—I just heard it on the radio."

People believed their radios. Houseman traced the hysteria to two things: The show's timing was perfect, coming about a month after the Munich meeting between Hitler and Chamberlain; also, on-the-spot radio coverage was then a fairly new device, a fact that the script used to manufacture, with great exactitude, the illusion of "real time." Many didn't believe the announcement of the attack on Pearl Harbor three years later because of the Martian landing hoax.

What the show had accomplished so brilliantly was using radio itself as a framework for Welles's little horror story. "It could have been carried off in no other medium than radio," Houseman said. "Not even the realistic theater observes the literal unities; motion pictures and, particularly, radio (where neither time nor place exists save in the imagination of the listener) have no difficulty in getting their audiences to accept the telescoped reality of dramatic time." He added, "If, that night, the American public proved 'gullible,' it was because enormous pains and a great deal of thought were spent on making it so." Welles had insisted on taking more time than some thought necessary to lull the listener into a sense that all was normal. Houseman went on: "At rehearsal, Orson stretched [the opening musical interludes] to what seemed to us, in the control room, an almost unbearable length. We objected." A lengthy interview with a rambling professor also "was dragged out to a point of tedium. We cried that there would not be a listener left on the air. Defiantly, Welles stretched [lines] out even longer. He was right. His sense of tempo that night was infallible." Once it was all over, Welles delivered what Houseman termed "a charming informal little speech about Halloween"—with that lovely line about the show just being "our way of jumping out of the bushes and saying Boo!"—hoping to settle everyone's nerves.

Houseman described Welles standing onstage the next day as photographers snapped his photo: "His eyes raised up to heaven, his arms outstretched in an attitude of crucifixion," pictures accompanied in the next day's tabloids by the headline I DIDN'T KNOW WHAT I WAS DOING! One actor said, "It was the only time I ever saw Orson *slightly* afraid." At the press conference (perhaps still acting) a fretful young Welles with the scruffy beginnings of a beard spoke somberly to reporters: "We are deeply shocked and deeply regretful at the results of last night's broadcast. One doesn't believe much in the radio audience—whether they're listening or not. Or what they're thinking. I had every hope that the people would be excited as they would be at a melodrama. But radio is new and we're learning about the effect it has on people. We learned a terrible lesson last night."

Houseman recalled, "We were on the front page for two days," not to mention the columns and editorials "only too eager to expose the perilous irresponsibilities of the medium." The FCC held hearings and passed a few regulations, and CBS apologized. The major casualty inflicted by the Martians was a young woman who fell and broke her arm running downstairs. The series wound up with a sponsor, Campbell's Soup, and the name of the show was changed to *The Campbell*

Playhouse. The company figured, Houseman remarked, "that if we could sell Martians we could also sell tomato soup."

No other single radio show zoomed an actor to stardom as *The War of the Worlds* did Welles, who was unknown to most Americans on Halloween, October 30, 1938; by October 31, the Martians had made him a household name. With typical Wellesian flair, he burst on the scene overnight. Welles liked to say he had planned the program as a Halloween trick, nothing more, but when he later recalled the event for the director Peter Bogdanovich, he admitted: "The kind of response [we got], yes—that was merrily anticipated by us all. The *size* of it, of course, was flabbergasting. Twenty minutes in, and we had a control room full of very bewildered cops. They didn't know who to arrest or for what, but they did lend a certain tone to the remainder of the broadcast. We began to realize, as we plowed on with the destruction of New Jersey, that the extent of our American lunatic fringe had been underestimated."

For Orson Welles it was the career move of a lifetime. "It put me in the movies. Thanks to the Martians, we got us a radio sponsor and suddenly we were a great big commercial program, right up there with Benny, Burns, Allen, and the *The Lux Radio Theatre* with C. B. DeMille. The next step was Hollywood."

The War of the Worlds was the single most famous program in radio history, superbly combining two scary genres—the extraterrestrial tale and the horror story. Because of it, radio frightened off all further pseudoreality outer-space shows. Those pesky Martians had triumphed after all.

WELLES LEFT A BIG FOOTPRINT in radio, but the dramatist who raised radio to its highest level, to indeed a new theatrical form, was Norman Corwin, a small-town ex-reporter whose magnificent CBS series of patriotic and poetic broadcasts on *The Columbia Workshop* and *Columbia Presents Corwin* are now, alas, largely forgotten and hard to find.

Corwin's works—shows like *We, the People* and *We Hold These Truths*—were sui generis, blending drama, history, journalism, verse, narrative, music, and sound into a kind of radio tone poem, using the finest actors, composers, poets, and special effects available. "If anyone deserves the title of Mr. Radio, it is surely he," wrote Charles Beaumont in an eloquent 1960 eulogy for radio.

Fusing pop culture and patriotism, a little like Ken Burns's works *The Civil War, Baseball,* and *Lewis and Clark* on PBS, Corwin set about creating challenging works that sought to invoke a flagging nationalism in the wake of the Depression and on the eve of world war. His stirring agit-prop verse dramas helped make the case for U.S. intervention in the war, most vividly and intensely in a celebrated parable by Archibald MacLeish called "Fall of the City," a futuristic antifascist allegory that, with disturbing prescience, foreshadowed events in Europe. The 1936 series' unabashed aim, noted an observer, was "to raise the nation's political conscience." *The Columbia Workshop* did just that. It was an experimental theater of the air that used every sort of broadcasting device—choruses, filters, weird sounds, echo chambers—and reconfigured others. It amounted to a kind of WPA, unsponsored but fully supported by the network, which paid new and untried writers a paltry $100 per script and underemployed actors $18.50 per half-hour performance.

During his years at CBS, Corwin had any writer-producer's dream assignment—a free hand to create what he liked without regard to sponsors or ratings. He worked less like a playwright than in the bold symbolism and broad strokes of an editorial cartoonist, sketching in vivid points not so much through character as by painting in a mood with voices, sounds, and music. A few felt he was too simplistic: "He has endless ideas and excitements but he rushes on breathlessly from one to the next without adequately digging into any of them," wrote a UCLA professor; a valid point, yet beside the point. Whatever his shortcomings—purple passages, heavy-handed irony, liberal bias—they were overcome by the programs' ambitions, impact, superior writing, and high production values.

Some thought he was adventurous; others, pretentious. A New York critic dismissed one work as a "dramatic recitation with sound effects." Perhaps, but the *Columbia* series attracted famous authors eager to have their work performed over the air. William Saroyan, W. H. Auden, Maxwell Anderson, and Stephen Vincent Benet all contributed. Corwin was a popularizer in the best sense, refusing to compromise respected writers just to make them palatable to the masses, cross-pollinating them with popular performers. He commissioned work from Pare Lorentz, Irwin Shaw, Dorothy Parker, James Thurber, and others; he produced T. S. Eliot and Aldous Huxley.

Some of his wartime work was propaganda, most significantly his series *This Is War.* Corwin restyled some of the techniques first heard on *The March of Time,* which dramatized news events, but he added heart, soul, and wit. He lightened the tone with occasional works of whimsy done in Ogden Nash–like verse, such as "The Undecided Molecule"; another satirized radio itself; a third became his first major success, "The Plot to Overthrow Christmas." Corwin was an innovator in every area. He used actors in new ways, such as blending speakers into an a capella chorus, and he blurred traditional dramatic boundaries, mixing politics and poetics, melodrama and irony; he persuaded stars to stretch and play against their image. In "The Undecided Molecule," about the scary future of nuclear fission, labeled "a rhymed fantasy," he cagily cast Groucho Marx, Vincent Price, and Keenan Wynn, with Robert Benchley as the rebellious molecule on trial; Groucho played a cosmic judge and Sylvia Sidney was a lobbyist for the animal kingdom. Told in comic doggerel, the play ponders whether atomic energy will be used for peaceful or hostile purposes. It's funny, informed, and pointed, political without being preachy, and, above all, accessible.

In a typical broadcast, "An American in England," the actor Joseph Julian played an imaginary Yank strolling through the streets of war-torn London commenting on the scene. The *New York Times* critic John K. Hutchens remarked that the program "finds Mr. Corwin once more writing with a poet's vision, a good reporter's clarity, and a technician's precise knowledge of his craft—three attributes that have made him pre-eminent in radio literature." The poet Carl Van Doren wrote that "Corwin was to radio what Marlowe was to the Elizabethan stage"—and a lot more prolific. In a series called *Twenty-six by Corwin,* he produced, wrote, and directed all twenty-six radio dramas in as many weeks; he called himself a "radiowright."

When listened to today (they were rebroadcast in a 1997–98 series of anniversary specials on National Public Radio), certain scripts may sound overwritten, overwrought, simplistic, or idealistic to modern ears. And, indeed, many of the plots are moralistic fantasies, often with a *Twilight Zone* flavor. As one Corwin scholar said, "He possessed an unusual ability to mix lofty, Olympian prose with everyday vernacular." Yet he fell short of achieving a vast popular following because, to quote Gilbert Seldes, "he lacked the dramatic instinct to make [characters] single individuals; they were more voices than people."

Nonetheless, Charles Kuralt, one of many broadcasters inspired by Corwin's programs and a man not unlike him in his fondness for all things American, remembered, "They had a book of Corwin's plays in the school library in North Carolina. I read it at thirteen and knew what I wanted to do with my life." Studs Terkel called him "the Bard of radio's Golden Age. It was no contest." And Ray Bradbury added: "Because of him I discovered Whitman, Wolfe and, indirectly, Shakespeare, and Shaw. In sum, he gave me the greatest gift any man can give another: to dare to speak in great tongues." The film director Robert Altman has said, "Anything I know about drama today comes more from Norman Corwin than anybody."

Corwin turned out a prodigious amount of work, from *Columbia Presents Corwin* to *Norman Corwin's Words Without Music,* a Sunday-afternoon series of socially conscious nursery rhymes. "I didn't know what I was getting into," he recalled much later. "I had to turn it out each week: not only conceive it, write it, direct it, and produce it, but get scripts out far enough in advance for an original score to be written. Sometimes I was into my fourth day before an idea or approach would take shape. In such a case I would practically have to turn out the script overnight." Between pages, he would cast, confer, rehearse, and revise. He often worked best when most pressured, revising a script so that, observed one writer, it looked as if it had been written by hand and corrected on the typewriter.

Noting that a TV pilot in 1979 cost about $400,000, Corwin recalled his own freedom on the air thirty-five years before: "Every word that I wrote, every sound effect, every musical score, every production would have been paid for by that pilot two or three times over. [And] some of my productions have had vast mural-size canvases. The most expensive production I ever undertook, which had a big orchestra and a big cast and sound effects and unstinting rehearsal—'unstinting' was like two days—must have cost $20,000 [most of it for ads]. I was on opposite Bob Hope, the number-one show in radio—so I was always hoping against Hope." Against Hope's 40 rating, Corwin drew about an 8.

Yet CBS took such pride in Corwin's shows the network bought double-page ads in *Fortune* to announce a new series, *Thirteen by Corwin,* later collected and published privately by CBS, with original engravings, and sent to government and advertising agencies; Corwin was a great promotional tool for CBS. He noted, "They went to pains. They had pride! It wasn't a bone to a dog. CBS in those days didn't say, 'Would you send us an outline of what you have in mind?' Or they didn't come to me and say, We'd like the program to be this and so, and we want it to appeal to the farmers in Kansas, we want it to be intelligible to a twelve-year-old. None of that. They didn't suggest anything. . . . They never asked, Can you cut down the size of that orchestra? Can we have fewer hours with the sound man in rehearsal?"

Corwin was a visionary. "There are a great many contributing elements to the art of radio," he said. "I use the word *art* very consciously and deliberately. The eye is such a realist. The eye is really the infantile organ. The eye has to be entertained in a way that the ear doesn't. Chases, automobiles hurtling from rooftop to rooftop, the obligatory mayhem that you see on TV—action! action! Whereas the ear is a refined sense. It is through the ear, after all, that we perceive the sublimest of the arts, which is music. We don't see the Beethoven Ninth." In Shakespeare, he noted, "the word has sovereign authority . . . the power to evoke imagery."

WHEN CORWIN ENTERED BROADCASTING in 1938, radio drama was already an established, popular form, but he broke its rigid theatrical mold. His work as a radio editor in Springfield, Massachusetts, rewriting wire stories for the air had taught him the crucial differences between writing for the eye and the ear. "It was a different rhythm—more conversational, simpler, punchier," he explained.

An amateur poet, he was appalled at the gloppy poetry he heard on the air, and volunteered to produce a better version, called *Rhymes and Cadences,* on a local station. It was the talk of Springfield, but Corwin was fired when he questioned a management memo ordering newscasts to cease reporting strikes. His brother got him a job in New York as a film publicist for 20th Century-Fox, and not long after that he convinced an experimental station, WQXR ("The Station for People Who Hate Radio!"), to let him do a show called *Poetic License,* in which he used several forms of poetry that he would later employ in his epic network works—nursery rhyme parodies, satirical verse on drunkenness, odes to the seasons.

An NBC show called *The Magic Key of RCA* invited Corwin to read his wry versions of "Mary Had a Little Lamb," which he recited as a radio commercial, as reported by the *New York Times,* as written by famous poets, and in *Time* magazine style. It was innovative enough to convince CBS's William Lewis to hire him to direct the newly formed *Columbia Workshop*—despite his lack of experience directing anything more than himself and his ignorance about the mysteries of the control booth or of how to put together a complex program. Lewis, hired by William Paley to elevate the network's image, also hired prestige directors like William Robson, Orson Welles, Irving Reis, the poet and playwright Archibald MacLeish, and composer Bernard Herrmann.

After some minor successes, he proposed a show called *Words Without Music,* to which Lewis affixed Corwin's name, flooring the newcomer. Critics praised his unique style, which CBS labeled, for lack of a better description, "vitalized poetry." In producing the works of Sandburg, Whitman, Benet, Edgar Lee Masters, Browning, Bret Harte, Swift, Poe, Woody Guthrie, and W. S. Gilbert, the series soon revealed Corwin's breadth and depth.

His career-making "The Plot to Overthrow Christmas," a whimsical morality play all in verse, is reminiscent of a Dr. Seuss poem, in which the world's meanies (Ivan the Terrible, Lucrezia Borgia, Caligula, Haman, Nero) conspire in hell to do away with Christmas. The piece, which featured Will Geer as the Devil and House Jameson (the head of *The Aldrich Family*) as Santa Claus, was unlike anything on radio. Among its admirers was Ed Murrow, who told Corwin it was the best lyric writing since W. S. Gilbert, further elevating Corwin's status within the CBS hierarchy.

In 1940, CBS's Irving Reis began *The Columbia Workshop,* for the purpose of nurturing new writers, directors, producers, and musicians, among them William Robson, Max Wylie, and Norman Corwin; Wylie later said Corwin "understood radio the first time he tried it." As a radio novice, he wasn't constrained by tradition, and pioneered such

devices as starting a show without a formal "opening," ca
tener's ear with just dialogue or sounds. In his first major
the gate, he created an antifascist piece in blank verse,
Through the Air with the Greatest of Ease," inspired by the Nazis
bombing of Guernica, Spain. It brought him immediate notice. The
New York *Daily News* called it "the best radio play ever written in
America," and *Time* accorded Corwin "a front-row seat among the
radio poets," never a crowded pew.

Corwin's work was outspoken for its time, when, he said, "it was
not yet fashionable to be antifascist," and it was gutsy of CBS to air
it. His biographer, R. LeRoy Bannerman, wrote that Corwin often
"would find himself at the center of various crises, charged with a mission to voice the feelings of the people. . . . He sang the song of America
in Whitmanesque cadences." A Detroit newspaper labeled him POET
WITH A PUNCH. He had, in any case, become the poet's champion.
Later, his verse dramas came to be called "word orchestrations." Arch
Oboler, one of his few peers, called Corwin the only writer in the history of radio he considered a "fine writer." Said Oboler: "I was a melo-
dramatist, he was a poet." Corwin's epic themes were an exploration of
the American experience, and the titles indicate their tone and sweep
and variety, such as "Pursuit of Happiness," which included everything
from a Paul Robeson ballad to a Robert Benchley piece on helping his
wife buy clothes to a Carl Van Doren portrait of Benjamin Franklin to
an essay on snake oil.

Corwin wanted to rediscover America on the air. He once devised a
kind of American fugue composed of random sounds picked up coast
to coast. First would be "the bells of the nation" from bells ringing out
on a buoy off the coast of Maine, to the Liberty Bell bongs, to a small-
town church bell, to mission bells of California. For a segment on "the
pulse of the nation," he imagined putting the nation's collective ear to
clocks from sea to shining sea—the wristwatch on Burgess Meredith's
arm, the giant tick-tock of the biggest clock in America, the clicks
inside a Chicago traffic light.

He seemed capable of anything, no matter the subject or mood,
whether dark or light, highbrow or low-, spiritual or irreverent. He
once created a wicked satire on national crazes, show business, and
hype in an unlikely fantasy called "My Client Curley," about a dancing

caterpillar who becomes a star overnight. Just when his agents worry that the furry worm is washed up, he turns into a butterfly to the tune of "Yes, Sir, That's My Baby." (This show was reborn as the Cary Grant–Janet Blair movie *Once Upon a Time*.) Corwin could charm audiences as well as inspire them; one critic said "a pixie [was] running wild" at CBS.

He was as much preacher as pixie, capable of a trilogy on the Bible or a program like "Descent of the Gods," with Henry Morgan as the God of Trivia. And he was a born showman. His "Pursuit of Happiness" featured, apart from journeyman radio actors, Jimmy Durante, Gene Autry, Betty Comden and Adolph Green, Ethel Merman, Abbott and Costello, Ethel Barrymore, Danny Kaye, and Bert Lahr. He did a show about a hillbilly harmonica player, "Lip Service," using Larry Adler. His "Mary and the Fairy" was a wry fantasy about a working girl who wins five wishes in a promotional contest for the Crinkly-Crunkly Bread Company, with Ruth Gordon and Elsa Lanchester. Sound essays, mystery parodies, patriotic paeans, musicals—the scripts poured out of him week after week for a decade—a reminder of the vast lost potential of radio.

The deadline pressures were helpful, he now realizes: "The beauty of a live production that has to be accomplished, start to finish, is that there is no time for intrigues, for the artistic shenanigans that too often occur when you have a production that runs over weeks and months. We had five to eight hours of rehearsal time for a half-hour broadcast."

It was war, however, that really created Corwin, whose vigor and inspirational temperament were perfectly in sync with the need to infuse America with passion and conviction. His timing wasn't bad, either: "We Hold These Truths," his landmark program to celebrate the 150th anniversary of the signing of the Bill of Rights, was aired a week after Pearl Harbor. On December 7, 1941, he was writing the script on a train to California when a porter told him about the Japanese bombing. He persuaded some of the country's best actors to participate, and the fervor of the time was again on his side: It would have been unpatriotic for an actor not to enlist with Corwin in his endeavors. He recruited people like Corporal James Stewart to narrate the show, along with Walter Huston, Edward G. Robinson, Lionel Barrymore, Marjorie Main, Rudy Vallee, Edward Arnold, and Orson

Welles, who called "We Hold These Truths" "one of the greatest scripts ever written for radio."

After Bernard Herrmann's overture, and cast self-introductions, Elliott Lewis recited a passage that is vintage Corwin: "One hundred fifty years is not long in the reckoning of a hill. But to a man it's long enough./One hundred fifty years is a weekend to a redwood tree, but to a man it's two full lifetimes./One hundred fifty years is a twinkle to a star, but to a man it's time enough to teach six generations what the meaning is of Liberty, how to use it, when to fight for it!" The show paid off in other ways: Corwin's price doubled and MGM's head of production, Dore Schary, was impressed enough to offer him a two-thousand-dollar-a-week contract, four times his CBS salary. But Corwin opted to stay in radio, where the freedom to write and produce what he wished, as he wished, he prized above money.

Corwin confronted wartime issues. Other shows, from comedies to sitcoms to soap operas, might make references or appeals, but as his biographer noted, "the steel-trap, hard-line, brutally frank approach to the cruel realities of the war was missing." The opening show in the wartime series began, "What we say tonight has to do with blood and with love and with anger, and also with a big job in the making. Laughter can wait. Soft music can have the evening off. No one is invited to sit down and take it easy. Later, later. There's a war on."

Corwin had become a one-man government agency, producing "America Salutes the President's Birthday Party" with Bing Crosby, Fibber McGee and Molly, and Dick Powell, and then a kind of one-man Voice of America. A show beamed to England, "Transatlantic Call," took Britons on a tour of the Midwest. He produced a star-studded pep talk for bond drives called "There Will Be Time Later," warning Americans against complacency on the eve of victory. Another, "The Long Name None Could Spell," told of Czechoslovakia's fall to Hitler. Other Corwin originals included a fantasia called "You Can Dream," about a dentist who finds himself peering into the mouth of a patient who looks like Adolf Hitler; a series dramatizing the undramatic lives of an elevator operator, a secretary, and a radio announcer; a version of Frank Sullivan's "Cliché Expert" with songs by Comden and Green; and "New York: A Tapestry for Radio," which included this funny, inspired stage direction to the sound crew: "an introduction descriptive of the annoyance of Fifth Avenue at having to cross Broadway in full view of 23rd Street."

His end-of-war masterwork, "On a Note of Triumph," opened in classic Corwin style, as narrated by Martin Gabel: "So they've given up!/They're finally done in, and the rat is dead in an alley back of the Wilhelmstrasse/Take a bow, GI./Take a bow, little guy/The superman of tomorrow lies at the feet of you common men of this afternoon/This is it, kid, this is the day, all the way from Newburyport to Vladivostok." Most critics praised it, but *Newsweek* thought it "better propaganda than art"—the old Corwin bugaboo. The *New York Times* filed a "minority report," and the poet Bernard De Voto called it "dull, windy, opaque, pretentious, false" and "saccharine," not to mention "cheap," "commonplace," and "vulgar."

Corwin was, by now, a public figure, but the specter of TV had begun to loom. Corwin's career, like radio itself, began its long, slow, sad decline. There was no more room in the log for "sustaining" programs, no matter how award-bedecked and soul-stirring. The accountants were running the show(s) by 1947, the date of Corwin's final major CBS piece, "One World Flight." Afterward, he took his own listeners' poll of what people wanted to hear, and reported, "They want more disc jockeys. What's radio coming to?"

Radio had fallen into the hands of not just DJs but congressional witch-hunters like J. Parnell Thomas, who first went after Reds in the movies and then turned his attention to Commies behind the mike. Corwin joined a resistance group called Committee for the First Amendment and produced "Hollywood Fights Back," a star-studded response to HUAC with some of filmland's leading liberals espousing freedom of speech. Corwin avoided the blacklist, despite his blatant one-worldism, probably saved by his patriotic wartime programs. After leaving CBS, he headed a special-projects unit at the United Nations, for which he wrote a piece called "Citizen of the World" and a six-part series, *The Pursuit of Peace.* HUAC claimed he belonged to some 150 Communist-front organizations, and it tried to nail him for his 1945 show entitled "Set Your Clock at U235" questioning the use of the atomic bomb, which was later read by Fredric March at a Madison Square Garden rally attended by such suspicious types as Helen Keller. He was cited in *Red Channels,* but Corwin shrugged off the yapping Red-baiters with a few defiant words: "I am not a Communist. I am not a fellow traveler. But I do have a contempt for irresponsible smear lists, whether issued by career crackpots or 'chicken-little' agents." He was called to testify before McCarthy, but after fifteen minutes of questioning the hearing ended and Corwin was dismissed from further appearances.

Brushed by the blacklist but never tarred, he later commented: "The postwar witch-hunt blunted my career but not as seriously as it did others'. I was on a gray list more than a black list. . . . I had a lot of gravel thrown in my face, but I was much luckier than others . . . I wasn't kicked out of radio, as so many were, because radio had kicked itself out by that time. I left CBS over a contractual dispute."

Apart from political scares, William Paley had been diverted from his high-minded aims to pursue the lowly dollar. Over lunch on a train to New York, Corwin found himself in an uneasy discussion with Paley, who grumbled over his salad that radio was "getting tougher," and added ominously, "Well, you know you've done epic things that are appreciated by us and by a special audience, but we've got to face up to the fact that we're in a commercial business. Couldn't you write for a broader public?"

Strange words for a man to hear who had made his reputation writing about the common man, but Paley was worried that the common man wasn't tuning in. Furthermore, the network wanted 50 percent of all commercial gains from the shows, which hurt, shocked, and depressed Corwin, who four years earlier had written a worried and (by late 1990s hindsight) prescient letter to an executive explaining why the network owed it to listeners to air unsponsored shows. In it, Corwin seemed to be arguing for CBS's soul: "The achievement which has most distinguished CBS from its chief rival has never been a sponsored comedian, or a variety show, or a mystery yarn, but the use it has made of its sustaining time—the *Workshop,* MacLeish, Shakespeare, Welles, Corwin, Murrow, *Philharmonic,* etc. . . . I am not one of those who spits kerosene on commercial radio. It is mainly good, it pays the bills, it makes it possible to bring Brahms and MacLeish and Chungking direct to the public. I am not sorry that we are making more and more money and selling more and more time—I rejoice in that. I am just sorry that along the way we may well lose the very stuff that made CBS what it is, a network of character."

By now, Corwin had defected to theater, TV, and movies, none of which came to much until he wrote the screenplay of *Lust for Life*, which won him an Oscar nomination. He also wrote *The Naked Maja*, with Ava Gardner, but was so unhappy with the film about Goya that he tried to get his name taken off it. Dispirited, he declined a chance to write the screenplay of *All the King's Men*. Movies never held much interest for him—not just the form, but the procedure itself. He found that the movies' "assembly line psychology" drained him. He gladly returned to CBS for a new series, on which the opening show was, of course, a satire of Hollywood.

For Broadway, he put together *The World of Carl Sandburg*, depicting the poet's life through his work, starring Bette Davis and Gary Merrill, but it ran only twenty-nine performances. Finally, inevitably, reluctantly, Corwin turned to TV in the 1960s, writing two programs of a twenty-six-part biography of FDR, a ninety-minute documentary, "Inside the Movie Kingdom," and a syndicated series on the oceans, *Seven Seas*. Westinghouse revived a dramatic anthology under its radio name, *Norman Corwin Presents*, and for Stanley Kramer he wrote a documentary, "Judgment," on the U.S. war crimes trial and the hanging of a Japanese general. He reworked old scripts for the stage and wrote a few new ones, such as *Cervantes*, which starred Richard Kiley, the original musical "Man of La Mancha." Some critics cried plagiarism.

Corwin became little more than a fading presence. In 1955, when CBS was about to dump shelves of Corwin radio shows, crudely labeled "air checks," he was alerted in time to rescue his *Columbia Workshop* shows from extinction. In his post-radio career, he has staged readings of his plays, written three books on pop culture—*Overkill and Megalove, Holes in a Stained Glass Window, Trivializing America*—and has continued to teach a course in radio production at UCLA into his late eighties as well as writing new works for NPR.

As for radio's future, he once said, "If it is to truly exist it must be worthy of its existence." Another time, he remarked, "Poets and teachers often thanked me 'for contributing to public awareness and appreciation of poetry'—a sort of midwifery, I suppose. But broadcasting can do a great deal for poetry, and vice versa. Too bad the telephone oracle and the singing commercial have preempted Frost, Benet, and others, including myself." Of radio itself, he misses now mainly "the camaraderie. The pride CBS took in its cultural accomplishments, the sense of eagerness to do good work, to expand artistic frontiers, to rush in where fools and NBC feared to tread." Of his own landmark contributions, he has remarked: "I was lucky enough to be part of a breaking wave at the full tide of radio's creativity. I like to think I ran up the shore a little way in helping the medium reach its high-water mark."

Since that time—those dozen dazzling years—Norman Corwin has been cherished, honored, praised, and draped with medals and awards of every kind by the medium that once decided, on the eve of its creative collapse, that it could do without him.

— 22 —
CRUNCH, CREAK, CRASH, WHOOSH, WHAM, AND WHOO-OOOO

SOUND EFFECTS WERE WHAT MANY RADIO SHOWS were really all about, and the sound men were the medium's great unsung heroes, who engaged the imagination almost as much as the adventures themselves—the Industrial Light & Magic miracle workers of their time. Tom Hanley, Bill James, Don Wingate, Eugene Twombly, Ross Murray, Berne Surrey, Ray Kemper, Frank Pittman, Keene Crockett, Charlie Forsyth, Wayne Kenworthy, Bud Tollefson, Terry Ross, Len Wright, Robert Mott, and Ray Erlenborn were among the most creative minds, hands, feet, and mouths in radio.

How sound men—there was only one prominent sound woman (Ora Nichols), plus a couple of girls, Sallie Belle Cox and Madeleine Pierce, who did bawling babies—could create sounds with such exact precision from a few simple household items fascinated listeners; it does still. For the crunch of shoes walking through snow, they would squeeze a handful of cornstarch; a balloon full of birdshot sounded like crashing thunder; a toilet plunger in a tank of water was a man falling overboard; a flapping glove became a bird on the wing; a speeding train was somehow reproduced by scraping a wire brush across tin; clinking ice cubes in a drink were created by tapping two flashbulbs together; fistfights were done by a man smacking his fist into the opposite palm so that the blows were in sync with the actors' grunts.

Mel Blanc, who knew from vocal effects, described the work of the sound men as a kind of controlled pandemonium: "During showtime, the sound-effects man resembled the Hindu god Shiva, appearing to have four arms in constant motion, creating thunder by violently shaking a piece of sheet metal, while simultaneously cueing up the next effects platter." Frank Pittman, the man responsible for creating the legendary jumble that went down in history as Fibber McGee's closet, over the years devised endless variations on his classic sound gag, at last topping each cascade of junk with a tinkling bell; often, nothing would

Overleaf: Sound-effects man Bud Tollefson and Fibber McGee's famous closet

happen for seconds when the door was opened, keeping listeners on the edge of their seats.

George Burns credited Jack Benny with integrating sounds into radio comedy, to give his show more dramatic texture, rather than just using noises like nightclub rim shots for explosive effect. Benny took weeks to find just the right sound of him strolling on the sidewalk in his neighborhood. Eugene Twombly of the Benny show worked with each cast member to create a distinct set of footsteps, experimenting with concrete slabs, blocks of wood, and makes and sizes of shoes. "Simulating footsteps," noted Blanc, "evolved into a veritable art form." Said one ex-sound man, "Footsteps have their own emotional context. Those of a woman walking off in a huff have a different sound and rhythm than they do if she is strolling or nervously pacing a hospital corridor awaiting the outcome of her lover's operation." He added, "A good sound-effects 'performer' did not deliver these sounds mechanically. He often literally put on a woman's shoes. If it was a horse, he became the horse, slapping his chest for a gallop, changing rhythm for a canter, using coconut shells for a slow trot or pawing the ground—and throwing in an occasional whinny or snort for good measure."

Sound men were often better paid than the actors. Because of the early network ban against recorded effects, a sound man in the 1930s working on a daily show could make ten thousand dollars a year simply by reproducing a wolf howl. Such a man was the aptly named Bradley Barker, who specialized in animal noises and scampered between several shows a day howling, growling, barking, wailing, and trumpeting; Barker lives on to this day as the roar of MGM's Leo the Lion, and he doubled as Pathé newsreel's crowing rooster. Donald Bain, another animal whiz, promoted himself in a brochure. "If you don't see what you want here, ask for it." When someone asked for a parrot, Bain asked, "Male or female?" He could mimic a dying mosquito and a catfight with three cats; some sound men were deft enough to mimic two people talking at once.

Music was a vital color in the sound man's palette. The theme music to *The Lone Ranger* and other programs provided audiences, especially kids, with their first (perhaps only) music appreciation course. Ferde Grofé's "On the Trail" from his *Grand Canyon* Suite is still remembered as the Philip Morris theme, with its restful, swaying, clippity-clop of donkeys descending into the canyon. Other shows used symphonic pieces (Saint-Saen's "Omphale's Spinning Wheel" for *The Shadow,* Sibelius's "Valse Triste" for *I Love a Mystery,* the march from Prokofiev's *The Love for Three Oranges* for *This Is Your FBI*), mainly because they often were in the public domain. Even so, the notion of scoring a western with a Rossini overture seems unusually inspired; after *The Lone Ranger,* it may never be possible to listen to the overture from *William Tell* for itself again.

Early on, orchestras played in studios separated from the performers. By the late 1930s, more economical, flexible Hammond organs took over and made life easier; an organist could expand or squeeze time by playing longer or shorter to cover, but an organ was the telltale sound of a low-budget operation—soaps, westerns, mysteries. Nonetheless, organists were capable of striking chords to suggest a vast emotional range of guiding lights, secret storms, and suspense. An organist might make a bold attempt to sound bouncy, but it was always a stretch. Radio organists—such stalwarts as Ann Leaf (nicknamed "Little Organ Annie"), Charles Paul, Bill Meeder, Rosa Rio, Paul Taubman, and Gaylord Carter—were at their most eloquent when they were heartrending. It's hard for anyone raised on radio to hear an organ, whether beautifully played or at a baseball game, without thinking of an overwrought Stella Dallas moaning about her ungrateful daughter, Laurel, or of a terrified character on *Suspense* pleading for mercy.

Rosa Rio, like many radio organists, had begun in movie theaters accompanying silent films on a Wurlitzer until the talkies put her and her colleagues out of business. Playing live organ over the air required an equally facile hand—the ability to improvise, fill, and change tempo in an instant with a "sting" or a bridge—not to mention having a vast repertoire of melodies to call upon to play a punning title on comedy and quiz shows. Organists, like actors, were forever flitting from show to show. Rio worked half a dozen programs a day in the 1940s, dashing from *My True Story* to *Mystery Chef* to *Ethel and Albert* to *Lorenzo Jones* to *Front Page Farrell.* "Rehearsal time was most limited and, in many cases, nonexistent," Rio recalled. "We had to roll with the punches. There was always an element of uncertainty in every situation. A radio organist had to be nimble of finger and fleet of foot to cope with the unexpected," such as directors indicating eight seconds of music only to suddenly cut that in half. "That happened many times on the air," Rio said. "An organist had to keep an eye on the script, director, actors, and clock all at once"—as did the sound men.

Aside from studio organists, networks and stations maintained vast libraries of recorded musical bridges that linked dramatic scenes. New York's WOR, reported Leonard Maltin, had some six thousand bridges with labels like "Wistful Yearning," "Ye Old English Countryside but Something Is Amiss," "There's a Face in the Window," "Quick! Follow That Car," "Marital Rifts," "Brotherly Love, Better World," "Big City," "Bigger City," "Slow Taxicab in a Traffic Jam," "Things Are Looking Up," and "Menacing Humor"—and even one labeled "Mommie! Mommie! Mommie! Daddy's Suitcase Is Gone!"

Mel Blanc's unique career straddled Warner Bros. cartoons and radio's comedy shows, where he was a staple of *The Jack Benny Program* and *The Judy Canova Show* (on which he once played seven characters on one program), but he popped up all over the dial in countless character roles, also as animals, automobiles, and other supposedly nonhuman phenomena. On a typical Sunday night during the 1944–45 season, Blanc performed on *The Jack Benny Program, The Great Gildersleeve, The Baby Snooks Show,* and *Blondie,* plus occasional appearances with Burns and Allen (as the dismal Happy Postman), on *Fibber McGee and Molly,* Abbott and Costello, Eddie Cantor, *Amos 'n' Andy,* and major variety shows. He also specialized in comic Mexicans.

No one starts out in life as a sound man (master sound man Ray Erlinborn once wondered aloud, "Why would anyone spend his whole life playing with toys?"), but Ray Kemper comes close. Kemper spent two decades as a sound-effects hand, after getting nowhere as a would-be actor and announcer. While working in the mail room at KHJ in Los Angeles, a Mutual outlet, the eighteen-year-old Kemper won an announcing audition in 1942 just in time to go into the service. When he came out in 1946, there were no announcing jobs left at the station so he took a vacancy on the sound staff.

At Mutual, he created sound for adventure shows like *Let George Do It, Johnny Madero, Pier 23, Voyage of the Scarlet Queen,* and *The Count of Monte Cristo,* for which he wrote a few scripts. He worked on *Suspense* and *The Jack Benny Program,* and had occasional gigs on *Amos 'n' Andy, The Whistler,* and others, but says, "Of all my sound effects days, *Gunsmoke* was my joy." When he began, recalls Kemper, "[producer-director] Norm Macdonnell told me he wanted this show to be a departure from anything else. He said, 'You'll be as much a part of this show as any actor.' Because he wanted to go for realism, we got time to build sound effects."

Kemper explains, "Until people like [actor-director] Elliott Lewis, Tony Ellis, Jaime del Valle, and particularly Norm took over, sound was kind of a bastard child. It was indicated [in the script] and then it was, 'Get out of the way and don't bother me.' The far-seeing people knew there was a great value [in good sound]. The voices and the actors furthered the drama, but the sound effects painted the picture." Most sound effects were live, but all outdoor night sounds—crickets, wind, storms—were recorded. "Good sound-effects people always do as many effects live as possible."

On one show he had to devise a distinction between the sound of beer and whiskey being poured. "We ended up using plain water, which has a hard sound, for whiskey, and warm soda pop for beer, because the bubbles give it a fuzzy, softer sound." He recalls a director known as a stickler for accuracy, William Robson. "He was a bit of a stinker to work for," Kemper laughs. "With Bill Robson, if the script called for the rattle of onionskin paper, you'd better damn well have onionskin paper." Sound men got used to the whims of demanding directors like Orson Welles, who once re-created the caverns of Paris in *Les Misérables* using the men's room walls.

Robert L. Mott, in his book on sound effects, told about a sound man who, asked to reproduce a train, demanded to know if the train was running or idling, express or freight, fast or slow, or steam or diesel. Likewise, the surface someone was walking, riding, or galloping across was crucial, and whether a crowd was angry, excited, or joyous. It was a far cry from the early days of radio sound, when a gunshot was produced by slapping a clapboard together and a shaking slab of tin had to approximate crashing thunder.

Once, short of time during a showdown scene, Macdonnell told Kemper, "Ray, just make that seven steps walking instead of twenty-one." Kemper, the purist, resisted: "Norm, he walked twenty-one steps going and he's gonna walk twenty-one steps coming back." Kemper won. "I think he cut a line instead."

Some sound men were better "step men" than others. Kemper could always tell a good step man by how consistent the steps were going up and down a flight of stairs. "Some sound men would do steps going up and down the same way," he explains. But a true sound artisan knows it's really *toe-heel, toe-heel* descending and *slide-slide, slide-slide* ascending. Some effects were indicated in great detail in a script, but many others were left to the sound man's whim, turning him into an amateur inventor tinkering endlessly to achieve the correct effect. "We built stuff as we went along, because we were always experimenting and trying to fake people out."

Being a sound man was filled with frustrations, for sounds—by nature elastic—tended to be expendable and normally were the first thing cut when a show ran a few seconds long. "They'd set up sound effects and then they'd cut them out during rehearsal," says Kemper. On comedy shows, sound effects were often removed, or muted, once the sound was established, so as not to interfere with a laugh or a line; cutting off laughs with a sound was a cardinal offense. Often, the frantic scurrying of sound men drew its own unintentional in-studio laughs, which accounts for some of those unexplained guffaws on comedy shows. Eventually screens kept studio audiences from watching or giggling at the sound men; sometimes effects were demonstrated to audiences before airtime, to prevent inappropriate laughter.

Kemper's greatest challenge came on *Gunsmoke,* where he and Tom Hanley spent weeks helping to create a realistic gunshot unlike the dead-sounding blanks of most westerns. "Gunshots had been a bogeyman since I started in 1946. We tried everything, even an echo chamber. It was terrible. It was nothing." It sounded more like a cap pistol than a six-shooter. In-studio shots were too loud for the mike because of something called a limiter, which protects a sound system from overly loud noise, so Kemper and Hanley spent two days in the desert with an arsenal of firearms to record the best gunshot imaginable, without luck. "The shots didn't have any bounce"—again, because "the limiter clips the sound and you lose the whole middle range, the guts, of the gun shot." Finally, in actor William Conrad's backyard in Laurel Canyon, they hit upon the magic bullet. Conrad's yard formed a natural amphitheater and created ideal acoustics for the perfect gunshot—a booming .45 blast that became the sound of *Gunsmoke* gunplay thereafter. "Those gunshots became the criteria," says Kemper, still proud of his creation. "Everybody else stole them."

A few of Kemper's other prized sounds were a baby-making machine he concocted for a science fiction show (a series of popping corks did the trick, suggesting infants popping off an assembly line) and, perhaps his second finest moment—or at least his favorite story— re-creating ten thousand drunk chickens. Kemper overdubbed a record- ing of clucking chickens with the sound of himself and partner Bill James hiccupping, speeded it up, and, to fool the director into thinking there actually *was* a recording of ten thousand tipsy fowl, slapped an official CBS label on the disc, and neatly printed on it 10,000 DRUNK CHICKENS.

Sound men were low down on the totem pole. "Until *Gunsmoke,* we always felt we deserved more credit than we got," says Kemper. He and Hanley were the first sound men to receive credit, after which other shows followed suit. Macdonnell also made good on his promise to treat sound men like actors by paying them not only for their sound work but as performers. "We'd do a few walla-wallas every show and he'd give us an actor's check." A "walla-walla" is radioese for crowd noises (*"walla-walla-walla-walla"*); Kemper adds with pride that there were no recorded crowd noises on *Gunsmoke.* Jack Benny also gave sound men an extra-actor's check. They earned the money, however, for sound men often did speak, via vocal effects. Kemper's specialty was cooing turtledoves, dogs, hens, and snorting horses; he could never do a whinnying horse, a separate talent. Mice were re-created by rapidly rubbing a wet cork over glass.

Watching a sound man in action reveals what a physically demand- ing, labor-intensive, and split-second job it is—timing a specific sound to occur at a precise moment, followed a second later with a very differ- ent, perhaps louder or more modulated, sound, everything timed to fit seamlessly into the action without calling attention to itself. "You become the actor's arms and legs," says Kemper. "I always felt we were actors, too—we just weren't vocal about it."

The effects crew would get a script about a week ahead of time and, then, prior to going on the air, load up all their equipment from a sound room that resembled Fibber McGee's closet and wheel it to the studio.

Bill Gordon, a writer for *The Cisco Kid,* liked to work close to deadline, and Kemper recalls, laughing, "You have no idea how many times we went on the air live and, while we were doing the first act, Bill was typing a stencil and running it off on a mimeograph. Then he would run in with the last pages as we were going. Sweat was running down Jack Mather [Cisco] and Harry Lang's [Pancho] foreheads. But he never missed a show."

Many effects, like gunshots, didn't sound authentic when simply recorded—rain, for example, which was re-created by running water under pressure through straw and then down a drainpipe. A rattlesnake's hiss sounds like escaping steam, but a sound man found a way to evoke it by taking the shell of a doorbell, attaching the buzzer to a cellophane bag, and then pressing the buzzer. "You'll have a reptile hiss that will make you jump right out of your chair!" he said. *Let's Pretend,* the kids' show, challenged CBS sound wizards to devise noises for fantastical things like flying carpets and shimmering moonbeams.

Radio lore is dotted with tales of botched sound effects, and Kemper has his own favorites, like the time a dam broke on an episode of *Straight Arrow,* and in place of rushing water, listeners heard the sound of twittering birds. If a sound man blew it in the pretape era, the entire segment had to be redone. When somebody new to *Inner Sanctum* mistakenly "fixed" its famous squeaking door by oiling it, sound man Terry Ross had to improvise the squeaky hinge with his voice.

That most famous of all sound effects—galloping hooves—was indeed created by dried-out coconut halves, with two holes drilled in the side for a strap attached to the sound man's wrist; each man had his own set of coconut shells. A so-called hoof box was a shallow eighteen-by-four-inch box filled with sand, dirt, a few pebbles and, just before air time, sprinkled with water to produce, says Kemper. "a nice clean dirt sound."

If nobody sets out to be a sound man, few also end up as one. "Our breed is dying out," notes Kemper, who, after *Gunsmoke,* became a music editor for a Rosemary Clooney–Bing Crosby show, then went into TV as a music mixer for Judy Garland and other shows. From 1963 until 1980, Kemper was a TV audio engineer and, although television finally bored him into retirement, his vivid sound waves survive.

— 23 —
THE UNSEEN AUDIENCE

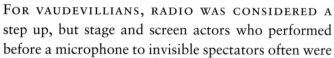

"I've done some pretty good acting for a buck and a half."

— PARLEY BAER

FOR VAUDEVILLIANS, RADIO WAS CONSIDERED A step up, but stage and screen actors who performed before a microphone to invisible spectators often were regarded like actors in TV movies today. Unless it was a prestige show like *The Lux Radio Theatre,* a guest shot on *The Jack Benny Program,* or a featured role on a series like *Suspense,* they were thought to be slumming, out for a fast paycheck, or doing hack work. But radio proved to be a mother lode for actors who had the style and the flexible vocal cords that allowed them to move from show to show, type to type, age to age, nationality to nationality, even race to race—often playing several roles at once while awaiting a movie or Broadway job. It was regular work, a lucrative living, and a godsend during the Depression.

Best of all, radio was visually an equal-opportunity employer. Many a homely, fat, or balding actor and dumpy or aging actress could play characters twenty years younger, taller, or slimmer. The classic case was that of squat, rotund William Conrad's gruff, macho Matt Dillon on *Gunsmoke.* Conrad sounded the way James Arness looked on TV. Conversely, pretty actresses could portray dowdy dowagers (Anne Elstner's Stella Dallas, say), and dashing leading men were handily recast as village crackpots, like handsome Carl Swenson's dotty inventor Lorenzo Jones.

Perhaps the most happily overworked actor of all was Marvin Miller, radio's man of a thousand voices, who finally came into his own on TV in *The Millionaire.* Miller not only played just about every show on the air, large or small, but frequently doubled as announcer or host, as many actors did. Radio was an incredibly democratic creative medium: actors directed, sound men wrote, announcers acted, writers produced. In *The Big Broadcast,* a Who's Who of radio, Miller has eighty-six entries after his name in the index. Under *Backstage Wife* alone, he bags four credits.

Others who worked everywhere included the mellifluously named

Facing page: The NBC Times Square studio in New York

Olan Soulé, who for ten years costarred with Barbara Luddy on *The First Nighter Program;* Les Tremayne, her other longtime costar; Raymond Edward Johnson (one of three Raymonds, the chillingly cheerful greeter on *Inner Sanctum*); Elliott Lewis, radio's renaissance man, who did dramatic roles, comedy parts, and also wrote and directed, called by many fellow actors the best of them all ("He could break your heart with a word," said actor E. Jack Neuman); and Alan Reed (aka Teddy Bergman). The major troupers also included Lurene Tuttle, Frank Lovejoy, Alan Frees (who later found semifame as the voice of TV's Fred Flintstone), Hans Conried (called by Gale Gordon "an actor-holic—Hans's idea of heaven would be to do a play that had thirty characters, men and women, and do them all"), Charlotte Manson, Ford Bond, Joan Alexander, Staats Cotsworth, Clayton (Bud) Collyer, Betty Lou Gerson, Mary Jane Higby, James Meighan, Santos Ortega, Jackson Beck, Beryl Vaughn, Virginia Dwyer, and Verna Felton, who specialized in battleaxes.

Many of them never found a starring niche, in radio or anywhere else (and many superb featured actors went uncredited on shows for years) but their names continue to ring a faint bell, and an occasional loud one—Macdonald Carey and Agnes Moorehead, for instance, as active in radio as they later became in films, not to mention the roster of movie stars-to-be who started behind a radio mike playing every sort of role: Shirley Booth, Don Ameche, Van Heflin, Dorothy McGuire, Gary Merrill, Dane Clark, Martin Gabel, Paul Ford, Richard Widmark, Edward Everett Horton, Burgess Meredith, Art Carney, Jose Ferrer, Paul Douglas, Howard Duff, and Mercedes McCambridge, to skim a few off the top. Widmark, the original "Front Page Farrell," once said: "I was probably the first actor to leave a house with a swimming pool to go to Hollywood." Cotsworth, a mainstay of radio drama, abandoned a respectable Broadway career playing opposite Eva LeGallienne, Maurice Evans, Judith Anderson, and Flora Robson for the financial security of *Casey, Crime Photographer* and *The Second Mrs. Burton.* He unashamedly called radio his life insurance. Actors like Frank Nelson were kept so busy in radio that they decided it just wasn't worth the hassle of scrambling for films. People in recurring roles felt obligated to turn up every week and didn't want to risk quitting a bread-and-butter part for a single movie job; commuting between a movie and a regular radio show was too tough.

For free-lance radio actors, according to *When a Girl Marries* lead Mary Jane Higby, the work was plentiful and almost around-the-clock; most shows were recorded twice live, once for each coast, doubling the actors' salary. The more prolific performers spent their days scampering from NBC to CBS to Mutual, which often required split-second timing, missed rehearsals, good luck and, in Manhattan, short-cuts through St. Patrick's Cathedral.

One busy actor, Matt Crowley—Dr. Brent on *Road of Life,* Jim on *Jungle Jim,* an announcer on *Pretty Kitty Kelly,* and John on *John's Other Wife*—would start work at 9 A.M. with a run-through for *John's Other Wife* at NBC, hire a stand-in to complete the rehearsal so he could grab a cab to *Pretty Kitty Kelly* at CBS, then hustle back to NBC for the East Coast repeat broadcast of *John's Other Wife.* At 10:14 A.M.—wearing his hat and coat—he would make his final announcement on the *Kitty Kelly* serial, rush out the door to a waiting elevator, tear two blocks to 50th Street, where a taxi, which stood with its motor running, would drive him a long block to Sixth Avenue, at which point he would leap from the cab and hoof it the rest of the way to the RCA Building and up another waiting elevator to the eighth floor for *John's Other Wife,* which went on the air at 10:15. More than one actor on a tight deadline hired an ambulance (it was legal then) to speed his way from one job to another; in one case, an actor recalls earning $1 for an appearance on *The Story of Myrt and Marge* that paid him $23, minus $15 for an ambulance, $5 for a rehearsal stand-in, and $2 to elevator operators to hold the door. In Richard Widmark's words, "It was a great life, but you had to be young to do it."

Moreover, radio didn't require a big investment for actors. They didn't need an agent and could make their own calls; casting agents were still relatively rare. On the other hand, radio actors (before they formed a union) could be written out of a show during rehearsals and never get paid. More benevolent producers found ways to shoehorn hard-up actors into shows, like the time Mercedes McCambridge needed rent money and Himan Brown wrote her in as an elevator operator.

Some actors were so busy working several shows that they would forget about the repeat broadcast a few hours later, go home, or wind up drunk in a nearby saloon. In such emergencies, they were rescued by colleagues who could mimic other characters—Art Carney was among the best—with listeners none the wiser. Hans Conried was a regular standby on Rudy Vallee's show for the often soused John Barrymore.

Actors seeking parts would congregate each morning in the third-floor lounge at NBC in Rockefeller Center, much like dock workers for the morning work lineup or a scene out of backstage movie musicals where the actor ambushes the producer on his way through the waiting room ("Anything for me in your next show, Mr. Ziegfeld?"). Or they would hang out at a favorite drugstore, bar, coffee shop, or poolroom and wait for their service to call.

Mary Jane Croft—who was married for thirty-one years to Elliott Lewis—says she never felt any rivalry with other actresses. "Oddly enough, it wasn't competitive. There was very little envy in radio. That's what was so wonderful. It was such fun every day just to come in and see people you knew—almost like a party. Well, we were young and in confined quarters, working so closely together. There was no ego in radio, because we were faceless. The work was not that hard. TV was work, but radio was fun. Of course, we never realized it at the time. Radio was a lovely, lovely lost world."

Radio acting required a specialized technique. Croft recalls, "Whenever a [motion] picture person came on, they were floored by our ability to do it. Movie people were not that fast. They would always say, 'How do you do this?' Movie stars were usually nervous, fidgeting and fumbling with their scripts, and kind of afraid they wouldn't be as good as the radio actors. Radio required a strange facility. Once you learned it, you got so you could grab the character immediately, whether it was a black person or a French person or whatever. We all had lots of voices. It's like jazz, like music—you needed a good ear." Parley Baer added, "The ability to fade in, fade out, or drop the voice was tantamount to an entrance or exit" onstage.

The only show Croft had less than rosy memories of was *Lights Out.* "I didn't enjoy working for Arch Oboler. It was never a happy atmosphere. He was not a fun man to be around, but then the shows he did were also dark and gloomy." Likewise, the intimidating presence at rehearsal of the soap-opera writing-producing team of Frank and Anne Hummert. If you displeased the Hummerts, you might be wise to consider a new line of work. They frowned on clowning around, late arrivals, or a breath of scandal, but when they liked an actor there were no more loyal employers; the couple slid their favorite actors from serial to serial like floating bars of Ivory soap.

For actors who took their craft seriously, radio was both a challenge and a continuing frustration. The work felt constrained and one-dimensional even to those who considered radio drama the equal of theater or films, but for just that reason radio demanded totally new and different performing skills—a dramatic shorthand that could give the outline of a character or a scene in a few bold brushstrokes and allow the listener to fill in the blanks, the details, and the colors. Directors would tell Parley Baer (Chester on "Gunsmoke"), "Just do your regular hillbilly." Orson Welles earned quick and easy money as a multivoiced radio character actor at $18.50 a job, eventually pulling down a tidy $1,500 a week—"skipping nimbly," he once recalled, "from one soap opera to another," often without bothering to rehearse. "I'd come to a bad end in some tearjerker on the seventh floor of CBS and rush up to the ninth (they'd hold an elevator for me), where, just as the red light was going on, somebody'd hand me a script and whisper, 'Chinese mandarin, seventy-five years old,' and off I'd go again."

Radio actors learned to make quick emotional shifts from scene to scene without the luxury of a day between movie scenes, or exits and intermissions between stage scenes. Actor/announcer Harry Bartell, a regular on *Sherlock Holmes, Nero Wolfe,* and other shows, said, "More than anything, live radio was stimulating and horribly challenging. You were working without a net." Elliott Lewis recalled the intense concentration involved, especially when last-minute cuts were needed as lines were hastily slashed and new ones inserted. "It's easy to get lost and people *would* get lost."

Theater people patronized their radio brethren—"stealing money," sneered many a Broadway performer—without realizing the subtleties of the craft. Many journeyman theater and movie actors who tried to slip in a fast radio show between Broadway and Hollywood jobs were unable to master the skill; nor did they like the tight time frame—three or four hours' rehearsal and then on to the next script, all within a cramped studio. It was literally performing in a box.

The veteran radio actor Joe Julian (who played Archie on *Nero Wolfe,* Sandy Matson on *Lorenzo Jones,* and had roles in several Norman Corwin plays), complained in a controversial piece for *Variety* in 1941 that radio acting created bad actors. Julian, who had higher ambitions and was an example of a good radio actor unable to break free of the medium, felt that radio thespians weren't taken seriously enough, that there was an "it's-good-enough-for-radio" attitude. Their "bag of tricks was acquired at a cost," he said. The busier actors became in radio, the more he said they degenerated as creative artists. Many radio actors, after winning auditions for roles in stage plays by impressing with facile first readings, had to be fired during rehearsals because they were incapable of going any further, adding new dimensions to their roles.

Due to so few rehearsal periods for most shows, there wasn't much time for direction in the traditional sense of searching for motivation and subtle meanings. A lot of it was logistics—making sure actors showed up on time and coordinating sound cues with lines. Directing actors on the air was like conducting an orchestra; some directors even used a podium. Bravura directors like Orson Welles and William Robson were studio Stokowskis. Jackson Beck adds, "Some [directors] blended subtlety and brass like an orchestra leader knows when to bring in the brass after the fiddles, knows when to take the brass, fade it out and bring the fiddles back with the cellos or the saxophones. What makes a great musical director made a great radio director because the whole thing was music in their ears."

The director-writer Jack Johnstone described the chore to Leonard Maltin: "Most directors directed from the control room. I directed in the studio, wearing a pair of earphones with heavy muffs on them so I couldn't hear the sounds directly. I'm thoroughly convinced it's the only way to direct a program. I could tell one actor to speed up just a little bit and another one perhaps even to slow down. If an actor was too close to the microphone, I could push him back gently or move him in closer. Sound effects cues were never missed when I was in the studio. It gave me much better control over the show."

Casts were so familiar with their characters and the show's pace and mood that one run-through was enough for timing and technical matters. After years together, actors fell into an easy groove and required little direction; a word here or a gesture there was enough to keep a show purring. It was like being part of a floating repertory company.

Radio's liveness accounted for much of its air of immediacy and visceral appeal, as if each show were being done explicitly just for you, as in live theater. Most TV is just a succession of little movies—*L.A. Law, Friends, Homicide,* and *Frasier* might as easily be watched in a movie house. Even sitcoms "filmed before a live studio audience" are in fact patched together from a series of interrupted movielike takes, then edited, and finally sweetened with laughter, with certain shots refilmed. But radio, through the 1920s, 1930s, and most of the 1940s, was pure and undoctored—what you heard was what you got, including spontaneity, ad libs, dead air, unplanned giggles, gaffes, missed cues. Spoonerisms were a constant booby trap, as when a cowboy on *Red Ryder* ordered someone to "Keep your tinger on the frigger."

Considering the possibilities for glitches in a live medium, it's astonishing how word-perfect the shows sounded—especially when you realize that most of the network programs were broadcast twice, once per coast, or three times if from Detroit. Most comedy, variety, and game shows were performed before a studio audience and went on the air quiveringly live, as did most of the dramatic shows before finally, in 1948, giving into "electrical transcriptions." By 1949, taping was still rare, except for commercials. Radio had to be timed to the second, a delicate tightrope act that allowed for no fluffs or other human error; Jackson Beck says it was like being in a spaceship for thirty minutes "and you've got to get back to land safely." Radio actors needed a tightly wound internal clock to stay in step with each show's tempo, as well as in time with the clock on the wall. When they had to stretch the last page to fill time, one performer recalls, it was like acting in slow motion. No wonder certain movie stars froze and veteran stage actors contracted mike fright: If a performer blew a line onstage, he might recover with a bit of stage business or repeat the line, but on-air errors were hard to cover, and often unsalvageable. There was a heady rush after finishing a show on time, under the gun, without a glitch.

Studio audiences were mesmerized by the logistics of a program, by the disparity between whatever they had envisioned at home in their heads and the organized, comparatively businesslike mood inside a studio, with actors sitting in rows of chairs awaiting their cue to speak, then calmly standing at a microphone reading lines off a page. It couldn't have been more lackluster—or more exciting for longtime listeners who had always wondered how it was all created; the most mundane mechanics of any show dazzled onlookers. At Fred Allen's show, the star worked in a loosened tie, chewing gum, often with his back to the audience, facing the cast. Usually, the orchestra on a comedy or variety show was also hearing the program for the first time, having rehearsed in another studio—partly because the musicians' laughter energized the cast and cued glassy-eyed audiences when to respond. Sometimes audiences became so entranced *watching* their favorite radio show live that they easily missed the jokes.

Despite these strict conditions, most radio actors loved the entire life—people like Shirley Mitchell, a veteran radio actress and comedy stalwart of *Blondie, The Great Gildersleeve,* Kay Kyser's show, etc. When Mitchell talks, it sounds as if she's remembering a bubbling cocktail party. "It *was* a party! I loved doing everything I did. Radio just wasn't cutthroat like movies and TV. I hated the summer, when the shows went off." Peter Leeds, who worked a lot with Stan Freberg, once told Mitchell, "Gee, it was all so easy, I wish we'd known it then." She replied, "I always knew it." Richard Crenna, of *Our Miss Brooks* and *A Date with Judy,* explains why radio actors had such affection for each other, and for radio itself. "I must sound like Little Orphan Annie, but there were no bad guys. People who were difficult got weeded out. There were so few of us that if someone was a pain in the ass, who was late, or who drank, it was all over town very quickly."

For comic actors, their voice was their fortune. "I'm kind of attached to it," quips Arnold Stang, whose quavery New York squeak engraved him in radio (and TV) audiences' minds for fifty years as the definitive nebbish. He calls his voice, identifiable still, "a personal logo. It's like you're Jell-O or Xerox"—a reliable brand name. Stang was acting at the age of nine on kids' shows like *Let's Pretend* and played countless variations on dramas and mysteries—"little killers," he calls them. A graduate of the Actors Studio who won an Oscar nomination for *The Man with the Golden Arm,* he states, "I didn't just do gags." Although he became a TV star on Milton Berle's show, he says, "I still get a lot of fan mail each week and none of it *ever* is about the Milton Berle TV show. It's all about my radio career."

While radio was the final resting place for many over-the-hill performers it was mainly a training ground for the young and untried like Croft and Stang. Disembodied performers learned how to act with their voice, shading it a hundred different ways and creating an instant intimacy, the way singers do. Many radio actors never developed a technique below the neck (a condition known in movies as "microphone feet"), but carved out long and lucrative careers treading the airwaves in more roles than most film actors could play in a dozen lifetimes. "I never took a drama lesson in my life," William Conrad told Leonard Maltin. "I never even thought about what it is to be an actor. All I thought about was the money that it was possible to make. I was just fucking lucky to have a voice that fascinated people," even if he never changed it. He was kidded by colleagues as "the man of a thousand voice."

Many acting stars tried to parlay their radio success into films, and vice versa: Nelson Eddy, Eddie Bracken, Mario Lanza, Billie Burke, even Fred Astaire had radio shows (but then so did Babe Ruth and Lou Gehrig one off-season). Radio actors like Don Ameche took a while to get their screen-acting legs. Rosemary De Camp recalled, "I was always terrified that I wouldn't handle the props correctly," so she would get to the set early just to work with props. Hollywood's *Grand Hotel* reopened on radio and the "Hardy Family" also moved in, with Mickey Rooney and Lewis Stone reprising their film series. Humphrey Bogart and Lauren Bacall costarred in *Bold Venture* in 1950 and 1951, with Bogey as the pirate-chasing owner of a Cuban hotel, and Frank Sinatra starred in *Rocky Fortune* during his famous fallow pre– *From Here to Eternity* period in 1953.

Most of the major comedy shows attempted films, which were little more than exploitation movies, curiosities to satisfy listeners' need to see their radio idols moving—in person, as it were. There were a handful of "Fibber McGee and Molly" films, RKO cheapies deservedly lost in time (with titles like *Heavenly Days, Here We Go Again,* and *Look*

Who's Laughing), just as there were quickie movies showcasing *The Great Gildersleeve, The Aldrich Family, Our Miss Brooks,* and others. Even quiz shows like *Take It or Leave It, People Are Funny,* and *Queen for a Day* were exploited for the screen.

THE VETERAN RADIO, TV, AND movie actor Jack Kruschen (nominated for an Academy Award as the doctor across the hall in *The Apartment*) was a staple of the *Dragnet* and *Gunsmoke* stock companies and helped found the Armed Forces Radio Service. He worked everywhere and, like his colleagues, retained a special affection for radio. In 1982, before a meeting of SPERDVAC (the Society for the Preservation and Encouragement of Radio Drama, Variety, and Comedy), Kruschen said: "Radio was a way of life that really doesn't exist anymore. When I first came into the business as a kid, I was taught by everyone around me that we all shared. We all helped one another."

Even so, actors loved playing jokes on each other on the air—setting fire to pages of someone's script, pulling an actor's trousers off during a show, cutting up his hat, or simply making funny faces. Steve Allen would insert gibberish in his announcer's ad copy. An actor playing a newsboy once bellowed a headline he had carefully devised: "Extra! Extra! Read all about it! Yellow cab driver marries white girl!" Casts would set the clocks ahead an hour without telling the director and go "on the air" with a show rife with missed cues, dead air, dropped words, and curses. The actor Dorian St. George is said to have removed organist Rosa Rio's blouse and unhooked her bra, then dropped his trousers while she tried to play the theme song.

During the last days of radio, budget cuts sliced into rehearsal time. On *Dragnet,* Kruschen recalled, "We walked in, picked up the script, did a run-through, and went on the air. There were times we'd pick up the script and go right on the air. They [Jack Webb and others in the company] were already doing television, so there wasn't time to do it all. We were a stock company and we all knew what the shows were, who we were, what we were gonna do. We'd walk in a little early and see the names of our characters, look at it and read ahead so we'd know where we were going."

The *Dragnet* stock company drew from some forty actors, with a nucleus of seven regulars. One was Kruschen, who didn't miss a show in eight years except when he left to make a film. "In those days, if you were any good you worked, unlike today, when there are so many good actors out of work. We had it better. Radio had no locked-in identity."

Yet for all of the family feeling, it wasn't that easy for outsiders to break into radio's tight circle, for there was a certain snobbery among the cliquish New York contingent—just as there is now—toward actors from Los Angeles. L.A. actors were equally wary of New Yorkers.

Kruschen once bluffed his way into an *Inner Sanctum* rehearsal, but producer-director Himan Brown took him outside and said, "Look in there. You see all those people. We're friends. We depend on each other. We do this show every week. If one of them dies, I might need you." Seven years later, when Kruschen had become a journeyman actor, Brown called him up and said, "It's Hi Brown," and Kruschen asked, "Who died?"

For Kruschen, "Every day, every show, was another lesson. I treated it like a class. I wanted to learn everything there was to learn about whatever it is I was doing, and I know everyone around me did the same thing. We knew as much about what went on in the booth as what went on in front of the microphone. We'd watch the sound-effects men and if they needed an extra hand we could step in and help. Even in the union days, the radio business was never like TV or motion pictures. If we stepped in and helped a sound-effects technician do his job, we never got yelled at. If we turned the pages for a musician, we never got yelled at. If we went to the booth if an assistant had to leave, we'd help back-time a show and nobody ever yelled at us."

Another of radio's foremost actors, Lurene Tuttle, played on virtually every major show—everyone from George Sand to Dolly Snaffle on *Duffy's Tavern,* Daisy June on *The Red Skelton Show,* and assorted characters on *Suspense, Lights Out,* and *One Man's Family.* She once played twins on a show and, on Norman Corwin's *Columbia Workshop,* to test her versatility, she did seven parts with different German accents. She performed often on *Dragnet,* was a librarian on *The Jimmy Durante Show,* and played opposite Dick Powell as his original costar on Louella Parsons's *Hollywood Hotel.*

A self-possessed woman, Tuttle made a crucial distinction between radio and theater training: "I had stage training, you see," she said in a 1980's interview. "Not only did I have something in the reading of the characters, but I had poise and presence. I want to make it clear that the Hollywood shows were not just studio shows. We were *performers* in radio. We stood out in front of audiences. You not only had to look well or look the part and dress well—be presentable, certainly, like you were in the theater. You had to be able to do comedy and get laughs out there in front of that audience."

Tuttle never felt radio actors got the credit they deserved, simply because they couldn't be seen and labored as formless voices. "On the air I could play a person I created visually, a whole flesh-and-blood human being. And I would come home and my little niece would say to me, 'I loved that lady you played with black hair with a bun in the back and long earrings and a green dress.' I created her so accurately there was no doubt in anyone's mind who I was playing. I was *not* doing a voice." So-called voice actors, she said, were able to switch on Voice 36 or Voice 12, but Tuttle tried for "the full person."

Betty Winkler Keane, another radio first lady, starred in half a dozen soaps—*Joyce Jordan, M.D., The Man I Married, The O'Neills, Girl Alone* (the first serial about an emancipated woman, a reporter)—and even appeared on the very first one, *Betty and Bob*. She recalls: "When I started, there were twenty-four of us who did it all. It was such easy money; I don't remember a struggle. Or maybe I wasn't bright enough to know it was so difficult. I know I wouldn't want to be a star in [today's] culture for all the tea in China."

Most of the shows Winkler worked on were broadcast from the top two floors of the Chicago Merchandise Mart, which became her radio household. "The sales department and the executives and the actors were all mixed up together all the time. We all socialized—I went out with a Kellogg's rep—but it was always respectable." Work was plentiful. "There was a lot of hustling, but I never had an agent in all those years. I had a good voice and I was very natural. And I was very pretty, and that didn't hurt. If I had a nickel for every time I was sexually harassed, my lord! You just laughed your way through it then. We had so many laughs in those days."

Peggy Webber, who specialized in gangster molls but played everything (babies, old women, foreigners), did as many as twenty-one shows a week. "They were first-nighters every show," she recalls. "During the broadcasts, we were under fire. It was like a war. The red light went on and the sponsors were there with blood in their eyes waiting for us to make a mistake. It was a lot of stress, but we supported each other. One night Peter Lorre got so excited he threw his script away, and we spent the whole next scene trying to ad-lib our way out of it."

One of radio's busiest child actors, Tommy Cook, played—simultaneously—Alexander on *Blondie,* Little Beaver on *Red Ryder,* and Junior on *The Life of Riley,* not to mention several Arch Oboler shows, *I Love a Mystery,* and *The Mercury Theatre on the Air.* Cook, now a slight, wiry, tightly wound man in his mid-sixties, has no bad memories of being a child actor on what he estimates at close to thirty-five hundred broadcasts. "They were the happiest times, not just for me but for my parents, who didn't have much money," he recalls. "My dad was an invalid. I helped put my sister through Stanford. But just to sit on my mom's lap and see the joy on their faces . . . I was a loner, in a way. My ma was the best agent I ever had, but she wasn't a stage mother. I told her to sit in the corner and mind her knitting and she did."

Cook adds, "I was a totally natural actor. I would just become that kid, whoever it was, and the words just flowed. Oboler called me a genius and didn't want me to woodshed [radioese for "rehearse"]. I resent very much when actors say they won't let their kids go into show business." Ivan Curry, a *Let's Pretend*-er who also starred as Bobby Benson, concurred. "I get so tired of adult actors who tell me, 'Don't you realize you missed your childhood?' I always say, 'But I knew the Shadow!' "

Another prominent child actor, Arthur Anderson, who wrote a book about *Let's Pretend,* on which he was a regular for several years, recollected, "We must have been hated by adult actors, because we just had to be cute or bring tears to your eyes and never had to rehearse as hard. I don't think kid actors get the credit they deserve." Dick Van Patten, who went on to fame in TV's *Eight Is Enough* and several film and video roles, recalls his radio days with unalloyed joy: "I loved it! What wasn't to enjoy? Thank God my mother *was* a stage mother and pushed me and my sister Joyce. Thanks to radio, I did a lot of Broadway."

Jackie Kelk, the legendary Homer on *The Aldrich Family* and the show's last survivor, was a seasoned Broadway child actor who ran the gamut of gawky radio teenagers, quadrupling as Jimmy Olsen on

Superman, Terry on *Terry and the Pirates,* Dick Tracy, Jr., on *Dick Tracy,* and Chester Gump on *The Gumps.* Kelk is much less romantic about radio than many of his colleagues: "I'd been on Broadway"—he was in Cole Porter's *Jubilee* with an equally youthful Montgomery Clift—"when they had footlights and all, so to me radio wasn't as exciting, just standing around a mike holding a script."

The character of Homer wasn't in Clifford Goldsmith's original Broadway comedy on which the Aldrich show was based; he was added when the play became a series. At the auditions, Kelk remembers, "Every kid in New York was there, and I thought, I'll never get this." On a whim, he changed his voice when he read the role. "I did that nasal voice—I don't know why, it just popped into my head—and everyone in the booth started cracking up." Kelk grew up in the role—indeed, his voice actually changed on the air during an *Aldrich Family* episode. "It scared me so much I cried, but I just carried on as if nothing had happened." Kelk doesn't feel that radio was so very different from stage or film acting, though he finally gave up performing to become a casting agent. "I just got tired of it; I'd been in it since I was eight. But some of the best picture actors came out of radio—Frank Lovejoy, Agnes Moorehead, Thelma Ritter. Listen, it's all acting."

— 24 —

We're a Little Late,
Folks, So Good Night

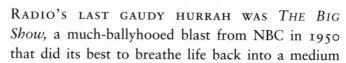

RADIO'S LAST GAUDY HURRAH WAS *THE BIG Show,* a much-ballyhooed blast from NBC in 1950 that did its best to breathe life back into a medium that had been scared silly by TV, and with good reason. Instead of developing its real strength—the spoken word—radio fell back into its old ways as electronic vaudeville, trying to compete against TV's exciting new in-your-face vaudeville.

The Big Show was a failed showbiz blitzkrieg that vainly attempted to outspectacular television, a radical move in many ways, beginning with the fact that it was produced not by an ad agency but by the network, NBC, supposedly a power play by Pat Weaver to take back control over radio and TV from the agencies; also, uniquely, it had several sponsors instead of just one. The show, a sort of prototype for TV's *Toast of the Town,* was a desperate effort to dismantle Jack Benny, who by then had also moved to TV but whose radio show still ran opposite NBC's extravaganza. Even NBC's sneaky maneuver of not taking a station break at the top of the hour, 7 P.M., didn't work; out of habit, people switched over to Benny anyway. *The Big Show*'s very name had a certain overhyped, hollow, straining-for-colossal television ring to it. It was hosted by Tallulah Bankhead, a big deal in her own right, but in the end, a miscalculation. It was a risky move—installing a woman to host a radio spectacular—but if any woman was up for it, the bigger-than-life Tallulah was that woman.

What radio didn't need in 1950, however, was a dusty Broadway diva who was herself on somewhat shaky career legs and seemed to symbolize both the past and radio's dubious future. Bankhead's *grande dame* persona, sprinkled with husky dirty laughs, wasn't enough to seduce listeners. In fact, she sounded outlandish and a little scary, not the sound you want in a fresh show meant to dazzle listeners. In the

Overleaf, from left to right: George Sanders, Peggy Lee, Portland Hoffa, Groucho Marx, Fred Allen, and Tallulah Bankhead (*The Big Show*)

wishful preamble of announcer Jimmy Wallington, *The Big Show* was "ninety minutes with the most scintillating personalities in the entertainment world . . . and here is your hostess, the glamorous, unpredictable Tallulah Bankhead!"

The slightly top-heavy ninety-minute circus, broadcast on Sunday nights at 6:30 P.M., was budgeted at $100,000 a show ("real TV money," snickered *Newsweek*). It featured Meredith Willson as Tallulah's music man—her bandleader and salaaming stooge ("Thank you, Miss Bankhead, sir") and the composer of the show's Hallmarkesque theme, "May the Good Lord Bless and Keep You," which became a hit, croaked by Tallulah at the end of each show while backed by Willson's forty-four-piece orchestra and sixteen-voice chorus. It was as close to a Broadway show as radio could whip together each week.

Bankhead was reluctant to host the show and only did it because she needed the money. "I succumbed to radio offers only when poverty-stricken," she once said. Yet she was flattered to be asked to take on such a massive enterprise, which was meant to blow TV out of its fairly shallow water. It was, as she noted, "a lofty project" but "a little frightening." At first, when she felt they were merely using her as an MC to announce the acts, she tried to back out. "Was I to be the sacrificial lamb, mute and disgraced, while the comedians and the singers had a field day?" she wondered. The producers were more alarmed when the great lady walked through rehearsals without any spark, but the first show proved everyone wrong. In her usual style, Tallulah surprised everyone, mostly herself.

"Guess what happened?" she later crowed in her memoirs. "Your heroine emerged from the fracas as Queen of the Kilocycles. Authorities cried out that Tallulah had redeemed radio. In shepherding my charges through *The Big Show,* said the critics, I had snatched radio out of the grave." Then she added, "The autopsy was delayed."

John Crosby, who had written radio off by then, was uncharacteristically ecstatic: "It was in practically every respect a perfectly wonderful show—witty, tuneful, surprisingly sophisticated and brilliantly put together . . . presided over and more or less blanketed by that extraordinarily vibrant lady known as Tallu." Crosby called it "one of the fastest and funniest ninety minutes in my memory." Picking up on the acerbic edge that Bankhead's banter lent to the proceedings, he wrote: "The passages between her and her guests were happily lacking in that overwhelming mutual esteem which marks the pleasantries between most MCs and guests."

Her grande-dameship described it thus: "My guests make scornful allusions to my age, my thirst, my romantic bents and frustrations. In turn, I deflate my opponents in scathing fashion." As she rightly observed, "This kind of calculated rudeness is rarely heard in either English or American radio programs. Usually the comedians drop sweetness and light, try to outdo each other in logrolling. *The Big Show* drips venom—ersatz venom. To the uninitiated, our conversations seem perilously close to a free-for-all."

The guest roster included every big name the bookers could nail down that wasn't otherwise busily ingratiating himself or herself to TV viewers—Broadway and London stage stars clearly meant to impress a radio audience, who, in the end, just weren't that interested. They had heard them all before. "We have nothing but the cream of show business," boasted Bankhead, from Edith Piaf to Gloria Swanson, and beyond—Dr. Ralph Bunche, Margaret Truman. You name it, *The Big Show* booked it.

Initially, the show was a hit, TV or no TV. Overnight, reported Bankhead, she was hooked by the notion that more people heard her in one show (30 million) than had witnessed her in thirty-three years in the theater. During each one-night radio stand, in less time than elapsed between curtains, she could log a virtual coast-to-coast tour—and was free from Monday through Friday to play. It must have all seemed a "simply *fa-a-a*bulous" idea at the time, but Bankhead was a stranger to radio, who, to younger listeners anyway, gave off the heavily perfumed scent of yesteryear. By the 1950s, all that precamp "Hel-loo, dah-h-h-lings!" stuff seemed archaic, silly, and even a touch embarrassing.

If radio was to go out with a bang, there was nobody who gave audiences a better bang than Tallulah Bankhead, but it was the wrong sort of explosion. Running scared, radio was trying to turn itself into TV, not that anything would have helped. TV then was far worse—ragged, raw, and stumbling—but it was something that radio could never be again: novel.

The Big Show was not just more grand than most radio shows—it was also more witty, smoothly produced, smart, and ambitious, with an interesting juxtaposition of guests, but it wasn't significantly different. It was just a more lavish, inflated revival of radio's earliest form—the variety showcase; you could almost hear the sequins. Listeners reveled in the interplay of celebrities, but radio had always been good at parading big names and parodying their images, such as Groucho singing "Some Enchanted Evening" in Italian, like some Catskill Caruso. It was all fairly sophisticated, but nothing could pry audiences from their expensive new glass boxes, and nothing could induce NBC to keep the lavish show on as a partly sustaining enterprise forever; it never did generate regular sponsors. NBC's sincere last-ditch effort was a lost cause, a white elephant that hung around for two seasons before folding its tent after incurring a $1 million loss. Jack Gould said it all when he gave *The Big Show* a backhanded compliment, calling the program "good enough to make one wish he could have seen it."

Radio's other final extravagant effort was NBC's *Monitor,* a 1955 forty-hour marathon that ran throughout the weekend, a kind of radio retrospective in a magazine format featuring some of its most famous names—Amos and Andy, Fibber McGee and Molly, Bob and Ray—reprised in five- to fifteen-minute snippets squeezed in among news, sports, and music: the ghost of radio-to-come.

By 1950, TV had begun to take a big bite out of listeners' time, but radio network sales remained steady ($183 million in 1950, just $15 million less than in 1948). There were some 5 million TV sets in use then, up from only 200,000 sets three years earlier, largely due to the advance work of Milton Berle, TV's greatest pitchman, who was rather swiftly knocked off the tube himself by TV's fickle audience. Berle's whirlwind tour of America via television lasted only six seasons before he wore out his wacky welcome.

TV ate up performers even faster than radio. Radio gobbled material, but it kept stars at a discreet distance, which preserved their aura. Even after a decade, a radio personality remained a voice in the void. By 1950, however, radio's major comics had been on for a generation or more: *Amos 'n' Andy* was a twenty-one-year veteran, Jack Benny had put in eighteen years and Bing Crosby, nineteen, followed closely by Burns and Allen, Bob Hope, and Edgar Bergen and Charlie McCarthy. Major soap operas were fifteen to eighteen years old, but unsponsored dramatic shows had all but left the air. Just as ominously, attendance at movie theaters, night spots, and sports events began to dwindle as people huddled around tiny screens. TV rolled over everything, and radio was flattened almost overnight, though it would die a slow, lingering death over the next decade as live orchestras were replaced by recorded music and star comics fired their writers and devolved into quiz-show MCs and panelists.

NOBODY KNEW HOW WELL RADIO'S established stars would do on TV. Berle was fearful in 1949, when he said, "What I have seen on my television set with the exception of one or two shows has been the worst kind of junk. It seems that the producers of this trivia have only one thing on their minds—is it cheap?" And the seemingly fearless Groucho Marx confessed, "With bloodshot eyes I watch this ogre night after night, bored but nonetheless fascinated by its potential. How long can I survive on radio against this new monster? When will I become a public charge?" Even Jack Benny, radio's megastar, underwent a sort of screen test to see how he would fare on camera.

Most of the early TV versions of radio shows were either literal or virtual simulcasts of themselves—shows like Benny's, Arthur Godfrey's *Talent Scouts, The Life of Riley,* and *The Goldbergs.* As Gertrude Berg recalled: "There were lots of people in radio who didn't want to believe the moving finger, and every control room was a little replica of a Hollywood movie studio when somebody mentioned TV. People said, 'It couldn't happen'; 'It wouldn't catch on'; 'It was a trick.' But as they talked they began to make other plans. It didn't take long for the halls and the studios to lose that feeling of excitement that made radio what it was." Composer Jerry Goldsmith recalled that people were playing to empty studios and sitting around reminiscing about the good old days.

Jackson Beck (the Cisco Kid, Philo Vance, etc.) made the switch to TV, unlike many of his colleagues, because he learned to memorize dialogue, a tortuous process that did in many longtime radio actors chained to mikes and scripts. "There were people who were marvelous radio actors and you never heard from them again," says Beck. "You'd be sitting around with other actors in a restaurant and someone would say, 'Where's so-and-so?' and you'd hear he was selling suits at Brooks Brothers." Beck didn't want to leave radio, but his agent got him a part on TV's *Edge of Night*, where he stayed eight years. "I felt at first like I was in a flying saucer—panic-stricken. I just figured they're gonna see how ugly I am, and how inept I am, and that'll be that."

Our Miss Brooks's Richard Crenna vividly remembers how radio actors "had to fight the stigma of being in radio. Movie people thought we couldn't walk and talk at the same time. It was a terrible shock to go out later and hear someone tell me, as they did when I auditioned for [the movie] *Wilson*, 'You don't look right for a college boy.' " Crenna made the transition from radio to TV, and also resisted typecasting, because, he says, "I didn't sound or look like Walter Denton. I could walk away from the character."

Compared to radio, TV was a far more expensive medium, closer to movies, involving sets and lighting designers, costumers, makeup artists, and wigmakers, not to mention cameramen, floor managers, cue-card people, etc. When the ad agencies, which had always controlled radio shows by packaging and running them, were no longer eager to take the financial risk involved in producing TV shows, the networks took over and advertising lost its longtime lock on programming. The TV studios were soon swarming with network guys in gray flannel suits dispensing advice.

William Paley, CBS radio's longtime cultural emissary, had liked devising shows himself rather than buying them from ad agencies, but even he was complacent about radio's primacy. "In 1949," said NBC program boss Pat Weaver, "Paley still seemed only minimally aware of television," one reason that Weaver eventually came up with a plan at NBC to create original network shows that CBS had yawned at. The comedy writer Bob Schiller recalls that one of the industry's major talent agencies didn't even have a TV department in 1949.

The arrival of *I Love Lucy* on CBS-TV October 15, 1951, signaled the true end of radio, symbolized by the fact that a sturdy radio transplant, *Lights Out*, was sent reeling into oblivion weeks later. "We were wiped out quickly," recalled Mike Dann, the NBC program chief at the time, who quickly took *Lights Out* to TV. "We never knew what had happened, but it happened and it happened fast."

People loved both *Lucy* and TV, and decided it was lights-out time for radio, though a few shows valiantly remained on the air until 1962. What truly frightened radio was when one of its hottest shows, *Stop the Music*, plummeted in 1950 from the fourteenth spot in the ratings to sixty-sixth; not even rowdy game shows and gimmicky giveaways (*Meet Your Match, Hollywood Calling, Chance of a Lifetime*) could hold listeners' once-loyal ears. Suddenly radio, like vaudeville before it, became the subject of not just good-humored ribbing but pointed ridicule. On Jackie Gleason's first TV show on the DuMont network, *The Cavalcade of Stars*, he played an inept radio sound-effects man, and on Jack Benny's final radio program Mel Blanc portrayed a desperate, overeager sound man who keeps bursting in with silly irrelevant sounds just to insert himself into the show.

Some of radio's biggest stars attracted little attention from TV moguls and were given a quick pink slip—Edgar Bergen and Charlie McCarthy and Ed Gardner of *Duffy's Tavern* quickly fell into oblivion. If even a hugely popular show had no TV future, it was coldly canceled by suddenly apathetic longtime sponsors. Adding to the insult were disastrous attempts to reproduce venerable radio shows on TV, such as *The Aldrich Family, The Great Gildersleeve,* and *Fibber McGee and Molly.* A few sitcoms were smuggled onto TV and survived—*The Life of Riley, The Goldbergs, Ozzie and Harriet*—but most were declared DOA and relegated to radio's mausoleum. TV was killing off radio headliners as efficiently as radio had dispatched so many vaudeville legends. Personalities and shows that people had listened to for their entire lives—ten, twenty, in some cases almost thirty years—and with whom they had formed complex relationships, were snuffed out overnight.

Nothing was more symptomatic of the scary changes overtaking radio than the fate that befell Clayton Collyer, who had played Superman on radio for fourteen years until he was suddenly laid low in the early 1950s, not by a glowing chunk of green kryptonite but by the even more lethal flickering raytheon tube. He was converted overnight into a toothy, jovial TV game-show host named Bud Collyer on shows like *Break the Bank, Winner Take All,* and *Beat the Clock.* As the broadcasting historian Thomas A. DeLong writes: "Once a TV set came into a living room, the radio, for the most part, was converted to an early morning wake-up device, transformed into a mealtime companion and positioned as a late-night slumber aid, while maintaining its position as a traveling mate in most cars."

"Television was already conducting itself provocatively, trying to get radio to pucker up for the kiss of death," wrote Fred Allen in the melancholy final pages of *Treadmill to Oblivion*. "Young men with crew cuts were dragging TV cameras into the studios and crowding the old radio actors out into the halls. Even without the coming of television, radio seemed doomed. The audience and the medium were both getting tired. The same programs, the same comedians, the same commercials—even the sameness was starting to look the same."

Like radio thirty years earlier, TV was inventing itself as it went along. All rules were off. No-talents were cashing in, legends were washing out. Everything, and everyone, was up for grabs. TV now was the new showbiz boomtown and the tube was littered with old radio corpses. Fred Allen, visiting friends at the Algonquin Hotel, noticed a basket of fruit on top of the TV set and said, "You know, that's the best thing I've seen on television yet." He wrote, "When television belatedly found its way into the home, after stopping off too long at the tavern, the advertisers knew they had a more potent force available for their selling purposes. Radio was abandoned like the bones at a barbecue."

TV didn't just eat up many radio comedians, like Allen. It exposed them in a new way that gave away all the comedy secrets they had so successfully kept hidden on the air. Jokes on radio didn't have to be established with a visual prop, which could kill them on TV. Matters left to listeners' imaginations now had to be solved, such as what Jack Benny's kitchen looked like and whether the refrigerator should have a lock on it. In radio, as Milt Josefsberg once explained, you could have a lock one week for a joke and then forget about it, whereas on TV if viewers *saw* a lock on the door, they would remember it. Thus every time Benny went to the kitchen, the lock had to be there, which might interfere with a new joke.

Sitcoms that had been so familiar and flavorful on radio now looked flat, one-dimensional, washed out, and strangely alien, bearing only a warped resemblance to the original show. As characters moved around needlessly, their facial expressions looked forced, painted on. The homes and rooms all looked the same, furnished in boring generic sit-com decor—much as they still do.

The writer-actress Peg Lynch was bothered by having to reinvent her laid-back radio comedy *Ethel and Albert* for a live audience on Kate Smith's TV show. "[Mine] was a quiet show," she recalled, "and I was not a stage person who was accustomed to performing in front of an audience, as comedians are. And I always felt it spoiled my timing. I would have to hold up for the laugh."

"The humor was almost entirely verbal," Larry Gelbart wrote in his memoirs. "It was as though we were trying to make the words *look* funny . . . Milton Berle had no intention of using TV as though it were only radio with a window. Berle *moved*." To which he now adds, "We were all pressing, thinking cartoony, as if writing for circus clowns. We'd put a 20-gallon hat on Hope instead of a 10-gallon hat. I don't think we ever did get it down [writing for TV]. After 280 shows with Hope, it was all still a bit crude, with everyone reading off cue cards and breaking up."

Sherwood Schwartz says the tension level in television was far greater than on radio, which he blames on TV writer-director-producer Garry Marshall (*Laverne and Shirley, Happy Days,* etc.), who changed TV gag writing. "It became joke-joke-joke," says Schwartz, the reason he left Hope's radio show. "I don't mind a page without laughs, people just talking normally," he says.

Bob Weiskopf, who made his fortune in TV, says radio was more kicks. "In many ways, radio was tougher, but it was never that difficult. The last two jobs I had in TV, I told my partner, Bob Schiller: No more. It destroys your morale. You feel it's bad enough if you need the money. My beef with TV is, the *people* aren't very funny—like, Jesus, this guy Tim Allen?"

By 1948, critics had begun to despair of the creeping grayness that pervaded much of radio, and left it ripe for television's takeover. Suddenly it seemed that everybody was piling on. John Crosby expressed a growing exasperation when he wrote, "Radio's social position remains low—lower even than the movies, which is about as far down as the social ladder goes." James T. Farrell accused radio of producing a "counterfeit" mass culture and of siphoning off "a large portion of the literary talent in America" to produce soaps and sitcoms, a charge long leveled against movies and TV. Ring Lardner's radio columns in *The New Yorker*, often written from a hospital bed, where he was forced to listen to shows he'd ignored before, regularly ridiculed radio's worst excesses.

Crosby, dubbed "the listener's critic," despaired that the medium had run out of steam, and in *Life* magazine he listed radio's seven deadly sins that, by midcentury, had led to its decline, among them: "Selling its soul" to advertising agencies; sticking to a few formulas (sitcoms, soaps, whodunits, quizzes, movie adaptations, etc.) and "not exploiting" its "enormous potentialities"; "pandering to the lowest tastes" but ignoring the highest ("While the America people listened to radio in vast numbers, they never quite respected it"); taking "false satisfaction from counting heads and assuming that they were contented heads"; failing to develop new talent and ideas; "created an insulting picture of the American people" by settling in New York and Hollywood, "two of the least characteristic cities in the U.S."; and acting too cowardly. "Rich and influential as radio was, it was timid."

Crosby felt a staleness had infected radio's comedy shows. Except for Fred Allen and Edgar Bergen, he wrote, "all these [other] comedians rely heavily on a formula invented almost fifteen years ago by Jack Benny." He said it felt as if the same twenty-four writers had been working all the shows for a decade or more, recycling ideas and jokes. A few comics—George Burns and the indomitable Ed Wynn—looked forward to the challenge. Wynn said, "I have fear, too, fear whether the public will accept me on television. But I don't fear TV itself." Burns, as it turned out, exploited TV better than most of his radio colleagues.

Yet when radio tried to throw listeners a literary crumb—such as Archibald MacLeish's landmark radio play "Fall of the City," produced and directed by Norman Corwin—it was considered pretentious by middlebrow critics. *Variety* grumbled that the program was "interesting to a few, exciting to a smaller few, a hopeless jumble probably to the masses." Radio couldn't seem to please anybody. It was no longer the darling of the masses; it had begun to seem a needy orphan.

By 1951, Corwin had become disillusioned, which led him to write a bitter piece in *The Writer* in which he advised would-be writers looking for success in radio to "be mediocre . . . safe, routine, unspectacular," and to "be willing to curb [their] imagination." Radio, he said, was "a trade outlet, not an art; it's a living." Perhaps, but by today's standards, radio was still incredibly vigorous in the early 1950s, with forty-four dramatic shows on the air, despite major budget cuts, the influx of shoddy giveaway shows, and the increasingly looming shadow of TV. In 1951, CBS cut radio advertising rates for the first time in its history.

Radio's brief life as America's main source of entertainment was just about over, a mere thirty years after it had first announced its arrival with a broadcast of the 1920 Harding-Cox presidential election returns, a short span for an age that had produced such a cornucopia of performing legends, had changed the face of pop culture in America—indeed, America itself—and created an audience of showbiz junkies, jingle-humming listeners, and swarms of news, sports, drama, music, and literature lovers. By the end of the last *Big Show,* the glory that was radio was gone, leaving only "the echo of forgotten laughter," in Fred Allen's bittersweet phrase.

To Paul West, TV didn't seem much of a real threat at first. "I remember once, when I first went to work at Columbia Square—the CBS complex in Hollywood—a program manager told me to go up to the conference room. He said, 'They have a TV set up there. Go up and give us your impressions.' It was just a little green screen, six by seven inches. But it shows you what they thought of television then: Here I was, a kid!—the bottom rung on the ladder—and they wanted *my* opinion. Nobody took it seriously. Then radio kind of whispered out the door and TV came roaring in. We had no idea radio would ever just die."

The Red-baiting of the early 1950s also drove good people out of radio. Senator Joe McCarthy waving a copy of *Red Channels* provided radio and TV with plenty of ready-made drama and bitter satire as it casually smeared scores of famous, even revered, radio names—from Himan Brown, Abe Burrows, and Martin Gabel to Morton Gould, Ben Grauer, and Orson Welles. It became a perverse honor to be on the blacklist, and almost more of a shame to be left off it. Several radio figures were blacklisted from TV, such as actors Philip Loeb of *The Goldbergs* and Jean Muir of *The Aldrich Family. Blacklist* was a vile word, so code words were devised; someone was said to be "unavailable" or "a controversial personality." An ACLU report claimed that the powerful ad agency Batten, Barton, Durstine & Osborn was fervent in keeping the blacklist alive. Plot lines were cleansed of any trace of pink, *peace* was a suspect term, and it was subversive to depict businessmen as heavies.

In radio's last days, some of its favorite shows suddenly found themselves sponsorless, padded with pallid public-service announcements that rubbed salt in an open wound. Since nobody was paying much attention, however, radio could loosen up and get away with more, as it had in its innovative youth, which led to such avant-garde programs as *Gunsmoke, Dimension X, The Henry Morgan Show, Escape, You Are There, The Stan Freberg Show*—and, in 1956, *The CBS Radio Workshop*, "dedicated to man's imagination—the theater of the mind," which aired adaptations of classic plays, novels, and poems. Elliott Lewis was told by a CBS vice-president, with a shrug, "Do whatever you want. You have a half hour." It lasted twenty months.

RADIO IN THE LATE 1990S seems as far removed from the radio heyday of the 1930s, 1940s, and early 1950s as did radio's heyday from the prim and primitive radio of the late 1920s. Radio today, oddly and ironically, echoes those first bland and hesitant years, killing airtime with words that make use of only radio's most basic forms of news, music, sports, and talk. Maybe the saddest part is that nobody seems to notice, much less care, primarily because few listeners under fifty-five realize that radio was ever anything more—that it once throbbed with theatrical life and exploded with laughter. People in their twenties, thirties, and even forties are scarcely aware that radio flourished with as much variety and vitality as TV does now, throwing its wide net over the full spectrum of human experience, knowledge, and entertainment.

Radio today, stuck on a relentless treadmill of news-music-sports, interrupted for warmed-over weather, commute, and stock updates every ten minutes, has once again shrunk the medium to a single-cell, one-dimensional organism. Hapless stations employ their listeners to entertain themselves with a babble of opinion, most of it mindless and mean-spirited, whipped on by shrill talk-show hosts. Even in its current distorted state, however, radio remains more the people's medium than television. "Talk radio is the last neighborhood in town," wrote Boston's conservative talk-show host David Brudnoy. "My listeners may not know who their neighbors are, but they feel they know me and the regular callers, like Bible Bob or Cheryl the libertarian insurance saleswoman." Pop music audiences are sliced into narrower and narrower marketing niches ("adult contemporary," "classic rock," etc.), with perhaps one classical, jazz, and "easy listening" station floating out there at the edge of the dial. While all of this goes on, as radio is reduced to a wisp of its once robust self, the Federal Communications Commission applauds with apparent satisfaction the idea that radio is serving the public.

In Britain, radio carries on as it has for seventy-five years under the BBC's original promise to "instruct, inform, and entertain." The BBC still takes the "entertain" part seriously, especially in its dramatic shows, but sitcoms, "sketch shows," and quizzes also thrive (only variety shows have gone out of business), not to mention the programs devoted to classical music, documentaries, magazine shows, and lectures—all for an annual tax of ninety-six pounds. "Radio has a protected niche here," says veteran radio critic Gillian Reynolds of the London *Daily Telegraph* (every nontabloid newspaper has its own radio critic). There is more radio now in England than there was in the '30s or '40s, she adds, ticking off such popular shows as *The Archers,* a daily thirty-minute serial now in its fifth decade that cuts across all ages and classes, a game-show parody called *I'm Sorry, But I Haven't a Clue,* and a popular situation comedy, *After Henry.* "It leaves American radio in the dust," to quote one U.S.-born Londoner.

A quick perusal of *Radio Times,* a weekly magazine in which radio has equal standing with TV and films, makes you want to move to London just to tune into BBC-4, which broadcasts a play a day. Writers like Harold Pinter and Tom Stoppard regularly write for radio, and British stage and film stars likewise cross over, as do theater and movie directors. A typical week's fare earlier this year on the BBC included the sixth in a series of adaptations of Trollope novels, a radio version of "A Clockwork Orange," a P. D. James mystery, an epic mini-series love story, a sci-fi satire, a three-part retelling of "The Snow Queen" on a weekly children's hour, a week of Victorian mysteries by Wilkie Collins heard on *Little Novels,* a horror tale on *Late Night Theatre,* a nightly reading on *Book at Bedtime* of Chekhov short stories—and, oh yes, a ten-part adaptation of *War and Peace.*

What survives of vintage American radio can be counted on two hands—the few shows and personalities that harken to an earlier, more intimate, congenial, and entertaining time: primarily, Garrison Keillor's *Prairie Home Companion,* which rediscovered radio in the 1980s and whose chromosomes contain the DNA of everything from *The Fred Allen Show* to *The Breakfast Club* to *The Kraft Music Hall.* A painstaking scan of the dial also turns up Paul Harvey's Bill Stern-like *The Rest of the Story;* Michael Feldman's hip yet folksy quiz show-cum-audience mingle, *Whad' Ya Know?;* Laura Schlessinger's take-no-prisoners shrink *Dr. Laura;* Charles Osgood's bemused *The Osgood File;* Tom and Ray Magliozzi's flip, funny, informative *Car Talk;* Harry Shearer's satirical riffs and NPR essayists Ira Glass, Bailey White, and David Sedaris; and, yes, Rush Limbaugh, who transcends his own desk-thumping right-wing diatribes with a unique persona and a clever use of radio's primary resources—voices, music, sound effects—and a satirical, albeit steeply tilted, conservative slant on events. Howard Stern, Don Imus, and their copycat trash-talkers across the land bend humor to their own perverse purposes, zinging celebrities in a volley of innuendo lobbed with raunchy bravado. Otherwise, National Public Radio's features, interviews, and commentaries are about all else that survives of classic round-the-clock radio of the sort that once made you want to reach for the dial again—not out of habit, duty, or desperation, but with delight and anticipation that something worthwhile, unexpected, moving, and amusing was in the air.

Radio has made a few thwarted attempts to return to those thrilling days of yesteryear, most valiantly in Himan Brown's *CBS Radio Mystery Theater* in the mid-1970s, hosted by E. G. Marshall. An aging Arch Oboler gave it a whirl as well. But like all great popular entertainment—most tellingly, the beloved popular songs and musical comedies of that same era—radio was too much of its time to be brought back or re-created. Whenever some well-intentioned diehard attempts to revive old radio, no matter how earnest or skilled the effort, it never sounds quite right; the voices, stories, music, and sound effects seem strained, contemporary, and strangely hollow. We can go back in our minds, but our ears are too postmodern. In the words of the critic James Wolcott, "Our nostalgia, like everything else these days, is filtered through ironic knowingness. These are the ideas we think we should have and would have if only we weren't such heathens, if only we weren't so damned hip."

In a 1979 speech, Norman Corwin said with feeling that radio drama could be revived within a week. "It's no great trick. It could be done tomorrow if radio was willing to do it. Golden Age II could be back tomorrow! There's no great mystery to it. . . . You don't *need* the set! You don't *need* the lighting! You don't *need* the wardrobe!"

David Mamet agrees, writing that "Radio is a great training ground for dramatists. More than any other dramatic medium, it teaches the writer to concentrate on the essentials. Working for radio, I learned how *all* great drama works: by leaving the endowment of characters, place, and especially action, up to the audience." He adds, "Good drama has no stage directions . . . The better the play, the better it will fare on the radio. Put *Streetcar, Waiting for Godot, Long Day's Journey, Lear* on the radio, and what do you miss? Nothing . . . Writing for radio forces you and *teaches* you to stick to the story. The story is all there in the theater—the rest is just packaging." Radio drama, he says, can be produced for next to nothing by anybody with a microphone and a tape recorder, and Mamet ends on an uncharacteristically upbeat note: "The time is auspicious for a rebirth of American theater, and radio would be a good place to look for it to happen."

Corwin refuses to eulogize a medium he considers very much alive but existing in a kind of coma, or perhaps just an arrested state of development, frozen in time in 1950. "Radio always meant a great deal to anyone who was ever in it, and it still means a great deal, but I'm afraid we've sort of swept it under the rug of our memories because we miss it so much. It was like losing a dear friend—better than that, a lover. It had a romance to it. It didn't die of natural causes, nor is it really dead."

Radiophiles agree, and remain convinced of the inherent superiority of a medium whose full-bodied return we await like members of some cult huddled in remote mountain outposts watching for signs of the true messiah, listening for the sound of NBC's welcoming door chimes—*bing! bang! bong!*—that ushered America into radio's home within a home. Unable to find anything truly entertaining on the air today, we're eager to buy our way back into old radio—literally, paying about six dollars a cassette for *The Jack Benny Program* or *Lights Out* or *Escape* or *Amos 'n' Andy* or a *Lux Radio Theatre* dramatization of *Mr. Deeds Goes to Town* with Gary Cooper. The pay-per-listen system delivers two half-hour shows or four 15-minute soap operas or kids' serials per tape.

The cassettes are hungrily scooped up by the bagful at conventions at airport hotels, swapped with fellow buffs, avidly bought through thriving mail-order houses, and purchased from dealers. "I got four *Gang Busters* out of the Library of Congress," someone was heard to crow at a meeting of the Friends of Oldtime Radio in Newark, New Jersey, the nation's largest annual gathering of the faithful, an odd collection of diehards, nerds, hustlers, bushy-bearded toothless mountain men, and polyestered Middle Americans, all fiercely protective of their favorite shows. "What was the outcome of *The Shadow* litigation?" somebody else inquires. "Hey, who owns the rights to *The Cinnamon Bear?*," asks a third.

Much of the action at conventions—apart from the precise re-creations of shows like *Meet Corliss Archer* or *The Cisco Kid* and the panel discussion love-ins—is the bustle of radio hounds sniffing out some long-lost episode of *I Love a Mystery;* a yelp of joy goes up when a man happens on an obscure tape of Frank Sinatra's action series, *Rocky Fortune.* Fan club booths and flyers invite one and all to join groups dedicated to preserving the memory of Rudy Vallee, Al Jolson, and Kate Smith. You name it and there's a fan club devoted to its furtherance: There is a *Vic and Sade* club, a *Lum and Abner* club, a *One Man's Family* club, also *Gunsmoke, Fibber McGee and Molly,* and *Suspense* clubs. There is an Eddie Cantor Appreciation Society, and the Arthur Godfrey Memorial Foundation of Whippany, New Jersey. There are massive logs that list every *Lux Radio Theatre* episode broadcast, and a show-by-show history of *Lux Presents Hollywood;* also, a fifty-dollar necrology of birth and death dates of some three thousand radio personalities, and small-press books about *Let's Pretend,* sound effects, and one by Fred Foy, the *Lone Ranger* announcer. Over dinner, war stories between old radio personalities are traded and mere listeners at the table tune in attentively. Ghostly yet vital visages wander the halls—

Janet Waldo (*Corliss Archer*), Jackson Beck (a now-stooped Cisco Kid), Les Tremayne (the still distinguished *First Nighter* star).

Everyone is an expert ready to display his knowledge of the fine points of *The War of the Worlds, Dragnet,* or *One Man's Family,* and actual experts mingle with the crowd—Carlton E. Morse's widow, or one of Eddie Cantor's daughters and his grandson busily pushing boxed cassettes of old Cantor shows. And look! There's Art Gilmore, the announcer. Wait, isn't that Rosemary De Camp? Someone just caught a glimpse of Sam Edwards—Dexter on *Corliss Archer.* Joe Franklin is here, of course, strolling down this most memory-choked of lanes, a showbiz pope moving among his throng. Old radio's caretakers channel all this fevered nostalgia and keep it purring—people like Jay Hickerson, Carl Amari, Anthony Tollin, Leonard Maltin, and the Gassman brothers, John and Larry, blind twins who run and wittily cohost SPERDVAC conventions in Los Angeles, the second-largest annual radiophile affair.

Most of the aging radio actors, directors, sound men, announcers, singers, engineers, ad guys, et al., who turn up are full of life and stories. They are a hardy band, joyful and generous souls. One icon, *Inner Sanctum*'s Raymond Edward Johnson, who, although crippled for many years, showed up at a 1997 gathering of the Friends of Oldtime Radio to deliver a spirited reading from a portable bed. Many a bent old-time actor will shuffle to the mike for a re-creation of, say, *Richard Diamond, Private Detective,* but once he is up onstage, script in hand, bifocals lowered, feet firmly planted before a mike, his voice comes alive again, resuming right about where it left off fifty years ago.

As William Faulkner put it, "The past isn't dead; it's not even past." Yet most traces are gone of the radio world that 100 million Americans once took for granted, before it vanished into thin air, whence it came, as the wise-guy insurance investigator of *Yours Truly, Johnny Dollar* signed his final expense account and it became the last network show to go off the air, on September 30, 1962—the night vintage radio drew its last breath.

Ⱥ(ⱧⱧOⱲⱢⱤDGⱮⱤNTꞦ

The secret collaborators in this venture begin with my editor, Robert Gottlieb, without whom there might be no radio book by me of any kind, let alone one so skillfully and affectionately edited. It was his private passion for, knowledge of, and insights into old radio that guided the book into print. He also saved me from going off the deep end more than a few times, and I quickly came to trust his judgment on every aspect, including an appreciation of shows he recalled better than I—*Easy Aces, Life Can Be Beautiful,* and *Our Gal Sunday,* to name three. I struck gold by stumbling onto Bob Gottlieb, not only for his justly celebrated editing gifts but for his own deep interest in the subject, the luckiest accident an author could hope to have.

Many other people played a smaller but integral part at various twists and turns along the way: Robert Taylor, Susan Stone, Steve Rubenstein, Kathy Philis, and Natalie Macris, all of whom graciously read a few chapters and gave me some early and crucial feedback; Jim Clark and Sue Heinemann of the University of California Press, who first read the entire manuscript and offered their helpful counsel; John and Larry Gassman at the Society for the Preservation and Encouragement of Radio Drama, Variety, and Comedy, who generously and patiently supplied phone numbers, contacts, and unfailing support; Marty Halperin, who gave me access to a glorious cache of photos from the crowded, dusty, but invaluable archives at Pacific Pioneer Broadcasters; San Francisco *Chronicle* librarian Johnny Miller, who let me copy a few hard-to-locate photos; Patricia Everett, who provided emergency computer aid; Ron Miller, who pointed me to several Los Angeles memorabilia shops and gave me the benefit of his ideas, nostalgic lust, and a link to Art Linkletter; Michael Johnson in London, who led me to two main sources on radio in Great Britain; Marshall Jacobs, my other English connection, who gave me his thoughts on British radio; Warren Debenham, who came up with obscure recordings from his vast collection of comedy tapes; Peter Mintun, who loaned me some rare books, photos, and contacts; Joel Selvin, Ricky Nelson's biographer and a former colleague, who gave me a glimpse into the Nelson household; Joe Franklin and Frank Bresee, who provided photos from their private archives; Ken Schneider, Bob Gottlieb's assistant, who crisply and ever cheerfully processed various logistical matters; editor Ed Cohen; the folks at Pantheon: Altie Karper, Susan Norton, Sharon Dougherty, and Kristen Bearse; designer Deborah Kerner; copyeditor Veronica Windholz, whose adroit queries, catches, and suggestions smoothed out more than a few bumps in the manuscript; Dana Rodriguez, my colleague on KALW-FM radio's weekly quiz show, who provided tapes, superb photos, a helpful book, and old-radio trivia; Leah and Jerry Garchik, who came up with contacts and moldy books on radio gleaned from their garage-sale exploits; Adam Green, who gave me data and insights on *Vic and Sade;* friends Rita Abrams, Linda Plack, and Morris Bobrow, who lent needed tapes and moral support; Jeanie Jordan, who put me in touch with sound man Ray Kemper; Anne Fadiman, who arranged an interview with her famous father, Clifton; Les Guthman, who led me to Norman Corwin; Kirsten Tanaka, of San Francisco's Performing Arts Library & Museum, who provided some good leads; Bud Cary, longtime host of San Francisco's *Old Radio Theater,* who supplied rare tapes and photos; Mary McGeachy, who did her best on my behalf at the Museum of Television and Radio; KQED radio's Michael Krasny, who turned over his *Forum* airwaves to further the cause; Howard Weinberg, who envisioned a documentary on radio's golden age; agents Charlotte Sheedy, Clyde Taylor, Robert Lescher, John Thorton, Barry Malzberg, Patti Breitman, and Bob Markel, who made me believe there might actually be a publisher out there somewhere; likewise, editor Rachel Klayman, who provided valuable contacts; Randy Poe, whose total immersion into old radio made me feel like a Johnny Dollar-come-lately, and whose keen, funny perceptions and enthusiasms about many shows spurred me on—as always; and, to be sure, Wendy Lu, who, raised in Hong Kong, never heard any of these shows but who nonetheless uncomplainingly listened to me rattle on about them and the book, and who offered savvy advice, serene reassurances, and gentle encouragement during some of the author's more fidgety moments.

INTERVIEWS

Mason Adams (New York, N.Y., 10-21-97); Gary Alexander (by telephone, 6-19-95); Lynne Waterman Ansara (Burlingame, Calif., 6-9-95); George Ansbro (by telephone, 1996); George Balzer (Van Nuys, Calif., 11-9-95); Jackson Beck (New York, N.Y., 10-22-97); Irving Brecher (by telephone, 12-10-94); Himan Brown (New York, N.Y., 5-4-95); Bill Burch (by telephone, 2-21-96); Bud Cary (Oakland, Calif., 1-27-95); Tommy Cook (Los Angeles, Calif., 11-12-94); Norman Corwin (by telephone, 9-17-96); Richard Crenna (by telephone, 12-11-97); Mary Jane Croft (by telephone, 11-28-94); Herb Ellis (by telephone, 12-5-95); Clifton Fadiman (by telephone, 10-29-97); Charles Flynn (by telephone, 2-4-95); Fred Foy (by telephone, 1-23-95); John Gassman (Los Angeles, Calif., 11-12-94); Larry Gelbart (by telephone, 6-4-98); Page Gilman (by telephone, 12-17-97); Art Gilmore (by telephone, 1-10-98); Lou Grant (Oakland, Calif., 10-28-94); Adam Green (San Francisco, Calif., 1-11-95); Ed Herlihy (by telephone, 9-15-95); Betty Johnson (Newark, N.J., 10-25-97); Larry Josephson (by telephone, 7-8-96); Hal Kanter (Los Angeles, Calif. 11-8-95); Betty Winkler Keane (New York, N.Y., 5-1-95); Jackie Kelk (by telephone, 12-11-94); Ray Kemper (by telephone, 6-10-95); Mort Lachman (by telephone, 2-21-96); Art Linkletter (by telephone 1-19-98); Naomi Cooks Mann (San Francisco, Calif., 11-1-95); Shirley Mitchell (by telephone, 11-22-94); Bill Owen (by telephone, 11-16-97); George Pirrone (Newark, N.J., 10-25-97); Abe Polonsky (by telephone, 6-2-97); Larry Rhine (by telephone, 9-5-95); Bob Schiller (San Francisco, Calif., 11-4-94); Sherwood Schwartz (Beverly Hills, Calif., 11-7-95); Hazel Shermet (by telephone, 9-5-95); Lon Simmons (by telephone, 12-30-97); Jo Stafford (Century City, Calif., 11-7-95); Arnold Stang (New York, N.Y., 10-21-97); John Stanley (San Francisco, Calif., 7-9-95); Gary Stevens (New York, N.Y., 5-2-95); Les Tremayne (by telephone, 1-9-98); Bea Wain (by telephone, 7-10-96); Mary Anna Waterman (Burlingame, Calif., 6-9-95); Bob Weiskopf (Santa Monica, Calif., 11-6-95); Paul West (San Anselmo, Calif., 7-7-95); Margaret Whiting (by telephone, 9-18-95); Barbara Whiting (by telephone, 12-19-95)

BIBLIOGRAPHY

Ace, Goodman, *Ladies and Gentlemen, Easy Aces,* Doubleday, 1970.

Allen, Fred, *Much Ado About Me,* Little, Brown, 1956.

———, *Treadmill to Oblivion,* Atlantic-Little, Brown, 1954.

Allen, Frederick Lewis, *Only Yesterday,* Harper & Row, 1931.

Allen, Steve, *More Funny People,* Stein and Day, 1982.

Andrews, Bart, and Ahrgus Juilliard, *Holy Mackerel!* E. P. Dutton, 1986.

Arce, Hector, *Groucho,* G. P. Putnam's Sons, 1979.

Auerbach, Arnold, *Funny Men Don't Laugh,* Doubleday, 1965.

Backus, Jim and Henny, *Forgive Us Our Digressions,* St. Martin's Press, 1988.

Balliett, Whitney, "Their Own Gravity" and "Two-Man Show," *The New Yorker,* September 24, 1973, and July 5, 1982.

Bankhead, Tallulah, *Tallulah,* Harper & Brothers, 1952.

Bannerman, LeRoy R., *Norman Corwin and Radio: The Golden Years,* University of Alabama Press, 1986.

Barber, Red, *The Broadcasters,* The Dial Press, 1970.

Barnouw, Erik, *The Golden Web,* Oxford University Press, 1968.

Beaumont, Charles, "Requiem for Radio," *Playboy,* May, 1960.

Benny, Joan, *Sunday Nights at Seven,* Warner Books, 1990.

Benny, Mary Livingstone, Hilliard Marks, and Marcia Borie, *Jack Benny,* Doubleday, 1978.

Berg, Gertrude, *Molly and Me,* McGraw-Hill, 1961.

Bergen, Candice, *Knock on Wood,* Random House, 1988.

Bergreen, Lawrence, *Look Now, Pay Later,* Doubleday, 1980.

Berle, Milton (with Haskel Frankel), *Milton Berle: An Autobiography,* Delacorte Press, 1974.

Blanc, Mel, *That's Not All Folks!* Warner Books, 1988.

Blythe, Cheryl, and Susan Sackett, *Say Goodnight, Gracie,* E. P. Dutton, 1986.

Brinkley, David, *David Brinkley, A Memoir,* Random House, 1995.

Burns, George (with David Fisher), *All My Best Friends,* Putnam, 1989.

Burns, George, *Gracie: A Love Story,* Putnam, 1988.

Burrows, Abe, *Honest, Abe,* Atlantic-Little, Brown, 1980.

Buxton, Frank, and Bill Owen, *The Big Broadcast,* Avon, 1966.

Cahn, William, *The Laugh Makers,* Bramhall House, 1957.

Campbell, Robert, *The Golden Years of Broadcasting,* Scribner's, 1976.

Cantor, Eddie, *Take My Life,* Doubleday, 1957.

Carroll, Carroll, *None of Your Business: Or My Life with J. Walter Thompson (Confessions of a Radio Writer),* Cowles, 1970.

Crosby, Bing, *Call Me Lucky,* Simon & Schuster, 1953.

Crosby, John, *Out of the Blue,* Simon & Schuster, 1952.

DeLong, Thomas A., *Quiz Craze,* Praeger, 1991.

———, *The Mighty Music Box,* Amber Crest Books, 1980.

Douglas, George H., *The Early Days of Radio Broadcasting,* McFarland & Co., 1987.

Dunning, John, *Tune in Yesterday,* Prentice-Hall, 1976.

Edmondson, Madeleine, and David Rounds, *From Mary Noble to Mary Hartman,* Stein & Day, 1976.

Elliott, Bob, and Ray Goulding, *From Approximately Coast to Coast . . . It's 'The Bob and Ray Show,' "* Atheneum, 1982.

Ely, Melvin Patrick, *The Adventures of Amos 'n' Andy,* Macmillan, 1991.

Fadiman, Clifton, *Party of One,* World, 1955.

Feldman, Ruth Duskin, *Whatever Happened to the Quiz Kids?,* Chicago Review Press, 1982.

Firestone, Ross, *The Big Radio Comedy Book,* Contemporary Books, 1978.

Gabler, Neil, *Winchell,* Vintage Books, 1994.

Gelbart, Larry, *Laughing Matters,* Random House, 1998.

Giddins, Gary, *Faces in the Crowd,* Oxford University Press, 1992.

Goldman, Herbert G., *Banjo Eyes,* Oxford University Press, 1997.

———, *Fanny Brice,* Oxford University Press, 1992.

Gottfried, Martin, *George Burns and the 100-Year Dash,* Simon & Schuster, 1995.

———, *Nobody's Fool,* Simon & Schuster, 1994.

Green, Abel, and Joe Laurie, Jr., *Show Biz—From Vaude to Video,* Henry Holt & Co., 1951.

Gross, Ben, *I Looked and I Listened,* Random House, 1954.

Halberstam, David, *The Fifties,* Ballantine, 1993.

Harmon, Jim, *The Great Radio Comedians,* Doubleday, 1970.

———, *The Great Radio Heroes,* Doubleday, 1967.

Havig, Alan, *Fred Allen's Radio Comedy,* Temple University Press, 1990.

Henderson, Amy, *On the Air,* Smithsonian Institution Press, 1988.

Higby, Mary Jane, *Tune in Tomorrow,* Cowles, 1966.

Hope, Bob, *Don't Shoot, It's Only Me,* Putnam, 1990.

Houseman, John, *Entertainers and the Entertained,* Simon & Schuster, 1986.

Jones, Gerard, *Honey, I'm Home!* Grove Weidenfeld, 1992.

Josefsberg, Milt, *The Jack Benny Show,* Arlington House, 1977.

Julian, Joe, *This Was Radio: A Personal Memoir,* Viking, 1975.

Keillor, Garrison, *WLT: A Radio Romance,* Viking, 1991.

King, Stephen, *Dance Macabre,* Berkley Books, 1983.

Klurfeld, Herman, *Winchell: His Life and Times,* Praeger, 1976.

Koch, Howard, *The Panic Broadcast,* Little, Brown, 1970.

Kronenberger, Louis, *Humor in America,* Harcourt Brace Jovanovich, 1976.

Lahr, John, *Notes on a Cowardly Lion,* Knopf, 1970.

Leaming, Barbara, *Orson Welles,* Viking Penguin, 1985.

Leider, Emily Wortis, *Becoming Mae West,* Farrar Straus Giroux, 1997.

Lembesis, Chris, and Randy Eidemiller, *Suspense,* self-published, 1997.

Leonard, Sheldon, *And the Show Goes On,* Limelight Editions, 1995.

Levant, Oscar, *The Unimportance of Being Oscar,* Putnam, 1968.

Linkletter, Art, *I Didn't Do It Alone,* Caroline House, 1980.

MacDonald, J. Fred, *Don't Touch That Dial!: Radio Programming in American Life from 1920 to 1960,* Nelson-Hall, 1979.

Maltin, Leonard, *The Great American Broadcast,* Dutton, 1997.

Mamet, David, *Writing in Restaurants,* Penguin Books, 1987.

Marx, Arthur, *The Secret Life of Bob Hope,* Barricade Books, 1993.

Marx, Groucho, *The Groucho Letters,* Simon & Schuster, 1967.

McCarthy, Joe, *Fred Allen's Letters,* Doubleday, 1965.

Metz, Robert, *CBS: Reflections in a Bloodshot Eye,* Playboy Press, 1975.

Mitz, Rick, *The Great TV Sitcom Book,* Perigee/Marek, 1980.

Morello, Joe, Edward Z. Epstein, and Eleanor Clark, *The Amazing Careers of Bob Hope,* Arlington House, 1973.

Morgan, Henry, *Here's Morgan!,* Barricade Books, 1994.

Morse, Carlton E., *The One Man's Family Album,* Seven Stones Press, 1988.

Nelson, Ozzie, *Ozzie,* Prentice Hall, 1973.

Oboler, Arch, *14 Radio Plays,* Random House, 1940.

Peters, Margot, *The House of Barrymore,* Knopf, 1990.

Pleasants, Henry, *The Great American Popular Singers,* Simon & Schuster, 1974.

Rhymer, Mary Francis, *The Small House Halfway Up in the Next Block,* McGraw-Hill, 1972

————, *Vic and Sade: The Best Radio Plays of Paul Rhymer,* Seabury Press, 1976.

Rockwell, Don, *Radio Personalities,* Press Bureau, Inc., 1935.

Seldes, Gilbert, *The Great Audience,* Viking Press, 1950.

————, *The Public Arts,* Simon & Schuster, 1956.

Selvin, Joel, *Ricky Nelson: Idol for a Generation,* Contemporary Books, 1990.

Singer, Mark, *Mr. Personality,* Knopf, 1989.

Stumpf, Charles, and Tom Price, *Heavenly Days!,* Woy Publications, 1987.

Taylor, Robert, *Fred Allen: His Life and Wit,* Little, Brown, 1989.

Teichmann, Howard, *Smart Alec,* Morrow, 1976.

Thurber, James, *The Beast in Me and Other Animals,* Harcourt Brace, 1947.

Vallee, Rudy, and Gil McKean, *My Time Is Your Time,* Obolensky, 1962.

Watkins, Mel, *On the Real Side,* Touchstone, 1994.

Weaver, Pat, *The Best Seat in the House,* Knopf, 1993.

Weiner, Ed, *Let's Go to Press,* Putnam, 1955.

Welles, Orson, and Peter Bogdanovich, *This Is Orson Welles,* Harper-Collins, 1992.

Wertheim, Arthur Frank, *Radio Comedy,* Oxford, 1979.

Zolotow, Maurice, *No People Like Show People,* Random House, 1951.

————, "Washboard Weeper," *Saturday Evening Post,* May 29, 1943.

Other major sources on the lives and careers of Walter Winchell, Jack Benny, Will Rogers, Roy Rogers, Al Jolson, Abbott and Costello, Fanny Brice, Arthur Godfrey, and Edward R. Murrow: *Biography,* on the Arts & Entertainment cable channel, and *American Masters* and *The American Experience* on the Public Broadcasting System. Various authors in SPERDVAC's "Radiogram" newsletter, especially Jim Cox's articles on soap operas.

Index

Page numbers in *italics* refer to illustrations.

David Sarnoff: *Archive Photos;* William Paley: *Archive Photos/Bert and Richard Morgan;* Ed Wynn: *NBC;* Jimmy Durante: *Photofest;* George Burns and Gracie Allen: *NBC Radio;* Kenny Delmar, Peter Donald, Minerva Pious, Parker Fennelley, Portland Hoffa: *Archive Photos;* Arnold Stang and Henry Morgan: *Courtesy of Arnold Stang;* Bob Hope: *Photofest;* Jo Stafford and the Pied Pipers: *Pacific Pioneer Broadcasters;* Jessica Dragonette and Rosario Bourdon's Orchestra: *Archive Photos;* Rudy Vallee: *Photofest;* Charles Flynn: *Courtesy of Charles Flynn;* Bud Collyer: *Photofest;* Nila Mack and the cast of *Let's Pretend: Archive Photos;* Brace Beemer: *Photofest;* Eve Arden: *Photofest;* Jackie Kelk, Ezra Stone, Katharine Raht, and House Jameson: *Photofest;* Gertrude Berg: *Bert Lawson/Photofest;* Hattie McDaniel: *Photofest;* Don Ameche: *Photofest;* Harold W. Arlin: *Archive Photos;* Ed Herlihy: *Ray Lee Jackson/Photofest;* Ken Carpenter and Don Wilson: *Photofest;* Freeman Gosden and Charles Correll in 1935: *NBC;* Freeman Gosden and Charles Correll in 1952: *CBS Radio;* Raymond Edward Johnson: *Photofest;* Arch Oboler and Alla Nazimova: *Photofest;* Bret Morrison and Gertrude Warner: *Photofest;* Jack Webb: *Photofest;* Joe Kelly and The Quiz Kids: *Photofest;* Ralph Edwards: *Pacific Pioneer Broadcasters;* Major Edward Bowes: *Archive Photos;* Arthur Godfrey: *Photofest;* Dorothy Powell: *CBS;* David Gothard and Julie Stevens: *Photofest;* Richard Leonard, Vivien Smolen, and Anne Elstner: *Photofest;* Page Gilman, Mary Adams, J. Anthony Smythe, and Russell Thorsen: *Pacific Pioneer Broadcasters;* Edward R. Murrow: *Pacific Pioneer Broadcasters;* Walter Winchell: *Archive Photos;* Bette Davis: *Photofest;* Orson Welles: *Photofest;* Norman Corwin: *Wide World Photos;* NBC Times Square Studio: *Archive Photos;* Howard Tollefson: *Photofest;* George Sanders, Peggy Lee, Portland Hoffa, Groucho Marx, Fred Allen, and Tallulah Bankhead: *Photofest*